BLOOMBERG

BLOOMBERG

A BILLIONAIRE'S AMBITION

CHRIS McNICKLE

FOREWORD BY
KENNETH T. JACKSON

Skyhorse Publishing

Skyhorse Publishing books may be purchased in bulk at special discounts for sales promotion, corporate gifts, fund-raising, or educational purposes. Special editions can also be created to specifications. For details, contact the Special Sales Department, Skyhorse Publishing, 307 West 36th Street, 11th Floor, New York, NY 10018 or info@skyhorsepublishing.com.

Skyhorse® and Skyhorse Publishing® are registered trademarks of Skyhorse Publishing, Inc.®, a Delaware corporation.

Visit our website at www.skyhorsepublishing.com.

10 9 8 7 6 5 4 3 2 1

Library of Congress Cataloging-in-Publication Data is available on file.

Cover design by Rain Saukas
Cover photo credit: New York City Municipal Archives

Print ISBN: 978-1-5107-2257-6
Ebook ISBN: 978-1-5107-2259-0

Printed in the United States of America

To Nick and Litna,
Danny and Ceci,
Katie and Becky

Acknowledgments

I have long had the good fortune to be friends with Mark Gallogly and Buddy Stein, who loyally read drafts of the manuscript for this book and shared good ideas for ways to make it better. Peter Cunningham, Charley Ellis, Joe and Mary Lynch, and Harvey Robins also read chapters or drafts and shared their insights. I am grateful for their help and lucky to have them as friends.

Many people involved with Michael Bloomberg, one way or another during the years he served as mayor, shared their precious time with me. I have listed their names in the sources section and I am grateful to them all. Howard Wolfson, Amanda Burden, Eduardo Castell, Fernando Ferrer, Linda Gibbs, Emily Mayrath, Seth Pinsky, Roberto Ramirez, and Marc Shaw were especially generous. None are accountable for the interpretations in this book, for which I alone am responsible.

At the City of New York Municipal Archives, Ken Cobb and Michael Lorenzini went out of their way to make my research easier, and at the City of New York Independent Budget Office, Doug Turetsky did the same. My agent, Erika Storella, worked diligently to find the right publisher, and Joseph Craig at Skyhorse guided the book into print. Frederik Bligaard, from a British Virgin Islands hilltop, tracked down a fact that a non-Danish speaker struggled to confirm. I thank them all for their help.

Fred Walters, who claims to have heard a live, real-time, audio version of the book since I recounted stories to him each day that I learned them, was a faithful companion throughout. Zack Stein and Alex Grimes, two talented young artists, one a playwright and the other a musician, graced our home at different times while I worked on the manuscript, and they cheered me on. The family members to whom this book is dedicated have been part of my New York life from the moment I entered the world in one case, and from the moment they did in three others. Two I met along the way when love and marriage brought them into our hearts. The constant love and support they all provide is beautiful.

Contents

Foreword
By Kenneth T. Jackson

New York, like America, is an idea. Russell Shorto captures this essential truth in *The Island at the Center of the World*: "If what made America great was its ingenious openness to different cultures, the small triangle of land at the southern tip of Manhattan Island is the birthplace of that idea: This island city would become the first multiethnic, upwardly mobile society on America's shores, a prototype of the kind of society that would be duplicated throughout the country and around the world." That is why New York matters so much more than other cities.

There have been 113 mayors of the great city at the mouth of the Hudson River—if we include the four chief executives of the Dutch West India Company, which controlled New Amsterdam before the English conquered it in 1664 and renamed it New York. For centuries, the job was not onerous and until 1834 the holders of the office were appointed rather than elected. They served only for a year or two, ended their terms with nice dinners and congratulatory toasts, and, with minor exceptions, did not leave deep footprints on the city.

Mayors who served after the consolidation of the five boroughs into one enormous municipality in 1898 had a more substantial effect on the metropolis. By then, New York stretched over three hundred square miles and was the second largest city in the world, after London, which was centuries older. New York's harbor was the busiest anywhere and its buildings the tallest. City government built roads, bridges, subways, schools, parks, and fire stations. It hired policemen and teachers, and had an annual budget greater than any state in the nation. For much of the last century, only the federal government spent more. Running the city was no longer a part-time job, and in some ways, all of the mayors of New York in the twentieth century were important figures in history.

But some were more important than others. Fiorello H. La Guardia, often called the "Great Mayor" of New York, took office in the depths of the Great Depression, when the unemployment rate reached a horrific 25 percent. Makeshift shelters and homeless encampments dotted the landscape; bread and soup lines were common, as was the spectacle of men in suits and hats selling apples and pencils on street corners. Through self-confidence, hard work, force of will, and engaging personality, La Guardia created an atmosphere of hope.

With Robert Moses, he attracted large federal grants to fund public improvements like the Triborough and Whitestone Bridges, the Henry Hudson and Northern State Parkways, and the renovation of Central Park. Their efforts employed tens of thousands of workers and helped the region recover from the worst financial crisis in its history. An airport, a college, a high school, and any number of institutions proudly wear La Guardia's name in honor of his memory.

Edward I. Koch also inherited a municipality in distress. In 1977, when he claimed City Hall, New York was technically bankrupt. White flight had reduced the number of middle-class families by the tens of thousands year after year, while corporations decamped to the suburbs or other regions altogether. Poor migrants from the American South and Puerto Rico seeking opportunities in the big city took their place. Tax rolls declined, welfare rolls grew, and the municipal treasury could not fund its obligations. Drug use and crime grew rampant. Koch, a supremely self-confident community leader from Greenwich Village, responded with dozens of hard decisions, and by the end of his third term New York was on its way back to the top of the world urban hierarchy.

Rudolph W. Giuliani ascended to the city's top job in 1994. Crime was already going down, but Giuliani made safe streets the centerpiece of his administration and by 2001, when he left office, homicide rates and major crime had fallen to the lowest levels since accurate record-keeping began. The perception of the city improved across the region and across the nation.

But on January 1, 2002, the future of New York looked grim. Just three months earlier, the city had suffered the worst terrorist attack in world history when two giant airliners crashed into the North and South Towers of the World Trade Center. Each building was 110 stories tall, and together they contained more office space than many entire cities. In less than two hours, 2,749 people lost their lives. The tragic day was especially hard on first responders, who had rushed toward the danger even as tens of thousands of others were running away. Three hundred and forty-three firemen perished. Despite overwhelming odds, they entered the inferno and climbed as far as they could, some with almost a hundred pounds of equipment on their backs, in a desperate effort to rescue people. Sixteen million square feet of office space were obliterated and upward of a hundred thousand people no longer had a place to work. Billions of dollars in economic investment had been lost. Giant plumes of smoke and stark steel girders were all that remained of a place once teeming with activity.

Giuliani's heroic response to the catastrophe earned him the title "America's Mayor," but the city still faced enormous difficulties. Predictions were common that the great metropolis was doomed. Businesses would flee lower Manhattan's "Canyon of Heroes," and tall buildings would soon be shunned in the spiritual home of the skyscraper. Downtown's emerging residential neighborhoods would be abandoned and public transportation would be avoided out of fear. The middle class would fly away.

Michael R. Bloomberg proved them all wrong. The leadership he demonstrated in response to the calamity he inherited, and the enduring impact the many policies that followed had on the city, make him, in my estimation, New York's greatest municipal executive and probably the most successful mayor the nation has ever known.

By 2014, when Bloomberg left office, the city was booming. Downtown's revitalization was underway, real estate values were soaring, construction cranes were everywhere, and public transit ridership reached a sixty-year high. The wealthy remained and demanded ever more upscale housing, resulting in a luxury building boom, and New York had become a mecca for young married couples with children, who created a new streetscape with their strollers and baby carriages. Immigrants arrived in the largest numbers since the 1924 McCarran Act limited newcomers, and more than fifty million tourists visited in 2013. The drop in crime that began under Mayor Dinkins in 1992, and that accelerated under Mayor Giuliani, continued. On Bloomberg's watch, New York became the safest large city in the nation, something no one could ever have predicted in the 1970s when subway crime, street violence, and personal safety fears were pervasive.

As Chris McNickle so effectively demonstrates in this carefully argued, well-written, and impressively researched book, Bloomberg led New York through an extraordinary period of effective government across the range of things that really matter to people living in a big city. Economic plans and land-use decisions, climate change policies and policing strategies, and radical reform of the school system and groundbreaking public health policies were among the many ways Bloomberg used his power to affect people's lives. That Bloomberg, one of the world's richest people, ever became mayor is itself quite a story, one that McNickle ably narrates. At the beginning of September 2001, most news media dismissed the billionaire's self-financed campaign as doomed. After 9/11, New Yorkers detected in him a sense of responsibility and business acumen his opponents lacked. The story of a self-made man who did not start out life rich appealed to a city that had always afforded newcomers the chance to prosper and to rise in status. The success of his company and the media empire it spawned provided evidence that he had the instincts and mettle to lead New York out of its crisis.

Great cities are resilient. London experienced a plague in 1327 that almost ended human life there. In 1923, Tokyo suffered an earthquake and fire that cost hundreds of thousands of lives, and bombing raids in 1944 and 1945 that flattened most of it. Today, both are again world-class cities. But the speed and intensity of New York's post-9/11 recovery are nearly miraculous, and Bloomberg is the primary reason. He proved a master manager, able to deploy the city's inherent strengths with rare skill, revitalizing "the island at the center of the world" at a time when it really mattered.

This book is the first full-length interpretative study of Bloomberg's mayoralty. It supports the view that Bloomberg is the city's greatest mayor, although McNickle pulls no punches when assessing the things he thinks Bloomberg got wrong. The volume reflects the unusual qualities that the author brings to his task. A Manhattan-born, Bronx-raised scholar with keen instincts for how the city where he grew up works, McNickle took a PhD in history at the University of Chicago, and then made his professional career in the financial industry rather than the university classroom. Yet, he obviously never lost his love for history or research. He first wrote *To Be Mayor of New York: Ethnic Politics in the City*, which Mayor Koch called a "primer for political histories yet to be written." McNickle followed that with, *The Power of the Mayor: David Dinkins, 1990–1993*, a careful analysis of the city's first African-American mayor. *Bloomberg: A Billionaire's Ambition* reveals rare command of the range of topics America's largest municipal government contends with, as well as knowledge of business that has helped the author to understand Bloomberg's reaction to some of the tough problems he confronted.

There are sure to be other books about Bloomberg's three terms as mayor. McNickle's engaging volume, rich in facts, statistics, and analytical insights, as well as first-person anecdotes that capture the human qualities of government decision-making, will serve as the place where other histories of Bloomberg start. The standard has been set high.

—Kenneth T. Jackson
Jacques Barzun Professor of History
and the Social Sciences, Columbia University
Editor in Chief, *The Encyclopedia of New York City*

Introduction—9/11

"Unbridled enthusiasm and belief that anything's possible may not be the real world, but trying things with low probabilities of success and big payoffs is a lot better than the alternatives," Michael Bloomberg once wrote. That outlook was reflected in the business Bloomberg built that restructured the $4.3 trillion global bond market with a plan the *Wall Street Journal* described in 1988 as, "almost too audacious." It is also what allowed Bloomberg to imagine he could be elected mayor of New York City in 2001 when objective analysis indicated otherwise—unless fate conjured up an alternate reality. That, of course, is what happened. On the day New Yorkers began to vote in primary elections to choose candidates for mayor, a plot devised half a world away by an evil genius caused a degree of physical destruction in lower Manhattan utterly unimaginable until it occurred. Among the many things the event transformed was New York City's political landscape.[1]

Clear blue skies and comfortably cool temperatures greeted New Yorkers as they awoke on primary day, September 11, 2001. Early risers headed to the polls which opened at 6:00 a.m. while workers for the six contenders—four Democrats and two Republicans—mobilized their supporters. Good weather promised high turnout.

At 8:46 a.m., an airplane crashed into the North building of the World Trade Center, one of downtown Manhattan's iconic Twin Towers. Speculation circulated that it was a small plane, perhaps a private one, maybe flown by an amateur pilot, a freak accident on a clear day. Seventeen minutes later another airplane crashed into the South building. Many people were looking up, watching the fire that had erupted after the first collision, and they saw the second one. A huge commercial airliner flew directly into the structure. Then everyone knew. New York City had been attacked in a deliberate act of terrorism. Less than an hour later, one building collapsed, and less than a half hour after that, the other. The pulverization of the twin skyscrapers that stood more than one hundred stories tall covered lower Manhattan in clouds of suffocating ash that caused the sun to disappear. Office workers blanketed with the toxic stuff fled north, away from the horrific catastrophe, creating the deeply disturbing picture of a retreating army of New Yorkers on Manhattan's streets. Before the buildings disintegrated, dozens of people trapped on the upper floors propelled themselves out of shattered windows to escape the intolerable heat of burning jet fuel. The desperate images seared themselves into New Yorkers' minds. Each jumper landed with a sickening thud, the sound of the bodies creating a drumbeat of death that echoed throughout the city.[2]

Mayor Giuliani and members of his staff were almost killed as they headed from a breakfast meeting toward the city's Emergency Command Center, lamentably located in the World Trade complex. They escaped with their lives, established temporary offices, and focused on disaster management with an extraordinary sense of purpose. Giuliani summoned steely nerves and remarkable personal courage. The crisis forced him to communicate with a deeply shaken public on the basis of partial information and constantly changing circumstances. He responded with sound judgment and perfect pitch. New Yorkers knew thousands had died, and many feared their own lives might still be in danger. Mayor Giuliani's actions and words reassured them that their government was in command, doing everything possible to protect them and to react to the unprecedented attack. At a moment of dire need, he embraced the wounded city with granite resolve and deep compassion. It was his finest hour.[3]

"When we get the final number, it will be more than we can bear," Giuliani warned. On September 11, 2001, 2,749 people were murdered in New York City, including 412 rescue workers—firefighters above all, police, and others. Another 247 people died that day in an airplane attack on the Pentagon in Washington, DC, and in a plane that crashed into a field in Pennsylvania when passengers tried to wrestle control of it from their hijackers. America was at war.[4]

The September 11, 2001, New York City primary never happened. By mid-morning the Board of Elections had the administrative judge in charge call it off, and shortly after noon Governor George Pataki canceled primaries statewide. The city's mayoral contests were rescheduled for Tuesday, September 25. On the one hand, the bloodied city had little appetite for the normal stuff of political campaigns. On the other, the commitment to follow democratic process had never seemed more important, and voters suddenly looked at the would-be mayors through the smoke still rising from the smoldering rubble at Ground Zero. Who could keep them safe? Who had a plan to rebuild lower Manhattan, one of the city's most important economic engines? Which leader had the best skills to see the city through tough budget years sure to come as the attack's devastation hit an economy already slowing down? On the morning of September 11, 2001, not a single New York City political strategist believed Michael Bloomberg could be elected mayor—including his own. Fifty-six days later, he won.[5]

Bloomberg would lead New York through an extraordinary period of active and effective government over the next twelve years. He launched a successful economic development strategy unlike any conceived by his predecessors and pursued a vision that converted prime parcels of underutilized property from wasting assets into catalysts for growth. He changed the rules of what could be built on more than a third of the city's land, transforming its zoning ordinance from a document that honored the past into a roadmap for a twenty-first-century metropolis. He implemented an unprecedented sustainability plan designed to ensure that the city's physical environment improved in tandem with the economy. He steered the city through two financial crises as severe as any in memory, save New York's near insolvency in the mid-1970s, and he left the city treasury stronger than any mayor before him. He seized control of a long-failing public school system and initiated radical reform. New Yorkers were safer when Bloomberg governed than at any time in memory, and healthier. His decision to ban smoking in workplaces sparked a national and international movement. Along with other groundbreaking programs, it contributed to extending the life-span of a typical New Yorker beyond the national average. It is hard to imagine a more profound impact by a public servant on a population. As a national leader, Bloomberg promoted campaigns to reduce gun violence, to reform education, to improve public health, and to respond to climate change.

Yet, a larger number and higher proportion of New Yorkers lived in poverty when Bloomberg left office than when he arrived. More lived in public shelters than at any time since the Great Depression after an ambitious plan to reduce homelessness failed. The New York City Housing Authority, long the model of an effective public housing program, descended into the worst state of disrepair in its nearly eighty-year history. Overly aggressive use of a basic policing tactic—stop, question, and frisk—caused a federal judge to rule the Bloomberg administration violated New Yorkers' constitutional rights. The city's jail system on Rikers Island descended into what federal investigators called "a culture of violence" worse than any they had ever witnessed.[6]

Bloomberg was the richest man in New York City and spent hundreds of millions of dollars on his elections, making a farce of the city's campaign finance rules. He disbursed hundreds of millions more in philanthropic contributions that bought political loyalty and silenced critics. The law limited him to two terms. Bloomberg used all the influence at his command to coerce a weak legislative body into rewriting the rules so he could perpetuate himself in power. Nearly nine New Yorkers in ten believed that the action disrespected their democratic rights, and then a majority reelected him to a third term anyway. He dominated New York City's politics like few leaders before him, and he left a legacy that will continue to shape events for decades to come.

This book tells the story of how Michael Bloomberg became mayor of New York and how he wielded power while in office. The first chapter recounts the early years of Bloomberg's life and his success as a Wall Street entrepreneur. Chapter 2 captures the drama of Bloomberg's election. Chapters 3, 4, and 5 lay out Bloomberg's management of three essential tasks of a mayor that affect the daily lives and futures of a city's people—fiscal solvency, public safety, and public education. Chapters 6 and 7 together capture Bloomberg's economic programs. They show how he and his team used the tools of government to support local commerce in ways that differed from any of his predecessors and that were vastly more effective. His strategies recognized globalization and technology as forces to harness rather than fight. His land-use policies, tax concessions, and infrastructure decisions sought to steer private investment in ways that took advantage of New York City's unique attributes in a world that had gone through a half-century of profound change with inadequate municipal response. The policies rejected the false choice between growth and a healthy environment. Bloomberg pursued both with vigor. Chapter 8 explores Bloomberg's ambiguous relationship to poverty in New York City, and policies he promoted to reduce it, with mixed results. Chapter 9 lays out how Bloomberg's billions affected city politics, and chapter 10 captures the dynamic of Bloomberg's third term, characterized by surprising management failures as well as successes that will leave New Yorkers profoundly better off. The final chapter assesses Bloomberg's legacy after twelve years as mayor of the world's most important metropolis, with implications for governing the United States and cities around the world.

Chapter One

The Making of a Billionaire

Michael Rubens Bloomberg was born in Boston on February 14, 1942. His family moved to the nearby working-class community of Medford, Massachusetts, a few years later, just about the same time that engineers at the University of Pennsylvania in Philadelphia completed work on ENIAC, the Electronic Numerical Integrator and Computer. ENIAC filled forty filing cabinets, each nine feet high, with eighteen thousand vacuum tubes and thousands of miles of wiring. Technicians had to replace tubes manually when they blew out, and they also removed by hand insects that occasionally crawled into the network and fouled it. They referred to this as debugging. The need to decipher secret enemy codes and to calculate missile trajectories during World War II led the United States government to fund the project. When the war ended, engineers sought commercial purposes for the new machine that calculated sums vastly faster than humans. By the mid-1960s, when Michael Bloomberg joined Salomon Brothers, banks, insurance companies, government agencies, and large corporations relied on computers to do work that once required thousands of clerical staff. Before long, handheld calculators with more power than ENIAC became commonplace. In 1981, IBM entered the personal computer market signaling the beginning of an age when every business, every home, nearly every person would own a computer. That was the year Salomon Brothers fired Bloomberg, the bank's chief technology officer.[1]

Up and Down on Wall Street

Bloomberg joined Salomon in 1966 after earning a master of business administration from Harvard Business School. It was no coincidence he joined a Jewish firm. Wall Street was still a place of clubby tribalism then. "Dress British, think Yiddish," was the way some at Salomon described the bank. At Goldman Sachs, a recruiter introduced the young MBA to "Mister Levy," the firm's legendary managing partner. At Salomon Brothers, he met "Billy," whose last name turned out to be the same as the firm's. Bloomberg felt he would fit in better with the more informal environment at Salomon, so he accepted their offer. He started at an annual salary of $9,000, plus a $2,500 bonus he negotiated with senior partner John Gutfreund in the form of a loan that would be forgiven over two years. The additional money was meant to allow the young professional to buy an acceptable wardrobe.[2]

Salomon humbled Bloomberg the summer he began, assigning him to work in "the cage," counting and stacking physical stock and bond certificates for delivery to other banks on the street as collateral for overnight loans. The junior bankers often conducted their work in their underwear since the bank vault where it took place lacked air conditioning. But after the requisite hazing, Bloomberg thrived in the fraternity-house atmosphere of Salomon's culture where the most commonly heard word above the chaotic cacophony of the trading floor was "fuck." He became an equity salesman, participating in the burgeoning practice of block trading, a highly profitable activity that propelled him upwards in the organization.[3]

Bloomberg was "the fair-haired boy," a "superstar in the most visible department of the trendiest firm on the Street," he wrote in his memoir, *Bloomberg by Bloomberg*. He "greeted all the important visiting customers, got interviewed by every newspaper that mattered, and had a great social life playing the role of Wall Street power broker to the hilt." He took the notion that he had become a high flyer literally, and learned to pilot airplanes and helicopters. He would test his own nerves twice later in life when equipment failures forced him to complete emergency landings, once in each type of aircraft. He "dated all the girls," and "skied and jogged and partied more than most," while always working a twelve-hour day. He had made it big, and he had become "more than a 'legend'" in his own mind. Some who knew him in those days say his memoir exaggerates his party schedule. They recall an ambitious man who enjoyed life, but who arrived at work earlier than most, and who often stayed late looking for a chance to share a taxi ride home with a senior partner for face time. In August 1972, many in Bloomberg's peer group made partner. To his astonishment, rage, and humiliation, he did not. He swallowed hard, went back to work, and was elevated three months later, off-cycle. While he claimed he never understood why, it is easy to imagine that the brash young Harvard MBA, cast among a crew of equally cocky streetwise kids from Brooklyn, Queens, and the Bronx, with less privileged educations, had rubbed some colleagues the wrong way.[4]

Financial markets follow profits with a shark's nose for blood. They tear apart inefficiencies of the kind that initially made block trading in equities so lucrative. By 1979, Bloomberg's department had run its course. He had lost the protection a high wall of profits offers a banker, and he had made some enemies. His partners exiled him to the computer room, assigning him responsibility for the firm's information technology systems. It was a critical function to be sure, but far removed from the glory of the trades and the deals that made the firm money. Two years later, in a surprise decision, Salomon merged with a little-known, publicly traded commodities firm called Phibro Corporation. The transaction freed wealth locked inside Salomon's partnership, so the firm's owners suddenly had access to riches that until then existed mainly in the abstract. Almost all who benefited remained to run the newly enlarged firm. A small number were handed large checks and asked to leave. Bloomberg was one of them.[5]

As chief of information technology, Bloomberg had challenged the prevailing organizational structure. He had argued strenuously for a single firm-wide computer system to facilitate cooperation across departments and risk management across products, and he objected to a change in hiring policy when the firm sought to attract senior "rainmakers" from other houses rather than grooming from within. His strongly held, readily articulated views caused colleagues to believe Bloomberg thought he could run the firm better than the Executive Committee. As he later put it, he "stirred the pot, lost the battle," and paid the price. At the age of thirty-nine, with ten million dollars in his pocket, Michael Bloomberg had to start over.[6]

A Child of the Fifties

When Michael was born, his father, William, was an accountant at a local dairy where he typically worked six or seven days a week. His mother, born Charlotte Rubens, had grown up in northern New Jersey, where as a young lady she worked during the day and earned a business degree from New York University at night, an achievement untypical of women in that era. She met her husband while working as an assistant auditor in a national dairy company. After she married and moved to Massachusetts, she kept house for her husband, their son, and a daughter, Marjorie, born a few years after her brother. Michael's paternal grandparents, both Jewish, were East European immigrants "who never had much money," Bloomberg recalled. He remembered his maternal grandparents, also Jewish, one born in Belarus, the other on Manhattan's Lower East Side to Lithuanian immigrants, as financially comfortable.[7]

Bloomberg thought of himself as simply "American." His high school had twenty-five Jewish students out of more than 680. It was a place where "we never felt any anti-Semitism," one Jewish classmate remembered, "but we were really a minority, and we all stayed together." All but Michael, who "was . . . on his own trip." During a carefree childhood and adolescence, Bloomberg displayed the classic profile of a bored kid who acted up in school and disrupted classes with childish pranks. He channeled youthful energy into the Boy Scouts, where he learned "to be self-sufficient and, simultaneously, to live and work with others." He became one of the organization's youngest Eagle Scouts, and also "a science nut, [who] went to the science museum, was into wild animals, electrical things," a childhood friend recounted to biographer Joyce Purnick. Sometimes, Bloomberg would bring home snakes. His sister frowned on this boyish practice since from time to time she would find Michael searching the house for one that had escaped from its cage.[8]

Bloomberg joined his high school debate team and the slide-rule club, and he worked after class, on weekends, and during summers for a small electronics company in Cambridge. He enrolled as an undergraduate at Johns Hopkins University planning on studying science. Rigorous data-gathering, dispassionate analysis, and tightly reasoned logic—hallmarks of the scientific method—became characteristic of Bloomberg's decision-making. He was intellectually curious, but with a pragmatic outlook, not an academic one. When he discovered he would have to study German if he majored in physics, he switched to electrical engineering. Technical matters continued to spark his curiosity throughout his adult life. On a helicopter tour of a windfarm off the coast of Denmark in 2009, he leaned over to ask mayoral aide Rohit Aggarwala if the machines below were generating AC current or DC. "Boss," Aggarwala replied laughing as he recounted the story, "I'm your policy guy. I have no idea." A Danish engineer answered the question: AC. Bloomberg's ability to grasp how the different elements of complex urban systems interacted, and his ability to tweak plans developed by experts to improve them, would impress city officials who worked with him.[9]

Bloomberg settled for academic mediocrity in college, focusing more on social activities than course work. He became Phi Kappa Psi's first Jewish member, and served as fraternity president and class president. His mother was unsurprised. She remembered him from a very young age as the family member who wanted to organize things, who wanted to be in charge. He applied to Harvard Business School, due to peer pressure as he recalled it, but there was more to it than that. Bloomberg described his father as "an average working-class guy from Chelsea, Massachusetts" who thought Harvard a "rarefied and almost unattainable waypoint on the trail to the great American dream." He thought Michael was "the most wonderful person on earth," and he died while his son was still in college. The desire to honor his father motivated Michael Bloomberg, as did his love for his mother. In many ways, she was the more forceful presence in his upbringing, and she knew him well. When he told her he had been accepted to Harvard, she responded, "Don't let it go to your head." Michael would call her most mornings throughout his adult life. She lived to be 102, and when she died, he said of her: "Our mother's unimpeachable integrity, fierce independence and constant love were gifts that profoundly shaped our lives. . . . Our family recognizes how truly blessed we have been to have her live such a long and full life, and to be able to carry her spirit with us forever."[10]

Bloomberg's reaction to one of the major concerns of his generation makes clear he was a child of the 1950s, not the more tumultuous 1960s. As his Harvard studies came to an end in 1966, so did his student deferment from the draft, which was no doubt part of his calculus to attend graduate school. He expected to be called to the armed forces and sent to Vietnam. He "didn't relish the thought of getting shot while walking through the jungle," he wrote, "but the thought of rebelling against our country never entered our minds. . . . Home, school, Boy Scouts, sports, politics, newspapers—everything in life taught us duty, loyalty, responsibility, sacrifice, patriotism." He applied for officers' training school, but a case of flat feet disqualified him. Political opponents would accuse him of dodging the war, but their charges were unconvincing.[11]

Bloomberg's attitude toward race relations also dates from the 1950s, when the civil rights movement was a quest for the equal justice of a color-blind society, and the concept of affirmative action to level a tilted playing field had not yet gained currency. He remembered his father writing out an annual donation to the National Association for the Advancement of Colored People, telling his son if people can discriminate against blacks, then they can discriminate against Jews and everyone else. The women's liberation movement had not yet emerged and Medford's married women kept house while the men worked. Bloomberg's formative years took place at a time when America was self-confident, and the white men who ran it felt secure in their power. "If . . . any of the extraordinary events of the [1960s] moved Bloomberg in any way, he had never let on," Elizabeth Kolbert would write in a *New Yorker* profile.[12]

America in the 1950s enjoyed a highly stable social and financial environment, but about the time Bloomberg joined Salomon in 1966, the financial system began to experience unusual stress. President Lyndon Johnson's pursuit of an expensive war in Vietnam and expansive social programs in the United States ignited inflation with far-reaching consequences. By 1979 prices were rising by more than 13 percent a year, and "no other issue could rival [it] as a pressure on the American mind," according to Theodore White, a shrewd observer of national politics. With the economy on the verge of crisis, Federal Reserve Board Chairman Paul Volcker forced interest rates up to frightening heights. The prime rate reached the unheard of level of 21.5 percent and a severe recession followed. The bold tactic worked, and by 1982 inflation subsided. The economy pivoted up, and a prolonged period of declining interest rates and renewed credit expansion began. A huge surge in financial markets followed. Americans held 17.5 million mutual fund accounts with $241 billion dollars in 1981. By 1985, the assets had doubled. By 2001, they had multiplied in size more than twenty-eight times, reaching

$6,975 billion, sitting in 245 million accounts, and they continued to grow from there.[13]

An Entrepreneur Unbound

Technology and finance were both in the midst of revolutionary changes in 1981, the year Salomon cashiered Bloomberg. As he contemplated options, he knew he had too much energy to retire on the fortune he had made, and he found the notion of returning to a trading desk somewhere else unappealing, so he decided to start his own company. "There were better traders and sales people," he acknowledged. "There were better managers and computer experts," as well. "But nobody had more knowledge of the securities and investment industries *and* of how technology could help them," he concluded. He would build a business, "around a collection of securities data, giving people the ability to select what each individually thought the most useful parts, and then providing computer software that would let non-mathematicians do analysis on that information." From his own experience, he knew how valuable securities traders would find it. So Michael Bloomberg, who had come to run the information systems at one of Wall Street's biggest trading houses by accident, set out to create an information technology business serving the financial industry at just the moment when both sectors were poised for explosive growth.[14]

Bloomberg had an entrepreneur's pluck. He rented an office, hired a team, and hustled to generate income through consulting assignments while building the technology system he imagined. At a crucial meeting, a Merrill Lynch executive asked his technology chief if he wanted the type of machine Bloomberg promised. "I think we should do it internally, build it ourselves," the man replied, but he had too many other commitments to start on the project for another six months. "I'll get it done in six months and if you don't like it, you don't have to pay for it," Bloomberg promised. The race was on. The team he assembled delivered the system against formidable challenges and secured Merrill Lynch as a client. Soon the firm made an investment in Bloomberg LP. The relationship brought the young enterprise tangible benefits and priceless credibility.[15]

Bloomberg's machines were carefully crafted to fit on a trader's desk. At first they provided selected, real-time market data through electronic feeds, focusing on bonds at just about the time Paul Volcker's decision to let interest rates rise made bond trading trickier than ever. The new technology steadily replaced quaint practices that involved someone, somewhere copying down rows and columns of numbers with a pencil onto pieces of paper and faxing them around to users. The new system worked faster and more accurately than human beings. In 1987, Bloomberg LP became the source of US government bond prices for the *Wall Street Journal* and the Associated Press, replacing the New York Federal Reserve Bank as the definitive provider of the single most important piece of financial information published in the United States. Until then, a runner holding two or three sheets of legal size paper with handwritten notes on front and back battled rush-hour traffic from downtown to midtown to allow the news services to meet deadlines.[16]

On September 22, 1988, the financial industry took public note of Bloomberg's company when Michael M. Miller and Matthew Winkler wrote a front-page article for the *Wall Street Journal*. "Michael Bloomberg, a breezy, profane former Salomon Brothers trader runs a small company with a high tech product," they informed their readers. "If Mr. Bloomberg has his way, he and his creation will transform the $4 trillion global bond market." The plan, they wrote, "seems almost too audacious." At the time, the company had 225 employees, $60 million in revenues and a chief executive with a "puckish sense of humor and a prodigious temper," the reporters wrote. "I do tend to break phones all the time," Bloomberg confessed. Staff learned to calculate the length of the cord attached to the receiver so they could stand outside its reach and avoid injury when the boss hurled it at them.[17]

Unlike the market for stocks, no exchange captured the price of a bond in a single place. Each investment bank arrived at its own calculation, complicating life for investors and at times leaving them at the mercy of traders who used the complex inconsistencies to engineer profits for themselves. The *Journal* explained the value of the little machine Bloomberg's company peddled in the terms of the industry it served. "A bond's value can be altered by dozens of arcane factors, ranging from early redemptions, to coupon reinvestment rates to principal repayment rates. The Bloomberg can calculate what a bond would be worth if any of these factors change." Users could also compare the value of different securities and see historical data. Rival services offered less data and cruder analytics. One client summed it up for the journalists and readers: "He has a product no one else has."[18]

Bloomberg, as CEO, did a little bit of everything in the company's early days. Securing the most important accounts was a paramount task, but for a time he signed every contract, paid every bill, did the hiring and firing, bought the coffee, sodas, cookies, and chips, wrote and handed out paychecks personally to each and every one of his company's New York City employees. "I used a screwdriver as much as a pencil," he wrote. "Amid old McDonald's hamburger wrappers and mouse droppings, a half dozen of us dragged wires from our computers to the keyboards and screens we were putting in place, stuffing the cables through holes we drilled in other people's furniture—all without permission, violating every fire law, building code and union regulation in the books," he reminisced in his memoir. "It's amazing we did not burn down some office or electrocute ourselves. At the end of the day, ten or eleven o'clock at night, we'd turn it on and watch what we'd created come alive. It was so satisfying."[19]

Bloomberg recognized that "from our first day" the company he founded "was making news with numbers." His data-centric business overlapped with the type of text-based information Dow Jones delivered to financial institutions in the United States and Reuters delivered in Europe. Either his company would displace the two installed giants, or they would smother his company, he reasoned. His response demonstrated the quality that sets apart the most successful entrepreneurs from others—the nerve to experience simultaneously the overwhelming fear of extinction and a fearless determination to destroy rivals. Ordinary people find the cognitive dissonance of such situations paralyzing. Bloomberg hired Matt Winkler, the *Wall Street Journal* reporter who had written about his company, to create a global news service. In time, with the seeming inevitability that follows the intense sweat of hard-won success, Bloomberg LP grew into a global media empire. Bloomberg News became "the chronicle of capitalism."[20]

Bloomberg combined the decision-making traits of an entrepreneur and a trader. Like most successful leaders of start-up businesses, he had little patience for process and cared only about results. "Whenever one of my employees designs a form or writes a memo, I walk out into the hallway and make a big deal of tearing it up," he once said. "The last thing we need are lots of forms and procedures and policies." His company did not use titles, had no private offices and no executive dining room. Instead he provided large fish tanks that he believed created a calm atmosphere, and free snacks. He found efforts by established news organizations to prevent his upstart company from securing press credentials or other rights typical of a media firm nothing more than thinly disguised exercises in self-perpetuating privilege. Obstacles and setbacks were parts of the landscape, to be avoided or overcome and passed by on the way to a goal, not topics to dwell on. Each transaction was a discrete event. As soon as one was complete, he moved on to the next with little introspective reflection. "He doesn't have self-doubts. There's no hand-wringing. It goes back to the trader's mentality. You take a shot, and if you're wrong, you go on to the next one," Bloomberg's friend, Morris Offit, would say of him.[21]

By the new millennium, the company Bloomberg created had become an indispensable component of the world financial system. The little machine that bore his name was nearly as ubiquitous as the telephone in the realm of institutional finance. It sat on the desk of virtually every capital markets trader, financial economist, professional investor, and central banker in the world, channeling data, graphs and tables, financial analysis, news stories, and later streaming videos, to the men and women who controlled the world's money. It became a status symbol among decision-makers because anyone who was anyone had one. By the end of 2000, Bloomberg LP employed 7,000 people, who ran seventy-nine news bureaus and ten television networks to serve 150,000 subscribers around the world. Its eponymous principal shareholder owned 72 percent of it and had become wealthy beyond imagination. *Forbes* reported his fortune worth over $4.0 billion in 2000 and ranked him number seventy-two on its list of the world's richest people. Shrewd analysts thought the figure hugely understated. By 2002, some reports valued Bloomberg's worth at $7.5 billion, making him, perhaps, the richest man in New York City. By the time Bloomberg left City Hall in 2013, he owned more than 90 percent of Bloomberg LP and estimates of his net worth exceeded $30 billion. A 2016 report put it at more than $40 billion.[22]

Restless

In 1976, Bloomberg married a British woman named Susan Brown. They had two daughters, Emma and Georgina. In 1993 they divorced with rare civility. "Nothing went wrong per se," Bloomberg wrote. "We just developed separate lives doing different things. One day, we looked back and found things had changed." Brown remembered it as her decision. She spent too much time home alone while Bloomberg built his business. The parents continued to raise their children together "as a unit," but at the age of fifty-one, Michael Bloomberg was once again a bachelor.[23]

With characteristic ambition, the businessman-media mogul began to navigate the social scene of Manhattan's elite, joining the boards of Lincoln Center, the Metropolitan Museum of Art, the New York Public Library, the Central Park Conservancy, and on and on. His nights became a series of black tie cocktails and charity dinners. The women who accompanied him sometimes towered over his diminutive five-foot-seven-inch frame. Gossip columnists recognized his dates as smart, attractive women successful in their own rights. They credited the man with good taste; the *New York Post*'s celebrity-focused Page Six awarded Bloomberg the title of "anti-bimbo billionaire." The tycoon cold-called New Yorkers of influence and invited them to lunch. Charlie Rose, who interviewed the good and the great of all stripes, taped his television show in Bloomberg's studios. The boss often stopped by to introduce himself to the guests and to chat with them. He described his life in a 1996 interview with the London *Guardian*. "Let me put it this way. I like the theater, dining and chasing women," he said. "I'm a single, straight billionaire living in Manhattan. What do you think? It's a wet dream." In time, he settled into a long-term relationship with Diana Taylor, a successful investment banker with a blend of beauty and brains that appealed to him. After he became mayor, at an event that included Lady Gaga, reporters questioned him about his flirtatious behavior with the theatrical diva. "The best kiss of the night came later, from Diana," he responded.[24]

It would be easy to interpret Michael Bloomberg's behavior as a rising outsider's quest for social acceptance. The first time the boy who had grown up in suburban Medford found himself dining at La Cote Basque, one of Manhattan's most elegant restaurants, he gawked at the opulence. A friend remembers Bloomberg as aspiring to crash New York's A-list parties. His driver's license claimed he was five foot ten. He himself once said, "All repetitively successful people have an inferiority complex." Yet, Bloomberg always seemed willing to do his own thing his own way. Once he had arrived, he seemed to take it for granted that he belonged to the city's social elite, and in fact thought it natural that he would lead it. For the most part, Bloomberg projected preternatural confidence. He liked parties, possessed a salesman's love of people and harbored genuine curiosity about any person of accomplishment. He also harbored restless ambition. Meeting the rich, the famous, and the powerful was interesting and fun, and bound to be good for business.[25]

The mogul also became a philanthropist, a decision he attributed to the values instilled in him as a Boy Scout, and by his parents at the family dinner table, where once a year his father read out loud for his children's benefit the names of friends who had contributed to important causes. A college friend recalled Bloomberg saying that the three most important jobs in the world were President of the World Bank, Secretary General of the United Nations, and President of the United States, because they had the power to make the world a better place.

Unsurprisingly, Bloomberg's riches drew politicians toward him. "As a wealthy Democrat who has given consistently to my party, I am called repeatedly by every Democratic candidate," he reported. All claimed to want his "insightful views," and to "tap my vast array of experiences," he wrote, "when what they really wanted, was a significant contribution to their campaign fund. . . . Do I give?" he asked rhetorically. "Of course. Democracy only works if we support it. The alternatives are untenable and I certainly want to leave a free, healthy country for my kids," he explained.[26]

For all his success, for all the gratification he experienced from his ability to do good things, and from the respect it earned him and the influence it gave him, Bloomberg remained ambitious. "Periodically," he wrote, "I get frustrated" with the bureaucracy that creeps insidiously into organizations as they grow. When that happened, Bloomberg would "dream of starting again." Yet, he had no interest in selling the company he built. The highly profitable enterprise generated vastly more cash than any rational person needed, so the money a sale would bring offered little incentive. And he asked himself, "What would I do if I sold it? Go into politics?" He knew himself well enough to know he had "no interest in being a legislator. The pace, the focus, and the compromises don't appeal to me," he wrote. Yet, when a *Financial Times* journalist interviewed him in London in 1997 during a promotional tour for his memoir published that year, he let on that someday he might very well run for mayor of New York City, an executive role. "I think I'd be great" at it, he bragged.[27]

Chapter Two

Restoration Interrupted

Bloomberg would not campaign for City Hall in 1997. "The challengers jockeying for position to win the Democratic primary for mayor are competing for the privilege of being shellacked in the fall" by Rudy Giuliani, *New York Times* columnist Maureen Dowd wrote early that year. Things turned out precisely as she predicted.[1]

Rudy's World

Giuliani, a former federal prosecutor, won the election for mayor in 1993 atop the Republican and Liberal party lines. Registered Democrats outnumbered Republicans five to one in New York City, and the Liberal Party's membership was tiny, so Giuliani's success was unusual. His margin of victory was the narrowest since 1905, and more or less mirrored the slim gap by which he lost in 1989 to the same opponent, David Dinkins, the city's first African American mayor. The 1993 voting statistics tell a stark tale of race relations in New York City. Giuliani won nearly 80 percent of white votes and almost 40 percent of Latinos. Almost no blacks voted for him. Dinkins won well over 90 percent of African American votes and more than 60 percent of Latino ballots. Just 23 percent of whites chose him. Two ethnic coalitions, one composed predominantly of moderate and conservative whites with some support from more conservative Latinos, the other composed predominantly of people of color plus the city's most liberal whites, had been competing for power in New York since the 1960s. By the time Giuliani and Dinkins confronted each other in their quests for power, the two coalitions' numbers were fairly evenly matched. Giuliani's victory came from barely more than half the city, amidst dispiriting accusations from blacks that racism explained the outcome.[2]

One aspect of Giuliani's mandate was undisputed. New Yorkers of every color and from every borough desperately sought relief from the onslaught of crime the city had suffered since the 1960s. William Bratton, Giuliani's first police commissioner, implemented the now-famous Compstat program. NYPD analysts mapped all the serious crimes reported in the city and, at Weekly Crime Control Strategy Meetings, police brass used the intelligence to hold local commanders relentlessly accountable for reducing lawlessness in their precincts. The smarter deployment of patrols discouraged crimes, and a crack-down on quality-of-life violations caused arrests for misdemeanors to surge. Aggressive use of the city's business licensing power crippled organized crime families that had dominated entire industries for decades. One year after his inauguration, Giuliani held a press conference with his highly popular police commissioner to announce crime in New York City had fallen in every impor-tant category during 1994. By the end of Giuliani's first term murders had fallen more than 60 percent, and the Federal Bureau of Investigation's index of seven major crimes fell by more than 40 percent in New York. Public places lost the sense of danger that had pervaded them for years, and people credited Rudy Giuliani with fulfilling his promise to restore order to a city at risk of spinning out of control.[3]

Giuliani responded to the $2.3 billion budget gap he inherited with cuts to every city agency except for the police and fire departments. In his 1995 State of the City address, he declared that he would require anyone who received city aid to work. A year later, the welfare roll was 18 percent lower, and by the time Giuliani left office it had fallen from 1.2 million to under five hundred thousand, fewer than at any time since 1966. With many "ifs, ands and buts," the executive director of the New York State Financial Control Board declared that Giuliani's early budget management made "very, very important progress toward fiscal stability." An economic surge and a spike in Wall Street profits boosted city tax revenues, creating a $1.3 billion surplus by June 30, 1997. The good fortune allowed Giuliani and the city council to write themselves an election year budget more than 7 percent richer than the year before, and they created a $500 million emergency pool as well. Moody's Investors Service announced a "positive" credit outlook for city bonds. In 1997, *Fortune* maga-zine rated New York the nation's most improved city for conducting business, just in time for Giuliani's reelection campaign.[4]

With the lowest turnout in memory for a Democratic primary, Manhattan Borough President Ruth Messinger, the darling of Upper West Side Jewish liberals, won just over 39 percent of the vote in 1997. That left her shy of the 40 percent required to win her party's nomination without a runoff against Reverend Al Sharpton, a champion of social justice to blacks and a racial rabble-rouser to whites, who came in second with 32 percent. A head-to-head contest loomed, but after counting absentee ballots and correcting some tabulation discrepancies, the Board of Elections ruled Messinger the winner with just over 40 percent. On Election Day, Giuliani trounced her, 57 percent to 41 percent. Whites voted for Giuliani and blacks against him by margins of roughly four to one. Giuliani won a modestly higher percent of Latino votes in 1997 than in 1993. The Republican's easy trot to victory in heavily

Democratic New York caused many to believe the city had entered a period of post-ideological politics. Abstract philosophical beliefs seemed to matter less to a majority of voters than effectiveness running a city bureaucracy that many had deemed unmanageable just four years before. Yet, despite the triumphant reelection, the stark racial voting pattern made it clear that on that most troublesome of American fault lines—race—the city remained as divided as when Giuliani first entered office.[5]

Nine days into his first term, a confrontation at a Harlem Mosque between the police and Louis Farrakhan's Nation of Islam set a negative tone for Giuliani's relationship with the city's African Americans, and it never recovered. Asserting he would not acquiesce to intimidation, Giuliani refused to meet with most African American elected officials or other black leaders throughout his two terms in office. The resentment his posture caused was extreme, and counterproductive when racially charged incidents occurred, like the brutal attack by a sadistic cop on a Haitian immigrant named Abner Louima in August 1997, and the police shooting of a West African man named Amadou Diallo in February 1999. The Diallo shooting had far-reaching political repercussions. The raw facts—forty-one bullets fired by four cops at an unarmed black man standing in the doorway of his own apartment, a man with no history of arrests and no connection to violence or crime—struck a public nerve. The tragedy caused a majority of New Yorkers, including most whites, to believe the Giuliani administration's approach to policing had gone too far and endangered people it meant to protect.[6]

By the time Giuliani delivered his second inaugural address, despite his successes and convincing reelection, a lot of New Yorkers had come to see him as strangely flawed. His ego seemed to make it impossible to share the spotlight with anyone. Despite William Bratton's remarkable record policing the city during Giuliani's first two years in office, the mayor forced him to resign after *Time* magazine ran a photo of the law enforcement official on its cover. Giuliani bullied popular Schools Chancellor Ramon Cortines into departing in June 1995, and after a somewhat extended honeymoon, engineered the dismissal of his well-respected successor, Rudy Crew. At the annual Inner Circle City Hall press charity show in 1997, he dressed up like a woman, replete with fishnet stockings, lipstick, and high heels. He would repeat the drag queen act several more times in various settings. Giuliani threatened to revoke funding for the Brooklyn Museum and to cancel its lease if it did not withdraw an exhibit he found offensive. Two-thirds of New Yorkers objected to the mayor's interference with artistic freedom. His administration lost twenty-seven of thirty-one First Amendment lawsuits brought by the American Civil Liberties Union. Bizarrely, in one speech Giuliani defined freedom "as the willingness of every single human being to cede to lawful authority a great deal of discretion about what you do and how you do it."[7]

Observant analysts realized that Giuliani's early commitment to reducing the municipal workforce and improving its efficiency had given way over time to renewed bureaucratic bloat and machine style politics. Ray Harding and the inaptly named Liberal Party he controlled became rich beneficiaries of city government largesse. Municipal judgeships, awarded by mayors Koch and Dinkins to candidates deemed qualified by an independent commission, became rewards for Giuliani loyalists without the benefit of professional screening. By the end of his second term, the city payroll Giuliani pledged to cut had ballooned to its highest level ever.[8]

Giuliani's personal life diminished public confidence in him as well. His wife, Donna Hanover, became nearly invisible after his first year in office. Rumors of a Giuliani romance with a City Hall staffer circulated for years amidst emphatic denials, only to be replaced by new ones involving a pharmaceutical executive named Judith Nathan. When he contemplated a run for the US Senate against Hillary Clinton as a stepping stone to the White House, his marital status became an issue. One afternoon, without alerting his wife or children in advance, Giuliani announced he would seek a divorce. He moved out of Gracie Mansion, the mayor's official residence, where his wife and children remained, and moved into the home of a longtime friend who shared an apartment with his gay lover. In April 2000, about the same time the marriage scandal began to develop momentum, Giuliani announced doctors had diagnosed him with prostate cancer, and he dropped out of the senate race.[9]

Shortly after his reelection in 1997, almost three-quarters of the city approved of the job Rudy Giuliani was doing, including more than half of its African Americans, even though most had voted for another candidate. By March 2000, the citywide approval figure had fallen below one-third, and a Quinnipiac College Poll in April of that year reported 91 percent of African Americans disapproved of Giuliani. The citywide approval number recovered to 55 percent by November 2000, but the mayor's combative personality had polarized the city, and were he allowed to seek a third term, just 41 percent would support him. A term-limit law that allowed most elected city officials to serve only twice had been adopted while Giuliani was mayor, so another term was not an option anyway. His time in office was coming to a close as primaries approached in September 2001. The Democratic contest would choose a candidate for the city's dominant party, and the Republican one generated more interest than usual because billionaire Michael Bloomberg had decided to run.[10]

Punch Line Candidate

Never in New York City history had one Republican mayor succeeded another, so as maneuvering for the 2001 mayor's race began, local politicians anticipated the restoration of City Hall to its natural state as a Democratic enclave.[11]

The New York City Republican Party primary rarely generated drama. The organization was a withered thing that lacked the tensile strength to hold on to a shape. Just 15 percent of Queens voters pledged Republican allegiance, and less than 12 percent in Manhattan, for the most part a shrinking sampling of Upper East Siders. Ten percent of Brooklyn voters and just 8 percent in the Bronx confessed to Republican affiliation. Tiny Staten Island had the largest proportion of Republican stalwarts, over 30 percent of citizens registered to vote. The organization offered candidates little beyond a line on the ballot. Rather than deliver resources to a chosen champion, it expected its nominees to self-nourish their campaigns. Its candidates for mayor often seemed indistinguishable from Democrats on matters that defined national fault lines. New York City Republican candidates for mayor tended to favor gun control and amnesty for undocumented immigrants, gay pride and abortion rights. Bloomberg supported all those positions.[12]

As early as 1999, Herman Badillo made clear that he would run for mayor in 2001, for the first time as a Republican. He ran as a Democrat in 1973, 1977, and 1985 but never won the nomination. In 1981 and 1993, he ended exploratory campaigns early after failing to gain traction. Orphaned at the age of five and raised by an aunt, Badillo had worked his way through high school, college, and law school, earning a certified public accountant's credentials along the way. He went on to become the first man born in Puerto Rico to serve as a city commissioner, to win election as borough president, and to win election to the US Congress. In 1993, he jumped on Giuliani's ticket to run for comptroller as a Republican, but lost. Afterward, he formally switched parties. As longtime observer of city politics Warren Moscow used to say, Republicans had been known to award their party's top spot in municipal elections without a primary to the "first loser who agreed to accept it." It seemed plausible Badillo would be selected, to go down in defeat yet again.[13]

Bloomberg's plans changed things. For years he had been discussing the possibility of a mayoral run with Patti Harris, an elegant and sophisticated woman who oversaw Bloomberg's philanthropic activities and was his closest confidante. She had served in the Koch administration on the city Arts Commission and had connections to government and politics that Bloomberg lacked. As it happened, in 1997 Senator Daniel Moynihan's chief of staff, Kevin Sheekey, reached out to her. The boyish looking political professional was primed for a career change, and as a result of work related to the Senate Finance Committee, he believed that government regulations would become increasingly important for Bloomberg LP. He told Harris the firm should hire him to represent it in Washington, DC. Harris had been discussing the need for a lobbyist with Bloomberg at the time, so she arranged for Sheekey and Bloomberg to meet. The two men "shot the shit" for an hour. "Do you think I should run for mayor of New York City?" Bloomberg asked early on. Sheekey responded, "I don't know anything about running for mayor of New York, but don't ever tell anyone you are not running since it's great promotion." At the end of the session Bloomberg asked, "When can you start, and how much do they pay for these sorts of things?" Sheekey "threw out a number" that twenty-four hours later he concluded was too low since it became his starting salary without negotiation.[14]

In the years that followed, Sheekey and Harris invited a range of academics and policy experts to school Bloomberg in the ways of city government, and they arranged for their boss to meet important elected officials, Democrats and Republicans. "You need to make your friends before you need them," Sheekey told Bloomberg. Douglas Schoen, Senator Moynihan's pollster, went on retainer with Bloomberg, and so did Bill Cunningham, a white-haired, blunt-talking political pro who had worked with Sheekey in Senator Moynihan's office, as well as on the staffs of governors Hugh Carey and Mario Cuomo. Cunningham had also been part of Cuomo's losing 1977 mayoral race and Richard Ravitch's forlorn quest for City Hall in 1989. "You learn a lot on losing campaigns," he concluded.[15]

At his first meeting with Bloomberg, a lunch that Harris and Sheekey joined, Cunningham asked Bloomberg why he wanted to be mayor. The confident man explained how he would bring his management acumen to the job. "That's not what I meant," Cunningham said. "You are wealthy. You have a nice life. You don't understand what guys like me do to guys like you in a campaign. The only thing worse than a billionaire is a landlord, so I'll give you that. But you'll be cut to pieces." At that point Bloomberg began yelling at Cunningham in the restaurant, telling him that guys like him were the problem with politics. At the end of the meal, Bloomberg summarily returned to his office. "That went pretty well," Harris and Sheekey assured Cunningham, to his surprise. The next day, Bloomberg called him and asked that they stay in touch.[16]

Bloomberg gradually ramped up his public speaking schedule, and Sheekey "plant[ed] plenty of stories about Mike thinking of running" for mayor. It was the kind of rumor the press loved to report, even though few political insiders took the idea seriously. Eventually, though, there came a "tipping point." A credible campaign would require a different intensity of activity. In January 2001, Bloomberg acknowledged it was time to decide, and he scheduled a dinner with Sheekey and Harris where he said the three of them would take a vote. Like Cunningham, the two loyal aides feared Bloomberg did not really understand how running for mayor would disrupt his life. They felt obligated to contrast their boss's extraordinary business, philanthropic, and personal circumstances to the downside of politics played ugly. They prepared for a detailed discussion to protect Bloomberg from making a naïve decision he might later regret. At dinner, each ordered a glass of wine. When the waiter served them, Bloomberg raised his and said: "Okay, so we're going to do this thing. I guess we should toast." Sheekey recalled he and Harris "looked at each other with our mouths open," as they realized Bloomberg had decided the matter with a "vote of one."[17]

The idea that Bloomberg might run for mayor created a stir among New York businessmen. Some had encouraged him to enter the arena. They worried that a Democratic restoration would return the city to policies that, in their view, had left it in sorry shape. Others who knew Bloomberg well, and who understood his impatience for getting things done, were unsure it was such a good idea. He did not seem to fit naturally atop a famously sprawling bureaucracy. Nor was it clear that the management skills and style he had developed as the head of a privately held company prepared him for the job. Bloomberg LP held no messy public shareholder meetings, it had no unions requiring tough negotiations, and included no independent board that could impose demands on its CEO the way big city stakeholders often imposed themselves on a mayor. Bloomberg had learned more about municipal affairs than the typical citizen, but he still had nowhere near the level of understanding required to run the city, or even to campaign competently. He talked to groups of employees all the time and had no reservations about public speaking, but he was not good at it. He recited information in a somewhat nasal, uninspiring monotone. He had never run for office of any kind, and he had never contended with the rough-and-tumble of New York City politics. Since consolidation in 1898, New Yorkers had never elected a businessman mayor. Bloomberg was virtually unknown outside the worlds of high finance and fancy philanthropy. To Bloomberg, none of that mattered. His belief that he could manage New York City government better than any of the likely contenders fueled his ambition.[18]

By the time Bloomberg made up his mind, his company had hired Edward Skyler, a sinewy six-foot-four-inch University of Pennsylvania history graduate who put himself through law school at Fordham at night while working in the city parks department press office, and then in City Hall as a deputy press secretary to Mayor Giuliani. He would serve as Bloomberg's campaign press secretary and in time become one of his most important deputies. Jonathan Capehart, a Pulitzer Prize–winning member of the *Daily News* editorial board, had also joined Bloomberg LP. He became responsible for developing the boss's policy positions. Peter Madonia, a streetwise New Yorker who grew up in the Bronx, who had served as chief of staff to Koch deputy mayor Nathaniel Leventhal and as first deputy commissioner in the fire department, among other city jobs, volunteered after Patti Harris reached out to him. A small cluster of former Koch and Giuliani officials also signed on. Just as no one at Bloomberg's company had titles, none of his campaign staff did. They operated like the "Knights of the Round Table," according to Cunningham, who found it odd that Bloomberg "hired political consultants, but then 'resisted' them." Challenged them might be a more precise word. It was the way Bloomberg, labeled "argumentative" by his high school classmates when asked to describe him for the yearbook in a single word, honed his thinking. Cunningham learned he and Bloomberg could disagree about something vehemently and shortly afterward move on to the next topic without residual rancor.[19]

Soon after Bloomberg decided to run, Patti Harris arranged to meet with David Garth, a living legend in New York City politics who had managed successful mayoral campaigns for John Lindsay, Ed Koch, and Rudy Giuliani. Harris and Sheekey sat down with him at a table hidden in an alcove way in the back of Café Des Artistes, the Upper West Side power restaurant of choice for Garth's generation of New Yorker. The political savant told Sheekey and Harris that he had been thinking about the upcoming mayoralty election and none of the Democrats appealed. In his judgment, none were up to the task of managing the city through tough days on the horizon. At the time, a national recession was gathering momentum with discouraging implications for the local economy and city revenue. Garth thought Bloomberg a better choice, and astonishingly, months before 9/11, Sheekey claims Garth was "fearful" New York City "may be subject to an attack." An inauspicious initial meeting between Garth and Bloomberg followed. "This guy was in love with himself," Garth told Joyce Purnick sometime later. "He's a prick, all right? But he has empathy for people—blacks and Jews, you know?" In any event, Garth figured it would be an interesting campaign, and lucrative. He signed on after cutting a "not inconsiderable deal" as Sheekey described it, adding wisdom and a welcome dose of credibility to the political novice's quest. Garth's relationship with Rudy Giuliani would also prove critical later.[20]

Bloomberg had quietly changed his political affiliation from Democrat to Republican late in 2000, shortly before the deadline for official registration that allowed a candidate to enter a primary contest in New York without special approval from party leaders. In one of his earliest interviews after deciding to run, Bloomberg explained his decision to switch. "The majority party always protects the insiders, the party faithful, the loyalists," he said. "Somebody like me as an outsider, would never get through the primary in the case of the

Democrats." Doug Schoen's polling had revealed Bloomberg had no chance to win a Democratic contest against a crop of well-established contenders. The numbers did not reveal a path to City Hall for Bloomberg on the Republican ticket either, but at least it offered the prospect of a general election ballot line. Ironically, the Republican Party's weakness appealed to Bloomberg. The feeble organization attracted less interest than Democratic contests from interest groups that wielded disproportionate power in low-turnout primaries, and that often used their influence to force promises in return for support. Bloomberg wanted to control his campaign himself.[21]

New York City enacted campaign finance laws in the years prior to 2001. The rules allowed for public funds to match all contributions up to $250 on a four to one basis—five to one if an opponent declined to participate in the system, later changed to six to one for up to $175. It capped the amount a candidate could spend in a primary and in a general election campaign, with higher limits for candidates who agreed to the voluntary program if an opponent did not. Bloomberg knew he would have to rely on his vast wealth to run a serious effort, so he declined to participate in the public program. Starved of resources, New York City Republicans often proved amenable to wealthy businessmen prepared to pledge their own money to mount a campaign. But the tactic hardly ensured success. In 1989, cosmetics heir Ronald Lauder spent nearly $14 million, five times more than Rudy Giuliani in the GOP primary, and he had the support of important party leaders in a bid that ended in humiliating defeat. In any event, Republican Governor George Pataki and party leaders welcomed Bloomberg with open pockets. Bloomberg hoped they could pressure Badillo to bow out, but the fiercely independent man would have none of it.[22]

The 2001 New York City Republican primary turned into a contest between two extraordinary self-made men, one a billionaire-businessman-Jewish-Democrat-turned-Republican, the other a veteran-politician-Puerto Rican-Democrat-turned-Republican. Such is the peculiar nature of New York City's GOP. Badillo, long a combatant in the city's political wars, had made his share of enemies and had joined a party that included few Puerto Ricans, his natural political base. He struggled to raise the funds needed to mount a serious campaign. Bloomberg lacked his opponent's baggage, brought with him suitcases filled with his own money, and played better with a party that preferred whites to candidates of color. From the beginning, pundits deemed him the likely winner and his campaign focused on the general election in November, not just the voters eligible for the September primary.[23]

The Republican nomination alone has almost never attracted enough votes to elect a New York mayor. Fiorello La Guardia and John Lindsay had both required additional ballot lines to provide disaffected Democrats a way to vote for them without supporting a Republican Party offensive to many New Yorkers at the national level. The same was true of Rudy Giuliani's first victory when the Liberal Party provided his margin of victory. The Bloomberg team sought a second spot on the ballot, and the Independence Party had one available. Founded to support Ross Perot's 1992 third-party bid for president, a somewhat nihilist group with an abstract commitment to an open political process had secured control of it in New York by 2001. Its leaders adopted the position that elections should be nonpartisan to eliminate the pernicious influence of party politics, an ironic mission for a political party. Bloomberg favored nonpartisan elections, and the idea fit with the rationale for his campaign—that he was an expert manager whose executive skill would serve the city better than party politicians pursuing power for its own sake. So he signed up to support nonpartisan elections and the Independence Party awarded him its nomination. The marriage of convenience came with a dowry. Bloomberg became the party's principal source of money. Inevitably, he had to explain his affiliation with an organization that included Lenora Fulani, a prominent party leader who had made some fiercely anti-Semitic remarks. Bloomberg simply rebuffed questions on the topic. "I'm not an anti-Semite, so why does this matter?" he said, adding that the party, not Fulani, had endorsed him. A few weeks later, after the *New York Times* reported Bloomberg belonged to four private clubs whose members were almost exclusively white, he defused the implication he was racially insensitive by resigning from them.[24]

Management competence was the simple—opponents said simplistic—reason Bloomberg thought himself qualified to be mayor. As the successful chief executive of a major corporation he had the administrative experience to run New York City government effectively. "The fact that I've shown that I do know how to manage something . . . seems to me to be an attribute," he told a reporter. He dismissed the experience of the Democrats running. "Let's get serious here. What skill does the public advocate or the comptroller or the speaker of the city council have to run the city?" he asked a reporter interviewing him. "There's absolutely nothing I can think of that they have done. Maybe they have a better knowledge of details of programs than I do, which is useful, but that's what you have your staff for!" he offered. He was running to be chief executive of the city, not chief operating officer.[25]

Bloomberg also emphasized that his extensive philanthropy demonstrated his love of New York City and his devotion to public service. In 2000, Bloomberg donated over $100 million to more than five hundred charities, two hundred of them for the first time and seventy-nine of those based in New York City. Critics accused him of a calculated effort to convert good will into votes, and of staging publicity events when newspapers showed him serving food to the indigent or helping to paint a school. He found the claims offensive, "total bull" he called them, since he had long been doing those sorts of things. Bloomberg also promoted the idea that he would owe no favors to interest groups because he would finance his own campaign. When asked by a journalist if he would spend as much as $30 million to pursue his quest, he responded the number was too high. "At some point, you start to look obscene," he observed.[26]

Bloomberg, like much of Manhattan's elite, was a social liberal. "You are not going to find much difference between any of the other four and me," he told a journalist, referring to the policy stands of the Democrats seeking the mayor's job. Education would be his top priority. He wanted to be the mayor who turned around the city's schools the way Mayor Giuliani had turned around the seemingly intractable problem of crime in the streets. And like the other candidates, he emphasized the need to improve relations between the police and black and Latino communities while maintaining public safety. His pitch suggested he had the management talent people liked about Rudy Giuliani, without the antagonistic personality.[27]

In June 2001, on the day after candidates filed petitions signed by registered party members to qualify for the primary ballot, working with media consultant Bill Knapp, Bloomberg's team launched biographical television ads to introduce him to the public and to develop name recognition. They featured him as "Mike" rather than the more formal Michael, and emphasized his middle-class roots, describing him as the son of an accountant who as a young man had parked cars to help pay his way through college and whose mother went back to work to pay the bills after his father died. He came to New York and worked hard, started a company, and made himself successful. A vote for Mike Bloomberg, the ads suggested, was a vote for the American Dream. From the beginning, they aired on Spanish-language television stations as well as English ones. To the surprise of local political veterans, on the day the campaign began, Bloomberg was out of state at a daughter's graduation ceremony in Princeton, New Jersey. That caused some reporters to view his approach to running for mayor of New York City as decidedly casual—"a remote control candidacy," that was little more than "a gold-plated pipedream," one called it.[28]

Candidate Bloomberg's relationship with New York's hardened political journalists started off bad and then got worse. Shortly after filing to run, clad in his financial executive suit and tasseled loafers, Bloomberg made his formal announcement for mayor. Then he took the first question from Gabe Pressman, dean of the City Hall press corps. After he answered, Pressman asked a follow-up. Bloomberg demurred telling the man he had been given his turn. Pressman lectured the candidate that at this type of event, custom allowed him one additional question. "Maybe that's how others do it and that's fine," Bloomberg told the man who had been covering New York City mayors for some fifty years by then, "but I'm going to do it my way and give someone else a chance. If we have time at the end, I'll come back to you." Pressman was incensed and his fellow reporters flabbergasted. The journalists proceeded to haze the candidate. His gaffes made it easy.[29]

Early in the campaign, Bloomberg declared sanitation men had a more dangerous job than the police. Long-term health data supported the claim, but the comment earned ridicule. When a Queens woman asked Bloomberg his views on school prayer, he replied that as a young student he had recited the Pledge of Allegiance and the Lord's Prayer every day as a boy and that it served to remind youngsters of "more important things." Strong local views on separation of church and state, particularly among Jews who no doubt wondered why one of their own favored a Christian prayer, made the comment impolitic and caused the candidate to look like an amateur. To press secretary Ed Skyler's politically attuned ear, Bloomberg's gaffes fit the classic definition of a campaign mistake: "When a politician says something that's true." The facts were not wrong, "but why would you go there?" the press secretary found himself wondering on a regular basis. Bloomberg lacked a politician's sensitivity for understanding how his words would be interpreted. "It was tough to keep him on message," Skyler found. When Bloomberg made a sarcastic remark suggesting that, as mayor, he would exile the City Hall press room to Staten Island, in addition to offending the reporters writing about him, he insulted the borough that housed the largest proportion of Republican voters. Unlike other candidates, he declined to release his tax returns. Late in the campaign, he would provide summary documents for journalists to review for a limited time. The materials reported his income as "over $500,000." When asked to justify his position when other candidates provided full disclosure, he blurted out, "It's because they don't make anything."[30]

"Politics, it seems, requires a set of skills, talents, and modes of discipline that everybody doesn't have," Michael Tomasky wrote in *New York* magazine. "Bloomberg shows no sign of acquiring those skills, and unless things change dramatically over the next five months . . . he's cruising toward not only losing, but becoming that thing every public person quietly fears becoming: a punch line." Tomasky's *New York* magazine colleague Michael Wolff had an even higher degree of disdain for the candidate. "I have to believe it is obvious to anyone who has given it any thought—there is no turn of events at all, no leap of logic whatsoever, that could make Michael Bloomberg New York's next mayor." He described the campaign as based on "the illusion of credibility," and dismissed Bloomberg's global media company as "an old-fashioned, single-function, almost idiot-savant-type business," providing data to the bond market. Bloomberg was closer to the Wizard of Oz than a heavyweight executive, Wolff contended. He was a man who should be treated by the press as "a pretender, or flake, or eccentric, or naked emperor," rather than a serious candidate for mayor. Another journalist called Bloomberg a "hologram."[31]

A short time later, on the eve of the Republican primary, Wolff published extensive excerpts from a gag gift Bloomberg's staff had given him on his birthday in 1990 entitled, *The Portable Bloomberg: The Wit and Wisdom of Michael Bloomberg*. It contained thirty-two pages of quotes that the often profane CEO had actually said. Politically incorrect does not begin to describe them. "Make the customer think he's getting laid when he's getting fucked," read the first. It went on from there. It provided Herman Badillo with a platform to call his Republican primary opponent, "a sexist, homophobic, racist individual who in my opinion should never be mayor of New York City." Brooklyn Congressman Anthony Weiner had his staff distribute copies of the document to the press, an action Bloomberg never forgave. In light of future developments, Weiner's apparent distress at crude remarks seems exquisitely hypocritical. His political career would implode as a result of revelations he tweeted photos of himself to young women in a somewhat aroused state, wearing only his underwear. Bloomberg dismissed the document as a bunch of lighthearted "Borscht belt jokes," and claimed disingenuously that he did not remember making them. Early on, when those who knew him warned Bloomberg that his salty language would torpedo his campaign, he dismissed the concern. If Bill Clinton's behavior did not stop the president, Bloomberg believed that his own behavior would not prevent him from becoming mayor.[32]

The vulgar document reminded people of three sexual harassment suits that had been filed against Bloomberg's company. Two had been dismissed and one the firm settled. The last accused Bloomberg personally of contemptible behavior, including saying to a woman on his staff, "Kill it, kill it," when she told him she was pregnant. "Great, number 16," he reputedly grumbled as he walked away, a reference to the number of his company's employees expecting to give birth at the time. He denied under oath that he made the comments, and he had taken a lie detector test to prove it, but the results had been sealed as part of the settlement. The news was old, and Bloomberg's press handlers had re-released it to the media in February 2001 in an effort to inoculate the candidate against the sort of negative campaigning sometimes launched at the last minute in close races. Despite his bawdy language that could make women uncomfortable, Bloomberg had a good record of promoting female staff, and he was never accused of seeking sexual relations with employees, so the issue did not bite.[33]

On September 10, despite the candidate's gaffes and the media sabotage, polls showed Michael Bloomberg with an unassailable lead over Herman Badillo in the Republican primary. He had outspent his adversary by a factor of about fifty times, more than $20 million to less than $400,000 according to reports filed ten days before the scheduled vote. The polls also showed that either of the Democratic front-runners would crush Bloomberg in the general election, as all the experts had predicted. It seemed there was only so far that a billionaire's money and ambition could take him in the rough-and-tumble of New York City politics, without some kind of drastic change.[34]

I'll Win, Unless There Is Some Big, Unexpected Event . . .

By September 2001, the Democratic primary had turned into a spirited contest between public advocate Mark Green and Bronx Borough President Fernando Ferrer. City Council Speaker Peter Vallone and New York City Comptroller Alan Hevesi also competed, but the two lifelong politicians, both white, middle-class homeowners like many of their Queens neighbors, struggled to gain a share of the public mind. During the early months of the campaign, polls showed Mark Green leading everyone by an ample margin. The candidate's youthful fifty-five-year-old face and full head of white hair had been familiar fixtures in New York City electoral politics since he ran for Congress in 1980 and for US Senate in 1986, dreaming of holding the seat once held by his hero, Robert F. Kennedy. He lost both times, became Mayor Dinkins's Commissioner of Consumer Affairs in 1990, and in 1993 he won election to the citywide post of public advocate, the successor role to the inaptly named and discontinued position of city council president. His responsibilities included serving as municipal ombudsman and he stood first in line to succeed an incapacitated mayor. Green won reelection in 1997, and continued to hold the post after losing yet another bid for US Senate in 1998.[35]

Green was one of Mayor Giuliani's most persistent critics, a one-man shadow government representing liberal Democrats while a philosophically antagonistic Republican ruled City Hall. A Harvard-trained lawyer who had worked in Ralph Nader's office protecting consumers between 1970 and 1980, the role of "advocate" came naturally to Green. He would choose the word to describe himself, citing his "Jewish outsider, argumentative DNA," as making him more comfortable challenging established authority than accommodating it. He was articulate and witty, energetic and telegenic. To his liberal Jewish neighbors in Manhattan, Mark Green seemed the perfect Democrat to run for mayor. Yet, almost no news article about him can be found that does not describe him as arrogant or brash, cocky or narcissistic. He was a lifelong Democrat, but he had not risen through the local party structure, either the regular organization or its reform wing with which he was philosophically more compatible. Some of his supporters viewed his independence from the local clubs and interest groups as an appealing trait but, despite his standing as one of the party's top officeholders, to Democratic power brokers Green remained an outsider.[36]

Bronx Borough President Fernando Ferrer followed a different trajectory to political power. He grew up in a Puerto Rican family in a tough South Bronx neighborhood. His mother and grandmother raised him and a sister while working as domestics at the Waldorf Astoria in Manhattan. Known to everyone as Freddy, Ferrer had shined shoes on 149th Street and Southern Boulevard as a boy while attending Catholic schools. He became a member of Aspira New York, an organization dedicated to providing Latino youths with opportunities, and he earned a bachelor's degree in philosophy and government from New York University at its Bronx campus. He worked as a staff assistant in the New York State Assembly and as housing director in the Bronx Borough President's Office before winning a city council seat in 1982. When Borough President Stanley Simon resigned in disgrace in 1987, under indictment for extortion amidst wide-ranging scandals among Bronx Democrats, the borough's council members chose Ferrer to replace him. The Latino political coming-of-age reflected the changed demographics of the borough and the city.[37]

Ferrer's close friend and ally, former New York State assemblyman and Bronx county Democratic Party chairman Roberto Ramirez, through force of personality and iron discipline reconstituted the local organization that had been shattered by scandal. By 2001 it rivaled the Queens organization as the most potent in the city, and it sat solidly in Ferrer's camp. News that Ferrer would run for mayor generated pride and excitement. If he won, he would be the first man of Puerto Rican descent to rule City Hall, and the first mayor from the Bronx since 1932. Yet, many members of New York's political class, even some who thought well of Ferrer, viewed his candidacy as fanciful over-reaching. The media discounted his chances, Democratic fund-raisers viewed him as a long shot, and union leaders sought evidence that Ferrer, who ran briefly in 1997 but then dropped out of the race, could mount a serious, city-wide campaign and go the distance. Others had a more negative view. The Bronx machine the Puerto Ricans inherited from Jewish politicians had been deeply corrupt. Even though no scandals had touched Ferrer or Ramirez, some thought little had changed beyond swapping Spanish for Yiddish.[38]

Ferrer's base was among Latinos and Green's was among Jewish liberals. Both sought to expand their bases by winning support among African Americans, who would cast about a quarter of Democratic primary ballots. Al Sharpton won most of them in the 1997 contest. Yet, as maneuvering took place early in 2001, it became apparent Sharpton would not join the race. "I didn't run to win office in 1997," he contended. "I ran because there was a constituency out there not being represented, and the Democrats needed to take note. I had already made the point, so I didn't need to run for mayor again." He had set his sights by then on a future presidential campaign. No other African American leader entered the mayoral contest, so without one of their own to claim their allegiance, African American voters became the contest's most sought-after prize, and Sharpton's endorsement a crucial step to win it.[39]

Green ran a highly energetic but cautious campaign designed to minimize controversy. He led in the polls and believed that if he kept himself top-of-public mind and made no mistakes, his party and city would anoint him their leader. He believed his background as the one-time editor of the Harvard *Civil Rights-Civil Liberties Law Review* and his long-standing record in favor of equal rights for people of color would win him support among African Americans, and he toughened up his image by securing the support of former police commissioner William Bratton. Ferrer leaned left with a bolder message, declaring himself champion of "the Other New York." For those unhappy with eight years of Rudy Giuliani's policies, he would be the remedy. His campaign sought a multicolored coalition of Latinos, African Americans, and the city's most liberal whites. Throughout the campaign Ferrer would emphasize that his message was meant to resonate broadly with everyone who recognized that a great city needed to provide for all its citizens. His opponents accused him of trying to polarize the city, his message a prescription for dividing New Yorkers, not uniting them.[40]

Early in the campaign, Ferrer trailed Green by as much as the others. By August, a drama-filled public courtship between the Ferrer camp and Reverend Sharpton culminated with Roberto Ramirez and Sharpton spending time together in a Brooklyn detention center. A federal judge had sentenced both men to prison for trespassing after they traveled together to Vieques, Puerto Rico, to protest the US Navy's training exercises dropping live bombs on the island. Every afternoon for nearly forty days, while they exercised in the prison courtyard, Ramirez told Sharpton, "you are the one who can make this happen . . . you can broaden your base . . . as a national leader you need to do this." It was during those talks, "with Roberto in my ear every day," that Sharpton agreed to back Ferrer. By early September he was campaigning with Ferrer in Brooklyn and around the city. With momentum building, Ferrer's team launched its radio and television campaign. Quinnipiac University published polling numbers that showed Ferrer suddenly ahead of Green 28 percent to 26 percent, a stunning change that put the two contenders in a statistical dead heat.[41]

Yet, despite Ferrer's strong momentum, Mark Green's private polls showed him still ahead with results in the mid-to-high thirties compared to the low thirties for Ferrer. Green had received endorsements from the city's most prestigious newspaper, the *New York Times,* and from the *Village Voice,* the tribune of the city's hard-core progressives. Former Mayor David Dinkins endorsed him too. Green doubted he would do well enough to avoid a runoff, but he expected to edge out Ferrer in the primary and to beat him by ten points in the head-to-head contest that would follow. Then he would trounce Michael Bloomberg in the general election to win the keys to City Hall. Mark Green's wife giggled the night before the primary when he reminded her of something he had said in September 1999 when he told her he planned to run for mayor. "I'll win," he declared at the time, "unless there's some big, unexpected event that changes everything . . ."[42]

It's a Brave New Political World

"Everything got blown up on September 11, literally and figuratively," a Democratic strategist told a journalist soon after the World Trade Towers attack. "It's a brave new political world." In particular, he said, "the popular assumption that Bloomberg would be an easy opponent in the general election next month no longer holds."[43]

After 9/11, candidates suspended their activities for a week during which Mayor Giuliani seemed to be everywhere. He appeared on morning television shows and in evening press conferences. He escorted the sister of a fallen firefighter down the aisle at her wedding in place of her brother, and he consoled the widows and families of police killed in the catastrophe. He stood next to foreign leaders who flew to New York to pledge their solidarity and escorted President George W. Bush to the top of the smoking funeral pyre of Ground Zero, where rescue workers afforded the mayor louder applause than the commander-in-chief. Among other things, the destruction of the World Trade Towers transformed Giuliani from a spent, lame-duck politician—recovering from cancer, homeless and sleeping on a friend's sofa in the aftermath of a nasty public divorce—into an international, national and, above all, local hero of near mythic proportion. He had become, "America's Mayor." When he drove down the West Side Highway from his emergency offices to the site of the crime, people lined the road and chanted "Ru-dy, Ru-dy," and then "four more years, four more years." At first the mayor dismissed the chant. He had work to do, no time for politics he said. Besides, the law forbade him a third term in office.[44]

Then the denials softened. The staggering scale of the work to clear the wreckage of steel, glass, concrete, and the corpses and body parts buried within it, caused the man and his staff to reconsider. They lacked time to complete the task they saw as their duty before Giuliani's term expired. Laws could be changed, and in an emergency they could be changed quickly. Governor Pataki contemplated postponing the primaries a second time and explored with key legislators the possibility of repealing term limits. He found little appetite for the notion. A more modest idea took form that appealed to Giuliani: a ninety-day term extension to allow a more measured transition from the experienced incumbent in the arena with a seasoned team, to one of the novitiates waiting in the wings. The September 25 primary would proceed surrounded by uncertainty.[45]

Despite the swirl of events, much of the primary contests' electoral logic remained unchanged. The demographic composition of the city's voters and the tactical lay of the land of endorsements, alliances, and field operations were the same after the attack as before, frozen in place by the crisis that dominated the news and people's minds.

On September 25, New York City's Republicans chose Michael Bloomberg as their nominee for mayor. Not quite seventy-three thousand registered members of the party, just 15 percent of the total, made their way to the polls where two lifelong Democrats turned Republican sought the GOP ballot line. About 10 percent of those cast write-in ballots for Rudy Giuliani. But more than forty-eight thousand voted for Michael Bloomberg, fewer than eighteen thousand five hundred for Herman Badillo. Michael Bloomberg's improbable quest advanced another step by a margin of more than two-and-one-half to one.[46]

Democrats gave Fernando Ferrer just under 36 percent of their votes and Mark Green a little over 31 percent. The two would face each other in a runoff on October 11. The voting pattern revealed the strengths and weaknesses of the two challengers left standing. Ferrer won over 70 percent of the Latino vote, which had surged to 23 percent of the electorate compared to just 8 percent in 1989 when David Dinkins first ran for mayor. African Americans made up 24 percent of the electorate and Ferrer won a majority of them. Among whites, who made up 48 percent of the September 25 Democratic electorate, Ferrer won a paltry 7 percent compared to 40 percent for Green. Among Jewish voters, Ferrer won just 7 percent compared to Green's 46 percent. Importantly, more than half of white New Yorkers voted for neither of the two front runners. They had cast ballots for Vallone or Hevesi.[47]

In these numbers lay the crucial pivot points for the runoff. In a one-on-one contest, Ferrer would win even larger proportions of Latino and black votes, but the vast majority of white voters who had supported Vallone and Hevesi were bound to cast their ballots for Mark Green. A Marist Institute Poll taken in the first few days of October showed Green and Ferrer in a dead heat with 45 percent of the vote each. Ferrer had the more loyal base. But when the pollster asked undecided Democrats which way they leaned, Green led by a margin of 48 percent to 45 percent.[48]

The day after the primary, Giuliani pursued his desire to extend his term. He met first with Michael Bloomberg. In private conversation with his staff, Bloomberg objected to the proposal. He felt ready for the job he sought even under the horrific conditions that had developed and he thought postponing the election would delay the compelling need to guide the city back to normal. Besides, disrupting the democratic process would constitute a terrorist victory of sorts. His pragmatic staff convinced him to take a different approach. The campaign strategy before 9/11 sought to portray Bloomberg as having Giuliani's positive management qualities without the polarizing negatives. His advisors hoped all along that they would secure the unpredictable mayor's endorsement and help convince a key group of voters, traditional Democrats who had opted for a Republican alternative against more liberal opponents in 1993 and 1997, to vote for Bloomberg. The incumbent's post-attack popularity raised the stakes dramatically. If Bloomberg did not offer support when asked, he was unlikely to get it when he needed it.[49]

The political calculation convinced Bloomberg to accept Giuliani's proposal. Publicly, he left the discussion to the mayor. "As you all know, I am not a professional politician," the candidate told the press after his meeting. "I don't deal in leaks and I don't violate confidences." He projected the image of a statesman in a time of crisis. By then, two weeks after the attack, his team had detected a shift in attitudes toward Bloomberg. Worry that the collapse of the towers would take the city's economy down with them was second only to the public's fear for its safety. Maybe a businessman mayor was not such a bad idea, many New Yorkers began to think.[50]

Giuliani met next with Mark Green, a man he detested as much as Green disliked him. The city's two top elected officials would sometimes pass each other in the corridors of City Hall and not so much as say hello. With discussion of an extension swirling in the press, Green issued a statement that said, "Because we are a nation of laws, we all have to obey the laws, and we do not change the law on the eve of an election. It did not happen in the Civil War and it did not happen in World War II and it's not going to happen now." As Giuliani argued in favor of a term extension, Green thought to himself, "Well that's pretty creative and chutzpadick." Giuliani pressed him to respond rapidly since the decision would set in motion a series of time-sensitive events.

By then it was the eve of Yom Kippur, the holiest day in the Jewish calendar when all Jews were required to fast and to spend a day atoning for their sins. Mark Green headed home for a final family meal. In the car, he took a call from Denny Young, a key Giuliani deputy. "A lot of New Yorkers want the mayor to stay," Green remembered Young saying. "You know the mayor is a tough guy," he continued. "You would not want to get him angry in a way that might hurt your campaign." The message was clear.[51]

At home, Green discussed the situation with his family, who argued unanimously in favor of accommodating the mayor's request. According to some accounts, his older brother, the real estate developer, thought it critical that he support the mayor. Giuliani had become the indispensable leader in the public mind, and challenging him would be bad for the city and bad for Green as a candidate seeking the votes of white moderates. Green marveled at how Giuliani had been transformed from "Nixon to Churchill," in the span of a few days. He got hold of a few members of his staff who also supported the extension, but the Yom Kippur observance prevented him from convening the full team that would normally advise on such a decision. Green made what he would call a strategic political decision to agree to the extension against his own gut judgment, and he called Denny Young to tell him.[52]

Next, Giuliani summoned Ferrer to the emergency command center, set up along piers on Manhattan's West Side, for the same conversation. The candidate brought Roberto Ramirez and other staff with him, passing through what Ramirez remembered as an "armada," the location flanked by police boats on the Hudson River and machine-gun wielding guards standing sentinel duty out front. "The whole thing seemed surreal," Ramirez recalled, "like a scene out of one of those futuristic end-of-the-world movies." Ferrer and the mayor met alone. Giuliani made his case, but Ferrer declined to commit. "Mike and Mark have already agreed," Giuliani told Ferrer during the conversation, and the mayor suggested he was being magnanimous. "I will have to convince the people who want me to stay for four more years to let me settle for just three months," he said, implying another term was his for the asking. The mayor's staff had circulated rumors that if all three candidates did not accept the extension, they would launch a full-court press for the repeal of term limits and seek four more years. Giuliani's comment struck Ferrer as a threat. "Yes, and if I agree, I'll have to explain myself to a lot of people who want you to leave now," came the frosty response from the man who had learned how to respond to bullies on Bronx streets.[53]

Back at his campaign headquarters, Ferrer fielded calls from powerful backers including union leaders. "If you don't accept Giuliani's request under these circumstances, your campaign is through," one told him. As *de facto* chairman of Ferrer's campaign committee, Roberto Ramirez asked everyone to leave the room. Then he turned to his longtime friend and said, "Make the case to me in favor of the extension, and then make the case to me against it. Try your hardest to convince me of each side." The candidate laid out the reasons for granting the request in coherent, logical terms. He then spoke against it, his conviction rising, his argument gaining force, pointing his finger at Ramirez and thumping the table. Anyone who was not prepared to take on the emergency was not prepared to be mayor, Ferrer said, and he was ready. "I guess you have your answer," Ramirez said to his friend. In the days that followed, Ferrer's decision to reject the term extension proposal made him look big, and more importantly as events unfolded, Green's made him look small. He had been a persistent critic of Mayor Giuliani and had run a campaign saying it was time to move beyond his policies. He had gone on record declaring an extension a terrible precedent, and then relented in response to political pressure.[54]

When Green's communications director, Joe DePlasco, learned of the decision, he erupted into the only screaming match he ever recalled having with Green. Philosophically, he thought the decision was just wrong, and as a practical matter, "there was this sense that this was going to blow up. It was going to play into the impression that Mark was just about politics even though he had spent his entire career in a different place." Sure enough, the next morning DePlasco's phone began to ring. "The entire liberal elite establishment that supported Mark was like, what the . . . ." Another senior advisor to Green, John Siegal, ran into an Upper West Side neighbor on the street as he emerged from synagogue at the end of Yom Kippur. "How could he do it!" she yelled at him before Siegal had even learned of the decision. The state legislature declined to act, the frenzy over term extensions subsided, and the normal stuff of politics resumed.[55]

Green made another bad mistake. In an early-morning telephone interview, a radio host asked him a version of the question about the three men vying to replace Giuliani that was on everyone's mind. "If you had been mayor during 9/11, how would you have done?" Clad in his bathrobe while sitting in his Upper East Side apartment, Green responded, "I actually believe that if, God forbid, I had been mayor during such a calamity, I would have done as well [as] or even better than Giuliani," he said. "Stupid answer," Green himself recognized after the fact. Later, Bloomberg's team picked up on the artless bravado and ran a series of television ads that quoted Green in his own voice against a black screen, followed by the single, silent word, "Really?" The brag came across as childish at a time when New Yorkers desperately needed a grown-up. It played into the view Green's arrogance would prevent him from governing effectively. Joe DePlasco remembered watching that "commercial over and over and over again." It was then that he began to realize how much money Bloomberg was "dumping into the campaign" and the impact it could have. Bill Cunningham remembered sitting in the pub in the Fitzpatrick Hotel on Lexington Avenue one night enjoying a Guinness when the ad played on the television. An Irish patron sitting within ear shot said to no one in particular, "What an eegit!" Well, Cunningham thought, when a television spot results in a stranger in a bar declaring his client's opponent an idiot, that's an effective ad. Green's comment so offended former Mayor Koch that he endorsed Ferrer in response.[56]

Before long, the formidable teachers' union and the largest municipal employees union, District Council 37, endorsed Ferrer, who already had the support of the hospital workers. In the context of a New York City political horse race, it was the trifecta. When an interviewer asked Koch why Green had not gathered more backing from traditional Democratic sources he responded, "He's obnoxious—that's the heart of it." With support from the three largest municipal unions and from Koch and Sharpton, polar opposites in politics and racial appeal, the Ferrer team could plausibly claim their candidate would unify the city.[57]

Yet, the Ferrer team faced serious challenges in the post 9/11 landscape. The candidate had featured himself as the remedy to Rudy Giuliani, but suddenly the incumbent's popularity had surged to unimagined heights. Ferrer's messages now required nuanced acknowledgement of the mayor's strong leadership, even as the candidate promised to lead the city in a new direction. Moreover, 9/11 had put fear in the air, and Ferrer's bid for a multicolor coalition like the one that elected David Dinkins scared many whites. Dinkins's mishandling of three racially charged events—a boycott by black militants of two Korean grocery stores in Flatbush, a riot between blacks and Lubavitch Jews in Crown Heights, and civil unrest in Washington Heights following a drug bust that left a Dominican drug dealer dead—had caused many to believe the city's only African American mayor refused to enforce the law against people of color. They associated the horrible levels of violence from that period with his rule. It did not matter that the crime wave preceded Dinkins's arrival in City Hall and that it crested and began to fall while he was there. The impression that chaos reigned when he governed persisted, and it fueled fears that a Puerto Rican mayor put in office by a coalition similar to the one that had elected Dinkins would cause the city to descend back into dismal days of deadly, violent crime. The message Ferrer sought to send was that he would direct more city government resources toward those who needed them most to make New York a fairer place. The message many whites heard was that Latinos and blacks were taking over.[58]

Joe DePlasco remembered attending meetings with Mark Green after Ferrer came in first in the primary. "There was a fundamental shift among the elite. Everywhere we went, whether it was real estate people, or financial services people, or publishers, or editorial board rooms, there was this sense

Freddy could win and it would be catastrophic." Safety was the issue, "not just as quality of life, but as the foundation of the economic vitality of the city." The intensity of the "fear" was "palpable" and "somewhat irresponsible" DePlasco thought, since there was nothing in Ferrer's career to warrant it. "People weren't just encouraging us, they were browbeating us to go after Freddy and it was all about linking Freddy to Sharpton to stop him." Green, to his credit according to DePlasco, refused to take the bait. Still, his campaign benefited. Editorial boards that had criticized Green for years suddenly found favor with him. "Before the 2001 Democratic primary, if you found one hundred articles about me in the *New York Post* you would find one hundred negative comments," Green told an interviewer, years later. But against Ferrer, the *Post* endorsed him, and so did the Patrolman's Benevolent Association, which had long viewed the man Giuliani once described as "the anti-police candidate" as their nemesis. The white, liberal outsider who had made his name as a perennial establishment critic suddenly became the favored candidate of the establishment because his opponent was a Puerto Rican.[59]

Four days before the runoff, Mark Green ran what he called "a clean negative" television spot that ended with a narrator asking ominously in the aftermath of 9/11, "Can we afford to take a chance?" Ferrer's team accused Green of invoking coded racism to frighten white voters. Journalists covering the runoff noted that the respectful tone that characterized the Democratic contest through the September 25 vote had turned. Racial crosscurrents, never far from the surface in New York's Democratic Party, were beginning to flood.[60]

On October 11, 2001, two days after American forces began bombing Afghanistan in preparation for invasion, by a margin of 51 percent to 49 percent New York Democrats chose Mark Green. The race-based pattern of the voting was as unmistakable within the Democratic Party as the contests between African American Democrat David Dinkins and white Republican Rudy Giuliani had been in 1989 and 1993. According to a *New York Times/ Edison Media Research* exit poll, white Democrats made up 47 percent of the electorate and Mark Green won 83 percent of them, Ferrer just 17 percent. Among Jewish voters the results were just as lopsided, 87 percent to 13 percent. Among Latinos, who cast 24 percent of ballots, it was almost precisely the reverse. Green won just 16 percent and Ferrer 84 percent. Twenty-three percent of votes came from African Americans. Green won 29 percent and Ferrer 71 percent. City Hall columnist Elizabeth Kolbert summarized the runoff and its impact aptly in the *New Yorker*. Green "won only because whites are still the largest group in the city electorate and they supported him by a margin of five to one . . . . the divisions that have once again been exposed seem likely only to widen."[61]

The Businessman or the Politician?

The Democratic runoff kept Mark Green highly visible for sixteen days. Bloomberg responded with an onslaught of television advertising that did the same for him. The week of September 26 to October 3, his campaign spent an estimated $1.2 million to air 338 advertisements. The two Democratic candidates combined spent just $800,000 and bought fewer spots between them than Bloomberg on his own. Pollsters usually work within a campaign's budget limits. In the case of Bloomberg's quest, none was set. Doug Schoen had the latitude to pursue a much finer level of detail in his telephone surveys than most campaigns can afford. In turn, the team could develop direct mail pieces targeted to small demographic groups with very specific concerns. The unusual degree of intelligence converted the typically blunt instrument of mass mailings into surgical strikes. Bloomberg would spend over $17 million delivering pamphlets and fliers with carefully considered images and messages to individual voters chosen to receive them on the basis of highly refined demographic analysis.[62]

Few New Yorkers found Bloomberg's private sector management experience a convincing rationale to elect him mayor at the start of the campaign. The contention, that big companies and municipal governments were simply two different sorts of large organizations that required skillful management to operate effectively, ignored what for many was a philosophical divide. New York City's liberal political heritage and its strong union tradition meant many of its voters viewed government as the counterforce that protected them against the inherent inequalities of market-based economies and the power of large corporations. But the devastation of 9/11 overwhelmed that outlook. Suddenly, the greatest imperative for government after protecting people from terrorism was to restore the business environment. "Before the attack, Bloomberg's resume didn't fit the reality of the job. Now it resonates much better with voters," Baruch College public affairs professor Doug Muzzio told a reporter. A Zabar's shopper buying Sunday brunch on the Upper West Side agreed. "After September 11 the priorities have changed," she told a reporter conducting an informal survey. "Things like education are still important, but getting the city back on its feet comes first. We have to convince companies to stay here." She planned to vote for the businessman. Before the crisis, the picture Bloomberg's team sought to draw of their candidate could barely be seen against the big city's bright lights. Against the dark backdrop of Ground Zero's ashes, the lines became suddenly clear.[63]

Public surveys taken immediately after the runoff showed Mark Green continuing to hold a substantial lead over Bloomberg. Privately, his experienced pollster, Mark Melman, told Green two things. He had never worked for a candidate as far ahead as Green who lost an election. But he had never worked against a candidate spending more than a million dollars a day who was gaining a point a day in the polls either. "You can't assume anything here," he told the candidate. The truncated general election campaign would unfold between October 12 and November 6, a span of twenty-five days. "We were not ready for the tidal wave that came at us," deputy campaign manager Jeremy Ben-Ami remembered.[64]

Democratic Dysfunction

The night of the runoff, Ferrer conceded to Green privately in a phone call, and then publicly pledged his support. The winner responded with equal grace. Then, everything changed. Stories surfaced that in the days just before the vote, the classic timing for negative campaign techniques, Green supporters in Brooklyn mounted automated telephone calls in Jewish districts highly hostile to Al Sharpton. The messages urged Democrats to vote for Mark Green to "stop Al Sharpton," and that "Sharpton cannot be given the keys to the city," so "please go to the polls tomorrow and vote against Fernando Ferrer and Al Sharpton." On the streets and outside the polls, Brooklyn political operatives distributed copies of highly offensive cartoons printed in the *New York Post* showing a fat-lipped Ferrer kissing the ass of a comically obese Al Sharpton and portraying the candidate as a puppet of the controversial preacher with a similar message about the need to stop them both from winning City Hall. The television spot, "Can we afford to take a chance?" now seemed part of a pattern.[65]

Green declared he had nothing to do with the offensive material distributed in Brooklyn, and denounced it as "reprehensible." He vowed he would remove from his campaign anyone involved and that they would play no role in his administration if the city elected him mayor. Years later, one senior member of Green's team remembered finding the episode incomprehensible. The fliers violated some of Mark Green's most fundamental beliefs, and as a tactic, it was "incredibly stupid. The *Post* had already published that stuff, it was out there, so why should we do it? Wasn't it obvious that it would backfire?"[66]

The unity rally that typically occurred the day after a primary did not happen, and Green's phone calls to Ferrer went unreturned for a time. After a week, and preliminary contact between Green and some of Ferrer's advisors, the losing candidate's office called Green to an evening meeting at his campaign headquarters. Ferrer was there along with Sharpton, Ramirez, and other staff. Mark Green was clad incongruously in white tie replete with tails since he had been at the annual Al Smith Catholic charity dinner. Richard Schrader, his campaign manager, accompanied him. The meeting rapidly turned tense. Green repeated his denunciations of the scurrilous literature that so offended the Ferrer team, and denied knowing anything about it until reports surfaced the day after the election. His campaign manager also denied any involvement in the activity. They defended the "Can we afford to take a chance?" ad as fair game in the context of a political contest in which government management experience had suddenly become crucial and denied any racist intent. Sharpton accused the two men in no uncertain terms of being racist liars. "We don't have to sit here and listen to this," Green and Schrader said. "No you don't," Sharpton replied. "We don't have to meet at all. You are asking for our support. If you don't want it you can leave anytime." Schrader stormed out leaving Green to rescue his campaign on his own. He hammered repeatedly on the point that nothing that happened in the runoff could justify actions that would leave Republican leadership in City Hall for the next four to eight years. Ferrer reluctantly agreed, and suggested another meeting the next morning with a broader group of his supporters for Green to address them and to commit to their common cause to restore City Hall to Democratic rule.[67]

The next day's meeting included former Mayor Dinkins, Green's most prominent African American supporter, and a broader group of black and Latino leaders from both camps. Toward the end of the caucus, Green told the people in the room that he did not view his relationship with them as a one-time transaction meant to elect him, but rather as a long-term commitment to work together for the good of the city. His exact words are a matter of bitter contention. According to a number of people, he told the political professionals assembled: "I don't need you to win. I need you to govern." The comment, as he heard it, infuriated Al Sharpton. It enraged Roberto Ramirez, who heard an arrogant white man dismissing the importance of the political organization dominated by Latinos and blacks that Ramirez had sweated for years to build. He heard that any respect granted to him and those counting on him was due to the magnanimous grace of the winner, and not because the Bronx organization had earned it and deserved its full share of political power. In his view, Green had stolen the runoff with nasty tactics that reduced his friend Fernando Ferrer to a racist caricature of the leader on whose proud shoulders rested the hopes of the city's Latinos and other citizens of color. If Mark Green were allowed to do that, it would grant permission for another candidate to do it again the next time. Ramirez, who had come to the Bronx from Puerto Rico as a teenager and worked as a janitor, who had put himself through college and law school, who had won election to the New York State Assembly and risen to become one of the most powerful politicians in New York City, felt disrespected and he would not tolerate it. Nor would Al Sharpton, who found Mark Green's arrogance "astonishing."[68]

Despite lingering hostility, Ferrer endorsed Green. He joined a Democratic unity rally that included labor leaders, the state's two Democratic US senators, dozens of elected officials and party leaders, where he said, "As between Mark Green and Mike Bloomberg, there is absolutely no comparison in my view. For Mark, the work of government is not a hobby . . . [it] is not something you do when you get bored—it's the job of his life." And Ferrer campaigned with Green in Brooklyn and elsewhere.[69]

Rudy to the Rescue

Green positioned himself as the proven commodity, a man whose public sector experience would allow him to seize the reins of power with confidence at a time when the city desperately needed its government to perform well. "Now more than ever, New York needs the experience that money can't buy," he said the night he won the runoff. At various points, campaign financing documents revealed Bloomberg's team spent $30 million, then $40 million, and then $50 million. Green accused his opponent of trying to buy City Hall and subverting democracy. Polls, press reports, and the Green campaign's own focus groups suggested the public did not particularly care. They were thinking about restoring the economy, fixing the schools, and above all public safety. Green claimed Bloomberg had no credentials in this last area that had taken on fundamental importance after 9/11. He featured his close ties to Bill Bratton to boost his standing on the topic, while simultaneously campaigning with David Dinkins and projecting respect for minority concerns about overly aggressive police practices. Bloomberg responded by attracting a former NYPD commissioner of his own to point out Green had no more security expertise than he did. Ray Kelly, a veteran of some thirty years on the force who had served as police commissioner under Mayor Dinkins, and in federal and private security roles afterward, defended Bloomberg as a competent manager who would know how to work with an experienced police professional. Bill Cunningham called the duel between the two chiefs the political equivalent of the "Ali-Frazier fight."[70]

Three of the city's biggest unions—the teachers, the hospital workers, and District Council 37—all endorsed Green, but he was a second choice, or in some cases, third. The members lacked enthusiasm, as did hospital workers union chief Dennis Rivera, who was deeply offended by the racist undertones he detected in the Green campaign. National Democrats, Bill Clinton, Teddy Kennedy, and others, announced their support for their party's candidate. But some prominent local Democrats never would come around, even after the unity rally. Former Mayor Koch and former Governor Hugh Carey both endorsed Bloomberg. At first, Green reverted to the front-runner strategy he had followed in the early days of the Democratic primary. He led Bloomberg and expected the numbers to stabilize with him in the lead if he focused on the topics that played to his strength. He redeployed key campaign staff to begin preparing transition papers, taking it for granted that he would be the city's next mayor. He avoided responding to comments Bloomberg directed to him and he downplayed the need for debates. Since Green had accepted public financing, he was obligated to participate in at least one, and to avoid criticism from editorial boards for limiting the public's ability to judge the candidates in direct comparison to each other, he agreed to a second.[71]

It was during one of the debates that Green remembered saying to himself of Bloomberg, "This guy is doing better than he should." Green was an experienced debater and expected to best his opponent. Bloomberg never did develop a feel for retail campaigning on city streets, but by the time of the debates, he had improved from "awful to competent" as a media candidate, in the judgment of his advisors. Bill Cunningham likened Bloomberg's journey to riding a bike. "You start out wobbly, but if you do it again and again, day after day, eventually you learn. By September Mike could ride the bike." Even prior to the canceled September 11 primary, candidate Bloomberg had found the voice he lacked early in the contest and came across as focused, clear, and confident in interviews. He was trying hard to address the most important question for his campaign: did the public believe that his success as a businessman was relevant to the job he sought? Did he have what it takes to be mayor of New York? One man above all others had the capacity to answer that question for New Yorkers: Rudy Giuliani.[72]

By mid-October Bloomberg's standing had improved substantially. Back in June, he trailed Mark Green by 40 points in polls. As the last few weeks closed in on the candidates, 35 percent or so of respondents said they would choose Bloomberg, and roughly 50 percent supported Green. But then Bloomberg's numbers stopped improving. He was stuck way shy of victory and his well-known temper flared in staff meetings. "When do our numbers move?" he asked time and again. His experienced team pointed out that although his numbers had reached a plateau, Green's standing continued to diminish. In the final days of the campaign, they asserted, a wave of undecided voters would break in Bloomberg's favor. Yet, no one dared believe they were ahead or on a path to victory. They desperately needed Mayor Giuliani's support.[73]

Before and after the short period when the desire to hold on to his office at City Hall bewitched him, managing the city's response to crisis absorbed Giuliani. It had taken up all his time, all his physical and emotional energy. He stayed out of the candidates' politicking that came across as petty in comparison to the tasks before the mayor, including a disheartening and seemingly endless series of funerals of firefighters, police, and others. Giuliani had no special relationship with Bloomberg, and as mayor he wanted to avoid anything that would cast a partisan tone to his efforts to lead a city still shaking from attack.

Concern for his reputation also made Giuliani reluctant to involve himself in the campaign. The mayor had endorsed Mario Cuomo for governor in 1994, who went on to lose against George Pataki, and over the years he had endorsed a number of local Republicans for state senate seats who lost. Endorsing losers diminished Giuliani's political standing, and he expected Bloomberg to lose, so the prospect held little appeal. "Rudy was always looking to see that we had a real campaign, that we were serious," Bill Cunningham remembered. The Bloomberg team's money, mail, and TV ads eventually had an impact. David Garth convinced Giuliani to allow him to film endorsement commercials, but with strict instructions they could not be used until Giuliani finally made up his mind.[74]

It was one thing for the man newly anointed "America's Mayor" to stay above the fray of local politics and to avoid criticizing Mark Green. It was another not to endorse his own party's candidate. By late October, he had not, and there came a moment when not endorsing Bloomberg began to be more of an issue than backing him. "If he doesn't," one aide said, "he'll look like petulant Rudy again." With constant prodding from Garth, Giuliani finally agreed, showing up seventy-five minutes late on the steps of City Hall on October 27, 2001 for a brief announcement during which the normally hard-charging mayor spoke so quietly reporters had to strain to hear him. His staff made clear he would not spend much time on the campaign trail.[75]

The very next day, with its unlimited budget, the Bloomberg team filled the airways with the Giuliani endorsement ads Garth had already filmed. The spots would continue right up until Election Day itself. Bloomberg ran a total of 6,500 television commercials. His team bought so much television time commercial rates rose, meaning Green could afford only 2,500 ads of his own. The *Daily News* described the thrust of Bloomberg's television campaign and direct mail pieces that complemented it as "a perfectly integrated message: Rudy and Mike—Mike as the logical extension of Rudy." Bloomberg also unleashed a torrent of negative ads warning that Mark Green fought against Rudy Giuliani's policies "every step of the way," and if elected, "he'll tear apart Mayor Giuliani's City Hall." The end of the campaign was, "a running gunfight," in Bill Cunningham's words.[76]

Some weeks before, Mark Green's team had developed a television spot meant to damage Bloomberg on the issue of character. It featured the accusation from years earlier by an employee who said that when she told Bloomberg she was pregnant, he had responded, "Kill it, kill it." The ad went on to declare the man unfit to serve as mayor. When Green first saw it, he deemed it offensive and inappropriate. His twenty-two-year-old daughter serving as his volunteer coordinator saw it and called it horrible. He told his staff he would not use it.

Then the race narrowed. A Marist Institute poll released November 2, 2001 showed Green's lead over Bloomberg had fallen to 4 percent or less, and that his backers were less committed than Bloomberg's. By November 5, the two were tied. One of Green's own polls showed him losing. "Green has to do something strong, decisive and critical to turn the tide," a pollster told a reporter when analyzing the trend. In an act of desperation, Green "reached for a sledge hammer," in the words of one adviser, and released the harsh ad on the last day before the election. Later he would regret the decision, and he would apologize to Bloomberg for it. Some senior members of Green's team thought the decision to air the ad had been a horrible mistake, and that its nastiness may even have driven voters away from their candidate.[77]

Meanwhile, on November 2, the *Daily News* revealed that the ugly politicking against Ferrer in Brooklyn had more connections to the Green campaign than anyone had acknowledged, more than Green himself had known. Two members of the "Green for Mayor" team had attended a meeting in Brooklyn where local political workers had discussed how to exploit Sharpton's endorsement of Ferrer in white neighborhoods. An infuriated Ferrer called Green and insisted that he fire the people involved. Green refused. "I couldn't do it," he would say. The men denied they had conspired with the people who proposed the tactic, and they claimed that when the topic came up they told the people who suggested it that Mark Green would never support the plan and did not want to run that type of campaign. To fire them under those circumstances and damage their reputations struck Green as a horrible violation of due process. Eventually it would surface that a nineteen-year-old volunteer acting on instructions from a mid-level staffer, who joined Green's campaign from another politician's office after the first round of the primary, had prepared the offensive cartoons.[78]

Ferrer found the posture maddening. The *Daily News* report made clear that two members of Green's team met with local political operatives and discussed race-based tactics. The resources for the blatantly racist activities against Ferrer, including distribution of the vulgar *New York Post* cartoons, had come from Green's campaign. Ferrer insisted someone be held accountable. Green heard Ferrer's anger loud and clear, and asked former President Bill Clinton to intercede and make peace. Clinton called Ferrer, but to no avail. The incensed borough president declined to attend a unity dinner the weekend before the election, his absence loudly noted by the city press corps.[79]

The matter had a tragicomic coda. Hollywood producer Harvey Weinstein was involved in sponsoring the unity dinner. His role was largely ceremonial, but the entertainment mogul took himself seriously and decided to try to heal the Democratic Party's wounds. Along with publicist Ken Sunshine, he invited Sharpton and Ramirez to a private hotel room in midtown Manhattan, and he asked Bill Clinton to come and broker peace between Ferrer and Mark Green, who Weinstein and Sunshine were trying to round up. Jeremy Ben-Ami, fielding Weinstein's calls for the Green campaign, felt like a character in a Tom Wolfe novel. "We had the Hollywood mogul, the black preacher, the former president of the United States, the political boss, and the two candidates, and it was all supposed to come together the last night of the campaign," he recalled incredulously. "I needed a drink." Green declined to participate and the summit meeting never happened.[80]

Mark Green's reaction to the Brooklyn cartoon flier episode contrasts sharply with the way the Bloomberg campaign responded to a similar incident that occurred on Staten Island. That borough's Republican chairperson produced pamphlets linking former Mayor Dinkins to Mark Green in a way meant to frighten white voters from casting ballots for the Democrat. When Bloomberg's team learned of it, they dispatched a senior advisor to fire the coordinator of their campaign's Staten Island field effort. "You may have had nothing to do with it," a Bloomberg advisor told the person, "but it happened on your watch so you are responsible." Bloomberg's staff ordered the local Republican leaders to withdraw the material from distribution and to destroy it, and not to engage in public criticisms of the decision or "we would have to determine how to deal with that." Bloomberg slammed a table in anger when he heard what happened. He felt personally insulted, and he called David Dinkins the next morning to apologize. And Green's decision to air the "Kill it, kill it," ad contrasted with another decision made by the Bloomberg team. Late in October five workers died when their scaffolding collapsed while they worked to repair construction flaws that had created a code violation in a building owned by Mark Green's brother Stephen. The Democrat feared Bloomberg's team would seek to use the tragedy for political gain. It never did.[81]

Don't Worry Mom, You Are Not Going to Be Embarrassed

On Election Day, Bloomberg's team thought their candidate still trailed by about 4 percent. Early exit polls showed Green ahead, and the always confident candidate called one of his deputies to discuss transition plans. Doug Schoen analyzed the early returns district by district, and concluded Green's margins in neighborhoods favorable to him were small. That meant Bloomberg would win when districts he expected to win reported results later in the day. Then technical problems called into question the accuracy of the exit polls, and confidence in them diminished. The Bloomberg team initiated a final round of get-out-the-vote calls in working-class districts where they polled well.[82]

Early in the evening, Michael Bloomberg telephoned his ninety-two-year-old mother and reported he did not expect to win, but the gap would be modest.

"Don't worry," he told her, "you are not going to be embarrassed." Ed Skyler was nearby at BB King's Blues Club prepping the room where Bloomberg would appear after the results were announced. He sensed that momentum had been with Bloomberg during the last weeks of the campaign, but feared "the clock [had] run out" before the team had secured victory. Then a co-worker reported from the candidate's suite that the vote had narrowed to a dead heat. "Which precincts have reported?" he asked. Everywhere but Staten Island came the reply. "Holy cow," Skyler thought to himself, "we're going to win."[83]

On Tuesday, November 6, 2001, nearly 1.5 million New Yorkers cast ballots for mayor. Michael Bloomberg won 744,757 votes and Mark Green 709,268 making Bloomberg the winner by a margin of 50.7 percent to 48.3 percent. The 35,000 votes that separated the two made it the closest election for mayor since consolidation of New York City into its modern form over one hundred years earlier. Green called Bloomberg to concede. "Well Mike," the defeated candidate told the man who vanquished him, "you're the Al Kaline of politics, winning the batting crown your rookie season." Euphoria broke out in Bloomberg's election night hotel suite. Rudy Giuliani, seated on a couch in front of the television when the news was broadcast, lifted his feet off the ground and pumped both fists in front of him with spontaneous emotion. Kevin Sheekey was stunned. "I went into this thinking this was going to be an honorable defeat, an honorable campaign, a good campaign . . . but winning was not something we ever talked a lot about or thought a lot about," he remembered. When the stunning victory was announced, he turned to David Garth and gushed: "Oh my God, we won." All throughout the campaign, Garth told Sheekey it was possible, but on election night he confessed, "I never actually believed it."[84]

In so close an election, every decision, every factor, every mistake, and every tactic can be said to have had an impact. "Honest to God, Mike Bloomberg won an election that was so close that if the wind had blown west to east instead of east to west on a particular day, I don't know how it would have changed things," was the way Sheekey characterized the narrowness of the win. Yet, two elements of the voting pattern stand out: almost all of the ballots cast by New Yorkers describing themselves as political independents went to Bloomberg, and the proportion of Latino ballots cast for the Republican candidate was exceptionally high. Rudy Giuliani's endorsement had an enormous impact on the first. Racial friction among Democrats caused the second.[85]

In response to a question in an Edison Media Research/Associated Press exit poll, 27 percent of respondents said Rudy Giuliani's support had made them more likely to vote for Michael Bloomberg. Rarely has a political endorsement had such an impact. Rudy Giuliani's elevation to hero status in the midst of the 2001 mayoral election converted what would have been an announcement of support like any other into an outcome-changing event. A post-election *New York Times* editorial called Bloomberg's "identification with Mr. Giuliani his strongest weapon." David Garth told the *New York Post*, "I think we won because of Rudy Giuliani." The triumphant candidate received more than 90 percent of the votes of people who described themselves in exit polls as independent. They made up more than a third of all the votes he won. Bloomberg of course had managed his campaign to appeal to those voters, but it was Giuliani's validation of him as fit to be mayor that sealed the deal.[86]

Bloomberg won as many Latino votes as Green, more according to some estimates. In 1989 David Dinkins won nearly 70 percent of Latino ballots and in 1993 just over 60 percent. During her discouragingly ineffective effort as the Democratic nominee against Rudy Giuliani in 1997, Ruth Messinger won 57 percent of the group's votes. Green won just 48 percent. Had he won the same proportion of Latino votes as Messinger did, he would have been elected mayor. It did not happen by chance. "The Bronx county Democratic headquarters was padlocked on election day. Whoever heard of such a thing?" one Bloomberg operative marveled. The metaphor was figurative, of course. Roberto Ramirez had opened the party office at 6:00 a.m., but he had sent out instructions: "brazos callados"—an order to his troops to stand down on political pay day when normally they pulled Democratic voters to the polls. "It was the logical consequence of the way Mark Green ran his campaign," the Latino boss declared. As far as he was concerned, Green had no one to blame but himself. Green viewed the "sit-down" strike by the city's Latino political leaders as "unprecedented," and "outrageous," an act of self-destructive defiance born of "personal petulance" that locked Democrats out of City Hall for more than another decade as things would turn out, on top of eight years of Republican rule the city had already experienced. Green could not fully fathom his predicament. "When you are attacked as obnoxious by Ed Koch, as racial by Al Sharpton, and egotistical by an opponent who's written a book called *Bloomberg by Bloomberg*, something is wrong," he lamented.[87]

Bloomberg won 59 percent of white voters overall, Green 39 percent. Each candidate won 49 percent of the Jewish vote. Jews typically vote for the Democrat in New York, and with greater enthusiasm when the Democratic candidate is Jewish. But in 2001, both the Democratic and Republican candidates were Jews who described themselves as liberal Democrats. Bloomberg had even declared himself a liberal in response to a reporter's question at a news conference when George Pataki endorsed him, to the Republican governor's "evident bewilderment." Several members of Green's team, and Al Sharpton as well, believed Green's decision to support Giuliani's term extension proposal damaged the candidate badly with the city's Jewish liberals.[88]

Bloomberg captured 22 percent of black ballots, Green three quarters of them. Al Sharpton sat out the election, never endorsing either candidate, and he characterized the African American vote for Bloomberg as higher than ordinary for a Republican. Not by much. By way of comparison, four years before, Giuliani won 20 percent of black votes against Ruth Messinger. Only when Giuliani ran against David Dinkins did his African American support drop below double digits. Had the percent of black voters casting ballots for Bloomberg fallen to the same level as Giuliani's four years earlier, Bloomberg still would have won the close race.[89]

Green managed to survive his run through his party's racial minefield and win its nomination, but just barely, and he left that battleground severely wounded as he headed for general election combat against a highly resourceful foe. Bill Cunningham summed up the primary tersely. "Mark Green's campaign broke on a rock named Freddy Ferrer. He mishandled almost every interaction between the two. He did everything he could to beat himself except move out of the state." Another Green supporter concluded, "had Mark Green won it would have been chaos. The campaign had burned every bridge. It would have been a catastrophe trying to govern." Al Sharpton saw it the same way. Had Green been elected, "We'd a 'bin fightin'," he concluded. Instead, he ended up talking, to Mayor Bloomberg.[90]

The Democratic Party race riot and Rudy Giuliani's crisis-intensified endorsement were critical for Bloomberg's victory. So was his vast wealth that allowed him to spend almost $74 million, four and half times the $16.6 million Green spent, after all the dollars were counted. Bloomberg's hard-earned business success provided a rationale for his campaign that resonated after the 9/11 attack, and his history of philanthropy demonstrated a commitment to the public good that gave him credibility as a candidate. His managerial skill allowed him to assemble a highly capable political team whose members worked together successfully and fully exploited his opponents' mistakes. The team broke new ground with its polling techniques, direct mail campaign, and television advertising strategy. Bloomberg committed no rookie error so egregious as to destroy his chances, and he deflected a number of potentially campaign-destroying attacks. "Three things usually separate the winners from the losers over the long term," Bloomberg once said, "time invested, interpersonal skills, and plain old-fashioned luck." And so it was that Michael Bloomberg won his bid to become mayor of New York City.[91]

At 4:00 a.m. on election night, Kevin Sheekey dropped the concession speech he had drafted for Bloomberg onto the bed in his hotel room. "That's the speech you wanted Mike to give," he said to his wife. On September 18 she had given birth to twins. Sheekey had promised her Bloomberg would lose, and he would take a month off to be with his family. His phone rang at 6:30 a.m. "We have a problem," Shea Fink, the campaign team's scheduler told him when he answered. "Mike is on his way to New Utrecht Avenue in Brooklyn. Chris Coffey is there now," she said referring to a young advance man, "and he says he has never seen so much press. All the morning shows are there. Skyler won't answer his phone and I don't know what to tell Chris." After being up for the better part of forty-eight hours, campaign press secretary Ed Skyler had passed out on his bed in exhaustion on election night, and his cell phone battery had died.[92]

Bloomberg was making good on a promise. Some weeks before he had been shaking hands at a Brooklyn subway stop while his team handed out fliers. A passer-by struck up a cordial conversation with him, but at the end of it declared: "You politicians are all the same. You come out here looking for our votes, but you never come back after the election." Bloomberg vowed to return, win or lose. The morning after his stunning victory, the event attracted more attention than any during the contest itself. Producers from a half dozen television programs asked for interviews. Coffey selected the *Today Show* since Katie Couric called herself, and NY 1, the local cable channel, for one-on-one attention. The rest had to settle for a scrum. A huge contingent of police, including senior brass, was there as well. The Brooklyn man who had challenged Bloomberg approached, but a policeman told him to move along. "He's here to see *me*," the man insisted incredulously. "Yeah, sure," the cop said, "He's here to see all of us. Move along." People from Brooklyn often express themselves in clear language. The level of communication rose and risked becoming a confrontation. A supervisor checked with Coffey, just to be sure, who recognized the man and ushered him in front of the cameras. "I love this guy," Anthony Santamaria gushed, hugging the billionaire. "This guy is different. He keeps his promises." Soon New Yorkers would find out if Tony from Brooklyn was right.[93]

Chapter Three
Money Manager

"Welcome to 'the Other New York,'" was how Fernando Ferrer greeted Michael Bloomberg as they sat down to a staged breakfast at a diner near the Bronx borough president's office the morning after the election. Bloomberg traveled directly there after keeping his campaign promise in Brooklyn. "You'd have beat me," he said to Ferrer, as newspaper photographers snapped pictures. That night, the same leadership instincts that led him to demonstrate his respect for the city's Latinos took him to a dinner of 100 Black Men, a group of the city's most successful African Americans, where Bloomberg made a point of acknowledging Reverend Sharpton. His political advisors had fretted over the event, debating how Bloomberg should handle the encounter. "I'll just shake his hand and that will be that," the mayor-elect replied. A few weeks after taking office, Bloomberg accepted Sharpton's invitation to address his National Action Network on Martin Luther King Day, where the overwhelmingly African American audience greeted him with warm applause.[1]

Two days after his victory, Bloomberg paid courtesy visits to Randi Weingarten, leader of the teachers union, and to Lee Saunders, trustee of DC 37, in their offices. "Don't underestimate this," Saunders told reporters, as he stood next to Bloomberg, who smiled for cameras after donning a green union T-shirt the labor boss gave him. "This is an extremely important signal the mayor-elect is sending us," he said of Bloomberg's visit. Weingarten, in an oblique reference to Giuliani's confrontational style, called it a "real breath of fresh air" that the new boss planned to work with, not against, the people who staffed city agencies and its schools. The day after those meetings, Bloomberg met with hospital workers union chief Dennis Rivera who was even more direct about the contrast between the last mayor and Bloomberg. "We're very gratified he's coming," Rivera said. "In eight years, Mayor Giuliani has never been here." A large room full of SEIU 1199 members cheered Bloomberg when he arrived. All three labor organizations had endorsed Mark Green. To the one-time Salomon Brothers banker, that was as irrelevant as a day-old trade. As the new boss of the municipal government he wanted an open dialogue with the leaders who represented the city's workers, and he hoped to earn their cooperation on tough management decisions to come. That would prove hard.[2]

The day after the election, Bloomberg announced that to avoid the appearance of a conflict, the media company he ran would forgo a $14 million tax concession the city had agreed to as an inducement to keep it in New York at a time when it was moving its headquarters. Before long he placed his ownership stake in Bloomberg LP in a blind trust. The action signaled that the new mayor had stepped away from managing the company he owned to focus on city matters, "even if, in reality, it was closer to a half-step," *New York Times* financial markets reporter Andrew Ross Sorkin would conclude sometime later. Bloomberg kept tabs on the company, and he would purchase Merrill Lynch's ownership stake in 2008, boosting his share of control beyond 90 percent.[3]

In the immediate aftermath of his election, observers hoped that the chief executive of a media empire would find more common ground with City Hall reporters than other mayors. It was not to be. Bloomberg displayed the same impatience with the press as mayor-elect and mayor that he had shown as a candidate. It particularly irked the City Hall press core that the newly elected public official they relied on to provide them with something to write about daily insisted on keeping some elements of his life private, including his whereabouts on weekends when he might jet off for a few rounds of golf in Bermuda, one of a dozen or so places where he owned a home. Journalists tried to turn his unwillingness to share his personal itinerary with them into a story by suggesting he needed to be on site in case of an emergency. Bloomberg dismissed the complaints. "If [my staff] have a question I should always be accessible 24 hours a day seven days a week. And I am," he said. He paid no attention when the *New York Post* printed a picture of him on a milk carton and declared him a missing person one day, and he continued to live in his elegant private town house on East 79th Street, using the mayor's official residence, Gracie Mansion, for occasional public events.[4]

The Mayor's Side of the Building

Like any newly elected mayor, Bloomberg had to form a government. To reassure a city still reeling from the 9/11 attacks, within a week after his victory he named Ray Kelly police commissioner. A short while later, Bloomberg named Patricia Harris Deputy Mayor for Administration. She would oversee the departments of Cultural Affairs, and Parks and Recreation, as well as public events in general. Insiders understood Harris would have influence beyond any formal rank. Unlike some men of his generation, Bloomberg, who had grown up in a household with a strong mother trained in business and accounting, was comfortable delegating power to capable women. The same day Bloomberg appointed Harris, he named Marc Shaw Deputy Mayor for Operations and Dennis Walcott Deputy Mayor for Policy.[5]

Shaw was an experienced city and state government official whose soft-spoken manner and easy smile belied the depth and breadth of his knowledge. He was the number two executive at the Metropolitan Transportation Authority when Bloomberg tapped him, and he had served as Mayor Giuliani's budget director for a time. Early in his career, he had been the city council finance director and also an analyst and assistant director for the New York State Senate Finance Committee. Peter Madonia, who Bloomberg named as chief of staff, recommended him. Twenty minutes into an interview where he met Shaw for the first time, Bloomberg put a short note on the candidate's resume and passed it to his transition manager, Nathaniel Leventhal. Later, Shaw learned what it said: "Hire this guy." Shaw accepted a substantial pay cut to take the job. "For whatever reason, I was a government service junkie. I was being offered Deputy Mayor of New York City. How could I turn it down?" he said of his decision. Shaw's skill as a budget "wizard," as one journalist termed it, would help the new mayor contend with the city's complex finances. Most city departments would report to Shaw, who coordinated oversight of day-to-day operations closely with Madonia.[6]

Walcott was a slimly built African American well versed in community-government relations. He was head of the New York Urban League, and had served on police review commissions and the Board of Education. He and Bloomberg had crossed paths several times, but they did not know each other well. At a 2001 Urban League forum to provide mayoral candidates a chance to present their ideas for helping the city's youth, Bloomberg asked Walcott about a pin he wore. It featured an equal sign set atop a Big Apple to symbolize fair access to opportunity for everyone in New York City, the Urban League's mission. "I like that," Bloomberg said. He reached to Walcott's lapel, removed the pin and placed it on his own jacket. "I'll wear this as long as I am a candidate," he said, "and if I win, I'll wear it as long as I'm mayor of the City of New York." He kept his promise. After Bloomberg won, Walcott ended up on the mayor's transition committee, which in theory rendered him ineligible for a role in the administration. But a back channel call invited him to an interview with Bloomberg, Harris, and Leventhal. A day or so afterward, while walking down Eighth Avenue at 35th Street, his phone rang. "Walcott," a voice barked with staccato diction. "Bloomberg here. Do you want to be my deputy mayor?" After talking to his wife, Walcott accepted. Bloomberg described Walcott as the right person "to make sure we understand who we are here to serve," when he announced the decision.[7]

By including a woman and a black in his first appointments, Bloomberg got high marks for inclusiveness. And by selecting the highly respected Harris, along with an experienced government professional, and a well-regarded community leader, neither of whom had much history with the mayor-elect, he made it clear merit would be the guiding principle of his hiring decisions. To the consternation of Republican loyalists hoping for jobs, all three were registered Democrats, punctuating how little party affiliation meant in Bloomberg's City Hall. Bill Cunningham became director of communications, Ed Skyler became press secretary, and the mayor named Kevin Sheekey a special advisor. Carol Robles-Roman, the director of public affairs for the state court system and an NYU Law School classmate of Roberto Ramirez, became deputy mayor for legal affairs, adding the diversity of a Latina to his senior team. By the end of 2001, Bloomberg named Daniel Doctoroff deputy mayor for economic rebuilding and development. He would become the forceful leader of many of the Bloomberg administration's most important initiatives.[8]

Throughout the transition period, and in later interviews for commissioners and senior staff, Bloomberg usually invited members of his leadership team to participate. He often began the sessions by asking candidates to explain why they wanted the job they sought. Sometime during the broad ranging conversation that typically followed, he might explain to a candidate that he and his leadership team were responsible for setting the tone and pointing the administration in a general direction, but he expected agency heads to bring ideas, pursue creative initiatives, and manage day-to-day operations with substantial autonomy. He rarely imposed a policy agenda on them, but wanted them to lead based on their knowledge and expertise. He often focused on some area of shared interest or common ground to connect with the candidate on a personal basis, and many successful interviews ended with a curt instruction: "Don't fuck up."[9]

His instinct to delegate did not prevent the mayor from keeping city officials on their toes. "Bloomberg here," he might bark into the transportation commissioner's phone: "There's a mess on the Henry Hudson Parkway. Clean it up." The officials he appointed knew it was wiser to dispatch a clean-up crew than to respond that Route 9A was a New York State road and not their responsibility. "What's all the mess," he might ask his parks commissioner, when he drove by an unkempt site and called to report it. Sometimes it was staging materials for a project in progress. Other times, it was a spot that needed attention. Once, he called the 311 telephone center he initiated to allow citizens to seek information or service from any city agency with a single call. After he shared his concern, the agent asked: "Would you like to leave your name?" "Bloomberg," he replied. "Could you spell that?" the unaware agent asked. He did, with wry amusement.[10]

Bloomberg organized the mayor's office in City Hall like a Wall Street trading desk. He put himself in a cubicle in the middle of the floor surrounded by his top deputies—the bullpen, he called it—reserving the mayor's corner office in the building's West Wing for ceremonial meetings and converting the conference room below it eventually into an emergency command center. When he proposed the unorthodox arrangement, his staff expressed concern. It was out of keeping with tradition. "This is the mayor's side of the building and I am the mayor, right?" he asked rhetorically, ending the discussion. The open office structure had powerful tangible and symbolic implications. Communications flowed readily, the mayor and his key advisors all had easy access to each other, and all could stay well informed about the range of issues affecting multiple deputies and departments. Brief discussions could resolve simple but important matters that might otherwise require formal scheduling and inefficient meetings. It also projected a visual sense of transparent government, the idea that the people's business would be conducted in the open for all to see. Under any circumstances, a mayor's decision to bring Wall Street ergonomics to City Hall would have been perceived as unusual. The contrast with Mayor Giuliani's closed circle of prosecutorial minded fellow-travelers with a penchant for secrecy made the move even more dramatic.[11]

The structure served purposes particular to Bloomberg's personality. He had little patience for process. He participated in senior staff meetings, and met weekly with some deputies and commissioners, but by temperament he was primed to execute transactions. If a matter required his attention, he expected his team to tell him so he could take care of it, not wait for a scheduled session. And he knew himself well enough to know his temper intimidated the uninitiated. He wanted the new members of his team to see the veterans yell back at him and hold their ground in an open forum, and then have the next discussion a short time later with no signs of hostility. It had worked that way at Bloomberg LP where the boss and Matthew Winkler "would occasionally disagree and end up in the middle of the floor yelling at each other . . . but at the end of the argument one of us would make a joke and we'd walk away smiling," Winkler told a reporter.[12]

Bloomberg's staff did not disappoint his desire to be challenged. Bill Cunningham's aggressive style created some fierce dust-ups, but the tension never lingered. Dennis Walcott had a deferential demeanor, but on occasion he too locked horns with the mayor. One day, during a senior staff meeting, a disagreement between the two became heated and neither side gave ground. The group stopped for a break, but the uncomfortable dialogue continued in the hallway. After a while, Walcott turned and walked away with the mayor in mid-scold, causing a flustered Bloomberg to shout: "Stop moving when I'm yelling at you." But the issue fell within the deputy's domain, so in the end Bloomberg accepted his judgment.[13]

Walcott and others thought the communication the unusual office configuration fostered was critical to the Bloomberg team's successes. Some were unsure about it, and others never really got used to it. Scott Adams, creator of the Dilbert cartoons that satirized office life in America, predicted that the unhappiest workers in New York City would be the ones sitting closest to the new mayor. Marc Shaw confessed he "used to get in trouble for ignoring the bullpen." He worked within arms' reach of Bloomberg and other top deputies whenever the mayor was present, and he acknowledged the practice had some benefits. Bloomberg "wanted to hear lots of voices and he wanted a certain group of people around him at all times, and to his credit it worked for him," Shaw realized. But to discuss sensitive budget and labor matters Shaw typically snuck off to a private office elsewhere in City Hall, and reporters and staff often spied the deputy mayor outside in City Hall Park, smoking cheap cigars while conducting business on his cell phone, away from potentially indiscreet listeners.[14]

Bloomberg took another important administrative step early on. In February 2002, he called all his commissioners and deputies together to lay out the ground rules. "You may not fight with each other privately or publicly," Bloomberg told them. He insisted it would not be tolerated. The message resonated with particular power in the catastrophe-charged atmosphere post 9/11, and it set the tone for cross-agency cooperation to a degree untypical of New York City government. Bureaucratic infighting did not disappear, but it diminished to as low a level as veteran city officials remembered. When asked what he had accomplished in his first one hundred days, Bloomberg answered, "I set the tone for the next one thousand . . . pick the team and set the tone."[15]

The Mayor Is the Lightning Rod

"New York is alive and well and open for business," Bloomberg announced from the victory podium the night of his stunning election. "We are clearly going to have enormous problems," he acknowledged, "but I know we are up to the task. We can do it." Unlike many political leaders who enter office bemoaning inherited ills, Bloomberg sought to reassure New Yorkers and the world that the city he would lead was fundamentally as strong the day after the Twin Towers went down as it had been the day before. He projected confidence and optimism at a time when both were in short supply. At the Citizens Union holiday party in December 2001, "everyone in the room seemed apprehensive," Michael Barbaro wrote in the *New York Times*, "everyone, that is, except for Michael R. Bloomberg," who declared New York's best days were still to come in a "peppy and sunny speech."[16]

On January 1, 2002, in Times Square, a few minutes after the glittering ball dropped signaling midnight and the start of a New Year, Rudolph Giuliani swore in Michael Bloomberg as mayor of New York City. Bloomberg's elder daughter, Emma, held the Bible. The high-profile public ceremony showed the world that the city had achieved an orderly, democratic transition of power despite the attack on it. Earlier, Bloomberg had actually been sworn in officially at the City Clerk's office, where the billionaire paid the fifteen cent fee required for the service in pennies, a New York tradition. The formal inauguration ceremony took place on the steps of City Hall on New Year's Day. "We will rebuild, renew and remain the capital of the free world," Bloomberg declared in his inaugural address. "We are the toughest, most resilient, and most determined people on the planet . . . . And there will be a better tomorrow," he insisted. "New York has been and will continue to be a magnet for people from all over the world. This is where the arts, business, research, and technology converge to create the world's foremost urban economy," he continued, and he cast his confidence in personal terms. "Based on my experience building a business here in New York, I can guarantee that New York is the best place in the world to do business. No city can match New York for its intellectual capital, financial know-how and cultural vibrancy." He addressed head-on a concern on people's minds. "To our corporate leaders, I urge you to strengthen your commitment to New York. This is no time to leave the Big Apple. Your future is New York. And New York's is better than ever."[17]

Amidst the cheerleading on behalf of the strong but battered metropolis, Bloomberg offered a sober assessment of the task ahead. "Rebuilding our city, restoring our infrastructure, continuing the fight against crime and reforming our schools will not be easy in the current economic climate. . . . We will not be able to afford all that we want. We will not even be able to afford everything we currently have," he warned. Yet, despite the challenges, New York would remain "a city of big dreams, of big ideas, big projects and a big heart . . . . We must never abandon the future," he insisted, telling New Yorkers that his administration would plan and develop for the long term even as it contended with urgent, short-term constraints.[18]

Bloomberg faced an enormous budget gap. All else in city government depends on fiscal solvency. A crisis mishandled causes deep reductions in essential municipal services, the quality of life deteriorates, the city becomes a less attractive place to live, and people and businesses leave. The tax base falls, more services are cut, and the downward spiral continues. It happened in New York in the 1970s with disastrous consequences that lasted for years. People were scared it would happen again. "I think the financial and economic problems the city has are potentially as severe as in the mid-1970s," outgoing City Comptroller

Alan Hevesi warned. Felix Rohatyn, instrumental in crafting the 1970s fiscal crisis rescue plan, feared the challenge would be much greater. The *New York Times* reported that "experts worried the situation was so dire there will have to be a takeover next year by Governor George Pataki."[19]

The fretting proved somewhat overblown. The city's local economy and the government's financial infrastructure were far superior to what they had been in the 1970s, and the gap Bloomberg inherited his first year at 12 percent of budget dollars was considerably lower than the 19 percent hole the city confronted during the 1970s meltdown. Still, the crisis was real enough, as severe as the worst David Dinkins contended with in the early 1990s. Bloomberg and his team responded with skill and political courage. In February 2002, the mayor presented a preliminary budget that would "hurt everybody," he acknowledged, but nobody "fatally." The plan had five components: expense reductions, revenue enhancements, project postponements, state and federal funding initiatives, and short-term borrowing. It included increases in the prices of some municipal fines and fees, but Bloomberg had promised during his campaign and reiterated in his inaugural address that he would not raise taxes. He kept his word in his first budget, except for a huge increase in the city sales tax on cigarettes from 8 cents to $1.50 a pack. He viewed the measure as a means to discourage young people from smoking while incidentally providing some money. "The numbers are clear," Bloomberg said. "You raise cigarette taxes, the kids smoke less."[20]

Capital expenditures were cut nearly 20 percent, but they were still higher than they had been a few years before, and the city would borrow $1.5 billion under state-authorized transitional bonds to get through the crisis. Bloomberg made it clear that he viewed borrowing money to cover operating expenses—a key cause of the 1970s fiscal crisis—an "extraordinary measure" related directly to the consequences of the terrorist-inflicted damage to the economy. He promised his administration would not borrow again to pay operating expenses. "I hope the rating agencies understand," he said. "We are not going to mortgage our future."[21]

The mayor's team negotiated the city budget with a substantially recast city council. Term limits forced the retirement of many longtime officeholders, so thirty-seven of the fifty-one legislators were new to their job. To lead them as speaker, they chose Manhattan Councilman Gifford Miller, a well-heeled and handsome Princeton graduate who had worked for Congresswoman Carolyn Maloney for three years before winning an electoral office of his own. He was thirty-two years old when he became the second-most powerful elected official in New York City government. "We are committed to going over this budget line by line to ensure we maintain important services," he said the day the mayor presented his plan. The centerpiece of the council's response was a proposal to address school overcrowding with $5 billion in construction financing supported by an income tax surcharge. It also called for restoration of a commuter tax discontinued in 1999, and for renewal of a stock transfer tax dropped in 2001, to fund some of the programs the mayor proposed to cut. But all three taxes required state legislature votes in a year all of its members were up for reelection. There was no chance any would win approval. Bloomberg dismissed the council budget as political posturing, and after modest bickering between Bloomberg, Miller, and their staffs, the council accepted the mayor's budget with a few compromises.[22]

America's federal system makes cities the creature of the state. The governor and the legislature in Albany exercise enormous power over matters that affect the daily lives of New York City residents, including the city budget. The conflict is institutional, and New York City mayors chafe at it. The often-mediocre caliber of state legislators and the extraordinary level of corruption at the state level intensifies the problem. But securing support from Albany is part of the job and every mayor must come to terms with it. In 2002, Republicans from outside the city dominated the state senate—they had for decades—and Governor Pataki was from Poughkeepsie. New York City Democrats controlled the assembly and in many ways looked out for the city's interests.[23]

Bloomberg managed negotiations with the state successfully during his first years in office. He relied heavily on Marc Shaw and Bill Cunningham, both well schooled in Albany's ways, and state elected officials seemed uncharacteristically high-minded in the post-9/11 atmosphere. It helped that Bloomberg was not Rudy Giuliani, who had developed an unconstructively contentious relationship with the state legislature. At his first meeting with the assembly's Democratic caucus, Bloomberg received a standing ovation simply for expressing his desire to work together for the good of the city. During key first-term budget negotiations Bloomberg, Assembly Speaker Silver, Shaw, and the speaker's key aide, Dean Fuleihan, dined regularly at the Prime Grill, a Manhattan steakhouse that served kosher food, which Silver required. Bloomberg complained good-naturedly to hate it. As a teen, he had sometimes rejected his family's kosher dinner in favor of Chinese takeout, served on glass plates his mother kept for the purpose. Bloomberg also developed a productive relationship with State Senate Majority Leader Joe Bruno, and on occasion the mayor and the two powerful political leaders worked together to outmaneuver Governor Pataki.[24]

In later years, Bloomberg would suffer a small number of high-profile failures in Albany that would stick in people's memories. And as time went on, he would end up at antagonistic odds with Silver, and with many state officials who expected to be treated with respectful deference as democratically elected officeholders. In some cases, their petty and dishonest behavior made it hard for Bloomberg to hide his disdain. In others, Bloomberg's arrogance caused the rifts. But in the first years after 9/11, an aura of good will prevailed.[25]

The state legislature approved the mayor's tobacco tax and other requests in his first budget and found additional money for the city's school system, reducing threatened cuts to education. Higher-than-projected city tax collections allowed $175 million of restorations in services, for which the council took credit. After modifications, Bloomberg's first budget totaled $43.5 billion, a little higher than the prior year. Inflation, plus uncontrollable expenses for things like debt service, pension and health benefits, and state and federal government mandates, meant that even after program cuts the city budget typically grew year after year, much to the dismay of fiscal conservatives and monitoring agencies.[26]

Ink on Bloomberg's first budget had barely dried when in July 2002 he instructed city agencies to find more savings. Baseline projections for the next year anticipated a gap of over $3 billion at first, but as the national recession lingered, profit forecasts for Wall Street turned dismal, and city revenue collections disappointed. The projected gap ballooned to an alarming $6.4 billion. Closing it through service cuts alone was impractical, so higher taxes would have to be part of the solution. At Marc Shaw's urging, Bloomberg presented the city council with a plan for closing the gap as part of an interim budget report in November 2002. Early implementation would allow savings from service cuts and increases from revenue measures to accrue sooner than if the city waited for the next fiscal year's cycle. It was the decision of a confident chief executive confronting a serious problem head-on.[27]

The mayor's plan challenged the city's municipal unions to find $600 million in productivity improvements, and it asked the city council to approve more than $1 billion in service reductions. It also called for a whopping 25 percent increase in the city's property tax rate, which had not been raised in ten years. Deputy Mayor Shaw knew that the budget crisis would require tax increases, and he had wanted to implement them as soon as Bloomberg took office. But the mayor had forbidden them for his first year to honor his campaign pledge. "It a little bit made me crazy," Shaw confessed, "because I knew we didn't have the resources we needed to provide the services I knew this mayor wanted to provide." He set his sights on a January 1, 2003 tax rise, the earliest his "marching orders" would allow.[28]

When Shaw first proposed the 25 percent figure, "it left my jaw on the floor," City Council Speaker Miller remembered, but in short order he helped choreograph what Shaw called, "a Kabuki dance." The city council would reduce the hike to 20 percent and claim credit for limiting the rise. After ritual protests and serious negotiations, the council approved an 18.49 percent increase, a number politicians would round down to 18 percent in public announcements, and $840 million in savings. It was just over a-percent-and-a-half short of Miller's promise, which made Shaw angry, but it began on January 1, 2003, which to him was, "really, really important." Applying the higher rate six months early generated an additional $800 million of badly needed money for the city's depleted coffers. The Municipal Labor Council agreed to $100 million in health-care cost savings, provided the city used the money to maintain payments to benefit funds that might otherwise be cut. The city's largest union, District Council 37, submitted an efficiency plan more comically self-serving than helpful. All of its proposals involved transferring responsibility from workers in other municipal unions to its own.[29]

Bloomberg proposed to raise more money with a "place-of-work" tax, an overhaul of the old commuter tax by another name that would require a state legislature vote. It was a bargaining stance with no chance to succeed. In addition to charging workers from New Jersey and Connecticut, it would have applied to voters who rode to the city from Long Island and Westchester, an unappealing prospect for New York State legislators from those regions who would have to approve the measure. And the plan's 2.7 percent top rate was six times higher than the old tax, an improbable leap. Bloomberg also proposed tolls on East River bridges to match the charges on other Manhattan crossings. There was little rhyme or reason for the different treatments other than history. At the time of consolidation in 1898, unrestricted access to Manhattan across the East River was seen as a means of uniting the five boroughs. Like many other local funding mechanisms, the proposal required state authorization. The idea gained no traction, but would return years later as part of a bid to implement congestion pricing in Manhattan.[30]

Between the time when the mayor presented a fully developed budget in January 2003 and the end of April, the New York State fiscal process ground to a dysfunctional halt. Governor Pataki rejected any tax increases at the state or local level and sought to resolve the state's own formidable budget problems with massive cuts and one-time gimmicks. The single-minded austerity program met fierce resistance in the assembly and the state senate. Bloomberg's effort to curry favor with Pataki—he hosted two fund-raisers for him and donated $1.2 million to the governor and to the Republican Party—bought no help. The mayor instructed his team to develop a fallback proposal that called for massive cuts and layoffs of up to fifteen thousand city workers. It smacked of the time-honored tactic of a budget so unpalatable it would scare people into action, even though in reality smarter choices could be made. Yet, the city had already undertaken several rounds of service cuts and raised the property tax.

If it did not get some relief, its options were limited. "The city from Day 1 has been talking about how big the problem is," Deputy Mayor Shaw said. "We did the labor part and the property tax part. The stuff that didn't need state action has been done. State help is the only part not done yet."[31]

The governor's stubborn recalcitrance caused the other two members of Albany's ruling troika to render him irrelevant to the negotiations. Assembly Speaker Silver and State Senate Majority Leader Bruno built a budget that undid the governor's cuts to education, Medicaid, and other important services that would have left New York City and other locales around the state suffering. To fund it, they applied a temporary surcharge to the state income tax, and to the state sales tax. And they passed a separate revenue bill that authorized the city to do the same locally to meet its needs. New York City residents making more than $150,000 per year would pay more income tax, and the local sales tax in New York City would rise by a quarter of a point. Legislative sunset clauses would cause the exceptional increases in city taxes to expire in three years. Assemblyman Silver's support had been key to secure the deal.[32]

At Deputy Mayor Shaw's urging, the legislature approved a state takeover of responsibility for bonds dating from the 1970s fiscal crisis, removing $500 million of obligations from the city for each of the next five years. A state entity would refinance those over a thirty-year period creating minimal debt service stress by extending bonds first issued in the 1970s into the year 2034. Paying for operating expenses incurred decades earlier with debt that spanned sixty years seemed ludicrously irresponsible, but the annual amounts were small enough that analysts did little more than take caustic note. As Shaw put it, the city "played the Albany game," and "got the money it wanted." The governor vetoed the state budget and the revenue bill, and went to court to prevent the bond refinancing proposal. The Democratic assembly and the state senate, controlled by the governor's own Republican Party, overrode his vetoes, and the court eventually ruled the refinancing plan legal without judgment about its prudence.[33]

Mayor Bloomberg found the money the city needed to manage through two years of crisis without deep, self-defeating service cuts. The outcome caused a sigh of relief, and might even have earned the mayor and his budget team a victory lap. Yet, the multiple tax increases made the mayor a political loser. They coincided with a decline in city gross domestic product from $434 billion in 2001 to $394 billion in 2003, so people who had less were taxed more. Fiscal conservatives feared the higher taxes would slow the economic recovery and complained that it would have been healthier for the city to cut services more. Others worried that the sales tax hike would hurt low-income New Yorkers most. Targeted layoffs were an essential element of the budget plan that antagonized municipal workers and union leaders. They were more important to demonstrate financial discipline to taxpayers than for the money saved, according to one senior advisor. "You can't [raise the property tax rate] 18.5 percent if you are not giving pain out across the board," he observed. And Bloomberg also raised water fees in 2003 to provide capital for long-delayed and federally mandated projects he deemed important to complete.[34]

Bloomberg's popularity ratings were high during his first few months in office—hovering above 60 percent. His competent but unpopular handling of the fiscal crisis caused his approval rating to plunge to 31 percent in July 2003 according to a Quinnipiac University poll. Just 24 percent of the city said it would reelect him. "The mayor is always the lightning rod," Press Secretary Ed Skyler observed. In time, he expected New Yorkers to acknowledge the mayor's accomplishments.[35]

Economic Recovery, Mayoral Recovery

About the time Bloomberg's popularity was reaching bottom, improvement in the national economy began to make its way from Main Street to Wall Street and New York City's economy recovered. In 2004, its gross domestic product surpassed its 2001 level. The budget outlook was less bleak than the prior two years, and then got consistently better. Steady growth over the next three years boosted personal and commercial income tax collections. City dwellers had more money to spend on homes among other things, so residential real estate values began to recover, and property tax collections along with them. Housing permits reached record levels, and construction workers went back on the job. Commercial real estate occupancy slowly began to rise, first in midtown, then downtown, and commercial rents began to recover before surging to new heights in 2007 and 2008. Higher income and higher real estate values led to a surge in deals that created transaction taxes. Tourists too frightened to visit the city immediately after 9/11 returned in record numbers from around the United States, and from overseas, beginning in 2005. Hotel occupancy rates rose and service employees began to find jobs again. Employment grew more slowly than the economy for a time, so at first the high salaries and bonuses of Wall Street masters and real estate titans fueled the recovery, along with high profits at the firms where they worked. By 2008, total employment finally surpassed the prior peak. The trends had strong positive implications for city revenues. Instead of gaping deficits, the city found itself with ample surpluses.[36]

The mayor was cautious at first. "We must be mindful," Bloomberg wrote in his January 2004 Financial Plan, "that the [projected] budget gaps beyond Fiscal Year 2005 remain significant and we must continue to be vigilant." He also noted that mandated increases in Medicaid, fringe benefits, pensions, and debt service were rising faster than forecasted growth in city tax revenues. They risked crowding out spending for essential services like education, public safety, affordable housing, and clean streets. But the fiscal tide had turned. Over the next three and a half years, the mayor and his team found that they could reverse cuts, expand city services, pursue new initiatives, and still have money left over to pre-pay some of the next year's debts while building up reserves.[37]

The surge in tax collections during the first half of 2004, and revenue estimates that followed made financing a full range of robust municipal services easy for the following year. It also allowed for a creative tactic designed to afford homeowners a measure of tax relief. Marc Shaw and Bill Cunningham hatched the plan one night in an Upper East Side bar with Cunningham intent on rehabilitating the mayor's popularity and Shaw determined to preserve city budget options. It called on the city to send every Class 1 homeowner, meaning New Yorkers living in one, two, and three family homes, and the owners of most cooperative apartments and condominiums, a one-time check for $400 without changing the tax rate or providing a rebate for others. The policy applied only to primary residences and it returned more or less entirely the 18.49 percent real estate tax increase experienced by small homeowners, who were among the most reliable voters and the most sensitive taxpayers. It left the rate intact on commercial property, large rental buildings, and other structures preserving roughly 80 percent of the revenue the tax hike generated. Shaw described it as one of the "best joint ideas" he and Cunningham hatched. The state legislature approved the plan for up to three years, subject to annual city council review, and then renewed approval for another three years. The first set of checks went out to about 650,000 homes in October 2004 just as the mayor and his team turned their attention to his reelection the following year. Another round of checks would go out in October 2005—just weeks before Bloomberg stood for reelection—and in 2006, 2007, and eventually in 2008 as part of a budget compromise between the mayor and the council before budget constraints led to their halt.[38]

The income and sales tax surcharges enacted with sunset clauses in 2004 expired as promised, lowering the local tax burden by 2007. That same year, Bloomberg added $500 million to a $1 billion reserve created the year before to begin funding retiree medical care. In addition to the $400 property tax rebate for all homeowners, the budget provided a one-year 7 percent reduction in the property tax rate itself, rescinding more than one-third of the earlier increase. Bloomberg's budget also reduced some fees that fell heavily on small businesses, generally the greatest source of job creation, and it eliminated sales tax on all clothing to make city stores competitive with shopping malls across the Hudson River in New Jersey. All in all, the budget provided a billion dollars in tax relief. The mayor's popularity recovered in line with the flush economic times.[39]

Storm Clouds

"There are storm clouds on the horizon," Mayor Bloomberg warned in the opening line of his January 2008 Financial Plan. During the summer of 2007, several banks that managed funds heavily invested in sub-prime mortgages got into trouble and refused to honor requests for withdrawals. A severe credit crunch followed. In the spring of 2008, Bear Stearns, an eighty-five-year-old investment bank that had survived the market crash of 1929 and the Great Depression without layoffs, failed spectacularly. In close conjunction with US Treasury and Federal Reserve Bank officials, JP Morgan acquired Bear Stearns to prevent a complete market meltdown. The event rattled Wall Street's nerves. Banks laid off staff and pared spending in preparation for a market shakeout.[40]

The mayor insisted on measured prudence in the executive budget he presented to the city council in May 2008. His Wall Street–honed instincts caused him to feel the pain of the city's most important financial engine, and he feared the consequences of tougher times for the industry so critical to municipal income tax collections. Lower profits for banks and lower bonuses for bankers meant less tax revenue for the city. A downward arc on Wall Street typically caused the same for the city's commercial real estate industry, and home construction as well. History suggested that the city weathered national recessions that began in the manufacturing sector fairly easily, and in the technology sector as well, but when the financial industry turned sharply down, the city suffered.[41]

"Bulls make money, bears make money, and pigs make shit," was among the earthy Wall Street sayings Bloomberg quoted occasionally. Smart traders profited in good times, and they could position themselves skillfully for bad times, but greedy traders who chased profits when tough times loomed lost out. Bloomberg anticipated a downward spike in the local economy and managed his budget responsibilities accordingly. Yet, in no small measure due to careful management when times were good, the city still showed a substantial surplus for the year ahead. Many council members objected to the mayor's conservative approach that included cautious cutbacks for a range of programs and reductions in social services when the city had the money to support them. The mayor's proposal also trimmed capital expenditures by 20 percent and required all agencies to pursue efficiencies. "Everything was given a little haircut," according to council finance chairman David Weprin.[42]

The mayor negotiated his budget that year with Christine Quinn, who became city council speaker after term limits forced Gifford Miller's exit in

2005. A one-time community organizer, Quinn's political career began when she served as campaign manager for Thomas Duane's city council race in 1991. Duane became the council's first openly gay member, and Quinn, also gay, took pride in her role in helping him win. When Duane moved on to the New York State Senate in 2001, Quinn won his Manhattan council seat representing Greenwich Village, Chelsea, Clinton, and parts of SoHo and Murray Hill. She earned a reputation as someone with strong views she was not afraid to defend, but ultimately a pragmatist, out to cut the most effective deals for her constituents and for the causes that mattered to her.[43]

Quinn responded to her members' demands for less austerity and more humanity by negotiating hard with the mayor in an effort to win a more generous budget. Discussions continued past the June 5 formal deadline set in the City Charter for budget approval, and up to June 26, just days before the July 1 start of the next fiscal year. In the end, with a few modest accommodations, the mayor persevered. "I don't have to tell anyone here that this is a difficult time and forecasts are worrisome," Bloomberg said when he and Quinn announced the plan. In prior years, after presenting the budget, the mayor and speaker had kissed. This time, they began walking away from the podium without honoring the sweet tradition until reporters reminded them.[44]

Brooklyn Councilman Bill de Blasio was among the legislators unhappy with the outcome. "I am disappointed that with a $4.5 billion surplus the mayor forced the council to cut funding for essential services, including homeless prevention, legal and mental health services, and workforce development," he complained. He also took exception to efficiency measures limiting support services at the New York City Housing Authority. "The mayor should not have put the city in this situation," he declared, "and these cuts will be deeply felt for years to come," he warned. In negotiations with the council, the mayor had offered the possibility of revenue measures to support an additional $1 billion in services. The council had declined to bear the political burden of that approach, so Bloomberg held his ground on the need for measured austerity.[45]

Less than three months later, on September 14, 2008, Lehman Brothers collapsed. It filed for bankruptcy as a consequence of large holdings of securitized mortgage bonds that had gone bad. That same day Merrill Lynch, a household name and a part of the financial lives of millions of Americans, announced it would sell itself to Bank of America in an act of desperation. It too had miscalculated the risks in its mortgage loan portfolio. Its leaders feared that panic over Lehman's collapse would lock it out of inter-bank borrowing markets and create a fatal liquidity crisis. Its chief executive opted to sell the firm for a fraction of what it was once worth rather than lead its iconic thundering herd through capital markets slaughter. Investors around the world discovered that trillions of dollars of bonds with AAA credit status, the safest designation offered by professional rating agencies, had risks they had not recognized. Assets thought almost as safe as cash could not be redeemed at any price for a time. Stock markets plummeted around the world. The United States Treasury took extraordinary measures forcing billions of dollars of government capital onto bank balance sheets to reassure depositors and creditors that the nation's largest financial institutions would not dissolve. The Federal Reserve Bank let flow unprecedented levels of liquidity in an effort to drown the panic.[46]

Wall Street had become the epicenter of a global financial crisis the likes of which the world had not seen since the Great Depression. After a call with Treasury Secretary Henry Paulson alerted him to Lehman Brothers meltdown and Merrill Lynch's surrender, Bloomberg canceled a scheduled trip to California. "The world is about to end tomorrow," he told Kevin Sheekey when informing him of the change in plans. He felt obliged to assess the damage to the city's most important business sector that he knew so well. He needed look no further than his own team to understand the consequences for those in the industry. His deputy mayor for economic development at the time, Robert Lieber, worked at Lehman Brothers before joining Bloomberg's administration. The bank's collapse was a devastating emotional and financial blow. Bloomberg took Lieber and his wife to dinner the night of the bankruptcy announcement in a gesture that Lieber would long remember. Many on his staff would tell similar stories about Bloomberg's loyalty to them in moments of duress.[47]

Bloomberg responded to the unnerving fiscal circumstances he faced in 2008 with the same sangfroid he displayed in 2002. In November, months before the formal budget process called for a plan, he presented one to the city council for action. It included a range of cuts and revenue sources, notably the early repeal of a one-year 7 percent across the board real estate tax cut meant to expire in June 2009. He also sought to cancel the $400 property tax rebates paid every year since 2004 that many New Yorkers had come to rely on. The council refused that request and allowed the popular largess a final time. During fiscal year 2009, New York City experienced a $3.3 billion decline in local revenue. Overall, the budget fell $1.8 billion as the city released reserves created during good times to mitigate the pain for the average New Yorker.[48]

City officials and residents feared a prolonged period of financial stress based on the seriousness of the crisis. "The economic downturn is in full swing. The global financial crisis has damaged the national and local economies," Bloomberg wrote in his January 2009 Financial Plan. He proposed measures to close a $4 billion gap for the next year and threatened to lay off thousands of city workers if adequate savings could not be found. But surprisingly, the city experienced a partial recovery in revenue collections that year, and by 2011 city revenues reached the previous high-water mark again. It would continue to grow afterward for the rest of Bloomberg's term. Federal government emergency measures to stabilize the financial industry worked. The purpose was to prevent a collapse of confidence in the world banking system that risked unleashing a second Great Depression. A consequence was that Wall Street profits and all that followed from them for the New York City economy recovered more fully and rapidly than many feared in the early stages of the crisis. The sales tax and other charges went up modestly, and Bloomberg's last three budgets contained more one-time revenue sources than earlier ones, attracting criticism from the Citizens Budget Commission among others. Discretionary social services support suffered noticeably, but New York City weathered the storm with less pain than anticipated and virtually no layoffs. The annual ritual where the mayor proposed cuts and the council restored some services continued. By fiscal year 2014, the last for which Bloomberg submitted a budget, spending totaled $73.8 billion.[49]

The special interest Bloomberg ignored the most when budgeting was the city's powerful real estate lobby. "He fucked them," was the succinct and non-judgmental summary of one senior advisor actively involved in the decisions. Commercial property taxes rose significantly and the real estate firms that paid them were left out of the small homeowner rebate program Bloomberg's top advisors developed with at least one eye on the politics of the decision. Some real estate executives thought the approach unfair. Yet, overall conditions for commercial real estate during Bloomberg's time in office were highly favorable, in great measure because of city policies. Developers and management companies were making so much money, that most industry executives viewed the higher taxes as a cost of doing business and well worth the trade-off.[50]

The Real Estate Board of New York did encourage Bloomberg to address a specific issue that large commercial owners of rental properties who dominated the board felt forced them to pay some $200 million more in taxes than was fair. It had to do with arcane rules that left luxury condominiums owned by individuals grossly undervalued, which led to higher taxes for corporate accounts to make up for the revenue reduction that resulted. As a practical matter, the policy delivered millions of dollars of subsidies to the super-rich owners, often foreign or out-of-town billionaires buying Manhattan trophy apartments as investments. So many sat in buildings on East 57th Street it became known as "billionaire's row." The mayor met with the board to discuss the issue, and when its staff produced a list of the names of the owners benefiting, he pocketed it for personal scrutiny. The board claimed the city had the authority to correct the problem, but Bloomberg's law department determined the state legislature would have to make the change, and no action followed.[51]

In Pursuit of Productivity

Managing relations with the city workforce is a key element of budget management. The adversarial nature of contract negotiations between the mayor and the municipal unions that represent New York City's army-sized workforce often creates acrimony. The Bloomberg administration experienced its full share, starting with labor leader hostility in response to post-9/11 fiscal crisis layoffs. During his initial campaign for office, and in his inaugural address, Bloomberg insisted that wage increases would have to be funded entirely with productivity gains. It was an aggressive starting point that provoked strong reactions. Bloomberg achieved only modest success on this front, most of it during his first term.[52]

On his first day on the job, Bloomberg got a taste of how complicated municipal labor relations could be when drivers at a city-subsidized private bus service went on strike. Labor commissioner James Hanley, a holdover from the Giuliani administration and the Dinkins administration before that, briefed him on the details. "Jim, let me get this straight," Hanley recalled the mayor saying in response to what he learned. "We pay the salaries and the operating expenses of these bus companies, and they provide lousy service, and they go on strike all the time?" he asked, obviously displeased. Hanley confirmed the sorry state of affairs. "Well that won't last very long," Bloomberg vowed. "With respect," Hanley replied, "mayors have been dealing with this since John Lindsay and nothing has changed." "We'll see about that," Bloomberg retorted. The next year, as part of his administration's first full budget cycle, Bloomberg's team negotiated the transfer of responsibility for the bus lines to the Metropolitan Transportation Authority, which was better equipped to manage them.[53]

Remarkably, when Bloomberg became mayor, no one could tell him how many workers the city employed. New York paid all or part of the salaries of staff that the mayor controlled directly, all or part of the salaries of staff at non-mayoral agencies like City University, and it did the same for private sector agencies independent of the city that provided important municipal services with heavy city subsidies. Bloomberg had his team codify the different categories, and by the time he created his first full year budget, the city could declare with long-overdue confidence that it employed 248,911 staff directly and a total of 306,590 full-time staff overall. Its three largest municipal unions were District Council 37, which in 2002 had some 125,000 members organized into an unwieldy structure of fifty-six union locals, the United Federation of Teachers, whose 120,000 members included 80,000 teachers and 40,000 educational support staff, and the Patrolman's Benevolent Association, the largest of the uniformed service unions with 22,000 members. The three represented roughly three-quarters of city workers.[54]

A tug-of-war over control of the educational workplace colored all of the Bloomberg administration's negotiations with the United Federation of Teachers. In return for hefty raises, and in response to public pressure, union chief Randi Weingarten agreed to important productivity improvements in 2005. In other years, few were forthcoming. Bloomberg inherited tense relations with the Patrolman's Benevolent Association. Until a rich budget and a concerted effort by Deputy Mayor Edward Skyler improved things in 2008, binding arbitration was regularly required to settle disagreements between the two sides. Effective law enforcement reduced crime and allowed Bloomberg to achieve cost savings by shrinking the size of the police force. Bloomberg closed six of eight firehouses he targeted in 2003 despite intense union and community opposition, including anonymous telephone calls threatening Marc Shaw's family. Bloomberg angered the fire department again when he declared the police would take charge at major catastrophes, putting an end to a long-standing feud that on occasion had created life-threatening interagency rivalry. And DC 37 accepted a contract in 2004 with small raises and reduced wages and benefits for new employees that constituted real productivity gains for the city. Later agreements were more generous and fewer productivity gains achieved.[55]

While Bloomberg governed, the city avoided one transit strike but suffered another. Toward the end of his first year in office, negotiations between the Metropolitan Transportation Authority and the Transit Workers Union remained tense as a December 31, 2002 contract deadline approached. The governor dominates negotiations with the MTA, and Bloomberg supported Pataki's strong stance in 2002 that ended in a last minute agreement. Bloomberg had counseled New Yorkers to prepare for a possible strike by buying bicycles. He led by example and bought one himself, but took tabloid flak for choosing a $600 model, beyond what many New Yorkers who relied on mass transit could afford. He got a little positive publicity later when he gave the bike to a boy in Brooklyn. In December 2005, the transit workers struck for sixty hours. New Yorkers responded to the short-term disruption with their usual resilience, and the action had little lasting impact other than damaging the union's finances and its leadership's credibility.[56]

In the aftermath of the world financial crisis and the Great Recession that followed, the Bloomberg administration reached no more wage agreements with municipal unions. During the initial phase of the frightening financial meltdown that occurred in the last quarter of 2008 and the first quarter of 2009, private sector companies froze wages, even cut them significantly in some cases while eliminating or reducing bonuses and laying off staff. Bloomberg reasoned that in such an environment city workers should not receive salary increases, and to avoid layoffs should offer up additional efficiencies. After the worst of the crisis subsided, the mayor declined to consider retroactive raises. The private sector by and large did not provide special consideration to workers who had suffered. The income private sector workers lost was the price people paid when the economy collapsed, no matter who was to blame, and the mayor did not see why public employees should be treated differently. He also declared flatly that the city could not afford to fund retroactive raises, especially when the cost of benefits continued their relentless rise.[57]

Bloomberg's refusal to hold public workers harmless from a worldwide financial crisis they had not caused angered many union heads. Municipal employees did not get the outsized bonuses bankers did when things went well, so they should not suffer financially when things went badly, labor leaders reasoned. The relatively generous wage increases of Bloomberg's middle years created expectations that added emotional baggage to the negotiations. As the mayor's third and final term unfolded, union leaders decided to wait him out and take their chances with a new mayor in 2014. "The unions didn't want to settle with him," Citizens Budget Commission President Carol Kellerman concluded. When Bloomberg left office, some 152 contracts covering virtually the entire city workforce had expired. It would fall to his successor to negotiate terms. In response to observations that Mayor Bloomberg left his successor a small budget surplus, critics pointed out that he also left municipal employees expecting very large retroactive raises that would cost the city billions. Others noted Bloomberg would face no more municipal elections, so he could grandstand without electoral consequences during his last term. By the end of his administration, at least one close observer described union heads at some of the city's largest public employee unions as "hating" the mayor. To Bloomberg, it was strictly business.[58]

Pension Peril

New York City government pension contributions exploded from $1.6 billion in fiscal year 2002 to over $8.3 billion in fiscal year 2014—growth of nearly 520 percent. The trajectory alarmed anyone paying attention to the city budget. Certainly it worried Bloomberg. Many of his annual five-year Financial Plans highlighted the unhealthy evolution of retirement benefit costs. "If we enhance the pension system and salaries, we can't afford to have as many employees or to provide as many services," the mayor told the city with simple logic. Pension contributions would crowd out libraries and parks, cultural institutions and environmental initiatives, schoolteachers and police officers. Yet, until late in his tenure his statements of concern had a ritual quality about them. The mayor saw the numbers, understood the arithmetic, and recognized the peril, but provided no serious strategy for responding to it. To the contrary, during Bloomberg's first two terms, the raises his administration granted to municipal employees drove a substantial portion of the increase in pension obligations—about 30 percent according to a *New York Times* analysis. Contracts that provided salary increases included no reforms to the benefits packages driving toward unsustainable outcomes.[59]

There was a reason. Since the 1970s fiscal crisis, New York State has held authority over city pension benefits while the city remains responsible for funding them. Incredibly, it is illegal for the city to address pension benefits during collective bargaining negotiations. The lack of accountability creates billions of dollars of fiscal mischief. Executive leadership by a governor might have provided the basis for change, but none emerged between 2002 and 2010. Governor Pataki set his sights on national office after 9/11, and in any event proved as captive to the state's public unions as any other politician. Governor Spitzer, elected in 2006, promised to "steam roller" adversaries into submission on policy matters, but a little over a year after taking office resigned in disgrace amid a sex scandal featuring high-priced call girls while accusations that he had misused his authority over state police to investigate political enemies swirled around him. Lieutenant Governor David Paterson succeeded Spitzer in the State House and proved generally inept, notwithstanding a decision to veto a pension fund extender bill in 2009. That decision ended an unhealthy thirty-two-year practice of ensuring new uniformed workers received the same benefits as older ones, despite a 1970s law that had changed the rules in a bid to make the system sustainable. Tough tactics by the city seemed pointless without support at the state level.[60]

The collapse of investment markets during the global financial crisis intensified concern about pension funding. The S&P 500, one broad measure of the value of US stocks, fell by over 50 percent between October 2007 and March 2009. New York City's pension system was better funded than most, but the city's chief actuary had been providing calculations since 2003 that projected huge deficiencies on the order of $50 billion. When Andrew Cuomo ran for governor in 2010, he identified public pension obligations as among the most important causes of New York State's fiscal woes, and he pledged to reform the system. "The numbers speak for themselves . . . . The pension system as we know it is unsustainable," Cuomo told New Yorkers when he announced a formal plan to address the problem. The city piggybacked on his leadership. Less than three months after Cuomo's November 2010 victory, Bloomberg delivered his 2011 State of the City address and declared pension reform his number-one priority for state legislative action. "In the 1970s, after years of fiscal mismanagement, the City was forced to ask Albany to step in and manage its affairs. Today, after years of responsible management, we have a different request from Albany: let us manage ourselves," he said. The mayor outlined a program with three parts: a series of obvious but contentious changes to benefits; consolidation of the city's five pension funds into a single integrated governance structure; and restoration of city authority to negotiate pension fund and other retirement benefits directly with city unions through collective bargaining.[61]

In March 2012, in a late-night session typical of Albany, legislative leaders passed a bill that achieved about two-thirds of the savings the city sought. Tensions between Mayor Bloomberg and Governor Cuomo were no less than with other mayors and governors, but Bloomberg awarded Cuomo "an A-plus" for persuading lawmakers to resist union pressure and enact "real reform" while still providing "a phenomenally generous plan," for future city workers. The legislature did not make the administrative change the mayor sought to consolidate the city's five pension investment funds, and the legislature also failed to return the power to include pension benefits in collective bargaining negotiations to the city. The 2012 pension reforms improved New York City's long-term financial outlook by an estimated $22 billion in savings over thirty years. It was a structural reform that left the city's predictable expenses better aligned than they had been with its annual revenues. It is the sort of unheralded decision that helps ensure New York City does not follow the fiscally fraught path of cities like Detroit and Chicago.[62]

New York City retiree health-care commitments, like pension fund obligations, increased dramatically on Mayor Bloomberg's watch. The annual cost of health-care insurance premiums grew from $2 billion in fiscal year 2002 to $4.8 billion in fiscal year 2012. By the time he left office the estimated value of the city's unfunded retiree health-care obligations, plus other post-employment benefits, totaled the staggering figure of $83 billion, double what they had been ten years before. Bloomberg did not make changing the city's healthcare policy a priority. Indeed, Bloomberg LP was one of the few large companies in New York City that continued to pay 100 percent of its employees' medical benefits, a telling indication of the mayor's outlook on the topic. During the flush years between 2005 and 2007, his administration set aside reserves to fund retiree healthcare—$2.5 billion—which was a start, and he was the first mayor to do so. But when the 2007–2009 financial crisis hit, he released the health-care reserves. The decision confirmed the worst fears of fiscal monitors who worried when the city created the account that it would be used as a general rainy day fund and not accumulate over time to protect the city's long-term fiscal integrity. The decision was one of the few where Bloomberg opted for short-term convenience over responsible long-term management.[63]

We Will Not Mortgage Our Future

Bloomberg's belief that successful enterprises constantly invest in themselves to grow and improve service is evident in his administration's management of New York's capital budget and borrowing capacity. "The city's infrastructure is the key to its future economic competitiveness and must take precedence over most tax-cutting proposals," Bloomberg told the Citizens Budget Commission as a candidate in 2001. Obligations with a direct claim on city revenue stood at $54 billion at the end of 2013, a little more than double the level at the time Bloomberg took office. Indirect obligations from various municipal entities boosted the number beyond $100 billion according to the Citizens Budget Commission, an overall increase in the debt level of about 80 percent. The Citizens Budget Commission also calculated the value of the capital investments Bloomberg made and compared it to investments under his predecessors, adjusted for changes over time in the cost of construction. Bloomberg invested $123 billion, more than twice what Mayor Koch spent in twelve often fiscally constrained years, and far more than mayors Giuliani and Dinkins invested during their collective dozen years in City Hall.[64]

Despite substantial increases in debt levels, Mayor Bloomberg left the city more creditworthy than when he found it. Debt grew, but the value of the city's real estate and its residents' personal income grew faster. As a percent of total city expenditures, annual debt service declined from 14.3 percent in 2002 to 11.6 percent in 2013. It is the job of bond rating agencies to assess all of the things that could affect a city's ability to repay its debt and to offer a judgment. When Bloomberg became mayor, the three main municipal rating agencies gave the city solid investment grade scores for general obligation bonds. In the aftermath of the 9/11 attacks, the agencies warned of a negative outlook. The mayor's competent if unpopular budget management through the fiscal crisis he faced his first two years allowed the city to escape downgrades. And by the time he left office, all three agencies rated the city's credit worthiness higher than when he arrived, stronger ratings than the city had ever received. In his first budget statement, when he announced he would raise debt to cover operating expenses in response to the extraordinary circumstance of the 9/11 terrorist attack, Mayor Bloomberg pledged his administration would not mortgage the city's future. He kept his promise.[65]

Die-hard fiscal conservatives looked at the growth of the city budget while Bloomberg governed—nearly 80 percent in nominal terms—and declared his fiscal stewardship disastrous. But Bloomberg's government grew in line with the local economy. As a candidate, Bloomberg's self-description as a man who would handle the city budget skillfully while remaining true to his beliefs as a liberal Democrat turned out to be true. He enhanced city government and expanded service delivery at the pace the city could afford. Just a few months before leaving office, Bloomberg explained his outlook to a journalist in characteristically salty terms. "The conservative columnists write, 'Oh, you should just tell the unions go fuck themselves!' You can't do that. You have to keep delivering services."[66]

Bloomberg understood the importance of efficient management and encouraged city officials to use resources effectively during good times and bad. He created reserves when money was flush and applied necessary discipline when the economy faltered. Yet, his decisions were guided by a belief that creating a positive environment for business, and an attractive quality of life for residents, would cause the city to grow and prosper more successfully than the low tax–minimum service approach conservatives preached. He rejected slash and burn budgets that pleased taxpayers in the short-term because he feared the lasting long-term damage such a strategy inflicts on a city. His willingness to enact unpopular tax increases to protect vital services reflected his instincts to invest in an enterprise to strengthen it. Small government advocates did not appreciate how firmly Bloomberg's entrepreneurial business philosophy was rooted in building something up and delivering service excellence for a premium price rather than in cutting costs, except when circumstances compelled it or analysis showed a program should be dropped. The disconnect revealed just how little New Yorkers really knew about Michael Bloomberg when they elected him—less than they had known about almost anyone they had ever elected mayor.

And among the many things they did not know about him was how he would police the city in an age of global terrorism.

Chapter Four

The Safest Big City in America

Michael Bloomberg had no experience policing a metropolis or managing anti-terrorist strategies when he took control of a city shell-shocked by the 9/11 attacks. He understood he had to move swiftly to demonstrate that he could handle this critical element of his job. During the first week after his election, he chose Raymond Kelly to serve as police commissioner. The decision would turn out to be one of his best. News accounts reported Bloomberg had considered appointing Bernard Kerik, Mayor Giuliani's last police commissioner, to reassure New Yorkers that the policies they associated with a dramatic fall in crime would continue. It was fortunate that did not happen. Kerik later wound up in prison on corruption charges.[1]

Kelly announced three priorities on the day Bloomberg swore him in. He would use police resources to prevent another terrorist attack on New York, he would improve relations between the police and the city's blacks and Latinos, and he would continue to drive down crime—both violent acts that create fear and minor ones that diminish the quality of life. He moved on all three priorities simultaneously.[2]

Ray Kelly Returns

Bloomberg consulted with Mayor Giuliani and former mayors Koch and Dinkins when considering Kelly, who by then had spent more than thirty years in the NYPD. "Kelly knows every button, lever and switch" in the department, was how one deputy chief once described him. He rose from first in his class of cadets in 1963, to commissioner when David Dinkins appointed him in 1992, stepping down in January 1994 after Giuliani became mayor. In the eight years that followed, Kelly led an international law enforcement initiative in the troubled country of Haiti, and served as US Treasury under-secretary for enforcement, responsible for the Secret Service and the Bureau of Alcohol, Tobacco and Firearms Control. He also served as commissioner of the Customs Service, and as vice president of Interpol, the international police organization. In an age when global terrorism would feature high among the NYPD's priorities, a police commissioner who knew how federal and international law enforcement agencies worked seemed a smart choice. Kelly had also served in the United States Marine Corps, including twelve months of combat duty in Vietnam, reaching the rank of colonel in the reserves. And he was highly educated, earning an undergraduate degree at Manhattan College in the Bronx, and law degrees from St. John's and New York University, and a master's degree in public administration from Harvard.[3]

Kelly had been police commissioner in February 1993 when radical Islamic terrorists hid explosives in the garage beneath the World Trade Towers that blew a seven-story hole in the structure, killing six people. That experience left Kelly keenly aware of the terrorist threat to New York City, and the September 11, 2001 attack had a personal quality for him as well. He was global head of security for Bear Stearns at the time and was living in Battery Park City, just west of the towers. The catastrophe destroyed his neighborhood and left him unable to return to his home for several weeks. When he got there, he could look out his window and see the smoldering scene of the crime.[4]

The department Kelly inherited in 2002 was larger and stronger than the one he left eight years before. The Compstat approach to policing that William Bratton pioneered, combined with a substantial increase in resources, allowed the NYPD to accomplish two goals that had long eluded American law enforcement agencies. The first was creation of a well-developed two-way flow of information. Priorities set at the top were clear to the cops on the streets, and the intelligence gathered on the streets traveled swiftly to headquarters. The second was to allocate police resources when and where intelligence indicated it would matter most, rather than rely on routine patrols. In great measure, the approach changed the goal of policing in New York City from catching criminals after the fact to preventing crime. The combination of more resources and smarter police tactics improved safety all across the city, in neighborhoods rich and poor, black and white, Latino and Asian.[5]

"Compstat reform has had a successful run," Professor Eli Silverman wrote in *NYPD Battles Crime,* published toward the end of Giuliani's rule. "But no show runs forever." The reduction in crime was so great, many experts believed it had reached a floor and could not continue to fall. And the departure of Rudy Giuliani—the man of legend who had seized control of an ungovernable city with "sword flashing" to "slay the beasts of business as usual" as one *Daily News* editorial put it—caused many to fear the evil forces that had plagued New York for years would return.[6]

Bloomberg knew that keeping the city safe was paramount. "Businesses do not want to locate in cities where crime is a serious problem and where they cannot attract an educated work force," Bloomberg told the Citizens Budget Commission as a candidate identifying his two top priorities. "Moreover," he continued, "families move to the suburbs taking their tax dollars with them when public schools are mediocre and public safety is a problem. New York has already made enormous strides in reducing crime and this record must be maintained," he asserted. When Bloomberg named Kelly head of the police department, he announced the role would report directly to him, highlighting the post's importance. He made it clear that the NYPD would continue to police "quality-of-life" crimes aggressively, referring to minor infractions that nonetheless diminished people's sense of security in public places.[7]

The control Compstat offered the NYPD's leader appealed to Kelly, who many considered a micromanager. At times he would deny it, but he confessed he did not consider the term pejorative. "I see it as paying attention to details when it's needed most," he said. He created a customized briefing document, *Police Commissioner's Weekly Agency Overview,* which grew to 263 pages by 2011 when a *New York Times* reporter got hold of one. It covered everything from the number of members in each major gang in the city (8,800 Bloods, 3,249 Crips), to the number of police horses in the department (59), to the number of artists in its database of graffiti offenders (11,108 chronic vandals) along with fifty pages of talking points on recent news topics. In his own mind, Kelly was a "situational manager," a leader who responded to the facts of each event. His style fit well with Bloomberg's, who would tell his staff at City Hall, "In God we trust, all others bring data." Kelly always did.[8]

Kelly also brought Bloomberg exceptional credibility on a topic where the mayor had none. The local police commissioner's background in national and international law enforcement arenas gave him unusual stature above and beyond the already high level of respect normally accorded to the leader of the largest police force in the United States. Colonel Kelly's Marine Corps command presence projected an aura of disciplined control over complex events. His vaguely bulldog-like face and close cropped hair screamed street-cop, but he dressed in custom-tailored suits and Charvet ties (bought on sale, he insisted) as befitted a powerful New Yorker. He explained arcane police and security matters with the simple clarity and clipped diction of an NYPD detective, but with the sophistication of a highly educated man. The combination, when added to his mastery of the relevant facts whenever he addressed important matters, made him the symbol of a New York City defiantly determined to crush criminals and thwart terrorists. Bloomberg, unlike his predecessor, embraced the credibility his commissioner provided. He appeared with Kelly as frequently as his role required, but was content to let Kelly represent the city's law enforcement positions when public concern did not require the mayor's presence. Kelly would become the city's longest serving police commissioner.[9]

The NYPD had just over thirty-nine thousand uniformed officers and almost fifteen thousand civilians in January 2002. Budget cuts over time caused the uniformed number to dwindle to about thirty-six thousand by 2005, and to thirty-four thousand by 2013, 20 percent lower than at its peak under Mayor Giuliani. Redeployment of one thousand or more officers into anti-terrorist work stretched resources even further. Kelly, like Bloomberg, had an affinity for technology and relied on it as a force multiplier. His department upgraded computerized maps of the city streets to track crime reports in real time. To respond to the information developed, he teamed-up two-thirds of his new recruits with experienced officers and deployed them in high crime areas— Operation Impact he called it. He installed thousands of security cameras in public places, initially in lower Manhattan to protect the financial district, then in midtown and elsewhere. His staff monitored them remotely 24/7 from an $11 million Real Time Crime Center at One Police Plaza, enhancing anti-terrorist and anti-crime management. Most of the information was available inside mobile communication units that could be positioned near trouble spots. The visual database the cameras created could be searched electronically. In a matter of seconds detectives could see all the footage of pedestrians in red shirts in a particular place for a specific time period, or the location of a particular car with a certain license plate number. Kelly also had radiation and toxic chemical sensors placed around the city and on patrol officers' belts to detect would-be terrorist threats. He built a counterterrorist bunker in Brooklyn with specialized training facilities and secure access to national security reports.[10]

The historic downward arc of crime in New York City continued, at a slower rate than in the 1990s, but still an impressive one. According to official records, 30 percent fewer crimes were committed in 2013 than in 2001, the year before the Bloomberg/Kelly law enforcement team took control. Murders fell by nearly half to 335, the lowest number since statistics were kept. The good news in New York between the end of 2001 and the end of 2013 happened while elsewhere in the United States crime rates reached a floor and stopped falling. For the first time in roughly a half-century, New York followed a different, safer pattern than the rest of the country. And while across the United States a record number of Americans were being incarcerated, the number of inmates sent to prison from New York City courts declined by about 36 percent. That meant some twenty thousand fewer New Yorkers were deprived of their liberty at the end of Bloomberg's rule than in the beginning. Bloomberg could declare accurately, that "New York has not only kept our city safer; we've done so while locking fewer people up."[11]

Early in his administration, Bloomberg took an important step to insure the integrity of the city's criminal and family courts by restoring a good-government practice Mayor Koch initiated and Mayor Dinkins followed, but that Mayor Giuliani abandoned. By executive order in March 2002, he created a judicial screening panel and charged it with presenting three qualified candidates for open appointments for judges. Bloomberg reserved the right to reject the committee's nominees if he found them lacking, but he would not appoint anyone it had not deemed fit to serve. And he would automatically reappoint sitting judges the panel deemed qualified to insulate them from political pressure. The provision also applied to interim appointments for civil court.[12]

Analysts checked the Bloomberg administration's extraordinary policing results against demographic information that sometimes explains movements in crime rates. They found the composition of the populations in Brooklyn, Queens, and the Bronx had not changed much at all, and crime rates in those boroughs dropped about the same amount as they did in Manhattan. Crime rates in Staten Island had long been lower than elsewhere in New York City and they remained so. Skeptics challenged the numbers and accused the police of underreporting incidents to make themselves look good. Undeniable evidence emerged that commanders cooked the books in at least three precincts. But careful studies by independent academics confirmed that crime went down substantially as claimed.[13]

Locking up twenty thousand fewer inmates saved the city almost $1.5 billion per year according to one independent academic study. Reducing the police force by five thousand officers saved an estimated $500 million more per year. Michael Bloomberg promised to make city government operate more efficiently. The NYPD and related law enforcement services did. And they did it while assuming direct responsibility for protecting the city from international terrorist threats, a function prior mayors had left to Washington, DC, with tragic consequences.[14]

The Anti-Terrorism Capital of the World

Seared into Kelly's mind on 9/11 was recognition that New York City could not rely on the federal government to protect it from foreign terrorist attacks. That lesson caused him to create a global intelligence division and a counterterrorism force. The audacity of the idea was breathtaking—a local police force with a worldwide perspective that could unearth terrorist plots wherever conceived and prevent them from reaching New York City. When Kelly proposed hiring a deputy commissioner for counterterrorism and another for a reconceived intelligence unit, Bloomberg approved it. "The world no longer stops at the oceans," the mayor said at the time. "We have to make sure we get the best information as quickly as we possibly can," he asserted. It was the same concept—accurate information delivered in real time to people making important, complex decisions—that had been the basis for Bloomberg's global business. Kelly had little trouble convincing his boss of the need, or the viability of the bold idea, even though at the time he had not yet developed a detailed plan.[15]

Kelly rapidly changed the status of the NYPD on the Joint Task Force on Terrorism that the FBI had been running in New York City since 1980. He named retired Marine Corps Lieutenant General Frank Libutti the first NYPD deputy commissioner for counterterrorism, and he increased the number of NYPD detectives assigned to the group from twenty to more than one hundred. By sheer presence, the additional manpower raised the level of intelligence available to the NYPD. "It's not brain surgery," Kelly would say when explaining how additional resources led to improved results. "We muscled our way in. . . . We wanted granular information—and we got it any way we could get it . . . grabbing it, pushing and shoving." But the attacks that took down the Twin Towers did little to remove the barriers to information sharing among sixteen different federal intelligence agencies, or between federal and local law enforcement departments like the NYPD. Official turf battles, the stuff of movie- and real-life legend, remained as intense as ever, putting New York at risk of a second wave of terrorist acts.[16]

Kelly recruited David Cohen to serve as deputy commissioner for intelligence. He was a thirty-five-year Central Intelligence Agency veteran experienced in operations as well as information gathering, who capped a controversial career with five years as the New York City field office representative, the city's CIA station chief. It was Cohen who had created a special intelligence unit to follow Osama Bin Laden and al-Qaeda globally in 1996, an approach that fell outside the typical geographic structure of the agency's projects. It was innovative, but ultimately unsuccessful in stopping the 9/11 attacks. One version of the story asserts that elected decision-makers and senior policy-makers failed to take actions Cohen's team recommended. Every morning Kelly met with his intelligence and his counterterrorism deputies, and the three men brainstormed about what actions to take.[17]

Initially, Cohen worked his CIA contacts to make sure his unit had the best and most up-to-date information possible about al-Qaeda and Osama Bin Laden, still at large and plotting attacks on America. As details emerged from terrorists interrogated as part of the federal government's rendition programs, Cohen learned of them rapidly, not always through formal channels. Yet, Cohen and Kelly knew that to be successful over the long-term they would need more structured access to intelligence. There was no such thing as information sharing among intelligence agencies, only information trading. If the NYPD wanted to know what others learned, it had to offer valuable information of its own. That meant creating a network of analysts and spies to gather it.[18]

Shortly after he started his new role, Cohen came up with a list of some fifty different languages and dialects the department would need—Egyptian Arabic and Moroccan; Caribbean Spanish and Mexican; Mandarin and Cantonese; Urdu and Farsi; and on and on. Kelly, who knew most everything there was to know about his department, knew where Cohen could find the linguists he needed. Police work in New York had long been an entry-level job for immigrants. Its officers came from 106 different countries and NYPD records listed 2,500 employees who spoke a foreign language. The team asked for volunteers and the Berlitz language school tested 1,800 who responded. Before long, the department had 700 employees designated as "expert," and about 200 who received perfect scores and became "master linguists." Forty-five of fifty languages were covered in a matter of months. The diversity of New York City's population, one of the reasons fundamentalist terrorists targeted it, gave it the raw material to defend itself. In a year when the total number of undergraduate degrees granted in Arabic from all of the colleges and universities in the United States was six, and when the FBI had thirty-three agents with "some proficiency" in Arabic, the NYPD had more than sixty fluent Arabic speakers across a range of dialects. At federal intelligence agencies, foreign born citizens and Americans whose parents came from abroad were considered security risks. The number of native foreign language speakers they could field was remarkably small. The speed with which the New York intelligence unit mounted a team of highly capable linguists stunned federal agencies.[19]

An NYPD cyberunit worked online with an effectiveness other agencies could rarely match. Hate blogs preaching *jihad* were terrorist recruiting tools. The NYPD infiltrated them with foreign-born officers who had grown up speaking local dialects and who had ties to their ancestors' countries. The terrorists knew to be suspicious when recruiting online and would lay traps to test a supposed sympathizer's authenticity. "You know the mosque that burned down last year . . ." they would probe. "I was visiting family there last year and it was still standing. What are you talking about?" would come the reply. School-trained linguists, even the rare ones who were fluent, lacked the local knowledge to fool terrorist recruiters that way.[20]

Cohen also attracted some of the best and brightest from the country's elite universities, gifted students who had chosen to study topics related to global violence and terrorist activity around the world. For decades, Washington, DC, had been the only place for them to work. Now New York City was an option. Academic experts, as knowledgeable as anyone in the United States about different terrorist groups, their history, motivation, and practices, were teamed up with streetwise New York City detectives and sent into neighborhoods around the city to determine if terrorist groups were plotting attacks. The initiative created formidable combinations of brains and experience. A Brooklyn born-and-bred twenty-year veteran who had worked New York's streets might be assigned alongside a Harvard Kennedy School/Harvard Law School graduate who had studied international terrorism and national security law before spending time at the Council on Foreign Relations and at the Organisation for Economic Cooperation and Development in Paris learning about France's nuclear energy industry.[21]

As effective as the local intelligence team would become, Kelly and Cohen knew they would need access to information from key locations abroad. They decided to place NYPD liaison officers in Scotland Yard in London, and with police intelligence units in other key cities where national agencies developed important insight about terrorist groups. The NYPD would eventually colocate with eleven key departments around the world. To avoid potentially complex discussions about jurisdiction and the use of public money far from New York City, Kelly relied on the New York Police Foundation for funding, a nonprofit organization that provided private money unrestricted by government rules. Some good-government groups viewed the practice as a dodge that avoided proper oversight of government decisions. To Kelly and team, the clear and present danger of ongoing terrorist threats made the approach imperative.[22]

The purpose of the international liaison program was to create a relationship of trust, "cop to cop," outside the bureaucracy of embassies and national agencies. NYPD officers would work with local police to develop intelligence on how different international terrorist groups operated. Each had a way of doing things that constituted a signature. The NYPD wanted to learn to recognize them, so if one showed up in New York it would have a chance to disrupt their plots. One NYPD officer stationed in Amman, Jordan, when terrorists bombed a train in India took the next plane to Mumbai and secured a meeting with the local police commissioner. Details of the bombing made their way back to New York with a speed and effectiveness no other agency could match. The department learned the bombs were assembled near the train station. The next day, the NYPD increased patrols around the city's 468 subway stops and instituted random searches of bags and backpacks on the New York system. New Yorkers reading the headlines knew their police department was working to protect them.[23]

The next year, after terrorists seized a hotel and other buildings in Mumbai, the NYPD returned. Within five days its team produced a seventy-five page report. The department briefed four hundred New York City building security directors on the events so they could develop defenses. Kelly concluded that his department lacked sufficient heavy weapons manpower to respond to a similar attack, and had 250 officers from the Organized Crime Patrol Unit trained. "It would take years to get a report like that from the federal government," one local law enforcement official remarked. Kelly knew terrorists strike at moments of their choosing without regard to the typical pace of bureaucratic decision-making. The "flash-to-bang" time working with him, the time it took to convert an idea into action, was "lightning speed," in the words of Michael Sheehan, who succeeded Libutti as deputy commissioner for counterterrorism in 2003. He was a former US Special Forces commander who had served on the National Security Council and as Ambassador-at-Large for Counter Terrorism during the Clinton administration.[24]

Federal law enforcement agencies resented the NYPD's expansion of its role into overseas territory. Gathering intelligence abroad for use inside the United States had been the exclusive province of the Federal Bureau of Investigation for many years. But from Kelly's perspective, the FBI "took in a lot of information, but it didn't let it out." Senior officials in Washington, DC, tried to block Kelly's team, but with Mayor Bloomberg's full support the NYPD proceeded without pause. Eventually, federal agencies realized they were fighting a losing battle and begrudgingly accepted the new normal in international law enforcement as it related to New York City. By 2004, Kelly could send letters to the CIA, FBI, Defense Intelligence Agency, and National Security Agency offering help with linguistics. It was a sincere offer, but also a clear statement. In time, other agencies came to recognize that the NYPD had information to share, information that would help other agencies to protect the United States better than they could without it.[25]

Kelly initiated a series of actions designed to instill confidence in the public and fear in terrorists. Every day, on short notice, he would send Emergency Service Units and well-armed Hercules teams—what most departments called SWAT teams—to specific locations that might be the target of an attack, along with over 150 officers plus captains and sergeants. The officers came in pairs in squad cars from each of the seventy-six precincts around the city distributing the load so the neighborhood of the training target did not lose its normal protection. The approach provided a continuous reminder for police in every precinct to remain alert for signs of a terrorist threat that could emerge anywhere, anytime. It had the same impact on the general public. The surges served an intelligence-gathering purpose as well. When crowds gathered around the site of one, plainclothes detectives watched to see if anyone reacted suspiciously to the show. And the tactic signaled to any group contemplating attacking the city that formidable resources were deployed against them. In response to one interviewer's question, Kelly revealed that the NYPD had developed the capability to shoot down an aircraft if an emergency called for it.[26]

The counterterrorism team enhanced general public awareness of potential threats with Operation Nexus, a program to enlist the support of a broad range of businesses. Items with many normal purposes, like hydrogen peroxide or nitrate fertilizers, cell phones that could be used as timers on homemade bombs, propane gas tanks, storage facilities where materials might be staged, and some eighty categories of businesses became of interest. The NYPD reached out to companies and shop owners in New York and beyond to encourage them to alert law enforcement officials if suspicious people came to their shop. The scope of the effort was formidable. For example, castor beans are part of the raw material required for the manufacture of a potentially deadly poison called ricin. When British police discovered a plot to produce it in London, the NYPD went on alert. Urban legend had it that in short order, Kelly knew the location of every castor bean in New York City. The department sent undercover teams to shops hundreds of miles outside the city to try to buy bomb-making materials to determine how hard it would be, and to learn if shopkeepers would report suspicious purchases. Most of the time they did. The department created training and information-sharing programs with neighboring police forces.[27]

The initial focus of the NYPD and federal agencies was on the foreign sources of terrorist plots. Yet, it became apparent in the years after 9/11 that al-Qaeda's philosophical commitment to violence and loose operating structure encouraged dangerous homegrown radicals. The NYPD analyzed the circumstances that caused otherwise "unremarkable" people to seek to kill innocent Americans. They published their findings in a ninety-two page report entitled *Radicalization in the West: The Homegrown Threat*. It reminded people that the 1993 World Trade Tower bombing and other plots to blow up city landmarks had been hatched in a Brooklyn mosque. It created a stir among Muslims who thought some of its conclusions distressingly general and inaccurate. In particular, the authors wrote: "Unfortunately, the city's Muslim communities have been permeated by extremists who have and continue to sow the seeds of radicalization." The report implied the city's six hundred thousand or more Muslims all represented a danger, rather than a small group within it. The Council on American-Islamic Relations, an advocacy group, issued a statement the day the report appeared. "Whatever one thinks of the analysis in the report," the organization said, "its sweeping generalizations . . . may serve to cast a pall of suspicion over the entire American Muslim community." Subsequent versions of the report included a two-page "Statement of Clarification," that acknowledged "the NYPD understands it is a tiny minority of Muslims" who represented a threat, and that its focus on al-Qaeda-inspired terrorism should not be "mistaken for any implicit or explicit justification for racial, religious or ethnic profiling." The de Blasio administration would remove the document from the NYPD website.[28]

On several occasions, including when police uncovered terrorist plots, Bloomberg cautioned New Yorkers against holding all Muslims responsible for the violent intentions of a few. In August 2010, he demonstrated the depth of his commitment. Imam Feisal Abdul Rauf, a Muslim cleric with a reputation for reaching across religious divides and for preaching a version of Islam that emphasized its spiritual side, arranged to buy land just two blocks from the site of the World Trade Towers. He intended to build an Islamic Center there that would offer religious and community services, as well as interfaith activities. Among other things, it was meant as a symbolic message that the 9/11 attackers who claimed religious justification for their murderous barbarism did not represent all Muslims. "It sends the opposite statement to what happened on 9/11," the imam said. "We want to push back against the extremists."[29]

A majority of New Yorkers opposed the idea according to polls, some stridently. Despite the imam's stated intention, detractors viewed it as an effort by Muslims—those who shared a faith with the attackers no matter how differently each group defined their beliefs—to claim the hallowed ground as their own. The controversy struck the mayor's nerves in several places. As a boy, Bloomberg's family had relied on a Catholic lawyer to purchase a home for them in Medford because the selling broker feared retribution if he sold it to Jews. Bloomberg believed deeply in property rights. "If somebody wants to build a mosque in a place where it is zoned for it and they can raise the money, then they can do that. And it's not the government's business," he said in response to efforts to pressure the city Landmarks Commission to stop the plan. Bloomberg had met the imam a year earlier and deemed him a decent man. When opponents sought to portray him as a radical, the character assassination infuriated the mayor. When the Jewish Anti-Defamation League came out against the plan, Bloomberg declared himself disappointed and called the decision "totally out of character with its stated mission."[30]

In a speech delivered on Governor's Island in New York Harbor on August 3, 2010, with the Statue of Liberty as his backdrop, Bloomberg stated his position in uncompromising language. "In rushing into those burning buildings," Bloomberg said, referring to the firefighters and other emergency workers who entered the World Trade Towers on 9/11, "not one of them asked, 'What God do you pray to?' . . . We do not honor their lives by denying the very Constitutional rights they died protecting. We honor their lives by defending those rights—and the freedoms the terrorists attacked." New York, he declared, is the freest city in the world. "That is what makes New York special and different and strong." Some wrote Bloomberg letters praising the speech. Many more attacked him, but Bloomberg stood his ground. With the unequivocal support of the mayor who had appointed all of its members, the city Landmarks Commission voted unanimously to allow the Muslim developers to proceed with the project.[31]

Yet, Bloomberg was hardly naïve about the nature of the Muslim fundamentalist threat, and he supported his police department's efforts to spy on potential terrorists. Unlike typical criminals, suicide attackers could not be deterred by fear of punishment after the fact. Only fear of being prevented from achieving their mission could discourage them from trying, and the only way to stop them was to learn of their plans in advance and to intercept them. That reality caused the NYPD to petition a federal court to ease special restrictions on political surveillance, including activity involving places of worship, that were part of the Handschu Guidelines, issued in response to a 1971 class action lawsuit that charged the department's intelligence gathering practices violated constitutional rights. A favorable decision cleared the way for the NYPD to create the Demographics Unit, whose mission was to "identify and map ethnic residential concentrations within the Tri-State area," of twenty-nine "ancestries of interest"—all of them heavily Muslim, according to a confidential document the Associated Press published. The unit's work included the controversial tactic of "deploy[ing] officers in civilian clothes throughout the ethnic communities" targeted. It included surveillance of student groups at a range of institutions including the University of Pennsylvania in Philadelphia, Rutgers University in New Jersey, and colleges all throughout New York City and state. NYPD activity at Yale prompted President Richard Levin to protest in an email. Bloomberg was unimpressed. "I don't know why keeping the country safe is antithetical to the values of Yale," he said in response.[32]

Some Muslims took offense to the Demographics Unit's work. Four members of a New Jersey mosque targeted for surveillance filed a lawsuit claiming the NYPD violated their rights under the First and Fourteenth Amendments to the Constitution. A New Jersey federal district court judge ruled otherwise, dismissing the case in February 2014. The intelligence-gathering activity had no tangible impact on any of the plaintiffs, he wrote, and the "motive for the Program was not solely to discriminate against Muslims, but rather to find Muslim terrorists hiding among ordinary, law-abiding Muslims." Bloomberg's successor would disband the unit and agree to civilian oversight of similar intelligence activities. A joint City of New York Inspector General and NYPD Inspector General report published in August 2016 would criticize the department for failing to follow guidelines designed to protect civil liberties, and a federal judge rejected proposed remedies as insufficient. Federal courts would continue to scrutinize NYPD anti-terrorist activity.[33]

Kelly was defiant in the face of criticisms leveled at his department for spying on Muslims in New York and elsewhere, and he responded to them in an interview on WOR-AM in April 2012. "Apologize for doing what I am paid to do, for being realistic about the way we protect this city, and what we know about the way radical Islam works? Not happening," he said. "The notion that the police department should close our eyes to what takes place outside the five boroughs is folly," he told Mike Lupica at the *Daily News*. Yet, the sensitive topic followed him. Kelly sat for an interview for a documentary film, *The Third Jihad*, which portrayed American Muslim leaders as wishing to "infiltrate and dominate" the country. The NYPD used the film in its training program for a time. When Kelly realized how xenophobic and paranoid the finished movie sounded, he expressed regret he had participated in it and the NYPD stopped screening it.[34]

Through a combination of aggressive police tactics and sheer luck, the NYPD and federal agencies disrupted sixteen terror plots aimed at New York City that Kelly called, "live, active conspiracies, perpetrated by people intent on mass murder," between the beginning of 2002 and the end of 2013. Some attempts were serious, others seemed more the stuff of vicious bunglers. Al-Qaeda was just not that good in the opinion of counterterrorism deputy Michael Sheehan, and Bloomberg declined to govern in constant fear of another terrorist attack, according to Edward Skyler. He was determined not to let obsession with terrorist threats distract from other priorities, even as he recognized that the seriousness of the risk justified his police department's intense vigilance. "When you catch a terrorist and you look at the map in his or her pocket, it is always a map of New York," Bloomberg said at one point. While he governed, the city did not let down its guard.[35]

Two Dead Unarmed Black Men

On January 24, 2004, Mayor Bloomberg found himself confronting the reality that police actions can ignite racial tensions. A white officer on routine patrol on the roof of a New York City Housing Authority project, shot and killed Timothy Stansbury, a nineteen-year-old black resident crossing the top of the building with friends in the early hours of the morning. They were taking a shortcut on their way back to a birthday party after gathering up some CDs. The cop, Richard Neri, had just started to open the rooftop door leading to the stairwell when Stansbury pushed on it from the other side. Neri was startled by the abruptness with which he came face-to-face with the young man. He had been patrolling with his gun in his hand and fired reflexively, killing Stansbury with a single shot.[36]

Stansbury was a model young man, a high school senior holding down a job at McDonald's with no history of violence or any interaction with police.

Neri, an eleven-year veteran, was a model cop who had never before fired his weapon and who had never faced disciplinary proceedings. A patrol partner had been with him when the shooting occurred and provided the police with the facts of the shooting. Commissioner Kelly held a news conference the day the tragedy occurred at which he said, "At this point, based on the facts we have gathered, there appears to be no justification for the shooting." He moved quickly, he would tell an interviewer years later, "because I feared the circumstances were so clear that unless we acted fast, there was a risk of retaliation, of someone ambushing a cop," to avenge the killing of an innocent young man.[37]

PBA head Patrick Lynch denounced Kelly for declaring the shooting unjustified so rapidly. When a reporter asked Bloomberg to comment he responded in a matter-of-fact way. "I think in this case it looked to us pretty obvious that a tragedy occurred, that there was no justification . . . and the public has a right to know." Brooklyn District Attorney Charles Hynes brought charges against the officer, but a grand jury refused to indict him after listening to his testimony. Following a department hearing, Kelly suspended the cop for thirty days and permanently stripped him of his weapon, assigning him to clerical duties. The city paid the family a $2 million settlement in 2007.[38]

Mayor Bloomberg and Commissioner Kelly visited the family of the slain youth, and Bloomberg spoke at the young man's funeral, quoting the Bible and speaking of his love for his own children. It was a "powerful" statement delivered to "a sea of black faces," Deputy Mayor Walcott would remember. African American leaders took note of the dramatic change in tone in comparison to the way the Giuliani administration responded to police shootings of black residents. Bloomberg was "praised in the fiery oratory" at Stansbury's funeral and by civil rights advocates. African American Councilman Albert Vann who represented the largely black neighborhood of Bedford-Stuyvesant declared, "This can be a defining moment. Things can happen differently in this city," and he thanked Mayor Bloomberg for having the courage to tell the truth. The way Bloomberg and Kelly responded to the tragedy was similar to the way they responded to an incident the year before when police tossed a stun grenade into the wrong apartment during a drug raid in Harlem. The mistake caused fifty-seven-year-old Alberta Spruille, getting ready to go to work at her city job, to suffer a heart attack and die. The mayor acknowledged the tragic error within days, and the city settled the lawsuit that followed with unaccustomed speed. Kelly transferred the head of the unit responsible and instituted policy changes to prevent a repeat of the tragedy.[39]

A more complex police shooting than the one that struck down Timothy Stansbury occurred on November 25, 2006. At a Queens strip club, a twenty-three-year-old African American man named Sean Bell had been celebrating with friends at his bachelor party. The NYPD had identified the place as a location of drug use, underage drinking, and prostitution. Illegal weapons had been confiscated there. Undercover cops were outside the club, and inside it as well. About 4:15 a.m., Bell and his friends who had been drinking, left the club and got into a fight with someone outside who gave the impression he was carrying a gun. The fight broke up with one of Bell's friends saying, "Yo, get my gun, get my gun," as they headed to Bell's car. By the time they got there and Bell began to drive, an undercover cop had approached the vehicle and positioned himself in front of it. It is unclear if Bell knew the man was a police officer, but he accelerated rapidly. His car brushed the cop and then crashed into an unmarked police van almost head-on as it converged on the scene. Bell backed his car across the street so fast he hit a metal gate covering a storefront, and then accelerated forward hitting the police van again. The officer who had first approached the car saw a man inside it twist around in a motion that could have been reaching for a gun. In the chaotic moment, he opened fire, provoking other officers to do the same in what police call contagion shooting. In a matter of seconds five cops fired fifty bullets.[40]

Sean Bell died on the day he expected to be married. Two friends suffered multiple wounds and went to the hospital. As it turned out, no one in Bell's car had a gun. In simple terms, that made it an instance of NYPD cops killing an unarmed black man. The tragedy stunned the city, and the sheer volume of bullets fired created the impression of trigger-happy cops. It evoked bitter memories of the Amadou Diallo killing. Two of the officers who fired shots were white, two were African American, and one a Latino.[41]

Mayor Bloomberg called Bell's fiancée to express condolences, and he met with her and Bell's family. He also convened a meeting of a group of the city's African American leaders, including Reverend Sharpton, who the family had named an advisor and who had already denounced the shooting. Bloomberg described Bell's killing as "an excessive use of force," and said that to him, as a civilian untrained in police tactics, it was "inexplicable how you can have 50-odd shots fired." He told the group he anticipated Queens District Attorney Richard Brown would impanel a grand jury to review the evidence and act accordingly. With Commissioner Kelly in the room, he pledged to review the city's policies to prevent a repeat of the tragedy. Some participants described the session as heated, while others acknowledged it as a far more constructive approach than the city had often taken in the past. Reverend Sharpton captured both sentiments when he said of the meeting, "We prefer talking to not talking, but the object is not a conversation. The object is fairness and justice."[42]

The day after the shooting occurred, Commissioner Kelly put the officers involved on administrative leave, which was typical, but he also ordered them to surrender their weapons, which was not. Publicly, Kelly took respectful exception to the mayor's characterization of the shooting. In an interview later the same day Bloomberg made his comments, Kelly told a television reporter, "The mayor is certainly entitled to his opinion. I think we need an in depth examination of all the facts," although he acknowledged the number of shots fired was unusual. The stakes for Kelly and the city were high. "Ray Kelly's word is seen as good in a lot of our community," Reverend Sharpton said. "But now his word is on trial." A few weeks later, as Christmas approached, Sharpton led a march he called "Shopping for Justice," down Fifth Avenue and across 34th Street. The size of the crowd it attracted made it clear that the shooting, like the one that killed Amadou Diallo, had struck a nerve. A demented city jail inmate tried to hire an assassin to murder and behead Commissioner Kelly and to blow up One Police Plaza in revenge for Sean Bell's killing. It turned out he was talking to an undercover cop.[43]

Kelly hired the Rand Corporation to review the NYPDs firearms training, including an analysis of ways to prevent contagion shooting. A department review took place as Bloomberg promised, and in 2007 the NYPD implemented twenty-three changes to policies for undercover operations at night clubs. Later, the city would agree to pay the estate of Sean Bell $7 million. A grand jury indicted the police involved on a range of serious charges. They were tried in Queens and acquitted on all counts in 2008. Major protests followed, but they were peaceful and wound down fairly rapidly. The police department held an administrative hearing. NYPD regulations forbid officers to fire at a motor vehicle, even one being used dangerously, unless another weapon was involved. They also require shooters to pause after three shots to reassess the situation and the imminent danger that led to the use of deadly force. In March 2012, the NYPD dismissed one of the officers who shot at Bell and forced two others to resign. One of the shooters had already left the department, and one who apparently had adhered to guidelines was exonerated. The lieutenant in charge of the operation was also forced to resign even though he had not fired his weapon. By the time the ramifications of Sean Bell's killing played out, Bloomberg and Kelly were caught up in a much broader clash of police tactics and racial tensions.[44]

Stop, Question, and Frisk, Mostly Young Men of Color

When a patrol officer sees a person who fits the description of a criminal suspect, or can "articulate . . . reasonable suspicion" that criminal activity may be "afoot," it is standard police practice to stop and question the person. If the officer has reason to fear the person stopped is armed and may pose a danger to the cop or others, then the officer is allowed to conduct a frisk—a pat-down on the outside of the person's clothing to see if there is a weapon. If the frisk gives reason to believe a weapon is present, then a full search of the suspect is allowed. In many ways stop, question, and frisk is at the heart of proactive policing. "It's a basic tool. It's the most fundamental practice in policing. If the police are not doing it, they are not doing their job," Ray Kelly would tell an interviewer. The United States Supreme Court has ruled the tactic constitutional.[45]

In a metropolis the size of New York, the scale of activity often dwarfs the numbers that seem reasonable elsewhere. In 1990, the NYPD reported stopping and questioning more than 40,000 people. Lax recordkeeping procedures at the time give reason to believe the number is understated. The practice rose fairly steadily during the 1990s as police tactics became more aggressive, but really took off following Kelly's return to the department. In 2002, the number totaled just under 100,000. By 2004, the number surged to more than 300,000, and by 2011 the police stopped and questioned more than 685,000 New Yorkers, a number larger than the population of Boston. They frisked more than half of the residents they stopped. Between January 2004 and June of 2012, dates referenced in court cases, the NYPD stopped more than 4.4 million citizens, and frisked some 2.3 million. Eighty-eight percent resulted in no further action. Six percent resulted in arrests, and 6 percent in a summons. In 1.5 percent of the cases the police found an illegal weapon. In just 0.1 percent of stops an arrest resulted in a conviction for a violent crime. Kelly asserts the numbers grew mostly because he insisted on accurate recordkeeping so he could be confident cops were policing the streets with the vigilance required to keep them safe. Any increases beyond that were the result of actions in the field by local commanders and officers doing their jobs, he claims, not a consequence of orders from One Police Plaza.[46]

The very small 1.5 percent of stops that led to discovery of an illegal weapon, multiplied by 4.4 million meant the police confiscated more than 66,000 deadly devices, mostly knives but also about 4,400 guns. Removing guns from the street was a huge priority for Bloomberg. In 2002, after an uptick in shootings, he announced an amnesty. The city offered to pay any New Yorker who surrendered a handgun, assault weapon, or sawed-off shotgun $100 with no questions asked. Bloomberg lobbied for stiffer federal controls on guns, and the NYPD sent undercover officers to forty gun stores in other states that had been traced as the sources of multiple weapons used in New York City crimes. In twenty-seven, the cops succeeded in buying guns in ways that the city claimed violated federal laws. New York City filed suit, winning the right in at least twenty-one instances to have a federal master oversee activities in the stores for several years and ensure federal rules were followed. The city also took gun manufacturers to court, but its suit was dismissed after Congress passed the Protection of Lawful

Commerce in Arms Act, exempting weapons makers from liability risks that applied to most companies, an action Bloomberg and other mayors denounced. Still, the stop, question, and frisk program was the centerpiece of efforts to reduce the number of guns on the street.[47]

Unsurprisingly, most of the stops took place in the parts of the city with the highest crime rates. That's where the benefits would be greatest. Since over 80 percent of New York City crime suspects, and 90 percent of violent crime suspects, were black or Latino according to police statistics, it is equally unsurprising that the neighborhoods most affected were heavily black and Latino. Those were also among the poorest districts in the city. Bloomberg and Kelly saw the aggressive stop, question, and frisk program as a commitment to ensure that poor New Yorkers of color who lived in neighborhoods with the highest incidences of crime received the same protection as other New Yorkers. It was an act of social justice in their minds. "If you look at a map showing where crime is, it is clearly concentrated in a couple of areas, and the people in those areas have a right to live in a safe neighborhood just like those who are lucky enough to do so today," the mayor said, when announcing that all of the police cadets in a new class about to graduate would be assigned to Operation Impact to patrol high crime districts. A *New York Times* editorial praised the decision. In a Citizens Crime Commission Survey published in January 2004, 59 percent of New Yorkers expressed strong support for police searches to ensure safety, 30 percent moderate support, and just 10 percent said they disapproved, although fear of terrorism seemed to drive the answers more than concern about street crime.[48]

Yet, as the number of street encounters grew, they became increasingly controversial. More than 80 percent of the people stopped were people of color, 52 percent African American and 31 percent Latino. Just 10 percent were white. The people stopped most often were young men between the ages of eighteen and thirty-four, the group most responsible for crime. Young men of color were also most often the victims of violent crime, so while the program seemed to target them, it also protected them more than any other group. The logic behind the practice and the numbers seemed clear to the mayor and to the police commissioner. "The NYPD conducts stops based on seeing something suspicious," the mayor said, not on "demographic data that would have you stopping old women as often as you stop young men." For his part, Commissioner Kelly declared, "crime is down, and stop-and-frisk is an important reason why." In an ABC News interview he claimed that the department actually stopped fewer African Americans than logic suggested, since 70 to 75 percent of criminal suspects were described by their victims as black. A Rand Corporation study he commissioned, "Analysis of Racial Disparities in the New

York Police Department's Stop, Question, and Frisk Tactics," examined the issue in technical detail and supported the claim. Kelly also denied repeatedly that the department engaged in racial profiling.[49]

Others saw it differently. Nearly 90 percent of the stops resulted in no suspicious findings, meaning hundreds of thousands, ultimately millions of law-abiding New Yorkers were stopped by police, and in many instances for no apparent justification other than they were young men of color. Critics of the program would point out that a statistic that showed 80 percent or more of suspected criminals were black or Latino was very different than a presumption that 80 percent of blacks and Latinos are criminals. As one grandmother put it after watching the police stop a small group of black youngsters playing ball, "All the kids are not bad." Others captured the mood in African American neighborhoods by accusing the police of treating "walking while black" as sufficient reason to suspect someone of a crime.[50]

The policy had a range of unintended and undesirable consequences. Young men of color not engaged in criminal activity felt singled out and discriminated against. It caused them to distrust the police and made them less likely to report crimes, according to the Vera Institute for Justice. Cases emerged where individuals were stopped, questioned, and frisked more than twenty times as they walked from the public housing developments where they lived to the local subway station where they caught the train to go to work. Since 1977, a New York State law had barred the arrest of people in possession of small amounts of marijuana provided it was not being smoked or displayed in public. In many instances, cops who found marijuana after stopping a person declared it on public display, even though it was the police officer's search that caused it to be pulled from a pocket or backpack. The practice became common enough to have a name: "manufacturing misdemeanors," cops called it. In 1990, one thousand low-level marijuana arrests occurred. By 2011, the number had risen to fifty thousand. Since most of the stops were of young black and Latino men, so were the arrests, even though studies showed whites, African Americans, and Latinos used marijuana in roughly equal proportions—Latinos a little less than others, whites a little more. The mayor was a case in point. During the 2001 election campaign, a reporter asked Michael Bloomberg if he had ever smoked marijuana. "You bet," he answered, "and I inhaled and enjoyed it." He later apologized for the comment.[51]

In most cases the charges were dismissed before trial, but the arrests created serious risks for many. They could disqualify people from working in law enforcement, joining the armed services, or from any employment that required a background free of criminal activity, like private security guard, or that required a city license, like cab driver. It could disqualify a person from a right to public housing and it could provide the basis for legal immigrants to be deported. It layered an additional obstacle to employment onto a class of Americans who traditionally struggled more than others to find steady jobs.[52]

Compstat intensified the impact of the policy. Every time a police officer stopped and questioned a person, the NYPD required completion of form UF-250 providing basic details, including the reason for the action based on a list of possibilities. Categories included things like "furtive movements," and "high-crime district," and "suspicious bulge." The number of stops conducted in each command was closely tracked by NYPD brass. That caused local commanders to insist that the cops patrolling in their precincts stop and question a lot of people. Patrolmen complained to reporters that they were being forced to stop innocent kids. Beginning in 2006, the NYPD created a database with all of the information gathered from its stop-and-frisk records, "to be used primarily by department investigators in the course of criminal investigations," Kelly informed the city council in response to questions. Of course, the vast majority of the names in the database were people who had done nothing wrong. But the database put their names on record as having been stopped by the police because of "reasonable suspicion" that criminal activity was "afoot," according to the standard that applied to the tactic. The potential for mischievous use of the information was obvious. In 2010, the state legislature passed a law forbidding the department to keep the records, and Governor Paterson signed it over Mayor Bloomberg's and Commissioner Kelly's strong objections while criticizing the practice as "not a policy for a democracy."[53]

Along the way, two class action suits developed, one with Jaenon Ligon as lead plaintiff, and the other with David Floyd in that role. They contended the NYPD's tactics were illegal. US Federal District Court Judge Shira Scheindlin heard both cases, and in separate decisions in 2013, found that the NYPD stop, question, and frisk practices violated the Fourth Amendment's protection against unreasonable search and seizure without due process, and that it violated the Fourteenth Amendment's prohibition against race based discrimination. Kelly denounced the trials as "horrendous," and bitterly criticized Scheindlin for disallowing the Rand Corporation's analysis of stop, question, and frisk racial disparities to serve as evidence. The Bloomberg administration protested the decisions, claiming Scheindlin took inappropriate actions to ensure she heard both cases out of a personal desire to rule against the police department, and not as a matter of administrative efficiency as she claimed. A three-judge panel censored Scheindlin for speaking publicly about the cases while they were in progress, and removed her from further responsibility for them. Bloomberg's law department petitioned the court to vacate Scheindlin's ruling as a result of the irregularities, and when that failed, it filed an appeal. After Bill de Blasio became mayor, the city dropped the suit and ordered the police to work with a court monitor to implement remedies.[54]

Scheindlin's opinion was forceful. "In their zeal to defend a policy that they believe to be effective," she wrote of the NYPD and the city, "they have willfully ignored overwhelming proof that the policy of targeting 'the right people' is racially discriminatory and therefore violates the United States Constitution." She also wrote: "One NYPD official has even suggested that it is permissible to stop racially defined groups just to instill fear in them that they are subject to being stopped at any time for any reason—in the hope that this fear will deter them from carrying guns in the streets." The comment was attributed to Kelly by State Senator Eric Adams, an African American former police captain who often sparred with the commissioner. Kelly called the accusation, "absolutely, categorically untrue." The racial element in the statement does not sound at all like Kelly. Yet, it is easy to believe he sought to create a generally hostile environment for people carrying guns in high-crime districts that happened to be predominantly black and Latino. He told a *Wall Street Journal* reporter, "If you don't run the risk of being stopped, you start carrying your gun, and then you do things people do with guns. And you see what you have in some other places in this country." Bloomberg told one church group, "By making it 'too hot to carry' the NYPD is preventing guns from being carried on our streets." His comment also suggested a policy-driven program, rather than event-driven stops consistent with constitutional requirements.[55]

As the court cases played out during 2013, the number of stops NYPD officers conducted fell by nearly two-thirds in comparison to the year before. To the surprise of many, the crime rate remained the same as before the significant cutback. And while the number of stops dropped by over 70 percent between 2011 and 2013, the number of murders fell by 35 percent, from 515 to 335, the lowest level on record up until then. Shootings declined as well. Kelly attributed the fall to a major anti-gang program, "Crew Cut," instituted about the same time. An assessment of the 5.1 million stops that occurred between 2002 and 2013 while Bloomberg governed and Kelly ran the NYPD, reveals that murder and major crime dropped with substantial consistency in years when the number of stops were relatively low and in others when they were high. There appears to be no statistical correlation between the number of stops and frisks and the pace of decline in crime rates. The numbers do not prove the activity did not deter crime, but no analysis to date demonstrates a clear connection between the scope of the tactic and a consequent decline in violence and lawlessness.[56]

The police department's decision to scale back stops came too late to avoid formal actions to restrict it. A Quinnipiac University poll showed that despite high confidence in the NYPD and Kelly, by April 2013 a slight majority of New Yorkers disapproved of the city's stop-and-frisk actions. Unsurprisingly, attitudes differed dramatically by race. Fifty-nine percent of whites supported the program, but only 24 percent of African Americans, and 36 percent of Latinos did. In June 2013, the New York City Council created an independent Inspector General to monitor the police department—a move popular sentiment supported by a 66 percent to 25 percent margin and a majority of all races polled—and it expanded the definition of bias-based profiling to make class-action suits easier for people who believed the department's policies discriminated against them. Kelly opposed both measures adamantly and criticized the city council for ignoring what he asserted was the compelling fact that the aggressive tactics protected young African American and Latino men from fatal violence. Mayor Bloomberg vetoed both bills declaring the issue a matter of "life and death." The council overrode his decisions. "Make no mistake," Bloomberg said in response. "The communities that will feel the most negative impact of these bills will be minority communities across our city, which have been the greatest beneficiaries of New York City's historic crime reductions." He defended the policy fiercely in op-ed columns. Fortunately, the tragic increase in violent crime that he, Commissioner Kelly, and conservative commentators predicted did not occur.[57]

The stop-and-frisk controversy is perplexing. In 2000, speaking of the Giuliani administration's policies, Kelly told an audience of attorneys at the New York City Bar Association: "A large reservoir of goodwill was under construction when I left the police department in 1994. . . . But it was quickly abandoned for tough-sounding rhetoric and dubious stop-and-frisk tactics that sowed seeds of community distrust." The day Bloomberg swore him in as commissioner, Kelly declared improving relations with the city's blacks and Latinos one of three key priorities. In March 2002, Kelly published a department-wide memo stating in strong terms that racial profiling had no place in the NYPD as a tool for arrests, car stops, or other enforcement actions. He claimed the memo simply put into writing what had been the department's policy all along, but that it was important to publish it to respond to African American concern on the topic. Just a month later, Kelly disbanded what remained of the Street Crime Unit that had been involved in the Amadou Diallo killing. He explained the decision as a housekeeping detail, but he knew it had symbolic significance for African Americans who viewed the unit as dangerously aggressive in black neighborhoods. On Kelly's watch, a majority of NYPD uniformed police officers became non-white, a huge shift aligning the department's demographics with the city that relied upon it. As federal Customs Commissioner, Kelly had ended practices that smacked of racial profiling and replaced them with thoughtful, more effective guidelines.[58]

In February 2002, when reporters asked Mayor Bloomberg what had changed in New York City since the Amadou Diallo shooting three years before to reduce the chance it would happen again, his response was, "Ray Kelly and Mike Bloomberg." Their open communication with the city's African Americans and their constructive attitudes were perceived as likely to ensure fairness and justice. "Not only is it a different tone," Al Sharpton said of the new administration at the time, "it's a whole new sound system." And the emotional climate in the city in the immediate aftermath of 9/11 seemed disposed to foster greater harmony. In response to a June 2002 *New York Times*/CBS survey, for the first time in fourteen years a majority of all races reported relations between their group and others were generally good, 53 percent of blacks, 56 percent of Latinos, and 69 percent of whites.[59]

Mayor Bloomberg and commissioner Kelly were both astute enough to realize that the scale of the police action and the intensity of resistance that developed toward it among African American leaders, elected officials, and civil libertarians was bad for the city, particularly after the emotional outpouring that followed the Sean Bell shooting. The way the "dynamic played out undermined the credibility of stop and frisk and what the goals were," in the view of a senior City Hall official. Another simply acknowledges, "I can't explain it." Pursuing the tactic as aggressively as they did for as long as they did seems at odds with their general recognition of the importance of maintaining strong relationships with New York's black and Latino communities—roughly half the city—and the leaders who represented them. Kelly asserts that community resistance came largely from advocates, and that his frequent visits to black churches were met with expressions of support. The statement may be technically accurate, but it ignores the broader truth that stop-and-frisk tactics were deeply unpopular among a supermajority of African American New Yorkers. Bloomberg and Kelly were guilty of the very things Kelly had criticized in his 2000 speech, depleting over time the goodwill that had greeted Bloomberg's election and Kelly's second tour as commissioner.[60]

Kelly's motivations are clear and admirable. In a speech at Reverend Al Sharpton's National Action Network in 2013 he said, "African-Americans aged 16 to 37, just 4 percent of the city's population, comprised 40 percent of those murdered citywide; 82 percent were killed with a firearm. As a city, we cannot stand idly by in the face of those facts." In testimony before the New York City Council he challenged his detractors to offer a better alternative for getting guns off the street and stopping shootings, with the clear implication that no one had one. He defended the scale of the program by pointing out that the seemingly huge number of stops amounted to less than one per officer, per week. Conservatives, like Heather Mac Donald at the Manhattan Institute, agreed with him that the numbers were not "out of whack" with a city the size of New York.[61]

Despite concerns about stop, question, and frisk, public confidence in Commissioner Kelly remained consistently high. Polls showed him the most popular official in New York City, with an overall approval rating as high as 75 percent at times, including a smaller but still comfortable majority among African Americans throughout his tenure. When asked during the height of the controversy if he had considered replacing Kelly, Bloomberg responded, "As God is my witness, never once." Kelly acknowledged he would have been unable to pursue the controversial approach without the mayor's political cover. One senior City Hall source told a reporter that he had never seen an agency head with such sweeping, unchecked power and who so intimidated other city officials. Bloomberg's support for Kelly was unequivocal to a degree that was unwise. A different civilian leader, more sensitive to democratic due process, might have recognized that the police have an institutional bias toward any action they believe reduces crime, at times at the expense of civil liberties. He might have provided his extraordinary police commissioner with a moderating influence and caused a better outcome for the city and the NYPD. After all, virtually none of the opponents of stop, question, and frisk sought to end the practice. They wanted it modified to adhere to constitutional norms and to avoid stigmatizing one group of New Yorkers in ways that caused symbolic and tangible damage. Lamentably, their sincere desire to protect New Yorkers in high crime districts caused Bloomberg and Kelly to descend into mutually reinforcing, highly stubborn arrogance in defense of unconstitutional tactics. Kelly would continue to defend the policy in his memoirs.[62]

Yet, when considered as a whole, the Bloomberg administration's policing record was extraordinary. The city experienced fewer murders and major crimes than at any time in its modern history, while spending millions of dollars less at the police department, and reducing the number of New Yorkers deprived of their liberty by more than one-third. Simultaneously, the city built the most effective counterterrorist and intelligence division of any local police department in the world. Protecting people and their property is the primordial purpose of government. At a graduation ceremony for a new class of NYPD cadets on December 27, 2013, days before he left office, Mayor Bloomberg declared, "New York's crime fighting strategies have made us America's safest big city— and one that cities across the globe want to learn from. Twelve years ago no one thought New York's crime rate could go any lower. But it did." He was right to acknowledge the remarkable achievement.[63]

Chapter Five

Creative Destruction in the School System

"If an unfriendly foreign power had attempted to impose on America the mediocre educational performance that exists today, we might well have viewed it as an act of war," the National Commission on Excellence in Education wrote to President Ronald Reagan's education secretary in April 1983. Its seminal report, *A Nation at Risk*, was a self-described "Open Letter to the American People" that called on citizens to reverse "the rising tide of mediocrity" in the nation's schools. Their deplorable condition, the report asserted, threatened the "once unchallenged preeminence in commerce, industry, science and innovation . . . that undergirds American prosperity, security and civility." The country's deep-rooted loyalty to local control of schools meant some fourteen thousand districts—of which New York City was the largest—would have to muster for reform. The fractured response that followed seemed less like a nation mobilizing to defend a vital interest than an undisciplined confederation of educational militias, each marching to the beat of its own school band.[1]

A decade later, little had changed. American Federation of Teachers leader Albert Shanker warned of a reckoning to come. He compared the state of the teaching industry to the American automobile industry a few years before. "They could see they were losing market share every year and still not believe that really had anything to do with the quality of the product. Then, when it was almost too late and they were about to go out of business, they pulled themselves together," he explained. "I think that we will get—and deserve—the end of public education through some sort of privatization scheme if we don't behave differently," he told his union members. "Very few people really believe that yet," he surmised ruefully in 1993.[2]

Shanker had been the head of New York City's United Federation of Teachers before he moved to the national stage. He had been a principal protagonist in the city's school decentralization battle that led to state legislation in 1969 creating a system one chancellor described as a two-headed monster. A central Board of Education was responsible for high schools, special education programs, and a range of administrative functions. It consisted of seven members appointed by six different politicians, two by the mayor and one by each of five borough presidents, virtually assuring incoherence. Thirty-two community school boards, each with nine elected members, exercised substantial control over elementary schools and junior high schools in their designated neighborhoods. In theory, the central board selected a chancellor who served as chief executive of the dual system. In practice, board members and thirty-two local school districts, teachers' and administrators' unions, school custodians, central office bureaucrats, education advocates, parents, local politicians, the governor, the mayor, and their deputies, and others with a stake in the system clawed the chancellor to pieces. Savvy New Yorkers had concluded that no one smart enough to do the job of chancellor was dumb enough to accept the position. Few lasted long, so even well-conceived programs typically lacked the administrative follow-through required for enduring improvement.[3]

Over time, many New Yorkers came to view the central Board of Education as a monument to inefficiency. Its structure made it impossible for members to provide the leadership the massive system required. Worse still, in many neighborhoods the community school boards degenerated into rats' nests of political patronage and corruption. At one point during the Koch administration eleven of the thirty-two—more than one-third—were under criminal investigation. Mayors Beame, Koch, and Dinkins asked for direct control over the schools, and Governor Mario Cuomo sought to deliver it at one point, but the politics that supported the status quo proved more powerful than the combined authority of the highest elected officials in New York City and New York State. Meanwhile, despite pockets of excellence and thousands of committed professionals, the majority of the million children enrolled in New York City public schools suffered. Wealthier citizens had choices and exercised them. They sent their children to private or religious institutions. Poorer citizens, primarily of color, were stuck with a failed system.[4]

Mayor Giuliani adopted an aggressive posture toward the Board of Education when he became mayor in 1994. "The whole system should be blown up and a new one put in its place," he said. Early on, he sought huge cuts in budgets bloated with hundreds of millions of dollars of unneeded administrative functions and politically motivated appointments. Later, he restored some funds and supported specific reforms. Like his predecessors, Giuliani sought control over the schools, and like them he failed to secure it. During his second term, school performance trended up, but at the end of his eight years in office, fewer than 40 percent of high school students passed New York State Regents exams. The same dismal percent of elementary and middle-school students achieved grade-level proficiency in English or math on city and state tests, and only half as many—19 percent to 22 percent—reached proficiency on more rigorous federal tests given by the National Association of Educational Progress in the years immediately after Giuliani left office. Barely half of all students graduated high school in four years and fewer than 70 percent graduated at all. A poll published by the conservative Foundation for Education Reform and Accountability a year after Giuliani left office revealed 80 percent of New York City public school parents, three-quarters black or Latino, would send their children to private or religious schools if they could afford the tuition.[5]

The Mayor Must Control the Schools

Prior to the terrorist attack, during the 2001 election campaign for mayor, every survey confirmed that improving the city's schools was the most important issue to voters. In his autobiography, Bloomberg had written that his "greatest love" as a philanthropist "was helping educational organizations." He told the Citizens Budget Commission that fixing the schools had to be a top priority because when they are broken people take their tax dollars to the suburbs and businesses do not want to locate where they cannot attract an educated workforce. He said he wanted to do for public education what Rudy Giuliani had done for public safety—restore it and make it work the way it was meant to work. The extraordinary decline in crime during mayor Giuliani's tenure boosted public confidence in city government and in the future of New York City as a place to live and to work. Real improvement in the school system would have similar far-reaching consequences, far beyond the positive long-term impact on the children themselves. In no small measure, the dire straits of the city's schools, and the extraordinary benefit improving them could have, motivated Bloomberg to run for mayor. He told voters he wanted them to judge him on how well he accomplished this goal. The challenge fit his disposition to take on big projects where the chance for success might be small, but the outcome so worthwhile that the risk and the work involved justified the time and resources invested.[6]

In the presence of New York's political classes assembled with unusual solemnity for his inaugural address in the aftershock of 9/11, Bloomberg declared: "We will test our students. We will test our teachers. But the real test is that of political resolve, the test of ourselves. The need is real. The time is now. Without authority there is no accountability. The public, through the mayor, must control the school system." On his very first day in office, Bloomberg took on the challenge of mayoral control that had defeated mayors Beame, Koch, Dinkins, and Giuliani over more than a quarter of a century. Within six months, he had accomplished it.[7]

The mayor's team, led by deputy mayors Marc Shaw and Dennis Walcott, submitted a proposal to the state legislature to restructure the system. Republican Governor George Pataki and Republican state senate leader Joe Bruno were favorably disposed. Greater accountability suited them philosophically, and control would go to a mayor just elected on their ballot line who had donated over $700,000 to the New York State Republican "housekeeping" account in 2001. New York City's Republicans worked the corrupt school system as shamelessly as Democrats, but the great majority of the city's local elected officials were Democrats, so restructuring the system would weaken their party disproportionately. Winning the support of the Democratic speaker of the assembly became the key to achieving the goal. Sheldon Silver favored the move, but Deputy Mayor Shaw knew that "without the union, Shelly would never agree to the change."[8]

The United Federation of Teachers contract had been expired for eighteen months when Bloomberg took office. During the first half of 2002, Shaw wrangled with UFT President Randi Weingarten over terms. Mutual respect and easy access characterized their talks. Shaw would often arrive at City Hall by 7:00 a.m., and sometimes, shortly after he got settled in the conference room he favored, his phone would ring. Weingarten, Shaw concluded, could see the window of the room where he sat from her downtown apartment, and when something was on her mind, she would call him as soon as the lights went on. Both knew that collective bargaining law forbid connecting school governance to contract negotiations. Both also knew that as a matter of practical politics, the two were inextricably linked. Bloomberg, prone to speak his mind and inexperienced in the political theater of municipal labor negotiations, said so at one point. Weingarten filed a complaint with the state in response. The governor declared the two matters separate. But in April 2002, speaking at a meeting of two thousand UFT members, Assembly Speaker Silver declared, "All the mayor can talk about is getting control of the schools. But I cannot move forward with a schools plan . . . unless this city's teachers get the contract and the pay raise they deserve." One journalist described his stance as "legislative blackmail." If so, the blackmail was mutual.[9]

Not long after Silver's comment, the union's delegates nearly unanimously authorized its leaders to seek the permission of its members to call a strike if necessary. It was posturing designed to increase pressure on city negotiators, and "to appease angry teachers who feel their union has not been sufficiently forceful in the long-stalled talks over a contract," according to the *New York Times.* "This is the level of frustration and demoralization that is in our membership right now," Weingarten declared, noting her disappointment that she and mayor Bloomberg had been unable to reach an agreement rapidly.[10]

By then, a state labor panel had proposed a generous settlement along lines Shaw found acceptable. It was not binding, but it raised the pressure on the parties to agree. Neither side rejected it. Negotiations over mayoral control had also advanced, consistent with the most important elements of the mayor's proposal. Among other efforts, Bloomberg testified before the City Council Education

Committee, and he spent two hours with key legislators in Gracie Mansion reassuring them of his motives and intentions in a way his predecessors never had. "Members of the caucus had more of a comfort zone with this mayor," Roger Green, an assembly Democrat who headed the Black, Puerto Rican and Hispanic Legislative Caucus told a journalist. On June 6, 2002, Bloomberg and Weingarten agreed to contract terms, and the same day the UFT announced its support for the mayor's plan to restructure the school system. On July 1, 2002, Mayor Bloomberg had control of the vast New York City school bureaucracy. Bloomberg's "negotiating prowess contributed mightily" to the outcome, a journalist wrote in the *New York Times*. Despite his success, one official involved in the discussions thought the process left Bloomberg feeling bruised. The mayor had expected to win school control on the merits of the issue, not in return for a contract settlement. It had been more than two decades since the CEO of Bloomberg LP had been forced to confront power equal to his own in that type of negotiation. The episode was part of the mayor's education.[11]

By the time Weingarten accepted mayoral control, she viewed it as inevitable. At the national level, in January 2002 President George W. Bush had signed landmark legislation known as No Child Left Behind designed to raise educational standards across the country. Other major American cities, including Boston, Cleveland, and above all Chicago, had shifted from decentralized school systems to mayoral control. Early returns suggested the change helped. The voices in New York City and New York State calling for improved public education were as loud as anywhere in the nation. If the UFT refused to support a proposal to fix a system universally perceived to be in desperate need of repair, the accusation of obstructionism would echo across the city and state, damaging Weingarten's reputation and her union's standing. The generous wage agreement the city offered the UFT, despite dire budget straits, boosted Weingarten's credibility with members angry they had not had a raise in three years. And Weingarten had been among the many to feud with Giuliani. Marc Shaw believed the union president welcomed the opportunity to demonstrate her willingness to collaborate with the new mayor in the post 9/11 environment while still delivering for her members. "In the end, it was not so hard," Shaw said modestly of the enormously important accomplishment he and Deputy Mayor Walcott engineered on Bloomberg's behalf. Weingarten agreed. "No one was going to give Giuliani control," but once he passed from power, the path to mayoral control was clear.[12]

The contract settlement boosted teachers' pay between 16 percent and 22 percent over thirty months in return for an additional hour and forty minutes at school every week. A proposal to develop formal teacher evaluation mechanisms linked to merit pay dropped out of the talks. The school governance law eliminated the thirty-two elected community school boards. It gave the mayor direct authority to select a schools chancellor, and the chancellor the authority to select superintendents for the local districts. Legal maneuvering by assembly Democrats later on would prevent complete elimination of the districts, but stripped of their elected boards and almost all of their authority, they lived on as legal artifacts, shells of their former selves.[13]

The law gave a greatly diminished Board of Education the ability to approve capital and expense budgets and some other things, but mostly it would have an advisory role. Importantly, the mayor would control eight of thirteen votes, seven appointments plus the chancellor as chairman. The five borough presidents would appoint one member each. Bloomberg renamed the body the Panel on Educational Policy to distinguish it from the former board that had been responsible for managing the system. Silver inserted a sunset clause that required the legislature to review the new structure in seven years—toward the end of a second Bloomberg term if there were one. Silver also included a provision that the city could not reduce its funding for education unless its revenues declined. While not exactly the structure the mayor sought, it was "a homerun with two men on. No other mayor could get to first base," in the words of New York City education expert Joseph Viteritti. Federal civil rights rules required formal acceptance of the law by the US Department of Justice, which was granted without drama.[14]

The Antitrust Chancellor and the Untrusting Union Leader

Mayoral control was a fundamental condition for improving the schools, but on its own it assured nothing. Entrenched stakeholders ensured powerful bureaucratic inertia. Bloomberg understood the depth of the challenge, and from the start he signaled his intention to force root change. In March 2002, projecting complete confidence he would win the authority he sought, he surprised the city with an announcement that he would make the newly renovated Tweed Building the new headquarters for the city's education department. "The first thing we are going to do," he told a group of children assembled for a press photo opportunity, "is we're going to move the central administration of the school system right next door to the mayor's office because it is the most important thing in this city." The building would include a school, so that every day the people responsible for running the system would be reminded "what their mission is." The symbolism of the move was exquisite. The Board of Education headquarters, at 110 Livingston Street in Brooklyn, had become the physical manifestation of the system's dysfunction. Closing it down and placing its occupants right beside City Hall announced the end of one era and the start of another. Dennis Walcott would declare himself eligible for "Frequent

Walker Miles" for the number of trips he made "back-and-forth, back-and-forth" between the two buildings.[15]

The schools chancellor was the highest-profile appointment Bloomberg would make other than police commissioner. Eva Moskowitz, chairperson of the City Council Education Committee, compared the chancellor's role under mayoral control to the first premier of the Soviet Union after its empire collapsed. The old, defunct system was all its people knew. Motivating them to do things differently would require leadership of the most forceful kind. It would have to be someone prepared to do battle with a recalcitrant system, and with the guile to maneuver successfully through the bureaucratic and municipal minefield in the way of the goal. Bloomberg considered educational administrators with national reputations, but feared professionals raised in the stale logic of a failing system would lack the mental agility to reform it. Instead, he chose Joel Klein, a lawyer who had served for just eighteen months as CEO of the United States operations of the German media company Bertelsmann. It was a surprising choice.[16]

Klein was the Bronx-born son of a postman father and a bookkeeper mother raised in Brooklyn and Queens. He attended New York City public schools, graduated *magna cum laude* from Columbia University and from Harvard Law School as well. He taught math for a few months to sixth graders in Astoria, Queens, where he had once gone to school himself. That experience, and a few years teaching law at Georgetown University, was the extent of his career as an educator. Klein clerked for Supreme Court justice Lewis Powell, helped found two law firms, and established a reputation as a highly skilled appeals court attorney before joining the Clinton White House as deputy counsel. He helped navigate the political minefield of the Whitewater Investigation, and went on to the United States Department of Justice where he rose to become the assistant attorney general for antitrust. On his watch, the division blocked or modified almost two hundred mergers, put fifty-two executives in prison, and collected some $2 billion in fines. Klein took on Microsoft, accusing it of abusing its monopoly power in computer operating systems. In a ferocious legal battle, he and his team prevailed against the technology giant in federal court and on appeal. Upon leaving government, Klein opted for something new, accepting the role with Bertelsmann for more than $2 million per year in guaranteed compensation.[17]

Klein had been among a group of professionals who served as informal education policy advisors to Washington, DC, Mayor Anthony Williams, and he had crossed paths with *Time* magazine correspondent Margaret Carlson, who knew Bloomberg well. When Bloomberg began looking for a schools chancellor unconstrained by ideas developed within the existing framework of public education and unafraid of enormous challenge, Carlson recommended Klein. By any standard, he was an impressive man with a record of success at the highest level. Yet, his executive experience was limited to eighteen months at Bertelsmann. The seven hundred attorneys Klein had overseen at the Justice Department was a rounding error in comparison to the 120,000 employees in New York's schools. He lacked pedagogical credentials, so his appointment would require a waiver from the New York State education commissioner. Nevertheless, shortly after interviewing Klein in a meeting with Nat Leventhal and deputy mayors Harris and Walcott, and a follow-up session with Marc Shaw, Bloomberg decided Klein was the one for the job.[18]

Observers pointed out that Klein had much in common with Bloomberg. They were of the same generation, two Jewish kids born to families unconnected to wealth or fame who worked hard and became successful, self-made men. Both boasted Harvard graduate degrees, analytical minds, and a willingness to tackle problems others found intimidating. But more than anything else, Klein's fearlessness confronting Microsoft is what convinced Bloomberg to select him. "Jesus Christ wasn't available . . . and I thought Joel was smart and tough as nails for a job that really required that," Bloomberg told author Steven Brill of his decision. And in the minds of many, the public school system was the ultimate monopoly in need of a trust-buster. Parents unable to afford private options had little choice of where to send their children to school, which in turn gave bureaucrats the power to persevere indefinitely despite repeated failure.[19]

During his interview, Klein made it clear that if Bloomberg named him chancellor, he would seek to slay the torpid leviathan and replace it with something completely different, not try to make marginal improvements by being a better bureaucrat. That suited Bloomberg perfectly, who would remain closely engaged in the high-profile effort he launched. Together with Deputy Mayor Walcott, he met with Klein weekly to review progress, and more often when circumstances required it. The terrain proved as hostile as promised. Missteps, of which there were more than a few, proved costly since so many critics stood poised to pounce on every one, none with greater purpose than UFT chief Randi Weingarten.[20]

Weingarten was born to a Jewish family in New York City in 1957 and grew up in Rockland County where she attended public schools. Her mother was a teacher, whose union went on strike for seven weeks when Weingarten was in the 11th grade. The job action cost strikers two day's pay for each one they did not work, a penalty Weingarten thought unfair. She also thought it unfair when her father's employer laid him off without notice, causing financial hardship and intense family anxiety. Weingarten would always consider layoffs cruel. After studying at Cornell University's School of Industrial and Labor Relations, serving as a legislative assistant for the Labor Committee of the New York State Senate along the way, Weingarten earned a JD from Cardozo School of Law. After she handled several arbitration cases on behalf of the United Federation of Teachers, she became counsel to UFT President Sandra Feldman in 1986. Union members elected her assistant secretary in 1995 and treasurer in 1997. Weingarten had chosen a legal career as a way to pursue important causes. At the UFT, she found herself at the intersection of the labor movement and public education, two institutions that gave "ordinary individuals [who] don't have any power on their own," a way to climb the ladder of opportunity. She believed the union she worked for allowed people living in a "capitalist democracy . . . who were not born with a silver spoon in their mouth . . . to actually have control over their own destinies and power over their own lives." When Feldman became the head of the American Federation of Teachers in 1998, Weingarten was her handpicked successor to head the UFT, and New York's labor chiefs selected Weingarten to head the Municipal Labor Council responsible for coordinating union activity with the city.[21]

For almost eighteen months after Bloomberg's election, Weingarten granted the new mayor a honeymoon and signaled support for his administration's efforts to reform the broken school bureaucracy. In May 2003, the romance ended and Weingarten became a combative foe. Yet, on specific occasions she proved a crucial ally agreeing to proposals that might have been expected to ignite fierce opposition. Her fans described her as a hard-working, intelligent union official committed to helping the public school system migrate from mediocrity to excellence at the pace her members could travel. Peter Cunningham, a US assistant secretary of education who dealt with Weingarten held that view. "Randi is unequivocally trying to support reform, but there is a militant wing in her union that will vote her out if she moves too fast," he said of her. "She is a negotiator, and negotiators need to get to the finish line, not create immovable obstacles." Weingarten's detractors denounced her as a cunning defender of a discredited status quo, a pretend-partner-in-reform who resisted the scope of change required to achieve real success for schoolchildren. Her wily cooperation consisted of the smallest concessions possible to secure the most generous benefits for her members. They viewed her call for collaboration as code for her desire to hold on to as many unjustifiable work rules as she could at a time when their corrosive impact on school performance had brought them under siege.[22]

The day Bloomberg announced that Klein was his choice to lead the schools, Weingarten told a journalist: "He's a non-traditional choice. We're going to give him a chance. We hope everyone else does as well." Despite the initial statement of goodwill, the selection process had put Weingarten on guard. Bloomberg had not involved her, which she took as a message that he did not see her as a full partner in school reform. "I knew there was going to be a problem," she would say years later. The relationship between Klein and Weingarten got off to a bad start during a lunch meeting shortly after the new chancellor's appointment. Klein asked the UFT leader how she thought the two could work together to fix the school system. Her answer was through "continuous, incremental change." Weingarten believed that other approaches to improving government bureaucracies invariably proved unsustainable. Klein believed only radical reform could fix New York City's schools. Early on, he took his bold agenda public declaring that the union contract's "three pillars of mediocrity: life tenure, lockstep pay, and seniority-based decision making," were the greatest impediments to developing excellent schools.[23]

Klein's statement constituted a frontal assault on work rules that union officials had negotiated over the years. He was correct that the contract provisions he sought to destroy contributed to the broad based failure of city schools. Yet, they had been implemented originally in response to management abuses only too real in the minds of teachers who had lived for decades in a politically corrupt system, and who had often struggled in daily working conditions no reasonable person would find acceptable. Securing agreement on the changes he sought would require a relationship of trust between city teachers and the department of education. The starting point for that was trust between Weingarten and Klein, which could not be sustained. The union chief responded to the chancellor's posture by accusing him of "scapegoating" her members. She dismissed his focus on specific contract provisions as efforts to distract New Yorkers from realizing that the chancellor had no experience running a school system and did not know how to fix the one now in his charge.[24]

The scope for real collaboration between Klein and Weingarten, narrow from the start, all but ended in 2003 when the city announced plans to lay off some 864 paraprofessionals who belonged to the UFT. Weingarten tried to avoid the job cuts by suggesting tactics often used in the past, like borrowing from city pension funds. Bloomberg declined to sanction "gimmicks" that satisfied short-term needs but compounded long-term problems, and Weingarten rejected proposals that teachers pay for part of their pension contributions or other benefits. Klein thought the layoffs unfortunate but necessary in the context of the post-9/11 fiscal crisis, and modest in comparison to cuts at other agencies at a time when none could expect to be spared entirely. Weingarten's ferocious reaction caught Klein by surprise. "Boom, boom, boom, boom, boom," was how he described the blows the UFT president delivered one after another in response to the layoffs. "I don't punch first," Weingarten said of the event, acknowledging with her choice of words that she viewed the layoffs as a call to combat.[25]

As Weingarten tells the story, her discussion with Klein over the fate of the paraprofessionals left her livid. "He called them 'thumb-suckers,'" she claimed, with evident anger, a charge Klein denies. "It was a terrible thing to do," she would say over and over again. "How dare you do this to low-wage workers," she thought. And there was a power equation to the episode as well. "Klein knew how passionate I was about averting layoffs," Weingarten said. She thought Bloomberg and Klein went forward with the move in part to show her who was boss. "It was clear that what they wanted to do was basically say, 'We run the school system. You listen to us, teachers. You do what we say. You do what we tell you.'" She accused the mayor and chancellor of treating the school system as if it was "their business" to run as they pleased, rather than a public good with a full range of stakeholders.[26]

The union filed a civil rights suit claiming racial discrimination against the predominantly African American and Latino workers who were fired, an act Klein dismissed as a public relations stunt. Suddenly, the chairman of the New York State Assembly Education Committee and sixteen other legislators gave support to a lawsuit claiming the Department of Education could not eliminate district superintendent roles as it had planned. "That was not an independently happening event," Klein surmised. Then, at her union's annual spring conference at the Hilton Hotel in Manhattan, Weingarten denounced the mayor and his chancellor. She listed a series of concerns the union had raised about the proposed education reforms and accused the city of responding to none. For effect, she mounted a goofy bobble-head doll on her speaking podium while a screen behind her projected her message in big letters: "They Just Don't Get It," it read. She derided the efforts of the "CEO mayor" and his "lawyer chancellor" accusing them of seeking to implement a "hierarchical, command-and-control" structure rather than respecting teachers as professionals.[27]

Bloomberg and Klein had many supporters among editorial boards, principals, teachers, and parents who viewed their commitment to change as offering the best chance to create a school system that worked. Yet, the view that a businessman and a lawyer lacked the knowledge to run the schools grew and intensified over time among educators and other critics. Diane Ravitch, a former US assistant secretary of education and renowned historian of the New York City school system, became one of the most prominent. She would point out that for nearly a century, between 1873 and 1969, when New York City mayors had sole authority to appoint all Board of Education members, the boards invariably chose an experienced educator as chancellor. Under Bloomberg, Ravitch wrote, "that tradition—in which a mayor relied on and respected the professional judgment of educators, was abandoned, and the city embarked on a form of intrusive and authoritarian control unprecedented in city history."[28]

The substance of the criticism was that the two men running the schools ignored decades of relevant experience about one of the city's most complex institutions. The emotional subtext attacked them as arrogant and disrespectful of educators who had dedicated their professional lives to developing programs to teach children and adolescents. In time, displaced and disenfranchised educators, union leaders, unhappy parents, community activists, and others coalesced into an anti-Bloomberg, anti-Klein coalition in opposition to their reforms. Given the stakes and the extent of the changes undertaken, resistance was unavoidable. Aspects of the two men's backgrounds and personalities contributed to the intensity with which the opposition emerged.[29]

After the layoffs, Weingarten concluded she could not trust Klein. She came to view him as a "trustbuster," working with a model that required "destabilizing" the school system. According to a union official familiar with what happened next, Weingarten concluded that working with Klein was unlikely to accomplish the things she thought important, so she developed a strategy of working around him. She nurtured her relationship with Mayor Bloomberg, and negotiated with sympathetic members of the education department when possible. When those channels proved inadequate, Weingarten appealed to allies in the city council and the state legislature, the governor or community activists. When Klein's department made mistakes, she was quick to seize opportunities to diminish his credibility. Periodically, she would call for the mayor to fire him. Bloomberg stood by his appointment with fierce loyalty. In a comment Klein would describe as "so Bloombergian," the mayor called him one morning to tell him, tongue in cheek: "I'm really upset. Randi just said you should be fired. Now I can't fire you even if I want to." It was a welcome statement of support from a boss "who had my back better than anyone I ever worked for," Klein said, although Bloomberg's temper would flare privately when Klein and his team blundered. The chancellor was grateful for the protection. The union leader who was one of the city's most skillful political tacticians had become his "most formidable foe." Klein and Weingarten would prove worthy adversaries.[30]

Power to the Principals

In October 2002, Klein launched a study called *Children First: A New Agenda for Public Education in New York City.* It was a plan for a plan, a road map that outlined a process for developing a new governance structure for 1,200 schools, many of them failing. It led to two fundamental conclusions. For schools to succeed, principals needed greater control over instruction and budgets, and parents needed to engage more deeply in their children's education. For principals to wield expanded authority effectively, they had to be well-trained, high-caliber professionals. Some were, many were not. Encouraging parent involvement with neighborhood schools had been one of the community school boards' primary purposes, but most failed at the task. Klein, and a new team he hired with active involvement from Deputy Mayor Walcott, set about developing plans to push the bureaucracy in the direction they wanted it to move.[31]

It is not unusual for a new leader of a large, complex organization first to centralize authority, and then to distribute it while retaining accountability for results. The initial phase allows the leader to understand the organization and to hire a competent and loyal team. Together, they develop a strategy and identify measures they will use to evaluate success. Then the leader can distribute authority for implementation, confident the team will lead in the direction desired, and that deviations can be spotted and corrected. That is what happened at the New York City Department of Education in three phases in 2003, 2007 and 2010, in a messier manner and with more uncertainty than a summary after the fact makes it sound.[32]

In a speech high on symbolism as well as substance, Mayor Bloomberg announced the first reorganization on Martin Luther King Day in January 2003 at the Schomburg Center for Research in Black Culture. The new structure "will be one, unified, focused, streamlined chain of command," dedicated "to instruction and instruction alone," he declared. Instead of thirty-two community school boards and eight more divisions, just ten Regional Superintendents, among the department's "top ten best educators," would report to a deputy chancellor for teaching and learning. They would sit together in the Tweed Building to "coordinate policy and provide direct accountability from the top down." Each would lead a Learning Support Center with ten Local Instructional Supervisors, and each of those would work closely with the principals at a dozen or fewer schools focusing exclusively on instruction. Every school in the system would have literacy and math coaches who would work with teachers, and a parent coordinator reporting to the principal, responsible for facilitating parent engagement with their children's education. Weingarten, still on her honeymoon with the mayor, praised the initiative. "The implementation is going to be tough," she cautioned, but "it is breathtakingly possible."[33]

Central control through Klein's hand-picked team put an end to the corrosive patronage politics of the old system. "When I go to choose my assistant principal, I don't have to buy tickets for the next dinner for some politician," one South Bronx principal told an interviewer gratefully. When local officials appealed directly to Klein for favors, he rebuffed them knowing the mayor would never undercut him. The new approach also reduced the administrative staff that swarmed community school boards from six thousand bodies down to several hundred. The resources freed went back into the classrooms and administrative effectiveness improved. Yet, the Regional Superintendents and the Local Instructional Supervisors turned out to be old-school in a literal sense. They behaved the way administrators did in the old system, exercising strict control, micro-managing principals and teachers, de-motivating them in the process and giving them the ability to blame failure on the supervisors' rules rather than their own decisions. In 2004 Klein asked Eric Nadelstern, a longtime Board of Education employee with a reputation for innovation and effectiveness, to figure out how to fix it. He responded by launching the Autonomy Zone.[34]

The Autonomy Zone began with twenty-nine schools placed at the top of the organization rather than the bottom in the belief that the principals who ran them, in consultation with teachers, parents, and sometimes students themselves, were best placed to make important educational decisions. It re-oriented administrators, superintendents, and other staff to think of themselves as working for the principals rather than supervising them. The role of the central office was to remove obstacles to instruction, not create them. In return for autonomy, principals had to accept performance contracts detailing the results they would deliver. The contracts typically included things like low truancy, the percent of students expected to pass citywide exams, and graduation rates. It was a prescription for "a system of excellent schools rather than for an excellent school system," Klein declared. It relied on three fundamental principles of effective management: leadership, empowerment, and accountability. Those attributes were part of Bloomberg's core beliefs about how to run an organization, and consistent with Klein's own management experience.[35]

For the new approach to work, principals had to possess the skills required to transform failing schools into successful ones. "If low-performing schools knew how to fix themselves, they would do it," one school superintendent pointed out in a statement of the obvious. There was little reason to believe the highly political selection process that had staffed the system's school leaders for more than thirty years had produced the talent required. Early on, Klein estimated about 400 of the 1,200 or so New York City Board of Education principals were "first rate." The new initiative would fail if two-thirds of school leaders proved unequal to the redefined task. In response, Klein and team adopted two key policies: annual performance reviews of principals designed to identify and force out the weakest ones, and specialized programs to train talented educators to become principals of the kind the new program required. Since 1997 school administrators had the authority to dismiss any principal with a record of "persistent educational failure." Klein's predecessors had not used the power, but he announced in December 2002 that he planned to fire the fifty poorest performing principals within a year if they did not improve. It signaled a new level of accountability and an intolerance of failure. Klein would make it an annual practice. He also created special training programs, a Leadership Academy in 2003, and later, programs that groomed administrators within the schools where they worked. The department also developed a close relationship with New Leaders, a national agency that trained teachers as principals and educational administrators.[36]

In the spring of 2006, Klein invited principals across the system to join the Autonomy Zone and 332 did. Beginning in the fall of 2007, Klein adopted the Autonomy Zone structure for the entire education system. Authority for instruction and school-based budgeting shifted directly to principals, with each entering into a contract detailing the results on which the department would judge performance. Superintendents evaluated progress, but they did not have day-to-day management authority over principals. The new structure also gave principals a choice of a dozen or so School Support Organizations offering different educational philosophies and a different mix of resources in support of classroom instruction. One was the Autonomy Zone itself, renamed the Empowerment Zone. Four were run by Department of Education Regional Superintendents deemed up to the task. Universities and nonprofit agencies ran the others. School leaders had to choose one, effectively identifying their school as philosophically similar to others that made the same choice. Most opted for one of the education department-run programs. School systems in other cities that had experimented with autonomy typically offered it as a reward to principals who had achieved excellent results. Bloomberg's Department of Education offered it prospectively, and on a scale unmatched anywhere in the nation.[37]

In 2010, Klein required each school to join one of about sixty Child First Networks. The decision linked together anywhere from eighteen to thirty-five like-minded schools for human resources, technology, and other administrative functions, pushing those support tasks closer to the institutions they served. Devolution to principals of instructional authority, budget control, and school management was greater than it had ever been, while accountability standards remained centralized. By eliminating the geographic structure of operational support—networks cut across two, three, or even four boroughs—Klein broke the last link to the city's political districts.[38]

The new structure mimicked in some respects the way entrepreneurs in a franchise system operate in local markets. Principals had become the leaders of department of education outlets. Klein and his team actively encouraged innovation designating two hundred schools part of an "iZone," granting them additional money to explore creative teaching techniques. Strong administrators unbound from bureaucratic tethers excelled in the newfound autonomy. But, "hundreds of new and inexperienced principals were left to figure out what to do on their own," critics contended. Teachers described principals as constantly "in crisis mode," according to a study of the impact the department's initial reorganization had on special education students. According to one instructor, the changes were "just too much, too fast without enough support." Klein felt the image his opponents drew of young, flailing administrators was a caricature that at best described inevitable outliers. He attributed resistance to bureaucratic discontent from the people losing power, and philosophical objections toward his drive for a merit based system. The School Support Organizations his department created included four run by veteran central office administrators. Principals who wanted the kind of traditional hands-on support the old structure had offered could get it, only now it was their choice, not a "decision imposed on everyone by central."[39]

Klein's approach to fixing the education system was at sharp odds with the model Weingarten's UFT favored. She believed schools worked best when administrators and teachers cooperated and collaborated among themselves and with parents and students. She imagined a system of neighborhood schools through which the broad range of resources needed to support educational success for disadvantaged students could be channeled. In her mind, Klein's drive for principal control and school autonomy disrupted the multiple connections between local schools and the neighborhoods they served. At best, it left it up to individual school leaders to pursue those connections. The two approaches were incompatible. "I could never convince him and he could never convince me," Weingarten would say of the ideological clash.[40]

Teacher Talent

Teacher talent rivals the importance of principal effectiveness in determining how well a school system educates students. The caliber of New York City's public school instructors had deteriorated as it had elsewhere in the country in the last decades of the twentieth century. Yet, diabolical procedures for firing even the most incompetent or malign educator, once tenured, protected misfits. The worst offenders ended up in "rubber rooms," places where they did no work while receiving full salaries as disciplinary procedures played out. Savvy administrators learned to avoid exhausting themselves by trying to force dismissal through a system designed to prevent it. If teachers were not dangerous, merely ineffective, principals harassed them until they left their school. But since the unwanted were almost never fired, they reappeared elsewhere—"lemons" they were called—typically in less-desirable schools run by less-shrewd leaders in tough neighborhoods where it was harder to attract instructors with other options. And since teachers decided which school they would work in on the basis of seniority until changes were negotiated in 2005, good schools in safe neighborhoods had become havens for experienced instructors, channeling callow novitiates into the toughest neighborhoods with the worst schools. The students who needed the most help tended to receive the least.[41]

A long-standing budget process intensified the injustice. The education department funded a school's roster of teachers as a starting point no matter the amount. Funds for all other purposes were then apportioned without regard to how much money had gone to a school to pay its instructors. The practice meant one school heavily staffed with experienced teachers might have a payroll as much as 50 percent higher than another school whose teachers had accumulated less time in the system. When Bloomberg's education department sought to change the approach and channel funds to follow students not teachers, with extra allocations for special needs, it hit a wall of resistance from the UFT in strong alliance with well-organized and highly determined middle-class and affluent parents. The union worried, with reason, the proposed plan would cause administrators to favor young teachers over experienced ones to save money. The parents feared their children's schools would lose the high-caliber educators concentrated in upscale neighborhoods. The intensity of opposition caused a retreat to a fallback strategy. The department would increase resources gradually to shortchanged schools over time without ever cutting budgets at others below a base year. The policy meant a slow march toward economic justice rather than rapid correction of an unfair process.[42]

The city tried to hit the collective bargaining reset button with the UFT in 2004. It suggested the union scrap its two hundred–page agreement and the eight hundred pages of additional documents that detailed teacher protections for an eight-page, high-concept approach. The short form proposed would have wiped out in one blow decades of hard fought provisions designed to give teachers control over their jobs. Weingarten called the idea "a kick in the teeth," and would have none of it. Contract talks continued until just a few weeks before Election Day 2005 when a labor fact-finding panel issued a report. Michelle Rhee, founder of the New Teacher Project, who would later become a highly contentious national figure as head of the Washington, DC, school system, testified for the education department. Her well supported testimony detailed the many ways UFT contract provisions impeded effective school management and recommended they be changed. The toughest issues involved control, not benefits.[43]

Bloomberg was seeking a second term in 2005, and polls showed him with a comfortable lead. Yet, his political advisors worried that if the UFT threw its support to his Democratic opponent at the last minute, it risked changing the momentum. Worse still, a teacher's strike could deal the election campaign an unpredictable wild card. Campaign staff encouraged Bloomberg to settle with the teachers "and put this thing behind him," Klein remembers. Bloomberg responded with bravado, offering the stock answer he often quoted when people warned him an unpopular decision could cost him his job. "My plan B," returning to life as a billionaire bachelor running a global media empire, "is better than anyone else's plan A." Yet, Bloomberg was hardly naïve or disinterested, and Weingarten believed neither the people of the city, nor her union, were prepared for a strike that could prove long and damaging. She also knew that if the UFT endorsed his opponent and Bloomberg won a second term, presumed to be his last due to term limits, her negotiating influence would collapse. So Weingarten accepted a relatively generous 14.25 percent raise in return for accepting some of the proposals the fact-finding panel recommended. Bloomberg, who had handled much of the negotiations with Weingarten personally, acknowledged, "the progress we made, we bought." Plain and simple, it was a "quid pro quo," he told an interviewer. The UFT typically endorsed the Democratic candidate for mayor. That year, they did not.[44]

The most significant concession the UFT accepted was elimination of "excess rules" that allowed senior teachers to choose where to work by "bumping" more junior staff out of a position. According to Weingarten, a majority of her union's members favored the change since for every member who benefited there was one whose working life was disrupted. Elimination of the rule meant principals, not teachers, would decide who worked in their schools. To Klein, it was a critical provision since without it school leaders could not control the most important resources they relied on for results. Unwanted teachers were left to look for a job in another school. If they did not find one, they could not be fired and the education department declined union suggestions that they be redeployed for special instruction or other purposes. Instead, they would go to an Absent Teachers Reserve where they would become permanent substitutes and eventually cost the department more than $100 million per year. Klein sought but failed to win an eighteen-month transition period after which unwanted instructors would leave the system. Failure to create an "exit ramp for the incompetent" was one of his biggest regrets.[45]

Weingarten knew the workplace concessions she accepted in 2005 would be controversial. "Vocal factions within the union are already working to convince the eighty thousand rank-and-file teachers to reject the agreement," the *New York Post* reported the day after the union chief announced its terms. Weingarten made the case for the package as persuasively as she could and won approval from 63 percent of her members, a comfortable majority by normal standards, but more than 30 percent lower than the 94 percent vote in favor of the 2002 contract, more typical for UFT-endorsed agreements. The significant proportion of teachers who rejected the reforms laid bare the leadership challenge Weingarten faced when supporting change. The vote was one of the reasons Klein felt the city had done about as well as it could in the 2005 negotiations. When the city and the union announced the contract, Klein gave Weingarten a hug. There would not be occasion for another. To win back disaffected members, Weingarten created a comically large three hundred–member negotiating team to participate in future discussions with the city. When negotiators claimed they could not find a room big enough to meet with the unwieldy group, the three hundred members created a fifty-person executive committee. By then, Randi "got very dug in," Klein would say. In later negotiations he failed to secure key concessions he sought on tenure and seniority rights.[46]

The relatively generous settlement, scheduled to run retroactively from July 1, 2003 until October 12, 2007, along with the wage increase negotiated in 2002, and another struck in 2006 to take effect between 2007 and 2009, raised starting salaries for first-year teachers to more than $45,000. The most experienced teachers with the right educational credentials could eventually make more than $100,000. The pay was competitive with jobs requiring comparable skills, and a long-standing gap between city and suburban teachers narrowed. The off-cycle 2006 agreement to raise salaries between 2007 and 2009 was highly unusual. The local economy had been on the upswing during the 2005 talks, and it kept on improving. Weingarten wanted to take advantage of the buoyant budget outlook and positive negotiating environment to secure additional wages for her members and to repair her credibility. When the administration needed the union to endorse a memorandum of agreement in support of the organizational changes Klein proposed in 2006, Weingarten seized the opening. In return for the provisions the chancellor needed, she locked in future salary increases.[47]

In parallel with negotiations to improve teacher quality by raising salaries and modifying work rules, the city moved aggressively to recruit new talent into the system that experienced high annual turnover. It built strong ties to Teach for America and the New Teacher Project, innovative programs that sought the best and the brightest college graduates from diverse fields who had not studied education. Both programs provided short, intense teacher training in return for a commitment to work in underserved areas for two years. The opportunities offered became particularly popular when unemployment soared in 2009 and 2010, and alternatives were hard to come by, even for top students from elite universities. Klein also intensified support for the New York City Teaching Fellows program, a variation on the New Teacher Project that trained experts from a variety of fields how to teach. It placed a higher premium on talent and subject matter knowledge than on educational theory, while providing practical training in classroom techniques. Klein's department sought to apply higher standards for awarding tenure, and it lengthened the process. The rules continued to insure the vast majority of teachers received the protection eventually, but only about half qualified after three years rather than over 90 percent as had been typical. The department had long had the power to do this, but UFT pressure and bureaucratic sloth had conspired to make third-year tenure virtually automatic. The change fell short of Klein's goal to deny a "non-trivial" proportion of teachers a job for life as a means of maintaining pressure on instructors to do their best work.[48]

The Substance of the Matter

Curriculum and pedagogy, the two critical elements of education that determine what and how students learn, challenged Joel Klein more than any other part of his job. "I was not a curriculum guy," he acknowledged. He had to rely more on his staff for decisions in these areas than in any other aspect of his work, especially early on. By his own account, it took him longer than he wished to develop real understanding of the issues and a vision toward which to point the huge bureaucracy he ran. Days after Mayor Bloomberg announced the Department of Education's restructuring in 2003, Klein declared that all of the city's schools would adopt uniform curricula for reading and math. He exempted the two hundred best-performing institutions, later increased to more than three hundred. The idea was to avoid disruption where things were working well, but otherwise to apply a single set of carefully considered topics and teaching methods to education's primary building blocks. It promised to bring coherence for the first time in decades to policies adopted in the past by forty different decision-making bodies. In theory, the new guidelines were not meant to limit teacher creativity in the classroom any more than providing a musical score would limit the ability of an orchestra conductor to render an interpretation of a symphony. The objective was to provide a framework for optimum impact and consistent, measurable results.[49]

Within days Klein found himself in an educational firestorm. Educators debated reading and math courses of study with the same animation others reserved for religion and politics. The reading program the city chose came down on the side of whole language disciples, inciting a call to arms among phonics crusaders. The one group, associated with political liberals, favored a holistic approach that sought to inspire a lifelong passion for reading. The other, championed more often by conservatives, believed traditional, highly structured methods that taught students to recognize sounds represented by combinations of letters a superior approach. Some evidence supported the claim. To Klein's dismay, phonics believers included senior advisors to President George W. Bush's United States Department of Education. Federal bureaucrats informed the city its decision put tens of millions of funding dollars at risk since the reading program it chose did not meet standards. "We can find no published research indicating this program has been tested with well-defined groups of kids and shown to be effective," G. Reid Lyon, chief of the Child Development and Behavior Branch at the National Institutes of Health told the *New York Times.* Klein's department revised the program sufficiently to allow it to cash Washington's check. The compromise left neither side in the reading wars enthusiastic, and the incident embarrassed the chancellor and mayor.[50]

Similarly, Klein's department chose a program that supported a constructivist approach to math that sought to engage students in practical experiences and intuitive learning processes. Others favored a more traditional computational approach and accused Klein's department of adopting a program that lacked rigor. One scholar shot off an email to the administrator responsible for the choice attacking the process used to select it. "The New York City schools system is the size of a small country," he wrote. "I find it remarkable . . . there is apparently no proper documentation of the considerations that went into that choice . . . no record of any comparative evaluation of candidate curricula, and no record of the expert testimony and opinion upon which you relied." The intensity of this debate also caught Klein off guard and left him feeling let down by his team. Within a year, his head of teaching and learning moved on. Her credibility had been hurt by her decisions and by a clumsy effort to place her husband in a high-level administrative job at the education department that caused Klein to fire her, with Bloomberg's strong encouragement according to some accounts.[51]

Bloomberg and Klein's commitment to insure public school graduates developed the skills to contend with college courses or meaningful jobs played a role in a controversial decision to end social promotion. After the third grade, instruction in New York City schools shifted from teaching children how to read, to using reading to teach children other subjects. Students who advanced from third grade to fourth without adequate language skills were at high risk of falling behind in all their courses. Many educators favored holding underachieving students back a year to ensure their reading capabilities were up to the tasks ahead. Others supported social promotion, advancing students who had not passed tests to keep them together with their peer group and avoid the emotional consequences separation could cause. Often believers in this approach supported special summer programs or additional resources for weak students to help them catch up. Bloomberg and Klein came down firmly on the side of advancing only students who had demonstrated the minimum level of skill to proceed to the next grade.[52]

The decision to end social promotion for third graders was the type of decision that the Panel on Educational Policy, created when the state legislature granted the mayor control of the schools, could vote on. The chancellor submitted a proposal, and the UFT opposed it, countering with a program to create special fourth grade classes with just fifteen low-achieving students as an alternative. The smaller class size would allow more intense instruction and help the challenged children improve, the union contended. It convinced a majority of panelists, including some appointed by the mayor, that it had developed a superior proposal.[53]

The day the panel was scheduled to meet and to vote on the education department's plan, Bloomberg dismissed two independent-minded appointees he had named and replaced them with loyalists. In a coordinated effort, the borough president of Staten Island did the same with his representative. The outcome of the vote became a foregone conclusion in favor of ending social promotion. Many criticized the heavy-handed tactic. Bloomberg dismissed the objections as easily as he had dismissed the wayward panelists. "Mayoral control means mayoral control, thank you very much," he told a journalist in response to a question. "They are my representatives, and they are going to vote for things that I believe in." The department created a rich summer program to help struggling students improve. It worked effectively enough that it was expanded over time to other grades without additional controversy. But students who failed to meet standards by the end of the added instruction periods repeated a grade. Critics accused the mayor and chancellor of holding weak readers back to boost fourth-grade test scores and make their reforms look better. Bloomberg and Klein dismissed the accusation out of hand. Both thought the pedagogical decision an important one. It had also become a contest over who would set school policy. Bloomberg made clear he would exercise the full range of the authority at his discretion. Critics contended he had overstepped the intended bounds of his powers.[54]

Choosing Schools, Choosing Sides

Giving parents a choice of schools where they could enroll their children emerged as a fundamental building block of the Bloomberg administration's reform agenda. The push for competition fit easily into the outlook of an entrepreneur mayor and an antitrust chancellor. The imperative overlapped with Klein's belief that some city schools, particularly some of the largest high schools, had deteriorated beyond salvage. He was convinced there were instances where the cultures of failure had taken such deep root for so long that digging them out was unrealistic. He moved to close those schools, and to establish several smaller ones in the buildings vacated, creating options.[55]

Klein believed smaller schools were inherently virtuous for struggling students. They allowed teachers and administrators to know their students personally and to direct individual attention to them. That very basic goal was impractical in institutions with thousands of pupils where teachers taught classes with as many as 170 different children in the course of a day. Critics countered that small schools lacked the critical mass to support special programs, things as traditional as high school football teams, theater groups and glee clubs, science laboratories and advance placement options, properly stocked libraries and art rooms. Lack of scale also meant that small schools were not well designed to provide dedicated classes for English language learners and special education students. For a time, Klein's department allowed the small schools to exclude these last two categories of students during their first two years. That decision and others that favored small schools made simple school-to-school comparisons difficult.[56]

Closing failed schools mimicked the creative destruction of a capitalist economy. The process sought to eliminate unsuccessful organizations and reallocate resources to more productive ones. The initiative was one of the major reasons the Department of Education spent over $27 billion on capital projects while Bloomberg governed. It shut 157 schools between 2003 and 2013 while opening 656 smaller ones during roughly the same period. Staying the course in the face of organized opposition required conviction. The working careers of staff were disrupted, and alumni felt their educations were devalued. Schools were associated with neighborhoods, so in some people's minds the closings stigmatized entire communities. Local leaders often protested and demanded burdensome analyses justifying the decisions. They accused the education department of creating self-fulfilling prophecies—opening new schools that siphoned off talented students leaving only the underachievers behind, ensuring failure over time. Some simply disagreed with the premise. Broken schools should be fixed, they insisted, not shut. The decisions generated intense resistance, and pursuing them required, "*enormous* amounts of political capital," remembered Howard Wolfson, Bloomberg's third-term deputy for intergovernmental affairs. The plan proceeded despite ongoing controversy. Anytime parents and students had a choice, a critical mass "voted with their feet" and chose the new, smaller schools. Students, coached by their parents, began to compete for the spots because there were never enough to meet demand.[57]

The application process for the new schools started out clumsy. Children had to apply to each one independently, the chances of success an unconnected series of up to five random lotteries. It required diligence and persistence. Some families proved better at it than others with lifelong consequences for children. The Department of Education responded by asking Harvard Business School professor Alvin Roth to design a better system. The result was a plan based on an algorithm he had developed to match aspiring doctors across the United States with their top choices for residency training. The process required every eighth grade student to list a series of choices—up to twelve—in order of preference on a single application. Once students submitted their applications, their preferences and records were assessed against the admissions criteria of each school. A computer program maximized the output, and by 2008 it awarded students one of their top three choices more than 80 percent of the time. Eventually the program expanded to cover other grades. In 2012, Roth would share the Nobel Prize in economics for the theoretical work that underpinned the optimization process he helped create.[58]

The drive to break up large failing schools into smaller ones overlapped with Bloomberg and Klein's support for charter schools—institutions that received public money but operated with greater autonomy than the school bureaucracy normally allowed. Charters were another pillar of the administration's effort to provide parents with educational choices for their children. To advocates, they were the country's best hope to replace a failed system with one that worked. To opponents, including the UFT, the movement in favor of them represented an existential threat to public education in America. The initiative created a polarizing debate that all but forced people to choose sides, even though by the end of the 2013–2014 school year, just 7 percent of New York City public school students attended 183 charters in a system which by then had grown to some 1,600 schools. Class consciousness compounded the tensions. Charters and other programs designed to bring competition to public schools captured the imaginations of some of America's most successful entrepreneurs and their philanthropies. Many union members and others with egalitarian sensibilities viewed a movement promoted by capitalist accumulators of vast wealth with suspicion. Diane Ravitch, once a strong proponent of charters, made an about-face that stunned many educators. She derisively dubbed the high-profile, rich advocates of charters like Bill Gates and Eli Broad "a billionaire boys club," and wrote: "There is something fundamentally antidemocratic about relinquishing control of the public education policy agenda to private foundations run by society's wealthiest people." In some respects, the charge applied to Bloomberg himself.[59]

Opening a charter school side by side with traditional schools in a single building raised the stakes all around. If parents with a choice preferred the charter, it delivered a loud message. If a charter drawing students from the same community as a traditional school outperformed, it challenged the status quo with demonstrative power nothing else could match. Klein understood this, and he also understood that if a charter had to build its own schoolhouse from scratch in New York City, it would add millions of dollars to the cost of establishing one. When Randi Weingarten applied for a charter for a UFT-managed school, Klein deliberately co-located it with a traditional school as a tactic to defang union objections to the practice. Opponents accused the education department of favoring charters in co-location sites, giving them preferential access to gymnasiums, auditoriums, and other shared facilities. As charters co-located around the city, the lines separating them from traditional schools inside single buildings became the schoolhouse equivalents of demilitarized zones. The debate over charter schools shows no signs of diminishing.[60]

Public Schools, Minus the Public

When the state legislature gave Mayor Bloomberg the authority to run the schools, it recognized that the new structure would require a means for engaging parents in their children's education. In the old system, community school boards were supposed to include parents in school management, and the superintendents' offices were supposed to offer local access to the senior administrator in charge. In some parts of the city the system had worked, and in the many where it did not, it had been a useful fiction. In the new system, "parents lost their primary avenue of appeal when their children were not receiving adequate services," one parent activist wrote in 2004. "I think they did a good job getting rid of the bad political stuff," a Bronx mother involved in her local school council said, "but they've gotten rid of everything else, too," she complained. A formal study by the Parthenon Group, a consulting firm, confirmed that the anecdotes spoke for many.[61]

Early on, Klein signaled parent involvement was meant to be a priority for his department. "We need to create an environment where parents are invited into the equation and not pushed aside," he told a journalist. When Bloomberg announced the first restructuring of the education department in January 2003, he talked of three key elements: structural changes, curriculum redevelopment, and parental involvement. "It's like a three-legged stool," he said. "If you don't have one the whole thing falls over." Appointment of parent coordinators at every school, accountable to principals and responsible for facilitating parents' participation in their children's educations, were meant to fulfill this need. And eventually each district had a family advocate responsible for offering parents a place other than their child's school itself to register concerns or complaints. Parents' councils and parent-teacher associations existed throughout the city. Klein made heroic efforts to respond to as many emails as he could from as broad a range of stakeholders as possible, including parents. He attended countless meetings in black churches on Sundays and talked with groups of concerned parents about school reform in living rooms around the city on weekday evenings. Some of his deputies also engaged regularly with parents.[62]

Taking a page from corporate governance practices, the Department of Education instituted annual satisfaction surveys among parents, students, and teachers beginning in 2007. Its first year, nearly six hundred thousand participated in the Learning Environment Survey and the number grew to almost one million by 2013. Results, fair at first, improving to good over time, were posted on the education department's website for all to see. They were analyzed in aggregate and made available at the school level so parents, teachers, and students could see how the specific institution that mattered to them rated in comparison to others. School Quality Reviews and annual Progress Reports were posted as well, along with state and federal accountability measures. Internet savvy parents had the same access to their children's records that teachers had. The information constituted "a remarkable wealth of school data and assessment tools," one team of policy analysts examining the city school system wrote in 2013.[63]

Yet, a broad range of critics accused the mayor and the chancellor of acting in secret when making important policy decisions. Klein denies the charge. He insists his department accepted input from diverse stakeholders, actively supported parent engagement in the education of their own children, and promoted school-based decision-making for many programs. His claims have merit, but it is equally true that Klein and Bloomberg declined to involve parent activists and other concerned citizens directly in core policy decisions. Tension between central management of the schools and community control was as old as public education in New York City with attitudes and practices shifting over time along a politically fraught spectrum. Bloomberg and Klein came down unequivocally on the side of central decision-making. In their judgment, involving large numbers of people in a management process was impractical and undesirable, even if all were well-intentioned and had legitimate stakes in the outcomes. They believed it would introduce more confusion than wisdom, slow things down and prevent progress. "In the end, it is my responsibility to say, 'I think this is the right policy,'" Klein told a reporter. "The mayor holds me accountable, and the city holds the mayor accountable. We should not have 'shared decision-making,'" he said. "That's what marks all unsuccessful school reforms."[64]

Bloomberg's and Klein's profiles as wealthy Manhattanites with elite educational and professional credentials contributed to the problem. They offered mutually reinforcing images of men whose lives had long been distant from the day-to-day realities of most New Yorkers. When clumsy implementation of changes in the school bus system left youngsters and their parents stranded curbside during a cold spell in January 2007, a reporter analyzing the episode wrote: "Parents and local officials called the mayor and the chancellor out of touch with modern family life and its architecture of careers, child care and commutes, particularly for parents outside Manhattan." Klein would remember the episode as "the most self-injurious thing we did." The often dismissive tone of the two men's communications exacerbated the problem as well. When a group of African American and Latino parents objected to the mayor's initial efforts to seize control of the schools, Bloomberg accused them of ignorance about how bad circumstances in their own neighborhood's classrooms really were. One councilman called the comment racist, and another characterized it as "patronizing, insensitive, condescending and denigrating." The accusations infuriated the mayor, and the council members who leveled them found city commissioners inaccessible for a time.[65]

Distrust breeds secrecy, and after May 2003 mutual suspicion defined the relationship between Chancellor Klein, union chief Weingarten, and the organizations they led. During various rounds of contract negotiations, the UFT organized mass demonstrations, ran public relations campaigns, and aired television ads designed to diminish confidence in the administration and its reforms. After the mayor flexed his political muscles to ensure the end of social promotion in 2004, Weingarten teamed up with Diane Ravitch to write a *New York Times* op-ed piece condemning him. "Public School Minus the Public," read the headline over an article declaring it time for the state legislature to reduce the power it had granted Bloomberg. It is unsurprising that the education department did not share works in progress with a union intent on ruining its credibility.[66]

The resentment Bloomberg's and Klein's management styles caused played a role in the 2009 hearings to renew the legislation granting the mayor authority over the school system. One group of activists organized the Parents Commission on School Governance and Mayoral Control. In the opening paragraph of a forty-page document it prepared for the state legislature, its members described themselves as parents of New York City public school children whose "voices have been excluded from decision making for the last seven years." They wanted a "real partnership . . . instead of the autocracy" in place. A second group, the Campaign for Better Schools, supported mayoral control with greater local involvement. In response to efforts to limit his authority over the schools, Bloomberg's team organized Learn NY, a coalition of some seventy community groups richly funded by the Gates and Broad Foundations, to make the case for unfettered renewal of the 2002 law.[67]

Political dysfunction in the state senate triggered the law's sunset clause, causing it to expire on July 1, 2009 without renewal. The Board of Education came "back from the dead, almost by accident," Javier C. Hernandez wrote in the *New York Times*. Borough presidents from Brooklyn, Manhattan, and the Bronx sought to manipulate the momentary chaos to revive their roles in the system. Despite criticisms and political maneuvering, before the 2009 school year began, a new law reestablished the mayor's authority, mostly the same as it was for six more years. Well-intentioned critics feared alienation of important constituents and their lack of support for Bloomberg's reforms would prevent the changes his team implemented from lasting past his time in office.[68]

The Amazing Disappearing Improvement in Standardized Test Results

The use of standardized tests to measure educational progress was as controversial in Bloomberg's New York as elsewhere in the United States in the early years of the twenty-first century. To the businessman mayor, test results constituted the educational bottom line. To his lawyer chancellor, they were the evidence that proved his department's programs were succeeding or made the case for appeal and reevaluation of a decision. What was the alternative, they asked in response to objections. No tests and no accountability? That hardly seemed smart. After some consideration, Klein decided to focus solely on English and math results for elementary and middle schools. He viewed them as crucial building blocks for learning in other subjects, and he built his evaluation systems of schools and principals around them. When he proposed to incorporate student progress on standardized tests into decisions to grant teachers tenure, he provoked intense resistance. The UFT took the issue to Albany where remarkably it convinced the state legislature to make the practice illegal. Sometime later, under pressure to support the city's application for federal Race to the Top educational dollars, the legislature reversed the decision.[69]

Unlike businessmen who relied heavily on profits as a single fundamental measure of corporate success, and litigators who won cases or lost them, educators dealt in the more highly nuanced world of intellectual development among children and adolescents. Almost all educators thought standardized exams designed to measure proficiency in a subject served a useful purpose, but a narrow one. They revealed how well students understood a certain body of knowledge at a moment in time. They could be used as a diagnostic tool to identify children at risk and areas requiring additional focus. What standardized tests designed to measure proficiency did not do, many believed, is determine how well a teacher had instructed a class, or how well a school had performed during a year.[70]

Many committed educators objected to Klein's decision to focus only on English and math. Testing just those two subjects out of context would not be very good indicators of preparation for academic success, they contended. "If [students] are not learning social studies, but their reading scores are going up, they are not getting an education," Diane Ravitch warned. Schools that favored a broad range of rich classes in history and science, the arts and music might fare worse than others more narrowly focused on exam topics. Critical success factors like school safety, parent engagement, and character development would be rendered invisible. Experienced educators feared the unintended consequences of relentless focus on specific tests. Time spent preparing for exams and taking them came at the expense of instruction in the subjects themselves, and created anxiety-provoking pressures on children and adolescents. The approach risked causing teachers to "teach to the test," and little else. Students, they feared, would become more accomplished test-takers, but not necessarily better-educated citizens.[71]

Moreover, the range of factors that contributed to student learning was so broad, and so much of it out of a teacher's control, that many thought evaluating success on the basis of standardized tests dangerous bureaucratic folly. Family structure, home environment, daily nutrition, medical care, neighborhood influences, school safety, ease of transportation, English language skills, classroom peer groups, cultural biases in tests, and more all played a role. Statistics made it abundantly clear that children with strong advantages across the range of factors that mattered, typically wealthier white ones, performed better on standardized exams than those who lacked them, typically poorer children of color. The discrepancies in scores across New York City neighborhoods were enormous, with the best boasting over 90 percent of students reading at grade level and achieving comparable success in math, while in the worst 20 percent or less met standards.[72]

Education department administrators understood the dangers, but believed schools with the right combination of instructional skill, determination, and accountability could teach disadvantaged children much more successfully than the belief that "demographics are destiny" implied. There were plenty of schools where underprivileged students suffering from the characteristics that typically limited achievement performed far better on standardized tests than others with similar challenges. Surely scaling across the city what the success stories proved possible was the correct goal, administrators argued. Holding principals and teachers accountable for outcomes was the only way to force failing schools to change, and standardized tests seemed the most practical way to do that.[73]

The Department of Education responded to the perplexing challenge to develop measures for year-over-year progress by developing a system that compared the results for each school to forty others with similar demographic characteristics—twenty immediately above it and twenty below it on factors that affected success. "Each school will receive a grade, from 'A' to 'F', on its year-to-year progress in helping students advance," Mayor Bloomberg announced in his 2007 State of the City address. "Personally, I can't think of a better way to hold a principal's feet to the fire than arming mom and dad with the facts about how well or poorly their children's school is performing," he told the city. Progress Reports, as they were called, established a level of accountability for educational results that had never before existed in New York City. It also created high institutional anxiety since the outcomes being measured were complex and calibrating judgments about them difficult. While many inputs mattered, and informative sub-scores existed, year-over-year results on standardized tests in English and math dominated the main score. For technical reasons, grades and standing within a peer group could swing wildly from one year to the next. Excellent schools that fell a notch received lousy grades. Awful schools doing a little better could get an A. Parents, teachers, and principals found it hard to interpret results and to respond to them. City grades were not well aligned with state standards, adding to the confusion.[74]

The evaluations were critical to Klein's strategy of empowering principals while holding them accountable for results. The annual grades became the linchpin in assessments of principal performance, school-wide bonus eligibility, certain budget allocations, and ultimately which schools to close down. The approach fit the framework of federal No Child Left Behind legislation, which included a mandate that states develop assessment standards for basic skills and test them annually. It required schools to demonstrate "adequate yearly progress" to continue to receive federal education funds. Those that did not were forced into an escalating regimen of improvement programs, and after five years of failure, risked being shut down.[75]

Between 2002 and 2004 the percent of New York City public school students deemed proficient in English in the grades tested rose modestly from 39 percent to 41 percent, and then surged in 2005 to nearly 52 percent. After hovering at that level for a few years, the number rose to 58 percent in 2008 and 69 percent in 2009. Math showed an even more impressive trajectory. Just over 37 percent of students in grades three through eight achieved proficiency in 2002. The percent rose reasonably steadily until 2009 when the city reported 84 percent of students tested could perform math at grade level. In addition, the discouraging achievement gap between white students and children of color diminished. The results were "nothing short of amazing and exactly what this country needs," Bloomberg bragged in 2009.[76]

Except the amazing scores did not reflect what their champions claimed. No Child Left Behind created a powerful incentive for states to make sure their school districts showed improvement on standardized tests every year. If they did not, federal money could be withheld. Since the states developed the tests and set the standards, many crafted exams that made it easy for grades to improve. "The gaming of the system . . . occurred all across the country," US Assistant Secretary of Education Peter Cunningham would remember. "It's almost criminal and it's not the fault of the cities/districts but the states." It certainly occurred in New York State. Exams were short, narrow in scope, and released publicly as study tools after they were used. The tests were so similar from one year to the next that students who studied from past exams found the ones they sat for easy. What the New York City and New York State results showed was not that students were learning more, but that the testing structure generated grade inflation.[77]

In the run-up to the 2005 mayoral election, analysts identified discrepancies between the results of city public school tests and federal exam scores that suggested less progress than the Bloomberg team claimed. Disappointing results for New York City students on nationwide standardized test scores raised doubts about the real pace of improvement again in November of 2007. By February 2008, and again in September of that year, experts advising New York State education officials warned in writing that the structure of the tests and the extraordinary importance attached to them was causing behavior that damaged their reliability, and they recommended audits. The state ignored the advice. City education department officials identified inconsistencies in scores on various tests that logic suggested should have been closely aligned if students understood the material. Klein took particular note that students who passed tests and graduated high school still required remedial courses in college. That meant the exams were too easy. To his credit, Klein raised his concerns with Richard Mills, the New York State education commissioner. No action followed.[78]

When test results circulated among members of the state Board of Regents in May 2009, one member who had taught and served as a principal and a superintendent in the Bronx for thirty years sounded the alarm. She called state chancellor Merryl Tisch and told her that the numbers were literally unbelievable and should not be released. Tisch declined to keep the test scores secret, but publicly acknowledged doubts about their accuracy. At the time, Bloomberg's education department had powerful incentives not to challenge the spectacular results publicly. The 2002 law granting the mayor control of the schools was under formal review. High test scores supported continuation. And by then Bloomberg had decided to run for a third term as mayor. He highlighted his successful management of the schools as a key reason to vote for him against his opponent, Democrat William Thompson, who was one of the last presidents of the old, discredited Board of Education. "Mike Bloomberg changed the system," one of his advertisements declared. "Now, record graduation rates. Test scores up, violence down. So when you compare apples to apples, Thompson offers politics as usual. Mike Bloomberg offers progress," his campaign declared.[79]

The state education department rescaled the tests beginning in 2010 and New York City's scores plummeted. The percent of students at grade level in English fell from 69 percent to 42 percent. Math proficiency sank to 54 percent, measurably better than when the mayor and his chancellor launched their reform program, but nothing like the 84 percent figure they had reported. The achievement gap between white students and others reappeared. The collapse in achievement on the standardized tests cascaded through to school Progress Reports, destroying their credibility. Bloomberg's school management, promoted as a spectacular success, suddenly boasted only modest gains after eight years of enormous effort, investment, and turmoil.[80]

The episode was embarrassing and damaging. "If four years from now reading scores and math scores are not significantly better, then I will look in the mirror and say that I have been a failure. I've never failed at anything yet, and I don't plan to fail at that," Bloomberg said as a candidate in 2001. In October 2004, he touted the statistics as proof his approach was turning the schools around. In January 2006, he held out his school reform program as an example of what was possible in America. "Because the eyes of our nation are on our efforts," he said, "our successes hold promise for schools across the land. What a wonderful gift for New York to share with the rest of our country," he boasted. After the release of 2007 results, he declared himself, "happy, thrilled—ecstatic I think is a better word. The hard work going on in our schools is really paying off."[81]

Bloomberg prided himself and promoted himself to New Yorkers as a man who understood how to use data to manage their complex government. In describing a typical meeting with Bloomberg, Klein wrote, "The mayor understood and devoured data. When others' eyes might glaze over at the numbers on a page, Bloomberg eagerly pored over charts with test scores, crime data, attendance, summer school results and anything else that would indicate how we were doing." Yet, when changes of the magnitude reported across New York City schools should have made it obvious something was wrong, Bloomberg's analytical instincts failed him. Critics have suggested that in the midst of his 2009 reelection campaign, he did not want to know the truth.[82]

Klein and Walcott defended themselves and Bloomberg by comparing New York City scores to other districts in New York State where students took the same tests over the same time period. Before and after recalibration, the city fared better than the others demonstrating "real progress" compared to a relevant peer group. "Comparing apples to apples," Klein, Walcott, and Bloomberg thought, "we've got something here . . . we're doing well." In Klein's view, the state's poor communication about the issue created the impression that the city education department had manipulated the results deliberately, which was untrue and unfair. Opponents, he believed, ignored the important message that even after recalibration real improvement had occurred. Yet, Klein did not doubt the episode hurt his department's credibility.[83]

Early in 2011, Klein returned to the private sector. He was the longest-serving New York City schools chancellor in more than a half century. His replacement, Cathie Black, turned out to be a disastrous appointment. Her selection, in the words of one City Hall insider, was simply "inexplicable." She was the chief executive of the Hearst Corporation, and a close friend of Bloomberg, but she had no credentials for the job. In an action that smacked of hubris, Bloomberg selected her on his own without following his usual practice of conferring with key advisors that had led to so many excellent staffing decisions. In April 2011, after three months of impolitic mistakes, the mayor asked Black to move on and asked Walcott to take over as chancellor.[84]

Walcott set about restoring order and morale at the department in the wake of Black's disruptive tenure, and he undertook important refinements of the strategy he had helped Klein set in motion. In particular, he established greater clarity around the lines of authority connecting the department's central staff at the Tweed Building with the relatively new structures that supported instruction and operations. He also sought to dial down tensions surrounding charter programs and decisions to shut failing schools, and it fell to him to implement the new curricula that accompanied the state's decision to adopt Common Core educational standards. Sometime before, Randi Weingarten became head of the American Federation of Teachers, the national union headquartered in Washington, DC, and Michael Mulgrew replaced her as UFT leader in New York. Unfortunately, the change in personalities at the top of the Department of Education and the local teachers' union did little to create more trust. Irreconcilable differences over teacher evaluation processes and accountability for educational outcomes continued.[85]

Mayor Bloomberg's Report Card

The plan Joel Klein and the Bloomberg administration followed in pursuit of educational excellence for New York City schools can be summarized in five parts: school choice; principal control; talented teachers; budgets that follow students and that allocate more money to needier children; and accountability. With fits and starts, the city made partial progress on all five dimensions of the program.[86]

Bloomberg challenged a deeply entrenched political status quo and a sclerotic bureaucracy failing its students for decades. His success securing clear responsibility for the system was fundamental for the program to have a chance to succeed. Without it, pursuit of a coherent strategy would have been impossible. "I don't think there was any issue that we pushed that the system did not push back against us with a well-financed, well-organized opposition," was how Howard Wolfson remembered school reform initiatives. "To his credit, he didn't blink," Joel Klein would say of Bloomberg's commitment to change. For that alone he deserves much praise. Dennis Walcott considered mayoral control the Bloomberg education team's most important and lasting achievement.[87]

School choice was a critical element of the plan, and it had a positive impact. Critics point out accurately that many of the small schools created when large failing ones were closed remained weak. Yet, careful assessments of the small schools indicate that overall, the innovation helped more students to graduate with a higher degree of learning than the system it replaced. MDRC, a think tank dedicated to evaluating social program effectiveness, analyzed the initiative in detail. Its president, Gordon Berlin, declared the program a success. "The evidence is clear," he asserts. "Students from the small schools are 15 percent more likely to graduate high school and 21 percent more likely to go to college. No one gets results like that," he said. "It worked for every sub-group we looked at." Since more students graduated, and fewer needed an expensive fifth year of high school, the initiative also proved cost effective.[88]

The commitment to charter schools also delivered positive results. Across the country, charters performed at about the same level as traditional schools, but in New York City they performed better. Analyses supporting that conclusion were controlled for demographic factors, and for charges that charters skimmed the best students out of the general population, declined to accept special needs students, and dismissed troublemakers. Rather than compare schools, analysts looked inside different schools to find students in the same neighborhoods with comparable backgrounds of race, language skill, income level, and other characteristics. The comparisons are imperfect, but convincing. Klein wishes he had promoted charters sooner and more aggressively. When he left, there were thousands more families applying for far fewer slots than were available. The gap makes it clear the charters were filling a perceived need. It was "an example of where we should have been bolder," Klein believed. The better outcomes that charters delivered obviously benefited their students directly. Perhaps even more important, the results created pressure on traditional schools to raise their standards. That offers hope that over time the positive impact of the charters will spark improvement across the entire system.[89]

The Bloomberg/Klein strategy increased principal control over the schools they ran. The 2005 agreement that allowed principals to choose the instructors who would teach in their schools was a critical development, despite union rules that continued to provide more protections to teachers than professionals in other industries, and despite what Klein called "a broken process for termination." The way the department selected the newly empowered principals received high marks from education professionals who reviewed it. The revised approach contrasted sharply with the corrosive politics of the one it replaced. On average, the crop of principals running New York City's schools in 2013 were better educated and better trained than the earlier cohort, although significantly less experienced. Bloomberg and Klein consciously opted for new blood in their effort to revamp a culture of mediocrity.[90]

Early returns on the impact of the dramatic change in the structure of the school system have been mixed. A careful assessment by academics at the Center for New York City Affairs found, "the network structure has allowed some effective principals to turn around failing schools . . . without bureaucratic interference." But it also concluded that "some principals are floundering without adequate support and guidance." A Parthenon Group analysis came to a similar conclusion. When Dennis Walcott became chancellor, he took steps to provide more centralized direction and support while retaining the basic premise of principal autonomy. New school leadership under Mayor de Blasio has restored formal authority to superintendents. It remains to be seen if this adds stronger guidance and support, or if it stifles creativity. Former chancellor Klein worries. "If the principals are not up to the task, micromanagement from central will not make them effective," he says. The debate continues.[91]

Teachers were better educated and better trained under Bloomberg than before. A 2010 study found "consistent descriptive evidence that the changes in teacher recruitment and selection in NYC have substantially changed the qualifications of its teachers and that these changes have had at least a modest impact on student achievement in the city's most-difficult-to-staff schools." The gap in teacher quality between high-poverty and low-poverty schools diminished, although it remained too high for complacency. Even within schools, the difference in teacher quality continued to be higher than desirable. In his famous essay "This Is New York," E. B. White wrote that to live in New York, a person had to be prepared to be lucky. Lamentably, the advice applies to children seeking an education in the city's public school system no less than others.[92]

True to his campaign commitment to make public education a top priority, Bloomberg invested heavily in the schools. In nominal terms the education budget grew over 70 percent between fiscal years 2002 and 2014 from $11.4 billion to $19.9 billion. In inflation-adjusted terms, that represented a 26 percent increase per pupil. The number of students served fell somewhat and a significant reduction in central administration allocations allowed more money for instruction. Substantial budget inequities continued to shortchange disadvantaged students, but to a lesser degree than when Bloomberg took office. His administration worked very hard to direct more budget dollars to schools serving underachieving students, and over time the commitment had an impact. And Bloomberg invested the huge sum of $27 billion to build new schools and to fund long-overdue capital improvements in existing buildings.[93]

Accountability was meant to be a hallmark of Bloomberg's education reforms. The confidence-killing inconsistencies in standardized tests between 2002 and 2013 crippled the effort. The National Assessment of Educational Progress, a congressionally mandated organization sponsored by the United States Department of Education, offers the most trustworthy data on the subject. Its numbers support the conclusion that New York City's education system delivered measurably better outcomes at the end of Bloomberg's three terms in office than at the beginning. In Klein's judgment, the Bloomberg administration made substantial progress. It merited, "Good marks. Not perfect marks, but good marks," he says. A 2010 Quinnipiac University poll found 46 percent of New Yorkers believed Klein's tenure as chancellor was "mainly a success," compared to 35 percent who deemed it "mainly a failure." "It's not a secret that the chancellor and I did not always see eye to eye on what's best for our children or fair for our teachers," Randi Weingarten told a journalist following the announcement Klein would leave, "but I never questioned his commitment." And she added, "I believe New York City's schools, despite the challenges they face right now, are better than they were a decade ago." Data for the full twelve years of Bloomberg's rule support the claim. Drop-out rates declined, scores on New York State Regents exams rose across five subjects, not just English and math, and school safety improved. High school graduation rates reached 69 percent in 2013 versus 50 percent a decade earlier, during a period when educators assert that New York State standards were rising. High school graduation rates among African Americans and Latinos rose significantly from below 50 percent in 2002 to above it in 2013, although only about 10 percent of blacks and Latinos were deemed college ready, and New York City's schools remained intensely segregated by race.[94]

Despite measurable improvement, the level of achievement of New York City public school students on NAEP tests remained disappointing. A little more than one-quarter of fourth graders were deemed proficient in reading and just over one-third achieved comparable competence in math in 2013. Among eighth graders, one-quarter qualified as proficient in each subject. Far more students—between three-fifths and three-quarters—achieved basic competence across the subjects and grades measured, but those students were not deemed well prepared for higher education or challenging jobs. New York City's scores matched the average results for fifteen large cities across the country, exceeding them modestly only for fourth grade math. Progress seemed to plateau along the way with no significant differences in any categories between 2008/2009 and 2013, suggesting the easy gains have been won and continued improvement will be hard. The better but still weak NAEP proficiency scores are consistent with 2013 New York City Common Core exam results that indicate 70 percent of New York City high school graduates lack proper preparation for college level study or twenty-first century jobs. City University of New York further confirmed the fact indicating 70 percent of public school graduates who entered its system required some remedial education.[95]

Klein is clear-eyed on the status of the school system he worked so hard to improve. "A system in which 30 to 35 percent of our kids are college ready . . . I think that's a system in crisis," he acknowledged in an interview. Mayor de Blasio's education department agrees. A report announcing organizational change in January 2015, *Strong Schools, Strong Communities,* declared: "The status quo is simply unacceptable. We are failing far too many of our kids, with dire consequences that ripple out far beyond individual families." Randi Weingarten, from her national perch as head of the American Federation of Teachers, diplomatically declines to declare New York City's school system in crisis. She offers the view that mayoral control and Bloomberg's commitment to providing the schools with ample resources created a historic moment when a system that had long suffered corrupt governance and chronic underfunding might have been fixed. Lamentably, she believes the moment was lost in a misguided approach to reform, heavy on sanctions and light on collaboration. The court of public opinion agreed. Roughly half of New Yorkers disapproved of Bloomberg's handling of the schools toward the end of his administration, while just a third or so approved of it.[96]

The New York City school system had been adrift for decades when Mayor Bloomberg seized control of it. He launched the herculean task of transforming the enormous failed institution into an education system committed to excellence for all its children. Progress occurred, and Mayor Bloomberg left the system better off than he found it. But the work that remains to achieve a "school system second to none" remains daunting. Klein assesses the progress made with admirable humility: "I think we covered about 30 yards out of 100 yards," he says. "There's more road ahead of us than the road we covered." The effort made, and the real progress achieved, make it uncharitable to conclude Bloomberg failed. Too much remains to be done to say he succeeded. The decades-long struggle to provide a quality education to public school children, and in particular African American and Latino students from poor families, continues to challenge America's premier metropolis, and indeed the nation. The implications for the future of New York City and the United States are enormous.[97]

Chapter Six

The Entrepreneurial City

Michael Bloomberg believed a flourishing private sector was essential for a city to thrive and that creating a favorable business environment was one of a mayor's most important tasks. He pursued it with muscular management of municipal assets, not *laissez-faire* policies. If Bloomberg followed an American political tradition, it was the activist version Alexander Hamilton promoted, not the limited one Thomas Jefferson romanticized. In a farewell salute to the mayor published in the *New York Observer,* urban policy expert Mitchell Moss, an informal advisor to Bloomberg, wrote: "Michael Bloomberg's mayoralty has been built on one simple fact. The City Charter gives the mayor . . . enormous power," power that Bloomberg used "aggressively" to influence "almost every aspect of civic life: health, transportation, public schools . . . parks, culture and economic development through bold rezoning and preservation policies."[1]

There was never any doubt Bloomberg would manage municipal government the way a corporate CEO manages a company. "I was elected largely on the basis of my business background," he said in his State of the City address after a year in office. "I think New Yorkers expect me to run City government in much the same way I ran my company. I am doing exactly that." One of his first projects was initiation of a 311 government information service that allowed New Yorkers to telephone one number for help on municipal matters from any of the city's dozens of agencies. It mimicked the call centers that private companies had long integrated into their customer service models. In 2008, in conjunction with public advocate Betsy Gotbaum's office, his administration launched a citywide customer satisfaction survey to learn what issues were most important to residents and how they evaluated their experience as city dwellers. The culture he established caused his commissioners to institute similar surveys for their departments. They used the data to improve the services city agencies provided to residents, just as private companies modified their offerings in response to customer feedback.[2]

Bloomberg had a vision for New York's future from the start of his administration that was shared by his influential deputy mayor for economic development and rebuilding, Daniel Doctoroff. In broad terms, it followed a concept that academics called the entrepreneurial city, an idea that emerged out of

America's painful restructuring from an industrial and manufacturing nation into one dominated by services and technology. As working-class jobs vanished between the 1960s and 1990s, many northeastern and midwestern cities fell into financial and spiritual deficit. Revival required a city's leader to think like an entrepreneur, urban theorists surmised. A metropolis was a service provider like any other—a Walmart store, a Disneyworld theme park, or a casino. City dwellers were customers who used the city just as shoppers, tourists, or gamblers used the destinations available to them for various purposes in life. People had choices about where to live, so for a city to succeed it had to offer an attractive user experience. In particular, it had to make life pleasant enough to retain its residents and to entice new ones to become loyal to the urban brand by moving in. The larger the number of residents enjoying the city, the broader the tax base and the bigger the pool of money to enhance services and to attract more people. The virtuous circle of growth known to successful businesses could be had by any metropolis with the right neoliberal outlook on life.[3]

The idea promoted the greatest good for the greatest number of people based on the premise that unless the city succeeded overall, none of its people would be very happy. Local government failure to maintain fiscal solvency causes such pervasive damage to every aspect of urban life that the entire population suffers. Certainly that was the case in mid-1970s New York, even if some suffered decidedly more than others based on personal circumstances.[4]

Not all customers are the same. Some generate more profit than others, so successful businesses segment their markets. They create goods and services designed to appeal to desirable consumers while fretting little about others. Cities, on the other hand, have an obligation to serve all their residents. Democratic sensibilities meant to value every citizen's intrinsic worth equally— one person, one vote—live awkwardly in entrepreneurial cities where public policies embrace capitalism—one dollar, one vote. Bloomberg had to reconcile his desire as municipal chief executive for market-driven development programs with the imperative he faced as New York City's highest elected official to treat all members of its impossibly diverse population fairly. His approach contained inherent tensions.[5]

New York on the Ropes

A resurgent Wall Street and buoyant stock market fueled the city's economy in the 1990s, but the growth in banking and related industries was narrow in scope. It left the city and its municipal revenue stream overly dependent on the fortunes of a single, volatile financial industry and the professional services firms that depended on it—lawyers, accountants, consultants, and the like. Even before 9/11, it had become clear that the lucrative financial sector would not be a source of robust job growth for New Yorkers. Changes in technology, consumer decision-making, and business practices had caused the share of securities industry jobs located in New York City to fall from 36 percent of the national total in 1981 to 23 percent in 2002. Since 1987, the city had created only 3 percent of the country's new securities sector positions.[6]

In the immediate aftermath of 9/11, Wall Street profits fell 60 percent and the city lost 130,000 private sector jobs. Lower Manhattan lost thirteen million square feet of prime office space and the market value of what remained fell by 25 percent. The outlook for promoting new industries in New York was not encouraging. Since the 1980s, companies with fewer than 100 employees created the vast majority of America's new jobs, but despite its storied history as a place where creative minds could turn ideas into dollars, New York City had become a tough field for dreams. In 2000, a West Coast economic think tank ranked it 169 out of 200 places in America to do business. The consulting firm Cognetics ranked it forty-six out of fifty as an "entrepreneurial hot spot." The tech boom inflated activity in Silicon Alley, the Manhattan district where software start-ups clustered, but momentum stopped dead after 9/11. Despite unmatched financial know-how and media creative talent, plus a critical mass of scientific research institutes, the city's software industry failed to evolve into an ecosystem to match Silicon Valley when it came to creating new technology businesses. New York City research institutes spawned about thirty biotech start-ups every year, but almost all launched outside the five boroughs. A huge crop of young, creative, and highly educated people had migrated to the city during the 1990s, contributing to vibrant boom years. Massive departures predicted after 9/11 did not occur, but a lack of jobs and lingering fears of another terror attack reversed the flow of attractive residents. Foreign workers had long been a persistent and self-renewing source of energy and stability for New York City. The number of immigrants entering the United States dropped by half after 9/11.[7]

For years New York City's economic development policies relied on an unofficial presumption that the metropolis remained the capital of the world and that the best and brightest would beat a path to Manhattan as a matter of course. The devastation of 9/11 and fear that the city had become the planet's most likely terrorist target triggered doubts. Shortly after the attack, more than seventy-five organizations banded together to create the Civic Alliance to Rebuild Downtown New York. Their working group papers cited "a mood of pervasive pessimism." In a study assessing the commercial impact of the attack, the New York City Partnership estimated it would cost the local economy $83 billion. In the Autumn 2001 edition of *City Journal,* Steven Malanga wrote: "It is impossible to overstate the danger facing New York right now. A devastated downtown, thousands of businesses struggling and some leaving, a steep drop-off in visitors and consumer spending, and a national recession," confronted the wounded city. "Until September 11, the compelling question in the campaign was how to carve up the city's $40 billion budget," Mitchell Moss told a journalist during the contest for mayor. "After September 11, the question became: how do we keep the city's $400 billion private economy intact?" Regional Plan Association President Robert Yaro remembered "talk about lower Manhattan never coming back. . . . New York was on the ropes."[8]

The Luxury City

Public confidence that Bloomberg was the leader who could navigate the city through its fraught economic circumstances was crucial to the conversion of his mayoral campaign from punch line to victory. He and Doctoroff focused intently on the issues threatening New York's economy, and they convinced Andrew Alper, Goldman Sachs' chief operating officer, to sign on as president of the Economic Development Corporation (EDC), the municipal entity responsible for promoting local commerce. With help from the Partnership for New York City, Alper brainstormed with working groups of senior business leaders, and he asked McKinsey & Company to help him understand the issues facing the city just as any new head of a complex private business might.[9]

The discussions yielded a number of insights, two in particular that influenced the Bloomberg administration's strategy. The first recognized that dense populations of workers in interrelated industries—what urban theorists call agglomerations—continued to make cities attractive places to do business. Yet, the shift toward an information economy and the technology revolution made it easier than ever for people to live and to work wherever they chose. That was true across the region and across the world. New York City competed with Westchester, Connecticut, and New Jersey for the best local talent, and it competed with London, Los Angeles, and Hong Kong to attract global firms and their well-paid employees. The second key insight was that the cost of doing business in New York would remain higher than elsewhere. Many factors ensured it: the city's geography and transportation needs, local real estate values, New Yorkers' respect for labor unions, the city's tradition of providing generous social benefits, along with expensive state mandates. Cutting municipal taxes would not change the cost equation much for most companies, even though many business leaders complained about them. Conservatives insisted that the path to prosperity was paved with tax relief. Bloomberg and team saw it differently. They believed that the painful lesson the city learned during the 1970s was that tax cuts that diminished city services would drive businesses and residents away.[10]

Since competing on price—lower taxes in the context of a municipality—was a sure loser, the city needed a different plan, one that played to its strengths. It had many. New York remained the world's most important financial center despite the rise of alternatives by 2002. And even though the number of immigrants entering the United States after 9/11 fell by half, those who did come continued to view New York as the city of choice for their energy and small-business entrepreneurship. No place compared as a major media capital. The depth and breadth of its universities and medical research centers had few equals, if any. The same was true of its cultural centers, its sources of entertainment, its restaurants and night life.[11]

Yet, one quality stood out above the others, in great measure a consequence of all the rest. New York City was a storehouse of human capital without equal anywhere in the world. Bankers and business leaders, artists and entertainers, professionals and elites of all stripes lived in New York because they liked to be among people like themselves. The more that people like them lived in New York, the more it attracted others. It was a wealthy and mobile class who could afford to pay a premium for the benefits of a vibrant, exciting city. Bloomberg and his team set out to develop policies that would make New York as attractive as possible for the world's elite—the city's new target market, to put it in business terms.[12]

In January 2003, at an economic forum at Rockefeller University, Bloomberg shared the vision. "I've spent my career thinking about the strategies that institutions in the private sector should pursue, and the more I learn about this institution called New York City, the more I see the ways in which it needs to think like a private company," the text of the speech read. New York "isn't Walmart," he said. "It isn't trying to be the lowest-priced product in the market. It's a high-end product, maybe even a luxury product," he declared. The billionaire mayor who made his fortune selling expensive technology to large financial firms found the concept comfortable. A little over two weeks later, in his State of the City address, Bloomberg elaborated on the idea. "Our unique 'value added' is our diverse eight million citizens and workforce. It is what makes us the best city to live in and do business," he declared. "To capitalize on that strength, we'll continue to transform New York physically . . . to make it even more attractive to the world's most talented people. We'll invest in neighborhood livability, cultural organizations, education, research and medicine." In Bloomberg's mind, government and business were in a *de facto* public-private partnership for the good of the city. His economic team would undertake projects to create "magnetic infrastructure," a memorable phrase used to describe the sorts of municipal assets that attract companies and people to a location. He pledged the program would encompass all five boroughs, and that the city would "imaginatively, aggressively and relentlessly market our cultural attractions and all our competitive advantages," around the country and around the world.[13]

In some ways, the term Bloomberg himself coined, "luxury city," with its connotations of serving only the elite, does a disservice to the holistic nature of the programs his administration developed. The mayor and his team understood that they would have to offer first-rate municipal services of all kinds to attract the full range of residents required for the strategy to work. "Companies come here because the people they want to employ want to live here," Bloomberg explained to a journalist. "Crime, garbage in the streets, and homelessness," are all "job killers," he said. "Cultural institutions, great parks, clean streets, safe streets—these are the things that get the workforce here." He understood that New York's middle class and workers living in upper Manhattan and the Bronx, Brooklyn, Queens, and Staten Island were essential for a luxury city to function, and that they had a claim on municipal government. He believed that by "investing in the conditions that create safe, vibrant and attractive places to live, work and visit," the city would be an appealing place to live for people at every level of the job pyramid. That in turn was a key element of his plan to make New York the preferred home of the world's elite, people prepared to pay a premium to reside in a luxury city, and whose tax bills would fund rich municipal services. In time, Bloomberg came to think of almost every policy in terms of its impact on his broad-based economic development strategy.[14]

Bloomberg's approach departed dramatically from other mayors in scope and thrust. He thought "about diversifying the economy in ways his predecessors hadn't," Regional Plan Association President Robert Yaro recognized. Mayors Koch and Dinkins lacked economic vision, and were handcuffed by fiscal constraints for most of their time in office. Doctoroff summarized Mayor Giuliani's strategy as "make it safe and they will come." It was "not necessarily wrong for the times," in his view. In addition to the obvious benefits of a safe city, Doctoroff thought the dramatic drop in crime made "the impossible, possible" in people's minds. It restored confidence that New York City could be governed and "set the tone" for Bloomberg's team "to be successful."[15]

Yet, to an even greater degree than Koch or Dinkins, Giuliani reacted to private sector requests for help rather than pursue original ideas. Tax breaks for big firms threatening to leave was the most important policy under all three mayors. Between 1988 and 2000, the city cut deals worth some $2 billion with 80 different companies. Corporate commitments to create additional jobs in return for the concessions often failed to materialize, and in many instances—roughly half, according to one analysis—divisions moved out of the city even when the headquarters stayed. Many observers thought companies with no intention of relocating bluffed city government suckers into forfeiting pots of rich tax dollars. Cynics thought it politically motivated corporate welfare—rewards for executives in the financial services, insurance, and real estate industries who made large campaign contributions. The best such an approach offered was a prop for the status quo. It did nothing to promote new industries or innovative business models.[16]

Bloomberg of course had been on the other side of the table—a businessman who had negotiated $14 million in concessions when constructing a new building for his expanding company. He had no intention of taking his firm elsewhere when he cut his deal, and it stayed put when he surrendered the benefits to avoid the appearance of conflict after his election. He knew his friends and peers who ran other important Manhattan businesses would not leave either, and he did not need their campaign contributions to pursue his political ambitions. Early on, he announced the era of corporate welfare had ended. For the most part, he kept his word with respect to tax favors for specific companies threatening to leave New York. His administration approved just five deals for individual firms during his first term, and it instituted measures to track compliance with the obligations that went with the agreements, recapturing some $85 million from wayward companies over time according to calculations by the Economic Development Corporation. A 2012 New York City Comptroller's audit would criticize Bloomberg's administration for lax oversight of relevant job commitments, but the case is unconvincing.[17]

Many found Bloomberg's move to end retention concessions counterintuitive. "Business decisions are being made now," a New York City Partnership report on the impact of 9/11 asserted. "Government must provide decisive leadership," because "the senior management of every business has had to reevaluate the geographic concentration of their talent and facilities." But Bloomberg understood with a confidence his predecessors lacked that local taxes were low on the list of the factors that caused businesses to choose a location. "If the only reason a business will stay is tax concessions, then they have no business," he asserted. Early on, he reversed a decision by Mayor Giuliani to provide $1 billion of city support to the New York Stock Exchange to build a new trading floor. The rise of electronic alternatives in an increasingly virtual financial world made the logic of that deal particularly suspect. Bloomberg and his team knew all about the subject, of course, and could not be fooled. Besides, Bloomberg would later say dismissively, "They're the New York Stock Exchange. Where were they going to go?" A controversial decision to award Goldman Sachs a $50 million tax concession not long after 9/11 to keep its headquarters in lower Manhattan was an exception that Bloomberg later regretted. Concessions for a Bank of America tower on 42nd Street also generated criticism. Doctoroff thought the symbolism of supporting the financial industry, so badly damaged in the 9/11 attack, important enough to justify the decisions at the time they were made.[18]

Bloomberg's team would use city resources, including tax concessions, to promote private sector development. But with a few exceptions—notably for stadium projects—they would be targeted to sectors expected to grow employment in high-value-added industries that the city's business environment favored, not toward specific companies looking for handouts. The policy also sought to diversify the local economy away from financial services and away from Manhattan's midtown business district. More contentiously, the city would provide incentives for real estate development that promised to create favorable physical conditions for business expansion—especially first-class office space in mixed-use settings designed to appeal to highly educated and talented professionals. Bloomberg thought of the government resources dedicated to these projects as a catalyst for private sector investment—an agent that accelerated market activity without otherwise interfering with it. The commercial expansion that followed generated jobs and higher tax revenues, which justified the use of public assets in his mind. "It was all about the economics," Doctoroff asserted.[19]

The mayor attracted his senior economic development team from the city's finance and real estate sectors. In a series of management changes in 2007 and 2008, Robert Lieber, a Lehman Brothers real estate banker, succeeded Andrew Alper at the Economic Development Corporation, and then succeeded Doctoroff as deputy mayor for economic development and rebuilding. Seth Pinsky, an investment banking analyst and real estate finance lawyer who joined the EDC a few years after 9/11, became the corporation's president when Lieber became deputy mayor. Toward the end of Bloomberg's third term, Pinsky returned to the private sector and hand-picked the EDC's chief financial officer, Kyle Kimball, as his successor. Kimball had been a banker at JP Morgan and Goldman Sachs. In 2010 Robert Steel succeeded Lieber as deputy mayor for economic development. Steel was a former Goldman Sachs vice chairman, Wachovia bank CEO, and undersecretary of the Treasury for domestic policy.[20]

"Michael Bloomberg was a manager. His talent was to attract talented people and to give them the rope to do bold things. A number of them did extraordinary things, and he backed them up," was how Robert Yaro described Bloomberg's team. Tom Wright, who succeeded Yaro as head of the Regional Plan Association, was even more emphatic. "Hands down, Bloomberg's team was the best and brightest," he said. Steven Spinola, the president of the Real Estate Board of New York, saw it the same way. "No question, with the talented people he brought there, he gave them phenomenal freedom to go do their job."

Kimball described Bloomberg's management model as, "find really talented people and let them run." Without exception, his economic development team would describe Bloomberg as a man who delegated power to them, supported them loyally, and in return expected—indeed, demanded—first-rate results.[21]

Marketing the Metropolis

A luxury-city strategy required New York to attract companies that hired well-educated, talented people, particularly in sectors where they needed to interact with others like them in a range of related fields. Relying on the well-established business precept that structure follows strategy, Alper created a division of sector specialists at the Economic Development Corporation. It was the approach investment banks deployed to cover important accounts. Specialists were assigned to sectors with the goal of convincing leading companies to locate and expand in New York City. To do that, a specialist had to understand the business, highlight what it was about New York that should appeal, and listen to complaints about obstacles that city policy could address. The strategy intended to send a clear message, reinforced regularly and powerfully by Bloomberg himself, that New York City government had adopted a business-friendly disposition in contrast to its long-standing reputation as an incubator for bureaucrats rather than entrepreneurs. "Taxpayers are our valued clients. We have to see how much we can help them," Alper told a city council committee when describing the approach.[22]

The Center for an Urban Future, a progressive think tank, praised the decision. Its director, Jonathan Bowles, testified before the city council that his organization advocated a sector approach, "partly because the city's longtime economic development strategies have not been working and partly because sector strategies have worked in numerous other cities and states." The Civic Alliance to Rebuild Downtown New York supported it, as did Kathryn Wylde, President of the Partnership for New York City. "In my time working with city government, since 1970, this is the most dramatic departure in economic development we have ever had," she said. Unlike past administrations that expected the economy to take care of itself, the Bloomberg Administration has said, "we have to have a strategy, we have to have tactics for achieving it, and the twenty-first-century economy is something we have to fashion in a proactive way."[23]

The sector strategy injected basic business principles into government economic development efforts. The idea was to make smart use of municipal resources to create a favorable environment for businesses that could benefit from the city's unique characteristics. Bloomberg and his team did not set out to pick winners and losers. They expected the market to determine which industries and which firms would thrive, but they recognized the compelling logic of adopting policies that favored industries likely to succeed in a high-cost location, rich in creative brain power. "New York is a place that competes on intellectual capital," Bloomberg told one audience. "If you want to plant corn, we're not the place for you. . . . We want to attract industries with high profit margins . . . ."[24]

Finance could not be ignored and Bloomberg was the sector's most prominent cheerleader. His support never wavered. When a lax regulatory environment appeared to be giving London financial firms an edge over New York's banks in 2006, Bloomberg teamed up with US Senator Charles Schumer to ask the federal government to respond. Even after the 2008 financial meltdown made bankers the target of deep public scorn, Bloomberg stood loyally by them. But the industries with the greatest growth potential were technology, media and film, fashion and design. Universities and hospitals, long staples of the local economy, had characteristics that made New York City a favorable location for continued growth. Bioscience was an industry Bloomberg cited specifically during his 2001 campaign as underrepresented in New York City.[25]

Despite a rich cluster of world-class medical research institutes, New York City's bioscience industry employed just two thousand people compared with over seventy thousand in California's Silicon Valley and twenty-five thousand in Greater Boston. An anti-commercial attitude among the city's medical scientists and a lack of adequate lab space seemed to be the two most important obstacles to growth. Andrew Alper responded by promoting development of a bioscience campus. The result was construction of a 1.1 million-square-foot facility on Bellevue Hospital's grounds, on Manhattan's East Side. It "came after decades of efforts by a succession of mayors and their economic development entities . . . failed to lure medical and research development institutions," the *New York Times* reported. The project anchored creation of the New York City Bioscience Initiative, a public-private partnership of a dozen world-class research institutions with the city and the state. The group worked with Columbia University in Manhattan and Downstate Medical Center in Brooklyn to create two additional bioscience incubators, and it developed plans for a fourth bioscience facility at the Brooklyn Army Terminal. The objective was to spark development of a new, high-value industry in New York City. Employment in the sector grew to over eleven thousand by 2010.[26]

When Bloomberg was elected, the local entertainment industry was flagging. Movies set in New York were being filmed in Toronto, which had created an environment that attracted cost-sensitive film production companies. Incongruously, a biopic about Rudy Giuliani was being shot in Montreal. Bloomberg asked the Brooklyn-born general manager of his company's radio and television business, Katherine Oliver, to return to New York from London to sort out the situation. She did, with programs small and large over the next dozen years. "Made in New York" was perhaps the most important. It was an initiative to level the playing field with Canada and various US states and cities that gave production companies tax concessions to film in their locations. It included a 10 percent New York State tax credit, upped to 30 percent following the 2008 financial crisis, plus a 5 percent local credit. "New York City is the greatest film set in the world and, this law will help . . . [ensure] that films that are set in New York City are actually filmed there," Bloomberg declared. Films and television series produced in the city were invited to display a "Made in New York" logo, fashioned after subway tokens familiar to residents of a certain age, as a proud symbol of urban patriotism. *Sex and the City* was the first to add it to its credits.[27]

Disruptive changes were well under way in the media industry when the global financial crisis happened. Internet-based news and entertainment was crushing the print industry. Cable TV was pushing the once all-powerful national networks to the margins. The convergence of entertainment and technology promised to destroy long-established business models, the sort of trend that allowed new geographic centers to displace old ones as the hub of an industry. New York's position as the country's traditional media capital was at risk. The Economic Development Corporation and the Mayor's Office of Media and Entertainment convened a high-powered group of the city's media companies, and hired strategy advisors Oliver Wyman and Co. and the Boston Consulting Group to help identify ways to support the sector.[28]

One program was a $40 million infrastructure investment at the Brooklyn Navy Yard. It supported a $700 million, fifty-acre backlot production site that Steiner Studios built there, the largest in the country outside of Hollywood. Its chairman described New York City as "the mating ground for entertainment and technology," which allowed the ecosystem for the media industry's transformation to evolve in a single place. The sector added forty thousand jobs in New York between 2002 and 2012 while media jobs shrank by roughly that number elsewhere. It provided work for some 130,000 people, ranging from celebrity artists and entertainers, to carpenters, stage hands, and electricians. Robert Yaro gave Bloomberg's team credit for ensuring New York remained America's second biggest television and movie production center after Los Angeles. "That was not preordained to happen," in his judgment.[29]

The 9/11 attack devastated tourism, an industry with high growth potential. It differed from other targeted sectors because many of its jobs offered entry-level work for low-skilled workers, immigrants in particular. Bloomberg knew ensuring security was critical to attract travelers back, so he made it clear the city had a terrorist prevention strategy, and that keeping the streets safe and reducing crime would remain top priorities.[30]

Bloomberg also knew that, "When you ask tourists why they're here, visiting a cultural institution is the number one thing they all talk about." Bloomberg himself "could not have cared less about the arts," one close advisor revealed. His friends knew he fell asleep at the opera, did not visit museums except to attend functions, and delegated selection of artwork for his dozen homes to decorators. Yet, he served as a private and public arts patron because he knew that "the arts and culture are the reason people want to live and stay here, and that they are strong economic engines," Patti Harris told people. During the crisis years of fiscal 2003 and 2004, Bloomberg philanthropies made up for some of the cuts to the Department of Cultural Affairs, and by fiscal year 2006, the department's operating budget had recovered to $138 million, more than the annual amount the National Endowment of the Arts spent. In a typical year, the city supported some two hundred different institutions. The multi-year capital account for cultural facilities was cut severely following 9/11, but restored when city revenues recovered. During Bloomberg's dozen years in City Hall, the Departments of Parks and Recreation, and Cultural Affairs, benefitted from $2.8 billion of capital funds. Only education, water infrastructure projects, and transportation programs received more.[31]

Deputy Mayor Harris oversaw parks and cultural affairs for the city, and managed Bloomberg's philanthropy as well, in close coordination with him. The combination made her responsible for hundreds of millions of dollars in annual allocations for a broad range of local, national, and international civic activities. She was a graceful woman and a force to contend with, as her insider nickname, "the velvet hammer," implied. Her keen esthetic eye and commitment to design excellence in city funded structures influenced many decisions. During her years at the city Arts Commission in the Koch administration, she had learned that bad design was often just as expensive as good design, and there was no reason for the city to tolerate it. She insisted on attractive municipal buildings—recreational facilities in parks, but also things as pedestrian as police security stands, municipal truck depots, and public comfort stations.[32]

Along with Commissioner of Cultural Affairs Kate Levin, Harris convinced Bloomberg to support high-profile events expressly intended to project New York City's image as a global culture capital. One of the most prominent was The Gates, a public-art project twenty-six years in conception, spurned by some of Bloomberg's predecessors. It came to the city in February 2005 for sixteen days. At the opening, Bloomberg unfurled the first of thousands of sixteen-foot-high gates composed of saffron colored fabric that created "a visual golden river" in the words of Christo and Jeanne-Claude, the husband-and-wife artists

Rudy Giuliani's endorsement was critical for Bloomberg's surprising 2001 election as mayor of New York City. Bloomberg's daughter Emma held the Bible as Giuliani, accompanied by Judith Nathan, swore Bloomberg in just after midnight January 1, 2002. *Photo Credit: New York City Municipal Archives*

Bloomberg's mother, who he called most mornings throughout his adult life, was ninety-two when she attended her son's inauguration as mayor of New York City. *Photo Credit: New York City Municipal Archives*

Bloomberg (top right) organized the mayor's side of City Hall into a bullpen resembling a Wall Street trading floor. He is speaking with Patti Harris. Bill Cunningham (bottom left) can be seen speaking with Kevin Sheekey, facing away from the camera. *Photo Credit: New York City Municipal Archives*

Bloomberg managed budget crises following 9/11 and the global financial meltdown of 2008/2009 with poise and skill. *Photo Credit: New York City Municipal Archives*

Patti Harris was Bloomberg's closest confidant. They are seen here watching the rescue of passengers aboard flight US 1549 that Captain Chesley Sullenberger landed safely in the Hudson River. *Photo Credit: New York City Municipal Archives*

Bloomberg's relationship with the municipal labor force was often tense. He is shown here with DC 37 president Lillian Roberts (left) and Labor Department commissioner James Hanley. *Photo Credit: New York City Municipal Archives*

Bloomberg maintained a dialogue with Reverend Al Sharpton throughout his three terms as mayor. The open communication eased tensions racially charged events caused. *Photo Credit: New York City Municipal Archives*

Getting guns off the street was a top priority for Bloomberg, and for Police Commissioner Raymond Kelly (left). *Photo Credit: New York City Municipal Archives*

Bloomberg with Deputy Mayor Dennis Walcott (far left) on their way to announce appointment of Joel Klein (center) as schools chancellor. Ed Skyler (front right) was press secretary and later deputy mayor for Operations. *Photo Credit: New York City Municipal Archives*

United Federation of Teachers President Randi Weingarten was with Bloomberg in his City Hall cubicle shortly before announcing agreement on contract terms and union support for mayoral control of the New York City school system in June 2002. *Photo Credit: New York City Municipal Archives*

Deputy Mayor Daniel Doctoroff led the Bloomberg administration's drive to bring the 2012 Olympics to New York City. The failed bid served as a vehicle for launching successful economic development plans. *Photo Credit: New York City Municipal Archives*

Amanda Burden (left) is with Bloomberg and Deputy Mayor Doctoroff at the opening of the High Line. Burden led the planning department that rezoned 38 percent of the city's land, a critical element of Bloomberg's vision of how the city should grow. *Photo Credit: New York City Municipal Archives*

who created the exhibit. Private sources paid the project's $20 million cost, which included a $3 million fee for the city. It attracted an estimated four million people, and it generated $254 million in business, according to a report by the Public Art Fund. Central Park purists declared it an abomination. The frugal thought it money foolishly spent. Others thought it a delightful way to brighten a bleak part of the year, "a worldly expression of the divine," in the words of one resident. To Parks Commissioner Adrian Benepe, it represented the culmination of New York's "spiritual recovery from 9/11. . . . All these people came from all over the world and said 'hey, not only is New York still there, but it's a great, cool place.'"[33]

In 2006, Bloomberg attracted brand management expert George Fertitta to serve as chief executive of NYC & Co., the entity responsible for promoting tourism in New York City. Fertitta launched an integrated global marketing campaign that ultimately leveraged a network of eighteen offices serving twenty-five countries. New overseas promotion centers opened in China, India, Brazil, and other locations mimicking the way private firms allocated more resources to growing foreign markets. He expanded the use of city bus stops and other public spaces for advertisements generating incremental city revenue as well as more opportunities to promote the city as a destination. And NYC & Co. swapped billboard real estate with other cities, allowing them to advertise their charms in New York in return for the right for New York City to do the same in their towns. By 2013, the number of tourists visiting New York climbed above fifty-three million, up from thirty-eight million in 2001, with growth in all five boroughs. Direct tourist spending rose from $25 billion in 2001 to $39 billion in 2013. Including the indirect effects on other businesses, the sector's total economic impact exceeded $57 billion. By then it employed 363,000 people, 84,000 more than when Bloomberg started.[34]

Game Changers

The 2008 global financial crisis, and the Great Recession that followed, raised the stakes for economic development in New York City even more than elsewhere because the local economy remained so dependent on financial services. "Until recently, the New Deal and the 1930s seemed like a distant memory—something we read about in history books," Bloomberg said during his 2009 State of the City address. "But last year, when the sub-prime mortgage write-down became a global financial meltdown, the bank panics returned and today more people are worried about their jobs, their savings and their homes than at any time since the Great Depression." He took it as an article of faith that it was government's job to respond, and turned a famous quote on its head. "When Ronald Reagan said government is not the solution, it's the problem—he was partly right. When government falls down on the job, recessions get compounded and recoveries delayed," Bloomberg told the city. He went on to assert that his government would respond with, "independent leadership, based on facts and pragmatism—not politics and ideology," in a thinly veiled swipe at the dysfunctional United States Congress. The Economic Development Corporation "didn't . . . just watch it happen," Kyle Kimball remembered, referring to the crisis. "There were quick responses . . . to try to keep the city moving."[35]

The boldest aspect of Bloomberg's announcement was a pledge to "retain as many jobs as possible now, and to create four hundred thousand new ones over the next six years." Responsibility for policies to support private sector job growth fell on Bloomberg's economic development deputies, Robert Lieber and later Robert Steel, who would describe the challenge as "a little like patting your head and rubbing your tummy at the same time. The mayor wanted to preserve jobs in the short term, but also to expand and diversify the economy in the long run."[36]

Bloomberg's team convened the good and the great from the city's fashion industry to explore ways to help it through the economic crisis, and it intensified city activities in the media sector, among others. It also adopted policies designed to limit the fallout to displaced workers in the financial sector. Yet, Seth Pinsky realized that to measure up to Bloomberg's charge, the team needed to find "game changers," ideas big enough "to move the dial" of an economy with some 3.3 million private sector jobs. To do that, the economic development team organized brainstorming sessions. Academics and entrepreneurs, business and community leaders, elected officials and others were asked a simple, compelling question: "If you could change one thing about New York City that would have the biggest impact on the city's economy what would it be?" The idea that captured imaginations was a proposal for a competition to create a world-class applied science institute in New York City. Despite its deep pool of research institutions and universities, the city's engineering schools lacked stature and scale. Fear that a shortage of local talent in computer and other technical skills risked limiting the city's growth was a common theme in conversations the mayor and his deputies had with local businessmen.[37]

The Economic Development Corporation researched what it would take for the project to attract top-tier universities, identified potential sites for a new campus, and organized the structure of a competition. But before the initiative gained traction, Deputy Mayor Lieber left the administration, and bureaucratic obstacles caused it to stall. Robert Steel arrived in August 2010. Among his other experiences, Steel had been chairman of Duke University's trustees. It was a "lens" that had made him a self-professed "Eds and Meds hawk." To most people, universities and hospitals were service centers. To Steel, they were also business sectors with very appealing characteristics. Both were growing industries. Universities and hospitals tended to have strong balance sheets, and the demand for education and medical care tended to be non-cyclical, far less exposed to economic volatility than the financial sector. They employed people "up and down the jobs pyramid." Staff typically included construction workers and maintenance teams, cafeteria aides and others, in roles Steel referred to as economic "on ramps for less skilled people." They also relied on different levels of administrators and business professionals, and of course universities employed professors while hospitals hired nurses and doctors. "These are all pretty good things" from the perspective of economic development policy, Steel recognized. The benefits universities brought to a city were the reason Bloomberg's administration supported Columbia University's expansion plans in Morningside Heights bordering Harlem, and New York University's development program in Greenwich Village.[38]

Steel described the applied science initiative in a way that highlights the Bloomberg administration's conception of a smart government project. First, an agency had to identify a need, and then it had to seek independent verification. Once that was accomplished, the government needed to put in a little money and the private sector a lot. Bloomberg frequently talked of government investment as a "catalyst." Ideally, a private sector entity with proper expertise and market incentives would manage the operation without government interference, but against a set of performance requirements that ensured the public would be served. Once an agreement was struck, it should be put in a "lockbox" to prevent arbitrary renegotiation after the fact if the electoral process caused a change in political leadership.[39]

Bloomberg's team also believed that the electoral process gave most politicians a powerful bias in favor of immediate consumption rather than long-term investment. This was especially true of legislators, like the 51 members of the city council who competed for attention. They wanted benefits delivered to their districts that they could point to before the next election. By contrast, the mayor commanded attention more or less whenever he sought it, had a citywide mandate, and in the case of Bloomberg, boasted "a Plan B better than anyone else's Plan A" for life outside City Hall, affording him the luxury of a long-term perspective. As a consequence, it fell to the executive branch "to put a thumb on the scale" in favor of investments with citywide implications that would take time to show results.[40]

In December 2010, Steel outlined the applied sciences initiative in a speech at Google's New York headquarters, and then launched it formally by issuing a Request for Expressions of Interest. Steel confessed to a bout of nerves when he hit "send" on the email inviting twenty-eight institutions from around the world to offer a plan. "My hand was shaking because you never know what you will get back," he said. Seventeen institutions responded, and seven made the cut to a second round. That constituted independent verification that the idea had merit. The city offered land—at the Brooklyn Navy Yard, on Roosevelt Island, or on Governor's Island—infrastructure improvements, and a commitment to streamline regulatory approvals. It also committed seed capital to help fund start-up businesses that emerged from the university's research in return for a commitment by the businesses to stay in the city for at least three years. Steel estimated the value of municipal assets dedicated to the project at "$250 million, max." Other estimates ran as high as $400 million.[41]

Until late in the contest, Silicon Valley's own Stanford University appeared to be the leading candidate. It dropped out the weekend before a final decision. A consortium of Cornell University and Technion-Israel Institute of Technology won the contest and the rights to open a graduate institution on Roosevelt Island. It pledged to build a two-million-square-foot, $2 billion campus in stages, opening in 2017 with completion scheduled for 2043. So the private investment was multiples greater than the public resources, and a highly respected private consortium would operate the school under a contract that transferred government resources in stages, based on performance targets. "A pretty good forty-yard pass," Steel called the project. "It would not have happened without him," in the view of Seth Pinsky, whose EDC was integral to the project's success. An urban affairs expert remarked of the project, "Only a mayor who had been chair of Johns Hopkins trustees with a deputy who had chaired Duke's trustees would have had the nerve," to pursue the competition. The two city government officials were declaring to the world what others knew, but would not dare say. Despite their stature in many other fields, the engineering departments at Columbia and NYU were not up to the task of leading New York into the twenty-first century.[42]

Cornell had secured a $350 million anchor donation from alumnus Charles F. Feeney, something it kept secret until the last moments of its final presentation, leaving the selection committee in stunned silence with the surprise. When Bloomberg announced the winner, a reporter asked what role he would play personally in raising money for the school. "You assume that when they make the phone calls, I'd be on the list," he said to laughter. Eventually Bloomberg philanthropies would commit $100 million to the project. New York University, Columbia University, and Carnegie Mellon had all submitted plans for the contest. All three secured city support for expanded technology programs leveraging the initiative beyond original expectations.[43]

Fostering technology-related businesses was an explicit part of Cornell NYC Tech's mission. It launched its initial year of studies in 2013 inside temporary facilities at Google's New York headquarters in Chelsea, one of Manhattan's trendier districts. Google's 2010 decision to buy the building had been another brick in the Bloomberg administration's efforts to build a technology industry in the city. The transaction signaled to other firms that New York possessed the critical mass of talent needed to attract first-rate technology firms. Google's New Zealand–born chief engineer, Craig Nevill-Manning, begged Google founders Larry Page and Sergey Brin to let him move back to New York City from California in 2003. He craved the lifestyle, and contended other talented professionals did too. The company agreed as an experiment. "If you can find fifteen really great software engineers that we wouldn't have hired otherwise, you can stay," the Google leaders told him. A personal relationship between Bloomberg and Google CEO Eric Schmidt also helped. By 2013 Google had 1,500 people working in New York. In 2012, Microsoft opened a New York research laboratory. Its director, Jennifer Chayes, would describe herself as a "big fan of Mayor Bloomberg's applied science research initiative." She told the *New York Times* that Silicon Alley, New York's first-class universities, and the city's policy initiatives are creating a "groundswell of technology in New York. And we want to be in the places around the world where there is great science and technology." Twitter, Facebook, and eBay would all open New York City engineering offices on Bloomberg's watch.[44]

When the financial crisis caused acres of commercial real estate to go vacant, and left large numbers of talented financiers without jobs, it created an opportunity that served several purposes. A smart program could fill empty offices, retain talented professionals in the city, and allow start-up entrepreneurs across all industries to pursue their ideas locally. "The next generation of successful employers is being developed now," Bloomberg declared as he announced the opening of a start-up incubator at 160 Varick Street. "No one can say for certain what they'll be. But we want to make sure as many of them as possible start and grow in New York City." The incubator offered space, basic business services, networking opportunities, and a mentoring program run by NYU's Polytechnic Institute. Applications exceeded spots many times over, so the EDC created more centers, sufficient to support five hundred firms eventually. Typically, the city negotiated favorable leases that covered the costs of the vacant space without profit for the owners. It took some effort to overcome industry resistance to the parsimonious offer, but once the depth of the financial crisis became apparent, denial gave way to economic reality.[45]

Recognition that technology had ceased to be a discrete industry like others, but was in the process of pervading economic sectors and transforming them caused Bloomberg's team to give tech start-ups special attention. Bloomberg himself hosted dinners for technology business leaders and attended press conferences with companies with as few as five and ten employees. "He knew what it would mean to them," Kathryn Wylde said of Bloomberg's attention, "and that word would spread." Jonathan Bowles agreed. "It was really different than with other mayors. If you ask people in the tech sector, they will tell you they really felt the embrace of New York City government . . . word got out. Mayor Bloomberg was on their side." Bloomberg's posture led "all of city government to make it clear to the tech industry New York was a player and wanted to be a player," according to Robert Yaro.[46]

Bloomberg's affinity for technology in particular, and for high-value businesses in general, contrasted with his personal outlook on manufacturing at first. In 2003, he told a *Financial Times* interviewer that New York City should not waste its time with the sector. After a false start, the Economic Development Corporation and Department of Small Business Services identified industrial niches still operating successfully in New York. There were certain sites where manufacturing and distribution continued to make sense. The Department of City Planning created Industrial Business Zones, sixteen at first and a few more later, and pledged not to rezone them for other purposes. The city also developed a tax credit program and other support for manufacturers displaced by zoning changes to help them relocate into the designated areas. Robert Yaro credited Bloomberg's policies for "essentially" turning the "moribund" Brooklyn Navy Yard into "an incubator for a range of manufacturing industries." One South Bronx development official said of the program Bloomberg's team developed, "We haven't had an industrial policy in this city for fifteen years. It may not be the quintessential policy, but we have a policy." By the end of Bloomberg's third term, evidence suggested that the long, steady decline of manufacturing in New York City may finally have reached bottom and stabilized.[47]

Some Bloomberg administration decisions created hostility among small-business owners. Efforts to raise non-tax revenues led to extreme enforcement of fine-generating regulations causing accusations that Bloomberg was an economic elitist, a mayor willing to allocate vast city resources to large real estate developers and high-value industries, but unwilling to give the little guys a break. Major development projects often involved relocating small businesses to make way for large buildings at great, sometimes crippling inconvenience to the enterprises forced to move. To the mayor and his team, the decisions were part of a much bigger picture, unfortunate perhaps for the enterprises affected, but unavoidable costs of progress and change. And despite the many aggravations small businesses faced in New York City, when the Kauffman Foundation dedicated to understanding and promoting entrepreneurship created a Main

Street index of small-business activity in the United States in 2014 just after Bloomberg left office, New York City ranked number one among big cities, ahead of San Francisco, Boston, and everywhere else.[48]

Zoning Rehab

The city zoning resolution that set out rules for what could be built where— a fundamental power of municipal government that in great measure determines how a metropolis grows—was as misaligned with the twenty-first century as the city's economic policies when Bloomberg took office. It had last been updated in a major way in 1961. One sarcastic scholar described the document as "unworkable rules to prevent developers from building what the market wanted." It led to exquisite negotiations that allowed "the richest, most patient developers to build what city planners and the 'community' think best," since virtually every major structure required approval of a variance.[49]

New York still thought of itself as a working-class city in 1961. Zoning rules generally restricted property to manufacturing or residential use, rarely allowing a mix, to protect residents from the noxious by-products of industry. But industrial businesses were moving out of New York continuously by then and the places reserved for them decayed. Provisions for cleaning them up and converting them to other uses were inadequate. In some neighborhoods individuals seized the initiative and illegally converted lofts and warehouses into places to live. Sometimes the results were creative and appealing, other times ill-advised and dangerous. In 2002, much of New York City's 520 miles of shoreline remained reserved for a shipping industry that had long since sailed away. Ideal locations for offices and apartment buildings with inspiring views were off-limits to builders. Large stretches of riverfront sat wasting, lined with decrepit piers, broken-down warehouses, and rusting structures that prevented access to the water. Four boroughs sat on islands and the fifth on a peninsula, making New York virtually an archipelago that boasted the longest and most-varied shoreline of any city in America. Yet, few New Yorkers thought of their home as a place for waterfront recreation, other than its public beaches.[50]

When Bloomberg was considering running for mayor, he reached out for advice to Amanda Burden, a close friend of Patti Harris, and a social acquaintance who lived on the same block as him on East 79th Street. Bloomberg knew Burden had been a New York State urban development official, and that she had earned a reputation as an exacting taskmaster for the oversight role she played at Battery Park City, the huge state-sponsored residential community in downtown Manhattan. She had also served for more than a decade on the city planning commission. Burden took Bloomberg to parts of the city that a Wall Street billionaire would rarely see—the tough Brooklyn neighborhood of Bedford-Stuyvesant, the community court in the equally rough area of Red Hook, the "somewhat dangerous" Greenpoint-Williamsburg waterfront. Bloomberg was predictably surprised at the degenerate condition of places a short limousine ride from the Upper East Side.[51]

Burden had well-developed views about ways to prime the city's physical space for life in the twenty-first century. Unsurprisingly, when Bloomberg won election, she wanted to be head of city planning, the dream job for anyone in the field. The function actually encompassed two roles, chair of the planning commission and director of the department of city planning, the administrative unit that housed the city's planning professionals. Bloomberg favored Burden, but he had already decided to name Doctoroff deputy mayor for economic development and rebuilding, and that role included responsibility for the planning department. Typically, Bloomberg let members of his team make their own hiring decisions. In this instance, he pressured his deputy to choose Burden. Doctoroff "fought it tooth-and-nail," one City Hall insider remembered. He feared Burden was a socialite looking for a hobby rather than a serious professional, and besides, he had a candidate of his own—renowned urban planning scholar Alexander Garvin, who had been collaborating closely with Doctoroff on his project to bring the 2012 Olympics to New York. But Burden persevered through three interviews. "I did extensive due diligence," Doctoroff would tell a reporter, "and what I found was someone who was strikingly substantive, passionate about her work, passionate about New York City and had a sense of where she wanted to take the City Planning Commission. I was very comfortable." Garvin would become the head of planning for the Lower Manhattan Development Corporation created to oversee rebuilding of the World Trade Center, the highest-profile public construction project in the world at the time.[52]

Burden possessed impressive command of the city's zoning code and keen appreciation of the role the city's local community boards played in the approval process. They had only advisory status, but from her perch as a member of the planning commission, she had watched neighborhood opposition pressure council members into derailing projects. The experience taught her to respect the views of the people who lived on the streets that city decisions affected. When she became chair of the planning commission, she often spoke with two or three council members a day searching for ways to respond to local concerns and to achieve consensus without compromising a project's goals or standards. In 2011, her department published the first comprehensive update of the *Zoning Handbook* in fifty years. The intent of the impressive guide was "to make zoning more accessible to all, and to help New Yorkers advocate for their neighborhoods. Planning initiatives are most successful when there is full participation by residents, elected officials and other stakeholders," she wrote in the preface. The description was more than platitudes. Periodically, the hard-driving Doctoroff would tell Burden that the professionals in her department knew better than the community what would work best and that they should drive decisions more forcefully. "I am just as ambitious as you are," she would respond, "but we have to do this my way."[53]

Over the next twelve years, Burden would lead the city through some 124 amendments to the zoning resolution, changing the status of 38 percent of the city's land by her reckoning. The ambitious effort set the stage for the conversion of New York City's physical landscape from an unintended monument to time-gone-by into a place where the future could happen. With just a small number of significant exceptions, notably stadium plans, Burden's ideas about how to rezone the city were highly compatible with Bloomberg's and Doctoroff's com-mitment to population growth and economic diversification. The Bloomberg administration "worked very quickly and aggressively to capitalize on the plan that we had because we came in with a vision of what we wanted," Doctoroff would tell an interviewer years later. Yet, the amendments were pursued a neighborhood at a time with active local input. It was the opposite of the tactic Mayor Giuliani's planning department followed for a 1990s proposal to revise the zoning resolution citywide that was defeated by broad-based resistance.[54]

Burden's objective was to allow growth "in the right places" and preserva-tion elsewhere. The decisions were subjective to be sure, but they were based on careful analysis and smart principles. Mass transportation was often key. Multiple subway lines and commuter rail connections made locations ripe for greater density. The opposite was equally true. More building where people relied on cars to get around made little sense in a traffic congested metropolis. So locations near transit hubs suitable for building were rezoned to encourage new housing in particular, and residential neighborhoods without transporta-tion networks were down-zoned. Other considerations included a range of over-lapping circumstances. Underutilized, low-density industrial zones were recast to promote development of prime office space, apartments, retail stores, and related amenities. Sites deemed suitable for industry were declared off-limits for zoning changes to prevent speculators from bidding up land values and making them unaffordable for low-margin businesses important to keep in the city. Mature commercial hubs in upper Manhattan, Brooklyn, Queens, the Bronx, and Staten Island were rezoned to spark revitalization. And rules applying to major stretches of New York's underutilized waterfront were changed to pro-mote development and access.[55]

High-profile projects to promote commercial real estate development cap-tured headlines, creating the impression they were the only important thrust of Bloomberg's rezoning efforts. The image is misleading. A report by the Furman Center for Real Estate and Urban Planning, a department of New York University's Wagner School of Public Policy, assessed seventy-six changes that took place between 2003 and 2007 across 188,000 of the city's 880,000 land lots. The study determined 14 percent constituted up-zonings that increased the buildable capacity on the affected sites by more than 10 percent. Some 23 percent were down-zonings, reducing buildable capacity by more than 10 percent. The remainder, more than three-fifths of them, were contextual only, meaning their provisions had little direct impact on building density. Rather, they meant to preserve the existing character of a neighborhood. That approach was particularly true of changes on Staten Island and Queens, and parts of Brooklyn. The study estimated the net effect on housing capacity was more than trivial, but not great, providing for perhaps two hundred thousand more people. Burden believed the study failed to appreciate the full impact of the transit-based strategy, and consequently understates the increase. But there is little doubt that the rezoning decisions changed where and how growth would occur. The new rules made more commercial sense and promised less unwise disruption to middle-class neighborhoods. Some feared the down-zonings went too far and would interfere with desirable density increases required to accommodate more people, particularly low-income residents searching for affordable housing. It would fall to Bloomberg's successors to contend with that problem.[56]

Zoning initiatives under Bloomberg supported an ambitious vision of how New York City should evolve to remain relevant in a world drastically different than the one the zoning resolution had been designed to serve in 1961. Bloomberg guided economic development policies in different directions than his predecessors, with enormous, positive impact on New York City. The leaders he recruited to city government transformed its economic development agencies. Doctoroff, Lieber and Steel, Alper, Pinsky and Kimball, Burden and the highly talented staffs they attracted, converted the departments they ran into high-powered, proactive resources that pursued clear goals with a sense of mission untypical for municipal bureaucracies. The team consciously set out to remake the city's image from a businessman's burden to an entrepreneur's friend, with significant success. The level of collaboration across agencies was "without precedent," according to Doctoroff, who applied standard business practices of setting goals, aligning priorities, and actively encouraging cross-agency communication in the departments he ran. "There was no tradition" of city departments talking with each other about shared or overlapping priorities when he arrived, according to Doctoroff. In his mind, the change in culture from turf protection to collaboration had a huge impact on the team's effectiveness. Lifelong government staffers worked effectively alongside professionals whose entire careers had been in business.[57]

Others confirm the claim of an unusual degree of cooperation among Bloomberg's staff, although it must be kept in perspective. It is easy to find stories of commissioners fighting with each other, budget office deputies holding hostage "certificates to proceed" required to disburse money for approved projects until some unrelated matter was resolved, and senior staff hanging up telephones on each other. The flip side of a team of talented people operating with a high degree of autonomy was that in Bloomberg's government it was not always easy to find a forum for resolving the conflicts that affect any large, complex organization, New York City government no less than any other.[58]

In any event, Bloomberg's team set the stage, and in some cases set in motion, a series of projects that leveraged overdue zoning changes, smart public infrastructure improvements, and other municipal resources to stimulate private investment. Many of the most important ones emerged from Deputy Mayor Doctoroff's dream of bringing the 2012 Olympics to New York City, a boldly ambitious plan that Bloomberg's entrepreneurial instincts caused him to support even before he took office. [59]

The World's Second Home

"All Olympics, all the time," was how City Council Speaker Gifford Miller remembered Bloomberg's first term. Deputy Mayor Doctoroff brought his plan to bring the 2012 Olympics to New York City with him to work his first day on the job in January 2002, and promoted it without pause until July 2005 when the selection committee chose London. Hundreds of people invested thousands of hours in the effort, not least Mayor Bloomberg himself, who lent it unequivocal support. He flew with Doctoroff to Singapore for the final decision knowing full well their pitch had slim chance to win. Just a few months earlier Ladbrokes of London, bookies to the world, reported the odds against their plan at fourteen to one. When the members of the International Olympic Committee cast just sixteeen votes for New York placing it fourth out of five contenders, Bloomberg told reporters with little emotion, "In the world I come from and Dan comes from, if you lose, it's another deal. You go on." In this instance, the lack of despondency in defeat was more than Bloomberg's trading personality shrugging off a transaction the moment it failed. The desire to win the Olympics had been real, but it was not essential to a broader mission.[60]

From the start, Doctoroff's plan rested on real estate–development alchemy designed to produce municipal gold before a shovel ever touched city soil. New York's Olympic bid committed the city to build a range of arenas and facilities. Wielding the hard deadlines the selection process imposed the same way

Olympic trainers used the dates of its events to motivate athletes, Doctoroff pursued site development projects and zoning changes related to the bid with unaccustomed urgency for city plans. The initiatives rendered the properties suitable for contemporary use. That raised the value of the properties significantly and promoted economic growth. It assured profits for real estate developers and higher revenues for the city, a key element of the idea all along. Supporters insisted from the outset that the plan would create the benefits regardless if the city won the games. For the most part, the communities near the chosen sites welcomed the improvements promised, with the dramatic exception of Manhattan's far West Side where the plan's flagship arena generated fatal opposition.[61]

Doctoroff was born into a Jewish family in Newark, New Jersey in 1958, and raised in a Detroit suburb. His father was an appeals court judge, his mother a psychologist. He left the Midwest to study government at Harvard, and returned to attend law school at the University of Chicago. When his wife landed a job as a marketing professional in New York City, he transferred to New York University School of Law, unenthusiastic about the relocation. A summer internship working on financial transactions for a law firm convinced him he would rather be a banker than an attorney, and he took a job as an analyst at Lehman Brothers. Before long, he moved to Oak Hill Capital Management, a private equity firm. Doctoroff set himself a goal of making a lot of money fast to give him the freedom to choose another career later. He did just that by developing expertise doing real estate deals and by becoming Oak Hill's managing partner, accumulating "infinitely more money" than he ever imagined possible.[62]

Doctoroff had youthful athletic aspirations, but his football career ended in ninth grade after he broke both thumbs in a Friday afternoon game, his collarbone in practice the following Monday, and then his arm as soon as he returned to the playing field after six weeks of recuperation. He was a tall, handsome, athletic adult who rode his bicycle around New York and bought part of a hockey team, but mostly he enjoyed sports as a spectator. In 1994, he attended a World Cup football match between Italy and Bulgaria on the New Jersey side of the Hudson River where the frenzied energy of the crowd swept him up. It struck him as extraordinary that two foreign competitors could create such intense excitement. Even more remarkable was the realization that the New York area's unmatched diversity meant that any pair of teams in the world would generate the same sensational reaction. The idea of bringing the Olympics to his adopted metropolis captured Doctoroff's imagination. It struck the Midwestern-raised transplant as incongruous that New York City, where public schools boasted children from 188 nations, had never hosted the world's foremost international athletic games. Eventually, the marketing tag line he would promote welcomed Olympians to their "second home." In language that might serve to narrate a gauzy documentary, the proposal submitted to the committee that would select the 2012 site observed that, "in a short ride on the No. 7 subway from Queens to Manhattan . . . you experience . . . a city that has been preparing to host the Games for nearly four hundred years."[63]

The roar of the crowd that set Doctoroff's blood running also started the wheels of his real estate banker mind turning. He conducted "intensive research" and learned how Olympic hosts—"some better than others"—had used the games, and the deadlines that a bid to win them created, to "really change the face of the city." He believed New York could have a similar experience, and it was time. "The fall-out from the conflict between Jane Jacobs and Robert Moses," two brilliant New Yorkers with irreconcilable visions of urban development, coupled with "nostalgia for New York's manufacturing past," left former industrial zones "largely untouched despite the fact that for a twenty-first century city they were in some of the best locations," Doctoroff believed. The idea of "adaptive reuse" of languishing prime real estate, much of it along the waterfront, made great sense. People had talked about the sorts of projects Doctoroff had in mind for thirty or forty years, but little had actually happened.[64]

In 1996 Doctoroff convinced urban design expert Alexander Garvin, author of *The American City: What Works, What Doesn't*, to sign on as managing director for planning of an organization whose mission was to bring the Olympics to New York. In his book, Garvin defined "successful city planning as public action that generates a desirable, widespread, and sustained private market reaction." Both men believed that the quest to bring the Olympics to New York City could serve as a vehicle to create momentum for major development ideas that had been floating in the New York skyline for years. The result would be dramatic improvements to the city's physical landscape. Doctoroff persuaded the city's business elite, and then Mayor Rudy Giuliani, to support the plan. Initially the goal was the 2008 games, but the United States Olympic Committee decided not to sponsor a bid that year, so the focus shifted to four years later, and the organization became known as NYC2012.[65]

About two weeks after Bloomberg's election, transition chairman Nat Leventhal approached Doctoroff in search of a deputy mayor for economic development. "I never had anyone else in mind," he would later confess. Doctoroff was "initially resistant." His professional commitments plus his leadership of NYC2012 had him working flat out. And the conversation came at a difficult personal moment. His father had recently been diagnosed with ALS, Lou Gehrig's disease. But it also came right after 9/11, which for Doctoroff was "a huge blow to everything New York represented, not just here but to people around the world." The attack caused his urban patriotism, already primed by his Olympic quest, to swell. When Leventhal approached a second time, he agreed to meet the mayor-elect. At the least, "it was a great opportunity to talk to [Bloomberg] about the Olympics," Doctoroff reasoned. Bloomberg had been among the many businessmen who had contributed to NYC2012, and the two men knew each other, but not well. Their shared backgrounds in investment banking, structuring deals, and doing business gave them common ground for conversation. By the end of the talk, Doctoroff concluded Bloomberg was prepared to invest the power and prestige of the mayor's office in the Olympic project. He realized that the position on offer would provide a singular chance to pursue his dream and to have a lasting impact on the future of New York City. "Over the course of an hour and a half, I decided it was something I wanted to do," he recalled.[66]

For a $1-per-year salary, Doctoroff signed on for a brief that included responsibility for the Economic Development Corporation, the City Planning Commission, and the Department of Housing, Preservation and Development. In time, his portfolio would expand to include other departments. The formal authority of the role combined with tenacity, intellect, attention to detail, and a persuasive personality made Doctoroff a force to contend with. Before long, comparisons with New York's master builder, Robert Moses, would circulate. Not all were complimentary. Doctoroff used to keep track of the number of days in a row he could work without losing his temper with his staff. At one point a journalist reported he made it to thirty-four and that the record was still mounting. Comparisons to Moses ignored at least one crucial point. Moses built sources of power independent of New York's elected officials. Doctoroff's authority depended entirely on Bloomberg, who gave his deputy unfailing support.[67]

The Olympics promote an extraordinary range of esoteric sports. Three of the proposed sites to host them sat on the East River, or upstream on the Harlem River where they separated the waterfront from surrounding neighborhoods in a way that left a marvelous natural resource wasting. The Hunters Point section of Long Island City, Queens, directly across from the United Nations, contained train depots, tired warehouses, and worn-out factories. Public and private initiatives had long sought to convert the area from an out-of-date, out-of-the-way industrial location into a residential neighborhood. A few buildings had gone up, but development remained limited. It became the proposed site for an Olympic Village to house sixteen thousand people—the athletes and their trainers. After the bid failed, the city assembled thirty acres of waterfront property, and approved plans for up to five thousand apartments on the rezoned site, the city's largest affordable housing development since the

1970s. Ground breaking on phase I, the first two residential buildings, seventeen thousand square feet of new retail space, a 1,100-seat school and a 5.5-acre waterfront park took place in March 2013. Construction continues under Bloomberg's successor.[68]

In the Brooklyn neighborhoods of Greenpoint and Williamsburg, aging warehouses, some converted into illegal lofts, deteriorating manufacturing buildings, and broken piers impeded development of a waterfront with magnificent views of Manhattan. To Amanda Burden, the site "was really an outrage," epitomizing the way the city had "turn[ed] our back on the waterfront." Early in her tenure, the planning department proposed to rezone the area for mixed use development, including a two-mile-long riverfront esplanade. NYC2012 proposed to use the site for a range of aquatic sports, including beach volleyball, diving, and synchronized swimming. A few weeks before the International Olympic Committee selected a 2012 host city, the zoning proposal won approval, with a few modifications sought by the local community board. The new rules promoted construction of residential high rises and affordable housing. Commericial activity on nearby retail streets surged, and the area experienced a revival.[69]

The decrepit Bronx Terminal Market, completed in 1935 as a food distribution center, sat within the poorest congressional district in the United States. The building that housed the once-vibrant trading center had declined over time to the point that the city had condemned the structure. The legal action was a means of wresting control away from an unscrupulous landlord who had secured a ninety-nine-year lease from the city on unjustifiable terms after reportedly handing a brown paper bag with tens of thousands of dollars in it to the staff handling Mayor John Lindsay's hopeless 1972 presidential campaign. Yet, plans to redevelop the property stalled. The Olympic bid renewed attention to the site. A private real estate firm with close ties to Doctoroff, the Related Companies, bought the property and swapped some land needed for the Olympics for a nearby city detention center scheduled for demolition. Development followed and brought the underserved area its first modern retail center with a host of popular stores millions of Americans take for granted: Home Depot, Staples, Toys "R" Us, Bed, Bath & Beyond among others. When it opened in September 2009, the headline in the *New York Times* read, "Exhilaration as Giant Mall Springs Up in a Strike Against Blight."[70]

The Terminal Market project included construction of a park along the nearby riverfront, more or less facing the 369th Regiment Armory on the Manhattan side of the river at 142nd Street and Fifth Avenue. The structure, once home to a famed African American United States Army unit nicknamed "the Harlem Hell Fighters," had been steadily deteriorating for years when

Doctoroff incorporated it into the Olympic plan. In the aftermath of the failed bid, substantial renovations turned it into an active community center. A project to build a pool and skating rink begun under Mayor Giuliani in Flushing, Queens, took on special urgency when the facilities became part of the Olympic proposal to accommodate water polo matches. The work done as part of the bid preparations pushed the project to completion, even though 2012 Olympians competed in London. The pool was the first the city had built in forty years.[71]

The Biggest Stadium New York Never Built

By far the most complex and controversial aspect of the bid was a proposal to build an Olympic stadium along the Hudson River, on the far West Side of Manhattan. It was the flagship of an enormously ambitious goal to extend the midtown business district. Organic growth should have allowed some fifty-nine blocks of land that touched 28th Street and Seventh Avenue on its southeast corner, and 43rd Street and Hudson River Park on its northwest to become an extension of the city's primary business center. Three things prevented it: low-density industrial zoning, Metropolitan Transportation Authority rail yards that put a grimy six-block hole in the middle of the area, and inadequate public transportation. The Javits Convention Center compounded the challenge. It sat between 34th and 39th Streets west of Eleventh Avenue. Boosters had hoped the convention center would draw the business district west after it opened in 1986, but the outcome disappointed. The center was too small to compete effectively with larger facilities in other cities, and lack of subway access left it isolated.[72]

The city undertook modest rezoning in the area over the years, but little development occurred. The neighborhood consisted of early-twentieth-century low rise apartments and local stores scattered among brick warehouses, old factories, and parking lots. Chelsea to the south and Hell's Kitchen to the north gentrified and enjoyed a revival. The neighborhood in between, which planners took to calling Hudson Yards, remained largely unchanged. The residents who lived there liked its edgy, urban feel. But as a use of riverfront real estate contiguous to the most productive central business district in the nation, it made little sense.[73]

Focus on the neighborhood surged in June 2001. A blue-ribbon panel dubbed The Group of 35, convened by US Senator Charles Schumer, issued a ninety-nine-page report entitled *Preparing for the Future: A Commercial Development Strategy for New York City.* It projected a need for an additional sixty million square feet of office space to accommodate economic growth over the next twenty years. A key recommendation called for rezoning waterfront areas designated for low-density manufacturing and industrial use into sites where high-density office space, apartments, and supporting retail shops could thrive. The far West Side was one of three locations highlighted as offering the possibility for a new or expanded major business district, along with downtown Brooklyn and Long Island City, Queens. The report captured the sense of the city's business elite that without substantial rezoning, New York would face a severe office space crisis. Mayor Giuliani's city planning department developed a proposal for Hudson Yards that Bloomberg's team inherited.[74]

First-class sports stadiums were also in short supply, according to the owners of three of New York's most important professional teams. Yankees owner George Steinbrenner complained that the Bronx stadium where his franchise played was substandard, and the location itself discouraged suburban fans from attending games. He threatened to leave New York for New Jersey just as the football Giants had done years earlier if the city did not build him an arena with an ample number of lucrative corporate hospitality suites on Manhattan's far West Side. He convinced Mayor Giuliani he was serious, but then Derek Jeter led the Yankees on a multi-year winning streak, attendance soared, and the argument became unconvincing. Still, during his last days in office, Giuliani committed substantial city support for a new Yankee Stadium in the Bronx, and he gave the Mets a similar commitment for a new stadium in Queens. Bloomberg put both initiatives on hold when he became mayor, declaring they would have to wait until the city recovered from the post 9/11 fiscal crisis.[75]

Meanwhile, interest in the West Side stadium emerged from across the Hudson River. Robert Johnson, heir to the Johnson & Johnson fortune, bought the New York Jets in 1999. His newly acquired team played in Giants Stadium in the New Jersey Meadowlands, the only shared arena in professional football. The arrangement had little emotional or commercial appeal to Johnson. He wanted the Jets to return to their New York City home in a stadium of their own, and he initiated discussions with city officials.[76]

Amanda Burden's Department of City Planning was already at work on an ambitious proposal to rezone the fifty-nine-square-block area on the far West Side. The department's initial response to the Group of 35 report was the point of departure for changes meant to promote development of a thriving mixed-use location connected to the midtown business district. Doctoroff liked the plan, and he proposed the construction of an Olympic stadium for seventy-five thousand to eighty thousand fans on a platform built over the Metropolitan Transportation Authority train yard, just as Park Avenue had been built decades earlier on a platform over rail tracks leading to Grand Central Terminal. The stadium would be fitted with a retractable roof, and a tunnel would connect it directly to the Javits Convention Center, which sat just a block north. Ten days a year or so, the stadium would serve as the Jets home field, and the rest of the time it would provide an additional two hundred thousand square feet of space for conventions. The idea complemented a separate city and state sponsored plan already under way to enlarge the convention center and to add amenities. To make the entire plan work, the MTA and city would agree to extend the route of the Number 7 subway to Eleventh Avenue and 33rd Street from its existing terminus at Times Square, 42nd Street and Seventh Avenue.[77]

The Jets announced they would invest $800 million in the stadium, and Governor Pataki and Mayor Bloomberg declared the state and city would provide $300 million each. The MTA was the logical source of financing for the Number 7 train extension, but there was a problem. Sometime before Bloomberg's election, onetime Lindsay Chief of Staff Jay Kriegel, the executive director of NYC2012 at the time and later its president, met with New York State Assembly Speaker Sheldon Silver to secure his support for the plan. He summarized the outcome of his meeting succinctly in a phone call to Doctoroff immediately afterward. "We're fucked," he said. Construction of the Second Avenue Subway meant to link the Upper East Side to Silver's downtown district had been stalled for decades. Silver told Kriegel in blunt terms that until the MTA finished the project that affected his district directly, there was "no chance" he would support allocating state funds to a different major capital commitment. Silver also had practical reservations about the subway plan as conceived.[78]

Doctoroff and team had already been working on innovative plans to make the entire Olympic bid, including the stadium and its related infrastructure as close to self-financing as possible. It included creation of a public authority that would issue bonds. The debts would be repaid from dedicated payments in lieu of taxes—PILOTS in municipal finance jargon—derived from the incremental revenues the higher real estate values rezoning would cause. After Silver's blunt rejection of support for the subway extension, they rolled its costs into their financing program. It would be the first time since creation of the MTA decades earlier that the city would fund a subway project on its own.[79]

Many community representatives and local activists did not like the rezoning plan or the stadium. They would force relocation of some 139 residences, more than four thousand jobs, and change the character of the neighborhood forever. In response, advocates pointed out that the rezoned area would generate vastly more apartments and jobs than would be displaced. The owners of Cablevision and Madison Square Garden, located just a few blocks southeast of the proposed stadium, feared the new arena would compete with their business. They launched an expensive publicity campaign to halt the project, $8.5 million worth according to one report. "You need that like you need a hemorrhoid," a Bloomberg ally told a reporter.[80]

The MTA, an agency with formidable financial challenges and subject to scrutiny by state legislators and private bond holders, expected to be paid for the air rights to build over its tracks. The arena proposal included $100 million payment by the Jets for the ethereal asset, and the city pointed to its financing of the Number 7 train as additional compensation. But one estimate put the market value of the building rights at $1.2 billion. Richard Ravitch had been chairman of the MTA years earlier when the property was assembled. "I created an asset for the MTA, it was very valuable, and I didn't think it should be given away," especially not for a Jets stadium which Ravitch deemed "a mistake." He also thought the details of the Number 7 train extension did not make sense because it lacked a connection to Penn Station at 33rd Street and Eighth Avenue. Ravitch met with Bloomberg privately to express his concerns, and then opposed the project publicly. Maneuvering by other opponents of the plan forced the price of the MTA air rights way up, making it clear the original bid had understated the value of the public subsidy. The mayor's critics chastised him roundly on the subject. Credible estimates put the total taxpayer bill for the stadium at about $1 billion and for the entire project at about $4.5 billion.[81]

Groups without an economic stake and in favor of the proposal to repurpose prime real estate to more valuable uses also raised serious objections. After more than a year's thorough analysis, the Regional Plan Association's professionals concluded the stadium was a foolish idea. It would add to traffic congestion, serve as a new obstacle to riverfront access, and stay vacant roughly 60 percent of the time even when attached to the convention center. "Mixed-use development on the site would do more to catalyze development throughout the district than a stadium," it concluded. Such a plan would provide improved waterfront access and better connections to the neighborhood. Quietly, professionals at the city planning department agreed with the critics. So did a majority of New Yorkers according to a May 2005 Quinnipiac University poll. Resistance to the arena was so great that Doctoroff asked the mayor if he wanted to abandon the plan to avoid the political repercussions during a year when he would stand for reelection. Bloomberg dismissed the notion. "We think it is the right thing to do," he said, and stayed the course. The argument for the arena was that it was more than a stadium. To Doctoroff and Bloomberg, it promised to convert the "pathetic" Javits Convention Center into a competitive, "close to world-class," location for huge exhibitions. The economic implications, including employment opportunities for low-skilled workers, were substantial. Still, most New Yorkers found the trade-off unappealing.[82]

While controversy swirled around the stadium proposal, the Department of City Planning secured city council approval for the fifty-nine-block rezoning plan, but the site for the arena sat over MTA property. Doctoroff and team had structured their proposal for it as a separate project to avoid forcing council members to take a position on it. A majority of the New York State Assembly and a majority of the state senate favored the arena, according to Doctoroff and others, but state support for the project required approval of an obscure agency, the Public Authorities Control Board. Like so much of New York State government, three men controlled the board: the governor, the leader of the state senate, and the speaker of the assembly. Each appointed one member and commitments required unanimous approval.[83]

Bloomberg tried to force a decision. Several times he declared it imperative that a vote take place by a certain date to show the Olympic Committee all necessary approvals for the project had been secured. Assembly Speaker Silver paid no attention. He shared many of the doubts others expressed about locating a stadium on Manhattan's West Side, and he objected intensely to an effort to allocate state capital to a new and controversial midtown development project when Ground Zero remained a huge hole that happened to be located in his assembly district. Public officials had to put "moral obligations" ahead of "ambitions," he said. He had little desire to allow himself to be labeled as the man who lost the Olympics, but he declined to be suckered into approving a dubious subsidy for a private sporting arena when it was likely another city would win the games. He also sought to avoid alienating two Democratic assembly members from the West Side, Deborah Glick and Richard Gottfried, who were implacable foes of the project.[84]

Early in June 2005, the Olympic committee released its appraisal of the competing bids in anticipation of a July decision. New York featured toward the bottom of the list. The senate and assembly PACB representatives voted no on the West Side stadium, and it vanished into the $300 million financing gap that resulted. Silver suggested arrogance had played a role in the outcome. Early on, before Bloomberg's election, Doctoroff had explored ways to bypass state legislative authority. Later, with the mayor's support, based on counsel from Governor George Pataki's office, he tried to finesse state approval by attaching an amendment to a bill relating to the Javits Convention Center. "I just think nobody's opinion counted until it counted," Silver said after the PACB vote. "They never talked to Senator Bruno, they never talked to me. And they just proceeded ahead, and they used this Olympic timetable as the hammer that was going to make everything that was wrong with the bid suddenly right." Silver's description ignored intense efforts by the city, Doctoroff, and Bloomberg himself to secure the speaker's endorsement, but it told a tale. When Bloomberg declared the day after the proposal's defeat that its opponents "had let America down," he did nothing to defuse accusations that his team's imperious attitude contributed to the plan's demise.[85]

Remarkably, within seventy-two hours, Doctoroff and others worked out a new deal with the Mets to accommodate the need for an Olympic stadium. Regional Plan Association President Robert Yaro marveled at the Bloomberg team's ability "to turn on a dime." A week or so after the stadium plan collapsed, Yaro was at a social event when Bloomberg arrived. They made eye contact, and Bloomberg walked across the room toward him, obviously a man on a mission. Yaro tensed up. After the RPA opposed the stadium, Doctoroff had treated Yaro personally to a ferocious telephone tongue lashing that went on for so long, with such hostility, that Yaro ended up holding the receiver at arms' length to spare his ear and his psyche. "Oh Christ," Yaro thought as Bloomberg approached. "Here it comes, public humiliation over this thing," and he braced himself for the dressing down he was sure would follow. Instead, Bloomberg asked him to breakfast the next day, where he told Yaro he understood the RPA had made an honest professional judgment about the West Side stadium, and that it was time to move on. He wanted to salvage the Olympic bid and he needed the RPA's help to win approval for the revised stadium project. Yaro signed on. His organization believed all along that a stadium in Flushing Meadows was a better idea. It would cost less than half of the estimates for the West Side arena, with a fraction of the public subsidy, in a more sensible location.[86]

The city made commitments at the same time to the Yankees for a new stadium in the Bronx to avoid the political fallout favoring one team over another would cause. The Olympic bid went forward to defeat despite the last-minute heroics, but without the deep embarrassment of an eleventh-hour withdrawal. In an interview sometime later, Doctoroff would reflect on what he had learned working for the city. "Lesson one, respect the state and the State Legislature. We made the presumption we could go it alone and that was a mistake."[87]

Zoning modifications required to take advantage of the site where the arena would have been built occurred in 2009 with active collaboration between the Regional Plan Association and the city. The global financial crisis halted new building construction for a time, but as the economy recovered, development on the far West Side reemerged. By 2015, the site was "just teeming with development" according to Tom Wright, who succeeded Yaro as RPA president. In a section planners named the Eastern Rail Yards, fast by the Number 7 subway stop, densely clustered commercial office space is rising. Density allowances terraced down with more housing units and open space anticipated in the Western Rail Yards, a long city block farther away from the business district and closer to the river. To the north, across from the convention center, the new rules called for a more balanced mix of commercial and residential building. Development in each area was meant to reflect the character of the adjacent neighborhood. When fully built out, the fifty-nine square blocks rezoned are expected to include more than twenty-five million square feet of office space and over thirteen thousand units of new housing. It will include more than one hundred retail shops and restaurants, a school, a hotel, a cultural center, and acres of public space in what one real estate company asserts is "the largest private real estate development in the history of the United States and the largest development in New York City since Rockefeller Center." The long-desired link of the area to the midtown business district may finally happen.[88]

The West Side project stood adjacent to another bold initiative, the High Line. Elevated railroad tracks built in the 1920s to carry freight to warehouses south of Penn Station had fallen into disuse. Parts were torn down in the 1960s and the rest had been scheduled for demolition. What remained standing was one government approval away from destruction when two local residents, writer Joshua David and painter Robert Hammond, started a movement to save the structure and convert it into a unique elevated urban park. It stretched from 34th Street near the Hudson Yards to Gansevoort Street, three blocks below 14th Street. Amanda Burden made the project a top priority and her planning department worked closely with community advocates to make it a reality. The space became a spectacular success, a tourist destination and a neighborhood resource that attracted thousands of visitors daily, more than six million during the course of 2014. The property alongside it surged in value, generating millions in city tax revenues.[89]

Power and Persuasion in the Neighborhoods

Interactions between Bloomberg's team and communities in areas of the Bronx, Harlem, and Queens affected by the Olympic bid were mostly cordial. Local representatives in long-neglected neighborhoods found the additional offices and apartments, shops, parks, and cultural facilities that rezoning promised appealing. Businesses displaced were of course angry, and the twenty-three still operating in the Bronx Terminal Market sued. They complained that the city's stingy relocation offer was woefully inadequate, and above all made no effort to keep their shops together as a market so retailers could buy rare ethnic foods all in one place. Their lawyers accused Bloomberg of pushing out working-class New Yorkers for the "fish and chardonnay" crowd. Urban planners lamented the rise of a sterile, suburban-style shopping mall where laborers would make minimum wage. When the mayor ran for reelection in 2005, *Daily News* journalist Juan Gonzalez and others wrote that the benefits the mall delivered to local residents were meager in comparison to the size of the subsidy for the private developer who built and operated it. Despite active support from Bronx elected officials, local community board members objected to many aspects of the Yankee Stadium plan, and analysts criticized the basic premise—city tax dollar subsidies for one of the richest teams in professional sports.[90]

In Williamsburg-Greenpoint, reactions were mixed. Some community residents welcomed the plans while others were displeased with the city's efforts to accelerate change in communities already on the rise. "Sometimes it seems like the ghost of Robert Moses donned some hipster sunglasses and started tearing up the neighborhood," one Williamsburg community journalist complained in response to extensive building in the area and displacement of local residents. Local filmmaker Su Friedrich captured the tension in her 2013 movie, *Gut Renovation*. Critics chastised the city for not doing more to retain working space for artists, and for failing to provide as much park space as promised. The latter problem emerged after a judge ruled that the city had to pay owners of land it planned to use for parks the post re-zoning value, which was several times higher than the money set aside to buy the properties based on pre-zoning estimates. The de Blasio administration would eventually make good on the commitment.[91]

South of Williamsburg, the colossal Atlantic Yards development generated great resistance and litigation. Forest City Ratner, a national real estate firm, built the Barclays Center near downtown Brooklyn on top of gritty MTA-owned railroad tracks. The major sports and entertainment arena would serve as home to the New York Nets. The plan included fifteen towers that would add huge high-rise apartments and offices to a low-rise neighborhood. Because the project stood mostly over state controlled land, the city's normal review process did not apply, causing many neighbors directly affected to feel shut out. "Bloomberg and Pataki—our only elected representatives with the power to force a real debate about Atlantic Yards—instead jumped aboard early and fastened their seatbelts," Chris Smith, who lived in the neighborhood, wrote in *New York* magazine. The city contributed $100 million in cash, infrastructure support, and tax abatements to the private project. Dissatisfied residents criticized Bloomberg and Doctoroff harshly for not engaging with neighborhood concerns, but since New York State had authority over most key aspects of the development, including controversial use of its right of eminent domain, it attracted most of the litigation and discontent.[92]

At Hudson Yards, conversations with community representatives and the city planning department were respectful regarding city-owned land, and some modifications occurred in response to neighborhood concerns. Many involved believed resistance to the stadium absorbed so much of the community's energy that little remained for the rest of the project despite its enormity. The irreconcilable conflicts relating to the stadium itself caused a classic battle over urban space. Opponents and promoters rallied their troops in public protests and demonstrations of support. Doctoroff pushed forward, prepared to persuade anyone who would listen and to bulldoze anyone who would not. In addition to berating Robert Yaro after the Regional Plan Association criticized the project publicly, Doctoroff made phone calls to the association's corporate financial sponsors and urged them to withdraw funding. His campaign cost the organization hundreds of thousands of dollars. "He was playing hardball," Yaro remembered. RPA staff joked among themselves that they needed to place any outside experts helping their analysis into a "witness protection program" to prevent Doctoroff from punishing them. Robert Johnson, the Jets owner, played good cop. He met with Yaro during the middle of the stadium controversy to say he would like to make a major donation to his organization. Yaro responded he would be happy to accept the financial support after all the decisions involving the stadium had been settled. Johnson never called back.[93]

Bloomberg stood by Doctoroff and chastised critics for standing in the way of thousands of construction jobs and thousands more office positions that would follow from the project. The mayor suggested opponents did not understand the importance of taking risks to secure the future, an attitude many found arrogant. Bloomberg and his deputy followed a simple calculus. They anticipated the public expense of the Hudson Yards project at $4.5 billion, and the long-term revenue impact for the city in the range of a projected $67 billion. If the plan were even a fraction as successful as they expected, it would be hugely beneficial to the city as a whole and would justify the disruption the citizens directly affected would experience. Far West Siders were being told to take one for the New York City team.[94]

Doctoroff is calmly unapologetic about his efforts. "Getting stuff done is not easy," he says, with matter-of-fact understatement about what it takes to move major projects through New York City's gladiator arena of interest groups. In a similar matter-of-fact tone that lacks the bite of arrogance, he declares his team's record without precedent. By his count, it completed 286 major initiatives with just three aborted, two at the hands of the state legislature—the West Side stadium and congestion pricing. It is too soon for an independent, systematic review of the many projects Doctoroff's team pursued and their impact. Many of the largest ones are still evolving and will be for years. But when time ripens the record, history is sure to credit Doctoroff and the rest of Bloomberg's economic development team with enormous success.[95]

Some urban policy experts criticized what they called the Bloomberg team's "big idea" approach to city planning. They recognized that Bloomberg's projects were nowhere as intrusive as the oft-criticized Robert Moses plans that bulldozed entire neighborhoods in the name of urban renewal. Still, they were often massive in scale and imposed on neighborhoods by government agencies from the top down. In certain instances—near Columbia University in Harlem, Willets Point in Queens, and other locations—the city supported or threatened the use of eminent domain powers to seize properties so developments could move forward. New York City's long-standing Uniform Land Use Review Process, known by its goofy acronym—ULURP—ensured transparent community access to development designs. It gave people ample opportunity to register concerns and objections, but the process provides advisory status only. In the end, a small number of city agencies that answered to the mayor, along with the city council and state officials, exercised decision-making authority. Advocates committed to community control objected to the lack of power sharing. Bloomberg's economic development team was more impressed with the ability of even small groups of well-organized opponents to obstruct development projects through the political process or the courts. To them, the structure in place gave communities real input while affording government the tools it needed to prevent democratic ideals from degenerating into paralysis and stagnation.[96]

Some developers found City Planning Commissioner Burden distressingly heavy-handed. She could hold up zoning variances or amendments as a means of pressuring builders to accommodate her vision of urban esthetics, passing judgment on specific design details that had little to do with land-use policy. Some capitulated pragmatically and hired only architects who shared her sensibilities. Yet, more common was the view that Burden's planning department and Bloomberg's highly professional economic development team worked effectively with local communities. One "good-government type" told a journalist that "except for the West Side," the Bloomberg administration was "completely open to community input." A longtime South Bronx activist praised the team from Bloomberg's Economic Development Corporation for "actually listening to us" when crafting the Hunts Point Vision Plan to integrate the area's industrial park and food distribution center more sensibly into the surrounding community. "It's a total change. I don't think under another administration this would have happened at all," he said. "Wow," Maria Torres, another Hunts Point activist, remembered thinking to herself shortly after Bloomberg's election. "You have a voice, you have the mayor's ear." Steven Spinola, president of the Real Estate Board of New York, agreed that Bloomberg's team took local concerns seriously. Burden shared with him a rezoning proposal for the 125th Street commercial district in Harlem. From the real estate industry's perspective, Spinola thought it was great. "But then it went through the process," he said, and the city modified it based on community comments. He objected to the new plan since it was less favorable to real estate development priorities. As far as Robert Yaro could tell, Burden never turned down a meeting from a civic organization or community group.[97]

By the end of Bloomberg's first term, rezoning decisions, momentum caused by the Olympic bid, and other pro-development policies spurred real estate development projects throughout the city. "We were beginning to see the fruits of success," Doctoroff recalled, "and we were trying to think comprehensively." It had become clear that the growth set in motion would continue for years. Managing it thoughtfully would be critical to fulfill Bloomberg's ambitious vision for a luxury city. That in turn led to development of the most far-reaching blueprint for managing New York City's resources ever prepared, with implications for virtually every city agency, every business, and every resident for decades to come.[98]

Chapter Seven

Healthy Economy, Healthy City

"Noxious uses on really interesting sites," is how Doctoroff described what he and his team kept finding as they thought broadly about city land use toward the end of Bloomberg's first term. A storage facility for salt used to melt winter ice on city streets sat on prime West Side real estate. A tow-pound occupied a parcel with a view of the Hudson River. But there seemed to be no good alternatives that would free the locations for higher-value purposes. Doctoroff decided the city needed a comprehensive review of land-use policies and options. In September 2005, confident that there would be a second term for Bloomberg, he organized a summit of his senior staff at Gracie Mansion to identify priorities.[1]

"What we eventually began to see [were] the interconnections between a whole set of physical attributes of the city in ways we never had before," Doctoroff remembered. "Whether it was parkland, housing, land use more broadly, brownfields, transportation, energy, water, air quality . . . we saw these things as increasingly completely intertwined. We started to unpack them and look at them individually, but we recognized that the connections among them were really where the complexity lay." At the time, Al Gore was promoting his documentary about the environment, *An Inconvenient Truth*. Consequently, "climate change was beginning to play a role in our thinking," Doctoroff recalled.[2]

As analysis progressed, city demographers projected New York's population would reach nine million over the next twenty-five years. That meant New York City would grow by more people in the span of a generation than already lived in San Francisco. It was startling news. Accommodating them all lay at the core of the Bloomberg team's economic development strategy. Doctoroff described it as resting on two pillars: steady growth in people and constant improvement in the quality of life. "Marginal revenues from the incremental people," whether visitors, residents, or workers, "are greater than the marginal costs, on average, because you've got a fixed infrastructure that you spent centuries building," Doctoroff explained in classic economic terms. The difference, "was additional profit," to reinvest in maintaining and improving the quality of life. People would only come, and residents only stay, if the city remained an attractive place. The environment that brought people to the city in the first place had to be preserved for the "virtuous cycle of a successful city" to continue. Without quality of life, Doctoroff knew, "the cycle goes into reverse."[3]

Moreover, the moment in the cycle had arrived when the infrastructure the city had built over centuries needed substantial renovation. Between 1960 and the early 1980s, the city's population declined. Population growth that occurred in the two decades prior to Bloomberg's 2001 election consisted of people coming to a city built to accommodate their numbers. Continued migration into the city meant it would grow beyond the size its infrastructure was designed to support. "It didn't take a huge leap of imagination to under-stand that if the city was already crowded, how much worse it would be if the population grew," Doctoroff reasoned.[4]

Shortly after Bloomberg's reelection, Doctoroff assigned a team to work across city agencies to develop a strategic plan for accommodating the projected population increase. The City Planning Department and many others had already begun working on the topic. By March 2006, the project had become complex enough that it needed a team of its own. Doctoroff's chief of staff, Marc Ricks, had worked at McKinsey & Company before joining city govern-ment. On the way home from a recruiting trip to the Wharton School at the University of Pennsylvania in Philadelphia in 2003, he shared a drink in the bar car with a McKinsey colleague he had not met before, Rohit Aggarwala. Rit—as everyone called him—had attended Columbia University for his undergraduate degree, MBA, and PhD in history, and had spent two years working for the fed-eral department of transportation before joining McKinsey as an infrastructure expert. Ricks telephoned him and asked him to join the city's effort to help it sort out complicated transportation issues.[5]

Aggarwala was reluctant to pursue the conversation, but his former colleague persisted. "Look Rit, for the price of an electronic resume you get an hour to tell the deputy mayor what he ought to do." So Aggarwala attached a curricula vitae to an email and hit "send." Two days later, he got a call from Doctoroff, traveling in Israel at the time. The deputy mayor's responsiveness impressed the potential recruit, and his "historical situating" of the city's infrastructure needs suggested serious thinking about New York's future was under way. In the interview that followed, Aggarwala challenged the premise of the project with a range of penetrating questions that left Doctoroff so impressed he asked him to lead the effort. Aggarwala became the director of what was eventually called the Office of Long-Term Planning and Sustainability. His decision to join was a "truly key step" in the evolu-tion of the effort from a strategic land-use study to a sustainability project, according to Doctoroff.[6]

Environment and Public Health Is Sort of the Same Thing

During Bloomberg's first term, protecting the city and resurrecting its economy after the 9/11 attack, along with education reform and the Olympic bid initiative, dominated the mayor's attention. His administration had little time for environmental concerns as typically defined. But many environmental issues had health implications, and Bloomberg did stake out a claim early on as a strong proponent of sound public health policies. In the early 1990s Al Sommer, the dean of Johns Hopkins School of Public Health, approached Bloomberg for a donation casting his pitch in business terms. Medicine saves lives retail, one at a time, he said. Public health saves them wholesale, millions at a time. The description captured Bloomberg's imagination and by 2001 he had provided so much support that Johns Hopkins named the public health school after him. Bloomberg understood that many public health initiatives sought to reduce disease by improving the environment, including creation of a social atmosphere that encouraged healthy behavior. "You can argue environment and public health is sort of the same thing," Bloomberg concluded.[7]

To head the city's health department, Bloomberg chose Tom Frieden, a public health specialist who had studied at Columbia and Yale, spent time at the Epidemic Intelligence Service of the national Centers for Disease Control, and had worked at the New York City Health Department years before. His staff described him as a micromanaging, workaholic genius with a penchant for numbers. Even before he assumed his new responsibilities, the soon-to-be commissioner had looked at the city's vital statistics and concluded that reducing smoking and improving food health were the most important steps the department he would lead could take to improve New Yorkers' lives. The impact would be far greater than anything else the city might do, including protecting people against bio-terror, the topic on everyone's mind after 9/11.[8]

The enormous increase in the tobacco tax that Bloomberg included in his 2002 budget proposal demonstrated to Frieden that he and the mayor thought alike when it came to smoking. The health commissioner wanted the city to follow the aggressive fiscal action with an even bolder regulatory initiative. He proposed New York City ban smoking in all workplaces, including restaurants and bars, to protect people from second-hand smoke. Ed Skyler, Deputy Mayor Shaw, and other top advisors opposed it. They worried about the economic consequences for tourism and hospitality, and they feared that the 22 percent of New Yorkers who lit up regularly—roughly 1.7 million people—would "despise" a government decision that interfered with their habit. The senior officials forced Frieden through an obstacle course of information gathering and analysis before reluctantly letting him take his case to the mayor.[9]

Bloomberg cut through the objections. The policy would save lives, so he favored it. To Marc Shaw, it was a case of Bloomberg, a former smoker, displaying the "zeal of a convert on the issue." Bloomberg instructed his deputies to get on board, and they did. The city council passed the ban despite howls of protest from restaurant and bar owners, and from personal freedom advocates who called it an unwarranted government intrusion into their lives. As it turned out, patronage in eating and drinking establishments went up, not down. The ban had no negative impact on tourism. Even many smokers acknowledged that offices, restaurants, and bars were more pleasant without the poisonous clouds that had filled them for decades. Eventually the city extended the ban to parks as well. The Smoke-Free Air Act, the cigarette tax that was raised again in 2011, and hard-hitting anti-tobacco advertising campaigns sought to convert smoking from a normal part of the city's environment into socially unwelcome behavior. The proportion of New Yorkers lighting up fell to 14 percent, before ticking back up after the *Mad Men* series made smoking cool again. Some 450,000 people dropped the death-inducing habit by 2013, and the health department estimated that the city's policies saved 50,000 lives over time. The astonishing number—over eighteen times greater than the number killed in the World Trade Tower attack—was unverifiable, but it was based on simple logic and basic math.[10]

The public smoking ban in America's largest metropolis, a place with a worldwide reputation as a town where anything goes, struck a latent national and international nerve. Other cities and countries began implementing similar policies, and second-hand smoke began to disappear in places near and far. Bloomberg embraced the cause wholeheartedly and spent at least $600 million of his own money combating smoking worldwide in the years that followed. He considered New York's smoking ban and the global movement it triggered one of his greatest achievements. He continued the crusade as a private citizen after he left office.[11]

Bloomberg knew that New York's poor, like the poor elsewhere in America, suffered more than others from life-limiting medical conditions. The New York City Health and Hospitals Corporation has long run the largest municipal health-care system in the nation. The eleven acute-care hospitals it operated in 2002, and its eighty-five local clinics were a primary source of medical care for impoverished New Yorkers. It treated huge numbers of Medicaid patients and provided most of the care for the uninsured. The nature of its mission and the politics that surrounded it left its finances constantly strained. The situation was particularly fraught when Bloomberg won election because Mayor Giuliani had tried to privatize the system, and when that failed, he starved it of funds.[12]

Bloomberg's commitment to sound public health policies made HHC a special object of his affections in the early days of his first term. Despite dire budget constraints, he raised city subsidies by hundreds of millions of dollars to help the public hospital system expand preventive care and to implement new programs. Quality standards improved, often exceeding state and national benchmarks, and HHC won national recognition for transparent publication of data few hospitals provided. Bloomberg went so far as to brag that the service levels in the Health and Hospital Corporation's facilities exceeded the quality of care in some of New York's best private institutions, citing Centers for Medicare and Medicaid Services data to support the surprising claim. The Great Recession tempered Bloomberg's generosity toward the city's hospital system, and budget cuts caused some performance measures to deteriorate, but on balance the neediest New Yorkers had better access to health care while Bloomberg governed than before.[13]

Bloomberg's education department instituted school-based health clinics at high schools across the city, and created a program called Connecting Adolescents to Comprehensive Healthcare (CATCH) that ensured access to medical service for youngsters without other options. Preventing teenage pregnancy was an important priority to Bloomberg, so public schools had mandatory reproductive health curricula. High schools and health clinics had condom distribution plans. When the Human Resources Administration ran edgy public service ads meant to discourage unmarried teens from having babies, protests flared. Bloomberg dismissed the objections to the relief of the agency officials responsible for the messages. His press office issued a statement declaring: "It's well past time when anyone can afford to be value-neutral when it comes to teen pregnancy." On Valentine's Day 2007—Bloomberg's 65th birthday—the health department introduced NYC CONDOMS, prophylactics branded with letters that mimicked New York City subway designations. The department promoted their distribution with a provocative ad campaign that urged New Yorkers to "Get Some." Over the following year, the city gave away more than 36 million of them as part of an effort to create a safe-sex environment to reduce AIDS, sexually transmitted diseases, and unwanted pregnancies.[14]

Some of Bloomberg's health initiatives were directed specifically toward poor children. Some 185,000 New Yorkers five and younger—nearly one in three—lived in homes that offered diminished chances for a productive life because of insufficient income in 2005. Half of the city's newborns entered the world poor, at higher risk than others of low birth weight, inadequate prenatal care, and infant mortality. Nearly 70 percent were Latino or African American. In response, the city expanded its investment in the Nurse-Family Partnership, a national program that connected trained medical professionals with impoverished expectant mothers having their first baby. The goal was to help ensure adequate health care for infants for the first two years of life.[15]

A public awareness plan called "Take Care New York" promoted steps people could follow to keep themselves and the environment around them healthy—everything from avoiding tobacco and excessive alcohol consumption, to pest control measures and screening for lead paint on apartment walls. The Health Department also adopted policies to bring healthy food to poor neighborhoods. In many, it was strikingly hard to find fresh produce and vegetables. Experts cited the problem as contributing to any number of diseases, most obviously obesity and ailments that followed from it. A 2007 city Health Department survey revealed more than 30 percent of the residents living in East Harlem were seriously overweight, compared to just 9 percent of New Yorkers living in the wealthier neighboring district of the Upper East Side.[16]

With council speaker Christine Quinn's strong support, the city hired a Food Ombudsman and created a Food Policy Task Force. The city improved the menu for some 217 million meals it served every year at schools, hospitals, jailhouses, and elsewhere. Low-fat milk became standard, deep-fried foods disappeared. The ombudsman's office worked with hundreds of bodegas in the South Bronx, Central Brooklyn, and Harlem to encourage healthy options on their shelves, and the city increased the number of food carts allowed in New York, but only for the sale of green vegetables and fresh produce, not the hot dogs, pretzels, and grilled meats that have long been sidewalk fare. Zoning changes that encouraged construction of new supermarkets in underserved areas, and that allowed larger stores if grocers committed to allocate space to fresh produce, held long-term promise. Bloomberg's health department also tried to convince food companies to reduce the amount of salt in their products with little success. Those who knew how generously the mayor salted his own food— particularly the popcorn he often snacked on in the City Hall bullpen—found the irony amusing.[17]

The Board of Health—all if its members appointed by Bloomberg—initiated a ban on trans fat and also insisted that restaurants publish the number of calories contained in the meals they served. Trans fat was a chemically modified ingredient found in prepared foods throughout the city that contributed to heart disease. The city ordered all but trivial amounts of it phased out of all foods in stages by 2008. Calorie counts were meant to encourage people to moderate their food intake and reduce obesity. With a recommended daily average of 2,000 to 2,500 calories per person, it came as a shock to some that a double hamburger with cheese from a well-known franchise delivered nearly 1,000 calories, and the order of French fries that inevitably went with it another 500. The 325 calories in the thirty-two-ounce container of soda that washed it down became a target of Bloomberg's wrath second only to cigarettes. To nudge New Yorkers away from the unhealthy amount of sugar that millions swallowed daily in big gulps without much thought, the Board of Health issued a regulation forbidding restaurants to serve sugary drinks in quantities larger than sixteen ounces. But courts ruled it beyond municipal authority to tell food purveyors what size portions to offer their customers. Political and legal combat over soft drinks, innocuous beverages in the mind of the average person, generated resentment about the way Bloomberg wielded the city's regulatory power. A clear majority of New Yorkers opposed the policy. His reputation as "Nanny Mike," a man prepared to tell others what is good for them and how to live their lives, grew.[18]

Like any informed American, Bloomberg knew that for decades the tobacco industry had invested heavily in a well-funded campaign of false science designed to confuse people about the link between smoking and cancer, and other serious diseases. A group of businessmen involved with carbon-based energy companies—most notably the Koch brothers—organized a similar campaign to create doubts about global warming and the impact of human behavior on the planet's environment. Climate change policies and other decisions President George W. Bush made during his first term, seemed to elevate science denial to national policy.[19]

Bloomberg's 2005 landslide reelection emboldened him and his team, and Kevin Sheekey began to organize a potential 2008 presidential campaign. Sheekey believed "sustainability was going to be the 'It' concept for a little while," according to an administration insider who knew his thinking, and encouraged Bloomberg to take a stand. The issue resonated. Bloomberg understood and respected the science surrounding climate change better than the average politician, and he objected to efforts to manipulate facts to confuse people. He began to use his bully pulpit, second perhaps only to the president's, to speak out. In May 2006, he delivered the commencement address at Johns Hopkins Medical School. "Today, we are seeing hundreds of years of scientific discovery being challenged by people who simply disregard facts that don't happen to agree with their agenda," he told the audience. "Some call it 'pseudo-science,' others call it 'faith-based science,' but when you notice where the negligence tends to take place, you might as well call it 'political science,'" he said pointedly. "You can see political science at work when it comes to global warming," he continued. "Despite near unanimity in the scientific community, there is now a movement—driven by ideology and short-term economics—to ignore the evidence and discredit the reality of climate change." The lack of commitment to develop a response to the challenge at the national level made it imperative in Bloomberg's mind that New York and other cities take action.

It would fall to the team working with Doctoroff on the city's strategic plan to offer recommendations that were business friendly, but also rooted in environmentally sound science.[20]

A seventeen-person advisory council Doctoroff created to help guide his planning process included environmental experts as well as a broad range of stakeholders to help build support for the initiative across the city. The staff working on the project met with dozens of community organizations to listen to proposals. Along the way, the team sent out more than a million pamphlets in English and Spanish informing residents of the initiative and encouraging them to visit a website to submit ideas. "It was substance and optics," Doctoroff recounted.[21]

In December 2006, Bloomberg spoke about the plan's objectives in general terms at an event in Queens as the first phase of a two-part communications strategy. To reinforce the message, during the week of Bloomberg's speech a special written supplement appeared in every Sunday newspaper challenging the city's people to embrace the initiative. The second phase took place on Earth Day, April 22, 2007, when the mayor invited some seven hundred civic leaders to the Museum of Natural History to hear him present *PlaNYC: A Greener, Greater New York*. It was a comprehensive framework for city development policies to "unleash opportunity," remove "tangible barriers to improving our daily lives," and to protect the environment New Yorkers lived in for the long term. It included ten broad goals and 127 implementation projects. Many of them updated and modified initiatives already launched by Bloomberg and prior mayors. Others were far-reaching new ones, including a pledge to reduce the city's greenhouse gas emissions 30 percent by the year 2030.[22]

PlaNYC—A Greener, Greater New York

Three explicit themes served as organizing principles for *PlaNYC*: the need to accommodate population growth, the importance of infrastructure maintenance, and the compelling reality of climate change. A fourth theme, the need to renew New York's physical plant to compete with other cities "like Chicago and Los Angeles . . . London and Shanghai" is marbled throughout the text. Urban centers around the world "are pushing themselves to become more convenient and enjoyable, without sacrificing excitement or energy. . . . [W]e must not only keep up with the innovations of others, but surpass them," the study declared.[23]

By the time the administration published an update in 2011, the fourth theme had become explicit in a prominent section of the introduction entitled "A Global Economy." It reminded New Yorkers that, "Today's mobility of people and capital has created a fierce competition among cities. We're competing for the best ideas and the most capable and highly-trained workforce. To thrive economically, we must create a setting where talented entrepreneurs—and the businesses they grow—want to be." The plan dealt with the "physical city, and the functionality of its infrastructure in New Yorkers' everyday lives." In concept, it complemented initiatives to control crime, improve education, reduce poverty, and provide adequate public health and social services. All were part of the overriding objective to make the city an attractive place to live on every dimension of municipal life, the document declared.[24]

Much of New York City's infrastructure was "a century old and showing its age," the study acknowledged. The government had often deferred maintenance of vital plant and equipment during the last half of the twentieth century. Bloomberg responded by investing $123 billion in capital improvements. After the department of education's investments in support of the mayor's school reform plan, and spending by the department of environmental protection that managed the city's water supply, transit projects attracted the most capital dollars during Bloomberg's three terms.[25]

Four of New York's five boroughs are on islands and one is a peninsula, posing unique transportation challenges. Some 789 city-owned bridges, plus another 600 run by public authorities or the state, six tunnels and nineteen thousand miles of road link the five boroughs to each other and to the rest of New York, New Jersey, and Connecticut. The Metropolitan Transportation Authority runs the city's bus and subway systems. It is also responsible for the Staten Island Railway and two suburban commuter rail lines, Metro-North and the Long Island Rail Road. PATH and New Jersey Transit run commuter lines that cross the Hudson River. The 1970s financial crisis caused underinvestment across the entire sprawling network, which hit bottom more or less literally in 1973 when a truck plunged through a hole in the West Side Highway. Some bridges became dangerous enough they had to be closed entirely or in part, and mass transit was in comparably abysmal shape. In 1981, the MTA ceased all work on expansions to dedicate resources to restoring safety and basic service.[26]

Things had improved dramatically by the time Bloomberg became mayor, but the city still failed to provide anything like acceptable transportation infrastructure. Commuters in Queens, Staten Island, the Bronx, and Brooklyn suffered the four worst commutes in the nation, and the greater region was home to thirteen of the twenty-five longest travel times to work in America. The Partnership for New York City estimated that traffic congestion caused $13 billion in lost productivity annually, which cost jobs, slowed emergency response vehicles, and added to health-damaging pollution. Roadway travel, already strained, was growing faster than the population. "Left unchecked, excess congestion and its consequences will stunt the region's capacity for sustained growth and innovation in the years ahead," the Partnership warned. New York was already the most mass transit–oriented big city in America. The Lexington Avenue subway line alone carried more passengers than the nation's second largest system, the Metro in Washington, DC. But public transit use in New York trailed Tokyo and Singapore, Hong Kong and Shanghai, London and Paris by wide measures. Those cities had recognized mass transit led to "a cleaner, healthier and more efficient urban environment," *PlaNYC* reported, and "New York City must keep pace."[27]

Two of *PlaNYC*'s ten goals focused on transportation. "Improve travel times by adding transit capacity for millions more residents, visitors and workers," and "reach a full 'state of good repair' on New York City's roads, subways and rails for the first time in history." It envisioned a broad range of initiatives for trains, roads, ferries and especially buses, including implementation of Bus Rapid Transit, a system where riders pay their fares at sidewalk kiosks and buses travel on dedicated lanes to speed trips. The transportation program was ambitious and creative, and with rare exceptions its proposals would cost enormous amounts of money. Without a well-developed financial structure, the plan risked suffering the same fits and starts that had plagued MTA and city transportation efforts for decades. Optimistic beginnings and high hopes were often followed by disheartening delays and disappointing outcomes because of revenue shortfalls. When the MTA broke ground on the Second Avenue Subway in 2007, it was the third time in thirty years that construction on that project began. Engineers estimated the city needed $15 billion of work just to bring its existing public transportation and roadway system to a normal state of repair. Desired improvements would cost $35 billion more. "The greatest factor in determining the success of our city in the 21st century," *PlaNYC* warned in 2007, "may be whether we can summon the collective will to generate the funds necessary to meet the transportation demands of the future." It asserted that New York City "is prepared to make an extraordinary commitment to ensure that we do."[28]

Legislative Congestion

Bloomberg proposed the creation of a regional financing authority to fund transportation projects. Capital would be allocated to the existing transportation agencies to allow them to manage construction and maintenance at the scale required. Bloomberg was prepared to channel an "unprecedented" amount of money from city sources into the agency, and called on New York State to do the same. He also proposed to raise an additional $380 million in the first year, and $900 million annually by 2030, with an innovative congestion pricing plan. Stockholm, Singapore, and above all, London had shown that congestion pricing could work. *PlaNYC* listed three favorable outcomes in those cities: less congestion and faster travel times; less pollution; and revenue to fund transportation network upgrades. Bloomberg proposed a three-year trial period to learn if congestion pricing's "tremendous" potential benefits could be captured in New York City. Federal transportation initiatives promised $354 million to fund the pilot program.[29]

Congestion pricing had been a topic of animated conversation inside the administration. Aggarwala challenged Doctoroff on the subject during his initial conversation with him. Was the administration prepared to consider "politically challenging moves like congestion pricing that they have in London? Would something like that be on the table?" he asked, with obvious skepticism. Doctoroff threw his hands up at the question, frustrated by the intensity of Aggarwala's doubts. "On the table? We're already running the numbers," he answered. More than anything else, that response convinced Aggarwala of *PlaNYC's* seriousness. Doctoroff and team believed the policy was a crucial element of an overall transportation and air quality strategy. Others were less convinced, including Bloomberg at first.[30]

Shortly after Bloomberg's 2005 reelection, New York City Partnership President Kathryn Wylde told a journalist she expected congestion pricing to be on the mayor's second term agenda. Bloomberg immediately clarified that it was not, "and Kathy got her hand slapped," one civic leader recalled. Bloomberg remembered that his 2002 proposal to toll East River bridges, when the city had a dire need for revenue, went nowhere. He knew the approval road congestion pricing would have to travel was littered with proposal-wrecking potholes. It required support from the city council, the governor, the state senate and the assembly, all in the context of a change to long-established public behavior. Bloomberg and Doctoroff discussed the political reality of the plan at great length. They knew it was fraught. "Don't break the Bloomberg administration," someone said to Aggarwala shortly before the plan was unveiled, fearing congestion pricing would place the mayor in the midst of an unmanageable political maelstrom and derail other initiatives.[31]

Bloomberg understood the stakes. He reviewed the details and challenged the analysis that supported it. In the end, he became convinced congestion pricing was the best way to achieve important objectives, so he approved it. When he did, he told his staff that he was not at all sure it would pass. But pursuing it was the right thing to do, he said, because even if it failed, giving it "our best shot," would lay the groundwork for a future effort by another team. He called congestion pricing "the elephant in the room" when he announced *PlaNYC*, and he confessed he had been doubtful himself. "But I looked at the facts," and concluded "asking New Yorkers," to pay a fee to drive in central Manhattan was the right thing to do.[32]

The mayor's initial plan imposed an $8 fee on all cars entering Manhattan below 86th Street between 6:00 a.m. and 6:00 p.m. For a commuter driving into the impact zone every working day, that amounted to roughly $2,000 a year. Trucks would be charged $21 or only $7 for low-emission models. Driving only within the zone would cost $4 for cars and $5.50 for trucks. As a matter of history, East River crossings charged no tolls. The bridges and tunnels connecting Manhattan to surrounding territory from other directions did. The mayor's plan proposed to deduct from the congestion fee the amount paid for tolls on the way to and from the impact zone. For New Jersey drivers, that meant no additional charge since a round trip across the bridges or tunnels connecting them to Manhattan already cost $8. Drivers from Westchester and the West Bronx entering from the north paid lower tolls and would receive partial rebates. The full weight of the congestion fee would be felt overwhelmingly by drivers from eastern Queens, southern Brooklyn, and parts of the Bronx. Most commuters from those neighborhoods trekked to their jobs daily on public transportation despite a journey that could take an hour or more in each direction. But those who traveled by car valued the convenience, and they had organized their jobs and their daily lives around the status quo.[33]

As a matter of pure logic, tolling East River bridges corrected a long-standing anomaly that forced drivers entering the city from some directions to pay more than those coming from others. As a matter of emotion, to those affected it felt unfair, a violation of tradition. "The concept was alien to the city," was how Steven Spinola, president of the Real Estate Board of New York and sensitive to the attitudes of city homeowners living outside Manhattan, described it. The classic example offered in opposition was of an elderly Queens resident, on a fixed income, forced to pay a high toll to travel to a Manhattan research hospital for specialized, life-saving care.[34]

Public opinion on the topic was complex. One Quinnipiac University poll reported 90 percent of New Yorkers opposed the fee when asked about it without context. Yet, by a margin of 67 percent to 27 percent, they supported it if they could be confident the funds collected would actually be invested in transit projects as promised. Class consciousness affected many people's views. Manhattan's wealthier neighborhoods would receive the most direct benefits. Their residents would breathe cleaner air and suffer less traffic congestion while bearing little of the cost. However high-minded the idea might seem to some, others thought it catered to the needs of New York's most privileged residents at the expense of a relatively small group of men and women trying to make a living and to feed a family. Fee exemptions for yellow taxis and cars-for-hire used mostly in Manhattan, and for cars circumnavigating the impact zone on its littoral highways, added to the sense that the plan levied its charges unevenly.

Tangible arguments in favor of better mass transportation for commuters in assembly districts across the city got lost in the enthusiasm for environmental benefits described in the accents of Manhattan's elite.[35]

Assembly Speaker Silver shared the concern about fairness. At one point Citibank Vice Chairman Robert Rubin, a former Treasury Secretary and former Goldman Sachs CEO, called Silver to encourage him to support the measure. Silver asked Rubin if he was in "one of those limo-type cars . . . that doesn't pay to be congesting," under the mayor's plan. He was. For the benefit of a journalist, Silver wondered aloud how much the proposal was motivated by the desire of Manhattan's moneyed class—people like Bloomberg and Rubin who could afford an $8 toll more easily than working-class commuters—to "get the riff-raff off the streets." The exemptions caused some opponents to argue the plan would not achieve its clean air and congestion reduction goals. Many also feared the money generated would make its way into general revenue coffers to be used for ever-expanding city operations. There were technical matters too. The city's transit system was already so near capacity that it could not easily accommodate more riders if significant numbers of drivers stopped commuting by car. And engineers raised doubts about the wireless technology required to make the plan practical.[36]

Despite arguments against the proposal, it developed strong momentum. Groups favoring improved mass transit and sound environmental policies, including many that received contributions from Bloomberg philanthropies, applauded it. It captured the imagination of community organizations and citywide agencies whose mission involved promoting commerce. Labor unions realized it would provide crucial funding for construction jobs. Some 135 civic groups came to support it as it wound its way through legislative processes. The editorial boards of the *New York Times,* the *Daily News,* the *New York Post,* and *New York Newsday* endorsed it. "A coalition of liberals and conservatives; environmentalists and business leaders; developers and preservationists: People who in the past could not agree on the time of day agreed that it was time to give congestion pricing a try," was how Bloomberg described the reaction.[37]

The 2007 state legislative session was far along by the time Bloomberg announced the plan. He flew to Albany with a private jet full of civic leaders to lobby the governor and other elected officials. Observers took note of the symbolically incongruous way the group promoting a plan to reduce carbon emissions traveled. Yet, the people Bloomberg brought with him had an impact on Governor Spitzer, elected just a few months before. "Mike," he said toward the end of a meeting, "all the people who endorsed me are on your side of the table." He pledged his backing. Other important stakeholders did not. Kevin Sheekey, by then deputy mayor for intergovernmental affairs, had expected to return home with the mayor at the end of a day of lobbying, but he stayed longer seeking additional support. "Buying underwear at Target in Albany at 9 o'clock at night," was about as "depressing as you can get" he would say of the experience.[38]

Regional transportation networks—the MTA, the Tri-borough Bridge and Tunnel Authority, and the Port Authority—opposed the idea. For better or worse, the current system allowed them to manage their own finances. The proposal would have created shared control with greater city influence over decisions, which they did not favor. Despite his reservations, Assembly Speaker Silver worked with his caucus searching for a formula that might gain support for the plan in a politically palatable way. In the Republican-controlled senate, Joe Bruno wanted to support the mayor's proposal, but he feared forcing party members representing Queens and Brooklyn to vote for it could cost them their seats. That in turn could allow Democrats to win control of the senate. Bruno tried to convince some Democrats to defect, but failed by the time the legislative calendar ran out in June 2007. Another chance to secure a vote emerged during a special session in the summer, and Bloomberg returned to Albany. But senate Democrats continued to oppose the change as a block, so Bruno never called for a vote. Bloomberg's aggressive lobbying style won him few friends. "His posture was not ingratiating," one Democratic senator from Brooklyn said of the mayor's efforts to persuade him. "He says he doesn't know politics, and he certainly bore that out by the way he behaved," the un-enamored politician told a reporter.[39]

The federal program that offered hundreds of millions of dollars of financing to pilot the project was set to expire if the state did not act. Assembly Speaker Silver helpfully organized a commission of city and state representatives headed up by former Deputy Mayor Marc Shaw, who had taken a private sector job by then, to review the plan for reconsideration in 2008. The tactic kept the proposal alive and created a reason for the federal government to extend its offer for another year. The commission developed a set of amendments that in the opinion of the *New York Times* editorial board, "markedly improved it." After intense lobbying from the mayor's office, the city council voted in favor of the revised plan by a margin of thirty to twenty. Despite the victory, the vote signaled danger. New York City's local legislature decides most issues by near unanimity, with the speaker enforcing outcomes when the issue itself does not generate consensus. Protest votes from a half dozen or fewer members unhappy with a particular policy or intent on making a statement are typical. Twenty dissenters are not.[40]

Resistance in Albany remained great. Bloomberg reportedly secured an agreement from Majority Leader Bruno to force a vote in favor of the revised proposal during the 2008 session. Some doubted Bruno could make good on the deal. Bloomberg contributed $500,000 to the Republican Senate Campaign Finance Committee that year, politically motivated generosity that alienated Democrats whose votes he needed, and his personal lobbying efforts appeared to make things worse. Political advisors concluded his involvement had become counterproductive. Consequently, he stayed clear of Albany during the 2008 session and instead made carefully targeted phone calls. "He just doesn't understand it when people say no to him," was one legislator's assessment of the situation.[41]

Speaker Silver endorsed the congestion-pricing proposal publicly, a position consistent with popular sentiment in his Manhattan district. But when he convened a series of meetings with the Democratic caucus to try to win support for the program, strong resistance from a critical mass of assembly members representing Queens, Brooklyn, and the Bronx persisted. In the end, Silver decided not to exercise his power to call a vote. He announced he would leave it to the assembly's Democratic majority to determine if it wanted to consider the issue. It was a passive-aggressive tactic that killed the proposal. With no vote in the assembly, Bruno had no reason to call one in the senate and was off the hook.[42]

A furious Bloomberg felt "he had been double-dealt," according to one deputy aware of the negotiations. When Silver announced his support for congestion pricing, Bloomberg thought he had secured a deal. "It takes a special kind of cowardice" to refuse to even call a vote on an issue that had been "debated, and amended significantly to resolve many outstanding issues," over the course of a year, he said after the speaker's decision. A *New York Times* editorial wrote of Silver: "Rarely does one man have a chance to do so much harm to so many." Bloomberg pledged to "push forward on the other 126 proposals" in *PlaNYC*, and traveled to Washington DC, the next day with Kevin Sheekey and Rit Aggarwala to announce federal support for other initiatives to emphasize the point. Aggarwala remembered the conversation on the way to Washington. The mayor and his team were incensed with Silver. "It was personal," he said.[43]

A strong governor might have forced the issue, but Eliot Spitzer resigned early in 2008 toward the start of that year's legislative session. His lieutenant, David Paterson, became the state's chief executive with no mandate and limited authority. After Bloomberg made a passionate appeal for support in a City Hall meeting, the new governor supported the congestion plan publicly, but accounts about the depth of his commitment vary. "The governor wasn't in a position to make it happen," according to Kathryn Wylde, negotiating in favor of congestion pricing on behalf of the New York City Partnership. Robert Yaro, working on the issue for the Regional Plan Association, was more emphatic. "The governor's office was supine," was his recollection.[44]

Collapse of the congestion pricing proposal in June 2008, and the bigger regional financing plan of which it was a part, left the MTA with a huge financial hole—an estimated $1.2 billion for the next fiscal year. In the fall of 2008 Governor Paterson asked Richard Ravitch to lead a commission to consider options. "The MTA was in deep shit. You didn't have to be a genius to figure out what needed to be done. You needed a revenue stream," Ravitch would tell an interviewer. He talked with business people, labor leaders, and politicians, and determined a payroll tax was the least objectionable option. He proposed a 0.34 percent levy on employers in counties the MTA served, moderate fare rises, and tolls on East River bridges south of 60th Street, a provision that would accomplish some of congestion pricing's goals. Ravitch had favored East River tolls for years. The proposal spread the pain of paying for mass transit among the riders who used the MTA, drivers whose roads would be unbearably crowded without it, and businesses that benefited from it.[45]

By the time Ravitch convened meetings, the global financial crisis had changed fiscal calculations everywhere. The MTA found itself forced to hike fares 20 percent to 30 percent and to initiate severe cutbacks, including shutting two subway lines and eliminating thirty-five bus routes. Without new sources of financing from somewhere, the large number of commuters relying on the system would experience even higher charges and worse service. With the stakes raised, Assembly Speaker Silver announced he would support East River bridge tolls of $2 in each direction, the same as the cash cost of a single ride on the subway at the time.[46]

Meanwhile, the state senate had descended into chaos. During the 2008 election Republicans lost their majority, but a shifting cast of New York City Democrats—Carl Kruger from Brooklyn, Hiram Montserrate from Queens, Pedro Espada and Ruben Diaz Sr. from the Bronx—refused to support their party's leadership without self-aggrandizing favors. Wheeling and dealing by the unscrupulous rebels allowed Republicans to claim control some days and Democrats others. "Government by circus," observers called it. A deal secured a bare majority for the Democrats, but a lack of party discipline prevailed and the situation remained unstable. Republicans protested that the Ravitch plan did not provide enough money for transportation needs upstate and voted against it as a block, which in alliance with a few Democratic defectors defeated the plan. One Albany staff professional actively involved in the negotiations contends the outcome was even uglier than it appeared. The vote was defeated because of "corrupt Democrats in the state senate," he told an interviewer. "If [the governor's office] had been willing to pay bribes, we could have got it done. We weren't, and so it failed." In later budget negotiations, the payroll tax Ravitch proposed was approved, along with a $1 surcharge for taxi fares and additional licensing fees to help meet MTA obligations. New York City's East River bridges remain free. In the years that followed, Carl Kruger, Hiram Montserrate, and Pedro Espada would be indicted, tried, and convicted of various felonies unrelated to the MTA budget negotiations. "I had three state senators who opposed my tolling proposal," Ravitch remembered. "I am pleased to tell you all three are now in the hoosegow."[47]

"The instability of financial support for New York City's transit system jeopardizes our economy and quality of life," the Bloomberg administration wrote in its 2011 *PlaNYC* progress report. Many transit initiatives would go forward, and the mayor's office of operations identified some thirty programs it urged the MTA to pursue to improve service. But the transit authority remained plagued by insufficient funds. New Yorkers continue to search for the regional and state leadership required to fund a transportation system worthy of a great city. After losing its bold transportation financing plan, the Bloomberg administration kept its contribution to the state controlled MTA to a minimum. The mayor lacked confidence the money would be put to good use and feared increases in city funding would provide excuses for other contributors to reduce their allocations. "I could never get the mayor to focus on the MTA because he could not control it," Robert Yaro of the Regional Plan Association lamented. "He had limited political capital and he wanted to spend it on things he controlled."[48]

PlaNYC 2007 made no mention of New York's airports even though they were as inadequate as the rest of the city's transportation network. JFK and LaGuardia sat on city-owned land, but the Port Authority operated both. It also ran Liberty International Airport which served the region from Newark, New Jersey. The three regional airfields were among the most delay-prone in the country. More than a third of flights took off or landed late due to congestion, and remarkably the cascade effect on connections made the New York area responsible for more than three-quarters of all flight delays nationally. A 2009 study sponsored by the Partnership for New York City estimated the annual cost of the problem in the billions. The personal aggravation experienced by travelers was beyond tally. In 2007, the Port Authority took control of Stewart International Airport, more than sixty miles north of Manhattan, with the intention of developing it into a fourth regional facility, but the financial crisis delayed progress.[49]

The intensified global focus of the 2011 *PlaNYC* update caused the city to acknowledge vital dependence on national and international connections "owned by other government or private entities." The Port Authority struggled to fulfill its many obligations even before the 9/11 attack destroyed the World Trade Center. Afterward, it became harder still. Near the end of Bloomberg's third term, the Port Authority planned runway extensions and other improvements at JFK, and adopted a program to build a new main terminal at LaGuardia to accommodate larger planes. In 2015, at Governor Andrew Cuomo's insistence, the Port Authority developed a far more comprehensive plan for LaGuardia. Along the way, the Economic Development Corporation collaborated with the Port Authority on a project to craft a plan for enhancing air freight traffic through JFK. "We should not be satisfied until the day when someone stepping off an airplane . . . in New York City feels like he or she has arrived at an airport . . . suitable for a world-class city," its report declared. That day remains far off.[50]

Interstate rail facilities in New York City were also in a state of disrepair. In 2010, New Jersey Governor Chris Christie canceled a joint New York–New Jersey federal construction program for a new rail tunnel under the Hudson River. Federal transportation secretary Raymond LaHood described Christie's decision as "a devastating blow to thousands of workers, millions of commuters and the state's economic future." In 2011, the Bloomberg team sought support for a plan to extend the number 7 subway line across the Hudson River to Secaucus, New Jersey, as an alternative, but the idea never gained traction. As predicted, train service for passengers living in or passing through New Jersey on their way to Manhattan deteriorated. Delays on New Jersey Transit trains in the summer of 2015 put the issue back into headlines. Governors Cuomo and Christie agreed to split half the cost of a new rail tunnel, looking to the federal government for the rest. Debate and delays for commuters continue.[51]

A Breath of Fresh Air

Just a few weeks after Bloomberg released *PlaNYC* in 2007, he announced Janette Sadik-Khan would become transportation commissioner. Michael Crowley would describe the new city official in a *New York* magazine profile as "equal parts Jane Jacobs and Robert Moses." For years, the transportation department had defined its role as promoting efficient and safe motor vehicle traffic while ensuring compliance with government regulations. Sadik-Khan embraced those goals, but had a broader conception of the mission. She believed streets were not just thoroughfares, but an important part of urban life that attracted people to New York City—"assets hidden in plain sight," she called them. Roads and streetsides belonged to spectators, walkers, and bikers, as much as cars, trucks, and buses. They were mutable objects, cast in concrete literally but not figuratively. They could be modified to "serve as public places in and of themselves" where people could mingle and talk, or just sit and enjoy life, much as they might in a park.[52]

Sadik-Khan had her team study thousands of New York City car crashes to learn who was getting hurt, where and why. That led to lifesaving modifications at more than a hundred dangerous intersections around the city. She also had her staff identify poorly utilized patches of street that could be put to better use. The transportation department launched experiments at several that attracted high volumes of pedestrian traffic. It closed them to cars with construction barrels and painted the road green to create the notion of a park. People gravitated to the reclaimed spaces, and sales at nearby retail businesses spiked. Residents and shop owners were pleased. Once the department deemed a location a success, it dressed the spot up with a few benches and concrete planters, or permanent bollards instead of construction barrels. In wealthy areas, Business Improvement Districts provided funds for the work and upkeep. In less affluent neighborhoods, the transportation department provided the money, often raised from private sources. Suddenly, untamable New York had pedestrian plazas just like many better-behaved European and American cities. Eventually, there would be sixty across the five boroughs. Regional Plan Association President Robert Yaro marveled at the decisions. "It was the first time in a hundred years that we actually took paved surfaces away from the automobile and gave them back to pedestrians," he said.[53]

Encouraged by early successes, Sadik-Khan decided to take on Times Square. Traffic fatalities took place in New York City at just one-quarter the rate of the national average, and they were declining, but the streets around Times Square were 140 percent more dangerous for pedestrians than a typical midtown block. Vehicles moved across its perpetually crowded intersection at just four miles per hour. Sadik-Khan's department conducted extensive computer modeling of the traffic patterns around the three-way intersection where Broadway crosses Seventh Avenue at 45th Street. Analysts concluded shutting Broadway north-south to motor vehicles would make the area safer for pedestrians. They also made a counterintuitive claim—the action would simultaneously improve cross-town traffic flow. A profanely skeptical Mayor Bloomberg agreed to allow a pilot program to close Broadway between 47th and 42nd Streets, provided results of the test could be accurately measured. The cross streets themselves remained open. A similar experiment took place at the same time near Macy's at Herald Square between 35th Street and 33rd Street, also on Broadway. It was another place of perpetual crowds, lured to the area by shopping and other attractions.[54]

"Green Light for Midtown" was how Sadik-Khan referred to the audacious experiment to convert "the cross-roads of the world" at Times Square into a pedestrian plaza. "It was like a *Star Trek* episode," Sadik-Khan would later say of the initial event, Memorial Day weekend 2009. People appeared in the vehicle-denuded street so spontaneously it was as if they had been beamed down from a spaceship. To provide amenities that could be easily removed if the plan proved disastrous, the department bought a few hundred lawn chairs and placed them in the newly reclaimed public space. The town went abuzz. "Lawn chairs on Times Square was all anyone could talk about," Sadik-Khan remembered. Many found the unorthodox approach creative and fun. Others thought it dopey and disruptive. In the months that followed, local retail sales soared, pedestrian accidents fell by 40 percent, and traffic flow improved modestly. There were complaints. Shops a few blocks outside the newly reconfigured space lost business, and more than a few taxi drivers grumbled. To the politically attuned, the most surprising thing was that Bloomberg allowed it in May of an election year when he was on the ballot. Surely it could have blown up, and it seems the mayor feared it would. Yet, he swatted down concerns and let the experiment proceed without politically motivated delay.[55]

By the end of the Bloomberg administration, permanent pavers and amenities were put into place. Tourists love the plaza. Some New Yorkers working in the area, and taxi drivers in particular, still complain about it. Performers clad in Disney character costumes took to posing there for photos with tourists in return for tips, sometimes with unseemly aggressiveness. In 2015, topless women with breasts painted patriotic colors began to do the same. The de Blasio administration found itself navigating free speech rules while seeking to retain a semblance of order at the world famous tourist destination. The city council restricted the aggressive commercial activity to specific zones and the NYPD enhanced the police detail there in an effort to restore control.[56]

Even more controversial was Sadik-Khan's aggressive pursuit of the city's bike master plan, an initiative launched years before that called for 1,800 miles of lanes for cyclists. Many thought of the project as offering welcome support for a healthy form of recreation. "Summer Streets," was an event that fit the image. The city closed major roads to traffic so thousands of bikers could peddle from the Brooklyn Bridge up to East 72nd Street on sleepy, August Saturdays, while an army of happy pedestrians marched alongside. But Sadik-Khan had something more in mind. She knew that places where bicycles were integrated into the transit network benefited from less congestion and less pollution, and that commuters exercised and saved money at the same time. She set out to convert cycling from a hobby and a means of transportation for a cult of true believers into a mainstream option. For that to happen, a fully developed, safe network that connected existing lanes to bridges and major corridors was essential. By the time Bloomberg left office, the transportation department had added four hundred miles of bike paths strategically chosen to strengthen key links. It brought the network total up to one thousand miles. The Citi Bike program that placed bicycles at various places around the city, and allowed users to rent them at one location and return them to another, added another dimension to the plan.[57]

Despite the benefits, some thought the bike lanes a mistaken priority. They claimed it denied the people who relied on cars to get to work access to hundreds of miles of streets to accommodate an environmentally conscious, exercise-obsessed elite. Tabloids ran controversy stoking headlines describing the "bikelash" Bloomberg's transportation commissioner inspired. "When I become mayor," brash politician Anthony Weiner said to Bloomberg one day, "you know what I'm going to spend my first year doing? I'm going to have a bunch of ribbon cuttings tearing out your fucking bike lanes." The opposition became intense. Sadik-Khan knew "culture eats policy for lunch," and she feared the cultural changes she was promoting provoked criticism so intense, it risked damaging the administration she was supposed to be helping. She headed for a meeting with the mayor at the height of the tension believing tendering her resignation might be the right thing to do. When she began to express her concern, Bloomberg cut her off. "Don't worry. Just keep going," he told her. She was among the many Bloomberg officials who described her boss as "having her back" when it mattered.[58]

Weiner was never elected mayor. The bike lanes are still there. The number of pedestrians and car passengers killed fell by nearly one-third between 2001 and 2013, and miles peddled by New Yorkers quadrupled with no rise in biker fatalities. A few months before the end of Bloomberg's third term, a *New York Times* survey revealed twice as many New Yorkers approved of the administration's bike lanes as rejected them. They liked the Citi Bike program by an even greater margin. The twin goals of making it easier and safer to move around the city appealed to people. The distinctive way Bloomberg's team thought about streets became something of a "clarion call" for other cities around the country. "Bike lanes became the new bling," for urban planners, Sadik-Khan declared.[59]

Bike lanes were part of a broader initiative to reduce pollution. New York's air quality had improved since passage of the Federal Clean Air Act in 1970, yet it still did not conform entirely to United States Environmental Protection Agency standards. On this fundamental dimension of city life, with profound long-term health implications, New York lagged seven of eight large American cities. The *PlaNYC* team had some 140 air quality meters installed around the city, which allowed the health department to estimate that pollution contributed to three thousand deaths per year in New York. It caused two thousand hospitalizations for lung and heart conditions, and sent six thousand patients to emergency rooms with asthma attacks. Bloomberg's plan set out to achieve "the cleanest air quality of any big city in America" by 2030 as one of its ten goals.[60]

Cars, trucks, and other traffic traveling some forty-eight million miles every day generated roughly half of the city's pollution, making transportation programs critical to achieve clean air. Analysts paid particular attention to taxis and car services since they motored around Manhattan almost continuously. *PlaNYC* team members wanted the city to require taxis to switch to fuel efficient hybrids. They drove so much that improved mileage would pay for the change in a reasonably short time, so the policy was economically and environmentally sensible. Bloomberg resisted at first. If the change would pay for itself, then rational owners should do it without regulation, he argued. He preferred market solutions to government action, unless someone could demonstrate the market had failed. Aggarwala explained to Bloomberg the economic misalignment that caused the inertia. Taxi drivers paid for the gasoline they used on their shifts, but most vehicles were part of fleets owned by businessmen, or at least rented out by the driver-owner when not on the road. So most of the savings would not go to the people making the incremental investment. The explanation led Bloomberg to approve the recommendation. Court cases followed, challenging the city's authority to trump federal emissions standards, but incentives and persuasion had an impact. By 2015, 60 percent of the yellow taxis were hybrids. The city also adopted clean fuel standards for ten thousand "black car" limousines and twenty-five thousand for-hire vehicles, along with six thousand Boro Taxis. Programs to replace and retrofit diesel trucks with cleaner fuel, and hybrid models for the city's own fleet of twenty-six thousand vehicles were also part of the plan.[61]

Buildings accounted for roughly one-third of particle pollution. Relying on the city's expanded network of air quality meters, the health department presented Bloomberg with maps showing pollution levels in different neighborhoods. It turned out that boilers burning dirty oil in just ten thousand structures, 1 percent of the total number in the city, accounted for over 80 percent of the problem. The city forced landlords to upgrade their systems and to decommission the poisonous ones as rapidly as practical. The move to eliminate dirty fuel from the city's atmosphere supported another *PlaNYC* goal: to "provide cleaner, more reliable power for every New Yorker by upgrading our energy infrastructure." Three main ideas drove the strategy: reduce consumption, expand the clean energy supply, and modernize delivery infrastructure. Exceptionally close collaboration between City Council Speaker Quinn and Bloomberg's team led to passage of four laws in December 2009 known collectively as *Greener, Greater Buildings* to improve energy efficiency. The team working on the legislative initiative recognized that at least 85 percent of the city's carbon emissions in 2030 would be generated by structures that already existed. A serious program had to apply to the 5.2 billion square feet of space in nearly one million buildings already in place, not just new construction.[62]

Despite some compromises struck along the way, the Real Estate Board of New York took exception to new burdens the legislation placed on building owners at a time when the financial crisis had caused cash flow to fall and financing to disappear. Steven Spinola fired off a letter of complaint. Bob Lieber was deputy mayor for economic development at the time. He gathered the facts, and along with Rit Aggarwala met with the mayor to review the issues. Bloomberg listened and then asked: "Are these the things we said we would do in *PlaNYC?*" They were. "Are they all still necessary?" They were. "Fine," he said and got up to leave. Lieber was unsure what that meant. "Do we do them?" he asked. "Yes," Bloomberg replied. "All of them?" Lieber asked, to be sure. "Yes!" Bloomberg responded again as he walked away, a little short-tempered at being asked to repeat himself. In Aggarwala's recounting, Bloomberg believed if his administration did not implement long-term policy decisions despite opposition, no one else would. As serious as the financial crisis was, Bloomberg viewed it as part of a business cycle. He knew that in the long run the real estate industry would be fine and the city better off as a result of the changes.[63]

A blackout in western Queens in July 2006 left thousands without electricity for nine days, highlighting the age and weakness of the city's power grid. It was one of the oldest in the nation, a key reason electricity in New York City cost more than almost anywhere else in America. Residents and businesses spent over $13 billion annually for it. The city accelerated planned improvements in public grid infrastructure and supported Con Edison's efforts to do the same. By 2011, two of the city's most important plants had been repowered to operate more efficiently and cleanly. Smarter peak load management reduced reliance on older, dirtier, and more costly sources called into service when demand spiked. The city also took steps to increase the supply of natural gas in the short term and adopted measures to promote solar, wind, and tidal power as future sources.[64]

Beyond the city's own actions, in July 2008 Bloomberg and Speaker Quinn asked the local chapter of the US Green Building Council to convene a task force to make additional recommendations. It issued a report in February 2010 with 111 recommendations based on Leadership in Energy and Environmental Design—LEED—standards. By the time Bloomberg left office, forty-six had been implemented and eighteen more were under active consideration. New York's air quality ranked fourth among large American cities in 2013, up from seventh. The city estimated 780 fewer people died and 2,000 fewer residents rushed to emergency rooms for respiratory and cardiovascular illnesses in 2013 than before efforts to clean the air began.[65]

City of Perpetual Housing Shortage

PlaNYC incorporated a goal set a few months earlier of creating "homes for almost a million more New Yorkers, while making housing more affordable and sustainable." It contemplated important interconnections with the city's energy and transportation strategies. People living in apartments with easy access to mass transit would drive less, which would reduce fuel consumption, lower congestion, and improve air quality. Residents would benefit from shorter commutes. That meant new housing should be built near public transportation, which in turn meant reversing recent trends when "many of our greatest areas of growth have been underserved by transit; many of our most connected urban centers have either lost population or experienced only modest growth."[66]

When New York City spiraled down during the mid-1970s fiscal crisis, many landlords simply walked away from properties that became uneconomic. The city finance department seized them for lack of tax payment and ultimately the housing department became the unwitting landlord of last resort for one hundred thousand *in rem* buildings, in more or less decrepit condition. Mayor Koch undertook to restore, or knockdown and replace, those buildings, and convert them to private ownership. For most of the next two decades, the scope and location of government-sponsored apartments under Koch and his successors was determined by city ownership of the distressed buildings. The program was a resounding success that spanned the administrations of four mayors.[67]

In 2005, in the midst of a booming economy, the city issued the last request-for-proposal for redevelopment of an *in rem* property. The next year the number of permits issued for housing construction hit a thirty-two-year high, but developers seeking maximum profits in a rapidly tightening market with rising land costs focused on expensive, high-margin units. "Not long ago, our greatest housing challenge was abandonment. But as our city's resurgence continues to attract record numbers of residents, the most pressing issue we face today is affordability," *PlaNYC* declared. In 2005, over half of New Yorkers paid more than 30 percent of their income toward housing, one of the highest rent burdens in the nation. A public poll discovered that nearly two-thirds of people who moved out of the city cited housing costs as a major factor. Housing availability and affordability would top the list of concerns cataloged in the city's 2008 satisfaction survey.[68]

In December 2002, Bloomberg launched the New Marketplace Housing Program. The initiative promised to create or preserve sixty-five thousand units of affordable housing to provide homes for two hundred thousand people. The case for producing more affordable housing was compelling. A city—even a luxury city—requires a solid population of workers across a range of skill levels, and therefore across a range of incomes. Housing costs that pushed New York's working class ever farther outside its boundaries in a region with long and unreliable commutes created an unviable trajectory. And the program fed the desperate need for employment in the aftermath of 9/11. Bloomberg expanded the program modestly to sixty-eight thousand units in 2005, in what one analyst described as an election year bidding war between the mayor and his Democratic opponent, Fernando Ferrer.[69]

In 2006, when the improved economy and strategic analysis made clear just how great a shortfall in affordable housing the city faced, Bloomberg expanded the program dramatically. He raised the target to 165,000 units, sufficient to house a half-million people. The program Housing Preservation and Development Commissioner Shaun Donovan's team developed targeted two-thirds of the apartments for households earning $50,000 a year or less, with others available to people with higher incomes, up to as much as $130,000 for a family of four. Some 30 percent of the apartments allowed for individual ownership, the rest were rentals. It was the largest municipal affordable housing program in the nation's history, with a $7.5 billion price tag. When the world financial crisis hit, Bloomberg stayed the course, and by the time he left office, the plan had met its goal. Even groups that criticized the program for failing to provide enough housing for New York's poorest workers making $20,000 to $40,000 acknowledged: "Mayor Bloomberg's [housing] plan is an impressive achievement that took great strides toward creating affordable housing opportunities for residents. . . . The mayor's commitment and perseverance, even through a severe economic downturn, makes the achievement all the more remarkable."[70]

The New Marketplace Housing Plan would accommodate about half of the population growth anticipated by 2030. Private sector initiatives were expected to build the rest. Yet, demand for affordable housing in New York City continues to outpace supply, a sign of the city's current appeal and a challenge to its continued vibrant growth. A 2014 study revealed the average rent for an apartment rose 11 percent in real terms and wages just 2.5 percent between 2005 and 2012. The vacancy rate in 2013 was a paltry 3.45 percent, below the 5 percent level deemed a housing emergency. Bloomberg's successor would launch a program of his own in 2014 designed to create two hundred thousand more affordable units.[71]

Shorelines, Playgrounds, and Parks

Two more Bloomberg administration goals captured in *PlaNYC* were "develop critical backup systems for . . . aging water networks," and "open 90% of our waterways for recreation." After a fire devastated Manhattan's downtown business district in December 1835, the city built a major aqueduct to bring water to New York from the town of Croton, some forty miles north of City Hall. In the early decades of the twentieth century, the city built a second system even farther away in the Catskill Mountains, and it completed a third called the Delaware System in 1964. The three systems fed two huge tunnels under the city's streets, one built in 1917 and the other in 1936. The city had long needed another, so the ones operating could be repaired when necessary. Slow progress on the third tunnel persisted. Creation of a Water Board in 1985 with special taxing authority provided dedicated financing. Early in his administration, Bloomberg's team undertook a disaster-planning exercise which concluded that a water tunnel collapse—from natural causes or others—was perhaps the most crippling risk to the city's well-being. "If you want to bring a city to its knees, turn off the faucets," was how Ed Skyler remembered the conclusion. That compelling insight, along with federal regulations requiring a filtration plant for the Croton system and ultraviolet disinfection technology for the Delaware and Catskill systems, caused Bloomberg to more than double the Department of Environmental Protection's capital budget to $16.5 billion in 2003, a tight budget year. In October 2013, the city activated the first stage of the long-planned third tunnel.[72]

The Croton System included High Bridge, an elegant structure resembling a Roman Aqueduct that sat astride the Harlem River. It was constructed in 1848 to extend water pipes from the Bronx mainland to Manhattan, and during an 1864 expansion the city built a walkway over the structure. It became a popular promenade that a Parks Department brief history referred to as a nineteenth century High Line. Over time, it was no longer needed for water, and the structure fell victim to disrepair and neglect. Safety concerns and budget constraints caused the city to close it to pedestrians by 1970. The Bloomberg administration renovated it beautifully, and the city reopened it in 2015. In addition to restoring a distinctive path with river views connecting parks on both sides of the span, it reestablished access for residents on the Bronx side to a city pool in Manhattan that had been out of reach for decades. For local residents, the impact was "huge" in the judgment of Bronx Borough President Ruben Diaz Jr.[73]

During the Dinkins and Giuliani years, the city made real progress toward reclaiming its long neglected waterfront, which was badly underexploited. By the time Bloomberg launched *PlaNYC,* the planning department had developed a holistic program for improvements, and in 2011 it published *Vision 2020: New York City Comprehensive Waterfront Development Plan.* It included wetlands projects to protect the environment, maritime projects to make the working waterfront more efficient for business, and major residential development and recreation initiatives to reclaim the water for human enjoyment.[74]

New York's waters were cleaner than they had been in one hundred years, *PlaNYC 2007* reported. The expanses of water safe for swimming, fishing, and boating were greater than in decades past. Yet, in some places, an archaic design continued to drain rain runoff into effluent sewer pipes. During heavy storms, combined sewer overflows floated untreated human waste into rivers and waterways. Programs to increase natural absorption by channeling rainwater into swales and reserve tanks for controlled disbursement, along with new construction rules, promised to mitigate the problem. The environmentally friendly approach emerged after consultation with advocates who opposed an initial plan that would have relied on expensive and disruptive engineering projects to solve the problem. The city launched programs to restore salt- and freshwater marshes, areas for bird nesting, rejuvenation of once-common plant life, and restoration of natural habitats. The city even began to experiment with creative uses of water-cleansing mollusks. New York Harbor was once filled with oysters. It may be again someday.[75]

The Bloomberg administration set itself the ambitious goal of "clean[ing] up all contaminated land in New York City." In some areas, industrial muck on the bottom of manmade canals or inland waterways that did not self-cleanse created unhealthy and unpleasant conditions. The city undertook expensive measures to try to remedy the situation without stirring up contamination. On shore, the city promoted an innovative program to reclaim brownfields exposed to toxic substances. The ugly industrial sites often sat in poor neighborhoods where unquantifiable liabilities prevented commercial development, locking blight into place for decades. Plans that defined clearly the environmental standards that would have to be achieved to allow development removed uncertainty and made restoration of some sites possible. In a 2014 update, the Mayor's Office of Environmental Remediation reported 3,900 units of affordable housing and sixteen million square feet of new building space on cleaned up brownfield sites.[76]

To address water- and shore-based contamination near Willets Point, Queens, adjacent to Citi Field, the city created a sixty-two-acre special-purpose zoning district. Fifty million cubic yards of ash had been dumped into nearby waters in the first decades of the twentieth century, leaving behind a toxic heap thirty feet deep. Later, auto theft chop shops regularly dumped oil, transmission fluid, and other contaminants in the water until a 2001 law enforcement sting shut operations down. The Economic Development Corporation worked with the Downtown Flushing Task Force composed of government officials, local business leaders, community board members, and developers, to create a plan. The result was a proposal to build 5,500 housing units on the site, 20 percent of them affordable, 1.7 million square feet of retail space, a convention center, hotels, offices, and parking.[77]

Businesses that the Willets Point plan proposed to displace sued the city, and their lawyers accused the Economic Development Corporation of violating some anti-lobbying provisions that applied to it. The EDC resolved the matter in a consent decree with the state attorney general, and its president, Seth Pinsky, restructured the corporation to avoid the problem in the future. The Willets Point proposal was a long-overdue improvement for the community and city, yet in 2015, a state court ruled the original action that allowed a stadium to be built on the property did not allow the sort of project the city proposed, and brought the project to at least a temporary halt.[78]

New York's population density left it with less green space per person than almost any other major American city, despite 29,000 acres of parkland. *PlaNYC* reflected a Bloomberg administration goal of ensuring "all New Yorkers live within a 10-minute walk of a park." The Parks Department would lead the city's biggest development program since the federally financed initiatives of the Great Depression. Some of the most dramatic projects faced the shoreline. "New York is re-embracing the waterfront for the first time in more than a century," Bloomberg declared in 2007 when announcing a city led project on Governor's Island, 172 acres of land that sits between the southern tip of Manhattan and the Brooklyn shore. The federal government had ceded it to the city and state some years before, but proposals for what to do with it went nowhere. Bloomberg's team developed imaginative designs for a public space on the island, and when work was complete in 2016, the results were magnificent. Writing in the *Financial Times* about just one of the island's new parks, Philip Delves Broughton described "The Hills" as a "Walt Whitman poem come to life, intimate and expansive, enraptured by New York and its endless possibilities." Underneath the Brooklyn Bridge, the city developed 85 acres facing lower Manhattan into a "spectacularly successful" site, according to *New York Times* architecture critic Michael Kimmelman. Parks Commissioner Benepe praised it for serving Brooklyn "in all its diversity." In total, Bloomberg's team created 320 acres of waterfront parkland.[79]

Upgrades to existing parks to make them usable for a broader range of residents, and converting streets and sidewalks into newly conceived public spaces were two more threads of the plan to give every New Yorker access to recreation sites. A third element was a decision to unlock school yards normally closed when students and teachers went home. The program was not new, but over the years, school bureaucrats fearful of weekend revelry and Monday morning messes resisted proposals to expand it. Bloomberg's control of the school system in conjunction with his administration's recreation space imperatives ended the resistance. Hundreds of school yards around the city became available to a broader community for more extended hours. The city also decided to undertake major improvements to a series of sites located across the five boroughs that professionals had long viewed as having high potential, but could never secure funds to develop. "We were pinching ourselves," Benepe remembered, as his department received approval to launch projects it had wanted to pursue for years. By the time Bloomberg left office, three-quarters of New Yorkers had access to a city park, and when federal and state parks were included, 97 percent of city residents met the ten-minute test according to the Trust for Public Land.[80]

Wherever possible, the city tried to create public/private partnerships entrusting local communities to fund and manage park maintenance. For high-profile sites, like the one under the Brooklyn Bridge, it was a fiscal measure. For most locations, the partnerships were more important as a means of engaging local residents in the care of a neighborhood resource. In all, the city added 870 acres of parkland and laid the groundwork for a total of 4,000 acres of new green space by 2030. The most ambitious will reclaim the Fresh Kills Landfill on Staten Island. The site where the city dumped its refuse for many years will be converted into 2,200 acres of parkland, an area nearly three times the size of Central Park. The City Planning Department promised it would "combine state of the art ecological restoration with extraordinary settings for recreation, public art, sports and programs." The project began on Bloomberg's watch. Like Central Park, it will take decades to complete.[81]

Sustainable City

"Collectively," *PlaNYC 2007* asserted, "these initiatives all address our greatest challenge: climate change." It dismissed the debate ideologues with a vested interest sought to perpetuate. "Scientists have now proven that human activities are increasing the concentration of greenhouse gases in the earth's atmosphere," it stated matter-of-factly. The plan declared that New York had a "special stake in this discussion—but also a unique ability to help shape a solution." The city's sheer scale meant it released some 0.25 percent of the world's total greenhouse gases. It was way too small an amount for the city to solve the problem, but it was big enough for the city to lead by example. The plan also declared that characteristics that defined the city—high density, smaller living spaces, and mass transit—meant the average New Yorker produced less than one-third the amount of greenhouse gas produced by the average American. "Growing New York is, itself, a climate change strategy," officials asserted.[82]

The city planned additional measures to complement the impact of improved transportation, more efficient buildings, cleaner power, and more thoughtful placement of new housing to achieve its bold goal: "to reduce our global warming emissions by 30%." Planting a million trees was the proposal that captured public imagination. Sometime earlier, working with US Forest Service officials, the city parks department provided an analysis that claimed for every $1 spent planting trees, the city received $5.50 of benefit. Increased real estate value was part of it, but the study also ascribed economic value to carbon dioxide absorption, and urban heat island mitigation. Bette Midler's New York Restoration Project was already at work planting trees on private land. As part of *PlaNYC*, Bloomberg's parks department took up the challenge to do the same, at scale, on city property. The million-tree project became a means of involving citizens in civic service as thousands volunteered for well-resourced and skillfully managed tree-planting events around the city.[83]

Incentives for buildings to place gardens on their roofs added more plants to the city's environment and covered heat absorbing tar at the same time. Reflecting paint was applied to roofs to reduce air conditioning needs and the energy use that went with it. Bloomberg advocated aggressive state and federal programs to respond to the rising challenge of climate change that no city could meet on its own. Environmentalists applauded the remarkable commitment to reduce the city's greenhouse gas emissions, even though many thought the scale of the aspiration beyond municipal reach. In a 2014 update, the city reported that its actions had reduced its own local government greenhouse gas emissions by 19 percent. A city comptroller audit insisted the number was 16 percent and that management of the initiative was sloppy. The report asserted New York would fall short of the goal of 30 percent reduction from government sources by 2017. Perhaps, but the program the comptroller critiqued had become a national and international model.[84]

When New Yorkers elected Bloomberg mayor in 2001, they feared their city was headed for prolonged economic stagnation and a serious decline in the quality of life. Bloomberg's first-term development programs were designed to reinvigorate the local economy in the short term and diversify it in the long-run. *PlaNYC* elevated city development initiatives into a holistic strategy to promote economic growth while creating a healthy environment that would sustain a higher quality of life for current residents and future generations. By the end of 2013, the New York City economy was stronger than ever, public amenities in better condition than at any time in memory, and environmental awareness greater than it had ever been. Updated zoning rules allowed the city's economy to follow the contours of a changed world so it could thrive in the twenty-first century. Sector-based promotion strategies supported employment in technology, fashion, film, arts, culture, higher education, and health care. The fifty-three million tourists who traveled to New York City in 2013 reflected a surging hospitality industry. Despite the global financial crisis, the city added nearly four hundred thousand jobs between 2010 and the end of 2013, more of them outside Manhattan than within it. Bloomberg's five-borough promise was real. Brooklyn added jobs at almost three times the pace of Manhattan. After decades of decline the population of the Bronx, the city's poorest borough, rose ever so slightly as jobs grew at double Manhattan's pace. Brooklyn, Queens, and Manhattan all attracted more people. The population of Staten Island, a bedroom community content to remain a quasi-suburban enclave, stayed about the same. New York City's gross domestic product exceeded $680 billion, its highest peak ever. Average income exceeded $80,000 per year, half again more than the average American. In 2012, New York ranked first among sixty global cities as the most attractive place to do business, according to an index prepared by A.T. Kearney and the Chicago Council on Global Affairs. The Citizens Budget Commission ranked the New York City metropolitan area's attractiveness as a home for human capital in 2013 against fifteen major American cities and concluded none surpassed it. Only Silicon Valley and Washington, DC, compared.[85]

Yet, despite the extraordinary success, critics declared Bloomberg's entrepreneurial city deeply flawed. Economic expansion swelled the wealth of the richest New Yorkers, but the poorest received not a trickle, they complained. Nearly one New Yorker in five—more than 1.5 million people—lived in official poverty, and just as many or more escaped it by so slim a margin, they too were poor by any reasonable standard. Left-leaning analysts complained that the rising tide of New York City's economic seas did little to lift the boats anchored in the mud at the lower end of its workforce, or that drifted unconnected to the job market. They claimed the city's programs contributed to a dispiriting and socially unacceptable—perhaps even dangerous—concentration of wealth. By 2013, when United States President Barack Obama declared income inequality "the defining challenge of our time," Bloomberg's critics thought his policies part of the problem—the billionaire mayor's economic vision of a luxury city a prime example of what was wrong.[86]

Chapter Eight
Rich Man, Poor Man

Michael Bloomberg was a Jewish kid raised in a middle-class family unconnected to power, fame, or fortune who grew up to become the richest man in New York City, and its highest elected official. He believed in the American Dream—with a little luck, a little talent, and a lot of hard work, anyone could succeed.

Bloomberg's attitude toward social welfare policy reflected the outlook of many liberals before the tumult of the mid-1960s. He wanted a tolerant and color-blind society to offer every child a decent education and every worker the opportunity to earn a living that would pay for a roof overhead and put food on the table. "It was a passionate part of his belief system that people need to have an equal shot," Deputy Mayor Walcott would tell an interviewer. "It's part of his DNA." If safety in some neighborhoods required more resources than others to make sure everyone could live free from fear of crime, if some children required special attention to learn, or if some families needed support to secure affordable housing and to have enough to eat, government had an obligation to help. So did wealthy citizens who benefited disproportionately from American freedom. Philanthropy was a form of patriotism to Bloomberg, but his antipoverty vision stopped way short of the Great Society philosophy that embraced affirmative action and programs to redistribute wealth. "Let's begin with the plain fact that the best anti-poverty program ever devised is a job," he declared when announcing a major initiative to reassess the city's programs for helping the poor. It was a statement that resonated with Heather Mac Donald, a fellow at the Manhattan Institute, and other conservatives.[1]

Antipoverty Entrepreneur

When Bloomberg became mayor, New York City's federally funded workforce training programs were poorly managed. Mayor Giuliani had viewed them with "undisguised contempt," one analyst wrote, and lumped them together with others that he believed undercut personal responsibility. New York had just a single center offering "one-stop" workforce services of a kind required to qualify for federal and state funds. Los Angeles had thirty-six at the time. After two rounds of analysis, in 2003, Bloomberg divided workforce programs into two categories. The Department for Youth and Community Development would handle support for aspiring workers between the ages of fourteen and twenty-one who were still in school or educational programs. The Small Business Services Department, a unit of the Economic Development Corporation, would handle workforce initiatives for adults, age eighteen and over. His administration would treat the programs as serious opportunities to channel people into gainful employment. "Training and education should be closely tied to the needs of city businesses and lead to real jobs," Bloomberg declared. Like Giuliani, he believed everyone receiving public help should work, but in a posture very different from his predecessor, he declared the city should provide childcare, job training, housing assistance, and substance-abuse counseling for workers struggling at the economic margin.[2]

Placing the adult division of workforce programs in the business services unit connected it with city workers already in active contact with employers. The move promoted a shift from supply-led decision-making to demand-driven approaches. The starting point for training became information from employers about the skills they needed. Program relevance improved, and credibility along with it. Bloomberg made it clear that he valued the work the unit did, raising badly depleted staff morale. The mayor's personal standing with business added to executive confidence that establishing and maintaining links to the long-maligned but newly energized system was worthwhile. In the three years following the 2003 restructuring, the city placed twenty-five thousand workers at an accelerating pace as it strengthened its department and the economy improved. Money that had been allowed to sit impotently in federal and state accounts as a result of the Giuliani administration's hostility to the programs was put to work for workers. Smart financing structures tied government training money to private sector financial commitments ensuring employers who benefited had skin in the game.[3]

An independent assessment of city policies concluded that the mayor's 2003 reorganization, "more than any other single event triggered the dramatic progress that the city has enjoyed on workforce development programming." Yet, it still fell short of a real transformation. "They did things that were low-hanging fruit," according to analysts at the Center for an Urban Future. Many of the jobs the career placement centers offered were low-wage retail positions without obvious career paths. Improvements in record keeping and accountability achieved within the adult workforce arena failed to translate into comprehensive information sharing and coherent case management across city agencies. Differing federal, state, and city social service funding sources—one analyst counted twenty-nine—and the rules that went with them, continued to impede integration of workforce training and social service support.[4]

By 2004, New York City's economic output had returned to its 2001 level, but job growth continued to lag, particularly among African Americans whose unemployment rate exceeded 10 percent. Bloomberg recognized the seriousness of the situation. During a public rally in support of his administration's West Side stadium plan, he began his pep talk by declaring three times loudly, "Jobs. Jobs. Jobs." The construction workers assembled for the demonstration cheered. Arm in arm with Harlem Congressman Charles Rangel in March 2005, joined later by Comptroller William Thompson and other leaders, Bloomberg created the Mayor's Commission on Construction Opportunity. Deputy mayors Doctoroff and Walcott chaired the group, which included the heads of seven city agencies and a total of thirty-four public, private, and union leaders. In October, just a few weeks before New Yorkers took to the polling booths to decide whether to reelect him for four more years, Bloomberg announced that the commission had agreed to ten goals. The most significant was a decision to dedicate 40 percent of coveted construction apprenticeships to specific groups traditionally underrepresented in the program or deemed especially worthy: women, unemployed youths not in school, graduates of New York City high schools, and veterans returning from overseas service.[5]

The confluence of an aging construction workforce and a mounting building boom created a rare opportunity for a large number of young people to move into solid jobs with lifelong earning potential. The posts were among the best paid for laborers with limited education. Bloomberg's commission was an effort to take maximum practical advantage of the moment and to achieve maximum political benefit in an election year. In an assessment of progress some two years after the launch, the Center for an Urban Future gave the stakeholders generally high marks for sticking to their commitments, including a pledge by the city to shield construction workers from exploitation. Many were immigrants with limited command of English, and little awareness of rules designed to protect them.[6]

By the time Bloomberg won reelection in November 2005, unemployment was trending down. The city's jobless rate fell to 5.5 percent in January 2006, and reached 4.6 percent by the end of that year, the lowest it had been since spring of 1988. Yet, not all were benefiting from the positive economic momentum. Official statistics, later revised down 1 percent, indicated more than 19 percent of New Yorkers—1.5 million people—lived in households with income below the federal poverty level. Another 1.5 million people lived in homes earning less than twice the official threshold, leaving them highly vulnerable to even modest financial misfortune. All told, three million or more of New York City's eight million plus residents were living on the economic edge. In the late 1960s, the poverty rate in New York City was barely higher than the national average. By 1979, and ever since, the local rate exceeded the national level. Among large American cities it ranked middle of the pack.[7]

As his second term began, Bloomberg's public safety, education, and economic recovery priorities all seemed on track, and the budget environment had turned favorable. He and his team had capacity for additional initiatives. *PlaNYC* was one major undertaking. Contending with persistent poverty became another. Three senior level departures at the end of the first term, Marc Shaw, Peter Madonia, and Bill Cunningham, created an opportunity for Bloomberg to reconsider how he organized his staff. He decided that bringing the city's social services agencies under a single deputy made sense, and he discussed the idea with various commissioners, including Linda Gibbs, who headed up the Department of Homeless Services during Bloomberg's first term. She was an experienced city administrator who had worked in the Koch and Giuliani governments in budgeting and policy roles, and also in the Administration for Children's Services, where she dealt with heart-wrenching social issues. During their conversation, Gibbs "screwed up her courage" and said she would like the deputy mayor job. The initial response, "hmph, hmm," was cryptic, but Bloomberg called her a short while later to discuss the role, and soon decided to appoint her. The portfolio included direct responsibility for social service agencies, and it came with a broad mandate. Bloomberg wanted the Deputy Mayor of Health and Human Services to explore ways to help people lift themselves out of poverty using all the resources of government, in cooperation with private sector and philanthropic partners.[8]

During his State of the City speech in January 2006, Bloomberg declared, "Men and women struggling to get out of poverty deserve our help—and so do their children." He committed his administration to achieving "a major reduction in the number of [New Yorkers] who live in poverty in this city over the next four years." To address the issue, he created the Mayor's Commission for Economic Opportunity, a public-private task force. Its mission was to "identify strategies to help more New Yorkers realize their aspirations by supporting their ability to secure meaningful employment at decent wages." In antipoverty vernacular, Bloomberg was looking for ways to offer a "hand up," not a "hand out." Two prominent African American New Yorkers, Richard Parsons, CEO of Time Warner, and Geoffrey Canada, founder and president of Harlem's Children Zone, served as cochairs. Some thirty-two leaders of businesses, social services agencies, academic institutions, and foundations served along with deputy mayors Linda Gibbs, Daniel Doctoroff, Patricia Harris, Carol Robles-Roman, and Dennis Walcott. The presence of five deputy mayors on the commission made it clear Bloomberg expected his entire government to engage in the mission.[9]

In September 2006, the commission delivered a report. The city faced a "stark" choice its authors wrote: "continue to shoulder the . . . costs of maintaining large numbers of New Yorkers in the dead-end of poverty, or . . . make long-term investments in offering increasing numbers of the poor access to economic advancement. . . ." It recommended the city focus on three overlapping populations that constituted seven hundred thousand impoverished New Yorkers: the working poor, young adults age sixteen to twenty-four, and children age five and under. The commission members believed that those three groups "can benefit most directly, immediately and dramatically from well-focused and coordinated interventions." When the commission contemplated how to act on its recommendations, the idea of creating a center in the mayor's office dedicated to achieving the report's objectives emerged.[10]

Bloomberg announced creation of the Center for Economic Opportunity in December 2006. Its goal was to reduce "the number of people living in poverty in New York City through the implementation of result-driven and innovative initiatives." Experimentation and evaluation would be hallmarks of the center's work, "very Bloombergian" characteristics in the words of Deputy Mayor Gibbs, to whom the center reported. One longtime antipoverty policy analyst described the effort as an attempt to "build a culture of evidence," for making decisions about programs to help the poor. It was a crucial development, "because we have such a long history of doing things that don't work," according to Gordon Berlin, president of MDRC, an organization dedicated to assessing the effectiveness of antipoverty programs.[11]

To Bloomberg, the new center was meant to operate as an "innovation lab" to test a "diverse new generation" of social programs, designed above all to combat the "cycle of intergenerational poverty." He expected the city to identify what worked in pilot studies, and then to scale them to have an impact. It was the strategy of an antipoverty entrepreneur. It mirrored the way venture firms build their portfolios—investing in a range of possibilities, knowing if even just a few really work, the payoff will be large. It was an effort to "disrupt" intergenerational poverty according to one senior advisor, sounding more like a Silicon Valley tech mogul than a big city social worker. Where practical, the projects included randomized control groups—populations similar to the ones being helped who did not receive benefits, so analysts could assess the impact. It mimicked the way scientists conducted their experiments. From the outset the CEO, as the center became known, intended to test ideas over time frames longer than the election cycle that so often drives public policy decisions. The new office would coordinate policy across public and private resources. Other cities operated partnerships with not-for-profit agencies, but none commanded the kind of cooperation among philanthropies that Bloomberg did.[12]

The CEO began operations with a $150 million Innovation Fund and took responsibility for some forty-one different initiatives its first year, thirty-one of them recommendations from the mayor's economic opportunity commission. Over time, it would experiment with many more. The majority were pursued by agencies not normally thought of as "poverty fighters," Deputy Mayor Gibbs remembered. Creation of the CEO reflected Bloomberg's belief that every city agency had an obligation to help lift the poor out of poverty. It was a holistic way of thinking about how government could deliver services to the indigent.[13]

Bloomberg insisted that the CEO use defined goals and accurate measures to evaluate its initiatives. His economic opportunity commission asserted that the federal poverty standard, developed in 1963 and not updated since 1969 except for cost-of-living adjustments, was "insufficient" for intelligent policy analysis. In 1995, Congress and President Clinton had instructed the National Academy of Sciences to develop more useful measures, which they did, but logic clashed with political agendas, and the official measures remained unchanged. After extensive study and review, New York City adopted the National Academy of Sciences recommendations, modified for "the realities of life in New York City," as Mark Levitan, a nationally recognized expert in the field who became the CEO's director of research, described it. New York City was the first government in the country to use the smarter measure. In 2011, spurred by New York's leadership, the US Bureau of the Census finally began releasing annual reports using a variation of the new calculation as a Supplemental Poverty Measure.[14]

New York's numbers determined that in 2006 a two-adult, two-child family living in the five boroughs needed $26,138 to meet minimum needs, compared to a federal threshold of $20,444. The cost of housing in New York was a major factor in the higher number. Using a broad definition of income that accounted for non-cash benefits as well as cash, when it netted out the higher threshold against the expanded income levels, the city concluded that 4 percent more city residents lived in poverty in 2006 than federal calculations showed. Later adjustments would determine the difference was closer to 2 percent—160,000 more people than the federal number identified. The city figures would trend consistently some 2 percent to 3 percent higher than federal numbers representing as many as 250,000 additional people. The conclusion that New York had even more poor than it previously acknowledged did not make Bloomberg happy, but "he didn't flinch," when Levitan gave him the news.[15]

Both sets of measures showed disproportionate poverty among African Americans, Latinos, and single-parent households, and both showed the highest concentration of poor in the Bronx followed by Brooklyn. Yet, there were relevant differences. City calculations showed more elderly lived in poverty than federal guidelines recognized—often as a consequence of high out-of-pocket medical expenses. The greater number of poor elderly included a relatively larger number of whites and Asians, with concentrations in Queens and Brooklyn. Immigrants also registered higher levels of poverty. In contrast, city figures offered the welcome news that fewer children lived in poverty than federal guidelines identified. Single-parent families suffered disproportionately from poverty, but benefit programs lifted more of them above the threshold than previously recognized. The information had important policy implications.[16]

If You Want to Work, We Want to Help You

"If you want to work, we want to help you," Robert Doar, who Bloomberg appointed commissioner of the Human Resources Administration in January 2007, told a community group meeting with the mayor in the Bronx. It was an apt summary of a key pillar of Bloomberg's antipoverty philosophy. He believed work gave structure and a sense of purpose to people's lives. It also provided hope. Once in the workforce, even at the most basic level, a laborer had an opportunity to move up. A person without a job had no chance to advance. Consequently, Bloomberg supported programs that removed obstacles to employment and that made work pay. He recognized that teen pregnancies, lack of child care, inadequate nutrition and health care, and deficient education and training deficits all placed limits on people's ability to secure and hold jobs. He saw it as government's role to invest in human capital to help people succeed in the employment market. Bloomberg also believed every person who could work had an obligation to do so. While he governed, he invested hundreds of millions of city dollars and hundreds of millions of his own money in efforts to move people into the labor market and up the job pyramid. At the same time, the number of people receiving direct cash payments under the federal welfare program, Temporary Assistance for Needy Families, shrunk from 430,000 in 2002 to 357,000 in 2013. Bloomberg was wary of creating a culture of dependency, and of unscrupulous people ready to abuse taxpayer programs.[17]

Private social service agencies thought his departments administered benefit eligibility rules with a heavy hand. Early on, advocates criticized Bloomberg for not quickly unwinding policies Mayor Giuliani implemented to make it difficult to apply for the Supplemental Nutritional Assistance Program—food stamps. Yet, between 2002 and 2007, the number of recipients in the five boroughs increased over 25 percent to more than one million. In the aftermath of the Great Recession, the number rose to nearly 1.9 million by 2013. Bloomberg viewed food stamps for parents with children, and food stamps for adults without children, very differently. In April 2006 when he learned his social services team applied for a special waiver to allow childless men and women to apply for the federal benefit, he ordered them to withdraw the request. "This potential policy change is not consistent with the mayor's goal of helping New Yorkers become self-sufficient," Gibbs said when announcing the somewhat embarrassing reversal. She affirmed the mayor's view that "every New Yorker who can work should work."[18]

Bloomberg also insisted on fingerprint imaging recipients of food stamps to prevent fraud. By 2012, New York City was the only major jurisdiction in the country outside Arizona to follow the practice. Critics accused Bloomberg of treating poor citizens entitled to benefits like criminals. He shrugged off accusations that the practice stigmatized people, saying "most companies fingerprint in this day and age." If workers tolerated the imposition, so too could New Yorkers relying on taxpayers' money. Eventually, Governor Andrew Cuomo overruled Bloomberg on the grounds that the practice discouraged needy New Yorkers from applying for benefits.[19]

Bloomberg was a vocal supporter of the federal Earned Income Tax Credit that has been one of the country's largest and most effective antipoverty programs. The thrust of it is to provide workers with children whose families fall below income thresholds with cash payments to supplement their wages. Roughly 80 percent of eligible New Yorkers applied for the benefit, but that meant 20 percent did not, often for lack of awareness. Bloomberg's finance department knew who they were because of city tax filings. The department completed amended tax forms on behalf of the residents who had missed out, and mailed the documents to them for verification and signature. The action resulted in some sixteen thousand New Yorkers receiving $10 million in otherwise unclaimed federal benefits the first year.[20]

At a Brookings Institute conference in Washington, DC, in 2006, Bloomberg praised the EITC for encouraging women to work, and for lifting children out of poverty. He criticized provisions that constituted a marriage penalty, allowing unmarried couples to receive higher benefits than the ones who tied the knot. But the most dramatic point he made was that "fathers are missing from our strategies to drive down the poverty rate." He proposed significant benefit increases to fathers not living with their children, provided they met thresholds for child support. The plan meant to encourage work in cases where accumulated financial judgments against fathers were so large in comparison to potential income that it discouraged them from seeking employment. Perversely, the situation sometimes motivated young men to take up criminal activity as a way to make money invisible to official eyes. The city would eventually launch a local pilot program to explore the impact of an EITC targeted toward unmarried fathers.[21]

The percent of New York City households living in poverty that had at least one person working—the working poor—had reached the alarming level of 46 percent by the start of Bloomberg's second term, way up from 29 percent in 1990. The city's Department of Small Business Services sought ways to help workers develop new skills and advance to higher salary levels. It recognized that drivers capable of steering freight-hauling equipment and other specialized vehicles were in short supply, so in 2008 it launched a program near JFK airport to train workers to fill the gap and to provide them with careers in the transportation field. The program generated jobs even as the economy turned down. That provided impetus to provide training in other fields likely to remain in demand during periods of weak employment, and initiatives in healthcare and specialized manufacturing followed. Evidence from Jobs Plus, a program officials described as a "place-based" program that had proved successful in other cities, also caught their attention. The initiative saturated public housing developments with job and career support, rent incentives, and other resources to create a critical mass of employment help in a specific location. Bloomberg's antipoverty team implemented it in New York City Housing Authority projects giving it "a second lease on life," according to Jim Riccio at MDRC, which in turn provided momentum to federal efforts to expand the program. The Department of Consumer Affairs created an Office of Financial Empowerment in 2008 that promoted financial literacy, negotiated with creditors on behalf of poor New Yorkers, and launched innovative programs with incentives to save money and avoid debt.[22]

Through various employment and workforce initiatives, the city placed up to twenty-five thousand people per year in jobs between 2008 and 2012, easing the impact of the Great Recession for many. These were in addition to between seventy-five thousand and ninety-thousand workfare positions staffed through the Human Resources Administration as a requirement for adults receiving cash welfare. Web-based research tools provided access to information about job programs and allowed users to screen their eligibility for over twenty city, state, and federal benefit programs in seven languages. Private agency referrals for social services added to the resources accessible through the city's 311 information call center in 2008 and made information available to needy callers in over 170 languages, twenty-four hours a day, seven days a week.[23]

New York City included 900,000 young adults between the ages of sixteen to twenty-four in 2006. Estimates of the number in that age group not working and not in school varied over the economic cycle and according to different definitions of employment. At any one time between 2006 and 2013, somewhere between 110,000 and as many as 200,000 or more young New Yorkers were disconnected from any formal productive activity. It was a population prone to high-risk sexual behavior, drug abuse, and crime. In its report to the mayor, the Commission for Economic Opportunity asserted that many were "one bad decision away from a lifetime of poverty." Of the fifty largest cities in the country, New York had the highest teenage unemployment rate. Analysts estimated that every high school dropout cost society on average almost $300,000 more than graduates in lower tax receipts, higher welfare payments, and incarceration expenses.[24]

Bloomberg's administration experimented with strategies to prevent teenagers and young adults from becoming disconnected in the first place, and to reconnect dropouts with educational opportunities. It also adopted policies designed to help the unemployed finds jobs and careers. The most successful, perhaps, was CUNY ASAP, City University of New York's Accelerated Study in Associate Programs. Left to their own devices, a dismal 11 percent of students who enrolled in New York City's community colleges graduated in two years, and a disappointing 22 percent after three years. CUNY's response provided more than one thousand eligible students with special help. It included remedial summer sessions, tuition waivers, small classes for a chosen peer group, block scheduling to facilitate competing obligations, free books, free public transportation, tutoring, counseling services, and job placement support. Students were required to enroll full-time, meet with advisors, and attend required remedial classes and tutoring sessions. The three-year graduation rate for challenged students nearly doubled to 40 percent, and because so many more earned diplomas, the cost per degree was lower for students in the program despite the substantial investment it required. "These are quantum leap results," MDRC president Gordon Berlin observed. ASAP's success caused Bloomberg's successor to embrace and expand it. A Young Adult Internship Program that placed out-of-school and out-of-work sixteen- to twenty-four-year-olds in paid internships, and a Young Adult Literacy Program that paid participants to achieve reading and writing goals also proved worthwhile.[25]

Yet, despite the specific successes, the number of disconnected youth in New York City remained discouraging. In his 2010 State of the City Address, Bloomberg told his audience that the city had to face some "very sobering facts about who is succeeding and who is not." Black and Hispanic young men "have a poverty rate that is 50 percent higher than young white and Asian young men. Their rate of unemployment is 60 percent higher. They are two times more likely to not graduate from high school, far more likely to become a teen father and—most troubling of all—more than 90 percent of all young murder victims and perpetrators are Black and Hispanic." He identified a compelling need to figure out how to "connect Black and Hispanic young people—especially young men—to the opportunities and support that can lead them to success."[26]

An August 2011 report to the mayor on the subject led to the launch of the Young Men's Initiative, funded by Bloomberg Philanthropies and George

Soros's Open Societies Foundations, among other sources. Bloomberg pitched the idea to his fellow billionaire philanthropist over lunch and asked him to contribute $30 million. Soros agreed, provided Bloomberg did the same. "Expensive lunch," Bloomberg mused. The initiative included more than thirty programs designed to provide a broad network of support that would "give young Black and Latino men a sense of opportunity that most of them do not have . . . to provide participants with a fuller sense of their options," was how one staff member put it. Three basic goals to help young men at risk generated several dozen programs to keep them in school, at jobs, and out of jail. By the end of Bloomberg's third term, it was too soon to know if the two-year-old program was working. Bloomberg's successor would align the initiative with My Brother's Keeper, a national program sponsored by President Barack Obama with many of the same goals.[27]

The mayor's economic opportunity commission also recommended expanded strategies to promote early learning, including universal pre-kindergarten. "Experience shows," the commission's report declared, that "investing in quality pre-school education at an earlier age is the most cost-effective strategy and yields the greatest results when targeted to at-risk populations." Later studies in other places would challenge the unequivocal conclusion. Yet, the city responded with ten thousand new full-day pre-kindergarten slots targeted for poor neighborhoods. Over thirty thousand four-year-olds would benefit from full-day pre-kindergarten programs by the end of the Bloomberg administration, either as a free service or one that included means-tested fees. Another twenty-six thousand were enrolled in half-day programs. Bloomberg's successor would expand the full-day program, mostly in middle-class neighborhoods. Bloomberg's approach constituted a targeted antipoverty campaign, while Mayor de Blasio extended the public's commitment to early childhood education to all New Yorkers.[28]

When the mayor announced creation of the Center for Economic Opportunity, he also announced the city would explore a concept called conditional cash payments never before tried in the United States, or any other rich country. Antipoverty initiatives in poorer and middle-income countries, in particular *Oportunidades* in Mexico, included cash disbursements to families that achieved specific goals intended to help poor people move out of poverty. School attendance, preventive health-care visits, and other activities were rewarded with money. The commission had not recommended the approach, but during conversations with antipoverty experts the bold idea captured Linda Gibbs's imagination. She promoted it with Bloomberg, who joined a field trip to Mexico to learn more about it. Evaluations suggested the program worked well there.[29]

The city's conditional cash payment experiment, organized with randomized control groups to allow careful evaluation of various strategies, generated some benefits, but outcomes were disappointing. In less-affluent countries where conditional cash transfers had a major impact, they often constituted the most important social welfare benefit. In New York City, where extensive existing programs covered most basic needs, their impact was marginal. Bloomberg understood all along that the program was a test. "We don't know if these initiatives will work," he said when announcing them, "but shame on us if we do not try new things" that might reduce poverty. As a well-structured test, the experiment was successful. As a plan for reducing poverty, it was not.[30]

The Limits of Small-Bore Experimentation

Bloomberg and his team were exceptionally proud of the administration's many important antipoverty accomplishments. In 2010, the federal government awarded New York money from its Social Innovation Fund to sponsor some of its most promising experiments in other cities. In 2012, Harvard's Kennedy School of Government named the Center for Economic Opportunity the winner of its Innovations in American Government Award. The Children's Aid Society honored Bloomberg for his leadership combating poverty at its November 14, 2013 fund-raising gala. Earlier that day, the mayor's office released an analysis based on US Census Bureau statistics. Between 2000 and 2012, poverty in twenty large American cities rose 28 percent on average. In New York, it remained flat. The city's poverty rate went from fifth highest to thirteenth. Poor New Yorkers withstood the Great Recession better than the poor elsewhere. Without its many programs the city contended, another 2.6 percent of the city's people—more than two hundred thousand additional New Yorkers—would have slid below the line. Taking the figure at face value, it represents a considerable reduction in misery.[31]

In his prepared remarks at the Children's Aid Society gala, Bloomberg praised his administration's economic development strategies for creating robust employment opportunities. The median level of income fell barely at all in New York City between 2000 and 2012, while it declined over 8 percent nationally. And he applauded his team's antipoverty initiatives. "I think it is fair to say that no American city has battled poverty more directly, or with more determination and innovation." Yet, when Bloomberg created his economic opportunity commission in 2006, 17.9 percent of New Yorkers lived in poverty by federal reckoning. The rate drifted down a little more than a point until 2009, when the impact of the Great Recession hit. It turned back up, peaking at 20.0 percent in 2012, where it stayed until the end of Bloomberg's third term, despite economic recovery locally and around the nation. The city's more relevant poverty measure was a few points higher and followed a similar pattern. By either standard, a higher proportion of New Yorkers were poor at the end of Bloomberg's third term than at the start of his second when he launched his antipoverty initiative, or when he became mayor. The city calculated twelve indices measuring different aspects of municipal life based on information gathered in its 2008 customer satisfaction survey. The Social Support Services Index received by far the lowest score. In 2013, at the end of Bloomberg's third term, the Center for Economic Opportunity reported that over 45 percent of city households—3.75 million people—lived on income that was 150 percent or less than the city-defined poverty level of $31,156 for a family of four. In his remarks at the Children's Aid Society, Bloomberg acknowledged the obvious: New York's poverty level remained unacceptably high.[32]

Even taken together, the Bloomberg team's successful initiatives, more impressive perhaps than any other set of municipal antipoverty programs, were not poised to scale in a way that would reduce the number of poor by anything like the level contemplated in the original antipoverty plan. David Jones, chief executive of the Community Service Society, a left-leaning anti-poverty agency, described them as "too small bore" to have a major impact. Mark Griffith, executive director of the Drum Major Institute, a progressive Manhattan think tank, saw it the same way. He viewed Bloomberg's programs as "isolated . . . concentrated interventions" that did little to address the systemic causes of poverty. Michael Katz, a University of Pennsylvania scholar of poverty in America, praised Bloomberg for "testing the limits of human capital and market-based strategies." Yet, he wrote, the many poor New Yorkers living outside or at the fringes of the labor market "remain untouched."[33]

David Jones questioned the premise of the Center for Economic Opportunity even though he had served on the 2006 commission that spawned it. "There's an assumption here that the problem in dealing with chronic poverty . . . is a lack of new ideas. In fact, New York, through its nonprofits and government, has been a laboratory for new ideas for generations," he told a reporter. His comment revealed a sense among experts long in the antipoverty trenches that Bloomberg, and the wealthy elite he traveled with, were naively spending time and money discovering things experienced people already knew. At least a few believed the mayor and his team responded to creative ideas the way children's eyes are attracted to bright shiny objects. Consistent allocation of adequate resources to help the poor was the main issue to these people. Advocates criticized Bloomberg when the financial crisis hit and he cut the Human Resources Administration budget to $8.1 billion in Fiscal Year 2011 from $8.5 billion the year before. City social services agencies resisted any weakening of eligibility standards for welfare in response to the economic catastrophe. Yet, when city revenues recovered and when federal stimulus money became available, the Human Resources Administration's budget surged to $9.4 billion in Fiscal 2012. The numbers make clear that budget discipline and a desire to alleviate poverty were both priorities during the Bloomberg administration.[34]

Where the Poor Live

Social service advocates faulted the mayor for homeless policies that led to record numbers of New Yorkers living in city sponsored shelters. The population seeking refuge had been fairly stable at around twenty-five thousand nightly in the early 1990s. It drifted down somewhat between 1996 and 1998, but had already tilted back up when a weak economy and the consequences of the 9/11 terrorist attack caused it to spike. The surge caused Bloomberg's team to set up temporary facilities for families in an old jailhouse near the city's notorious Emergency Assistance Unit in the Bronx. It was an effort to comply with a court injunction that forbade the city from leaving families to sleep on the floor of the administrative office where staff processed applications for shelter, a fate many families faced their first nights in the system, particularly when demand rose. The symbolism of sending destitute women and children to a former jailhouse was already something of a public relations disaster when it turned out the paint on the prison walls contained lead. The realization forced the city to send families with young children back to the agency offices to sleep, in violation of the court order after all. In 2005 Bloomberg's team revamped the intake process and moved it to a temporary facility. In 2011 it opened a new one that met the expectations for professional delivery of social services far better than the one it inherited.[35]

The injunction against using administrative offices to house families overnight was just one of many legal restrictions on homeless policy that some forty-one court orders imposed on the city. They defined the services for the homeless so specifically that officials complained they lacked the discretion necessary to manage the shelter system sensibly. In January 2003, the Bloomberg administration reached an agreement that converted twenty years of legal combat with advocates into a partnership of sorts. The city and the Legal Aid Society agreed that a jointly-appointed three-person Special Master Panel would review city policies for homeless families and make decisions that might otherwise be mandated by judges. The new approach meant common-sense exceptions to legal requirements would not cause violations of court orders and that officials could explore creative service options without filing court papers. The change in tone from the Giuliani administration was palpable and mutual suspicion between city officials and homeless advocates diminished modestly for a time. After two years of involvement the masters wrote: "We do not believe it appropriate . . . with all the changes that have occurred, for this court to remain in perpetual supervision of the system for homeless families. The City of New York has earned the right to go forward into a new era." Despite that conclusion, the Legal Aid Society would not agree to allow the court to rescind its orders. An irate Bloomberg accused it of acting in bad faith. Years later, the Legal Aid Society finally accepted terms and, within the bounds of defined policies, the city regained the right to control the homeless shelters its taxpayers financed.[36]

First term Chief of Staff Peter Madonia had worked in the Koch administration when homelessness first became a high-profile issue. He had watched it consume the mayor's office many days, and feared it would do the same to Bloomberg's team without a smart plan for contending with it. Over objections from other advisors, who sought to distance their boss from the intractable problem, Madonia and homeless services commissioner Gibbs won Bloomberg's support to launch a major initiative. They convened a forty-one-person coordinating committee that cut across business, academia, social services, and city government to conduct a comprehensive homelessness study. After conferring with hundreds of experts, in June 2004 the group published a report entitled *Uniting for Solutions Beyond Shelter: The Action Plan for New York City*. In the introductory letter, Bloomberg asserted his conviction that "every individual and every family deserves safe, affordable housing." He described the plan as addressing "the challenging issue of homelessness at its core, rather than manage it at the margins."[37]

Advocates and analysts praised the initiative. "Bloomberg brought in people interested in making things happen," Maureen Friar, executive director of the Supportive Housing Network told a reporter. "There was a real openness and willingness to learn," she said. Thomas Main, who studied welfare and social service policy at Baruch College, declared the plan "showed a lot of guts. It seemed to be the thinking of a business person, interested in solving problems rather than muddling through." The plan identified nine objectives to be implemented through sixty initiatives. It included an ambitious goal: reduce the number of people relying on city shelters by two-thirds in ten years. When Gibbs and her team presented the strategy to Bloomberg, he collapsed the timeline. "I told them I'm not going to be here in ten years, do it in five. Let's not leave it for somebody else to finish." Responsibility for the bold plan would fall primarily on Gibbs. For a time, the program she championed showed signs of progress.[38]

The city announced it had accomplished 86 percent of the plan's specific tasks in 2008. It also claimed that, since 2002, it had placed a total of 175,000 people into permanent housing or prevented them from losing their homes. Advocates questioned the data, but HomeBase, the main program that helped struggling tenants and doubled up families avoid eviction or displacement, was generally considered a success. It began in six target districts and later went citywide. Homeless living on the streets dropped by 25 percent, according to the city's one-night-a-year census, and single homeless individuals in the system fell 22 percent. But families accounted for most of the shelter residents, and the number of families in the system declined by just 3 percent. That meant despite real progress on a range of dimensions, the overall impact of the major effort was modest, and nothing close to the progress the high-profile plan promised. Then the Great Recession hit, and "positive moves by Bloomberg's homelessness team began playing out against a souring economy and problems with other aspects of the mayor's policies," Diane Jeantet wrote in a five-part series that appeared in the progressive online publication, *City Limits.* The combination prevented the mayor from achieving the success he targeted in 2004, and "created a deeper homelessness crisis than existed when he proposed his bold plan," she concluded.[39]

In 2004, New York City stopped relying on federal Section 8 vouchers as a key resource for helping homeless migrate to permanent housing. The decision was meant to discourage people from entering the system to become eligible for the benefit faster than they might qualify through other channels. And in any event, the New York City Housing Authority that administered the program needed all of the vouchers it received to support its own operations. From 2004 forward, Bloomberg's team experimented with three different options for transitioning shelter residents to permanent housing. The first two disappointed, leading to a third that Deputy Mayor Gibbs asserts was "working . . . the numbers were just starting to come down" when New York State withdrew funding for it in 2011 to contend with a budget crisis of its own. Federal money connected to the state's commitment also disappeared as a consequence. The gap amounted to some $140 million, two-thirds of the program's total cost.[40]

Unwilling to respond to the state's action by forcing city taxpayers to absorb the difference, the Bloomberg administration discontinued the program, and suddenly there was no provision to help people transition from shelters into permanent housing. Gibbs would describe the state's decision to withdraw support for the program as her greatest regret. The shelter population, which had been hovering for a time in the range of thirty-five thousand to thirty-seven thousand nightly, surged. "If you don't have any type of program to get out of the shelter, people are going to get stuck," a Brooklyn city councilman told a reporter, in a statement of the obvious. More than fifty thousand New Yorkers resided in city shelters by the time Bloomberg left office, more than at any time since the Great Depression. When asked why the numbers were growing, Bloomberg said improvements in the quality of the services offered made living in the shelters "a much more pleasurable experience," so shelter residents were in no rush to get out. Pleasurable was hardly the word that came to mind for anyone directly involved with the system.[41]

In December 2013, the *New York Times* published "Invisible Child," a wrenching five-part series written by Andrea Elliott on the life of a homeless eleven-year-old girl named Dasani Coates and her family. It described the city-owned shelter where Dasani lived as "a place where mold creeps up walls and roaches swarm, where feces and vomit plug communal toilets, where sexual predators have roamed and small children stand guard for their single mothers outside filthy showers." It blamed the surge in homelessness on Bloomberg's drive to reorder the city around the "whims of the wealthy" and the failure of his social policies. The harsh, accusatory tone of the article caused deputy mayors Gibbs and Wolfson to pen a response in the *Wall Street Journal.* "No city in the country has devoted more energy and resources to combating homelessness and poverty than New York City," their piece contended. "No mayor has been more personally committed and invested in this fight than Mr. Bloomberg, who in addition to dramatically increasing city spending on antipoverty efforts, has donated more than $320 million of his own money to helping those New Yorkers most at risk of getting trapped in poverty," they wrote in defense of Bloomberg's record.[42]

The lack of rental units poor New Yorkers could afford was one of the root causes of the long-standing homeless crisis. Bloomberg's impressive affordable housing program provided few apartments for the truly impoverished. New York City rent-restriction programs—control and stabilization—put in place in response to a post-World War II housing emergency that never ended, covered over a million New York City apartments when Bloomberg became mayor. Complex provisions allowed landlords to remove limits from units they owned when rents reached certain thresholds, and landlords could boost monthly charges by up to 20 percent when a tenant vacated an apartment. Another provision allowed rent increases when landlords made capital improvements. The increases were so generous in comparison to required investments, that landlords took full advantage of the program, often boosting rents beyond the ability of existing tenants to manage when they did. Evictions sometimes followed. Weak enforcement allowed unscrupulous landlords to claim large increases even when improvements did not meet standards. Lax reporting requirements made it difficult to keep track of the decline in rent-restricted apartments, but a Community Service Society study published in 2009 showed that more than half of new tenants in Manhattan south of Harlem moved into rent-restricted units in 2002, but fewer than one-third in 2008.[43]

Gentrification was a logical consequence of the city's vibrant economy between 2004 and 2008 as workers migrating to New York sought housing they could afford. *Governing* magazine assessed the pace of the trend nationwide. Its analysts identified census tracts that moved from the bottom 40 percent of the country on income and other measures, to the top third between 2000 and 2010. Thirty percent of New York's neighborhoods made the journey. As more middle-class professionals moved into impoverished communities, more private services and demand for public amenities followed. Yet, the blessing was mixed. People who had survived for years in communities with sub-optimal resources lamented undeniable improvements because they signaled changes that might force them from their homes. The influx of better-paid neighbors, "mothers with strollers that cost as much as a Chevy and their banker husbands," as Morgan Freeman's character put it in the 2015 film, *5 Flights Up*, risked pricing local residents out of places where they had long lived.[44]

The single greatest source of apartments for impoverished and near-poor residents of the five boroughs was the New York City Housing Authority. The average income of NYCHA leaseholders was roughly $23,000. Rent was capped at 30 percent of household income and averaged about $436 per month. The housing authority depended on federal and state subsidies, but it is a local agency and the mayor appointed all of the board members and controlled its operations. More than 400,000 people lived in NYCHA's 179,000 units. A half million more wanted to move in. For the vast majority of the 227,000 families and individuals on the waiting list, it was a hopeless wish. In any given year, only some 5,500 dwellings became available in "the projects," as they were called. Priority was given to victims of domestic violence, working families, and other categories; after 2005, homeless applicants were no longer included. On average, before the policy change, 1,600 families moved from shelters to NYCHA over the course of a year. Afterward it dropped to about 100.[45]

Leaders in many large cities around the country deemed federally sponsored public housing a failure. NYCHA had long been an exception. It dwarfed other programs and was one of the few big city programs that operated successfully. Most of its buildings were constructed between the 1940s and 1960s and were showing their age. Beginning in the 1960s, NYCHA depended primarily on federal subsidies to make up the difference between rental revenue and the annual cost of operations. It also received federal money for capital expenditures. Over the years, New York State and New York City also provided subsidies of lesser, but still significant amounts.[46]

By Bloomberg's second term, NYCHA faced a mounting financial crisis. The federal government's attitude toward public housing had been on a downward arc since the 1970s, and federal subsidies for NYCHA fell steadily under President George W. Bush. New York State also contributed to the problem. Its cash-welfare policies included an explicit shelter allowance that the legislature failed to adjust for inflation between 1989 and 2003. For fourteen years it was stuck at $286 for a family of three, while energy costs, salaries, pension contributions, health benefits, and other non-discretionary items drove NYCHA's operating expenses steadily higher. In 2003, the state legislature raised the shelter allowance for a three-person family to $400 per month, but the operating cost of a New York City apartment ranged upwards of $800, so a huge expense gap persisted. And New York State gave NYCHA families on public assistance reduced shelter allowances. In the late 1990s, New York State discontinued its direct support for NYCHA, and in response to the fiscal crisis the city faced in 2002 and 2003, the Bloomberg administration cut city subsidies. It also increased fees it charged NYCHA for certain services, particularly special police support.[47]

To contend with the shortfalls, NYCHA cut staff and social programs, instituted some efficiencies, and released reserves. But it was the housing authority equivalent of a cabin-bound mountain man burning the furniture to survive the winter. It was unsustainable, and by 2006 NYCHA confessed it faced a $168 million operating deficit. It had run out of ways, even ill-considered ones, to manage the rising gap on its own. In response, NYCHA developed a "Plan to Preserve Public Housing" and the Bloomberg administration provided $100 million of transitional support. The proposal was unconvincing when presented, and in any event, it failed. The American Recovery and Reinvestment Act and other Obama administration policies provided some relief, but they were temporary and insufficient. NYCHA's structural deficit—the difference between its reliable revenue stream and its operating expenses—continued to range between $50 million and $100 million annually. Its capital plan called for some $15 billion of investments and its repair log contained more than 330,000 complaints—roughly two years' worth. NYCHA administrative failures left nearly a billion dollars of federal money available for capital improvements unspent, adding embarrassment to the already difficult situation.[48]

A 2011 Boston Consulting Group study identified a range of management changes that could improve service and reduce the operating deficit, but to many analysts the essential problem was pure and simple. The authority did not have enough money to pay for its operations. The federal subsidy NYCHA depended on fell from $420 million in 2001 to $290 million in 2011 while its expenses steadily rose. Bloomberg blamed the federal government for the problem, and fearful that a commitment of additional city money would provide Washington with an excuse to cut back even more, showed little appetite for addressing the problem. It was the same approach he took with other agencies that shared authority among different branches of government.[49]

"By 2011, NYCHA reached a point where it might have qualified as the city's largest and worst landlord," the staff at the Community Service Society wrote. "The neglect was surprising given the scale of the problem," in the view of the society's senior housing analyst, Victor Bach. The ongoing crisis was clear by the time Bob Steel became deputy mayor for economic development with responsibility for the city's housing programs. In an effort to improve governance and save costs, he revamped an outdated board structure and came up with a plan to take advantage of underutilized assets. At some NYCHA locations, zoning rules allowed additional building, and at others, more space was allocated to parking than necessary. Steel proposed to make housing authority property available to builders to construct new apartments at market rates, with 20 percent reserved for affordable units. Eventually, the plan would provide NYCHA with a steady revenue stream of some $50 million or more a year. The proposal responded to what Bronx City Councilman Ritchie Torres, who grew up in a housing project, described as the only two options facing the city: "NYCHA generates more revenue, or you're condemning public housing to demolition by neglect."[50]

Yet, skeptics denounced the program as a plan to privatize public assets and enrich private developers with scant benefits for NYCHA residents. It gained no traction and Bloomberg's team withdrew it. Lack of trust seemed to be the heart of the matter. Mayor de Blasio inherited NYCHA's financial crisis. In the words of one politically astute Bloomberg-era official: "There is clearly no political will to fund [NYCHA] the way it needs to be funded," at the city, state, or federal level. "I hate to say any problem is unsolvable, because you are in government to solve problems, but I don't understand how NYCHA gets fixed given the politics."[51]

The American Dream Is Not Working . . .

By Bloomberg's third term, the debate about poverty in New York City and across the nation had shifted. Fallout from the global financial crisis and the Great Recession raised public awareness of a discussion already under way among economists and policy analysts for years. A growing school of experts believed structural flaws in the country's capitalist system were driving the rise of indigence, not specific failings of particular groups. Some local leaders and labor advocates called on the city to respond with a living-wage law. Bloomberg accused them of communism.[52]

"I've always wanted the marketplace to set the wages," Bloomberg told *Daily News* reporter Adam Lisberg the day after Labor Day, 2010, in response to a question about a living wage bill before the city council. "Government should not be in the business of doing that. The last government that tried that doesn't exist anymore. That was the Soviet Union." Discussing the issue on a radio program sometime later, Bloomberg would repeat his objection: "The last time we really had a big managed economy was the USSR and that didn't turn out so well." Something had flipped a switch in the normally pragmatic mayor.[53]

The idea of a living wage is simple. A full-time worker's salary ought to pay for life's necessities. Movements across the country between 1994 and 2006 established living wage provisions in roughly 140 locales. Coverage was in some instances extremely limited—a few dozen or a few hundred workers might qualify. Others were more expansive. Some applied to city contracts only. Some included any workers at a project that had received a public subsidy. In New York City, a 1996 initiative led by the Industrial Areas Foundation, a network of religious congregations and civic associations devoted to community organizing, secured living wage status for food service workers, security guards, office cleaners, and temporary office staff. Mayor Giuliani accused the activists of "trying to rebuild the Berlin Wall," but the city council passed the bill and overrode Giuliani's veto. The advocates did not think their aim was so grand. "We started with a pretty simple idea," one told a journalist. "If you work full time you shouldn't be poor." In November 2002, Mayor Bloomberg signed a living wage ordinance covering principally home healthcare and childcare workers employed by private companies under city contracts. It required the firms providing those services to pay their staffs a minimum of $8.60 an hour if health insurance was included and $10.10 if not. The amounts rose to $10.00 and $11.50 by 2006. Independent Budget Office analyst Doug Turetsky estimated the various provisions covered as many as sixty thousand city contract workers.[54]

In broad terms, the living wage concept was consistent with the 2006 report of the mayor's Commission for Economic Opportunity. "Playing by the rules and being rewarded for hard work must be the ticket to financial security for our city's families," the report said. It went on to lament that "an ever-widening skills gap and stubborn wage stagnation," often left honest, hardworking New Yorkers poor. "Consideration must be given to increasing household income through higher wages and tax reductions in working poor households," the report asserted. When Bloomberg announced the commission's recommendations, he acknowledged "there are some 340,000 working New Yorkers—people who regularly set the alarm clock and punch the time clock—who nevertheless live in poverty. For them, the American Dream of working your way out of poverty is not working—not yet anyway. . . . I agree with the commission that for these and other New Yorkers, we now need to make work pay."[55]

Living wage provisions tend to be highly specific and create different policy considerations than broad-based minimum wage laws, but the two are cousins in government efforts to ensure basic levels of income for low-wage workers. In general, Bloomberg viewed minimum wage laws as an undesirable government distortion of economic markets. Yet, he sometimes took a pragmatic view of them. In 2007, when Congress raised the federal minimum wage for the first time in ten years to $7.25, Bloomberg endorsed the decision. "Those that are working at the minimum wage are just, you can't possibly . . . feed your family. There is no reputable economic study that says that it would hurt . . . . Businesses will be able to absorb it and we just have to do something," he said at the time. The syntax was unartful, but the concession clear. A few years later, he would endorse a proposal to increase the state minimum wage, although he would have preferred "the federal government to act to keep us competitive."[56]

Bloomberg's 2007 comment seemed an oblique reference to a well-known study conducted by economists David Card and Alan Krueger that showed New Jersey suffered no negative consequences in employment conditions when it raised its minimum wage, even in counties bordering Pennsylvania where wages remained unchanged. Economists studying similar cases confirmed the finding repeatedly. At the low end of the wage ladder—roughly half the local median—businesses seemed able to absorb boosts of about 20 percent without an impact on employment, at least in the short term. Some studies questioned the longer-term consequences, raising concerns that minimum wage hikes would, over time, cause businesses to hire fewer workers, younger ones in particular.[57]

The topic of a living wage gained currency in New York City in 2009 as part of a redevelopment plan for the Kingsbridge Armory, a hulking structure that had been sitting more or less idle for decades in a somewhat gritty Bronx neighborhood. The Bloomberg administration sought to put the wasting asset to use and negotiated with the Related Companies to build a shopping mall there that would provide residents of the underserved neighborhood with the types of retail outlets the real estate developer had brought to the Bronx Terminal Market near Yankee Stadium a few miles south. One of the criticisms of that project was that the jobs it created were overwhelmingly low-skill, low-pay retail positions. Most offered minimum wage, weak benefit packages, and limited career paths. Local leaders formed the Kingsbridge Armory Redevelopment Alliance (KARA) to seek a different outcome for the project in their neighborhood. Discussions were under way when Bloomberg called a special election to fill a vacancy in the Bronx borough president's office, giving candidates thirty-one days to make their case to the people.[58]

On the far side of the Bronx, Assemblyman Ruben Diaz Jr. launched a blitz campaign for the vacant office. KARA's leaders met with Diaz in his campaign headquarters, and the candidate concluded their demands fit his economic platform: "projects done *with* the Bronx, not just *in* the Bronx." The issue offered Diaz a chance to broaden his appeal with voters who did not know him, and whose favor he suddenly needed. He pledged his support. By the time he won the special election, Bronx Community Board 7 had voted in favor of the shopping mall plan, with recommendations for improvements addressing neighborhood concerns. Diaz took a more aggressive stand and voted against the project to force negotiations on KARA's demands. While his opposition had only advisory status under city land-use rules, by custom, the city council respected the borough leader's wishes in such cases.[59]

Diaz invoked a simple equation when considering the topic. "If you want a public benefit to your project, then your project has to benefit the public," he said. Since the private developer would receive public support worth an estimated $50 million, applying living wage rules to the jobs created would make for a more democratic sharing of benefits. Other cities had adopted living wage rules for subsidized projects without damaging consequences, and the Bronx was the most impoverished of the city's five boroughs. Some 42 percent of its workers had low-wage jobs, compared to 31 percent citywide. Its unemployment rate at the time was 13.3 percent, the highest in the state. In the 2008 citywide customer satisfaction survey, its residents were the unhappiest with the support they received from municipal government. Its people needed the help, and felt they deserved some. Analysts ran numbers assessing the financial impact of the provisions KARA demanded and suggested some compromise was possible. Diaz "thought we could get there." Despite obvious reluctance among the city's negotiators, he had the impression all parties, including the Related Companies, were working to strike a bargain. About 11:30 p.m. the night before the city council voted on the deal—"literally the eleventh hour"— Diaz learned the city had rejected the demands.[60]

Deputy Mayor Lieber had approached Bloomberg with a plan he thought would satisfy the local politicians without placing onerous burdens on companies moving into the mall. But in the end, the mayor rejected the living wage concept outright. He declared it unacceptable government interference with the private market. "I was surprised at the intensity of the resistance," Lieber recalled. Economic Development Corporation President Seth Pinsky was surprised as well. He thought a compromise should have been possible. The amount of money involved was not that great. The mayor's position confused and disturbed the living wage advocates. From their perspective Bloomberg was plenty willing, even eager, to interfere with markets to deliver rich concessions to real estate developers. The companies involved, and the professionals who worked at them, made millions off of city assets. At the start of his second term, Bloomberg had declared reducing poverty a top priority and his economic opportunity commission had identified the working poor as a target population for action. Yet, he declined to approve a living wage policy.[61]

To Bloomberg, a bright red line was being crossed. He was no particular fan of the living wage provisions in city-service contracts that he had signed earlier, but in his mind, when the city hired outside firms to provide city-sponsored programs, the third-party companies were vehicles of convenience. It fell to the city to determine how much it was willing to pay for delivery of those services, and what the provisions of its contract should be, similar to the city negotiating directly with its own staff. If the city insisted on certain wage levels and was prepared to live with the implications for the cost of the service a living wage provision implied, that was within its contractual rights. One hoped the higher wages would attract higher caliber staff, boost morale, reduce turnover, and deliver a better program. Evidence suggested it was so.[62]

On the other hand, telling private sector companies selling their services to the public at large, on a commercial basis, what salaries they could pay, was a degree of market intervention Bloomberg would not tolerate. He felt the same way about efforts to force large employers to provide all employees with health insurance, or to provide paid sick leave, or to include same-sex partners in benefit packages even though personally he supported gay rights including same-sex marriage. Moreover, Bloomberg viewed city subsidies to promote business deals differently than his critics. To him, they were not rewards to be divided up among various participants according to some definition of fairness, but rather "catalysts." Channeling municipal assets to make a transaction happen was wise when it led to job creation and greater revenues for the city. But the catalyst was not meant to create a permanent change in the market economics that determined the prices of goods and services, or the price of labor, after the deal was done. To Bloomberg, a government decision to impose a wage level on certain private sector employers related to a specific project constituted central planning, a highly undesirable feature of communism and an integral reason for its failure as an economic system.[63]

Beyond Bloomberg's philosophical outlook, or perhaps because of it, he believed the living wage subsidy would have tangible negative consequences at the Kingsbridge Mall. In theory, fewer workers would be hired, fewer jobs created. He feared the higher cost of opening an outlet in the Kingsbridge Mall would make it uncompetitive with alternate sites—opening up across the street, for example, where the living wage would not apply. That would deter companies from locating in the mall, effectively punishing the Related Companies for doing business with the city. The overall message to businesses would be that that New York was becoming less friendly for commerce. He feared the precedent it would set.[64]

Economic literature on the market impact of living wage provisions was mixed, but the weight of the evidence supported the advocates' view that Bloomberg's concerns were overblown. The effects on employment and growth were statistically insignificant according to one nationwide study that compared conditions in fifteen cities with living wage provisions to sixteen similar cities without them. But credible economists presented studies that left the issue in doubt. In a 2004 paper prepared for the National Bureau of Economic Research, Jared Bernstein, senior economist at the Economic Policy Institute, concluded, "supporters and opponents can both point to studies that support their cause." In the end, the city council rejected the administration's Kingsbridge Armory plan because it did not include a living wage provision, and they overrode Bloomberg's veto of their decision by a vote of forty-eight to one. The development died.[65]

The tensions surrounding a living wage captured in narrow gauge a broader controversy that spread across the country in the aftershock of the 2008 collapse of financial markets. The general population began to take serious note of income inequality and the concentration of wealth. In the years before the recession began, the richest 10 percent of households kept nearly half of America's income; the top 1 percent about 20 percent. The richest 1 percent of Americans controlled more of the nation's wealth than the bottom 90 percent of Americans combined. The American economy and New York City's had grown throughout the 1980s, 1990s, and during the early years of the twenty-first century, but only a sliver of people had benefited significantly.[66]

Mark Levitan, who became the director of research at the Center for Economic Opportunity, identified the problem with respect to poor New Yorkers in an article he co-authored with Susan Weiler. "Despite gains in employment, income and educational attainment, New York City experienced a rise in poverty from 1969 to 1979 and a continued high rate from 1979 to 1999," the authors wrote. Demographic changes explained part of the problem, but "dwarfing the impact of the demographic changes . . . was a dramatic increase in income inequality from 1979 to 1999 driven by a widening disparity in wages," they concluded. Their assessment of New York City mirrored studies of national trends. The policy implications were significant. "Our findings support the view that fewer New Yorkers would be poor if more of them lived in working two-parent families," the authors wrote, addressing the demographic component of their research. But "any comprehensive effort to address poverty in New York, and the nation, cannot ignore the need for labor market policies that raise earnings for workers on the lower rungs of the wage ladder." Wage theft made things even worse. A report by the National Employment Law Project in 2010 indicated more than half of New York City's low-wage employees were cheated out of earnings on a regular basis. In some cases employers did not pay overtime. Some restaurants paid no wage at all to waiters and waitresses, leaving them to rely entirely on tips, in violation of the law.[67]

Wage stagnation and income inequality affected New York's middle class as well. The average income in New York City was way higher than the average across the country, but the median—the income level that the same number of New Yorkers fell below or above—slightly lagged the national level. Between 1975 and 2007, wages adjusted for inflation rose 1.1 percent in Queens, 1.7 percent in Brooklyn, 2.5 percent in Staten Island, and 8.6 percent in the Bronx. In Manhattan, they rose 96 percent over the same period. Manhattan's millionaires and billionaires were what drove New York's average income so much higher than the median, and Manhattan's wealth drove city prices up for a range of everyday needs. Telephone service in New York cost twice what it cost in San Francisco, groceries cost more than anywhere in America except Hawaii, gasoline and utility prices were among the highest in the nation. In the third quarter of 2008, just over 10 percent of the homes in the New York City region were deemed affordable for someone earning the median income of $48,631. The comparable figure for Chicago was nearly 50 percent, and over 70 percent for Atlanta. A New Yorker needed over $123,000 to match the lifestyle of a Houston resident making $50,000. New York's middle class found it increasingly difficult to live in Bloomberg's luxury city. "I can't vote for Bloomberg again," a middle-class resident of Queens told a reporter just before the 2005 election. "He hasn't done anything to make it less expensive to live here."[68]

The trajectory for improvement was mixed. Bloomberg had taken measures to support development of a range of high-value-added industries other than financial services. But redirecting an economy the size of New York City's takes time. Of the top ten job categories analysts expected to grow the most between 2009 and 2014, only two—nurses and executive secretaries—were expected to pay salaries above $28,000. The number-one growth sector, retail salesperson, offered $20,690 for a full-time worker, well below the poverty level for an adult with children. By 2014 evidence suggested that Bloomberg's long-term perspective was paying off. The Independent Budget Office projected robust job growth in the years following Bloomberg's reign, much of it in mid-range positions paying $50,000 to $100,000 and above, with just 30 percent coming from low-wage sectors. But during the last years that Bloomberg governed, nearly half the jobs created were on the bottom tier.[69]

To free-market champions, the price of labor set by supply and demand accurately reflected an individual's economic contribution. That outlook on life made it only logical that those who ran swiftest in capitalism's most competitive arena—Wall Street—would sit atop the highest piles of gold. That was what justified the $139 million in compensation Richard Grasso, chief executive of the New York Stock exchange, received in 2003, not including a $40 million special bonus. It was the logic that justified Bloomberg's income, estimated by one analyst in 2006 at roughly one billion times more than the $1 he received for serving the city—92 cents after payroll taxes, he liked to remind people. The number probably rose to over $2 billion by 2013, although the company remained privately owned so few knew for sure. Bloomberg's net worth would exceed $30 billion by the time he left office. A 2016 estimate would peg it at over $40 billion.[70]

Economic theory argued that laborers who received small wages were being rewarded at the level their production justified. Productivity improvements in the years between World War II and 1970 had been shared between owners of capital and labor with workers gaining ground. Since then, workers received almost none of the gains. The incremental benefits went overwhelmingly to the rich and especially to the very rich. By 2012 the purchasing power of the federal minimum wage had fallen to its lowest level in fifty years. The implications of businesses paying employees less than it cost to live came under scrutiny. If people with full-time jobs earned so little they were eligible for housing assistance, earned-income tax credits, childcare support, and food stamps, it meant taxpayers were propping up business profits, analysts asserted. Programs meant to support people in times of need and to boost people out of poverty had become *de facto* permanent business subsidies required to make up for substandard wages. The 1.9 million New Yorkers on food stamps by 2013 captured the scale of the problem.[71]

The 99%

By 2011 many people around the country and the world were fed up, New Yorkers no less than others. Many banks laid off staff and shareholders suffered losses in the first two years of the financial crisis, but the senior executives in charge still awarded themselves big bonuses. In *Rolling Stone* magazine, Matt Taibbi captured the public mood when he described Goldman Sachs as a "great vampire squid wrapped around the face of humanity, relentlessly jamming its blood funnel into anything that smells like money." Bloomberg defended the financial industry, so important to the city's economy and to Bloomberg LP.

Incredulously, he absolved his company's clients of any responsibility for the meltdown. "It was not the banks who created the mortgage crisis," Bloomberg told a crowd in November 2011 at a panel discussion with former mayors Koch and Dinkins. "It was, plain and simple, Congress who forced everybody to go and give mortgages to people who were on the cusp." To *New York Times* journalist Michael Powell, Bloomberg sounded like "a man trapped inside his 1 percent golden roost," unable to transcend his class. Powell pointed out that the Government Accountability Office came to a drastically different conclusion than Bloomberg did after careful research on the subject. So did economists at the Federal Reserve Bank. In his memoirs, Federal Reserve Board chairman Ben Bernanke wrote, "With inadequate oversight, greedy and unethical lenders had made hundreds of thousands of bad mortgage loans. Those loans would ultimately expose the vulnerabilities of a fragile financial system."[72]

Evidence surfaced of conflicts of interest at ratings agencies, fraud at mortgage financing companies, and conspiracies by banks to manipulate interest rates and foreign exchange markets. Large fines were leveled against the offending institutions, effectively punishing unwitting shareholders, but very few financial executives were prosecuted or jailed. Protests sprouted around the world. They coincided with the popular movements of the Arab Spring that toppled governments in Tunisia, Egypt, and elsewhere, demonstrating the power of direct action democracy. A Canadian countercultural group published ads that called on people to occupy Wall Street.[73]

Activists declared September 17, 2011 the day for action. Early that morning, they pitched their tents in Zuccotti Park, across the street from Chase Manhattan Bank. It was a private space, and arcane local ordinances left police with no basis for action without a request from the owner. "We are the 99%," the occupiers declared, contrasting themselves with the 1 percent who had accumulated such a disproportionate share of the country's economic growth over the past generation. The group, heavily populated with anarchists and socialists, governed itself with an ambiguous mix of general assemblies and experienced organizers. It denounced income inequality and corporate corruption of the political process, but arrived at no consensus regarding formal demands. The movement was a "voice" and an "experience" in the words of some participants who claimed to speak for it. The protests attracted media attention and it became apparent that the fringe movement reflected the emotions of a much broader population than the activists in the park. Similar protests emerged in cities across the country and in financial capitals across Europe and elsewhere.[74]

Bloomberg reacted initially with aplomb. "People have a right to protest, and if they want to protest, we'll be happy to make sure they have locations to do it," he declared. He was equally clear that he did not support the group's message or tactics. Relying on social media, the movement created traffic snarling protests at locations around Manhattan. Occupy became a matter of daily concern to the mayor and his public safety team. Deputy Mayor Howard Wolfson tried to negotiate with the group, but no one seemed to be in charge, and in any case the demonstrators were uninterested in talking with him. The occupation endured for nine weeks with all of the tragicomic street theater that occurs between police and demonstrators during mass protests.[75]

Generators and fuel tanks appeared at the site to provide electricity and to power cooking facilities. The private owner, Brookfield Properties, expressed worries to the city about the developments. In the early morning hours of November 15, 2011, on Mayor Bloomberg's orders, a large police contingent assembled by the Brooklyn Bridge about 1:00 a.m. and traveled in vans the few blocks to the park. They secured the area around the campers denying access to anyone, including journalists, and a helmet-clad police captain ordered the activists to "immediately remove all private property" from the park on the ground that they had turned it into a health and safety hazard. The city would allow the protestors to return, he said, but not to pitch tents, install equipment, and sleep there, because it made the park unusable for anyone else.[76]

Most of the demonstrators refused to leave, and one by one police officers arrested 142 people and removed them, for the most part without incident. Police arrested another 50 to 60 people on the streets nearby. Activists took the city to court the same day, but a judge ruled the action well within legal bounds. Some in the press cried foul even though the NYPD action was more restrained than similar police operations elsewhere. In Oakland, the police used tear gas to disperse occupiers, creating cries of brutality and widespread hostility toward that city's mayor. Protests followed in New York and elsewhere for a time, but the movement had run its course. Public opinion polls made it clear many New Yorkers' sympathies lay with the protestors and thought the city's reaction heavy-handed. Not the people who lived and worked in the neighborhood, however. Journalists saw pedestrians walking by the park the day after the police cleared it, flashing patrolmen the thumbs-up as they passed.[77]

Bloomberg's personal profile made him uniquely unsuited to deal with the occupiers. People were angry at Wall Street bankers and politicians. Bloomberg of course had been both. Income inequality was the focal point of the protests. Bloomberg was the richest man in New York City. "There is no easy answer," he told journalists at one point. "But there is a right answer and the right answer is to allow people to protest, but at the same time to enforce public safety . . . and quality-of-life issues, and we will continue to do that." He emphasized his disagreement with the occupiers and in the same breath his sympathy for their right to protest. "My personal view is, why don't you get out there and do something about the things that you don't like, create the jobs that are lacking, rather than just yell and scream," he told a reporter. Yet, he also said, "There's nobody that's more of a defender of the First Amendment than I am." It was an exaggerated claim to be sure, but Bloomberg found a better balance responding to the occupiers than many other politicians.[78]

The financial crisis reduced the concentration of wealth and income inequality for a short time since rich people lost more money and income than others. But the federal stimulus program and the Federal Reserve Bank's extraordinary measures caused assets to recover and the incomes at the top of the economic ladder to surge upwards again. In 2012, the highest paid 20 percent of New Yorkers earned more than twenty-six times the poorest 20 percent. In Manhattan, the numbers were still more unbalanced. The top 20 percent earned forty-two times what the poorest 20 percent made in 2012, the highest level of inequality of any county in the nation. Measured by the Gini coefficient, a statistical calculation economists use to calibrate income inequality, poor New Yorkers fell further behind rich New Yorkers while Bloomberg governed, more or less in proportion with the rest of the country.[79]

Toward the very end of Bloomberg's third term a French economist named Thomas Piketty, who spent several years teaching and studying at the Massachusetts Institute of Technology, published a book called *Capital in the Twenty-first Century*. The long, deeply researched study became a surprising best-seller on both sides of the Atlantic. The book provides extensive evidence that since the industrial revolution, the return on capital has been greater than the economic growth rate in the rich countries of the world. That meant that wages typically lagged behind. Even in a low-growth environment, also typical for most of post-industrial history, over extended periods of time, an enormous concentration of wealth developed. It explained the state of the industrial world at the end of the nineteenth-century in Europe, the United States, and Japan, when robber barons in America and aristocracies elsewhere dominated national economies.[80]

The have-nots had begun to make their dissatisfaction known with reform movements on both sides of the Atlantic when World War I, the Great Depression, and World War II destroyed enormous amounts of wealth. Economic discontent and political unrest led to highly progressive income and estate taxes, labor laws and the rise of unions, national healthcare, public housing initiatives, and other policy decisions across the rich countries of the world. After World War II, global economic predominance fueled higher growth rates than historic norms in the United States, and countries in Europe and Japan rebuilt their devastated economies at a much faster rate than their original development. The combination of progressive economic policies and rapid growth caused wages to grow faster than the return on capital for several decades. It led economists, most notably Nobel Prize winner Simon Kuznets, to believe that an increasingly skilled and educated workforce using ever-more-sophisticated technology would receive steadily higher wages. Everyone actively engaged in the workforce would do better, optimistic economists believed. Income inequality would diminish somewhat, and in any event remain within socially acceptable bounds.[81]

It was so for a time, and then it was not. During the 1960s and 1970s income and estate tax rates in rich countries dropped dramatically, social welfare support ceased to grow, union strength diminished, and by the 1980s the belief that virtually any government regulation of markets damaged a country's economy took hold. Growth continued at a rapid pace for a while, but the benefits once again accrued to a narrow elite as they had in the eighteenth and nineteenth centuries. By the dawn of the twenty-first century, concentrations of wealth and income inequality had returned to the levels of late-nineteenth-century Europe and 1920s America. Increasing numbers of workers in the rich world found they benefited little from economic growth. Many discovered that even working full-time, they could not reach a basic standard of middle-class life.[82]

Piketty took note of the political implications of a social structure that created such enormous concentrations of economic power. It would lead to a system, he surmised, where the very rich would control the political process.[83]

Chapter Nine
The Politics of a Billionaire Mayor

Bloomberg's wealth allowed him to manage the politics of the mayor's office differently from any of his predecessors. All the rest needed other people's money to win City Hall and stay there. Bloomberg financed his own campaigns, affording him unmatched independence. Yet, his vast wealth did not eliminate conflicts, it reversed their direction, as historian Fred Seigel has put it. Bloomberg outspent his rivals many times over, disbursed hundreds of millions of dollars of philanthropy that bought loyalty, and deployed the resources of an incumbent mayor with exceptional skill. The combination made him a formidable candidate. Unpopular decisions early in his first term made him appear vulnerable partway through it. Economic recovery and shrewd politicking allowed him to win a landslide victory for a second term. His bold ambition caused him to seek a third, even though New Yorkers had twice voted convincingly to limit city elected officials to two terms.

Not Feeling the Love

Like most newly elected politicians, Bloomberg enjoyed a honeymoon. His approval rating in February 2002 was 65 percent, and still 57 percent in July after his first round of budget negotiations. In November of his first year, a charter reform proposal he backed won, an indication of sorts that voters trusted his judgment. The new provision affirmed the role of the public advocate as acting mayor if the incumbent were incapacitated, but instead of serving for the remainder of a term in progress, the period was limited to just sixty days, followed by a special election. A few weeks after that vote, Bloomberg proposed a 25 percent property tax rate increase along with other revenue-raising measures, and his romance with voters turned to tears. Just 41 percent approved of his performance following the announcement, less than the 46 percent who told pollsters they did not like the way the mayor did his job. After budget negotiations in July 2003, nearly twice as many people disapproved of the mayor as favored him, 60 percent versus 31 percent. Only 24 percent would have reelected him. It was the lowest level of support for a mayor since David Dinkins's unhappiest days. Bloomberg's decision to raise taxes to help balance the budget rather than rely on fiscal gimmicks and quality-of-life damaging service cuts was good for the city, but bad for him. It required conviction and courage. Bloomberg did what he believed was right and took the hit.[1]

In August 2003, a power failure that started in Michigan and Ohio spread into Canada and across the northeast United States. The largest blackout in history arrived in New York City with startling swiftness. Bloomberg demonstrated deft emergency management skills. "Since 4:11 p.m. Thursday, Mayor Bloomberg has emerged as a highly visible and unifying figure in a city shaken by its sudden loss of electricity, subways and normal daily routines. He has sought to project calm in the face of adversity. He has sought to convey toughness at the very hint of lawlessness," *New York Times* reporter Winnie Hu wrote of the mayor. The *Times* editorial board agreed, describing Bloomberg as leading "the city relatively unscathed through a situation rife with potential disaster. He did it with a reasoned calm that was commanding, catching and for those fortunate enough to have a working television, seemingly omnipresent." But when the Quinnipiac University Polling Institute surveyed New Yorkers a few weeks after the power companies switched the lights back on, director Maurice Carroll discovered, "Bloomberg is still in the approval basement, and voters say almost 3 to 1 they want a new mayor."[2]

That November, New Yorkers crushed a charter reform Bloomberg championed. Seventy percent voted against the proposal to replace the city's deeply ingrained party primary system with nonpartisan elections, an approach followed by forty-one of the fifty largest municipalities in the United States. The measure was designed to reduce the influence of party bosses and to give voters who were not registered Democrats more influence in a city where the dominant party's primary often determined the outcome of general elections. Bloomberg had long believed in the nonpartisan approach, and he had promised to pursue it when he won the support of the Independence Party. He tried to place the referendum on the ballot in 2002 when a race for governor brought a mass of voters to the polls, but opponents blocked it. It appeared in 2003 when only a few local contests were in play, so turnout was low and skewed toward party loyalists, who opposed the change. Some New Yorkers feared that it would boost the ability of super-rich candidates, like the mayor himself, to dominate political outcomes, and resented Bloomberg's investment of millions of dollars of his own money in favor of it. In some respects, the rejection was personal. "Voters appeared to have made the decision, at least in part, based on their feelings about Mr. Bloomberg," Jonathan Hicks wrote in the *New York Times*.[3]

In 2004, at the end of August, the Republican National Convention came to New York. Hosting a political party's self-congratulatory celebration of its presidential candidate is always a public relations coup. It shines a bright light on the national standing of a city and its mayor, and the attention and hoopla it brings with it generates millions of tourist dollars. Immediately after his election, Bloomberg's team began lobbying hard for the Republicans to hold their convention in New York as part of the campaign to assert the city's post-9/11 resilience. Kevin Sheekey left City Hall officially in 2003 to dedicate himself virtually full-time to the effort. The symbolism of the decision suited incumbent President George W. Bush since it provided him with a stage at Madison Square Garden, just a few miles north of the World Trade Center site, where he could declare his post terror-attack leadership kept the country safe.[4]

It was the first time in the nation's history that New York hosted the Republican convention. There was a reason. Democrats had long outnumbered Republicans in the city. Seventy percent of New Yorkers disapproved of President Bush on the eve of the event, and many objected to the wars he had launched in Afghanistan and Iraq. Only the significance of 9/11 created a rationale for the GOP to hold its convention in politically hostile territory. The NYPD braced itself for an even larger wave of protests than normally accompany political conventions. It sent investigators around the country and around the world eighteen months in advance to spy on organizations it feared might disrupt the event. Undercover officers gathered intelligence on a small number of groups contemplating illegal action, and a much larger number of people preparing to protest peacefully against war and other policies they found offensive.[5]

On the Sunday before the convention began, several hundred thousand people, organized by a coalition called United for Peace and Justice, marched past Madison Square Garden. Disturbances were minor and the NYPD earned praise. Later in the week, things changed. The most controversial confrontations occurred when police reacted to protests in several locations by rounding up everyone in the vicinity with orange nets normally used to fence off construction sites, and arresting them all. Perpetrators of illegal acts, peaceful demonstrators, and innocent bystanders alike—more than 1,800 in total—were removed to Pier 57 on the far west side of Manhattan. The onetime Maritime and Aviation building was by then an abandoned bus depot pressed into service by the NYPD as a temporary jail. Porta-potties were the only concession to sanitary norms or comfort.[6]

The police, facing what intelligence chief David Cohen called a "tripartite threat of international terrorism, anarchist violence and widespread civil disobedience," learned through public sources that protestors had been told to carry false identification to frustrate efforts to keep track of them. As a consequence, the police insisted on processing and fingerprinting every detainee, a practice untypical for the sort of mass arrest that occurred. In many instances more than twenty-four hours passed between the time of detention and the time of release, violating the law. In the end, 90 percent of the cases were dismissed, but not before hundreds of detainees felt their rights had been compromised. Lawsuits followed, and a federal appeals court ruled the NYPD had broken state law and breached the Fourth Amendment. Nearly a decade after the convention, during Bloomberg's final days in office, the city finally agreed to an $18 million settlement covering almost all the individual and class action cases the event caused. When added to more than $16 million the city spent defending itself, the episode cost taxpayers almost $35 million.[7]

Not long after the Republicans left town, Bloomberg's reelection campaign began in earnest. The first checks under the property tax rebate that Bill Cunningham and Marc Shaw devised went out to virtually every private homeowner in October 2004 with the mayor's name in four different places— on the envelopes, on the stationery of the cover letter, in the signature block, and on the check itself. The $400 each homeowner received spoke for itself, as money always does. But "symbolically," Ed Skyler thought it sent a message that Bloomberg understood New Yorkers had been through hard times, and "now that we have a little bit of a surplus, we can give some back." It was meant to demonstrate that he was not so out of touch as critics claimed. Bloomberg's approval rating had generally been trending up for a time by then. Shortly after mailing more than $250 million to over 650,000 homeowners, 49 percent of New Yorkers liked how Bloomberg handled his job. Yet, they still told pollsters that they believed former Bronx borough president Fernando Ferrer cared about people like them more than Bloomberg-the-billionaire did, and that they preferred Ferrer for mayor.[8]

Kevin Sheekey moved to Bloomberg's reelection campaign full-time in November 2004. Bill Cunningham followed in March 2005. Doug Schoen built on the work he did in 2001 as Bloomberg's chief pollster. In an unprecedented tactic, he would survey virtually every likely voter in the city, identify issues that resonated with highly refined demographic groups, and segment them for targeted messages. It was a conscious effort to reach beyond party, race, and ethnic heritage as driving forces in voting decisions to appeal to people's interests in a far more precise manner. "It's the difference between going from X-ray machines to M.R.I.'s," Cunningham said of the more advanced process. As in 2001, Bloomberg declined to sign on for the city's public funding rules for campaign finance, and he set no budget. He expected his team to take every possible measure to make sure he won.[9]

Bloomberg would claim, with some justification, that he did his job without regard to public opinion. He held a simplistic view of democracy. The voters elected him to run the city, and it was up to him to do what he thought was right. If the people disapproved, then they could vote him out of office when he came up for reelection. The approach suited Bloomberg's temperament and followed easily from years as the chief executive of a company he owned. Yet, there was a difference. If Bloomberg LP did well, the owner received the benefits automatically. If things went well for the city, the mayor only benefited if people attributed the success to him. In November 2004, that was the crux of the matter. A strong majority of New Yorkers—nearly 60 percent—thought the city was heading in the right direction, but fewer than half approved of Bloomberg. Making sure the mayor got credit for the good things happening in New York became the thrust of the reelection campaign.[10]

"The progress we're making in reforming our schools, reviving our economy, driving crime down, and in enriching our quality of life didn't just happen. It's a product of independent leadership, a commitment to the kind of government New Yorkers deserve," Bloomberg said in his January 2005 State of the City Address, entitled "Building a City of Opportunity." He delivered it at Hostos Community College in Fernando Ferrer's home borough of the Bronx, where he acknowledged local heroes, surrounded himself with flags and patriotic words, paid homage to the city's ethnic groups, and spoke a few words of Spanish, as best he could. In her *New York Times* column, Joyce Purnick lamented that "the once defiantly apolitical business executive" had learned to play the game. Politics would drive many of the mayor's decisions and statements in the months leading up to the election, even as he continued to hold on with stubborn courage to some unpopular initiatives he deemed important.[11]

The Challengers

While Bloomberg set out to persuade the city he deserved credit for its positive direction, rivals maneuvered for position. None doubted the mayor would mount a formidable campaign, but there was a sense that Bloomberg's 2001 election had been a fluke. The extraordinary impact of 9/11 was a once in a lifetime event, and the hero status it bestowed on Rudolph Giuliani had faded. He no longer had the power to catapult a candidate into office. The candidates recognized the self-destructive nature of the unintentional race riot the Democrats waged in 2001, and were determined not to repeat it. Registered Democrats continued to outnumber other party members by huge margins, and polls revealed a vulnerable mayor. Fernando Ferrer, Council Speaker Gifford Miller, Manhattan Borough President Virginia Fields, and Congressman Anthony Weiner, whose district straddled Brooklyn and Queens, prepared to challenge Bloomberg. All agreed to abide by the city's rules for candidates to be eligible to receive public funds. Except for Weiner, all would wage primary campaigns that diminished their standing.[12]

Ferrer hoped to reassemble the coalition that nearly won him the Democratic nomination in 2001. An early March 2005 Quinnipiac poll showed him leading all Democrats and ahead of Bloomberg, 47 percent to 39 percent. His position changed abruptly after he spoke to a group of police sergeants in the Bronx. One asked Ferrer if he still maintained that the Bronx district attorney had been right to charge the officers who shot Amadou Diallo with murder. Ferrer had been one of the public officials most active in denouncing the tragedy. In a long and somewhat rambling answer, he described the decision as an attempt to "overindict." A firestorm of criticism followed. The comment was at such odds with his earlier posture that it "short-circuited" Ferrer's narrative and followed him throughout the campaign, according to Roberto Ramirez. Journalists wrote that it fit a pattern of flip-flopping they detected in Ferrer, adopting more conservative positions some years, and more liberal ones in others to suit the politics of the moment. Ferrer remained the Democratic front-runner despite the self-inflicted wound, but by a diminished margin. After the episode, he adopted a low-key posture designed to avoid controversy. Privately, he spoke by telephone with Amadou Diallo's mother and told her he was sorry for his careless comment. She was the one person he felt he owed an apology.[13]

The damage Ferrer did to himself, among blacks in particular, worked to the advantage of Manhattan Borough President Fields, the only African American in the race, and the only woman. As Ferrer's numbers fell in March, hers rose. In an effort to broaden her appeal, Fields's election team produced a flier that showed her in the midst of a diverse group of New Yorkers. But it turned out the piece was Photoshopped. If the politician was truly a champion of diversity, many asked, why couldn't she find an authentic photo to use? Fields and Joe Mercurio, a veteran New York City political strategist advising her, ended up in a public tiff on the matter. Fields fired Mercurio, or he quit, and in any event the episode made the borough president look like an amateur. Her strong support among African Americans kept her in second place ahead of Miller and Weiner through most of the race, but she never did regain traction.[14]

Council Speaker Gifford Miller got into trouble when his staff spent $1.6 million of city council money, almost the entire budget set aside for all fifty-one members to communicate with their districts, on a mailing that featured him. The transparent use of public money to promote the speaker's candidacy called into question his judgment and his integrity. Clumsy efforts by his staff to deny the scale of the problem compounded it. Miller raised money effectively and campaigned energetically, but despite generally high marks for his hard work and intelligence in the second most powerful job in city government, he had never won an election bigger than his council district. In June 2005, a majority of New Yorkers were unfamiliar with his name according to a confidential poll commissioned by Ferrer's team.[15]

Anthony Weiner alone among the Democrats ran a campaign that captured voters' imaginations. He pledged to cut taxes for small businesses and the middle class, raise them on incomes over $500,000, hire more police, and make it easier for small businesses to afford health insurance. He told the voters Bloomberg was about money and that he was about ideas. The policies he offered were designed to make him the champion of middle-class voters like the ones he represented in Brooklyn and Queens. He was the only Jewish Democrat in the race, and the candidate most likely to appeal to Italian, Irish, and other non-Hispanic Catholics.[16]

By the middle of July, the Democratic race turned into two contests. Ferrer led Fields in the competition for black and Latino votes. Weiner and Miller vied for whites. In the third week of August, an increasingly aggressive Weiner launched a series of television ads and surged in the polls. One survey showed him in a head-to-head tie with Ferrer, the two contenders with 30 percent of the vote each, far ahead of their fading rivals. On primary day, election gods toyed with Ferrer. The Election Board declared he won 39.949 percent of the vote, a sliver shy of the 40 percent needed to avoid a runoff. Weiner polled 29 percent. Fields came in third and Miller fourth. For twelve hours city Democrats braced themselves for a party-bruising runoff. But after consultation with Senator Charles Schumer, a longtime Weiner mentor, the runner-up dropped out. For a few days more after Weiner exited, confusion reigned. Election law required the runoff take place whether Weiner wanted it or not. Publicly, Democrats sweated. Privately, Ferrer claims he did not. The veteran politician had assessed the voting pattern on primary day and concluded the official count would put him over the top. His confidence proved apt. The Board of Elections completed their recount and declared Ferrer the winner with 40.15 percent of the votes.[17]

Turnout for the Democratic primary had been low. The race had been unusually civil, possessed of none of the divisive drama that ripped the Democrats apart four years before. Ferrer won a strong majority of Latino voters, and outside of Virginia Fields's Manhattan home base, a higher proportion of African American voters than he won in 2001 despite the Diallo dust-up. He won between three and four times the paltry 7 percent of white votes he polled in 2001 when racial hostility characterized the campaign. The number of white Catholics casting ballots was particularly low, the absence of one of their own on the ballot eliminating one of the reasons people go to the polls. The other explanation, more ominous for Ferrer, was that they expected to vote for Michael Bloomberg in the general election and saw no point in picking a Democrat they planned to abandon.[18]

The Advantages of an Incumbent Billionaire

While Democrats engaged in primary battle, Bloomberg made sure he would not face one among Republicans. Former Queens city council member Thomas Ognibene mounted a challenge and submitted the signatures required by New York State election law to qualify for a primary. Bloomberg's team challenged their validity and knocked him out of the race. The year before, during the 2004 Republican presidential primary in New York, Bloomberg had denounced the arcane tactic when opponents tried to use it against his friend, Senator John McCain. "It's time to end this 'gotcha' kind of technique where lawyers comb petitions to find some technical violation," he said at the time. When asked about it in 2005, he declared, "The law is the law. You either follow the law or you don't."[19]

Bloomberg had become the chief benefactor of the Independence Party, which delivered fifty-nine thousand votes for him in 2001, more than his margin of victory. In 2004 he contributed $250,000 to the organization, and in 2005 it endorsed him. Lenora Fulani remained a member of the party's executive committee and her unapologetic history of anti-Semitic rants surfaced again. Bloomberg's opponents tried to tie him to her bigoted remarks, with little success. He denounced the comments, and pointed out that if candidates refused to accept party nominations from organizations that included people who said offensive things, all of them would be off limits. The controversy swirled for a time and finally the party removed Fulani and five allies from leadership positions.[20]

On the sorts of issues that typically matter in mayoral campaigns, Bloomberg "had a record, and the record was very good," according to Ed Skyler. "Any time there was a trade show, or a convention, cultural [events] or sports, anything . . . that reestablished New York's role as a vibrant city, a safe city, a place where people wanted to do business, that was a validator of his record, and we promoted the heck out of those things." By 2005 the economy was growing, and crime was shrinking. There had been little of the high-profile racial violence that marred his three predecessors' terms in office, and Bloomberg had handled the episodes that occurred with tension defusing tact. Everyone agreed the school system remained in crisis, and Democratic challengers cited dismal statistics designed to call the mayor's management of it into doubt. But they failed to provide persuasive cases that they could do better. Bloomberg had secured control and shut down the local school boards that most recognized as disastrous. New Yorkers were inclined to accept that the mayor had a plan, and they were "prepared to give him more time," Skyler recalled. In September 2005, by a margin of 52 percent to 32 percent, voters approved of Bloomberg's education record.[21]

In May, the council approved the mayor's rezoning plan for the Brooklyn waterfront, a headline-generating victory. By contrast, the West Side stadium proposal remained unpopular. Even New Yorkers who favored hosting the Olympics thought committing a huge amount of public funds to a sports arena a mistaken priority. The mayor stood by the controversial plan, even in an election year. Detractors used the optics it created to support accusations that Bloomberg's development strategy favored Manhattan while ignoring the rest of the city. The mayor refuted the accusations forcefully, challenging his critics to name another mayor who invested $2 billion in the other boroughs. Independent assessments by the Regional Plan Association and the Center for an Urban Future validated his claims. Fortunately for Bloomberg, the stadium issue became irrelevant when state legislative leaders killed the project in June 2005. Deputy Mayor Doctoroff, Bloomberg and his team, were disappointed because they put so much effort into the project, but politically, his campaign team knew "it was a win." The lack of progress at Ground Zero captured press attention from time to time during 2005, embarrassing everyone involved. Governor Pataki, the Port Authority he controlled, and private developer Larry Silverstein attracted most of the blame. Bloomberg deflected criticisms by declaring he would take a more active role in the project during a second term.[22]

On other matters, Bloomberg proved politically pragmatic. Staten Island was the most heavily Republican borough. In January, the mayor announced the Department of Education would establish seven specialized and elite schools there. In March, he announced the city would build the borough a fourth police station. In April, Bloomberg agreed to a service increase for the Staten Island Ferry, a measure he vetoed the year before citing budget concerns. When he announced plans for a huge park in line with Staten Islanders' wishes at the site of the Fresh Kills Landfill, a reporter wrote: "Though the announcement was an official City Hall event for the mayor, it could easily have been mistaken for a campaign stop." In September, he announced the Metropolitan Transportation Authority would build Staten Island a third bus depot in response to demands for more service. "The decision helps to shore up Mr. Bloomberg's support in Staten Island, where strong turnout is critical for any Republican seeking city-wide office," a journalist pointed out at the time.[23]

New York is the only big American city without a major rail-freight system. Its overreliance on trucks congests its streets, pollutes the air, and adds cost to the economy. In 2004, based on an Economic Development Corporation analysis, Bloomberg endorsed construction of a federally sponsored railroad tunnel from Jersey City to Bay Ridge, Brooklyn, which would connect to a proposed trucking terminal in Maspeth, Queens. Local residents objected to the heavy traffic the project would bring to their neighborhood. In a politically motivated about-face, Bloomberg announced he opposed the tunnel at a March 2005 community meeting in nearby Middle Village, causing the crowd to respond with "boisterous cheers."[24]

Bloomberg would cede no voters easily. Ferrer had solid support among his fellow Puerto Ricans, and there was a presumed, if less certain, affinity for him among the city's rising Dominican population based on common Spanish and Caribbean heritage. In March 2005, Bloomberg appointed a special liaison from the NYPD to the Dominican Republic declaring: "The fortunes of New York City and the Dominican Republic are closely linked." When the occasion arose, he would gamely speak Spanish in an accent that often left listeners smiling with good-natured bemusement. Blacks would constitute more than 20 percent of general-election voters. Bloomberg's team took steps to weaken Ferrer's chances to forge the black-Latino coalition he sought. Early in 2005, Bloomberg traveled to the Allen AME Church in Jamaica, Queens, where its influential pastor, former Congressman Floyd Flake, endorsed him. In April, Bloomberg's campaign hired Terence Tolbert for $15,000 per month to head up operations to win African American votes. Tolbert was chief of staff to Harlem Assemblyman Kenneth T. Wright and had been responsible for mobilizing blacks in support of Senator John Edwards's Democratic presidential primary campaign in New York in 2004. It was the first time in the political veteran's twenty-year career he agreed to work for a Republican. Other strategists who normally worked for Democrats showed up on Bloomberg's payroll even though he had a fully staffed team. It was a well-funded tactic to deny expertise to potential opponents.[25]

The responsibilities of incumbency kept Bloomberg in the news. Like other mayors, Bloomberg spoke to the city every Saturday morning on WNYC, until August when campaign rules would have required the station to give his opponents equal time. When a retaining wall that supported an apartment building in upper Manhattan collapsed onto the Henry Hudson Parkway on a Thursday afternoon in May, Bloomberg was there with city engineers. He promised the road would be "back in business at an adequate level" before the Monday morning commute. "Did he really say that?" David Burney, commissioner of the city's Department of Design and Construction, who would be responsible for completing the task, thought to himself at the time. But the job got done and everyone looked good. "Let's just say he gave me all the shovels I needed," the dry-witted architect told a journalist when asked how Bloomberg had helped.[26]

At 3:00 a.m. one morning at the end of June, a group of young white men set upon three black men in Howard Beach, Queens. Two fled. One tripped and the attackers fractured his skull with a metal baseball bat, stole his sneakers, and ripped an earring from his ear. The event bore a disturbing similarity to a 1986 attack that took place just a few blocks away. In that episode, a gang of whites chased three blacks causing one to be struck by a car and killed while fleeing. It set in motion months of citywide racial acrimony. When Bloomberg learned of the 2005 event, he traveled with Commissioner Kelly to the 106th police precinct where the mayor told reporters, "The reason that we're here is that hate crimes will not be tolerated." He had already delivered the message personally to Reverend Sharpton, who led the 1986 protests. One suspect had been arrested by then and the police were on the verge of capturing the others. Queens District Attorney Richard Brown made it clear that he would prosecute the attackers vigorously. The racial atmosphere in the city had changed dramatically for the better in nineteen years. Reverend Sharpton did mount a modest protest in the neighborhood, but the ugly incident passed without the denigrating drama and political repercussions the earlier episode had caused years before.[27]

By spring of 2005, credit agencies had raised their ratings of New York City general-obligation bonds to their highest levels ever. S&P attributed the decision to "steady fiscal and economic recovery since 2001 and strong budget management by the Bloomberg administration." At the end of June, the mayor and city council approved a good-news budget that ultimately increased spending over the prior year by a whopping 12 percent, helping everyone running for reelection. The budget included a 1 percent additional wage increase for the workers of DC 37, the city's biggest union. An earlier contract provision allowed for the raise, provided productivity gains had been achieved. Election-year accounting made it so. A few weeks later the union, which had backed Ferrer in 2001, endorsed Bloomberg. The rank and file, many African Americans and Latinos among them, would vote for whomever they wanted. But the leadership's decision denied the Democrats a potent political field operation that normally worked for them, and put it to work for the mayor.[28]

Bloomberg fortified the strength of an incumbent atop a rising economy with the advantages that accrue to a billionaire. His philanthropies gave over $140 million to some 843 organizations and groups, up from 653 groups and $135 million the year before. Bloomberg's campaign released the list of the lucky winners in August 2005, just a few hours before the Democratic primary candidates held a debate. It was a transparent and successful attempt to dominate the day's news cycle. Many organizations that received Bloomberg's largesse were national or global. Many others were decidedly local. "For the fourth consecutive year, through the generosity of an anonymous donor, Carnegie Corporation is making small grants to small-and medium-sized New York City arts and social service institutions in all five boroughs that contribute to the culture, health, welfare and vibrancy of the city," the corporation's president, Vartan Gregorian, announced in July 2005. It was an open secret to anyone concerned that the anonymous donor was named Bloomberg. Some two hundred local groups received anywhere from $10,000 to $100,000 each during the year leading up to Bloomberg's reelection.[29]

Observers speculated logically that groups receiving money would be unlikely to criticize the donor, even if they disagreed with his policies, for fear they would lose financial support. The goodwill was not left entirely to chance. When a number of Manhattan arts patrons bought tickets to a Gifford Miller fund-raiser, Deputy Mayor Patricia Harris called them and "demanded to know what they were thinking." There was no need to remind the recipients that Harris was the deputy mayor responsible for dispensing city money for cultural institutions and also in charge of the mayor's philanthropic commitments. The two pools of cash, more or less equal in size, totaled over a quarter of a billion dollars a year. Bloomberg himself made some similar calls to Ferrer contributors.[30]

Bloomberg asked his friend Steven Rattner, whose firm he would later appoint to manage some of his wealth in a blind trust, to lead "Democrats for Bloomberg." Rattner was a prolific donor to Democrats at the national level, and his wife, Maureen, chaired the finance committee of the Democratic National Committee. Rattner sought public endorsements for Bloomberg from high-profile givers to Democratic causes, with two purposes in mind. One was to make it politically correct for committed Democrats to vote for Bloomberg. The other was to starve the mayor's opponents by rounding up the city's politically active elite and discouraging its members from nourishing any of the Democratic campaigns for mayor.[31]

Bloomberg and team took steps to refute accusations the billionaire was out of touch. The mayor kept his home telephone number listed in the white pages. He told New Yorkers that after rising about 5:00 a.m. on a typical day and exercising on a treadmill in his home, he rode to work by subway most mornings. He did not mention that often, a large Chevrolet Suburban, with a chase car behind, chauffeured him from his 79th Street town house to the express stop at Lexington and 59th. To refute the impression Bloomberg cared only about Manhattan, one ad featured him in an open-collared shirt, wearing a brown bomber jacket rather than his typical banker's gray pinstripes. "To build a business, you have to make smart investments," he said. "As mayor, that's what I'm doing for New York City: building infrastructure to bring jobs to long-neglected neighborhoods. A borough-by-borough plan."[32]

By May, Bloomberg led all challengers in the polls even before he started advertising. By late June he had spent $15 million, three times more than his four Democratic rivals combined. The mayor and his team "are building a tank, financially, politically, operationally," Mark Green told a journalist. And the Democratic nominee would be "like that brave Chinese student standing in front of the tank in Tiananmen Square." By July, even Democrats approved of how Bloomberg did his job by a margin of 58 percent to 32 percent. Shortly after Ferrer won the Democratic primary in September, polls showed Bloomberg beating him by fourteen to sixteen points. Some 121 Democrats actually wrote Bloomberg in as their choice for party nominee, swamping Donald Trump and Mickey Mouse who received one write-in vote each. Yet, analysts noted that Bloomberg's formidable position came at the end of a summer the mayor spent working the benefits of incumbency and spending millions—$50 million according to an early October filing—on mailings, fliers, posters, radio and television ads singing his own praises while the Democrats competed with each other. It was no surprise he led the field.[33]

A Political Juggernaut

The ghost of the self-defeating 2001 battle had kept the Democrats competing for their party's nomination for mayor on their best behavior, so their contest generated little acrimony. With a runoff avoided, and a champion to rally round, an appeal for party loyalty from national leaders to local Democrats who outnumbered Republicans by greater than five to one had the potential to change the campaign's momentum. Voters continued to say they believed Ferrer cared about people like them more than Bloomberg did, giving the challenger an opening. "I always thought Bloomberg was vulnerable," Roberto Ramirez remembered, because the Manhattan billionaire "wasn't what New York City was." Demographers reported the 2005 November general election would be the first in which non-Hispanic whites were not a majority of the New York City electorate. "Rodriguez" had become the most common name on voter registration rolls, an encouraging development for a Puerto Rican candidate. In mid-September, a Ferrer victory still seemed a possible dream. Certainly, experienced observers believed the gap would narrow.[34]

Goofy mistakes worked against Ferrer. A staff member posted a biography that said the candidate had attended New York City public schools for most of his education when primarily he was educated in Catholic institutions. Bloomberg's team spotted the gaffe and waited for just the right moment to share it with the press to distract from a Ferrer campaign event. Bill Cunningham mischievously milked the credibility-damaging error for all it was worth. "I happen to be a proud graduate of an excellent private parochial school, and I can't imagine why anyone would try to hide such a fact," he said, ascribing deceptive motivations to the mistake. Later that same week, Ferrer spoke to students in a New York

City public high school about the importance of civic duty. The event violated education department rules against politicking in its buildings. The *New York Post* gleefully printed a front-page picture of Ferrer wearing a dunce cap. A few weeks later, from inside a school, Bloomberg announced a new educational program to counter Ferrer's criticisms of his management of the system. The Ferrer team cried foul, but the incumbent was responsible for the schools, so he had cover.[35]

Bloomberg's campaign team was adept at leaking negative news to reporters. Day after day, his staff would share negative tidbits about his opponent. "You could set a clock to it," Ferrer campaign manager Nick Baldick would recall. "Stu's first shot would be at 4 p.m., his second shot would be about 5:15," he said, referring to Stuart Loesser, who worked for the Bloomberg campaign and later became the mayor's press secretary. Loesser hardly denied the claim. "We would send it out earlier," he clarified. The objective was to force the opponent's campaign team to spend its time defending its candidate, rather than delivering a message of its own. The afternoon leaks provided enough time for journalists to meet the deadlines for the nightly news or the next day's print edition, but not enough time to put to rest a matter that might be of scant consequence once all the facts were known, despite an ugly appearance at first glance. Bloomberg's team dominated the news cycle with rare skill, bumping the Democrats from the headlines time and again. It was a surround-sound strategy that all but ensured New Yorkers heard only what Bloomberg wanted them to hear, and not his opponent's message.[36]

Bloomberg continued to benefit from the power of his office in ways large and small. Twice Ferrer's team identified vacant lots in poor neighborhoods covered with trash and scheduled press conferences at them to criticize the mayor for neglect. In each instance, by the time the candidate and reporters arrived, city workers had cleaned them up. Ferrer championed a far-reaching housing program. Bloomberg announced one of his own, "adopting language strikingly similar to that used by Mr. Ferrer," a journalist reported. In October, another round of property rebate checks went out, hundreds of millions of dollars to hundreds of thousands of homeowners, just weeks before the election. In a concession to appearances, in 2005 they went out under the finance commissioner's signature rather than Bloomberg's. But his advertisements gave Bloomberg full credit for the taxpayer bounty. The mayor remained on message. "By improving our quality of life, driving down crime, attracting private investment and replacing outdated zoning laws, we are continuing to build a city of opportunity for all New Yorkers," he told voters.[37]

Education remained an important issue in voters' minds. Ferrer reminded them continuously that the city's graduation rate remained unacceptably low and accused Bloomberg of overstating it. The teachers had been working without a contract for three and a half years as the election approached. Many were angry with the mayor, and the politically potent United Federation of Teachers had made no endorsement. Ferrer hoped to gain momentum-changing late support from the union. Bloomberg's team viewed a teachers' strike as the most dangerous threat their candidate faced. In early October, the mayor and union chief Randi Weingarten came to contract terms, and her organization's political forces that typically supported Democrats remained neutral. A little later, the mayor settled contract negotiations with sanitation workers and firefighters, adding to the sense that labor relations were improving.[38]

Ferrer spent precious campaign time locked in a room making fundraising telephone calls. Often, his appeals were rebuffed by Democrats Bloomberg's team had dissuaded from supporting their party's candidate. And as the days passed, the expectation rose that Bloomberg would prevail and remain the mayor who power brokers would need to work with for the next four years. That made support for his opponent an unwise investment. Virtually every elected official in the country of both parties thought of Bloomberg as a potential campaign donor. The national Democrats who endorsed Ferrer did it ever so quietly. When former president Bill Clinton stood with his party's candidate for mayor on Charlotte Street in the South Bronx to declare his support, his staff would not allow the Ferrer team to arrange loudspeakers at the event. Reporters strained to hear the praise offered by the man whose wife would run for reelection to the US Senate in New York the next year.[39]

An "October surprise" worked to Bloomberg's advantage. Based on meager intelligence, the Department of Homeland Security alerted the city to a possible attack on New York's subways. Bloomberg declared a terror alert, and the NYPD deployed a highly visible contingent of police. At least one federal official expressed astonishment at the city's reaction. Inevitably, skeptics charged Bloomberg with "wagging the dog," deliberately overreacting to a security threat to remind voters that he was the public official they relied on to keep them safe. He dismissed the accusation out of hand, but observers took note that the October 6 announcement coincided with a mayoral campaign event at the Apollo Theater in Harlem that Bloomberg declined to attend. His announcement overwhelmed any news of it. No attack occurred, and the details of the plot that emerged suggested the idea never made it beyond the imagination of a single man in Iraq. In his 2015 memoir, Commissioner Kelly recounts sixteen foiled terrorist plots. The October 2005 event is not among them. In response to an interviewers question, he recalled that the bombing of London's transportation system on July 7, 2005—their 7/7 counterpart to New York's 9/11 disaster—made the possibility of an attack on New York's system seem plausible enough to command a response.[40]

Bloomberg took a highly public subway trip to show the trains were safe. His bravado had an impact. "After his dramatic announcement of a possible threat to the city's subway system, and coverage of Commander-in-Chief Bloomberg riding the subway, his numbers went through the roof," Quinnipiac University pollster Maurice Carroll reported on October 12, 2005. Bloomberg's lead spiked to 28 percent on the back of a security alert that would remain cloaked in doubt. "When I saw those numbers, that's when I knew I would lose," Ferrer recalled. "From that point on, my goal was to deliver a message: city government has to serve all its people. And I wanted to finish out the campaign with dignity."[41]

Meanwhile, the onslaught of advertising Bloomberg's unlimited checkbook could afford continued. In addition to English and Spanish TV and radio ads, his team aired spots on foreign language cable channels in German, Polish, Italian, Russian, Greek, Yiddish, Chinese, Korean, and Haitian Creole. His website included a feature that translated its messages into all those languages. Even for polyglot New York it was extraordinary. All four of New York's daily newspapers endorsed Bloomberg. As Election Day approached, Bloomberg's lead over Ferrer swelled to as high as 38 points according to one poll.[42]

The candidates met for two televised debates late in the campaign. Ferrer beat the mayor soundly in the first. One journalist called it, "his best day so far in his race for mayor," and wrote that Ferrer, "showed there is an alternative to the Bloomberg juggernaut in the Nov. 8 election." But the challenger's "feisty" performance delivered no knockout punch, and it came so late that many voters had already made up their minds. "I could have stood naked in Times Square at that point, and no one would have paid attention," Ferrer later lamented. On Election Day, by a margin of 59 percent to 40 percent, Bloomberg swamped his challenger.[43]

Bloomberg won 70 percent of ballots cast by white voters. He and Ferrer split black votes more or less evenly, a huge victory for a white Republican running against a Puerto Rican Democrat. Some 30 percent of Latinos cast ballots for the mayor, a credible showing against a Puerto Rican opponent. Turnout was low—some 1.2 million New Yorkers voted for mayor that year compared to 1.4 to 1.8 million in higher-turnout years. Still, the result was a huge endorsement of Bloomberg's many innovative policies and his muscular management of New York City government. The achievement was highly personal. By large margins New Yorkers reelected Betsy Gotbaum to the citywide office of public advocate, and William Thompson comptroller, both Democrats. Their party continued to dominate the city council.[44]

After paying campaign staffers generous bonuses, Bloomberg spent some $85 million dollars in his reelection effort, roughly $170 a vote. He bought an additional $140 million of good will in the year before the 2005 election with philanthropic largesse. Like any incumbent, he took credit for many millions of city government dollars spent on programs administered by the agencies he ran, including more than $250 million in tax rebates late in 2004, and again weeks before the election in 2005. He faced no primary. He used all the influence in his power to discourage New York City's Democratic elite from contributing money to his opponents. Ferrer benefited from public money, and had $14 million to spend in the four-way primary and the general election, a sum Roberto Ramirez described as "puny," in comparison to what Bloomberg spent. The mismatch made a farce of the campaign finance law's intention of neutralizing the impact of money on New York City elections. No reasonable observer could think the election fair. Ferrer understood life often is not. He conceded to Bloomberg graciously the night of the election. By 8:00 a.m. the next morning Bloomberg was at the same Brooklyn subway station he had gone to the day after his 2001 victory. He thanked passers-by for giving him a second chance to serve them. That evening during rush hour, he thanked commuters boarding the Staten Island Ferry for their support. No one could claim he had not worked for the victory.[45]

A Man for All Parties

Bloomberg had even greater ambition for his second term than he did for his first. Sound fiscal management, controlling crime, and combating terrorism remained non-negotiable imperatives of the job. He would continue to pursue school reform, bold development projects, and fundamental zoning changes. To that imposing list of priorities he added the antipoverty goals of the Center for Economic Opportunity, and the extraordinary breadth of the initiatives related to *PlaNYC,* including an enormous affordable housing program. To ensure a sense of urgency, he had a red digital clock installed in the bullpen at City Hall. Underneath a sign that read "Make Every Day Count," it ticked off the number of days remaining in Bloomberg's second term, presumed to be his last due to term limits.[46]

Most of his senior team stayed to help implement the program. Marc Shaw and Bill Cunningham, both family men with children headed for college, left government for private-sector jobs that would allow them to afford tuition payments. Peter Madonia became the chief operating officer of the Rockefeller Foundation. Despite the impressive talent pool that remained, the three who left were a significant source of the administration's knowledge and experience in city and state government affairs. Patti Harris took on the role of first deputy, exercising the mayor's powers when he traveled out of the city. In December 2007, Dan Doctoroff made plans to return to Wall Street. Bloomberg kept him within his sphere by convincing him to become president of Bloomberg LP.[47]

Edward Skyler was thirty-two years old when Bloomberg named him deputy mayor for operations at the start of his second term, a huge promotion from his press secretary job. He wanted Skyler to stay on board, and he offered him expanded responsibilities, but none of the other options they discussed appealed. Skyler made a case for himself. As press secretary, he had built relations with all of the city's commissioners. More important, he had been with Bloomberg "for every important decision for the past four years. I knew the way he thought, I knew what his values were, I knew what he expected. . . . I had pretty good attenae for what he wanted because I had watched him for years, so I was pretty comfortable I could do the job in a way that would fit him." Bloomberg was "a little reluctant" about the decision, and warned Skyler, "If things aren't working in a couple of months, I'll have to make some changes," but the young man with "something to prove" thrived in the role.[48]

Skyler worked demanding hours, focused with exceptional intensity on an exhausting array of daily responsibilities, and earned a reputation as an excellent hands-on manager. Some ninety-five thousand city employees reported up to him, including police, fire, and sanitation workers. His active engagement in labor negotiations, along with rich city budgets, improved the administration's relations with municipal unions for a time. Among other things, he helped restore the starting salary for police cadets, cut in earlier negotiations to provide money for veteran officers. Ray Kelly and Skyler both feared the decision would prevent the city from recruiting the quality officers the NYPD needed, and it risked fueling corruption. City Hall staffers took to calling Skyler "Batman" after he chased down and tackled a thief who swiped a BlackBerry from a lady on a city street one day. Irreverent journalists who knew him well privately called him "deputy mayor for bags of shit," because of the many undesirable tasks no one else wanted to touch that he cleaned up. When a steam pipe exploded near Grand Central Terminal, Skyler oversaw the repairs. When a putrid swamp of rodent-infested below-grade land in the poor Mott Haven section of the Bronx became an issue, Skyler got it drained. When workers found body parts amidst the rubble at the World Trade Center years after the attack, it was Skyler who oversaw an exhaustive search for remains.[49]

In 2008, within weeks of each other, two construction cranes fell from midtown Manhattan perches, killing nine people and wounding others. The tragedies highlighted longstanding problems in what one journalist called "the chronically dysfunctional—and sporadically corrupt—Buildings Department," intensified by a construction boom. Deaths at worksites rose from eleven in

2006 to fifteen in 2007 to twenty-five in 2008. Skyler channeled more resources to the department and hand-picked a new commissioner to reorganize it and increase its focus on reducing worksite danger. An extensive analysis by outside experts of high-risk construction safety protocols followed. Building fatalities dropped to five the next year, and stayed low for the remainder of Bloomberg's time in office. Skyler became one of Bloomberg's three most important deputies, along with Patti Harris and Kevin Sheekey.[50]

From the start, Sheekey had been part of Bloomberg's inner circle, but he had floated during much of the first term without a formal role equal to his talent or ambition. To some, he appeared "forlorn." At the start of the second term, he became deputy mayor for intergovernmental relations. In theory, that meant managing business with the city council, state government in Albany, and federal government in Washington, DC. Yet, it became evident those responsibilities would not be his priority the day after Bloomberg's landslide victory. During a live television interview, NY 1 newscaster Dominic Carter asked Sheekey about the mayor's political future. "Obviously, Bloomberg 2008—we'll roll right into the presidential as we move forward. . . . Don't you think the mayor should run for president next with his unique view on how to solve the problems in urban America?" Sheekey asked his stunned host on the air.[51]

A Democrat and experienced Washington hand, Sheekey developed strong ties with important GOP leaders during his work to bring the Republican National Convention to New York. In his well-informed judgment, Bloomberg had no chance to win the presidential nomination of either major party. He was too liberal for Republicans on emotionally charged issues like immigrants, women's rights, abortion, gay marriage, gun control, and climate change. He was too closely associated with Wall Street and too conservative on economic issues for Democratic primary voters. So Sheekey began plotting a path to the White House for Bloomberg as an independent. He floated the possibility every chance he got, declaring his boss could spend as much as he wanted—maybe a billion dollars—to become president. In December 2006, working with venture capitalist James Robinson IV, Sheekey founded a company called the Symposia Group, "expressly to support a presidential run by Michael Bloomberg." The company conducted polls and analyzed voter attitudes, and a representative claimed in an interview with *New York Sun* reporter Grace Rauh, "empirically, [Bloomberg] can win." Sheekey also organized a campaign-team-in-waiting for a national run.[52]

Doug Schoen, working on a book describing the decline of America's two-party system and the rise of independent voters, took up the cause as well. "I believe that a third-party candidate running on a platform of coherent compromise, tough-minded conciliation and candid, clear-eyed bipartisanship can achieve much to help resolve the seemingly intractable differences that exist between the two parties," he wrote. The idea was to pull disaffected voters from both major parties away from the ideological wings toward the pragmatic center. Schoen claimed his book was not meant to promote any particular candidate, but on the same page he offered that disclaimer, he wrote, "I also could not be more supportive of the work of Mayor Mike Bloomberg in New York City . . . who has put into action many of the principles outlined in the book." Bloomberg, of course, could have put an end to the speculation and preparations by uttering the single word, "stop." He did not.[53]

When reporters asked if he would run for president, Bloomberg said no. When they asked again, he replied pedantically, "What letter of no don't you understand?" Yet, he began promoting policies he pursued locally on the national stage. He declared his innovative environmental and antipoverty programs models for the country and the world. Cynics charged he had taken up those causes at the start of his second term with his national ambitions foremost in mind. He created a national group, Mayors Against Illegal Guns, to counter the influence of the National Rifle Association, and he shared his conviction on public health matters and his strategy for education reform in a range of national forums. He emphasized time and again his belief in the importance of independent, centrist political leadership, and in June 2007 dropped his Republican Party registration to declare himself an independent. Allowing himself to be talked about as a potential presidential contender was a no-lose position for Bloomberg. It enhanced his stature and, among other things, prevented him from suffering the loss of power that attends a lame duck mayor, unable to run for reelection because of term limits.[54]

Bloomberg seemed genuinely ambivalent about running for president. There is little doubt he wanted the job, but he was unconvinced any third-party candidate could succeed, and he had doubts about his personal viability. He remained an uninspiring speaker. His claim to power was competent management—entirely appropriate for the prose of governing but not to the poetry required of presidential campaigning. He laid out his own vulnerabilities in his typical blunt manner. "What chance does a short, Jewish, divorced billionaire" have on the national stage? he asked one supporter rhetorically. He was proud to be Jewish, but unreligious, and uncomfortable pretending otherwise in a country that expects its president to pray—to date only in Christian churches. He only wanted to run if he could win, and he especially did not want to become a spoiler responsible for the unintentional election of a right-wing president. One analysis suggested that the best Bloomberg could hope for was to win enough support to prevent anyone from winning the Electoral

College. That would throw the election to the House of Representatives, where the majority party would surely select its own candidate, who would be forced to govern the country with a crippled mandate.[55]

The disingenuous dance continued until February 2008 when Barack Obama won the Iowa Caucus, and then the New Hampshire primary. He began to appear less like a far-left long shot and more like a serious contender to become the nation's first African American president. His profile made him enough of a Washington outsider to keep Democrats disenchanted with their party's role in a dysfunctional national government inside the tent. John McCain, despite his many years in the senate, had a similar position as a maverick among Republicans. By the time Obama and McCain became their parties' leading candidates, the idea of an independent centrist running and winning had faded. On February 28, 2008, Bloomberg wrote in an op-ed piece in the *New York Times* that he had, "listened carefully to those who encouraged me to run, but I am not—and will not be—a candidate for president." Sheekey was not yet done. He promoted his boss for vice president. He implied Bloomberg could accept the nomination of either party and spend "between $0 and one billion dollars" on a campaign. It is not clear if the spot appealed to Bloomberg. It turned out not to matter. Neither campaign offered him the role. Bloomberg sat out the race, declining to endorse either candidate.[56]

Power, the Currency of a Billionaire's Price

"I will not go back to the company," a sixty-three-year-old Mayor Bloomberg told the *New York Times* in a 2005 interview that touched upon what life after City Hall might be like. "Eventually I will sell because if I don't my estate will have to, and I want to run a foundation," he said. The comment set off a flurry of activity among private equity investors seeking to buy Bloomberg LP. In the end, Bloomberg kept his shares, but the valuation exercises that followed revealed the company was worth $22.5 billion, far more than the estimates that circulated when its eponymous owner first ran for office. Bloomberg's 72 percent stake meant his personal wealth was about $16 billion at the time, from the company alone. Eyebrows rose at the uncomfortable reality that the mayor of New York's personal fortune seemed to explode while he was in office. In days gone by that was a sure sign of corruption. In Bloomberg's case, there was not the slightest whiff of old-fashioned impropriety. Yet, the blending of money and power, in so obvious and intense a manner, concerned people, and increasingly offended.[57]

When Bloomberg won reelection, the *New York Times* rained on his parade even though it had supported him. "In our endorsement, we said that one day Mr. Bloomberg could rank among the city's greatest mayors. The defect that threatens to overshadow all the good he has accomplished, is the obscene

254 • Bloomberg: A Billionaire's Ambition

amount of money he has spent on this reelection effort." In the midst of the 2005 campaign, the *Times* editors dressed Bloomberg down. "The sum total of the campaign budgets of all the mayor's opponents combined cannot begin to match what Mr. Bloomberg appears prepared to spend." The mismatch, by so enormous an amount, "makes him look less like a leader than a bully," they wrote.[58]

After the reality of America's two-party system crushed Bloomberg's presidential hopes by early 2008, he faced the reality of New York City's term limits. He was forbidden by law to seek a third term as mayor in 2009. Inevitably speculation emerged that he would run for governor, but Albany's corrupt corridors whistled no siren song for Bloomberg. While mayor, he had often said, "My plan B," life as a billionaire media-mogul-cum-philanthropist, "is better than anyone else's plan A," except he was not yet ready to surrender his A-game. Money could not buy Michael Bloomberg, but power could. He did not want to leave the office the law said he must. Most people, when confronted with a reality they do not like and cannot sensibly hope to change, respond with a range of human behaviors that allows them to cope with anger, frustration, and disappointment. Entrepreneurs respond by aggressively seeking to change reality in ways most people would not dare. That is what Bloomberg did.[59]

For most of its history, New York City placed no restrictions on the number of terms a mayor or other elected officials could serve in office. Mayors La Guardia, Wagner, and Koch each served three. In 1989, Ronald Lauder, billionaire heir to his family's cosmetics fortune, undertook a feckless effort to win the Republican nomination for mayor. He went down to an embarrassing defeat and came to believe that the ability of incumbents to hold on to their offices for as long as they liked limited democracy in the city. In his view, it gave incumbents sinecures and access to patronage that allowed them to perpetuate themselves in office more or less indefinitely, no matter how inept or corrupt they might be. Limiting the city's elected officials to two terms, he decided, would shake up the political establishment and restore a healthy dose of competition to city politics.[60]

The New York City Charter allows the public to express its will through citywide referendum. Lauder succeeded in placing his two-term-limit proposal on the ballot in 1993 when a tense race for mayor between David Dinkins and Rudy Giuliani created high turnout. He promoted the initiative with a few million dollars of his own money, and despite opposition from party leaders and many others who viewed the measure as an undesirable limitation on democracy, it passed by a whopping 59 percent to 41 percent margin. In 1996 the council passed a law extending the limit to three terms, but the prevailing interpretation of the charter called for a mandatory referendum to validate the change. Voters rejected it by a solid 54 percent to 46 percent margin. At that point, there was no mistaking popular will. Later court cases ruled the city council could amend the term-limit rules by a simple vote, but after two citywide decisions a majority of politicians were reluctant to go there. The city council made an exception for a technical fix pertaining to members who had been elected for truncated two-year terms under transition provisions included in 1989 charter reform.[61]

From the time he first became a candidate for mayor in 2001, until his presidential balloon burst in 2008, Bloomberg defended the term-limit law without exception as representing the will of the people. From time to time, council members would propose extending the limits to three terms instead of two. Some were motivated by a legitimate belief that the rule ensured an inexperienced and therefore ineffective council. Others simply wanted to hold on to their jobs. In any event, in response to one such initiative in 2002, Bloomberg said on WNYC radio: "The people themselves have twice explicitly voted for term limits. We cannot ignore their will. They want the openness new faces bring. And they will get it. We will not go back." He vowed "to oppose any change in the law that a legislative body tries to make." In 2005, the council began to consider a change that would allow its members three terms. Bloomberg's office issued a statement saying he "opposed any change in the term-limits provision." At other times, he said eight years was enough for elected officials to learn their job, be effective, and then move on to allow for fresh blood. On occasion he called efforts to change the rule without a referendum a "disgrace," or an "outrage." Term limits helped elect Bloomberg. Without them, the city likely would have reelected Rudy Giuliani amidst the groundswell of support he received for leading the city through the 9/11 crisis.[62]

So it came as a shock to his three closest advisors, Patti Harris, Kevin Sheekey, and Ed Skyler, when Bloomberg raised the possibility of a third term with them shortly after he bowed out of the race for president. All three opposed it. They feared ignoring two citywide referendums would be viewed as an undemocratic end-run around voters and taint Bloomberg's legacy. They also knew that historically third terms had been tough on New York City mayors. The job exhausts the person who holds it and the team around him. They feared that holding on to top talent for four more years would prove difficult. In a rare display of public dissent from Bloomberg's inner circle, their objections eventually hit the press.[63]

A referendum that put the question to the voters a third time was the respectful way to approach the topic, but a private poll Bloomberg commissioned revealed it would suffer the same outcome as the first two. A council vote seemed the only viable option. Powerful business leaders like real estate magnate Jerry Speyer and Bloomberg's good friend and financial advisor Steven

Rattner encouraged Bloomberg to run. Process seemed less important to them than keeping Bloomberg's talents in City Hall, even if it meant overruling the people. Rumors circulated and reporters asked questions. Bloomberg became coy. "It's a council decision," he said.[64]

Like Bloomberg, City Council Speaker Christine Quinn had declared she would not violate the people's will by changing the term-limit rule. "I will not support the repeal or change of term limits through any mechanism," she said in December 2007. She called that her "firm and final position," on the topic. Also like Bloomberg, during the course of 2008, she began to think a change might suit her after all.[65]

Quinn had expected to run for mayor herself in 2009 and to make history as the first woman and the first openly gay person to hold New York City's most powerful office. An ethical lapse threatened her plan. In April 2008, the *New York Post* reported that during the budget process, the city council allocated money to phantom organizations as a way to park funds for projects council members favored for their districts, pending final negotiations between them and the speaker. Many of the projects ultimately approved were worthy, some were sketchy, but in any event, the process smacked of secrecy and manipulation of public funds. A federal investigation followed and two council staff members were indicted. The event made Quinn damaged goods for a 2009 citywide run. A term-limit extension would allow her to bide her time as speaker for four more years in the hope of putting the reputation-soiling event behind her and allow her to pursue her dream in 2013. And very importantly, Quinn hoped Bloomberg would endorse her as his successor.[66]

So was born a crass marriage of ambitions. The billionaire politician, against the advice of his three most trusted advisors, urged on by New York City oligarchs, wanted to hold on to power beyond what the rules allowed. The city council speaker wanted to make history by becoming the city's first woman and openly gay mayor. Together, the two would conspire to violate the will of the people both had pledged to honor. By early September it had become clear Bloomberg would seek to overturn term limits. The Citizens Union, the New York Public Interest Group, and others announced their opposition to changing term limits by law and not referendum. Mark Green declared Bloomberg risked crossing into "Putinland." Ronald Lauder sought to protect the cause he had championed and began financing a television ad campaign. "Politicians are a lot like diapers," the narrator of the spot said. "They need to be changed regularly. And for the same reason." It urged voters to "tell politicians, messing with term limits stinks."[67]

In the meantime, the global financial crisis came to a head. The September 2008 collapse of Lehman Brothers and the panic that followed gripped New

Yorkers. Bloomberg had been marching steadily toward a third term bid for months by then. In August, he had met with the editors of the leading newspapers and secured their support. By the end of September, the *New York Post* and the *Daily News* ran editorials under the same headline: "Run, Mike, Run." The *New York Times,* never in favor of term limits, also supported a change that would let Bloomberg seek another term. Until the financial crisis, the rationale for a third term floated in abstract discussions of process. It balanced respect for two citywide votes against the notion that term limits were inherently anti-democratic since they prevented citizens from voting for elected officials they might want to keep. The financial crisis moved the discussion from philosophy to reality with the force of a global economic catastrophe. Suddenly, Bloomberg had a ready-made rationale for holding on to his office. He was the man to lead the city through the tough times ahead.[68]

On October 2, 2008, Bloomberg held a press conference at which he announced, "I love the city as a place to raise my family, to build my business from scratch and to give back. There is no greater honor than being able to make a difference in people's lives and to me that is what public service is really all about." He went on to reference, "unprecedented challenges" the nation and city faced and said, "as a businessman with expertise on Wall Street and in finance, and as a mayor who has balanced budgets and delivered services," he understood how serious the crisis would be for New York. The thrust of his message was that he was uniquely qualified to lead the city through the trial to come, and as a consequence he had made a decision about term limits. If the city council passed a law allowing him to seek a third term, he would sign it and run. A remarkable 87 percent of New Yorkers told pollsters the term limit issue should be resolved by a referendum, not a city council vote. When placed in the context of the emergency the financial crisis created, New Yorkers were split. One poll showed opposition to an exception for Bloomberg by a 51 percent to 45 percent margin. Another showed 46 percent in favor with 44 percent opposed and 10 percent undecided.[69]

Once Bloomberg committed, his team went to work using all of his official and unofficial influence to win support for the change he sought. Community organizations around the city that depended on Bloomberg for funding received calls asking them to lobby their local council person to support the change in the term limit law. Opponents launched a counter campaign, which also gained traction. Meanwhile, Bloomberg sought to defuse Ronald Lauder's objections, and the two men reached an agreement. To allow Bloomberg to stay in office and manage the city through the financial crisis, Lauder would support a one-time, temporary change that would let Bloomberg and other elected city officials serve once more. Afterward, the limit would revert to two terms. Yet, when the city council revealed its rule change, it proposed to make a three-term limit permanent. Lauder protested publicly and threatened to re-energize the opposition. He met with Bloomberg again and the two agreed Lauder would support the change in 2008, and in 2010 the mayor would appoint a charter revision commission with the intent of restoring the two-term limit and requiring a referendum to change it. That is what eventually happened, by a citywide vote of 74 percent to 26 percent, although the provision grandfathered sitting elected officials and allowed them to serve a third term. In any event, when Lauder dropped his opposition, the movement lost its main source of financing. The deal, struck between two billionaires to determine a matter of democratic principle for more than eight million people, offended.[70]

Council members crafted two bills. The one Bloomberg and speaker Quinn backed allowed a third term by a simple vote. The other, supported by Bill de Blasio, Letitia James, and others would have put the issue before voters in a referendum in the spring of 2009. After a heated debate, the council voted twenty-nine to twenty-two in favor of allowing the mayor and themselves to serve three terms instead of two without a citywide vote. Had four council members switched sides, the bill would have been defeated. One political insider claims the vote was closer still. It stood at twenty-seven to twenty-four when two members who realized they were on the losing side agreed to change their votes in return for favors Bloomberg's team dangled. Of the twenty-nine votes, twenty-three came from council members scheduled to surrender their seats in 2009. "The people will long remember what we have done here today," Councilman Bill de Blasio said, "and the people will be unforgiving. We are stealing like a thief in the night their right to decide the shape of their democracy." When the results were announced spectators shouted "shame on you," and "the city's for sale." City Comptroller Bill Thompson, who had remained friendly with Bloomberg throughout the seven years the two men had served the city in their respective roles, declared the decision an "affront to New Yorkers." He vowed to run for mayor as he had long planned despite the dramatic change in the political landscape. Anthony Weiner too denounced the move and declared he would run again for mayor.[71]

Custom has long allowed any New Yorker to attend the public signing of a local bill and to offer an opinion on the measure about to be made law. Usually, a handful of people appear. On November 3, 2008 some 137 people showed up, and more than half subjected the mayor to protests of outrage. "You have exploited the power of your office to overturn the express will of the people," one said in anger, capturing the sentiment of many. Another spoke with his back turned on the mayor in indignation. One forty-year veteran of City Hall theater could recall nothing like it. Bloomberg sat and endured the face-to-face confrontation for four hours. At the end, he made a brief comment explaining that the time it takes to learn how to be effective in public office had convinced him three terms makes more sense than two. "With that," wrote Michael Barbaro and Fernanda Santos, covering the event for the *New York Times*, "the left-handed Mr. Bloomberg picked-up a black and gold pen, and with the flick of a wrist, rewrote New York City's term-limits law."[72]

This Will Be Really Hard

Campaign funding and philanthropy money, along with the power of the incumbent, were at the core of Bloomberg's third term bid no less than his second, but the context for the 2009 contest differed from the earlier one in dramatic ways. The city faced a frightening economic downdraft rather than a buoyant commercial upswing, and Bloomberg's third-term power play damaged his ability to portray himself as a high-minded public servant. It provided opponents "a moral, ethical and principled reason" to run against him, as one Democratic political analyst put it. His own team thought the decision hurt Bloomberg more than it might have another politician because it was so "off-brand," so at odds with the image Bloomberg had established over the prior seven years. And after that time in office, many New Yorkers were simply fatigued by Bloomberg's personality, a common occurrence for high-profile elected officials. Bloomberg's team understood. Shortly after the council vote, Sheekey, Harris, and Skyler met with their boss to discuss campaign strategy. "This will be really hard," one told him.[73]

The team needed someone they trusted to run the reelection operation. Yet, there was a fear that anyone actively involved in the 2005 campaign would be inclined to mimic its approach when fresh thinking was needed to confront the vastly different context of 2009. The role fell to Bradley Tusk, who had managed the successful 2002 citywide campaign to change the succession provision in the City Charter. After that, Tusk led an initiative to catalog all of Bloomberg's campaign promises and report on them publicly, a project that appealed to the mayor's instincts for accountability. Tusk left the Bloomberg administration in 2003 to become deputy to Illinois Governor Rod Blagojevich, who federal prosecutors indicted when he tried to sell the US Senate seat Barack Obama vacated after winning the presidency. Tusk moved on untainted by the scandal, and landed at Lehman Brothers, which collapsed a short while later. Kevin Sheekey, always on a hunt for talent, recruited him back into Bloomberg's orbit. Tusk took charge of the campaign to secure council approval for revised term limits, and that made him the logical choice to spearhead the third-term reelection effort. As campaign manager, he would direct a tightly controlled operation that included offices in all five boroughs, worked paid staff hard, and attracted an army of volunteers across the spectrum of city dwellers—students and youths, senior citizens, and others. To mount an aggressive "shock and awe" communication offensive, meant from the very start to scare off potential opponents and their backers, Sheekey called Howard Wolfson.[74]

Sheekey had "admired and feared" Wolfson since the mid-1980s when both worked as congressional staffers in Washington, DC. Raised in Yonkers, after graduating from the University of Chicago and then Duke where he earned a master's degree in history, Wolfson spent time as a political reporter for a local newspaper in Virginia and then went to work for Westchester Representative Nita Lowey on Capitol Hill. He worked on Senator Charles Schumer's 1998 election campaign, and in 2000 on Hillary Clinton's race for US Senate from New York. When Clinton ran for president and lost to Barack Obama in the Democratic primary in 2008, Wolfson served as director of communications. During that battle, Wolfson was often the source of harsh anti-Obama messages that went on long after Clinton's chances to win had turned remote. At one point, Chris Matthews told him on television, "You're like one of those Japanese soldiers that's still fighting in 1953." His work earned him some enemies, and when Obama won, Wolfson ended up in the White House doghouse, somewhat despondent according to reports. "I basically took to my bed," was how Wolfson described his situation after Clinton lost.[75]

Along the way, Wolfson had worked against Bloomberg in several public battles. Cablevision hired him to help de-rail Bloomberg's West Side stadium plan, and working for the New York State Democratic Party, he helped to stop Bloomberg's push for nonpartisan elections for mayor in 2003. In an internal memo written as part of a Democratic Party strategy to defeat Bloomberg in 2005, Wolfson described the mayor as "an out of touch billionaire who can't relate to the problems of ordinary New Yorkers." He attacked Bloomberg for spending so much money on his reelection campaign that it "distorts the terms of the debate," and he even took a potshot at The Gates exhibit that Bloomberg brought to Central Park, dismissing it as "shmattes on sticks," in a colorful mix of Yiddish and English. "As you probably know," Wolfson said to Sheekey when he called and asked Wolfson to join the campaign, "I have said some rather unkind things about Mike over the years. I'm surprised that you are asking me." He wondered what Bloomberg would think. Wolfson's ability to diminish an opponent was precisely why Sheekey had called him. "All Mike will care about is if you can support him going forward," he responded.[76]

A series of conversations followed, and at one point Sheekey asked if Wolfson thought any of the Democrats would be a better mayor than Bloomberg. "No," he replied, and his decision was made. After meetings with Bloomberg and later Tusk, Wolfson signed on. He also met with Patti Harris, who made sure the new team member understood that the campaign he had joined would work differently from others. Wolfson was soon impressed at how well the Bloomberg machine ran in comparison to the barely controlled chaos and personal maneuvering among campaign staff typical of political quests for office. Some Democrats viewed Wolfson's decision as selling out for money and betraying his beliefs and friends. Wolfson claimed it was not the $40,000 per month consulting fee that motivated him, but "an evolution among rank-and-file Democrats in recognizing [Bloomberg] as a great mayor." In 2005, Wolfson had worked for Thompson's reelection campaign for city comptroller, and many presumed he would sign on to help Thompson run for mayor in 2009. In one motion, Sheekey's deft recruiting move added the talented Democratic operative to Bloomberg's team and denied his skills to opponents.[77]

Anthony Wiener's spirited 2005 run and credible showing in a four-way Democratic primary for mayor made it clear he could be a contender in 2009. His urban populist politics and streets-of-Brooklyn style contrasted sharply with Bloomberg's staid image and made him a logical alternative for voters ready for a change. Early polls showed him the Democratic front-runner. If he won the primary and the party remained united, he would win large majorities from African Americans and Latinos who typically vote for the Democrat in a New York City contest for mayor, and he would appeal to "white ethnics, Jewish, Italian and Irish" more naturally than a candidate of color like Thompson. In January and February 2009, Weiner lobbed verbal attacks at the incumbent signaling coming combat. Bloomberg's political pros viewed Weiner as a lightweight legislator, but a dangerously talented campaigner. If he were their opponent, they anticipated one of two things would happen: "He would have imploded and we would have won by 25 percent, or he would have beat us."[78]

Neutralizing the challenger who posed the greatest threat to Bloomberg became the campaign team's first task. Tusk and Wolfson were both fresh off career disruptions making them highly motivated to prove their worth. They invested "a lot of time and money," in what Tusk described as "an entire sub-campaign" to scare Weiner out of the race. Staff researchers surfaced illegal campaign contributions from foreign fashion models and linked them to Weiner's support for legislation that favored the industry. They spun Weiner's support for a hospital at risk of closing into a political favor for a donor. They turned Weiner's participation in a hockey league into a story about a congressman who missed votes to play games, and provided the *New York Post* with the photo that proved it, and on and on. "We threw everything at him we could," Tusk acknowledged. To Weiner, it seemed not a day passed without his office receiving a 4:00 p.m. call asking for comment about some purported misdeed, teed up perfectly for tabloid headlines and the evening news. By March, Weiner lowered his profile, hoping to duck below the Bloomberg team's cross-hairs. He stopped his attacks on Bloomberg and wrote to supporters that he would make up his mind about running for mayor by the end of May. The tactic did not work. The assault continued and the maligned "quasi-candidate," as Weiner called himself, held a news conference on the steps of City Hall to denounce the "daily Dumpster diving" Bloomberg's team engaged in to damage his image.[79]

A few weeks later, Weiner sounded a full retreat and declared he would not run for mayor. On the *New York Times* op-ed page, he claimed the main reason was that a national economic emergency in combination with the election of a Democratic president made his work in Washington, DC, particularly important. The more convincing explanation was that Bloomberg was sure to spend $80 million or more to win reelection. That was roughly ten times what finance campaign laws would allow his challengers to spend in a primary. "In this case, a sports analogy is apt," Weiner wrote. "If one football team has 110 players on the field, the team with 11 has a hard time getting through the blocking and tackling on the crowded turf." Weiner did not believe the public would hear his message against an opponent so able to dominate the media. Wolfson and Tusk were unsurprised by the decision. They had hired a pollster who had once worked with Weiner's pollster and aligned their tracking surveys with the schedule they knew he would follow. They were confident that if they could show Bloomberg ahead by 15 percent or more by Memorial Day, Weiner's adviser would urge him to drop out. Two days before the article appeared, their results showed their candidate with a 17 percent lead. They celebrated their "first scalp of the season," as one reporter termed it, with a steak dinner at Peter Luger's restaurant in Brooklyn.[80]

Weiner was not the only New York City politician who became cranky in the spring of 2009. Bloomberg did too. A passer-by brushed up against a wheelchair-bound reporter named Michael Harris, knocking his tape recorder to the floor and switching it on just as Bloomberg was about to start a press conference to announce his support for gay marriage. Harris's limited mobility caused him to struggle awkwardly for about a full minute to retrieve the machine and turn it off. Bloomberg, "glowering and sighing," scolded the reporter for the interruption. The mayor behaved as if "an unpardonable act of lèse-majesté had been committed," Clyde Haberman wrote in the *New York Times*. A spokesman delivered a halfhearted apology. A few weeks later, Bloomberg announced some positive economic news. Azi Paybarah, a reporter for the *New York Observer,* asked if the improved financial trajectory diminished the rationale for his third term. Bloomberg dismissed the question out of hand, ended the session abruptly, and as he stepped away from the microphone, he looked the reporter's way and sneered, "You're a disgrace." He took to rejecting reporters' questions as "wastes" and "ridiculous."[81]

New York Times editorial board writer Joyce Purnick was working on a biography of Bloomberg in 2009. Some of his closest friends explained to her why they thought he was in such a foul mood. "He's a different guy than he was a year ago," one confided. "He breached his own code of ethics. He was deceptive, he did what he criticizes others for doing—and it bothers him." Bloomberg's deputies dismissed the comment as "pop psychology." None ever heard Bloomberg second-guess his decision, and they did not find it surprising that a candidate in a reelection campaign proved cranky from time-to-time. If Bloomberg suffered remorse, he kept it well hidden, and it did nothing to temper the intensity of his commitment to win a third term.[82]

Bloomberg secured Republican Party support without opposition, despite his 2007 decision to leave the GOP, and the Independence Party once again awarded their generous patron their ballot line. He donated $1.2 million to the political organization. The campaign ignored editorial-board and public-interest-group scoldings about the scale of Bloomberg's spending, and by July the amount reached $37 million. By October, it was $50 million and rising. His philanthropy continued to buy loyalty from supporters and silence from potential critics. Most organizations and unions that supported Bloomberg in 2005 did so again in 2009, or stayed neutral.[83]

The Politics of Resentment

Weiner's exit effectively left the Democratic nomination to New York City Comptroller William C. Thompson Jr., who crushed Queens Councilman Tony Avella by seventy points in a non-event of a Democratic primary. Bloomberg scheduled a big rally for the day of the Democratic Party vote to distract news media from his opponent's success. The contrast between Thompson and Bloomberg was great on any number of dimensions. Billy Thompson, as many called him, grew up in Bedford-Stuyvesant, Brooklyn, the grandson of black immigrants from the Caribbean islands of Nevis and St. Kitts. His mother was a public school teacher and his father a politician, at different times a city councilman, a state legislator, and a New York State Supreme Court Judge, Appellate Division. Thompson attended local public schools and Tufts University, where he graduated with a degree in political science. He worked in the office of a Brooklyn congressman, and then as deputy to Brooklyn Borough President Howard Golden. He was the youngest person to fill the role, which at the time wielded significant power over city decisions. After a fleeting career at an investment bank, in 1994 Thompson lobbied his old boss to name him Brooklyn's representative on the central Board of Education. Not long afterward, his fellow board members named him president.[84]

Over the course of his career, Thompson earned a reputation as a quietly effective government official, able to find common ground among disparate parties to secure agreements and get things done. When he ran for the city-wide office of comptroller in 2001, it came as something of a surprise. It was the first time he presented himself for an elected position. He beat Herbert Berman, chairman of the city council finance committee in the Democratic primary 54 percent to 46 percent, a greater margin than anticipated. Thompson maintained his composure even during the final weeks of the campaign when the contest turned acrimonious. He sailed to an easy victory in the general election, and in 2005, no Democrat mounted a primary challenge. Thompson won reelection with more than 90 percent of the vote against a Republican name placed on the ballot as a matter of form. As comptroller, Thompson collaborated with the mayor as a partner in government rather than confronting him as an institutional rival. Sometimes the two played golf together. A cautious leader, Thompson did little to distinguish the comptroller's office and nothing to diminish it. In every respect, his career reflected the slow, steady rise New York City's Democratic political organizations offered its competent, loyal soldiers.[85]

From the moment Fernando Ferrer lost in 2005, Thompson made clear he planned to run for mayor. When rumors first circulated that Bloomberg would try to change the rules so he could stay in office, Thompson's team did not believe it. Eduardo Castell, Thompson's campaign manager, said they viewed Bloomberg as a man who "exemplified" the idea of doing the right thing for the city, not the sort who would seek to perpetuate himself in power in such a heavy-handed way. To a man like Thompson, who owed his success to playing politics by the rules, Bloomberg's move constituted "one of the greatest displays of self-interest we have ever seen in this city." And it stood in sharp contrast to what he called "the greatest display of democracy America has ever seen," when the very next day after Bloomberg signed into law the provision that allowed him to run again, Barack Obama won election as president of the United States. The normally temperate Thompson denounced Bloomberg for "hijacking democracy," and "betraying" the public trust. "I think the mayor can be beat and I think he can be beat now—in 2009," he told journalists, surprising people who viewed him as inherently cautious with his decision to take on the incumbent billionaire, by any definition a formidable opponent.[86]

As comptroller, Thompson had some incumbent powers of his own to work with. His office audited city government, and in the spring and summer of 2009, it issued reports criticizing the mayor's management of various agencies—mistakes at the Health and Hospital Corporation, lack of follow-up at restaurants with health department violations, sorry conditions at family homeless shelters, huge cost overruns at the Croton Reservoir filtration plant in the Bronx. The criticisms had merit, but little sting. They were the sorts of problems people expected in a city as complex as New York City, and confidence in Bloomberg's competence as a manager remained undiminished.[87]

Most of the Democratic Party lined up behind Thompson early since he faced such a weak primary opponent, but the party was moribund. Governor Spitzer's scandal-ridden resignation and Governor Paterson's feckless leadership limited the ability of the state apparatus to help the Democratic candidate for mayor. Congressman Rangel was under investigation for tax evasion relating to a condominium he owned in the Dominican Republic. Senator Schumer would go through the motions expected from a party leader of his stature and endorse Thompson, but he had little interest in fighting with someone as wealthy and powerful as Bloomberg, who had supported Schumer's reelection in 2004. In August, after signing a new contract and after budget negotiations were final, DC 37, the city's largest union endorsed Thompson, giving his field operation a much-needed boost, and the *New York Times* wrote him a warm endorsement for the Democratic nomination.[88]

By temperament, Thompson was a low-key campaigner with "a lackluster stump style," one journalist had written of the candidate in 2004. Thompson's team knew he needed to reserve his money to finance a general election battle against a foe with limitless resources, so he ran no ads during the primary. The confluence of events—an uncompetitive primary election, a weak Democratic Party, a candidate who lacked charisma, and limited funds caused a desultory result. Turnout for the Democratic primary was the lowest on record, about 11 percent of registered party members. Normally, after a primary victory, a winner gets a positive bounce in the polls. Thompson got none. Bloomberg had an eighteen-point lead in the first Quinnipiac poll taken after the vote.[89]

The politics of resentment was the one lever working for Thompson. Intense economic distress caused many citizens to fear losing their jobs. Few believed the richest man in New York City felt their pain. A rising chorus of analysts expressed concern about the social impact of income inequality and the concentration of wealth. Bloomberg responded with tin-eared temerity, declaring: "We like billionaires in New York. We wish more would move here." The man who built his fortune delivering data to bank trading desks refused to temper his cheerleading on behalf of the financial industry, even as details of reckless behavior by highly paid executives mounted, and the stacks of money redistributed from taxpayers to financial firms grew by the billions. The resentment was not limited to middle-class and poor New Yorkers. One Bloomberg strategist remembered attending a meeting with "like, thirty-two grand poobah real estate guys," at the Real Estate Board of New York. The developers loved Bloomberg's policies, but "in kind of a weird way, it was a tense meeting." As it progressed, the political pro did a calculation in his head. "All of them together weren't worth half of what Bloomberg was worth. Their power came from being the rich guy in the room and being able to bully the politician," the fellow surmised. When Bloomberg was mayor, it wasn't so, "and in some ways," he realized, "they resented that."[90]

The resentment that trumped all the others was Bloomberg's manipulation of the political process to grant himself the chance for a third term. It revealed itself in many ways. One that made an impression on Bloomberg's strategists occurred just after the city council approved the term-limit change in November 2008. Bill Knapp moderated a focus group for them among Latinos in Brooklyn. The participants were "really angry," one campaign advisor remembered. Strongman politics was one of the things many had hoped to escape when they came to America. "This is the shit they pulled in my home country," was the sort of thing the participants said. "This is not a small problem," the strategist remembered thinking. "This is a big problem."[91]

Thompson sought to channel the anger into votes. During the last week in October, with a little more than a week to go before Election Day, he delivered his best speech at Hunter College. "Tonight I want to talk to you about what I believe is a key issue in this campaign—Republican Mike Bloomberg's self-serving desire to do away with the term-limits law that New Yorkers voted for not once, but twice. He ignored New Yorkers' voices and votes in a clear violation of the will of the people." Thompson went on to embrace fundamental American beliefs. "I grew up in Bedford-Stuyvesant . . . in a household where we were taught a deep and abiding respect for the law—and for the freedoms so many fought so hard to secure for us," he told the audience. "And I learned from my father that no one—regardless of their skin color, their income level, or their neighborhood is above the law." He reminded his listeners that Abraham Lincoln, Martin Luther King Jr., and others fought to protect people's rights. He fast-forwarded to 9/11 and the judgment that despite a crisis, indeed because of it, democratic process had to be respected. He quoted Bloomberg's comment that it would be a "disgrace" to overturn term limits without a popular vote in favor of the change. Toward the end of the speech he asked, pointedly, "Does the richest man in New York get to live by one set of rules—while the rest of us live by another?" Thompson asked the same question during televised debates where he stood shoulder to shoulder with Bloomberg.[92]

The Power of Perception

From the very beginning of the campaign, Bloomberg's political pros worried that the climate of resentment swirling around the city in 2009 could cause New York power brokers, even the ones who had benefited from Bloomberg's policies, to unify against the mayor. Bankers and real estate moguls, political organizations and unions, industry groups, and other institutions were used to exercising influence at City Hall in ways they simply could not while Bloomberg governed. A mayor with a more typical profile would restore their status. Bloomberg's team decided early on that creating an aura of invulnerability was the smartest way to prevent formation of a dangerous coalition of the disaffected.[93]

From the time he secured the chance to run for a third term, and in every poll that followed, Bloomberg led all challengers by double digits. Yet, even as he appeared headed for an easy victory, Bloomberg's team maintained a full-court press. Television ads, radio spots, and mail fliers continued without pause. Volunteers went door to door and left handwritten notes when no one answered. They made telephone calls and followed-up with letters. They met with every community newspaper publisher in search of local support in every language polyglot New York City offered. Every day from March 24 to the end of the campaign, seven days a week, they announced another endorsement, many consequential, others entertainingly narrow in their scope of support—the Korean Dry Cleaners Association, for example. To casual observers, it looked like overkill—Bloomberg the bully running wild. In fact, his team was running scared. Its members understood the depth of resentment against Bloomberg, and they had noticed that no matter how high the percent of voters who approved of his management of the city—consistently above 60 percent and as high as 75 percent some months—the percent who declared themselves willing to vote for Bloomberg never rose much above half, barely enough to ensure victory.[94]

Bloomberg's political pros believed that the Democratic candidate for mayor—any Democrat—would win 45 percent of the vote from a committed core of voters. In the classic arithmetic of big city politics, Bloomberg had no strong natural base he could rely upon. Against an African American he would do well with white voters, and especially among his fellow Jewish New Yorkers, but his wealth distanced him somewhat even from them. It was a vulnerable position for a candidate who had to win almost all of the 55 percent that remained against a credible Democrat, including a stubborn cluster of undecideds. It ranged between 15 and 20 percent at times, and the outcome could hinge on them. Pros in both camps knew it, and they also knew that after almost eight years to evaluate Bloomberg's performance as mayor, anyone still unconvinced was searching hard for an alternative. That meant Bloomberg's lead in the final weeks was not comfortable double digits as headlines suggested. One pro watching from the sidelines estimated the gap at 5 to 8 percent. Public realization of that fact alone could have caused a shift in sentiment that would have energized Thompson's supporters. It risked unleashing powerful opponents who had stayed away from the race because they were afraid to cross a mayor they expected to rule for four more years.[95]

Part of the Bloomberg campaign's inevitability strategy was to make potential Thompson supporters believe their candidate was so far behind, there was no point to go the polls. Thompson's team tried hard to convince influencers it was not so, but the resources arrayed against them were formidable, and had been at work for months. When Thompson's campaign made mistakes, journalists saw in them proof that he could not be elected. Goofy errors—press releases that misspelled words including the candidate's name, tag lines on television commercials that displayed typographical errors, staffers' social-media whines about campaign dynamics—were cast as reflections of a lost cause. Thompson campaign advisor Eddy Castell accused *New York Times* reporter Michael Barbaro of being played for a fool by Bloomberg's team when he showed him a draft article that described Thompson's effort as in disarray. But the facts in the article were accurate, and it went to press.[96]

What Bloomberg's advisors feared most was a visit from Barack Obama. Still riding the crest of his extraordinary victory the year before, the charismatic president was enormously popular in New York City in 2009. The intense excitement Obama created among African Americans, young voters, and liberals of all stripes was precisely the electricity Thompson needed to charge up his supporters and motivate them to go to the polls. Obama "could have been an incredibly powerful endorsement for Thompson if he really worked it," Bloomberg's team knew. He could have converted the low-energy candidate into a cause by telling Democrats he was an important partner in a bold national movement to secure the country's economic future and to reform its politics.[97]

"We had this whole campaign to keep the White House out of it," Tusk recounted. We worked "every relationship we could tap—Rahm and Mike had a pretty good relationship at the time," he said, referring to White House Chief of Staff Rahm Emanuel and Bloomberg. "Geoffrey Canada and Valerie Jarrett were close." Geoffrey Canada's Harlem Children's Zone had received hundreds of thousands of dollars of support from Bloomberg. Valerie Jarrett was an influential personal advisor to President Obama. "Basically every single tentacle to the White House we had, we used to make the case," that Bloomberg was going to win reelection, so endorsing his opponent was a foolish move. Bloomberg's staff reminded Obama's that during the 2008 presidential election, Bloomberg had declined to endorse John McCain even though the two men were personal friends. Now, Bloomberg wanted the president to stay neutral in the mayor's race. National healthcare reform was President Obama's top priority, and in 2009 he still hoped to win bipartisan support for the ambitious goal. He wanted Bloomberg to endorse it. As a longtime Democrat, erstwhile Republican, and declared independent who had contributed money generously to members of both major parties, Bloomberg had unusual standing as a leader who could appeal to politicians across party lines. He could also write large checks in support of important public policy campaigns, like affordable health care. Working through their aides, the two powerful politicians cut a deal.[98]

On a Friday afternoon, late in the campaign, the White House issued the most tepid of endorsements. It came from Obama's press secretary, not the president. In response to a reporter's question, the spokesman said the president supported his party's candidate for mayor of New York City. He did not even utter the name. Thompson made the most of it. He held a press conference at City Hall to trumpet the almost silent support, and he produced posters of himself and Obama. Speaker Quinn, who hoped to have Bloomberg's endorsement to succeed him some day, followed a similar script. She offered Thompson her endorsement late in the contest in a contrived conversation with a reporter. Her posture so offended Thompson he declined to be seen with her.[99]

On Election Day, two days after 70 percent of New Yorkers reported to a pollster they approved of the way Michael Bloomberg did his job, just 51.1 percent voted to reelect him mayor. He beat Thompson, who received 46.5 percent of the votes, by a margin of just 4.6 percent. An Edison Research exit survey reported the racial and ethnic breakdown of the results. More than two-thirds of white voters cast ballots for Bloomberg. Among Jews it rose to three-quarters. Some 43 percent of Latinos and 23 percent of blacks favored him. More than three-quarters of African Americans, well over half of Latinos and almost 30 percent of whites, voted for Thompson, who took a strong majority in the Bronx, the city's poorest borough, and a slight majority in his home borough of Brooklyn. Bloomberg won Manhattan, Queens, and Staten Island. A strong majority of voters making $50,000 or less favored Thompson. Most making more than that cast ballots for Bloomberg.[100]

Thompson advisor Eddy Castell believed their team did a good job of giving voters a reason to "fire the incumbent," but fell short of convincing them "to hire the other guy." Turnout was low, suppressed in part by the Bloomberg team's efforts to portray Thompson as a lost cause, not worth the trip to the polling booth. Fifteen per cent of voters said they cast ballots for a candidate because they disliked the other guy more. Of those, nearly 80 percent voted against Bloomberg. Forty-five percent reported that Bloomberg's term-limit maneuver had made them less likely to vote for him. Exit poll anecdotes confirmed that many New Yorkers who cast ballots for Bloomberg did so reluctantly. They objected to his arrogant and autocratic ways even though they admired his management skill. The $108 million Bloomberg spent after distributing bonuses of $400,000 each to Patti Harris, Howard Wolfson, and Bradley Tusk, among other campaign staff payments, was a new record. Officially, he spent six times the amount Thompson did, and he disbursed a similar amount in philanthropy. One calculation estimated he paid about $2,000 for each vote in his margin of victory.[101]

Celebrating his win the night of the vote, Bloomberg was ebullient. He portrayed his reelection as a great reaffirmation of his administration. Many Democrats interpreted things very differently. The narrow margin of his victory despite spending more than $100 million meant his third term was barely legitimate to them. Several elected officials told reporters that had President Obama and other senior Democrats campaigned for their party's candidate as they should have, Bloomberg would have been defeated. Bloomberg remained the mayor, and the richest man in New York City, but his stature had been diminished. Jay Leno lampooned him on NBC's *Tonight Show*. "Well, congratulations to New York City Mayor Michael Bloomberg on the purchase of his third term," the comedian said in his opening monologue the evening after the vote. "Bloomberg spent $100 million to get reelected. Do you realize that's the most money ever spent on a New Yorker that's not playing for the Yankees?" came the punch line. One council member told a reporter "there is a lot of resentment" and that "a lot of members will be prepared to take him on." Under the headline, "Mayor No Longer Seems Invincible," Michael Powell and Julie Bosman wrote in the *New York Times*: "For the first time in years, Mayor Michael Bloomberg finds himself governing New York City from an unaccustomed vantage point: Vulnerability."[102]

Superstition has it that a curse haunts third-term mayors in New York City. It punishes them for hubris, for believing they have mastered the impossible burdens of the job, for thinking they are indispensable, the only one who can tend to the infinite daily demands eight million people place on their government. Fiorello La Guardia developed cancer. Robert Wagner's wife Susan died, and he became dispirited. Edward Koch became so despondent at the corruption scandals that swirled around him, he contemplated suicide. The governments they ran lost their edge. In his victory speech, Bloomberg addressed the myth. "Now, conventional wisdom says that historically third terms have not been too successful. But we've spent the past eight years defying conventional wisdom," he bragged. He cited post 9/11 economic recovery, crime reduction, and school reform as among the ways that "we've proven the experts wrong again, and again, and again. And we're not stopping now," he said, poking the air with the index finger of his left hand for emphasis. "If you think you've seen progress over the past eight years, I've got news for you," Bloomberg told his supporters, "You ain't seen nothing yet."[103]

Chapter Ten

Third-Term Disasters and Triumphs

She killed forty-three New Yorkers. Her murderous journey began off the west coast of Africa, where she mustered her forces before traveling across the Atlantic Ocean to strike Jamaica, and then Cuba, before heading north. She might have veered east and dissipated her power harmlessly out at sea, but a high-pressure system blocked her, and a low-pressure system intercepted her, adding to her size and power. The combination converted the hurricane into a post-tropical cyclone, and steered her west where she struck the Jersey Shore. Then she roared into New York Harbor the evening of October 29, 2012. Her eighty-mile-an-hour winds were formidable, but New York had withstood others more than half again as fierce. The half inch of rain she released was trivial. Other storms had dropped fifteen times as much water on the city. But never before had New York City experienced a flood surge that compared with Superstorm Sandy. She hit the harbor at high tide, and during a full moon. The water level at Manhattan's tip rose fourteen feet, higher by far than at any time in recorded history. In neighborhoods on Staten Island's east and south shores, the Brooklyn-Queens waterfront and elsewhere in South Queens and Southern Brooklyn, the flood surge was up to 40 percent above earlier high-water marks. It was an unprecedented natural catastrophe.[1]

Water covered more than fifty square miles of New York City's densely populated land, half-again more than federal estimates of the impact a once-in-a-hundred year storm might have. A six-year-old child and two ninety-year-olds were among the dead. Nearly ninety thousand buildings were in the flood zone. Hundreds were destroyed entirely, thousands severely damaged. Almost two million people were without power for several days, tens of thousands for longer. Hospital staff evacuated thousands of patients. More than a million children could not attend school for a week. The surge flooded dozens of subway stations, the Hugh L. Carey Brooklyn-Battery Tunnel, the Holland Tunnel, and other transit lines, disrupting the daily routes of 11 million travelers. Analysts estimated the economic loss at $19 billion.[2]

City, state, and federal officials had taken emergency measures, including shutting down transportation networks and some power facilities in advance of the storm. They issued evacuation orders for areas at greatest risk. The steps protected many and sped recovery. But New York City's defenses were unequal to the task of sheltering its residents from a natural disaster unlike any before. Bloomberg's government was keenly aware of weather-related risks. It had highlighted them in *PlaNYC 2007,* and to understand them better it had used LIDAR technology to map the city's topography with state-of-the-art accuracy. It had asked the Federal Emergency Management Administration to use the information to revise its Flood Insurance Rate Maps. The official documents, which identified flood zones and imposed standards on structures built within them, had last been examined in 1983. The project was a few months from completion when Sandy hit. The new maps confirmed that far more of the city was at risk than federal officials had acknowledged. Various runoff improvement projects, waterfront development designs, and bulkhead construction programs initiated as a consequence of *PlaNYC*'s imperative to make the city's environment more sustainable helped at the margins. But Sandy made clear that a serious effort to limit damage from ferocious storms would require an entirely different scale of commitment.[3]

Bloomberg responded by creating the Special Initiative for Rebuilding and Resiliency and tasked it with developing a plan "to provide additional protection for New York's infrastructure, buildings, and communities from the impacts of climate change." He instructed the team not to limit their analysis to the specific circumstances that caused Sandy, but to address the issue in its broadest dimensions. Deputy Mayor Steel called Seth Pinsky back from paternity leave to lead it, and he in turn recruited Marc Ricks back from the private sector to oversee some thirty-five staff. Working with the New York City Panel on Climate Change, a group of scientists and other experts charged with making projections to determine how weather patterns would affect the metropolis over time, the city published *A Stronger, More Resilient New York* in June 2013. In 437 pages of highly accessible language, the remarkable report identifies key elements of the city's infrastructure, and the likely impact of climate change on each one by the decades 2020 and 2050. The city proposed 257 initiatives to reduce damage and to insure rapid recovery from future catastrophes. Before the end of the Bloomberg administration, $15 billion of funding had been earmarked out of a total of $19.5 billion required, allowing work on most of the projects to begin. The plan provides a roadmap for improvements that will take decades to complete. It acknowledged candidly that "nature's force" is such that extreme weather events will "overwhelm" the city's preparations at times, but the measures planned will protect it better and allow it to rebound faster. Urban experts expect the program envisioned to prove as important to New York's long-term evolution as *PlaNYC*.[4]

Critics faulted Bloomberg and his team for not protecting the city better from Sandy, particularly since *PlaNYC* made clear the rising danger of natural disaster from climate change. The critique was unfair. The fact that federal floodplain maps had not been updated in the quarter century before *PlaNYC* is a reflection of the lack of attention paid to weather-related risks prior to the focus that Bloomberg team's put on them. Its sustainable city projects were long-neglected movements in the right direction. Bloomberg did slow certain *PlaNYC* initiatives after the global financial crisis in order to bank budget savings. But the work to harden the infrastructure at risk, and to protect people better, were multi-year projects. Little of it would have been finished by the time Sandy struck in any event.[5]

Bloomberg created the Mayor's Office of Housing Recovery Operations to coordinate help for storm-devastated communities. It launched NYC Rapid Repairs, a program that assigned general contractors to specific neighborhoods and authorized them to do the work necessary to restore power, heat, and water to any home affected at government expense. The plan relied on more than $600 million of Federal Emergency Management Agency money, but short-circuited its general practice of financing temporary relief only. Rather than spend millions on mobile generators and hotel rooms, the program secured special approval to invest in permanent fixes. Within just a few months, the city repaired more than twenty thousand homes more cost effectively than typical FEMA programs, according to city officials. In June 2013, the city launched Build It Back, a program to provide another round of financial support for additional home repairs and reconstruction of dwellings Sandy damaged or destroyed. It got mired in what a city Department of Investigation report called "a confusing, multi-layered application process," characterized by poor communication, inefficiency, inadequate coordination across stakeholders and contract delays. Years passed with no results from the program.[6]

Third-Term Blues

Bloomberg's third term was a mash-up of bad and good, more mixed than his first eight highly successful years in office. To a greater degree than ever before, he found himself reacting to events rather than driving them. His final term included a well-developed response to the global financial crisis, diligent pursuit of the many ambitious initiatives already under way, and a heroic and ultimately successful effort to ensure Ground Zero rose from its ashes. But it also included his two worst appointments—Cathie Black and Stephen Goldsmith—and epic fraud related to a major technology project. Problems long simmering, like inflated school test scores, failed policies to contend with homelessness, and degenerating conditions at NYCHA, all came to a boil during the third term. So did stop and frisk, and a federal lawsuit that charged the Fire Department with hiring practices that discriminated against blacks and Hispanics. Scandalous conditions emerged in the city's jail system. When Bloomberg left office, all three of the city's major public safety departments—police, fire, and corrections—were under Department of Justice oversight or on the verge of it.

After his 2009 reelection, some fifteen senior officials departed. Patti Harris stayed and remained Bloomberg's closest confidant. More than anyone other than Bloomberg himself, it was she who assured the senior team worked together collaboratively, focused on issues rather than personalities, and sought results on behalf of the city's people. Bloomberg would reward her loyalty and competence with a $1 million donation in her name to her alma mater, Franklin & Marshall College. Ray Kelly would serve as police commissioner until the very end. His reputation would remain stellar despite the stop-and-frisk controversy that soured the Bloomberg administration's relationship with African American communities. Kevin Sheekey returned to Bloomberg LP as head of communications and government affairs, where he remained available for counsel whenever Bloomberg sought it. Howard Wolfson stepped seamlessly into the role of deputy mayor for intergovernmental affairs. Edward Skyler's departure to become head of public affairs for Citigroup was more troublesome. During Bloomberg's second term, he had been the hands-on manager responsible for daily oversight of many important city agencies. He was also among the few who had the temperament and credibility to confront the mayor effectively on sensitive topics.[7]

To replace Skyler, Bloomberg named Stephen Goldsmith deputy mayor for operations. As mayor of Indianapolis between 1992 and 2000, Goldsmith earned a national reputation as an innovator who brought new ideas to government. He streamlined outdated bureaucracies, outsourced municipal functions, and incorporated technology into service delivery. At first blush, it seemed Bloomberg expected his new deputy to reinvent New York City government as his administration's last hurrah. But Goldsmith fit uncomfortably with the rest of Bloomberg's team and never did develop an intuitive grasp of how things worked in New York City. One City Hall colleague thought him "a brilliant guy, miscast in the role," a smart man who lacked the instincts required of a "hands-on operations guy."[8]

When a winter storm dropped twenty inches of snow on Central Park the day after Christmas 2010, the Sanitation Department that typically plowed city streets effectively seemed unable to do the job. It was the sixth-biggest storm in 141 years of records and the snow was uncharacteristically powdery for the region, causing disorienting drifts—one side of a street piled high with the stuff, the other side bare and clean. But the city made mistakes. It failed to declare a snow emergency. That would have kept nonessential vehicles off the streets and prevented them from getting stuck in place, which in turn crippled plowing efforts. Improper use of snow chains on sanitation vehicles exacerbated the situation. The failures caused speculation that workers had engaged in a deliberate slowdown, perhaps in retaliation for efficiency measures Deputy Mayor Goldsmith championed. The rumors turned out to be false, fueled in part by an irresponsible councilman.[9]

Both Bloomberg and Goldsmith were out of town when the snow fell. As the deputy directly responsible for making sure the city did its day-to-day job, Goldsmith called in and decided things were fine; when it turned out they were not, New Yorkers wondered if their city was being run by absentee managers. Several months later, in August 2011, Goldsmith was arrested in Washington DC, on charges of domestic violence. The episode was a misunderstanding, and the charges were dropped, but it was enough to cause Bloomberg to announce that Goldsmith had decided to leave. Caswell Holloway, a Harvard College and University of Chicago Law School graduate who had been Ed Skyler's chief of staff, and then the commissioner of the Department of Environmental Protection, stepped into the role of deputy mayor for operations for the rest of Bloomberg's last term.[10]

It was on Goldsmith's unfortunate watch that a scandal surfaced which had been slowly growing almost the entire time Bloomberg governed. CityTime was a project to migrate municipal workers from paper-based management and old-fashioned time clocks to a more automated system. A band of thieves would use the twenty-first-century technology project the same way Boss Tweed and his ring of conspirators had used their infamous nineteenth-century courthouse. As long as the project remained incomplete, invoices could be passed through the city payment system for more work. And incompetent oversight allowed those payments to be diverted to corrupt conspirators. The money stolen reached the staggering amount of $700 million before Juan Gonzalez's *Daily News* investigative reports, Letitia James's city council hearings, and City Comptroller John Liu's audits forced a halt to the looting. The episode contained a double irony. One was that a technology entrepreneur as successful as Bloomberg ended up responsible for a city government technology project that he himself described as a "disaster." The second was that a project whose main purpose was to prevent city employees from committing petty fraud served as a vehicle for city contractors to engage in massive fraud.[11]

The long-running scandal came to a public head in December 2010 when federal prosecutor Preet Bharara's office indicted six people involved with the scheme. Another set of charges followed in June 2011. "The crimes alleged in today's superseding indictment are truly jaw-dropping," Bharara told the press, "epic in duration, magnitude and scope." Since at least 2003, continuing until well into 2010, "there existed a massive and elaborate scheme to defraud New York City," the prosecutor reported. The extent of the kickbacks and thievery exceeded by far anything in modern New York City history. Eventually SAIC, the main firm involved in the fraud, agreed to repay more than $500 million to the federal government, of which $466 million reverted to New York City. Other money, either recaptured or never disbursed, meant New York recovered over $500 million of $652 million, not including payments to other shell companies involved, which added a few tens of millions of dollars more to the net loss. The city would complete a new payroll system by the time Bloomberg left office. In a spectacularly charitable conclusion, the mayor told the city that the new technology cost less than it would have without the fraud because so much money was recovered.[12]

A second major technology project, the Emergency Communications Transformation Program to upgrade the city's obsolete 911 phone system, also came under scrutiny. No one claimed fraud with respect to the multi-billion dollar initiative, launched after the 2003 blackout overloaded the system and revealed its dangerous fragility. But a 2015 Department of Investigation report prepared by the de Blasio administration "found significant mismanagement, internal control weaknesses, and contractor performance deficiencies that created the conditions for the substantial delays and rising costs which have plagued the project." It described the effort as a decade behind schedule and hundreds of millions of dollars over budget, concluding "the project has yet to fully deliver on its promise of a modernized 911 system that will more effectively respond to the health and safety needs of New Yorkers." The report lacks perspective, and its conclusion is wrong except in the most pedantic sense. The city's upgraded emergency 911 system was up and operating effectively by the end of the Bloomberg administration. The major cost increase and additional time to complete the project came from a strategic decision during the course of development to build a backup call center in a newly constructed facility in a secure, remote location, rather than renovate an existing site. There were other issues as well, some serious, but nothing peculiar for a complex technology project, and they were dealt with sensibly when they surfaced.[13]

The Crime of Punishment

The CityTime scandal cost the public treasure. Scandal at the city run jailhouses on Rikers Island caused human misery measured in blood.

Important aspects of prison administration were well managed during Bloomberg's three terms. Between 2001 and 2012, the number of New Yorkers incarcerated declined by almost twenty thousand people, a drop of 36 percent while the national rate drifted up 3 percent during the same period. Innovative programs that included community service sentences, day-custody for people who committed misdemeanors, and treatment for non-violent felony drug abusers helped cut the prison population. But the single most important reason for the trend was the decline in serious felonies. For years, many law enforcement officials believed that the key to reducing crime was locking up criminals, particularly repeat offenders, and above all "predators," loosely defined as young men, often of color, who had gone down a path of lawless violence. The New York experience reversed the logic chain. Instead of locking up more people to control crime, the NYPD sought to prevent crime from occurring in the first place, reducing the number of people who had to be locked up. How much of the decline resulted from policing strategies and how much from other factors remains a topic of debate among criminologists, but policy implications are profound.[14]

Bloomberg's team also undertook a major initiative to rationalize youth detention. In his 2010 State of the City Address, the mayor announced consolidation of the Department of Juvenile Justice into the Agency for Children's Services. It was the culmination of a three-year effort by Deputy Mayor Gibbs that brought coherence to different agencies with overlapping goals. It dovetailed with development of risk-assessment instruments that provided judges with tools to help them make informed decisions about which arrested youths compelled incarceration, and which could be released safely to their homes without fear of flight or violence. The approach reduced the number of youngsters detained by 20 percent, and the number in various forms of Office of Family Services oversight by as much as 60 percent according to one analysis. In the hope of reducing recidivism, the city gained greater control over prison placement for convicted youths and put young offenders in city facilities, rather than send them upstate where they became disconnected from their families and communities. The success of the various programs was sufficient in scale to allow the city to close a notorious juvenile center located at Spofford Avenue in the Bronx.[15]

Yet, an appalling rise of violence inside the city's detention centers occurred during Bloomberg's twelve years in office. The number of New Yorkers subjected to severe physical abuse in the jails sky rocketed during his second term, and then spiked even higher during his third. Beatings by guards on inmates, and inmates on each other, were frequent and severe, systemic and undeniable. They caused permanent injury and deaths. The level of violence was beyond what any city calling itself civilized could accept in its jails. Deputy Mayor Gibbs and Bloomberg's criminal justice coordinator, John Feinblatt, shared oversight responsibility for the corrections department and were focused on the problem. But one City Hall insider insists that despite headlines on the topic in New York's daily newspapers during Bloomberg's third term, the topic "just was not on the radar" for the mayor and the rest of his team.[16]

New York City runs one of the largest jail complexes in the United States. About three-quarters of the inmates reside in ten buildings on Rikers Island, a 415-acre spit of land that sits in the East River between the Bronx and Queens. The principal purpose of "The Rock," as many inmates called the place, was to house people who were accused of crimes but not yet tried or convicted. Roughly 80 percent of its inmates were in pretrial detention waiting for judicial hearings on their cases. Others had been convicted and locked up locally because their sentences were shorter than a year. Some were waiting to transfer to state or federal facilities to serve longer terms. While Bloomberg governed, typically one hundred thousand or more inmates passed through Rikers jails annually. Some twelve thousand to fourteen thousand were present on any day. The population was highly troubled. More than one-third were emotionally disturbed, and many were accused of serious crimes.[17]

Over the decades, violence inside Rikers' jailhouses was often extreme. Conditions were awful when Rudy Giuliani became mayor, and in 1995 he asked Michael Jacobson, then the city's probation commissioner, to add the corrections department to his responsibilities and to restore order. A sociology PhD and government whiz kid who had worked in the city's budget office, Jacobson responded with three key programs. He instituted TEAMS, the same sorts of data-driven tactics the NYPD was pioneering on city streets with Compstat. He identified gang members and guards with potential gang connections, and transferred them from one jailhouse to another every two or three days to prevent them from organizing trouble. And he instituted a broad range of in-jail activities to prevent idle hands from doing the devil's work. Between 1995 and 2002, Jacobson and his successors drove down inmate slashings and stabbings from over one thousand per year to just twenty-nine. When Giuliani left office, the jailhouses were as under control as the nature of the beast allowed.[18]

Martin Horn, a respected corrections professional who had run Pennsylvania's prisons for five years, became New York City probation commissioner in 2002, and corrections commissioner as well in 2003. For his first few years on the job, violence at Rikers continued to decline. In time, the general pressures of running the jails, budget issues, and, above all, conflict with Norman Seabrook, the combative head of the Corrections Officers Benevolent Association, wore him down. The jails were never a Bloomberg administration priority, but throughout the first term, Chief of Staff Peter Madonia was Horn's key City Hall contact, and among other things he enjoyed a certain "camaraderie" with Seabrook. The two men had worked together on Bloomberg's

2001 election campaign, and Madonia made a conscious effort to maintain the relationship. As it happened, both lived in the Bronx. So from time to time, on his way home from work, Madonia would swing through Morris Park and stop by the Pine on Bronxdale Avenue, the union leader's favorite "hangout," where Seabrook would confide in him over a tall glass of vodka. Sometimes Madonia would support an action Seabrook sought, or explain in person why he could not. An occasional favor, and the psychic support access to the mayor's chief of staff provided, made Seabrook feel he was "an important player" and helped keep him "inside the tent."[19]

Madonia's departure was part of the second term shake-up that led Bloomberg to name Linda Gibbs deputy mayor of Health and Human Services with a portfolio of responsibilities that included the corrections department. Her background and broad mandate over social service agencies made her well placed to support delivery of programs for the jails, but the essential jailhouse functions of care, custody, and control were the commissioner's responsibility. Gibbs made no pretense of expertise in those areas, nor did she have the kind of relationship that Madonia had with Seabrook. Other deputies had formal responsibility for labor matters.[20]

Seabrook had been a Bronx juvenile delinquent who joined the city corrections department as a young man, and in 1995 won election as president of the union representing its officers, a position he held throughout Bloomberg's three terms. He was the only major municipal labor leader to endorse Bloomberg as a candidate in 2001, and he fancied himself a kingmaker. He constantly reminded Horn he had the mayor's cell phone on speed dial, and easier access to him than the commissioner. At the merest hint of a slight, he would threaten to disrupt the jails, or to send hundreds of officers to protest in front of City Hall, or to seize control of the single bridge that connected Rikers jails to Queens and lockdown the island and the city's courts. He desperately sought parity for his department with the NYPD, and for himself with the city's most respected union leader, Randi Weingarten. Once, when the city closed a handful of schools during a flu scare, Seabrook called Horn and told him if the city was closing schools it had to close the jails too. Horn rejected the absurd request, but according to a city official familiar with the event, it was one of the few times Horn spoke directly with the mayor, and the instruction he received was to "kiss Norman's ass," to defuse the situation.[21]

Budget issues intensified the challenges of running the jails. Reacting to the decline in the number of inmates incarcerated, analysts called for staff reductions. The number of uniformed officers fell from over 10,600 in 2002 to fewer than 8,500 in 2011. Civilian support dropped by another 200 employees. Despite the job's stresses, overtime became mandatory, more than doubling between 2006 and 2013. Guards unable to cope called in sick. The absences forced the staff in place to remain on extended duty, wearing down more officers. A rising proportion of the smaller number of inmates were emotionally disturbed. Increasingly, instead of providing therapy, troublesome ones were placed in solitary confinement for twenty-three hours a day. Prisoner resentment toward guards grew. So did inmate attacks on them. Fatigue, frustration, anger, and fear rose among the harried keepers of a violent and troubled population. Acknowledged use of force by guards on inmates, low when Bloomberg became mayor, and somewhat lower still between 2002 and 2005, spiked from roughly 70 per thousand in 2006 to 130 by 2009.[22]

In November 2008, Horn warned the budget office in writing that "further cuts were impossible without jeopardizing the safety of everyone in the jails." His protest got lost in the ritualistic communication between a municipal line agency and the Office of Management and Budget, where the one pleaded for more resources and the other for more efficiency. Typically, an agency head confronted with that kind of situation would ask the deputy mayor responsible to arrange a meeting with the mayor to appeal the decision. Surprisingly, Horn never brought the matter to Gibbs. He had lost confidence by then that he would find support at City Hall. "There was very little interest in expending political capital or financial capital on the jails," he would later tell *New York Times* journalists Michael Schwirtz and Michael Winerip. Gibbs disputes the charge. In any event, a series of events during the first half of 2009 caused Horn to conclude that he "could not trust" the staff he relied on to control the jails. He filed for his pension, and retired to academia.[23]

By the time Horn left, things were bad. In one cell block, guards and supervisors organized inmates into a gang to maintain order and to run an extortion racket. It was so well developed it had a name, "The Program." When eighteen-year-old Christopher Robinson refused to "get with the Program," the gang beat him on instructions from corrections department staff, and killed him. The inmates were convicted of the murder, and three corrections officials involved were convicted on other charges. It was the second case brought against guards for running the gang. While Bloomberg was mayor, at least seven lawsuits were filed accusing corrections officers of beating detainees or ordering other inmates to inflict brutal violence on them. Sometimes guards opened cells to let enforcers in. In other instances, they instructed targeted inmates to enter rooms that lacked surveillance cameras where they were met with vicious attacks.[24]

Excessive use of isolation cells as punishment for infractions had inhumane consequences. Jennifer Gonnerman told the story of Kalief Browder in a *New Yorker* magazine profile. He was a sixteen-year-old African American accused of being one of a group of teens who stole another boy's backpack in May 2010.

Browder denied involvement. He had been arrested at least once before when some friends took a truck for a joyride and crashed it into a parked car. Browder claimed he had only watched, but he had no defense, so he copped a plea. Since he had a record, the judge in the backpack case set bail at $3,000, far more than his family could raise. Astonishingly, for a case that all agreed was straightforward, the dysfunctional criminal justice system kept Browder in pretrial detention for three years, much of it in psychologically damaging isolation before the charge was dismissed. The Bronx District Attorney's Office appears to have dragged out the pretrial period deliberately in the hope of coercing Browder to plead guilty and improve conviction rates. The young man tried to kill himself several times while in prison. Tragically, two years after his release in June 2015, he succeeded.[25]

Dora Schriro, who had run the Missouri and Arizona jail systems, and who served briefly in the federal Department of Homeland Security on detention related matters, became New York City's corrections commissioner in 2009. She focused on mental health–related violence and sought more resources for the department with modest success, but she proved unequal to the task of taming the jailhouse, dominated increasingly by Seabrook, who broke with Bloomberg when the mayor sought a third term in 2009.[26]

When Schriro tried to institute a program to search officers entering the complex for contraband, Seabrook blocked it despite evidence many were a source of the problem. He sabotaged proposals to screen corrections department job applicants for gang-related connections. In an effort to humiliate Schriro, he had one of his guards dress as the children's cartoon character, Dora the Explorer, and follow the commissioner around the jailhouse while she led a group on a tour. The union boss took every opportunity to denounce the department's chief investigator when she began to suspend guards for unnecessary violence, and refer cases to the Bronx District Attorney for prosecution instead of treating them as departmental violations. Armed with some $500,000 of annual contributions to New York State legislators, Seabrook succeeded in getting both houses to vote to transfer responsibility for prosecutions at Rikers from the Bronx to Queens, where he hoped for more favorable treatment. Governor Andrew Cuomo declined to sign the bill. Schriro was no match for Seabrook's corrupt politicking and thuggish tactics.[27]

While the battle for jailhouse control raged, cases of corrections officers assaulting inmates or allowing them to die with sadistic callousness continued to surface. The New York City Board of Corrections, a watchdog agency, met with members of Bloomberg's staff to talk "about the prevalence of violence by correctional staff toward prisoners, and they did not respond," according to board member Dr. Robert Cohen. "Bloomberg did nothing to restrain his out-of-control workforce at Rikers," was how Mary Lynne Werlwas, a Legal Aid Society lawyer, described events. Gibbs, Feinblatt, and Schriro were working to respond to the perplexing issues, and with other agency heads and outside experts they conducted an extensive study of mentally ill inmates searching for more humane ways to manage them. But the efforts lacked the urgency the situation required, and in any event were ineffective. The *New York Times* got hold of a confidential study by the Department of Health and Mental Hygiene that documented 129 cases between January and November 2013 of inmates who suffered injuries from guards too serious for the jail's clinic to handle. In some 80 percent of the cases, the inmates claimed that their beatings took place after they were handcuffed.[28]

The most serious challenge to the city's control over Rikers occurred in November 2013, toward the very end of the Bloomberg administration. A twenty-one-year-old inmate, Dapree Peterson, filed charges against two guards for assaulting him and covering it up. On the day of the trial, corrections staff declared all of the department's buses unsafe and refused to drive detainees to court. Drivers cited things like a broken taillight, an expired fire extinguisher, a "check engine" light, and an inaudible back-up signal as the reasons the vehicles were too dangerous to use. In addition to disrupting Dapree's trial, the action prevented some 750 inmates from appearing in court, and forty-nine more from receiving scheduled medical care.[29]

An enraged Bloomberg convened a group of senior city officials to determine how to discipline the conspirators. One of them remembered the scene. "There was this incredible resistance. Everybody was complicit . . . they weren't on [Seabrook's] side," but they all had a reason why their department could not pursue the powerful union leader and the militia he controlled. "You can't prove he told them to do it," one said. "You can't file administrative charges for this sort of thing," said another. "I don't know if you want to do that to Norman," said a third, fearful of escalating the conflict. "I don't give a shit," Bloomberg screamed, pounding the table. "Take him to court. File charges. Do it." The city sued the union, won the case, and docked the treasonous guards two days' pay. It was all the city could do. The union reimbursed in full all the officers who paid fines, rendering the punishment irrelevant.[30]

Almost two years earlier, in January 2012, US Attorney Preet Bharara's office began investigating the serious, persistent public charges that male adolescents at Rikers Island were subjected to excessive violence. The details of the investigation were deeply disturbing even to those familiar with the sort of barbarity that occurs far too often in American jails. "Force is used against adolescents at an alarming rate and violent inmate-on-inmate fights and assaults are commonplace, resulting in a striking number of serious injuries," the Department of Justice report stated. The incidence of "broken jaws, broken orbital bones, broken noses, long bone fractures and lacerations requiring sutures" made it clear that inmates were "at constant risk of physical harm while incarcerated." An experienced consultant the Department of Justice hired to help it assess the situation had "never observed a system with such frequent inmate-on-inmate violence." Corrections officers relied on beatings as punishment and retribution, and in response to verbal altercations, especially in places without video camera surveillance. Specialized teams that responded to disturbances—on average three a day—were especially brutal. To mask their attacks and provide false justifications for them, corrections officers would yell "stop resisting," while they pummeled adolescent prisoners curled up in the fetal position. Intimidation tactics caused many assaults to remain unreported. Senior corrections department officials falsified reports to cover up the extent of the violence.[31]

The federal investigation covered the period from 2011 to 2013, but findings were sent to the city officially in August 2014. It fell to the de Blasio administration to contend with the vicious environment that reemerged in the city jails while Bloomberg governed. A subsequent federal lawsuit claimed virtually the entire city corrections system engaged in abuses similar to the ones Bharara's office documented at the youth detention centers, and that the city had responded to the unacceptable conditions with "deliberate indifference" over an extended period of time. A settlement called for a federal monitor to ensure implementation of a long list of remediation measures. In the meantime, city undercover officers demonstrated illegal contraband could be smuggled into Rikers' jails, making Seabrook's opposition to guard searches untenable. Surveillance improved. The city showed that lax hiring and inadequate personnel assessment practices allowed the department to hire officers connected to gangs. Objections to improved employment screening measures lost credibility. Federal officials subpoenaed financial records from Norman Seabrook's union and launched an investigation into potential misuse of union funds for personal benefit, and in 2016 the US Attorney's Office indicted Seabrook. A senior Bloomberg official, speaking years after leaving office, expressed regret that no one realized they had an "either/or decision on their hands." Either "buy Seabrook off," with favors for his union, "or get rid of him." There was no other way to control the city's jails.[32]

Ground Zero's Indispensable Man

At the start of Bloomberg's third term in January 2010, Ground Zero remained a huge hole and the single greatest threat to the city's economic future. Without redevelopment at the site, downtown Manhattan could not recover and New York's second-most-important economic engine—the nation's fourth most important business district—would sputter ineffectively. By September 12, 2013, a dozen years after the 9/11 attacks, speaking at a breakfast held at 7 World Trade Center about the recovery effort, Mayor Bloomberg could tell the Alliance for Downtown Manhattan. "Today, I think it is safe to say together we succeeded beyond what anyone thought was possible." He had reason.[33]

In the fear and uncertainty immediately following the collapse of the Twin Towers, "there were serious people with serious discussions about whether we had any future at all," Bloomberg reminded his audience. "As the wakes and funerals stretched on for weeks and months, many people wondered whether the final eulogy would be for the city itself." Even years later, when the city's revival had been assured, doubts about lower Manhattan lingered. "Progress, in all fairness, we have to admit it, has not followed a straight line," Bloomberg told the audience, acknowledging with polite understatement that the neighborhood's reconstruction had been fraught with conflict. Yet, on the verge of Bloomberg's departure from office, the work completed, construction under way, and above all the revitalization of the area around the site, was legitimate cause for pride. For years, redevelopment had been crippled by legal claims, technical complexities, greed, incompetence, overlapping authority and accountability, and, above all, lack of political will. Along the way, it became apparent that no person and no combination of leaders involved in the reconstruction of the World Trade Center had the power, skill, or money to make something rise on the city's unhealed wound. Until Michael Bloomberg set his mind to it. More than anyone else, it was he who provided the essential leadership to make it happen.[34]

A century before Bloomberg's talk, the Woolworth Building opened for business. It was the tallest skyscraper in the world in 1913 and New Yorkers heralded it as the Cathedral of Commerce, a testament to their city's role as the center of global business. It stood just south of City Hall on Broadway, some blocks north of the Customs House at the southern tip of Manhattan that overlooked a harbor bustling with ships. The House of Morgan's new headquarters at 23 Wall Street completed that same year, and the New York Stock Exchange across the street from it, were likewise just a few blocks away from the new tower. At the time, none doubted downtown Manhattan was the place where New Yorkers and the world did their business.[35]

Another building that opened in 1913, Grand Central Terminal on Park Avenue at 42nd Street, would have a powerful impact on the city's commercial geography. "Even before it was finished, Grand Central became the impetus for an extraordinary urban renewal and repurposing of nearby property," Sam Roberts wrote in his 2013 celebration of the train station's centennial. The project included a decision to enclose the tracks that ran for miles down the east side of Manhattan on Park Avenue inside a tunnel, transforming what had been a source of blight for decades into the nation's most elegant address.[36]

Unlike downtown, almost exclusively the site of commercial and government offices, midtown had department stores and retail shops, museums and cultural centers, restaurants and evening distractions. It offered life during lunch hour and after work in a way Wall Street did not. Rich executives bought Park Avenue apartments and sought offices within walking distance. Businesses set up shop near Grand Central Terminal, and commuters arriving in the station found less reason by the year to make a second train journey downtown. Contractors built new offices in midtown to meet demand. The downtown structures, even elegant ones with inspired designs, became tired and out-of-date places to work as their insides aged. In the years after World War II, midtown became the place to be. In her 1961 classic, *The Death and Life of Great American Cities,* Jane Jacobs wrote Wall Street's nearly uniform use for commercial purposes explained why, "firm after firm has left for mixed-use midtown." They had to, a real estate broker told Jacobs, "otherwise their personnel departments can't get or keep people who can spell 'molybdenum,'" a serious deficiency, one supposes, for commodities traders.[37]

Despite the trend, in 1955 Chase National Bank decided to build a new office tower downtown. The inclination of so many other banks to migrate north, and the steadily declining pool of Class A office space in the lower Manhattan district, made it clear the downward spiral would continue if something did not change. When David Rockefeller, grandson of the nation's first billionaire, became president of a greatly expanded Chase Manhattan Bank a few years later, he decided it would be a good idea to build a World Trade Center in the neighborhood. He envisioned a huge office complex to make it easy for foreign companies looking to open shop in New York to rent suitable space downtown. Local companies doing business with foreign entities could move there as well. The project would reaffirm New York's role as the hub of international commerce at a time when the global direction of big business was accelerating. Rockefeller commissioned McKinsey & Company to study the idea. They did, and concluded it made no sense. Rockefeller suppressed the report, and realized the project would require public financing to move forward.[38]

The Port Authority of New York and New Jersey was created in 1921 to manage the infrastructure needs of the natural harbor that sat between the two states and the transportation links that connected them. The governors of New York and New Jersey appointed the authority's executives and board members, with each essentially controlling construction and operations on their side of the Hudson River. Since downtown Manhattan bordered the port, and since the center Rockefeller imagined was meant to promote international trade, creative minds could convince themselves it met the terms of the Port Authority's mandate. Conveniently, the governor of New York was David Rockefeller's older brother, Nelson. Unsurprisingly, he supported his sibling's project. The design that emerged called for two enormous towers 110 stories high, each story a full acre in size, and each tower the tallest building in the world when complete. They would be surrounded by five additional office buildings, each a skyscraper in its own right. McKinsey warned the scale proposed would glut the downtown market and make building anything else there infeasible for years.[39]

The superblock assembled as a platform for the towers, and the gigantic office buildings erected on them, reinforced with spectacular intensity the single-use, single time-of-day function at the heart of the area's decline. When the mid-1970s fiscal crisis arrived and New York City descended into some of its darkest days, acres of trade tower real estate remained unrented for two decades despite subsidies that poisoned the market for private developers. For years the World Trade Center served as a symbol of the folly that followed when government involved itself in initiatives best left to market forces.[40]

Slowly, things changed. Eventually the buildings became fully leased and tens of thousands of people worked in them daily. Millions visited their observation deck annually. The Twin Towers replaced the Empire State Building in the climactic final scene of *King Kong* in a 1976 remake of the 1933 classic, and they featured in countless Hollywood movies. They entered the popular culture and billions around the world recognized them as defining images of New York City's skyline. At some imperceptible moment, they became the iconic symbols of New York City as the place for global commerce, just as David Rockefeller had hoped. Ironically, it happened even though the towers did not sit in their own city's primary business district. Downtown still served as home to a critical mass of investment banks, but the term Wall Street had ceased to be a description of a physical location by the time the towers went up. It had become instead a metaphor for the city's financial industry and for high finance in general.[41]

Even in their more popular incarnation, the towers contributed to downtown Manhattan's sterile atmosphere. During the 1980s and 1990s, Battery Park City went up on landfill taken from the towers' site and deposited along the Hudson River shoreline just west of the business district. That brought a significant residential population and some services back to the area. It was an important start to creating a mixed-use neighborhood around the periphery of the massive state sponsored project. By the end of the 1990s, lower Manhattan had begun to do what Jacobs said worked best in cities. It had begun to organize itself. Buildings no longer suitable for their original purposes were being converted into attractive places to live, and shops and services to support the people moving into them were beginning to emerge. Urban planners with sharp, future-focused vision could just begin to see the fuzzy outlines of a revitalized multi-purpose neighborhood when the attack pulverized the towers and left a huge physical and spiritual hole in the middle of it. It fell to New Yorkers to find a path from a smoldering site of mass murder and devastating destruction to a place where people could once again work and live, smile, and play in defiance of evil inflicted upon them.[42]

The Port Authority owned the sixteen-acre patch of land on which the towers and related buildings once stood. The 9/11 attack killed its executive director and more than seventy members of the Port Authority's staff. The agency would have five leaders over the next dozen years. During that time, nine governors would come and go in New York and New Jersey, creating policy incoherence at the highest level of the dual-state governance structure. Despite the fundamental tangible and emotional significance the site had for New York City's people, their mayor had scant legal standing over it beyond responsibility for a few streets. Early on, Deputy Mayor Doctoroff tried to change the dynamic by proposing a swap of city-owned land at JFK and LaGuardia airports that were leased to the Port Authority for the World Trade Center site, but the proposal went nowhere. Governor Pataki preferred to maintain control over the high-profile construction site and the many photo opportunities it was sure to generate. Nevertheless, over time, Bloomberg was the only senior public official still in power with a stake in the project. Improbably, he became the indispensable man.[43]

Nineteen public agencies exercised some measure of control over various parts of the site, including complex transit infrastructure underneath it. It was also a state and federal crime scene. Just weeks before the 2001 attack, the authority had leased the World Trade Center for ninety-nine years to Larry Silverstein, a private real estate developer who journalist Deborah Sontag described as "a chauffeur-driven, cuff link wearing resident of Park Avenue," who had started life on the "not . . . very commodious nor sweet smelling" top floor of a Bedford-Stuyvesant walk-up. His contract gave him redevelopment rights over the site, and he owned the private insurance policies that would provide billions of dollars of critical funding.[44]

It would have surprised no one if a new mayor elected just weeks after September 11, 2001 had insisted on a major role in the rebuilding process. As late as early November of that year, Democrat Mark Green remained the presumptive winner of the contest, much to Republican Governor Pataki's consternation. Ostensibly to provide coherence to the decision-making scrum in formation, a few days before the election, Pataki announced creation of the Lower Manhattan Development Corporation to oversee a comprehensive

Bloomberg had to negotiate with four different New York State governors during his twelve years as mayor. He is shown here with Governor George Pataki (right) reviewing architect Daniel Liebeskind's proposal for rebuilding the World Trade Tower site. *Photo Credit: New York City Municipal Archives*

New York State Assembly Speaker Sheldon Silver provided critical budget support for New York City following 9/11. He and Bloomberg ended up at antagonistic odds over a controversial proposal for a West Side stadium, and over congestion pricing. *Photo Credit: New York City Municipal Archives*

When Governor Andrew Cuomo made pension reform a priority for state workers, Bloomberg made sure city pension plans were also covered. *Photo Credit: New York City Municipal Archives*

Bloomberg taxed tobacco heavily and instituted smoking bans in all workplaces, public buildings, and parks. He considered the national and international movement his initiative sparked one of his most important achievements. *Photo Credit: New York City Municipal Archives*

Bloomberg's sustainability initiative, *PlaNYC*, promoted economic growth and an environmentally healthy city as complementary goals. Rohit Aggarwala, shown here with Al Gore and Bloomberg, was instrumental in the plan's development. *Photo Credit: New York City Municipal Archives*

Bloomberg's Commission for Economic Opportunity set the stage for a range of creative antipoverty initiatives. Deputy Mayor Linda Gibbs (left) oversaw the study. Richard Parsons (right) co-chaired the commission with Geoffrey Canada (not pictured). *Photo Credit: New York City Municipal Archives*

Bloomberg traveled to his second inauguration on January 1, 2006 by subway with his companion, Diana Taylor. *Photo Credit: New York City Municipal Archives*

Howard Wolfson (center) played a critical role in Bloomberg's 2009 reelection to a third term and became deputy mayor. Stuart Loesser (right) served as Bloomberg's press secretary during his second and third terms. *Photo Credit: New York City Municipal Archives*

An ebullient Bloomberg the night of his reelection to a third term as mayor of New York City.
Photo Credit: New York City Municipal Archives

Surrounded by religious leaders, with the Statue of Liberty as backdrop, Bloomberg defended the right of a Muslim cleric to build a religious center near the World Trade Tower site. City Council Speaker Christine Quinn can be seen behind him. *Photo Credit: New York City Municipal Archives*

Lack of political leadership coupled with financial shortfalls prevented reconstruction at the site of the World Trade Towers until Bloomberg intervened. *Photo Credit: New York City Municipal Archives*

Bloomberg supported cultural events because they attracted people to New York City. He is seen here clowning with the cast of a skit during an annual presentation of the Mayor's Culture Awards. *Photo Credit: New York City Municipal Archives*

Mayor Bloomberg at work in his cubicle at City Hall. *Photo Credit: New York City Municipal Archives*

reconstruction plan. The timing of the announcement and the composition of the organization's board made it clear the decision was motivated by what one of its directors would refer to as "a game of keep away" from Mark Green. The new agency added another entity to the already cumbersome mix.[45]

Emotions compounded complex technical and legal matters. The families of the thousands murdered there knew that it contained the remains of people they loved. Recovery of body parts gave some a means of holding a burial and coming to closure. Many lacked even that. Everyone in the city and everyone in the nation had an emotional claim on the land, as did many foreigners as well. Citizens from eighty-two different countries had perished in the attack. Debate raged about what to do next. Rebuild it immediately, "taller, bigger, stronger," to demonstrate to the terrorists they had failed, defined one end of the spectrum. Recognize it as the cemetery it had become and build nothing on it, defined the other. In 2004, Governor Pataki declared that the footprints of the two fallen towers would be reserved to remember the dead. Building could take place on the rest of the site.[46]

In December 2002, not long before a round of redevelopment plans was scheduled for public view, Bloomberg outlined a comprehensive program for revitalizing lower Manhattan. It covered most everything except the site itself to make clear his views on how the rebuilt center should fit into the city around it. He approached the topic with admirable candor. "When the World Trade Center was first built, it was hailed as a cure-all for everything that plagued downtown," he told the crowd at a breakfast hosted by the Association for a Better New York, one of the city's premier business advocacy organizations. "But, if we are honest with ourselves," he said, "we will recognize that its impact on our City was not all positive." He reminded listeners that the towers had disrupted the local real estate market for a long time. The post 9/11 economic slowdown caused many to fear rebuilding massive amounts of office space would repeat the mistake. The enormous complex had also neutered the local neighborhood. The right approach to rebuilding, Bloomberg insisted, was to make lower Manhattan, "an even more vibrant global hub of culture and commerce, a live-and-work-and-visit community for the world." The public sector had a compelling responsibility "to catalyze" the neighborhood's transformation "by making bold investments," Bloomberg said. It needed to do so with a sense of purpose and urgency equal to the enormous task that confronted a resourceful but wounded city. "To be effective," the businessman mayor argued, public "investments must trigger a response by the private market that will—through joint public/private initiatives—create the kind of lower Manhattan we want." The place Bloomberg envisioned was filled with "people who reflect all the diversity and drive of New York," a place where remarkable people would want to visit, live, and work.[47]

Bloomberg's vision committed the city to sponsor affordable housing projects, new schools, a library, and other amenities. The projects were meant to spearhead development of two new neighborhoods downtown, one near Fulton Street east of Broadway and another south of Liberty Street on the west side. The city would also initiate zoning changes designed to encourage private development of housing and retail shops. Improved transportation flow and renovation of public spaces to take full advantage of the harbor near Battery Park and elsewhere were also contemplated. The taxpayer cost of the various initiatives was expected to exceed $1.5 billion. One major project, to build a direct "one-seat" mass transit link from JFK to the downtown business district for nearly $9.0 billion, would never get beyond the planning stage. The rest of the proposals moved forward.[48]

By the time Bloomberg announced his plan, the city working with the Port Authority and other agencies had already cleared massive amounts of debris from the site of the attack. Temporary infrastructure restored public transportation. Larry Silverstein won a $4.3 billion award from insurance companies in 2004 after several years of litigation, and he moved rapidly to raise a new skyscraper at 7 World Trade Center on the periphery of Ground Zero, outside of the complicated emotional and technical concerns entangling the core. Beyond that, little reconstruction occurred for years. Site plans were solicited, designed, ridiculed publicly, rejected, redone, approved, rejected again for security reasons, redone and approved again between 2002 and 2005. After an elaborate public contest, the Lower Manhattan Development Corporation accepted a Daniel Libeskind site plan that called for six buildings. The tallest would reach a symbolic height of 1776 feet counting the antennae on top of it. Governor Pataki named it the Freedom Tower.[49]

Many detected a *de facto* division of labor between the mayor and the governor on New York City's two biggest development projects. The mayor and the city pursued the Olympic bid and the huge midtown development at Hudson Yards, while the governor and Port Authority oversaw the downtown project at the trade tower site. Since the governor held most of the power over the downtown site, the arrangement seemed sensible. Moreover, Pataki was determined to see substantial progress rise from the ashes of 9/11 before the end of 2006 when his third term in office expired.[50]

Yet, despite Pataki's clear motivation, by the fall of 2005 the highest-profile development project in the world, which sat walking distance from the mayor's office at City Hall, was badly stuck. It had become a public embarrassment and a source of frustration to all involved. In May 2005, the *New York Times* editorialized that Bloomberg's "obsession" with the West Side stadium had left the rebuilding of Ground Zero "in the shadows." In *New York* magazine,

Kurt Anderson wrote that the reconstruction process at Ground Zero "whip-sawed between unfortunate private sector extremes governed by commercial and bureaucratic banalities on the one hand and blustery emotion and meta-physics on the other." Fixing it "would require our governor and mayor to behave like real leaders," he wrote. On November 1, 2005 the New York Metro Chapter of the American Planning Association issued a statement speaking for themselves and other organizations that opened with the line: "The sad and growing disarray at Ground Zero has recently been cited on the front pages and the nightly news." A lawyer "close to Governor Pataki" described the situation as "a fucking mess."[51]

A concerned Mayor Bloomberg asked for a briefing on the project. Deputy Mayor Doctoroff arranged for Lehman Brothers and the Urban Land Institute, a nonprofit organization, to collaborate with the city's Economic Development Corporation to analyze the problem. Robert Lieber, still at Lehman Brothers at the time, was part of the bank's team. Seth Pinsky, then a vice president at the Economic Development Corporation, and later its president, worked on the report for the EDC. The study recognized that coordinating construction of a huge memorial and museum, fifteen different subway and commuter train lines, and several major office buildings on property controlled by multiple agencies and a private developer created enormous technical and bureaucratic challenges. Yet, more than any other matter, the study concluded the problem was money. "What we realized," Pinsky later said, "was that unless someone came from heaven with a big bag of cash, there was no way financially to rebuild the entire site."[52]

The report Bloomberg ordered raised the possibility of a disaster. If Silverstein went ahead with his plans to launch reconstruction of ten million square feet and ran out of money before completing his projects, he might pocket what money he could, declare bankruptcy, and walk away. The Port Authority, and the city, and state, would be left with a huge, incomplete construction site in the heart of Manhattan's downtown business district that would remain mired in legal battles for years as creditors sought to recapture their share of the assets.[53]

Any diminishment in the amount of space rebuilt would diminish Silverstein's economic standing. It would also reduce the value of the site to the Port Authority, which remained the ultimate owner of the property. Silverstein had insisted from the first days after the catastrophe that he would rebuild the full scope of real estate destroyed, and he had continued to pay the Port Authority $120 million in annual rent as his lease required, even though the land was barren. Yet, the $4.3 billion insurance payout he received, large as it was, would cover less than half the cost his ambitious plan implied. He could not raise additional private funds since he could not secure anchor tenants. Renters feared that the site, and especially the Freedom Tower, would become the most appealing terrorist target in the world the day it opened for business. Moreover, according to the city's analysis, based on projected rates for office space, even fully rented, Silverstein's plan was "a financial impossibility" owing to the high cost of infrastructure and security at the site. Loath to surrender any of the space he controlled, Silverstein had been negotiating stubbornly for the Port Authority to absorb a greater share of the cost of rebuilding. He also called on the city and state to allocate to his redevelopment plans billions of dollars of tax-exempt Liberty Bonds authorized by the federal government to assist with rebuilding at the attack site.[54]

Bloomberg went public with his team's report and suggested progress would be easier without Silverstein involved. At the very least, he insisted, a major restructuring was needed to force the cash-constrained developer to surrender his rights over some of the buildings. He made his increased concern clear by appointing Deputy Mayor Doctoroff and other senior members of his team to represent the city on the Lower Manhattan Development Corporation. In the high-profile setting of his 2006 State of the City Address, Bloomberg drew attention to the stalled project, insisting that Silverstein and the Port Authority "push aside individual financial interest and do what's best for our city." The Port Authority adopted the mayor's posture and Governor Pataki set a mid-March 2006 deadline for agreement on a new plan. Weeks of ferocious negotiations followed. The date came and went, but instead of announcing an agreement, negotiators offered the public ugly recriminations. Finally, in April, Silverstein ceded control over the Freedom Tower and one other skyscraper to the Port Authority. With that and other provisions, the city and state allocated $3.35 billion in Liberty Bonds they controlled to Silverstein and the Port Authority on agreed-upon terms. The Port Authority rushed to lay down steel on the Freedom Tower before Pataki left office. The governor told an interviewer that he had read *The Power Broker*, Robert Caro's masterful history of Robert Moses and "how he got things done." Once construction was under way, Pataki knew his successor would find it impossible to stop the project and leave it unfinished. (And people say historians serve no practical purpose).[55]

The restructuring agreement established a schedule for rebuilding, including a series of deadlines and penalties for missed dates, but problems continued to plague the site. Controversy emerged surrounding cost estimates for a museum and a memorial selected through a complex, highly public design contest. Calculations suggested it would take $1 billion to construct what had been proposed, and $60 million annually to operate it. By comparison, the Vietnam War Memorial in Washington DC, had cost $8.4 million. In May

2006, former Goldman Sachs CEO John Whitehead, the chairman of the museum and memorial foundation, resigned. Other key people involved left and the memorial plan appeared at risk. Building offices on the site without a remembrance was unimaginable. No memorial meant no reconstruction project, which meant the huge wound in downtown Manhattan would continue to cripple the district indefinitely. So Bloomberg took responsibility for the museum and memorial.[56]

There is every reason to believe that Bloomberg took control of the task because he thought he was the only person who could get it done. In many respects, it was a surprising decision. Bloomberg's instincts were always to move on after a failure or disappointment, and he had said so in the context of 9/11. In a meeting with the design jury empaneled to select the memorial, Bloomberg described himself as "a believer in the future, not the past. I can't do anything about the past," he said. He made it clear in various settings that he would prefer to use valuable downtown real estate for schools, parks, and housing—services for the living—rather than a memorial for the dead. Yet, chaos at the memorial project meant stagnation at the building site. Bloomberg found that prospect unacceptable, and so he stepped up. Some saw it as a power grab. It is more accurately understood as an indispensable man assuming an obligation he would rather have avoided.[57]

Bloomberg's involvement in the memorial and museum gave the city a major role at the site. Its design covered half the surface area and construction had to be integrated into infrastructure decisions. It provided a platform for Bloomberg to intervene at key points. He contributed $15 million of his own money to the memorial and museum foundation, and he raised hundreds of millions of dollars from the network of wealthy friends he had developed through years of mutually supportive philanthropy. In great measure, the cash flowed in because his involvement restored confidence the project would succeed. He insisted that the memorial plans be revised to reduce the construction costs, and despite his personal attitude about dwelling on the past, he resolved emotional issues that others had found intractable, notably how the names of the people murdered would be displayed on the memorial.[58]

Despite commitments detailed in the restructuring agreement, construction fell way behind schedule. Silverstein could not proceed with certain obligations because the Port Authority had to rebuild infrastructure first. It proved incapable of doing so. Engineering decisions that needed to be made holistically crisscrossed the legal structure of the site and the leadership to sort through them was lacking. Pataki's term expired at the end of 2006. Governor Spitzer came and went in a little over a year, characterized more by drama than progress at the World Trade Center no less than in other aspects of his aborted term. The situation remained unacceptable.[59]

When David Paterson became governor, he sought to distance himself from his predecessors' failures. He asked around for a person he could appoint as Executive Director of the Port Authority to start his tenure over the troubled site with a clean slate. The name that emerged was Christopher Ward. He had served as Bloomberg's commissioner of environmental protection between 2002 and 2006, and he had worked at the Port Authority from 1997 to 2002, rising to chief of strategic planning and external affairs. At one point, he was tasked with project management of the effort to build the Air Train, a rail link from JFK airport to the city's transit system that cut through the middle-class African American neighborhood of Jamaica, Queens. His work on the project earned Ward high credibility with local African American politicians who recommended him to the accidental governor.[60]

Paterson's secretary, Charles O'Byrne, called Ward to Albany several times to discuss the job. "David really only knows one thing about the Port Authority right now and that is that the World Trade Center project is a disaster," Ward remembers being told. "It's the worst-kept secret that it's way over budget, and the schedules are all screwed up. You need to get in there immediately and turn that around. David isn't going to own Eliot Spitzer's problem or George Pataki's problem." Spitzer's team had insisted repeatedly that the project was on schedule. It was a public-relations strategy designed to keep pressure on the various contractors working at the site. Yet, all involved recognized the claim was disingenuous, so rather than motivate faster completion, the approach simply damaged credibility. Paterson's staff told Ward they expected him to keep their office informed of significant developments across the agency—"no surprises or we will be really pissed"—but they promised to trust Ward's experience and judgment on policy matters, and that the governor would avoid the sort of political interference that had contributed to the sorry state of affairs.[61]

Ward understood that in the mind of the governor who appointed him, the job was "the World Trade Center, the World Trade Center, the World Trade Center." During his first few months he responded to what he called "a willing suspension of disbelief" about the project by hitting the reset button. He issued reports that made it clear reconstruction would take more money and time than previously acknowledged. In a press conference releasing one of the earlier reassessments, the agency avoided specifics. Paterson slapped down questions pressing for details. "Here's what we're not going to do. We're not going to give any phony dates or timetables at this point and then follow it up with phony ribbon-cuttings and encouraging words and no follow-up," he said in thinly veiled reference to the way Pataki and Spitzer handled the matter. Ward brought a measure of badly needed discipline to the complex project, but conflicts continued and progress was slow.[62]

Bloomberg met with Ward and expressed his judgment that the Port Authority had to complete construction of the memorial in time for the tenth anniversary of the 9/11 attack in 2011, otherwise "the project would not survive." If people could not see tangible, visible progress after a decade, Bloomberg believed the reconstruction effort would be declared a failure in the court of public opinion. Other government agencies would seek to seize control. He told Ward, "the hole in his city" would remain an ugly impediment to progress in lower Manhattan. Bloomberg persuaded Ward of his view, who in turn worked with his engineers in a series of hot, late summer nights to develop a plan that constructed key elements of the site from the ground down rather than from the foundation level up to accomplish the goal.[63]

Despite signs of progress, in May 2009 another stalemate between the Port Authority and Silverstein put the deadline at risk. Bloomberg took matters into his hands. He called Ward, Port Authority Chairman Anthony Coscia, and their two bosses, Governor Paterson and New Jersey Governor Jon Corzine, to a summit meeting at Gracie Mansion, along with Larry Silverstein, Assembly Speaker Sheldon Silver, and Deputy Mayor Robert Lieber. As best people can remember, one of Silverstein's top staff and one of Governor Paterson's aides also attended. Bloomberg made clear to the small group of powerful men in no uncertain terms that he continued to expect the memorial to be completed in time for a commemoration ceremony on September 11, 2011. He spoke in his usual matter-of-fact tone, but there was no mistaking the view that the mayor expected everyone involved to find a way to break the impasse.[64]

Once again, the issue was money. Silverstein did not have enough to pursue even his revised plan, and wanted more from the Port Authority. The Port Authority's budget had been pummeled by the reconstruction effort and consequently a broad range of other pressing needs was suffering. It had already taken on major responsibilities at the site, and Ward could find little policy justification for allocating more public money to Silverstein's obligations. It was not a case of a public investment leveraging private money, but rather a public subsidy for a private developer. Bloomberg's team was sympathetic to Ward's argument, but they could think of no place else for the money to come from, so as a practical matter they wanted the Port Authority to raise its commitment. In a separate conversation, Assembly Speaker Sheldon Silver communicated the same message to Ward. Despite the pressure, Ward refused, and Governor Paterson, the one man who might have forced the matter, tacitly stood by his appointment's decision. Ward knew that Bloomberg "must have been as mad as a wet cat." When the mayor calls a Gracie Mansion summit, it is supposed to end with a mayoral victory. The assembled group could offer the press only platitudes that the discussions had generated progress.[65]

The meeting did not lead to a resolution of all issues, nor did it reduce conflict between Silverstein, the Port Authority, and the city. But the memorial deadline that Bloomberg pursued and reasserted forcefully at key moments provided a clear objective around which a range of contentious decisions could be organized. In Ward's mind, it allowed him to tell everyone else "to get the fuck in line." Importantly, after a blistering conversation with Deputy Mayor Lieber, it caused Larry Silverstein to recognize that he would have to contribute several hundred million dollars more of his own capital to preserve his position.[66]

The memorial opened on time and "received almost universally positive reviews from critics," Elizabeth Greenspan would write in *Battle for Ground Zero: Inside the Political Struggle to Rebuild the World Trade Center*. She would quote at length Martin Filler's assessment published in the *New York Review of Books*. The "inexorably powerful, enigmatically abstract pair of abyss-like pools, which demarcate the foundations of the lost Twin Towers, comes as a surprise to those of us who doubted that the chaotic and desultory reconstruction of Ground Zero could yield anything of lasting value," he wrote. "It is generally held that great architecture requires the participation of a great client," he continued, "but just how this stunning result emerged from such a fraught and contentious process will take some time for critics and historians to sort out." Michael Arad, the memorial's designer, seemed to know the answer. "It wouldn't have happened without him," he said of Bloomberg's involvement. "We'd still be arguing about what kind of memorial we should have," he told Greenspan, years after the fact. Christopher Ward shared the assessment. "He was absolutely indispensable," he said of Bloomberg.[67]

Larry Silverstein rebuilt 7 WTC by 2006. In November 2013, shortly before Bloomberg's third term ended, 4 WTC opened with city, state, and federal government agencies as anchor tenants. The museum and 1 WTC that Pataki designated the Freedom Tower opened just about a year later. 3 WTC is under construction, scheduled for completion in 2017. 2 WTC is also under construction, and 5 WTC is expected to be built at a later date. A colossal transit station on the scale of Grand Central Terminal, designed by famed architect Santiago Calatrava, is also under construction. Parts were opened in 2016. Slowly the wound is healing. Silverstein continues to negotiate with city, state, federal, and Port Authority officials for more money to finish his parts of the job at public expense.[68]

Throughout the decade-long drama that unfolded around reconstruction at the World Trade Center, Bloomberg's 2002 lower Manhattan redevelopment plan proceeded. In a 2006 progress report, Deputy Mayor Doctoroff observed that "thoughtful people had been prescribing the same remedy" for downtown Manhattan for many years, "a vibrant, highly accessible, twenty-four-hour community where people work, live and visit." The area "never lacked possibilities, or even a vision. What it lacked for decades was the will and the leadership." After 9/11, Michael Bloomberg proved the leader the district needed. "Nearly every inch of Lower Manhattan is being rebuilt, reinvented or reused and most of it will be done by the time we commemorate the tenth anniversary of 9/11," Doctoroff predicted optimistically in 2006, but accurately as it turned out. Downtown Manhattan is "on the verge of becoming the first modern commercial district to emerge in New York City in over a generation," Regional Plan Association head Tom Wright told a journalist in 2014. "It's going to be really remarkable."[69]

In 2013, Bloomberg declared that the vision he outlined in 2002 "has come to life in spectacular fashion. . . . The ghost town that was Lower Manhattan on weekends . . . has been replaced by a dynamic neighborhood that is one of the most sought-after places to live in our city." He cataloged the achievements. More than sixty thousand people lived downtown south of Chambers Street compared to some twenty-three thousand in 2001. Families could move there because the city had added 4,300 seats in five new schools. Another was on its way. Public spaces made the area "home to baseball and soccer fields . . . playgrounds and picnic gardens, bicycle lanes and pedestrian plazas, riverfront esplanades . . . and public art," Bloomberg bragged. "Even miniature golf is down here now," he told his audience. The waterfront was revitalized, twelve new hotels had already opened with another twelve expected to welcome guests within another two years. Just six had been operating in the area in 2001. Moribund city-owned buildings that had outlived their usefulness were transferred to private-sector owners, refurbished and repurposed. Employment in the area had grown modestly, even as the financial services industry shrunk in the aftermath of the global financial crisis. Media and technology professionals in particular had replaced bankers.[70]

In Bloomberg's mind, downtown Manhattan's revival was simply the highest-profile example of the way he managed the city's development priorities. His administration invested "in the conditions that create safe, vibrant, and attractive places to live, work and visit . . . across the five boroughs." He took pride declaring the city did not "spend the last twelve years trying to protect the financial industry—or any other industry—from the rising tide of globalization and technological change. . . . Instead we created the conditions that would allow a broad range of industries and entrepreneurs to capitalize on those market changes and to help us build a stronger and more diverse economy." The result was that New York remained not only "a global financial capital, but more than ever . . . a global capital for tech, for tourism, fashion, film, arts, culture, higher education, health care, entrepreneurialism of every kind," he bragged. "The future is not preordained," Bloomberg told his audience in September 2013. "It is ours to shape and strengthen as best we can."[71]

Chapter Eleven

Legacy

New Yorkers traumatized by the September 11, 2001 terrorist attack elected Michael Bloomberg to rescue the city from the risk of economic disaster and to keep them safe. He accomplished both tasks, and many more, with exceptional skill. Tactically, Bloomberg owed his election to four things. In the aftershock of 9/11, Mayor Rudy Giuliani's heroic status gave his endorsement of Bloomberg extraordinary power, particularly among political independents. Racial tension divided the Democratic Party and allowed Bloomberg to win unprecedented Latino support for a New York City candidate running for mayor on the Republican ticket. Bloomberg assembled a talented campaign team that projected the rationale for his election with rare effectiveness, and took maximum advantage of his adversary's mistakes, of which there were many. Vast wealth, which helped him to attract his team, allowed Bloomberg to arm it with $74 million, many times more than his opponents. On the morning of September 11, no New York City political strategist could be found who thought Michael Bloomberg could be elected mayor, including his own. Eight weeks later, he won.

A theory has gained some currency among political strategists that Republicans only win an election for mayor of New York when the city is in crisis. Certainly the 2001 contest fits the criterion. So does Fiorello La Guardia's 1933 victory during the Great Depression. The case for crisis as the context for the elections of John Lindsay and Rudolph Giuliani is more ambiguous. It is true that Lindsay's 1965 win took place during a mounting sense of deteriorating conditions in New York City and across urban America, and New Yorkers elected Rudolph Giuliani at a time when an extraordinary level of crime cast a shadow over the city. Yet, the challenges of those moments were surely less severe, for example, than when Edward Koch won election in 1977 as a Democrat against a backdrop of existential fiscal meltdown and blackout-induced summer riots.

Democrats only lose City Hall when the party fractures. To succeed, non-Democrats must win votes from major voting blocs—racial and ethnic groups—that normally cast ballots for the city's majority party. La Guardia pulled Italians and Jews away from Tammany Hall's Irish-dominated coalition.

Liberal John Lindsay ran disproportionately well among blacks and Jews in 1965, and Irish Catholic William Buckley won 13 percent of city ballots running on the Conservative party line that year, taking white ethnic votes that traditionally went to the city's Democrats in those days. Had Buckley not run, Abe Beame would have beat Lindsay. Giuliani won a strong majority of white Jewish votes, and a healthy share of Latino votes in his 1993 victory over African American David Dinkins. Crisis does intensify the chance of racial, ethnic, and party strife. But periodic assertions that we have achieved a post-racial society, and that ethnicity is an outdated means of understanding voting patterns in New York City, are greatly exaggerated. Conflict within the Democratic Party caused half or more of Latino voters to cast ballots against the Democratic candidate in 2001. Without that support, Bloomberg would not have been elected. And the Jewish vote also split, between two Jewish candidates who described themselves as liberal Democrats at heart. Many who chose Bloomberg were independent-minded voters more impressed by Giuliani's endorsement than by Green's campaign, and others were the sorts who had cast ballots for Ed Koch and Rudy Giuliani, liberal on a range of cultural issues perhaps, but more comfortable with Bloomberg's pragmatic, business-oriented version of liberalism than Green's ideological commitment.

Bloomberg's victory brought to City Hall a man who understood business, finance, and economics like no New York City mayor before him. His background as one of the world's most successful entrepreneurs, as an investment banker, and Harvard MBA set him apart from all of his predecessors. He attracted an unusually talented economic-development team, delegated to them boldly, and backed them loyally. He and his team steered city policy in new directions, combining bold rezoning decisions and repurposing of prime locations with revitalization initiatives in commercial districts across all five boroughs. The plans freed New York City from legacy constraints imposed by zoning rules adopted decades earlier when the city was a working-class, light-industry, and manufacturing metropolis. Aggressive management of city land-use authority and rich public investments in infrastructure readied underutilized assets to achieve their potential in a twenty-first century economy. Shrewd collaboration with private businesses leveraged the newly valuable properties. The strategy boosted private sector growth and raised municipal tax revenues. New York City persevered through the post-9/11 crisis and survived the 2007–2009 financial meltdown successfully, despite being Ground Zero for the first and the epicenter of the second. The city created jobs and maintained wage levels more effectively than the rest of the nation. Overall, economic growth lagged national levels because of 9/11 losses and the restructuring and reduced profitability of the financial industry so important to local commerce, but what was accomplished is impressive.[1]

To Bloomberg the entrepreneur, growth was an essential ingredient of success. To achieve it, he followed an old bond trader's maxim: the trend is my friend. He steered the city in the direction cast by globalization, the technology revolution, and the rise of creative talent over muscle as the source of economic value. That meant attracting to New York City the world's best and brightest, its most successful businessmen and bankers, its artists and entertainers, the elite of all stripes. He managed the tasks that followed from the strategy with rare skill, deploying municipal resources as deftly as he had his own when he set out to transform the world's financial markets. His policies provided a favorable business environment for media, telecommunications, and technology, for fashion and design, for bio-medicine, the healthcare industry and higher education, for tourism, entertainment and related services. He consciously sought to diversify the economy by business sector and geography, and made progress on both.

Bloomberg knew that keeping city streets safe, and its people free from the fear that terrorists could attack it at will, was essential for his plan to succeed. His administration's public safety record is remarkable. New York City suffered no successful post-9/11 assaults while he governed, and sixteen attempts failed. Major crimes, including homicides, fell to the lowest levels on record while across America crime rates plateaued. He accomplished the goal while shrinking the police force by five thousand officers, and reducing the number of New Yorkers in prison by twenty thousand, more than a third, while elsewhere United States inmate populations drifted up to record levels. New Yorkers of every class and every color, in every neighborhood around the city, reaped the tangible and psychological benefits of a safe city.

Bloomberg's vision required world-class cultural centers, plenty of parks, clean air and water, plus other amenities. On all those dimensions, he succeeded beyond any mayor in memory. His administration supported projects big and small, humble and grand, from the High Line in Manhattan to High Bridge in the Bronx. *PlaNYC* harnessed breathtaking ambition and set New York City on a growth path to maintain and improve the quality of life while the economy expanded. It destroyed the false choice between development and environment. The benefits of its initiatives—less pollution and fewer respiratory illnesses, more access to water for recreational use, more homes within walking distance to parks, more apartments near mass transit, and on and on—are tangible and speak for themselves. Collectively, they are the credible response of a global metropolis to the ever-more-obvious risks of climate change. Bloomberg's engineering training and understanding of science—another unique quality for a New York City mayor—caused him to embrace the far-ranging program. His business acumen gave him confidence it could be accomplished without compromising economic progress. The credibility his leadership lent the plan was critical to attract the broad support required to implement it. It became an instant model for cities around the United States and around the world. The extraordinary report of the Special Initiative for Rebuilding and Resiliency that followed Superstorm Sandy set in motion an array of projects to protect New Yorkers from future weather-related disasters.[2]

Bloomberg understood that the city he imagined required a large pool of capable workers who could staff businesses and deliver government services, build skyscrapers, repair bridges and tunnels, deliver laundry and clean hotel rooms. The laborers needed to make the city work migrated to it in ample numbers while he governed, so in the broadest and simplest sense Bloomberg succeeded in this dimension of his program as well. New York's population rose and the metropolis thrived. Yet, his record in delivering the municipal services particularly important to workers—affordable housing, effective mass transportation, quality public schools, and social services for those struggling at the bottom end of the labor pool—is decidedly mixed. He ruled over as many failures as successes. When the Citizens Budget Commission assessed the New York City metropolitan area's attractiveness as a home for human capital in 2013, the two areas of greatest weakness were rent affordability and commuting time, issues that affect workers and the poor, not the wealthy elite.

Bloomberg's $7.5 billion affordable housing plan produced enough places to live for some five hundred thousand people. It was the biggest municipal affordable housing plan in the nation's history. It worked well for New Yorkers making between roughly $35,000 and $130,000, the lower end of the expensive city's middle class. Yet, rents rose faster than middle-class incomes while Bloomberg governed, and New York's perpetual housing crisis persisted. The city's ability to accommodate more people and to continue to grow is strained. Supporters contend the problem is the inevitable consequence of Bloomberg's success. The city needs more housing because more people want to live in a vibrant place. Critics emphasize the erosion in workers' standards of living as a result of spending ever more of their monthly income on a place to live, and ever more time in long commutes. Both perspectives are accurate. In sum, Bloomberg's affordable-housing program, as impressive as it was, proved insufficient for the need. And it offered little help to the poorest New Yorkers.[3]

The bold gambit to create a regional financing authority to fund repairs of city roads, alleviate metropolis-limiting traffic jams, and convert its mass transportation system from a struggling relic into a world-class network failed. It is remarkable that Bloomberg came as close as he did to implementing congestion pricing, given the political minefield that lay in its path. The decision to try demonstrated political courage. But after it failed, no policy emerged that responded to the compelling issues it was meant to address. City residents and commuters were left with an inadequate transportation network. In 2015, Governor Andrew Cuomo came to negotiations with Mayor de Blasio armed with a "crowbar" in the words of one knowledgeable official, and secured a five-year, $2.5 billion commitment from New York City toward the MTA capital budget.[4]

Bloomberg inherited a school system in crisis. After twelve years, it remained so. During his first campaign for mayor, he asked the city to judge him above all on his success converting the dysfunctional bureaucracy that had failed the majority of its children for decades, most of them black and Latino, into a first-rate system. Strictly speaking, Bloomberg failed in that effort. Such a binary conclusion is unfair. His success ridding the system of the horrible hybrid that governed it for more than three decades was a fundamental change, and essential for any chance of turning the organization around. Deputy Mayor Walcott would declare it one of the administration's most important and lasting achievements. Bloomberg and his team pursued a vision, raised teachers' salaries, empowered principals, and invested some $27 billion in capital-budget dollars. They worked tirelessly and made measurable progress in a heroic effort. Charges that Bloomberg and Klein, neither one an educator, ignored important insights professionals had to offer, and got the politics wrong of managing change through so complicated a network, are true. The criticisms support the view that the outcome was a huge, missed opportunity. New York City, no less than the rest of America, continues to search for a formula for delivering first-rate public education, especially to children in poor urban neighborhoods.

Despite insufficient success on affordable housing, and modest progress on transportation and schools, the evidence is compelling that New York's professional classes, and the majority of its workforce and their families, were better off while Bloomberg governed than at any time in memory across the broad range of conditions that affect people's happiness in a big city. Among the many data points that support the contention is Bloomberg's favorite: the life expectancy of New Yorkers grew by 3.2 years between 2001 and 2010, compared to 1.8 years across the country. Bloomberg's health department attributed 70 percent of the improvement to reductions in cancer, heart disease, and HIV infection. City health initiatives played a role in all three. Audiences typically laughed when Bloomberg told them: "If you want your friends and relatives to live long, healthy lives, tell them to move to New York City." But the evidence supported the brash claim.[5]

Whether the city's 3.75 million poor and near-poor in 2013, most of them African American and Latino, were better off when Bloomberg governed is a more complicated matter. At the time New Yorkers elected him, 18 percent of city residents lived below the federal poverty line. When he left, the figure was

304 • Bloomberg: A Billionaire's Ambition

20 percent. The city's smarter measure of who was poor showed a similar pattern with slightly higher numbers. The trend applied to the near-poor as well. It is a particularly discouraging outcome considering the strength of the city's economic recovery after 2010. Yet, in comparison to the rest of the United States, the record is enviable. The poverty rate between 2000 and 2012 rose 28 percent in big cities across the country, and in every one of the twenty largest except New York, where it remained flat. In Chicago and Houston it rose 22 percent, in Philadelphia 17 percent, in Los Angeles a more modest 5 percent. On a relative basis New York improved from having the fifth-highest proportion of poor among twenty big cities to thirteenth. Median income in New York City remained stable while declining 8 percent across the United States. Mayors govern within the context of national policies and global markets over which they exercise scant control. Measured by the federal poverty standard, the poor survived the two economic crises of the first decade of the twenty-first century better in Bloomberg's New York than elsewhere in America. That is an achievement to praise.

Bloomberg's antipoverty programs, narrowly cast, focused on two priorities. He sought to protect children, including younger teens, from poverty's pernicious impacts; and he sought to help adults, including older teens, to earn their way out of its dispiriting clutches. The Center for Economic Opportunity claimed the Bloomberg administration's many initiatives lifted two hundred thousand people out of poverty who otherwise would have stayed stuck there. Stability in the proportion of New Yorkers impoverished compared to the rising trajectory in other large US cities supports the claim. And it is only part of the story. The modest but measurable progress in the city's schools helped the poor disproportionately. Many of the city's most important public health commitments did as well. The campaign to reduce teen pregnancy, steps to ensure that the millions of meals the city delivered annually were nutritious, incentives for bodegas and supermarkets in underserved areas to carry fresh produce, support for the Health and Hospitals Corporation, and other programs Bloomberg's team pursued with urgency were especially important to New York's most vulnerable residents. Smoking restrictions and the trans fat ban helped everyone, but even those initiatives helped the poor a little more than others. The lives saved by the sharp drop in homicides, and the misery avoided by the decline in shootings and violent crimes protected young black and Latino men and their families more than anyone else. The twenty thousand–inmate decline in the number of New Yorkers in state and federal prisons, and local jails, caused a dramatic improvement in the quality of life for the same population. The life expectancy of New Yorkers living in poor neighborhoods increased by nearly half-again as much as it did in rich neighborhoods between 2001 and 2010.

On average, poor New Yorkers lived almost five years longer than the poor living in Detroit. By other measures as well, health inequalities shrunk. Relative to the plight of poor Americans elsewhere, New York's did well between 2002 and 2013.[6]

Yet, rent is not paid in relative data and food is not put on the table with comparative statistics. The 2 percent rise in the proportion of New Yorkers suffering poverty meant some 160,000 more people were struggling economically at the end of Bloomberg's twelve years than at the beginning, in addition to the millions who benefited not at all from his economic policies. In New York City, as elsewhere in America, the primary reason was that wages at the lower end of the economy were insufficient to lift even full-time workers above the poverty threshold.

Bloomberg resisted living wage proposals and other programs meant to respond to the discouraging reality of rising income inequality. He believed market forces should set wages and generally rejected suggestions that government had a role to play in influencing them for social benefit. Instead, he supported food stamps for families and earned income tax credits for the working poor as ways the government could supplement inadequate wages without direct market interference.

Income inequality, worse in Manhattan than anywhere else in America when New Yorkers elected Bloomberg, got worse while he governed, more or less in line with the rest of the country. Bloomberg feared local measures to respond to the issue would make New York City uncompetitive for business, and that it was not a problem for a mayor to address, perhaps not a problem at all. One of his deputies would say somewhat plaintively, "by definition" billionaires are unconcerned about concentration of wealth. The strident way Bloomberg opposed even modest redistribution proposals played into caricatures of him as heartless and out of touch, damaging his stature and diminishing his authority. He lost the public relations battle on the topic. To be sure, there are limits to what a mayor can accomplish on matters dominated by national economic decisions and global market trends. But if income inequality is the defining issue of our time, as President Obama and many economists claimed, Bloomberg's complacency is a sin of omission.[7]

There is much to cheer about Bloomberg's policies toward the poor. There are also policies Bloomberg followed that reveal a dispiriting pattern of calculated negligence toward the most disadvantaged. He disinvested in the New York City Housing Authority, where more than four hundred thousand of the city's most financially challenged live. He left it in a deplorable state of disrepair. Conditions at Rikers Island went from manageable, to unacceptable, to barbaric while he ruled. Some ten thousand inmates, overwhelmingly men of color, lived in a jailhouse environment beneath the dignity of a civilized city at the end of Bloomberg's tenure. The federal government felt compelled to intervene. His program to reduce homelessness failed during his third term and left more than fifty thousand men, women, and children living in shelters, often in conditions of life-disrupting squalor. The constitutional abuses of stop, question, and frisk took place overwhelmingly in neighborhoods where poor people of color lived. One loyal aide confesses: "I think about this a lot. If I could go back in time . . . I wish with what I know now, I could have given the mayor a memo that said stop-and-frisk numbers are a disaster and you need to do something about it . . . . [and] you made a promise around homelessness to reduce it. You haven't reduced it. It's going up, and we need to figure that out. . . . I wasn't smart enough or prescient enough . . . to do that."[8]

Despite a cluster of policies that had pernicious impacts on dark-skinned New Yorkers, race relations while Bloomberg governed were less tense than at any time in memory—since at least the 1960s. Police shootings of unarmed black men—in particular two high-profile events—were handled with deft sensitivity. Mayor Bloomberg was not racist, nor was his police commissioner, nor any of his deputies. In part, ignorance explains the negligence inherent in some of Bloomberg's policies. He grew up in 1950s suburban America, attended Johns Hopkins and Harvard in the 1960s, and worked on Wall Street after that. African Americans and Latinos were rarities in all those places. So was real poverty and the denigrating impact it can have on people living in it and surrounded by it. David Jones, an African American who had long straddled the worlds of the city's elite and its needy as president of the Community Service Society, attended a dinner party one evening at Bloomberg's opulent East 79th Street town house. During the course of the evening's conversation he was struck by how little Bloomberg and the crowd he ran with understood the lives of the people Jones's organization served. Bloomberg did not fully realize the consequences of his administration's policies for the single mother with two small children forced to walk up several flights of stairs in a urine-soaked housing development stairwell because the elevators did not work. Or the impact on the minimum wage worker with no paid leave, forced to attend a hearing for possession of marijuana during working hours, even if the charges were eventually dismissed. In June of 2013, as his administration began to wind down, a Quinnipiac University poll revealed Bloomberg maintained a 51 percent citywide approval rating versus 41 percent who were disappointed with his performance, highly credible numbers for any elected official in the twelfth year of office. The margin among whites was 57 percent to 38 percent, among Latinos 52 percent to 38 percent, but among blacks, 45 percent versus

48 percent. More African Americans disapproved of Bloomberg's reign than approved of it.[9]

There is another disturbing reason for policies that left the poor to suffer. Businessmen segment their markets by profitability. In Bloomberg's New York, the target market was the elite. The middle class and even struggling workers appealed. The dysfunctional poor did not. A city that becomes a refuge for the indigent spirals down, just as a business with too many unprofitable customers stagnates and fails. New York "becomes Detroit" if the direction of things did not change, Ed Koch once declared in the early 1990s. Cold calculations place the poor at the bottom of an entrepreneurial city's priorities. Bloomberg's policies make it clear he had little interest in making life in New York City too comfortable for dysfunctional residents. One can make a strong case it is America's failing rather than the fault of any one mayor, but the picture it paints is ugly wherever it appears.

In certain respects, Bloomberg's policies toward New York's poor, in particular the innovations pursued by the Center for Economic Opportunity, reflect Bloomberg's science-heavy background as much as his understanding of economics. From his second term on, he sought to find a cure for the condition, like a medical researcher looking for a way to eradicate a disease. It was a clinical approach, not an emotional one. Bloomberg lacked the palliative empathy of a practicing physician, the humbling recognition that at times the best science can offer is relief from painful symptoms, and that it is humane to do so.

A loyal and admiring deputy pressed to identify Bloomberg's weaknesses cites a failure to project empathy. "We were meeting with people after Sandy," he recounted. The point was to show people whose homes were pummeled by the horrific storm that the mayor understood their plight. A series of communities had been targeted and media alerted. "After an hour the mayor says: 'I get it. Lots of water, lots of damage. Now let's get back to City Hall where we can do something about it,'" suggesting they cancel the rest of the sessions. "Can you imagine if Bill Clinton were meeting those people?" the Bloomberg aide asked rhetorically. "He'd say, 'It must have been horrible. How long have you lived here? Did you lose personal effects, things with sentimental value? You didn't deserve this, but you are strong.' He'd hug them. He'd say, 'We are going to help you.'" Bloomberg's staff insisted the mayor keep to the planned itinerary.[10]

Bloomberg's data-driven approach to problem-solving served him well in many realms—economic development plans and infrastructure management are prime examples. In areas deeply rooted in difficult-to-quantify human behavior and emotion—like the subtleties of the learning process, or the psychological impact on innocent people of color stopped repeatedly by police on the streets of their own neighborhood—the approach got him into trouble.

The efforts to reduce teacher evaluations, or annual progress at a school to a single grade, were naïve and ill considered. Bloomberg ignored a well-known characteristic of societal interaction known as Campbell's Laws: "The more any quantitative social indicator is used for social decision making, the more subject it will be to corruption pressures and the more apt it will be to distort and corrupt the social processes it is intended to monitor." The insight explains what happened with New York City's school-testing program. It explains how the NYPD approach to stop, question, and frisk, a necessary police tactic that even Al Sharpton did not want to discontinue altogether, turned into an unconstitutional violation of civil rights. Bloomberg's intellect was far more developed than his emotional instincts.[11]

Bloomberg was the canniest of businessmen, and his overreliance on numbers may have followed from his experience running his firm, which he understood so completely. The economics he had created were brilliantly simple. While serving as mayor, anytime he wanted to know how Bloomberg LP was doing, he called its chairman, Peter Grauer. "What's the number?" he would ask. Grauer would read the answer from an electronic monitor mounted in a conference room. It was a real-time accounting of the number of subscriptions the firm had booked. Bloomberg could multiply the number in his head by the annual cost of his company's service, and then by the profit margin of the business. With those simple calculations he could estimate the run rate of his company's annual income with remarkable accuracy. He behaved as if he could rely with similar confidence on test scores that dealt with a topic as subtle as the intellectual development of a million different children and teenagers, from within a complex system as diverse as New York City itself, that had evolved over more than a century, in a field with which he had no formal training.[12]

Numbers are of course essential when managing a budget, a fundamental task for a mayor at which Bloomberg excelled. He proved a master at raising revenue for city government without damaging private sector momentum. One Lindsay-era City Hall official likened Bloomberg's economic programs to a municipal Federal Reserve Bank. Policies that caused the value of prime real estate to rise increased tax revenues—the equivalent of a central bank's unique power to create money. Bloomberg also had the political courage to raise the real estate tax rate over 18 percent in 2003, a huge increase that provided the funding he needed to deliver the services his vision of the city required. He initiated income tax and sales tax surcharges when circumstances called for it. He challenged his deputies and commissioners to operate efficiently in good times and bad, and he sought productivity improvements from city workers. On that front, he achieved some successes during his first term, very few afterward. He supported tax rebates when the treasury was flush and allowed surcharges with sunset clauses to expire rather than extend them and spend more money simply because he could. He managed the capital budget with similar skill, approving projects when times were good, paring them back when times were tough, but investing steadily in infrastructure to maintain the city's vital plant and equipment, improving it over time. He left his successor with a budget surplus, the only mayor in memory to do so, and he left the city's capital accounts in better condition than when he found them, the strongest position in decades. "The next mayor is going to inherit from us a government that has been well run and fiscally responsible, and doesn't have any buried things," Bloomberg told Ken Auletta, writing a valedictory profile of Bloomberg's reign for the *New Yorker*. It was so.[13]

When Governor Andrew Cuomo initiated pension reform at the state level in 2011, Bloomberg seized the moment to accomplish helpful changes at the city level. But he yielded to temptation and reversed reserves he created to fund retiree health-care benefits when short-term imperatives made it convenient to do so. The city's long-term unfunded liabilities surged while Bloomberg governed. They remain a threat to the city's financial future. It will be up to Bloomberg's successors to make sure New York City does not become the next generation's Chicago. Bloomberg's critics delight in pointing out that the CityTime computer project was a budget debacle and management failure of the highest order. It is true. But the expensive embarrassment is an exception to Bloomberg's highly competent management of the city treasury and resources. And neither he nor any of his senior staff ever stood accused of corruption.

Bloomberg had a tough relationship with city unions during his first term when he offered most of them stingy increases and demanded productivity gains. Richer budgets during his second term led to higher raises and fewer demands for givebacks. Relationships improved for a time. During his third term, in the years that followed the Great Recession, Bloomberg held the line on raises and municipal labor relations turned bitter. The entire municipal labor force was without contracts when he left office. Critics charge that the cost of the settlements that followed overwhelmed the surplus he left. The charge lacks context. Bloomberg and other mayors before him also inherited expired contracts covering huge numbers of municipal employees, and they came accompanied by budget gaps, not surpluses. Moreover, the local economy was so robust, in significant measure because of Bloomberg's policies, that his successor's first budgets absorbed the additional costs with ease.

Bloomberg was a highly skilled talent manager who created a culture of competence throughout the government he led. Ability, creativity, and results counted for a lot, patronage and political standing for relatively little. He delegated authority boldly, often with excellent results, and he was fiercely loyal.

But at times he over-delegated, and at times he was loyal to a fault. Some of his administration's worst failures were overseen by staff who served for twelve years.

Loyalty was a personal instinct that came easily to Bloomberg, and it was also a carefully considered management tactic. There are many stories that support the point, but two capture his sentiments and his thinking. A junior staff member, normally visible in the bullpen, had to check into the hospital for several days for a medical condition. Embarrassed about missing work, he tried to keep the matter under wraps. But Bloomberg learned of it, and stopped by the fellow's hospital room. He spent twenty-five minutes cheering the man up, and he called the next day to see if he needed anything. In an unrelated matter, a deputy complained to Bloomberg that a staff member in another department was not up to standards and should be removed. Bloomberg agreed with the assessment, but not the conclusion. If he interfered with senior officials inside their domains, it would make it hard to recruit top-notch staff, he explained. Since attracting talent was a manager's most important job in his view, he was prepared to tolerate a few underachievers in order to reach a higher goal. Bloomberg's most likely reaction to criticism about another city employee was a dressing down for trash-talking a member of the team. He was forgiving of mistakes if made in reasoned pursuit of ambitious objectives, and he was reflexively protective when anyone attacked his staff, even if he spanked them himself privately when they erred.[14]

Bloomberg managed the politics of the mayor's office differently from others. He claimed apolitical independence. It was in some ways true, and in others not. Bloomberg needed no one else's money. He governed free from the imperative to curry favor with rich supporters that afflicts most elected officials in a deeply denigrating aspect of American democracy. Yet, the way Bloomberg used his money to win three elections corrupted New York City politics in a different way. He spent more than $250 million in direct campaign expenses in 2001, 2005, and 2009, multiples more than any of his challengers. Beyond that, he dispensed hundreds of millions of dollars in philanthropic contributions which bought loyalty from a range of agencies. Over twelve years, the amount invested likely exceeded $1.5 billion. He exercised the power of the incumbent to direct city resources to constituents whose support he coveted as ruthlessly as the toughest Tammany boss. When he flexed his political muscles to secure the right to run for a third term, something that the city forbade on the basis of two citywide referenda passed with ample majorities, he disrespected the will of the people he represented. He ignored the objections of his three closest advisors to take an action he himself called "disgraceful" and "outrageous" until he decided to do it. His contention that the maneuver did not violate democratic principles because voters still had to reelect him is disingenuous sophistry offered by a powerful incumbent who proceeded to outspend his rival by six times in campaign funds, and another six times in philanthropic largesse.[15]

Successful businessmen are often amoral when it comes to commerce. They view the law as a set of rules which must be obeyed, and part of their job is to seek every opportunity the rules offer to improve their company's position. If the rules are unfair or unwise, it is the job of the political process, not of the businessman, to fix it. The outlook is apparent in Bloomberg's defense that the democratically elected city council passed the law that allowed him to seek a third term. He behaved as if his efforts to persuade the council to pass legislation he favored were no different than anyone else's efforts to convince it to support a policy proposal, as the democratic process allows. In the unique circumstance of a mayor as wealthy and powerful as Bloomberg seeking to perpetuate himself in power, the perspective is willfully obtuse and highly undemocratic. There are New Yorkers so appalled by the fundamental abuse of his position that they will remain forever hostile toward Bloomberg despite his extraordinary accomplishments.

Bloomberg's unapologetic use of his money and power to perpetuate himself in office reveal he is a man of his times. Wealthy Americans have coopted the political process. They have used their money to dominate the United States Congress and to protect their interests in many statehouses around the country. On October 15, 2015, the *New York Times* reported 158 super-wealthy families were responsible for contributing nearly half of all the money for the presidential campaigns then under way in a nation of 320 million people. Some 138 of them contributed to Republicans, 20 to Democrats. Bloomberg differs from most in important ways. He did not seek surrogates he could control, but sought political office himself. The policies he advocated were reasoned positions designed to make America the country he would like it to be, not crass efforts to protect his financial interests narrowly defined, or to enact an ideological agenda with near religious conviction. Still, he is a leading member of the "overwhelmingly white, rich, older and male" billionaire class orchestrating a highly anti-democratic moment in American history, when in great measure we have displaced "one person, one vote" with "one dollar, one vote." The 2016 presidential campaign suggests a reckoning is unfolding.[16]

Bloomberg groomed no successor to serve as mayor of New York City. He conferred with businessmen and others, but found no takers to carry his City Hall mantle forward. Christine Quinn began 2013 as the favorite to win the Democratic nomination, but like Gifford Miller, she discovered that despite a council speaker's citywide influence, her campaign for mayor rested on a political base no bigger than a single district, just one of fifty-one in the city. Quinn's support for Bloomberg's third term, and her own, alienated a significant portion of the electorate. The council-funding scandal that surfaced on her watch also hurt, as did revelations that she possessed an unappealing, vindictive streak. Democrats disillusioned with Bloomberg by the end of his third term viewed Quinn as corrupted by her close support for his policies. Her public standing eroded fairly steadily between February and July, when she still led the polls, but by an ever-decreasing margin.[17]

Anthony Weiner was a disgraced former congressman by 2013. After claiming that his Twitter account had been hacked when photos were posted of a semi-aroused man in his underwear, further revelations forced him to admit that he had sent the pictures. Shortly afterward, party leaders forced him to resign from the House of Representatives. Despite the reputation-damaging scandal, he decided to run for mayor anyway. He began to gain traction until it turned out he continued to engage in the lewd behavior, even after his outing. New Yorkers rejected him as it became increasingly apparent he was a disturbed man. Comptroller John Liu sought the Democratic nomination as well, but he suffered a campaign financing scandal that sent two of his staff to jail for fraud and damaged his credibility.[18]

Former Comptroller Bill Thompson ran again. His tepid campaign style did little to energize supporters. Bill de Blasio, the city's public advocate, offered New Yorkers three messages: He would tax the wealthy to fund pre-kindergarten for all four-year-olds, he would use all of his power as mayor to address the overarching issue of income inequality, and he would end stop and frisk as practiced under Mayor Bloomberg and Police Commissioner Kelly. His ideas had just begun to resonate, and he was catching up to Quinn from way behind, when he aired a television commercial early in August. A black teenager sporting a magnificent Afro hairstyle talks to the camera. Headline images of de Blasio's campaign promises appear. Happy scenes of the candidate in the company of an African American woman follow. The candidate is shown walking down a Brooklyn street next to the youngster who opened the commercial, as he continues to offer reasons to vote for de Blasio. "And I would say that even if he weren't my dad," was the surprising punch line. De Blasio, a white man of mixed German and Italian ancestry, was married to the African American woman in the ad, Chirlane McCray. The teen in the ad was their fifteen-year-old son, Dante. They also had a daughter, Chiara. The impact as one Bronx politician put it with only slight exaggeration, was that "de Blasio out-blacked Billy Thompson."[19]

De Blasio won the primary with just over 40 percent of the vote, enough to avoid a runoff after a few days of doubt. Thompson won 26 percent. The two politicians each attracted slightly more than 40 percent of African American ballots. White Democrats also gave de Blasio some 40 percent of their votes in the four-way race, but Thompson only 19 percent. De Blasio ran somewhat ahead of Thompson among Latinos. Quinn won just 16 percent of Democratic ballots, Liu 7 percent, and Weiner just 5 percent. In the November general election, running as the remedy to Michael Bloomberg, de Blasio crushed Joe Lhota, a former Giuliani deputy mayor running on the Republican ticket, by a whopping margin of 73 percent to 24 percent. The long-awaited restoration of City Hall finally occurred. A Democrat would rule New York for the first time in twenty years beginning January 1, 2014. De Blasio treated his huge general election victory as a mandate for his policies. He ignored the message of the primary vote: 60 percent of Democrats voted against him.[20]

Bloomberg received rough treatment at de Blasio's inauguration. Brooklyn Councilwoman Letitia James won election as public advocate. She invited Dasani Coates to join her when she took the oath of office. The presence of the young girl featured in the long, highly critical *New York Times* series on Bloomberg's homeless policies that appeared just a few weeks earlier was meant as a human rebuke to the outgoing mayor. A Jewish rabbi, a Catholic priest, and a Muslim imam delivered blessings. So did Reverend Fred Lucas Jr., an African American protestant minister, who invoked his hope that "the plantation called New York City," would become a city of God. De Blasio invited octogenarian entertainer and civil rights activist Harry Belafonte to speak. Fixing stop and frisk was "only the tip of the iceberg in fixing our deeply Dickensian justice system," he said, while Bloomberg listened impassively. It fell to former President Bill Clinton to remind listeners that Bloomberg had made the city stronger before administering the oath of office to de Blasio on a Bible once owned by Franklin Roosevelt. The new mayor had the grace to call Bloomberg's record on public health and the environment, "a noble legacy," before offering his own vision for the city. "We are called on to put an end to economic and social inequalities that threaten to unravel the city we love," de Blasio told New Yorkers.[21]

Bloomberg began to live his plan B as a billionaire philanthropist. Many of his senior staff joined him at his foundation. Patti Harris had long been running Bloomberg philanthropies, committed to making the world a better place by funding projects in the arts, education, the environment, public health, and government innovation, along with founder's projects dear to Bloomberg's heart. Bloomberg became the United Nations Secretary General's Special Envoy for Cities and Climate Change. At a time when political dysfunction in the United States and in other countries at the national level made solving problems challenging, Bloomberg believed cities would be the places where strong leaders could make smart decisions on controversial issues. He pledged millions for

Every Town for Gun Safety, a consortium of US organizations promoting gun control, and to others pursuing educational reform. He took his anti-tobacco zeal overseas with efforts to reduce smoking in places as far-flung as Turkey and Uruguay. He bought another residence in London, where rumors circulated for a time that he would run for mayor someday, which Bloomberg denied. Years earlier, Bloomberg said he would not return to his company, but before long he did. Reports suggested he was dissatisfied with the company's evolution while he tended to the needs of the city. It is equally easy to believe he simply could not resist the itch to return to the head of the company he created and owned.

As America turned its attention to the 2016 presidential election during the second half of 2015, polls showed extraordinarily high disapproval ratings for Hillary Clinton on her way to the Democratic nomination, and for Donald Trump, on his way to a shocking victory for the Republican nomination and the presidency. Observers pointed out that Bloomberg was an independent centrist, with a track record running the nation's largest city successfully through a fraught period of economic anxiety and terrorist-created fear, similar to what the national electorate was feeling. "No fucking way," Bloomberg reportedly responded when first approached by others to run for president. But as the prospect loomed of a disreputable Donald Trump confronting a deeply unpopular Hillary Clinton in the general election, Bloomberg reconsidered. He took a national poll. His political advisors leaked news that Bloomberg had authorized steps to prepare a campaign to secure a ballot line in all fifty states in case he decided to mount an independent bid for president. Yet, in March 2016 Bloomberg concluded, just as he had in 2008, that he could not win as an independent. He declined to run, and denounced Trump as unfit to lead the nation from the speakers' podium at the Democratic National Convention where he endorsed Clinton.[22]

Yet, no matter what else Michael Bloomberg does or accomplishes, his legacy as mayor is assured. "The challenge in telling Mike's story," Edward Skyler counsels, "is that there are so many areas that he really pushed and broke ground . . . . He changed the expectation people have of their government." Bloomberg proved that well-managed government can promote private-sector growth, generate jobs, keep people safe, protect the environment, build infra-structure, contribute to society's cultural sensibilities, accomplish dramatic improvements in public health, and ensure the quality of life for millions. He did not diminish government services and cut taxes to achieve his goals, the only policy prescription that America's conservative ideologues believe works. He was an activist executive who used government assets boldly and wisely for the greatest good, for the greatest number of people.[23]

"Mayors will be breaking ground on projects Bloomberg began for decades to come," urban expert Mitchell Moss has said. In 2015, Bloomberg joined his successor at a ceremony launching construction of Cornell NYC Tech's Roosevelt Island campus. At Hudson Yards, on the far West Side of Manhattan, a development is rising that on its own is the size of a small city. A vibrant neighborhood is emerging around the office towers at the World Trade Center site, the place where a devastating attack cut a deep wound into a great city. With history's disregard for unintended consequences, the event created the alternate reality that allowed Bloomberg to be elected mayor of America's premier metropolis. It is a place where a poignant memorial reminds visitors that freedom conquers terror. For those who know its history and Bloomberg's role, it is also a reminder that who we elect to govern us and how they use the power we entrust to them matters. It is a fitting monument to Michael Bloomberg's ambitious rule of New York City. The twenty-first century, for which he prepared New York, relies on Twitter to capture life in 140 characters or less. While Bloomberg governed, tweets became a thing. It seems apt to end a history of him with one. #bloomberglegacy: "Bloomberg. Entrepreneur Mayor. Who says government can't work?"

Author's Interviews

Titles or affiliations are the one most relevant to events. Interviews took place between April 2014 and January 2017.

Rohit Aggarwala, director, New York City Office of Long-term Planning and Sustainability

Victor Bach, Community Services Society

Jeremy Ben-Ami, Mark Green campaign advisor

Adrian Benepe, commissioner, New York City Parks Department

Gordon Berlin, president, MDRC

Jonathan Bowles, director, Center for an Urban Future

Amanda Burden, chair, New York City Planning Commission and director, Department of City Planning

Eduardo Castell, William Thompson campaign advisor

Chris Coffey, Michael Bloomberg campaign advisor

Peter Cunningham, assistant secretary for communication and outreach, US Department of Education

William Cunningham, Michael Bloomberg campaign advisor

Joe DePlasco, Mark Green campaign advisor

Ruben Diaz Jr., Bronx borough president

Robert Doar, commissioner, New York City Human Resources Administration

Daniel Doctoroff, deputy mayor for economic development and rebuilding

Fernando Ferrer, 2001 and 2005 candidate for mayor of New York City

David Fischer, Center for an Urban Future

Dean Fuleihan, secretary for programs and policy to the speaker of the New York State Assembly and secretary to the Assembly Ways and Means Committee

Linda Gibbs, deputy mayor of New York City

Mark Green, 2001 candidate for mayor of New York City

James Hanley, commissioner, New York City Department of Labor

Caswell Holloway, deputy mayor of New York City

Martin Horn, commissioner, New York City Department of Corrections

Michael Jacobson, commissioner, New York City Department of Corrections

David Jones, president and chief executive officer, Community Services Society

Carol Kellerman, Charles Brecher, Maria Doulis, Citizens Budget Commission

Raymond Kelly, commissioner, New York City Police Department

Kyle Kimball, president, New York City Economic Development Corporation

Joel Klein, chancellor, New York City Department of Education

Jay Kriegel, president, NYC 2012

Robert Lieber, deputy mayor of New York City

Ronnie Lowenstein, George Sweet, Doug Turetsky, New York City Independent
Budget Office

Heather Mac Donald, John M. Olin Fellow, Manhattan Institute

Peter Madonia, chief of staff to Mayor Michael R. Bloomberg

Steven Malanga, senior editor, *City Journal*

Emily Mayrath, Bloomberg Philanthropies

Gifford Miller, speaker, New York City Council.

Mitchell Moss, Henry Hart Rice professor of urban policy and planning,
director of Rudin Center for Transportation Policy and Management, New
York University Wagner School of Public Policy

Patrick Muncie, Michael Bloomberg campaign advisor

Seth Pinsky, president, New York City Economic Development Corporation

Roberto Ramirez, Fernando Ferrer campaign advisor

Richard Ravitch, fiscal expert, lieutenant governor of New York State

James Riccio, director, Low Wage Workers and Community Policy Area, MDRC

Janette Sadik-Khan, commissioner, New York City Department of Transportation

Richard Schrader, Mark Green campaign advisor

Rev. Al Sharpton, civil rights activist and Fernando Ferrer campaign advisor

Marc Shaw, deputy mayor of New York City

Kevin Sheekey, Michael Bloomberg campaign advisor

Hank Sheinkopf, Mark Green campaign advisor 2001; Michael Bloomberg
campaign advisor 2009

John Siegal, Mark Green campaign advisor

Edward Skyler, deputy mayor of New York City

Seth Solomonow, Bloomberg Philanthropies

Steven Spinola, president, Real Estate Board of New York

Martha Stark, commissioner, New York City Department of Finance

Robert Steel, deputy mayor of New York City

Timothy Sullivan, chief of staff to Deputy Mayor Robert Steel

Bradley Tusk, Michael Bloomberg campaign advisor

Dennis Walcott, deputy mayor of New York City

Christopher Ward, executive director, Port Authority of New York and New Jersey

Tom Waters, Community Services Society

Randi Weingarten, president, United Federation of Teachers of New York

Howard Wolfson, deputy mayor of New York City

Tom Wright, president, Regional Plan Association

Kathryn Wylde, president and CEO of the New York City Partnership

Robert Yaro, president, Regional Plan Association

Sources

City of New York, Official Documents

Bond Official Statement Archive, 2002–2013.

City Planning Commission. "Application by the New York City Economic Development Corporation and the Department of Housing, Preservation and Development for Zoning Amendments to Create a 'Special Willets Point District.'" September 24, 2008/Calendar No. 14, N080382ZRQ.

Center for Economic Opportunity. "Strategy and Implementation Report." 2007.

_____. "The CEO Poverty Measure." August 2008.

_____. "The CEO Poverty Measure, 2005–2013." April 22, 2015.

_____. "Early Achievements and Lessons Learned." 2008.

_____. "Evidence and Impact." 2009.

_____. "Local and National Impact." 2012.

_____. "Replicating Our Results." 2011.

Department of City Planning. "Zoning Handbook: Guide to the Zoning Resolution of the City of New York." 1961.

_____. "Zoning Handbook 2011 Edition." 2011.

_____. "The New Waterfront Revitalization Plan." September 2002.

_____. "Comprehensive Waterfront Plan." 1992.

_____. "Vision 2020: New York City Comprehensive Waterfront Plan." March 2011.

Department of Citywide Administrative Services. "Determination of Violation of Civil Service Law 210 By Certain Correction Officers In the Department of Correction Transportation Division." December 11, 2013.

Department of Education. "Children First: A Bold, Common Sense Plan to Create Great Schools for All New York City Children, Updated 2008–2009 School Year." 2010.

_____. "Citywide Question-By-Question Survey Results for General Education Schools." New York City School Survey 2006–2007 through 2012–2013.

_____. "Learning Environment Surveys Citywide Results." 2007 through 2013.

_____. "Strong Schools, Strong Communities: A New Approach to Supporting New York City's Public Schools and All of Our Students." January 2015.

_____. Hehir, Thomas et al., "Comprehensive Management Review and Evaluation of Special Education," Report submitted to the New York City Department of Education, September 20, 2005.

Department of Health and Mental Hygiene. "Agency Biennial Report, 2007–2008." 2009.

_____. "Air Pollution and the Health of New Yorkers: The Impact of Fine Particles and Ozone." New York City Department of Health and Mental Hygiene, Lisa Millay Stevens, 2011.

_____. "Are You Pouring On the Pounds?" Undated.

_____. "Eating Well in Harlem: How Available Is Healthy Food." 2007.

_____. "Epi Research Report: Firearm Deaths and Injuries in New York City." April 2013.

_____. "Epi Research Report: Health Care Reform in New York City—Access to Primary Care Before Reform." November 2011.

_____. "Epi Research Report: Life Expectancy in New York City: What Accounts for the Gains." March 2013.

_____. "Health Bulletin: Choose Less Sodium." Volume 12, Number 1, February/March 2006.

_____. "Health Bulletin: NYC Condoms: Get Some." Volume 6, Number 1, 2007.

_____. "New York City Community Health Survey Atlas, 2010."

_____. "New York City Healthy Bodegas Initiative." May 2010.

_____. "NYC Vital Signs: Preventing Hospitalizations in New York City." Volume 11, Number 3, October 2012.

_____. "Sugary Drinks: How Much Do We Consume?" 2011.

_____. "Take Care New York: 10 Steps To a Longer and Healthier Life." Health Bulletin, Volume 8 Number 7. 2004.

_____. "Take Care New York: A Policy for a Healthier New York City." Volume 28, Supplement 5, September 2009.

_____. "The Regulation to Phase Out Artificial Trans Fat In New York City Food Service Establishments (Section 81.08 of the New York City Health Code)," February 2007.

Department of Homeless Services. "A Progress Report on Uniting for Solutions Beyond Shelter: An Action Plan for New York City." Fall 2008.

Department of Housing, Preservation and Development. "The New Housing Marketplace: Creating Housing for the Next Generation 2004–2014." 2006.

_____. "Housing New York: A Five Borough, Ten Year Plan." 2014.

Department of Investigation. "An Investigation of NYPD's Compliance With Rules Governing Investigations of Political Activity," August 23, 2016 and "New York City Police Department Final Response," August 23, 2016.

_____. "Investigation Into Allegations of Possible Slowdown By Department of Sanitation During Blizzard of December 2010." June 2011.

_____. "Report on Security Failures at City Department of Correction Facilities." November 2014.

_____. "Report on the Recruiting and Hiring Process for New York City Correction Officers." January 2015.

_____. "Status Report On Build It Back." October 9, 2014.

_____. "Preliminary Report On Investigation Into Delays and Cost Overruns Connected to the City's Emergency Communications Transformation Program 'ECTCP.'" August 6, 2014.

Department of Transportation. "Sustainable Streets: Strategic Plan for the New York City Department of Transportation for 2008 and Beyond 2008." 2008.

_____. "Greenlight for Midtown Evaluation Report." January 2010.

_____. "Sustainable Streets: 2009 Progress Report." 2009.

New York City Charter

New York City Council. "Fiscal 2003: Preliminary Budget Response." April 2002.

New York City Council Committee on Public Housing. "Preliminary Hearing on the New York City Housing Authority's Fiscal 2011 Capital and Operating Budget." March 28, 2011.

Office of the Comptroller. "Audit Report on the Contract of Basic Housing, Inc., with the Department of Homeless Services to Provide Shelter and Support Services." July 17, 2009.

_____. "Audit Report on the Department of Environmental Protection Oversight of Costs to Construct the Croton Water Treatment Plant." September 1, 2009.

_____. "Audit Report on the Department of Health and Mental Hygiene Oversight of the Correction of Health Code Violations at Restaurants." July 20, 2009.

_____. "Audit Report on the Follow-up of Violations Issued by the Department of Buildings." June 23, 2008.

_____. "Audit Report on Inventory Controls Over Noncontrolled Drugs at Coney Island Hospital." June 25, 2009.

_____. "Audit Report on the New York City Industrial Development Agency's Project Financing, Evaluation and Monitoring Process." March 19, 2012.

_____. "Audit Report on the Office of Payroll Administration's Monitoring of the Oversight of the CityTime Project By Spherion Atlantic Enterprises LLC." September 28, 2010.

_____. "Comprehensive Annual Financial Report of the Comptroller." Fiscal Year 2002 through Fiscal Year 2013.

_____."Municipal Employee Compensation in New York City." City of New York, Office of the Comptroller, Frank Branconi, Winter, 2011.

_____. "Sustainable or Not? NYC Pension Cost Projections Through 2060." June 2011.

_____. "The $8 Billion Question: Analysis of the NYC Pension Costs Over the Past Decade." April 2011.

_____. Bureau of Fiscal and Budget Studies. "Fiscal Year 2014 Annual Report on Capital Debt and Obligations." December 2013.

Office of the Mayor. "A Stronger, More Resilient New York." June 2013.

_____. "City of New York Financial Plan." Fiscal Years 2002–2006 through Fiscal Years 2014–2018.

_____. "Mayor Bloomberg Looks Back at New York City on September 12, 2001 and Outlines Progress on Economic Recovery, Major Growth in Population and Historic Decrease in Crime." September 12, 2013.

_____. "Mayor's Management Report." 1993–2014.

_____. "Mayor's Management Report Fiscal 2001 Supplement: Reengineering Municipal Services 1994–2001." 2001.

_____. "One New York: The Plan for a Strong and Just City." 2015.

_____. "Ready to Launch: New York City's Implementation Plan for Free, High Quality, Full-Day Universal Pre-Kindergarten." January 2014.

_____. "Remarks by Mayor Michael R. Bloomberg: Major Address on Education at New York Urban League's Dr. Martin Luther King, Jr. Symposium." January 15, 2002.

_____. "Speech by Deputy Mayor Daniel Doctoroff: New York City's Vision for Lower Manhattan: Vision to Reality in Ten Years." September 6, 2006.

_____. "State of the City Address." 2003, 2006–2013.

_____. "Uniting for Solutions Beyond Shelter: The Action Plan for New York City." 2004.

_____. "*PlaNYC*: A Greener, Greater New York." April 2007.

_____. "*PlaNYC*: A Greener Greater New York, Update." April 2011.

_____. "*PlaNYC* Progress Report: Sustainability and Resiliency 2014." April 2014.

Office of the Mayor and Office of the Public Advocate. "NYC Feedback Citywide Customer Survey: Report of Survey Results." December 2008.

Police Department. Crime Statistics. 1993–2014.

_____. "Crime and Enforcement Activity in New York City." January 1–December 31, 2013, Appendix C, New York City Police Department Census, C-1.

_____. Stop, Question and Frisk Report Data. 1998–2013.

_____. "Transition Memo: Muslim Advisory Council." December 1, 2013.

_____. "Executive Summary: New York City Republican National Convention." June 24, 2004.

Center for an Urban Future Reports

"New York By the Numbers: Five Borough Economic Report." Volume 1, Issue 2, September 2008.

Bowles, Jonathan. "A Case for a Sector Based Economic Development Strategy—Testimony of Center Research Director Jonathan Bowles before the New York City Council's Economic Development Committee." June 2002.

_____. "Beyond the Olympics." 2005.

_____. "Economic Development Overview: A Look at Economic Development Issues Likely to Face Our Next Mayor." May 2001.

_____. "Giving Small Firms the Business." Testimony before the city council by the director. June 2005.

_____. "Testimony of Jonathan Bowles, Research Director, before New York City's IDA Board on the Question of New York Stock Exchange Financing." October 2001.

_____. "The Start of a NYC Manufacturing Revival." March 2014.

Bowles, Jonathan and Joel Kotkin. "Engine Failure." 2002.

Bowles, Jonathan, Joel Kotkin, and David Giles. "Reviving the City of Aspiration: A Study of the Challenges Facing New York City's Middle-Class." 2009.

Fichtner, Aaron and K. A. Dixon. "Dressed to Skill." December 2003.

Fischer, David Jason and Neil Scott Kleiman with Julian L. Alssid. "Rebuilding Job Training from the Ground Up: Workforce System Reform." August 2002.

Fitzgerald, Joan. "Retention Deficit Disorder." March 2002.

Fischer, David Jason. "Training Wreck." April 2002.

_____. "Testimony of David Jason Fischer, Project Director, before New York City Council Committee on Economic Development Oversight Hearing: New York City Workforce Investment Board, CY 2005 Strategic Plan: Where Are We Today?" February 13, 2007.

_____. "Mike Has the Right Idea on Welfare Reform." June 11, 2002.

_____. "Testimony before the General Welfare Committee of the New York City Council: Transferring Workforce Programs to the Small Business Services Department." June 2003.

_____. "Off the Cuff: Something to Build On." February 2008.

_____. "The Big Idea: Black Male Unemployment in NYC in 2004." August 2004.

_____. "Work in Progress." June 2007.

_____. "The Many Faces of Poverty: Disconnected Youth." September 2006.

Gerend, Jennifer. "The Outrage Over New York's Storefront Awning Ticket Blitz Is Justified—But So Are the Limits." August 2003.

Giles, David. "Behind the Curb." February 2011.

Hilliard, Thomas. "Subsidizing Care, Supporting Work." January 2011.

Keegan, Robert, Neil Kleiman, et al. "Creative New York." 2005.

Kleiman, Neil Scott. "The Sector Solution: Building a Broader Base for the New Economy." January 2000.

Laney, Kahliah, David Giles, and Jonathan Bowles. "Innovations to Build On." November 2013.

"New York By the Numbers: Low Wage Jobs." Vol. 2, Issue 5, December 2009.

Powers, Laura Wolf. "Twilight Zoning." November 2003.

Citizens Budget Commission Reports

"7 Things New Yorkers Should Know About Municipal Labor Contracts in New York City." May 2013.

"10 Myths About Balancing New York City's Budget and 5 Ways To Lower the Cost of Government By $1 Billion Per Year." December 7, 2002.

"A Poor Way to Pay for Medicaid: Why New York Should Eliminate Local Funding for Medicaid." December 2011.

"A Review of the 2001 Financial Plan of the City of New York for Fiscal Years 2002–2005." March 29, 2001.

"Crime, Police and the Community." July 2001.

Doulis, Maria. "Competiveness Scorecard: Assessing NYC Metro's Attractiveness As a Home for Human Capital." February 2013.

"Everybody's Doing It: Health Insurance Premium-Sharing by Employees and Retirees in the Public and Private Sectors." January 2013.

Hayashi, Andrew. "Options for Property Tax Reform: Equitable Revenue Raising Reforms for New York City's Property Tax." 2013.

"Managing Economic Development Programs in New York City: Lessons for the Next Mayor from the Past Decade." December 2013.

"Managing the Budget in the Bloomberg Administration: A Background Paper Prepared for the Citizens Budget Commission Conference on 'New York City's Changing Fiscal Outlook.'" IBM Executive Conference Center, Palisades, New York, December 7–8, 2001.

"Old Assumptions New Realities: The Truth About Wages and Retirement Benefits for Government Employees." April 1, 2006.

"New York City Is Not Alone." November 17, 2011.

"Planning After *PlaNYC*: A Framework for Developing New York City's Next Ten Year Capital Strategy." December 6, 2013.

"Police and Public Safety in New York City." January 2004.

"Six Figure Civil Servants: Average Compensation Cost of New York City Public Employees." January 2009.

"Testimony Submitted to the City Council Finance Committee." Maria Doulis, Director of City Studies, June 6, 2012.

"The 40 Hour-Week: A Proposal to Increase the Productivity of Non-Managerial Civilian Municipal Workers." December 2002.

"The Candidates on Fiscal Issues: 2001 Mayoral Election, City of New York." April 2001.

"The Case for Redesigning Retirement Benefits for New York's Public Employees." April 2005.

"The Explosion in Pension Costs: Ten Things New Yorkers Should Know About Retirement Benefits for New York City Employees." April 2009.

"The First Priority in the New Year—Pension Reform." January 2012.

"The Myth of 'Uncontrollables': Four Ways New York City Can Take Control of Its Financial Future and Save $2.5 Billion per Year." May 2005.

Manhattan Institute *City Journal*, online version
Gelinas, Nicole. "Construction Safety Woes." Summer 2008.
_____. "Eminent Domain as Central Planning." Winter 2010.
_____. "Transit for Tomorrow." July 8, 2009.
_____. "Ungridlocked." Spring 2012.
Glaeser, Edward I. "Houston, New York Has a Problem." Summer 2008.
_____. "Start-up City." Autumn 2010.
Howard, Paul. "The Medicaid Monster." August 2009.
Hymowitz, Kay S. "Getting Dads Back on the Job." September 8, 2009.
Kagann, Stephen. "New York City's Vanishing Supply Side." Autumn 1992.
MacDonald, Heather. "New York's Indispensable Institution." July 7, 2009.
_____. "Courts v. Cops." Winter 2013.
Malanga, Steven. "How to Rebuild New York." Autumn 2001.
_____. "The City's Finances, Part 1: Life in Taxopolis." July 10, 2009.
_____. "The Coming Budget Crunch." Special Issue, 2013.
_____. "Union Power Comes in Many Forms." Spring 2011.
Miller, Judith. "Counterterror and the Crunch." August 14, 2009.
_____. "New York 9/11/11." Summer 2011.
Salins, Peter D. "Liberating Development." July 10, 2009.
Schulz, Max. "Energize." August 6, 2009.
Stern, Sol. "A Solution for Gotham's Reading Woes." Summer 2011.

_____. "A Teacher's Contract for a New Era." July 21, 2009.

_____."Can New York Clean Up the Testing Mess?" Spring 2010.

_____. "E.D. Hirsch's Curriculum for Democracy." Autumn 2009.

_____. "The Curriculum Reformation." Summer 2012.

Vanderkam, Laura. "Where Did the Korean Greengrocers Go?" Winter 2011.

MDRC Reports

Bifulco, Robert, Rebecca Untermann, and Howard S. Bloom. "The Relative Cost of New York City's Small Public High Schools of Choice." 2014.

Bloom, Howard S. and Rebecca Untermann. "Sustained Progress: New Findings About the Effectiveness and Operation of New Small Public High Schools of Choice in New York City." August 2013.

Bloom, Howard S., Saskia Levy Thompson, and Rebecca Untermann. "Transforming the High School Experience: How New York City's New Small Schools Are Boosting Student Achievement and Graduation Rates." June 2010.

Greenberg, David, Nadine Dechausay, and Carolyn Fraker. "Learning Together: How Families Responded to Education Incentives in New York City's Conditional Cash Transfer Program." May 2011.

Miller, Cynthia, James Riccio, and Jared Smith. "A Preliminary Look at Early Education Results of the Opportunity NYC Family Rewards Program." June 26, 2009.

Nunez, Stephen, Nadita Verma, and Edith Yang. "Building Self-Sufficiency For Housing Voucher Recipients: Interim Findings From the Work Rewards Demonstration in New York City." February 2015.

Pardoe, Richard and Dan Bloom. "Paycheck Plus: A New Antipoverty Strategy for Single Adults." May 2014.

Riccio, James, Nadine Dechausay, et al. "Toward Reduced Poverty Across Generations: Early Findings for the New York City's Conditional Cash Transfer Program." March 2010.

Riccio, James, Nadine Dechausay, et al. "Conditional Cash Transfer in New York City: The Continuing Story of the Opportunity NYC Family Rewards Demonstration." September 2013.

Untermann, Rebecca. "Headed to College: The Effects of New York City's Small High Schools of Choice on Post-Secondary Education." Policy Brief, October 2014.

New York City Independent Budget Office Reports

"Analysis of the Mayor's Preliminary Budget for 2015." March 2014.

"As Medicaid Enrollment Has Surged, Composition of the Caseload Has Changed." June 2003.

"Budget Outlook: A Bright Budget Picture: Jobs Increasing, Tax Revenues Rising, Budget Gaps Shrinking." December 2014.

Campion, Sean. "A Profile of New York City's Industrial Workforce." June 2014.

"Debt Affordability Metrics," special analysis in possession of the author, prepared 2014, courtesy of Doug Turetsky and Ana Champeny.

"Early Learning Takes Its First Steps: City's Redesigned Subsidized Child Care System Still Faces Challenges." December 2012.

"Examining NYCHA's Plan to Preserve Public Housing." April 2006.

"Federal Aid to New York City in the Aftermath of September 11: How Much and for What?" Testimony of Ronnie Lowenstein, Executive Director, IBO Before the Joint Hearing of the City Council Finance, Lower Manhattan Redevelopment and State and Federal Legislation Committees, February 2002.

"Fiscal Brief: How Much Is Too Much? Debt Affordability Measures for the City." April 2006.

"Fiscal Brief: Toward a State of Good Repair? City Capital Spending on Bridges, 2001–2012." April 2014.

"Growth in New York's Medicaid Enrollment and Costs: While Enrollment Highest in the City, Recent Increases Mostly in the Suburbs and Upstate." October 2013.

"Is It Getting Fairer? Examining Five Years of School Allocations Under Fair Student Funding." April 2013.

Lowenstein, Ronnie, Directors. "Letter dated August 25, 2010 to Hon. Letitia James, Council Member."

"Medicaid, Employer-Sponsored Health Insurance & the Uninsured in New York: Regional Differences in Health Insurance Coverage." October 2014.

"Memorandum dated 1/25/10 To: Ronnie Lowenstein, From: James Murphy, Re: Comparisons between Schools Slated for Closing and All Other Schools, transmitted to Council Member Robert Jackson, January 25, 2010."

"New York City By the Numbers: Fiscal History Table." December 10, 2014.

"New York City Public School Indicators: Demographics, Resources, Outcomes." May 2013.

"Testimony of Brendan Cheney, Budget and Policy Analyst Before the City Council Committee on General Welfare on the Uniting for Solutions Beyond Shelter: The Mayor's Five Year Plan to Reduce Homelessness by Two-Thirds." September 23, 2008.

"Testimony of George Sweeting, Deputy Director, to the New York City Council Committee on Contracts on Intro 251-A, Fair Wages for New Yorkers Act." November 22, 2011.

Turetsky, Doug, and Peter Madden. "Twenty-five Years After S7000A: How Property Tax Burdens Have Shifted in New York City." December 5, 2006.

Turetsky, Doug. "Living Wage Again." November 30, 2011.

"Working Together to Accelerate New York's Recovery: Economic Impact Analysis of the September 11th Attack on New York City." November 2001.

Civic and Public Agency Reports, and Other Sources

Agaton, Kathleen, and Donna Taper. "The New York City Young Men's Initiative: Working to Improve Outcomes for Black and Latino Young Men." Metis Associates, June 2014.

"Agreement, Board of Education of the City of New York and United Federation of Teachers, Local 2, American Federation of Teachers, AFL-CIO covering Teachers, July 1, 2003–October 12, 2007."

Alliance for Downtown New York. "A Surge of Bits and Bytes: The State of Tech and Innovation in Lower Manhattan." October 2013.

_____. "Turn the Page: Lower Manhattan's Moment Has Arrived." Annual Report, 2013.

_____. "Lower Manhattan Real Estate Year in Review, 2013." 2013.

American Civil Liberties Union. "Victory in Unlawful Mass Arrest During 2004 RNC the Largest Protest Settlement in History." January 15, 2014.

American Council for Energy Efficient Economy. "Case Study: New York City Green Codes Task Force." January 2014.

Annie E. Casey Foundation. "Building Family Economic Success: the Earned Income Tax Credit (EITC)." August 2005.

Armstrong, Amy, Vicki Breen, Josiah Madar, and Simon McDonnell. "How Have Recent Rezonings Affected the City's Ability to Grow?" Furman Center for Real Estate and Urban Policy, New York University, March 2010.

Associated Press publication of NYPD documents. "Albanian Location of Concern Report."

Associated Press publication of NYPD documents. "Target of Surveillance: Majid Omar, Paterson, N.J."

Associated Press publication of NYPD documents. "The Demographics Unit."

Association for Neighborhood and Housing Development Inc. *Real Affordability: An Evaluation of the Bloomberg Housing Program and Recommendations to Strengthen Affordable Housing Policy.* 2013.

Austin, James, and Michael Jacobson. "How New York City Reduced Mass Incarceration: A Model for Change?" JFA Institute, Vera Institute of Justice and Brennan Center for Justice at New York University Law School, January 2013.

Avery, Robert B. and Kenneth P. Brevoort. "The Subprime Crisis: Is Government Housing Policy to Blame?" Finance and Economics Discussion Series: 2011–36, Division of Research and Statistics, Board of Governors of the Federal Reserve System, Washington, DC, August 3, 2011.

Bach, Victor and Tom Waters. "Strengthening New York City's Public Housing: Directions for Change." Community Service Society. July 2014.

Banks, David and Ana Oliveira. "Young Men's Initiative: Report to the Mayor from the Chairs." August 2011.

Beacon Hill Institute at Suffolk University. "The Impact of the Republican National Convention on the New York City Economy." June 2004.

Bharara, Preet et al. "CRIPA Investigation of the New York City Department of Correction Jails on Rikers Island." US Department of Justice, United States Attorney Southern District of New York. August 4, 2014, and "Transmittal Letter to Hon. Bill DeBlasio and New York City Department of Corrections Commissioner, Joseph Ponte."

Bloomberg, Michael R. "Rebuild, Renew and Remain the Capital of the Free World." Inaugural Address, Mayor of New York City, January 1, 2002 as published in the *New York Times,* January 2, 2002.

Board of Elections of New York City, *Annual Report* 1993, 1997, 2001, 2005, 2009.

Boston Consulting Group. "Evaluating NYC Media Sector Development and Setting the Stage for Future Growth: Final Report." May 8, 2012.

Boston Consulting Group. "Reshaping NYCHA Support Functions." August 2012.

Boyd, Donald J. "A Simulation of Business Taxes in New York City and Other Locations." New York: Citizens Budget Commission, June 2, 2007.

Boyd, Donald, et al. "The Narrowing Gap in New York City Teacher Qualifications and Its Implications for Student Achievement in High Poverty Schools." Cambridge, MA: National Bureau of Economic Research, June 2008.

Bram, Jason, Andrew Haugwout, and James Orr. "Special Issue: The Economic Effects of September 11: Has 9/11 Affected New York City's Growth Potential." *Economic Policy Review,* Vol. 8, No. 2.

Brenner, Mark D., Jeanette Wicks-Lim, and Robert Pollin. "Measuring the Impact of Living Wage Laws: A Critical Appraisal of David Neumark's 'How Living Wage Laws Affect Low Wage Workers and Low-Income Families.'" Political Economy Research Institute, University of Massachusetts, Working Paper Series Number 43, 2002.

Brown, Jeffrey R., Roger Clark, and Joshua Rauh. "The Economics of State and Local Pensions," *National Bureau of Economic Research.* Working Paper 16972, February 2011.

Callahan v. Carey (1981).

Caps, Kristen. "Why Billionaires Don't Pay Property Tax in New York." *Citylab,* May 11, 2015.

Center for Constitutional Rights. "Racial Disparity in NYPD Stops-and-Frisks: The Center for Constitutional Rights Preliminary Report on UF-250 Data from 2005 Through June 2008." June 2009.

Center for Constitutional Rights. "Stop and Frisk: The Human Impact—The Stories Behind the Numbers, the Effects on Our Communities." New York, 2012.

Center for Research on Educational Outcomes at Stanford University. "Charter School Performance in New York City Schools." 2013.

Citizens Budget Commission and Partnership for New York City. "Out of Balance: A Comparison of Public and Private Employee Benefits in New York City." December 2009.

Coalition for the Homeless. "Briefing Paper: Five Years Later: The Failure of Mayor Bloomberg's Five-Year Homeless Plan and the Need to Reform New York City's Approach to Homelessness." June 23, 2009.

_____. "State of the Homeless 2013: 50,000." March 2013.

Cole, Richard, et al. "Assessing the Early Impact of School of One: Evidence from Three School-Wide Pilots." New York: NYU Steinhardt School of Culture, Education and Human Development, The Research Alliance for New York City Schools, June 2012.

Community Service Society and the Center for an Urban Future. "Closing the Gap: A Blueprint for Preparing New York City's Workforce to Meet the Evolving Needs of Employers." 2010.

CTL Engineers and Construction Technology Consultants, P.C. "Report for Buildings Commissioner Robert D. LiMandri: High Risk Construction Oversight Study." June 5, 2009.

CUNY-TV 75. "City Talk: Katherine Oliver, Commissioner, Mayor's Office of Film, Theater, Broadcasting." June 25, 2011.

Deputy Mayor Bob Steel. "Making NYC's Pension System Sustainable." Presentation to the Citizens Budget Commission. July 14, 2011.

District Council 37, AFSCME, AFL-CIO. "We Can Do the Work: How the City Can Save Over $600 Million Without Cutting Services: DC 37 Recommendations for Fiscal Year 2003 Savings for the New York City Budget." Submitted by Lillian Roberts, Executive Director, May 2002.

Dunn, Christopher, Donna Lieberman, et al. "Rights and Wrongs at the RNC: A Special Report About Police and Protest at the Republican National Convention." New York Civil Liberties Union, 2005.

Dunn, Christopher, Sara LaPlante, and Jennifer Carnig. "2013 Stop and Frisk." American Civil Liberties Union, New York, August 2014.

Eldredge v. Koch (1983).

Fernando Ferrer Campaign Documents, Hunter College Institute of Puerto Rican Studies.

Fernando Ferrer Tracking Polls and Top Line Polls, 2001 and 2005, courtesy of Fernando Ferrer and Global Strategy Group, in author's possession.

Floyd et al. v. The City of New York, 08 Civ. 1034, Opinion and Order, August 12, 2013.

Fratello, Jennifer, Andres F. Rengifo, and Jennifer Trone. "Coming of Age with Stop and Frisk: Experiences, Self-Perceptions and Public Safety Implications." New York: Vera Institute for Justice, 2013.

Fruchter, Norma, and Sara McAlister. "School Governance and Accountability: Outcomes of Mayoral Control Schooling in New York City." Annenberg Institute for School Reform at Brown University, October 2008.

Gardner, David P. , et al. "A Nation At Risk: The Imperative for Educational Reform." Washington, DC: National Commission on Excellence in Education, April 1983.

Gaumer, Elyzabeth, and Sheree West. "Selected Initial Findings of the 2014 New York City Housing and Vacancy Survey." New York City Department of Housing, Preservation and Development, February 9, 2015.

Golden, Megan, and Cari Almo. "Reducing Gun Violence: An Overview of New York City's Strategy." Vera Institute of Justice, 2004.

Governor's Press Office, New York State. "Governor Cuomo Introduces Pension Reform Legislation." Press Release, June 8, 2011.

Green, Jonah. "Off the Record." Documentary about the 2001 mayoral race.

Group of 35 Task Force. "Preparing for the Future: A Commercial Development Strategy for New York City." New York, June 2001.

Hacer Dinler et al., plaintiffs versus The City of New York et al., defendants, United States District Court, Southern District of New York, No 04 Civ. 7921 (RJS) (JCF) Consolidated RNC Cases, Opinion and Order, September 30, 2012.

Hales, Mike, and Adres Mendoza Pena. "2012 Global Cities Index and Emerging Cities Outlook." A.T. Kearney and the Chicago Council on Global Affairs, 2012.

Hassan et al. v. The City of New York. United States District Court for the District of New Jersey, Civ. No. 2–12.341.

Hemphill, Clara, Kim Nauer, Andrew White, and Thomas Jacobs. "Building Blocks for Better Schools: How the Next Mayor Can Prepare New York's Students for College and Careers." New York: The New School, Education Funders Research Initiative. November 21, 2013.

Institute for Politics, University of Chicago, May 27, 2014:
    Off-the-Record Forum: The 2001 New York City Election for Mayor
    Howard Wolfson, moderator
    David Axelrod, campaign advisor to Fernando Ferrer
    Maggie Haberman, *New York Post* city hall reporter
    Douglas Schoen, pollster for Michael Bloomberg
    John Siegal, campaign advisor to Mark Green
Jones, Dr. Delores Brown, Jaspreet Gill, and Jennifer Trone. "Stop, Question and
    Frisk Policing Tactics in New York City: A Primer." Center for Race, Crime
    and Criminal Justice, John Jay College of Criminal Justice, March 2010.
Kelly, David N., and Sharon L. McCarthy. "The Report of the Crime Reporting
    Review Committee to Commissioner Raymond W. Kelly Concerning
    Compstat Auditing." New York City Police Department. April 8, 2013.
Kelly, Raymond W. "Letter to Honorable Christine Quinn, Speaker, New York
    City Council." May 16, 2012.
Kemple, James J. "The Condition of New York City High Schools: Examining
    Trends and Looking Toward the Future." NYU Steinhardt School of
    Culture, Education and Human Development, The Research Alliance for
    New York City Schools. March 2013.
Kucsera, John, with Gary Orfield. "New York State's Extreme School
    Segregation: Inequality, Inaction and a Damaged Future." The Civil Rights
    Project. March 2014.
Landrum and Brown. "JFK Air Cargo Study." Prepared for the Port Authority
    of New York and New Jersey, January 2013.
_____. "Environmental Assessment: Runway 4L22R Improvements,
    John F. Kennedy International Airport." Prepared for the US Department of
    Transportation Federal Aviation Administration, November 2014.
Lester, T. William, and Ken Jacobs. "Creating Good Jobs in Our Communities:
    How Higher Wage Standards Affect Economic Development and
    Employment." Center for American Progress, November 2010.
Ligon et al. v. The City of New York, No. 12 Civ. 2274 (2013), Opinion, January
    8, 2013.
Madar, Josiah, and Mark Willis. "Creating Affordable Housing Out of Thin
    Air: The Economics of Mandatory Inclusionary Zoning in New York City."
    NYU Furman Center, March 2014.
Mark Green for Mayor, Selected Campaign Papers, in author's possession.
*Mark Nunez et al. v. City of New York et al., Memorandum of Law In Support of
    the United States of America Motion to Intervene*, 11 Civ. 5845 (LTS) (JCF),
    December 11, 2014.

Marsh, Julie A., et al. "A Big Apple for Educators: New York City's Experiment with Schoolwide Performance Bonuses: Final Evaluation Report." Santa Monica, CA: Rand Corporation, 2011.

McCain v. Koch (1983).

McKinsey & Company. "Sustaining New York's and the US' Global Financial Leadership." 2006.

MDRC. "Reforming Underperforming High Schools." March 2013.

"Memorandum of Agreement Between the Board of Education of the City of New York and United Federation of Teachers, Local 2, American Federation of Teachers, AFL-CIO Covering Teachers." Dated November 6, 2006, covering October 13, 2007 through October 31, 2009.

Monahan, Amy. "Public Pension Plan Reform: the Legal Framework," University of Minnesota—Twin Cities School of Law, Education, Finance and Policy, Vol. 5, 2010, Minnesota Legal Studies Research No. 10–13, 7–10.

Morelix, Amobio, Joshua Russell, Robert W. Fairlie, and E.J. Reedy. "The Kauffman Index: Main Street Entrepreneurship 2015." Ewing Marion Kauffman Foundation, December 2015.

Moss, Mitchell L. "How New York City Won the Olympics." New York: Rudin Center for Transportation and Management, Robert F. Wagner Graduate School of Public Service, NYU, November 2011.

Move NY. "The Move NY Fair Plan." New York, February 2015.

National Alliance to End Homelessness. "Community Snapshot: New York City." July 2005.

National Assessment of Educational Progress (NAEP). "The Nation's Report Card: Trial Urban District Snapshot Report, New York City Department of Education Public Schools, Reading Grade 4 and Grade 8 and Math Grade 4 and Grade 8." US Department of Education, Institute of Education Sciences, National Center for Education Statistics. 2002, 2003, 2008, 2009, 2012, 2013.

Neumark, David. "How Living Wage Laws Affect Low Wage Workers and Low-Income Families." Public Policy Institute of California Report # 156, 2002.

New York City Campaign Finance Board: CFB Rules.

_____. "An Election Interrupted . . ." Executive Summary, September 2002.

New York City Commission for Economic Opportunity. "Report to Mayor Michael R. Bloomberg: Increasing Opportunity and Reducing Poverty in New York City." 2006.

New York City Economic Development Corporation. "Fashion.NYC.2020." 2010.

New York City Economic Development Corporation and Oliver Wyman. "Media.NYC.2020." 2010.

New York City Economic Development Corporation. "New York City Industrial Policy: Protecting and Growing New York City's Industrial Job Base." January 2005.

New York City Family Homelessness Special Master Panel. "Family Homelessness Prevention Report." November 2003.

New York City Housing Authority. "The Plan to Preserve Public Housing." April 2006.

New York City Partnership and Chamber of Commerce. "Working Together to Accelerate New York's Recovery: Economic Impact Analysis of the September 11th Attack on New York City." 2001.

New York City Taxi & Limousine Commission. "2014 Taxicab Fact Book." 2014.

New York Metro American Planning Association. "A Statement from the New York Metro Chapter of the American Planning Association, New York New Visions, Civic Alliance for Downtown New York, and the Labor Community Advocacy Network." November 1, 2005.

New York State Constitution.

New York State, Department of Labor, "New York City Current Employment Statistics, 2002–2013."

New York State Department of Labor, Division of Research and Statistics, Bureau of Labor Market Information. "New York's Motion Picture Industry: A Statewide and Regional Analysis." June 2014.

New York State, Office of the Attorney General. "An Investigation Into the NYPD's Stop and Frisk Practices." 1999.

_____. "A Report on Arrests Arising from the New York City Police Department's Stop-and-Frisk Practices." 2013.

New York State, Office of the Comptroller. "New York City Department of Education Administration of the Early Grade Class Reduction Program, 2005-N3." March 16, 2006.

NYC & Co. "New York City Tourism: A Model for Success." New York, 2013.

NYC2012. "The Olympic Games in the World's Second Home." New York, Volume 1.

Obama, Barack. "Speech by President Barack Obama Sponsored by the Center for American Progress on the Economy and Income Inequality." December 4, 2013.

Parent Commission on School Governance and Mayoral Control. "Recommendations on School Governance." Final Report, March 2009.

Parrot, James. "Building Up New York, Tearing Down Job Quality: Taxpayer Impact of Worsening Employment Practices in New Construction in New York City." Fiscal Policy Institute, December 5, 2007.

Parthenon Group. "An Assessment of the New York City Department of Education School Support Structure." November 2013.

Partnership for New York City. "Grounded: The High Cost of Air Traffic Congestion." New York: February 2009.

_____. "Growth or Gridlock? The Case for Traffic Relief and Transit Improvement for a Greater New York." New York, December 2006.

_____. "NYC Jobs Blueprint." New York, 2013.

Port Authority of New York and New Jersey. "The Economic Impact of the Aviation Industry on the New York–New Jersey Metropolitan Region." October 2005.

Quint, Janet C., et al. "New York's Changing High School Landscape: High Schools and Their Characteristics, 2002–2008." New York: MDRC, 2010.

Regional Plan Association. "Urban Development Alternatives for the Hudson Rail Yards." New York: December 2004.

_____. "Study Shows Mixed-Use Development Outperforms Stadium on Far West Side." February 3, 2005.

Ridgeway, Greg. "Analysis of Racial Disparities in the New York Police Department's Stop, Question and Frisk Practices." Santa Monica, CA: RAND Corporation, 2007.

Rivlin, Alice, and Rosemary Scanlon. "Working Group Reports Prepared for Civic Alliance to Rebuild Downtown New York." New York, September 2002.

Roistacher, Elizabeth. "How Much Do Taxes Matter? What Economists Can—and Cannot—Tell NYC Policy Makers." New York: Citizens Budget Commission, December 11, 2006.

Rostker, Bernard D., Lawrence M. Hanser, et al. "Evaluation of the New York City Police Department Firearm Training and Firearm-Discharge Review Process." Santa Monica, CA: RAND Corporation, 2008.

Sadik-Khan, Janette. "TED Talk: City Transportation Expert." September 2013.

Seattle Police Department. "The Seattle Police Department After Action Report: The World Trade Organization Ministerial Conference, Seattle, Washington, November 29–December 3, 1999." April 4, 2000.

Second Supplemental Report of Jeffrey Fagan, Ph.D. in the matter of *Floyd et al. v. The City of New York 08 Civ. 01034 (SAS)*.

Shedd, Carla. "What About the Other 99%? The Broader Impact of Street Stops on Minority Communities." Research Paper presented at Urban Institute Justice Policy Center forum on Key Issues in Police Use of Pedestrian Stops and Searches, August 2012.

Siman, Nina. "Digital Collaboration and Classroom Practice: Educator Use of ARIS Connect." New York: NYU Steinhardt School of Culture, Education and Human Development, June 2014.

Silber, Mitchell D., and Arbin Bhatt. "Radicalization in the West: The Homegrown Threat." NYPD, 2007.

Terry v. Ohio, 392 US 1 (1968).

United States of America v. Faisal Shahzad, Official Complaint, filed May 4, 2010 with US District Court, Southern District of New York.

US v. Mazer et al. Superseding Indictment, June 20, 2011.

Villavicencio, Adriana, Dyuti Bhattacharya, and Brandon Guidry. "Moving the Needle: Exploring Key Levers to Boost College Readiness Among Black and Latino Males in New York City." NYU Steinhardt School of Culture, Education and Human Development, The Research Alliance for New York City Schools. July 2013.

Villavicencio, Adriana, and William H. Marinell. "Inside Success: Strategies of 25 Effective Small High Schools in NYC." NYU Steinhardt School of Culture, Education and Human Development, The Research Alliance for New York City Schools. July 2014.

Waller v. City of New York, New York State Supreme Court, Index Number 112957/2011, November 15, 2011.

Waters, Tom, and Victor Bach. "Destabilized Rents: The Impact of Vacancy Decontrol on Low-Income Communities." Community Service Society, June 2009.

Weingarten, Randi. "First Things First." Speech Given at United Federation of Teachers Spring Conference, 2003, in author's possession courtesy of Randi Weingarten.

Whitehurst, Grover (Russ) with Sarah Whitfield. "School Choice and School Performance in the New York City Public Schools—Will the Past Be Prologue?" Brown Center on Education Policy at Brookings. October 2013.

Media, Press Release Sites, and Polling Institutes

American Federation of Teachers

Associated Press

Bloomberg News

Carnegie Reporter

Centers for Disease Control and Prevention

City of New York, Department of Health and Mental Hygiene, Press Releases and Reports

City of New York, Office of the Mayor, Press Releases and Reports

City of New York, Office of the Comptroller, Press Releases and Reports

CNN

Digital Hollywood

Edison Media Research

FoxNews

Gotham Gazette

Indianapolis Star

Marist Institute for Public Opinion

Metropolitan Transportation Authority Press Releases

New York City News Service

New York Economic Development Corporation, Press Releases and Reports

New York Magazine

New York Police Foundation

New York Sun

NYC & Co.

Rolling Stone

The American Spectator

The Atlantic

The Brooklyn Mail

The Daily Beast

The Economist

The Financial Times

The Guardian

The Nation

The New Yorker

The New York Daily News

The New York Observer

The New York Times (NYT)

The New York Post (NYP)

The Related Companies

The Trust for Governor's Island

The Village Voice

The Wall Street Journal

United States Attorney Southern District of New York

Vanity Fair

Quinnipiac University Polling Institute

WNYC

WPIX 11 News

Books, Periodicals, and Other Published Sources

Angotti, Tom. *New York for Sale: Community Planning Confronts Global Real Estate.* Cambridge, MA: MIT Press, 2008.

Bagley, Katherine, and Maria Gallucci. *Bloomberg's Hidden Legacy: Climate Change and the Future of New York City.* New York: David Sasson, ebook edition, 2003.

Barrett, Wayne, assisted by Adam Fifield. *Rudy! An Investigative Biography of Rudolph Giuliani.* New York: Basic Books, 2000.

Bellush, Jewel, and Bernard Bellush. *Union Power & New York: Victor Gotbaum and District Council 37.* New York: Praeger Publishers, 1984.

Bernanke, Ben S. *The Courage to Act: A Memoir of a Crisis and Its Aftermath.* New York: W. W. Norton & Company, 2015.

Black, Cathie. *Basic Black: The Essential Guide for Getting Ahead at Work (and in Life).* New York: Crown Business, ebook edition, 2007.

Blake, Mathew. "Bloomberg's Poverty Party." *The Nation,* undated, accessed online September 18, 2015.

Blinder, Alan S. *After the Music Stopped: The Financial Crisis, the Response and the Work Ahead.* New York: Penguin Press, 2013, ebook edition.

Bloomberg, Michael, with Matthew Winkler. *Bloomberg by Bloomberg.* New York: John Wiley & Sons, 2001.

Brands, H. W. *Reagan: The Life.* New York: Doubleday, ebook edition, 2015.

Brash, Julian. *Bloomberg's New York: Class and Governance in the Luxury City.* Athens, GA: University of Georgia Press, 2011.

Bratton, William, with Peter Knobler. *Turnaround: How America's Top Cop Reversed the Crime Epidemic.* New York: Random House, 1998.

Brill, Steven. *Class Warfare: The Fight to Fix America's Schools.* New York: Simon & Schuster, ebook edition, 2011.

Brooks, Fred. "The Living Wage Movement: Potential Implications for the Working Poor." *Families in Society,* 88 (3) 2007.

Burrows, Edwin G., and Mike Wallace. *Gotham: A History of New York City to 1898.* New York: Oxford University Press, 1999.

Cannato, Vincent J. *The Ungovernable City: John Lindsay and His Struggle to Save New York.* New York: Basic Books, 2001.

Dickey, Christopher. *Securing the City: Inside America's Best Counterterror Force—the NYPD.* New York: Simon & Schuster, 2009.

Dwyer, Jim, and Kevin Flynn. *102 Minutes: The Untold Story of the Fight to Survive Inside the Twin Towers.* New York: Times Books; Henry Holt & Company, LLC, 2005.

Edgerton, Jesse, Andrew F. Haughwout, and Rae Rosen. "Revenue Implications of New York City's Tax System." *Current Issues in Economics and Finance, Second District Highlights,* Volume 10, Number 4, April 2004.

Elkind, Peter. *Client 9: The Rise and Fall of Eliot Spitzer.* New York: Penguin Publishers, 2010.

Fainstein, Susan S. *The Just City.* Ithaca, NY: Cornell University Press, 2010.

_____. "The Return of Urban Renewal: Dan Doctoroff's Grand Plans for New York City." *Harvard Design Magazine,* Spring/Summer 2005.

Farley, Tom, MD. *Saving Gotham: A Billionaire Mayor, Activist Doctors and the Fight for Eight Million Lives.* New York: W.W. Norton & Company, 2015.

Freeman, Joshua. *Working-Class New York: Life and Labor Since World War II.* New York: The New Press, 2000.

Freeman, Richard B., Joni Hirsch, and Lawrence Mishel, eds., *Emerging Labor Market Institutions for the Twenty-first Century.* Chicago: University of Chicago Press, 2004.

Fryer Jr., Roland. "Financial Incentives and Student Achievement: Evidence from Randomized Trials." *Quarterly Journal of Economics* 2011; 126 (4), 1755–1798.

Garvin, Alexander. *The American City: What Works, What Doesn't.* New York: McGraw Hill, 1996, third edition, 2014.

Geist, Charles R. *Wall Street: A History.* New York: Oxford University Press, 1997.

Geithner, Timothy. *Stress Test: Reflections on Financial Crises.* New York: Crown Publishers, 2014, ebook edition.

Gilens, Martin, and Benjamin I. Page. "Testing Theories of American Politics: Elites, Interest Groups and Average Citizens." *American Political Science Association*, Vol. 12/No. 3, 564–81, September 2014.

Giuliani, Rudolph W., with Ken Kurson. *Leadership.* New York: Miramax Books, 2002.

Glanz, James, and Eric Lipton. *City in the Sky: The Rise and Fall of the World Trade Center.* New York: Time Books Henry Holt and Company, LLC, ebook edition, 2013.

Goldberger, Paul. *Up From Zero: Politics, Architecture and the Rebuilding of New York.* New York: Random House, 2005.

Goldsmith, Stephen. *The Entrepreneurial City: A How To Handbook for Urban Innovators.* New York: The Manhattan Institute, 1999.

Goldstein, Dana. "Behavioral Theory: Can Mayor Bloomberg Pay People to Do the Right Thing?" *The American Prospect*, August 14, 2009.

_____. *The Teacher Wars: A History of America's Most Embattled Profession.* New York: Doubleday, ebook edition, 2014.

Gordon, John Steele. *Empire of Wealth: The Epic History of American Economic Power.* New York: HarperCollins Publishers, 2004.

Green, Mark. *Bright, Infinite Future: A Generational Memoir on the Progressive Rise.* New York: St. Martin's Press, 2016.

Greenspan, Elizabeth. *Battle for Ground Zero.* New York: Palgrave McMillan, 2013.

Hackworth, Jason. *The Neoliberal City: Governance, Ideology, and Development in American Urbanism.* Ithaca, NY: Cornell University Press, ebook edition, 2014.

Hammett, Jerilou, and Kingsley Hammett, eds. *The Suburbanization of New York.* New York: Princeton Architectural Press, 2007.

Heckman, James J., and Alan B. Krueger. *Inequality in America.* Cambridge, MA: MIT Press, 2005.

Hemphill, Clara, and Kim Nauer, et al. *Managing by the Numbers: Empowerment and Accountability in New York City's Schools.* New York: Center for New York City Affairs, Milano, The New School For Management and Urban Policy, 2010.

Investment Company Institute. *Investment Company Factbook 2013*, 53rd edition.

Isaacson, Walter. *Steve Jobs.* New York: Simon & Schuster, ebook edition, 2013.

Jacobs, James B., with Coleen Friel and Robert Radick. *Gotham Unbound: How New York City was Liberated from the Grip of Organized Crime.* New York: NYU Press, 1999.

Jacobs, Jane. *The Death and Life of Great American Cities.* New York: Vintage Books, 1961.

Jeantet, Diane. "A Brief History of Homelessness in New York." *City Limits,* March 13, 2011.

_____. "Bloomberg's Plan Was Incredibly Ambitious." *City Limits,* March 13, 2011.

_____. "As Homeless Numbers Rose, Clashes Over Policies." *City Limits,* March 13, 2011.

Johnson, Richard W. "Pension Underfunding and Liberal Retirement Benefits of State and Local Workers." *National Tax Journal,* 1997, 50 (1): 113–142.

Kahlenberg, Richard. *Tough Liberal: Albert Shanker and the Battles Over Schools, Unions, Race and Democracy.* New York: Columbia University Press, ebook edition 2007.

Karmen, Andrew. *New York Murder Mystery: The True Story Behind the Crime Crash of the 1990s.* New York: New York University Press, 2000.

Keane, Thomas H., Lee Hamilton, et al. *The 9/11 Commission Report: Final Report of the National Commission on Terrorist Attacks Upon the United States.* New York: WW Norton and Company, 2004.

Kelleher, Maureen. *New York City's Children First: Lessons in School Reform.* Washington, DC: Center for American Progress, 2014.

Kelly, Raymond W. *Vigilance: My Life Serving America and Protecting Its Empire City.* New York: Hachette Books, 2015.

Kerik, Bernard B. *The Lost Son: A Life in Pursuit of Justice.* New York: HarperTorch, 2002.

Kirtzman, Andrew. *Rudy Giuliani: Emperor of the City.* New York: Harper Collins, 2001.

Klein, Joel. *Lessons of Hope: How to Fix Our Schools.* New York: HarperCollins, ebook edition, 2014.

Kroessler, Jeffrey A. *New York Year By Year: A Chronology of the Great Metropolis.* New York: NYU Press, 2002.

Kuznets, Simon. "Economic Growth and Inequality." *American Economic Review 45,* No. 1, 1955, 1–28.

Lachman, Seymour P., and Robert Polner. *The Man Who Saved New York: Hugh Carey and the Great Fiscal Crisis of 1975.* Albany: State University of New York Press, 2010.

Levitan, Mark, and Susan Weiler. "Poverty in New York City, 1969–1999: The Influence of Demographic Change, Income Growth, and Income Inequality." *FRBNY Economic Policy Review,* July 2008.

Livin-Waldman, Oren M. "Local Labor Markets, Income Inequality and Institutional Response: The Case of New York City." *Regional Labor Review.* Fall 2001, 36–46.

Mandery, Evan J. *The Campaign: Rudy Giuliani, Ruth Messinger, Al Sharpton, and the Race to Be Mayor of New York City.* Boulder, Colorado: Westview Press, 1999.

McNickle, Chris. *The Power of the Mayor: David Dinkins 1990–1993.* New Brunswick, NJ: Transaction Publishers, 2012.

———. *To Be Mayor of New York: Ethnic Politics in the City.* New York: Columbia University Press, 1993.

Mollenkopf, John. *A Phoenix in the Ashes: The Rise and Fall of the Koch Coalition in New York City Politics.* Princeton: Princeton University Press, 1992.

———. *Contentious City: The Politics of Recovery in New York City.* New York: Russell Sage Foundation, 2005.

Mollenkopf, John H. and Manuel Castells, eds. *Dual City: Restructuring New York.* New York: Russell Sage Foundation. 1991.

Monahan, Amy. "Public Pension Plan Reform: the Legal Framework." *Minnesota Legal Studies Research,* No. 10–13, Vol. 5, 2010.

Morris, Charles. *The Cost of Good Intentions: New York and the Liberal Experiment, 1960–1975.* New York: McGraw Hill, 1980.

Nadelstern, Eric. *10 Lessons from New York City Schools: What Really Works to Improve Education.* New York: Columbia University Teachers College Press, ebook edition, 2013.

Newfeld, Jack. *The Full Rudy: The Man, the Myth, and the Mania.* New York: Nations Books, ebook edition, 2007.

Nocera, Joseph. *A Piece of the Action: How the Middle Class Joined the Money Class.* New York: Simon & Schuster, ebook edition, 1994.

O'Day, Jennifer A., Catherine S. Bitter, Louis M. Gomez, eds. *Education Reform in New York City: Ambitious Change in the Nation's Most Complex School System.* Cambridge, MA: Harvard Education Press, 2011.

Oreskes, Naomi. "The Scientific Consensus on Climate Change." *Science,* 3 December 2004, vol. 306, 1686.

Oreskes, Naomi, and Erik M. Conway. *Merchants of Doubt: How a Handful of Scientists Obscured the Truth on Issues from Tobacco Smoke to Global Warming.* New York: Bloomsbury Press, 2010.

Ouchi, William G., with Lydia Segal. *Making Schools Work: A Revolutionary Plan to Get Your Children the Education They Need.* New York: Simon & Schuster, ebook edition, 2003.

Pecorella, Robert F., and Jeffrey M. Stonecash, eds. *Governing New York State.* Albany: SUNY Press, 2012.

Piketty, Thomas (translated by Arthur Goldhammer). *Capital in the Twenty-First Century.* Cambridge, MA: The Belknap Press of Harvard University Press, ebook edition, 2014.

Piketty, Thomas, and Emmanuel Saez. "Income Inequality in the United States, 1913–1998." *The Quarterly Journal of Economics,* 118, No. 1 February, 2003: 1–40.

Plunz, Olivier. *A History of Housing in New York City.* New York: Columbia University Press, 1990.

Podair, Jerald E. *The Strike That Changed New York: Blacks, Whites and the Ocean Hill-Brownsville Crisis.* New Haven: Yale University Press, 2002.

Pollin, Robert, and Stephanie Luce. *The Living Wage: Building a Fair Economy.* New York: The New Press, 1998.

Popp, Trey. "Street Fighter." *The Pennsylvania Gazette,* March/April 2016.

Purnick, Joyce. *Mike Bloomberg: Money, Power, Politics.* New York: Public Affairs, 2009.

Quinn, Christine. *With Patience and Fortitude.* New York: HarperCollins, 2013.

Rayman, Graham A. *The NYPD Tapes: A Shocking Story of Cops, Cover-Ups and Courage.* New York: Palgrave Macmillan, 2013.

Ravitch, Diane. *The Great School Wars: A History of New York City Public Schools.* New York: Basic Books, 1988.

_____. *The Death and Life of the Great American School System: How Testing and Choice Are Undermining Education.* New York: Basic Books, 2010.

Ravitch, Diane, et al. *NYC Schools Under Bloomberg and Klein: What Parents, Teachers and Policymakers Need to Know.* New York: Lulu, 2009.

Ravitch, Richard. *So Much To Do: A Full Life of Business, Politics, and Confronting Fiscal Crises.* New York: Public Affairs, 2014.

Roberts, Sam. *Grand Central: How a Train Station Transformed America.* New York: Grand Central Publishing, 2013.

Rosensweig, Cynthia, and William Solecki. "Climate Change and a Global City: Learning from New York." *Environment,* Vol. 43 Iss. 3, April 2001.

Saad-Lesser, Joelle, Teresa Ghilarducci, and Laruen Schmitz. "Are New Yorkers Ready for Retirement?" Schwartz Center for Economic Policy Analysis and City of New York, Office of the Comptroller, January 2012.

Sadik-Khan, Janette, with Seth Solomonow. *Street Fight: Handbook for an Urban Revolution.* Viking Press, New York, 2016.

Safir, Howard, with Ellis Whitman. *Security: An Inside Look at the Tactics of the NYPD.* New York: St. Martin's Press, 2003.

Sagalyn, Lynne B. *Times Square Roulette: Remaking the City Icon.* Cambridge, MA: MIT Press, 2001.

Schaller, Bruce. "New York City's Congestion Pricing Experience and Implications for Road Pricing Acceptance in the United States." *Transport Policy* 17 (2010) 266–73.

Schneider, Nathan. *Thank You Anarchy: Notes from the Occupy Apocalypse.* Berkeley, CA: University of California Press, 2013.

Schoen, Douglas E. *Declaring Independence: The Beginning of the End of the Two-Party System.* New York: Random House, ebook edition, 2008.

Schreiber, Sylvester. "Political Economy of Public Sector Retirement Plans." *Journal of Pension Economics and Finance.* April 2011, 10 (2): 269–290.

Sharpton, Reverend Al, with Karen Hunter. *Al on America.* New York: Dafina Books, 2002.

Sheehan, Michael A. *Crush the Cell: How to Defeat Terrorism Without Terrorizing Ourselves.* New York: Three Rivers Press, 2008.

Shefter, Martin. *Political Crisis/Fiscal Crisis: The Collapse and Revival of New York City.* New York: Basic Books, 1985.

Siegel, Fred. *The Future Once Happened Here: New York, D.C., L.A. and the Fate of America's Big Cities.* New York: The Free Press, 1997.

Siegel, Fred, with Harry Siegel. *The Prince of the City: Giuliani, New York and the Genius of American Life.* San Francisco: Encounter Books, 2005.

Silverman, Eli B. *NYPD Battles Crime: Innovative Strategies in Policing.* Boston: Northeastern University Press, 1999.

Soffer, Jonathan. *Ed Koch and the Rebuilding of New York City.* New York: Columbia University Press, 2010.

Sorkin, Andrew Ross. *Too Big to Fail: The Inside Story of How Wall Street and Washington Sought to Save the Financial Systems—and Themselves*. New York: Viking Penguin, 2010, ebook edition.

Taylor, Clarence. *Civil Rights in New York City From World War II to the Giuliani Era*. New York: Fordham University Press, 2011.

Thabit, Walter. *How East New York Became a Ghetto*. New York: New York University Press, 2003.

Ungar-Sargon, Batya. "Decisions New York's Next Mayor Will Face on Public Housing." *City Limits,* April 18, 2013.

Vallone, Peter F. *Learning to Govern: My Life in New York Politics, From Hell Gate to City Hall*. New York: Chaucer Press, 2005.

Viteritti, Joseph P. *Across the River: Politics and Education in the City.* New York: Homes and Meier, 1983.

Viteritti, Joseph P., ed. *When Mayors Take Charge: School Governance in the City.* Washington, DC: Brookings Institution Press, ebook edition, 2009.

Watson, Robert T. and Core Writing Team. *Climate Change 2001: Synthesis Report, United Nations Environmental Program and World Meteorological Organization*. Cambridge, UK: Cambridge University Press, 2001.

Weikart, Lynne A. *Follow the Money: Who Controls New York City Mayors?* Albany: State University of New York Press, 2009.

Wong, Kenneth K., and Francis X. Shen. *Mayoral Governance and Student Achievement*. Washington, DC: Center for American Progress and the Broad Foundation, March 2013.

Wynn, Jennifer. *Inside Rikers: Stories From the World's Largest Penal Colony.* New York: St. Martin's Griffin, 2001.

Zimring, Franklin E. *The City That Became Safe: New York's Lessons for Urban Crime and Its Control*. New York: Oxford University Press, 2013.

Endnotes

Introduction

1   Michael Bloomberg with Matthew Winkler, *Bloomberg by Bloomberg* (New York: John Wiley & Sons, Inc, 1997), 151; Michael M. Miller and Matthew Winkler, "Plugging-In," *Wall Street Journal,* September 22, 1988.

2   Thomas H. Kean, Chair and Lee H. Hamilton, Vice Chair, et al., *The 9/11 Commission Report* (New York: W.W. Norton & Company, 2004), 1–14.

3   Rudolph W. Giuliani with Ken Kurson, *Leadership* (New York: Miramax Books, 2002), 3–25; Andrew Kirtzman, *Rudy Giuliani: Emperor of the City* (New York: HarperCollins, 2001), 289–306.

4   Giuliani with Kurson, *Leadership,* 25; Jim Dwyer and Kevin Flynn, *102 Minutes: The Untold Story of the Fight to Survive Inside the Twin Towers,* (New York: Times Books, 2005), xxi–xxiv; Kean and Hamilton, et al., *9/11 Commission Report, 1–14.*

5   Board of Elections of New York City, "Annual Report," 2001; Adam Nagourney, "A Day of Terror: The Elections; Pataki Orders Postponement of Primaries Across State," *NYT,* September 12, 2001; Adam Nagourney, "Primary Rescheduled for September 25, With Run-off, If Necessary, Set for Oct. 11," *NYT,* 2001; Clyde Haberman, "NYC; Reaffirming Democracy, Here and Now," *NYT,* September 22, 2001.

6   Preet Bharara et al., "CRIPA Investigation of the New York City Department of Correction Jails on Rikers Island," US Department of Justice, United States Attorney Southern District of New York, Letter to Honorable Bill De Blasio, New York City Department of Corrections Commissioner Joseph Ponte and New York City Corporation Counsel Zachary Carter, August 4, 2014, 3–14.

Chapter 1

1   John Steele Gordon, *An Empire of Wealth: The Epic History of American Economic Power* (New York: HarperCollins Publishers, 2004), 407.

2   Bloomberg with Winkler, *Bloomberg by Bloomberg,* 22–4; Elizabeth Kolbert, "The Mogul Mayor," *The New Yorker,* April 22, 2002.

3   Bloomberg with Winkler, *Bloomberg by Bloomberg,* 22–4; Author's recollection.

4   Bloomberg with Winkler, *Bloomberg by Bloomberg,* 29–36; Elizabeth Kolbert, "The Mogul Mayor," *The New Yorker,* April 22, 2002.

5   Bloomberg with Winkler, *Bloomberg by Bloomberg,* 37.

6   Bloomberg with Winkler, *Bloomberg by Bloomberg,* 37.

7   Bloomberg with Winkler, *Bloomberg by Bloomberg,* 204–06; Joyce Purnick, *Mike Bloomberg: Money, Power, Politics* (New York: Public Affairs, 2009), 10.

8   Bloomberg with Winkler, *Bloomberg by Bloomberg,* 11, 204; Purnick, *Mike Bloomberg,* 10–12; Dean E. Murphy, "Bloomberg: A Man of Contradictions, But With a Single Focus," *NYT,* November 26, 2001.

9   Bloomberg with Winkler, *Bloomberg by Bloomberg*, 12; Purnick, *Mike Bloomberg*, 8; Richard L. Stern and Jason Zweig, "Michael Bloomberg," 296 in Charles D. Ellis with James D. Vertin, *Wall Street People: True Stories of Today's Masters and Moguls* (New York: John Wiley & Sons, Inc., 2001), 295–7; Author's interview, Rohit Aggarwala, October 29, 2015; Author's interview, Janette Sadik-Khan, September 14, 2016.

10   Bloomberg with Winkler, *Bloomberg by Bloomberg*, 12, 205; Purnick, *Mike Bloomberg*, 14–20; Beverly Ford, Kenneth Lovett, Reuven Blau, Kathleen Lucadama, "Charlotte Bloomberg, Mayor Bloomberg's Mother, Dies at 102," *Daily News*, June 19, 2011; Dean E. Murphy, "Bloomberg: A Man of Contradictions, But With a Single Focus," *NYT*, November 26, 2001.

11   Kolbert, "The Mogul Mayor," *The New Yorker*, April 22, 2002; Bloomberg with Winkler, *Bloomberg by Bloomberg*, 14; Purnick, *Mike Bloomberg*, 12.

12   Kolbert, "The Mogul Mayor," *The New Yorker*, April 22, 2002; Bloomberg with Winkler, *Bloomberg by Bloomberg*, 14; Purnick, *Mike Bloomberg*, 12.

13   Charles R. Geist, *Wall Street: A History*, (New York: Oxford University Press, 1997), 299–328, *passim*; Joe Nocera, *A Piece of the Action: How the Middle Class Joined the Money Class* (New York: Simon & Schuster), 177, *passim*; Investment Company Institutute, *Investment Company Fact Book 2013*, *53rd* edition, online. Table 1: Total Net Assets, Number of Funds, Number of Shareholders, and Number of Shareholder Accounts of the Mutual Fund Industry.

14   Bloomberg with Winkler, *Bloomberg by Bloomberg*, 42.

15   Miller and Winkler, "Plugging-In," *Wall Street Journal*, September 22, 1988; Meryl Gordon, "Citizen Mike," *New York*, April 16, 2001; Michael Bloomberg with Matthew Winkler, *Bloomberg by Bloomberg*, 50.

16   Miller and Winkler, "Plugging-In," *Wall Street Journal*, September 22, 1988.

17   Miller and Winkler, "Plugging-In," *Wall Street Journal*, September 22, 1988.

18   Miller and Winkler, "Plugging-In," *Wall Street Journal*, September 22, 1988; Kolbert, "The Mogul Mayor," *The New Yorker*, April 22, 2002.

19   Bloomberg with Winkler, *Bloomberg by Bloomberg*, 59.

20   Bloomberg with Winkler, *Bloomberg by Bloomberg*, 75–89; Meryl Gordon, "Citizen Mike," *New York*, April 16, 2001.

21   Kolbert, "The Mogul Mayor," *The New Yorker*, April 22, 2002, 140, 143; Meryl Gordon, "Citizen Mike," *New York*, April 16, 2001; Bloomberg and Winkler, *Bloomberg by Bloomberg*, 56, 91.

22   Elisabeth Bumiller, "An 'American Dream' With an Eye on City Hall; Self-Made Billionaire Considers Running," *NYT*, January 18, 2001; Pagesix.com Staff, "Mike's Money Tops List," *NYP*, February 12, 2002.

23   Bumiller, "An 'American Dream'," *NYT*, January 18, 2001; Bloomberg with Winkler, *Bloomberg by Bloomberg*," 213; Maggie Haberman, "An Extremely Supportive Ex," *NYP*, January 6, 2002.

24   Gordon, "Citizen Mike," *New York*, April 16, 2001; Purnick, *Mike Bloomberg*, 59–61; Andrea Bernstein, "New York Remade: Before and After Bloomberg," WNYC, December 27, 2013.

25   Purnick, *Mike Bloomberg*, 56; Stern and Zweig, "Michael Bloomberg," 297 in Charles D. Ellis with James D. Vertin, *Wall Street People: True Stories of Today's Masters and Moguls*.

26 Bloomberg with Winkler, *Bloomberg by Bloomberg*, 232.

27 Bloomberg with Winkler, *Bloomberg by Bloomberg*, 186, 231–2; Purnick, *Mike Bloomberg*, 81.

Chapter 2

1 Maureen Dowd, "Worms in the Apple," *NYT*, February 20, 1997.

2 Chris McNickle, *The Power of the Mayor: David Dinkins* (New Brunswick: Transaction Publishers, 2012), 2–3, 24–9, 36–44, *passim*.

3 William Bratton with Peter Knobler, *Turnaround: How America's Top Cop Reversed the Crime Epidemic* (New York: Random House, 1998), xi, 152–4, 233–9; Fred Siegel with Harry Siegel, *The Prince of the City:Giuliani, New York and the Genius of American Life* (San Francisco: Encounter Books, 2005), 141–50, 166–72; Michael Tomasky, "The Day Everything Changed," *New York,* September 28, 2008; City of New York, Office of the Mayor, "Mayor's Management Report Fiscal 2001 Supplement: Reengineering Municipal Services 1994–2001," 5, 12–3, 15–6, 53–65, 191; Giuliani with Kurson, *Leadership*, 197–99; James B. Jacobs with Coleen Friel and Robert Radick, *Gotham Unbound: How New York City Was Liberated from the Grip of Organized Crime* (NYU Press, 1999), 42–3, 271–2, 382.

4 "Excerpts From Transcript of Giuliani Budget Speech," *NYT*, February 3, 1994; Steven Lee Myers, "Giuliani Outlines a Budget to Cut Government Size," *NYT*, February 3, 1994; Alison Mitchell, "New York City's Budget: News Analysis; Surprisingly, No Gridlock," *NYT*, June 22, 1994; Steven Lee Myers, "New York City's Budget: the Overview; Giuliani's Budget Wins the Support of Council Chiefs," *NYT*, June 22, 1994; Steven Lee Myers, "New York City's Budget: The Overview; Council Leaders and Mayor Reach Accord on Budget," *NYT*, June 14, 1995; Steven Lee Myers, "New York City's Budget: The Impact; Critics Maintain Budget's One-Time Savings Could Bring More Pain Later, *NYT*, June 15, 1995; Siegel and Siegel, *Prince of the City*, 153; Tomasky, "The Day Everything Changed," *New York*, September 28, 2008; Giuliani with Kurson, *Leadership*, 161–3; Vivian S. Toy, "After Late Flurry of Changes, City Council Approves Budget," *NYT*, June 13, 1996; Editorial, "More Budget Pain for the City," *NYT*, April 20, 1996; Editorial, "Budget Agreement at City Hall," *NYT*, June 12, 1996; David Firestone, "High Marks for Giuliani From Budget Watchdogs," *NYT*, July 18, 1997; Editorial, "The Next City Budget Debate," *NYT*, June 6, 1997; Clifford Levy, "Council, As Expected, Approves $33.4 Billion Budget Deal," *NYT*, June 6, 1997; City of New York, Office of the Mayor, "Mayor's Management Report Fiscal 2001 Supplement: Reengineering Municipal Services 1994–2001," 89–90, 111, 117–8, 257.

5 Evan J. Mandery, *The Campaign* (Boulder, CO: Westview Press, 1999), 272, 360; Kirtzman, *Rudy Giuliani*, 21; Siegel and Siegel, *Prince of the City*, 210.

6 Jerald Podair, "The Struggle for Equality in Rudy Giuliani's New York," 213 in Clarence Taylor, *Civil Rights in New York City* (New York: Fordham University Press, 2011), 204–18; Bernard Kerik, *Lost Son: A Life in Pursuit of Justice* (New York: HarperTorch, 2002), 309; Wayne Barrett assisted by Adam Fifield, *Rudy!: An Investigative Biography of Rudolph Giuliani* (New York: Basic Books, 2000), 335–7; Siegel and Siegel, *Prince of the City*, 273–4; Kirtzman, *Rudy Giuliani*, 68–73, 232, 272–5, 284; Peter Vallone, *Learning to Govern: My Life in New York City Politics,*

From Hell Gate to City Hall (New York: Chaucer Press), 242; Quinnipiac College Polling Institute, "Quinnipiac College New York City Poll," April 8, 1999.

7   Associated Press, "Giuliani in a Dress: Will Voters Care?" April 15, 2007 as published on FoxNews.com; Kirtzman, *Rudy Giuliani*, 221–6, 261–6; Jack Newfield, *The Full Rudy: The Man, the Myth, the Mania* (New York: Nation Books, ebook edition, 2007), locations 74, 77.

8   Siegel and Siegel, *Prince of the City,* 296–7; Barrett assisted by Fifield, *Rudy!,* 448–449; Tom Robbins, "Hard Time for Harding," *The Village Voice,* July 19, 2005; Diane Cardwell, "Giuliani Warns Candidates that Tax Increases Would Hurt City," *NYT,* March 24, 2001; Marcia Van Wagner, "Giuliani's Budget," *NYT,* August 24, 2001; Citizens Budget Commission, "A Review of the 2001 Financial Plan of the City of New York for Fiscal Years 2002–2005," March 29, 2001; Richard Perez-Pena and James C. McKinley, "Mountain of 90's Debt Looms As City and State Feel Pinch," *NYT,* February 21, 2002; Celeste Katz, "Ray Harding, Power Broker and Former Liberal Party Leader, Dead at 77," *Daily News,* August 9, 2012.

9   Kirtzman, *Rudy Giuliani,* 149–53; Frank Rich, "Journal; 1 Mayor, 2 Guys, 1 Shih Tzu," *NYT,* August 4, 2001.

10   Kirtzman, *Rudy Giuliani,* 222, 275; Tomasky, "The Day Everything Changed," *New York,* September 28, 2008; Siegel and Seigel, *Prince of the City,* 274, 277; Quinnipiac College Polling Institute, "Quinnipiac College New York City Poll," April 19, 2000.

11   New York City Board of Elections, "Annual Report," 2001.

12   Meryl Gordon, "Citizen Mike," *New York,* April 16, 2001.

13   James Traub, "A Minority of One," *New York Times Sunday Magazine,* October 31, 1999.

14   Author's interview, Kevin Sheekey, September 6, 2016.

15   Author's interview, William Cunningham, May 12, 2014; Author's interview, Kevin Sheekey, September 6, 2016; Tom Robbins, "The Best Campaign Money Can Buy: Team Bloomberg in the Chips," *The Village Voice,* October 30, 2001; Gordon, "Citizen Mike," *New York,* April 16, 2001.

16   Author's interview, William Cunningham, May 12, 2014; Author's interview, Kevin Sheekey, September 6, 2016.

17   Author's interview, Kevin Sheekey, September 6, 2016.

18   Gordon, "Citizen Mike," *New York,* April 16, 2001; Purnick, *Mike Bloomberg,* 81–4.

19   Author's interview, William Cunningham, May 12, 2014; Author's interview, Kevin Sheekey, September 6, 2016.

20   Author's interview, Kevin Sheekey, September 6, 2016; Joyce Purnick, *Mike Bloomberg,* 89.

21   Gordon, "Citizen Mike," *New York,* April 16, 2001; Elisabeth Bumiller, "An 'American Dream' With an Eye on City Hall; Self-Made Billionaire Considers Running," *NYT,* January 18, 2001; Off the record interview; Author's interview, Kevin Sheekey, September 6, 2016.

22   New York City Campaign Finance Board, CFB Rules; New York City Campaign Finance Board, "An Election Interrupted . . ." Executive Summary, September 2002, vii–xiv; Adam Nagourney, "Molinari Rides Into the Sunset as Bloomberg's Sidekick," *NYT,* July 18, 2001; Frank Lombardi, "Cash Can't Always Buy a Victory," *Daily News,* November 7, 2001.

23   Author's interview, Bill Cunningham, May 12, 2014; Author's interview, Edward Skyler, September 12, 2016.

24 Chris McNickle, *To Be Mayor of New York: Ethnic Politics in the City* (Columbia University Press, 1993), 35–41, 195–8, 208; Adam Nagourney, "Bloomberg Says Elections Should Be Nonpartisan," *NYT,* June 8, 2001; Dean E. Murphy, "Bloomberg Says He Quit 4 Clubs Because They Resisted Diversity," *NYT,* July 26, 2001.

25 Gordon, "Citizen Mike," *New York*, April 16, 2001; Bumiller, "An 'American Dream' With an Eye on City Hall; Self-Made Billionaire Considers Running," *NYT,* January 18, 2001.

26 Meryl Gordon, "Citizen Mike," *New York*, April 16, 2001; Bumiller, "An 'American Dream' With an Eye on City Hall; Self-Made Billionaire Considers Running," *NYT,* January 18, 2001; Purnick, *Mike Bloomberg,* 87.

27 Gordon, "Citizen Mike," *New York*, April 16, 2001; Bumiller, "An 'American Dream' With an Eye on City Hall; Self-Made Billionaire Considers Running," *NYT,* January 18, 2001.

28 Robert Hardt Jr., "Silent Mike Will Have to Explain Why He is Running," *NYP,* June 5, 2001; Author's interview, William Cunningham, May 12, 2014; Author's interview, Edward Skyler, September 12, 2016.

29 Author's interview, William Cunningham, May 12, 2014.

30 Dean E. Murphy, "Bloomberg Mentions Prayer, And His Opponents Pounce," *NYT,* July 20, 2001; Clyde Haberman, "NYC; The Reporters Who Call Him Call Him Boss," *NYT,* June 23, 2001; Author's interview, William Cunningham, May 12, 2014; Author's interview, Edward Skyler, September 12, 2016;

31 Michael Tomasky, "Wealth vs. Wisdom," *New York*, July 9, 2001; Michael Wolff, "Bloomberg News," *New York,* August 27, 2001.

32 Michael Wolff, "Chairman Mike," *New York,* September 17, 2001; Dean E. Murphy, "Campaigning for City Hall: Controversies; Questions Raised Over a Gag Gift to Bloomberg from 1990," *NYT*, September 8, 2001.

33 Gordon, "Citizen Mike," *New York,* April 16, 2001.

34 Author's interview, William Cunningham, May 12, 2014; Eric Lipton, "Bloomberg's Spending Is at $20 Million and Counting," *NYT,* September 1, 2001.

35 Author's interview, Mark Green, April 21, 2001; Marist Institute Public Opinion Poll, March 7, 2001 in the possession of the author, courtesy of Lee Miringoff; Adam Nagourney, "Dinkins Gives His Support to Green, Not Ferrer," *NYT,* May 16, 2001; Elisabeth Bumiller, "Faith, Hope and Hardball; In Mayor's Race, Vallone Can't Always Be Nice," *NYT,* April 12, 2001; Adam Nagourney, "Closing In on a Moving Target; As Mayoral Primary Nears, the Democrats Inject a bit of Drama," *NYT,* August 26, 2001; Elisabeth Bumiller, "An Advocate With an Eye for the Next Job; Mayoral Ambitions Thrust Green Into an Early Campaign Sprint," *NYT,* November 19, 1999; Eric Lipton, "Different Lives, Different Politics, But Greens Unite in Mayor's Race," *NYT,* August 13, 2001.

36 Author's interview, Mark Green, April 21, 2014; Author's interview, Joe DePlasco, May 12, 2014; Bumiller, "An Advocate With an Eye for the Next Job," *NYT,* November 19, 1999.

37 Bruce Lambert, "Man in the News: New Bronx Chief Hopes to Restore 'Faith': Fernando Ferrer," *NYT*, April 16, 1987.

38 Author's interview, Roberto Ramirez, April 16, 2014; Filkins, "In Bronx Revival, Ferrer is Credited With Only a Supporting Role," *NYT*, August 5, 2001; Jack Newfield, "Out Front," *New York,* October 15, 2001; Jonathan Hicks, "Leading

Bronx Politics Like the Bosses of Old; With Force and Fervor, Roberto Ramirez Helps Restore a Faded Democratic Organization," *NYT,* August 8, 1998; Clifford J. Levy, "As Ferrer's Gray Eminence, Roberto Ramirez Is a Force, and a Potential Power Broker," *NYT,* October 7, 2001.

39 Author's interview, Al Sharpton, May 23, 2014; Adam Nagourney, "Sharpton Gives Ferrer a List of Conditions," *NYT,* May 9, 2001.

40 Nagourney, "Closing In on a Moving Target; As Mayoral Primary Nears, the Democrats Inject a Bit of Drama," *NYT,* August 26, 2001; Author's interview, Joe DePlasco, May 12, 2014; Author's interview, Fernando Ferrer, April 14, 2014; Author's interview, Roberto Ramirez, April 16, 2014; Jack Newfield, "Out Front," *New York,* October 15, 2001; Adam Nagourney, "Entering Race, Ferrer Focuses on Giuliani," *NYT,* June 28, 2001; "Ferrer Defines the 'Other New York,' and He Discusses His Plans to Help It," excerpts from an interview with Fernando Ferrer conducted by several editors and reporters of the *New York Times, NYT,* July 27, 2001.

41 Author's interview, Roberto Ramirez, April 16, 2014; Author's interview, Al Sharpton, May 23, 2014; Eric Lipton, "Sharpton and 3 From Bronx Are Jailed in Vieques Protest," *NYT,* May 24, 2001; Rev. Al Sharpton with Karen Hunter, *Al On America,* (New York: Kensington Publishing Corp., 2002), 156–63; Dan Barry, "Leaving Prison, Sharpton Again Takes the Stage," *NYT,* August 18, 2001; Author's interview, Fernando Ferrer, April 14, 2014; Nagourney, "Closing In on a Moving Target; As Mayoral Primary Nears, the Democrats Inject a Bit of Drama," *NYT,* August 26, 2001; Dexter Filkins, "The Ad Campaign; Ferrer's Vision of the 'Other New York,'" *NYT,* August 30, 2001.

42 Author's interview, Mark Green, April 21, 2014.

43 Robert Hardt Jr., "Tragedy of Twin Towers Made Campaign Schizo," *NYP,* October 11, 2001.

44 Giuliani with Kurson, *Leadership,* 341–80; Jennifer Steinhauer, "In Crisis, Giuliani's Popularity Overflows City," *NYT,* September 20, 2001.

45 Dan Barry, "Giuliani Presses for Time; 2 of 3 Candidates Say Yes," *NYT,* September 28, 2001; Jennifer Steinhauer, "The New York Primary: The Incumbent; Giuliani Explores a Term Extension of 2 or 3 Months," *NYT,* September 27, 2001; Jennifer Steinhauer, "Giuliani May Try to Keep Job After Term Ends in December," *NYT,* September 24, 2001.

46 The Board of Elections of the City of New York, "Annual Report," 2001; Nichole M. Christian, "Voters Focus on Better Schools; A Changing Canarsie Wants Mayor to Ease Crowding," *NYT,* August 30, 2001.

47 Michael Cooper, "The New York Primary: The Democrats; Ferrer and Green Divide the Spoils of Their Rivals," *NYT,* September 27, 2001; Edison Media Research, "Exit Poll," September 25, 2001.

48 Marist Institute for Public Opinion, "Research Poll," October 5, 2001, in author's possession courtesy of Lee Miringoff.

49 Author's interview, Off the record; Author's interview, Edward Skyler, September 12, 2016.

50 Author's interview, Off the record; Robert Hardt Jr., "Tragedy of Twin Towers Made Campaign Schizo," *NYP,* October 11, 2001.

51 Author's interview, Mark Green, April 21, 2014; Author's interview, Jeremy Ben-Ami, May 26, 2014; Steinhauer, "The New York Primary: The Incumbent;

Giuliani Explores a Term Extension of 2 or 3 Months," *NYT,* September 27, 2001; "Off the Record," Jonah Green documentary about the 2001 mayoral race.

52 Author's interview, Mark Green, April 21, 2014.

53 Author's interview, Fernando Ferrer, April 14, 2014; Author's interview, Roberto Ramirez, April 16, 2014; Elizabeth Kolbert, "Around City Hall: The Long Campaign," *The New Yorker,* October 22, 2001.

54 Author's interview, Fernando Ferrer, April 14, 2014; Author's interview, Roberto Ramirez, April 16, 2014.

55 Author's interview, Joe DePlasco, May 12, 2014; Author's interview, Jeremy Ben-Ami, May 26, 2014; Author's interview, John Siegal, June 5, 2014; Author's interview, Hank Sheinkopf, July 1, 2014; Wayne Barrett, "The Giuliani Dilemma: How Freddy and Mark Used Rudy To Define Themselves," *The Village Voice,* October 2, 2001; Richard Perez-Pena, "Giuliani's Quest for a Term Extension Hits a Wall in Albany," *NYT,* October 2, 2001.

56 Author's interview, Mark Green, April 21, 2014; Author's interview, Joe DePlasco, May 12, 2014; Author's interview, Bill Cunningham, May 12, 2014; Timesvideo, *"Really?"* October 28, 2009; Dexter Filkins, "Ferrer Is Endorsed by Koch, Who Also Criticizes Green," *NYT,* October 3, 2001; Adam Nagourney, "Political Memo; Ferrer Gains Sudden Momentum In Latest Twist of the Campaign," *NYT,* October 3, 2001.

57 Robert Hardt Jr., Tom Topousis, and Maggie Haberman, "Ed's in Fred's Corner," *NYP,* October 3, 2001; Dexter Filkins and Michael Cooper, "Teachers' Backing Gives Ferrer Labor's Triple Crown," *NYT,* October 5, 2001; Abby Goodnough, "Backing Ferrer, Union Focuses On Teacher Pay," *NYT,* October 6, 2001.

58 Author's interview, Fernando Ferrer, April 14, 2014; McNickle, *The Power of the Mayor, passim.*

59 Author's interview, Joe DePlasco, May 12, 2014; Author's interview, Mark Green, April 21, 2014; Adam Nagourney, "Squirming in Sharpton's Embrace; Fidgeting Without It," *NYT,* October 5, 2001; Hardt Jr., "Tragedy of Twin Towers Made Campaign Schizo," *NYP,* October 11, 2001; Jill Nelson, "The Race Factor: A View From Behind the Scenes," *The Village Voice,* October 23, 2001.

60 Author's interview, Mark Green, April 21, 2014; Author's interview, Joe DePlasco, May 12, 2014; Author's interview, Fernando Ferrer, April 14, 2014; Author's interview, Roberto Ramirez, April 16, 2014; Author's interview, Al Sharpton, May 23, 2014; Author's interview, Off the record; Michael Cooper and Randal C. Archibald, "Green Broadcasts Runoff Campaign's First Negative Ad," *NYT,* October 9, 2001; Michael Cooper and Randal C. Archibald, "The Ad Campaign; Ferrer Returns Fire, With Help From Some Prominent Names," *NYT,* October 10, 2001.

61 Jonathan P. Hicks, "Green's Campaign Angers Backers of Ferrer," *NYT,* October 13, 2001; Kolbert, "Around City Hall: The Long Campaign," *New Yorker,* October 22, 2001; Jill Nelson, "Race Counts: White Voters Play the Race Card, Again," *The Village Voice,* October 23, 2001.

62 Author's interview, William Cunningham, May 12, 2014; Mark Green, "The Almost Mayor," *New York,* August 27, 2011; Dean E. Murphy, "Bloomberg Plows Ahead In Changed Political Landscape," *NYT,* October 8, 2001.

63 Murphy, "Bloomberg Plows Ahead In Changed Political Landscape," *NYT,* October 8, 2001; Tom Topousis, "Terror-wary Voters Give Bloomy a Boost," *NYP,*

November 7, 2001; Author's interview, William Cunningham, May 12, 2014; Author's interview, Edward Skyler, September 12, 2016; Michael Kramer, "The Last Word: Zabar's Poll," *Daily News,* November 5, 2001; Robert Hardt Jr., "Call Him: Bloomy Wins in Stunning Upset," *NYP,* November 7, 2001.

64 Author's interview, Mark Green, April 21, 2014; Author's interview, Jeremy Ben-Ami, May 26, 2014.

65 Author's interview, Fernando Ferrer, April 14, 2014; Adam Nagourney, "The New York Runoff: The Democrats; Green Beats Ferrer in Democratic Mayoral Runoff," *NYT,* October 12, 2001; Hicks, "Green's Campaign Angers Backers of Ferrer," *NYT,* October 13, 2001.

66 Author's interviews, Off the record; Adam Nagourney, "The New York Runoff: The Democrats; Green Beats Ferrer in Democratic Mayoral Runoff," *NYT,* October 12, 2001; Jonathan P. Hicks, "Green's Campaign Angers Backers of Ferrer," *NYT,* October 13, 2001.

67 Author's interview, Mark Green, April 21, 2014; Author's interview, Fernando Ferrer, April 14, 2014; Author's interview, Roberto Ramirez, April 16, 2014; Author's interview, Al Sharpton, May 23, 2014; Author's interview, Richard Schrader, June 26, 2014.

68 Author's interview, Mark Green, April 21, 2014; Author's interview, Fernando Ferrer, April 14, 2014; Author's interview, Roberto Ramirez, April 16, 2014; Author's interview, Al Sharpton, May 23, 2014; Author's interview, Richard Schrader, June 26, 2014; Author's interview, John Siegal, June 5, 2014.

69 Adam Nagourney, "Ferrer Formally Concedes to Green in a Democratic Show of Unity," *NYT,* October 20, 2001; Sharpton with Hunter, *Al On America,* 170; Author's interview, Fernando Ferrer, April 14, 2014.

70 Author's interview, Joe DePlasco, May 12, 2014; Michael Wolff, "The Ad Man," *New York,* November 19, 2001; Michael Cooper and Eric Lipton, "Bloomberg Sets a $41 Million Spending Record," *NYT,* October 27, 2001; Adam Nagourney, "The 2001 Elections: Mayor; Bloomberg Edges Green in Race for Mayor; McGreevey Is An Easy Winner in New Jersey," *NYT,* November 7, 2001; Elizabeth Kolbert, "Around City Hall: The Long Campaign," *The New Yorker,* October 22, 2001; Author's interview, William Cunningham, May 12, 2014; Author's interview, Jeremy Ben-Ami, May 26, 2014; Michael Cooper and Adam Nagourney, "Green Aides Say Bloomberg Can't Assure City's Safety," *NYT,* October 23, 2001.

71 Michael Tomasky, "The Union Label," *New York,* October 22, 2001; Dean E. Murphy, "Clinton Backs Green, and Koch and Carey Give Their Support to Bloomberg," *NYT,* November 2, 2001; Author's interview, Jeremy Ben-Ami, May 26, 2014; Author's interview, John Siegal, June 5, 2014; Michael Saul, "Koch and Carey Backing Bloomy in Slap At Rival," *Daily News,* November 2, 2001; Joel Siegel, "Bill Helps Give Mark Flashy Finale," *Daily News,* November 2, 2001; Tom Robbins, "Labor's Election Day Flop: The Coalition That Wasn't," *The Village Voice,* November 20, 2001.

72 Author's interview, Mark Green, April 21, 2014; Author's interview, Bill Cunningham, May 12, 2014; Author's interview, Edward Skyler, September 12, 2016; "CBS Channel 2 News Interview by Ernie Anastos with Michael Bloomberg," August 30, 2001, video tape on file in Fernando Ferrer Campaign Documents, Institute of Puerto Rican Studies, Hunter College; Joel Siegel, "Mark

& Mike Trade Barbs in Last Debate," *Daily News,* November 2, 2001; Michael Kramer, "Can They Lead? It's Debatable," *Daily News,* November 2, 2001.

73 Author's interview, William Cunningham, May 12, 2014; Marist Institute of Public Opinion, "Survey," August 16, 2001, in author's possession courtesy of Lee Miringoff.

74 Dean E. Murphy, "In Homestretch of Campaign, Mayor Endorses Bloomberg," *NYT,* October 28, 2001; Nagourney, "Bloomberg Puts Eggs in a Basket: Giuliani's," *NYT,* October 28, 2001; Author's interview, William Cunningham, May 12, 2014; Joel Siegel, "Bloomy Nearly Tied with Green; Giuliani's Support Helps Him Slash Double-Digit Deficit," *Daily News,* November 3, 2001.

75 Murphy, "In Homestretch of Campaign, Mayor Endorses Bloomberg," *NYT,* October 28, 2001; Nagourney, "Bloomberg Puts Eggs in a Basket: Giuliani's," *NYT,* October 28, 2001; Author's interview, William Cunningham, May 12, 2014.

76 Author's interview, Joe DePlasco, May 12, 2001; Author's interview, William Cunningham, May 12, 2001; Michael Kramer, "The Numbers Could Add Up," *Daily News,* November 1, 2001; New York City Campaign Finance Board, "An Election Interrupted . . ." Executive Summary, September 2002, 6.

77 Author's interview, Mark Green, April 21, 2014; Author's interview, Jeremy Ben-Ami, May 26, 2014; Author's interview, Off the record; Marist Institute of Public Opinion "Poll," November 2, 2001 and November 5, 2001, in author's possession courtesy of Lee Miringoff; Michael Kramer, "Bloomberg's Riding the Trend, But Will It Go Far Enough," *Daily News,* November 3, 2001; Joel Siegel, "Heading for Wire Mike & Mark Tied," *Daily News,* November 4, 2001.

78 Scott Shifrel and Larry Choler-Esses, "Green Aides Met with Dems on Ferrer-Sharpton Plan," *Daily News,* November 2, 2001; Author's interview, Mark Green, April 21, 2014; Author's interview, Fernando Ferrer, April 14, 2014; Author's interview, Richard Schrader, June 26, 2014; Larry Cohler-Esses, "Ferrer Tells Green: Fire 'em," *Daily News,* November 5, 2001.

79 Scott Shifrel and Lary Choler-Esses, "Green Aides Met with Dems on Ferrer-Sharpton Plan," *Daily News,* November 2, 2001; Author's interview, Mark Green, April 21, 2014; Author's interview, Fernando Ferrer, April 14, 2014; Celeste Katz, Greg Wilson, and Larry Cohler-Esses, "Green in Race-Vote Storm: Ferrer Snubs Fund-Raiser; Rev. Al Threatens Black Boycott," *Daily News,* November 3, 2001.

80 Author's interview, Mark Green, April 21, 2014; Author's interview, Roberto Ramirez, April 16, 2014; Author's interview, Al Sharpton, May 23, 2014; Author's interview, Jeremy Ben-Ami, May 26, 2014; Sharpton with Hunter, *Al On America,* 171–174.

81 Author's interview, William Cunningham, May 12, 2014; Author's interview, Edward Skyler, September 12, 2016; Adam Nagourney, "A Brutal Final Weekend in the Race for City Hall," *NYT,* November 5, 2001; Derek Rose and Larry Cohler-Esses, "Republicans Blast Dinkins in Anti-Mark Flyers on S.I.," *Daily News,* November 5, 2001; Deane E. Murphy, "Bloomberg Recipe: Luck, Lots of Cash and a Hands-on Role," *NYT,* November 11, 2001; Maki Becker and Derek Rose, "Sharpton Won't Back Green," *Daily News,* November 6, 2001; Author's interview, Mark Green, April 21, 2014; Charles V. Bagli, "Run By Green's Brother, Building Had Been Cited," *NYT,* October 25, 2001.

82 Author's interview, Mark Green, April 21, 2014; Author's interview, Jeremy Ben-Ami, May 26, 2014; "Off the Record," Jonah Green documentary about the 2001

mayoral race; Author's interview, Edward Skyler, September 12, 2016; Purnick, *Mike Bloomberg*, 117.

83 Author's interview, Mark Green, April 21, 2014; Author's interview, Jeremy Ben-Ami, May 26, 2014; Author's interview, Edward Skyler, Spetember 13, 2016; "Off the Record," Jonah Green documentary about the 2001 mayoral race; Purnick, *Mike Bloomberg*, 117.

84 Board of Elections of New York City, "Annual Report," 2001; Author's interview, Mark Green, April 21, 2014; Author's interview, Kevin Sheekey, September 6, 2016.

85 Author's interview, Kevin Sheekey, September 6, 2016; Edison Media Reasearch and Associated Press, "Exit Poll," November 6, 2001, as reported in *Daily News*, November 7, 2001.

86 David Seifman, "Mike Gets Ride on Rudy's Rep," *NYP*, November 7, 2001; David Seifman, "Campaign Wiz Works His Magic Yet Again," *NYP*, November 8, 2001; Edison Media Research and Associated Press, "Exit Poll," November 6, 2001, as reported in *Daily News*, November 7, 2001; Joel Siegel, "Bloomy Nearly Tied With Green; Giuliani's Support Helps Him Slash Double-Digit Deficit," *Daily News*, November 3, 2001; Joel Siegel, "Mike Beats Mark, Wins City Hall," *Daily News*, November 7, 2001; Michael Kramer, "Terror Attack + Rudy = Mayor Bloomberg," *Daily News*, November 7, 2001; "Mayor-elect Michael Bloomberg," *NYT*, November 7, 2001.

87 Author's interview, Mark Green, April 21, 2014; Author's interview, Roberto Ramirez, April 16, 2014; Seifman, "Mike Gets Ride on Rudy's Rep," *NYP*, November 7, 2001; Edison Media Research and Associated Press, "Exit Poll," November 6, 2001 reported in *Daily News*, November 7, 2001; Lisa L. Colangelo, "Stunned Democrats Face Deep Racial Divide," *Daily News*, November 8, 2001 cites a NY1 poll showing Bloomberg with more than half the Hispanic vote; Kirsten Danis, "Runoff Voters Abandoned Dem," *NYP*, November 7, 2001.

88 Edison Research Media and Associated Press, "Exit Poll," November 6, 2001, reported in *Daily News*, November 7, 2001; Author's interview, Joe DePlasco, May 12, 2014; Author's interview, Richard Schrader, June 26, 2014; Author's interview, Al Sharpton, May 23, 2014; Joel Siegel, "Mike Beats Mark, Wins City Hall," *Daily News*, November 7, 2001.

89 Edison Research Media and Associated Press "Exit Poll," November 6, 2001, reported in *Daily News*, November 7, 2001; Joyce Shelby, "Rev. Al Warns Green: Black Nod's In Doubt," *Daily News*, November 4, 2001; Frankie Edozen, "Minority Coalition Splinters," *NYP*, November 7, 2001.

90 Author's interviews, Off the record; Author's interview, Al Sharpton, May 23, 2014; Author's interview, William Cunningham, May 12, 2014.

91 New York City Campaign Finance Board, "An Election Interrupted . . ." Executive Summary, September 2002, vii–xiv; Michael Cooper, "Final Tally: Bloomberg Spent $75.5 Million to Become Mayor," *NYT*, March 30, 2002. The figure includes several million dollars for transition and inauguration expenses; Bloomberg with Winkler, *Bloomberg by Bloomberg*, 222.

92 Author's interview, Kevin Sheekey, September 6, 2016; Author's interview, Chris Coffey, September 12, 2016.

93 Author's interview, Kevin Sheekey, Sepember 6, 2016; Author's interview, Chris Coffey, September 12, 2016.

Chapter 3

1 Author's interview, Fernando Ferrer, April 14, 2014; Author's interview, William Cunningham, May 12, 2014; Author's interview, Rev. Al Sharpton, May 23, 2014; Maggie Haberman, "Mike's Off to a Running Start—Has Meetings With Ferrer and Rudy," *NYP,* November 8, 2001; Maggie Haberman, "Bloomy Gives Rev. Al A 'Fair Shake,'" *NYP,* November 9, 2001; Jennifer Steinhauer, "Initial Steps by Bloomberg Show Contrast With Giuliani," *NYT,* November 10, 2001; Kirsten Danis, "3 Days: That's How Long It Has Taken Michael Bloomberg to Embrace New York's Left-Wing A-List," *NYP,* November 10, 2001; Karen Hunter, "Mike Vows A Fair Shot for Blacks," *Daily News,* November 8, 2001; Michael Saul, "Bloomberg Reaches Out to 2 Key Union Leaders," *Daily News,* November 8, 2001.

2 Adam Nagourney and Stephen Greenhouse, "Bloomberg Visits Head of 2 Unions Over Fiscal Fears," *NYT,* November 9, 2001; Maggie Haberman, "Mike Shows Some Unity With Unions," *NYP,* November 9, 2001; Jennifer Steinhauer, "Initial Steps by Bloomberg Show Contrast With Giuliani," *NYT,* November 10, 2001; Steve McFarland, "Unions Hope He'll Ease Labor Pains," *Daily News,* November 8, 2001.

3 Brian Kates, "Mike Rejects 14M in City Tax Breaks," *Daily News,* November 8, 2001; Andrew Ross Sorkin, *Too Big To Fail* (New York: Penguin Books, 2010), 147.

4 Frankie Edozien, "When Gracie Mansion Just Isn't Good Enough," *NYP,* November 8, 2001; Jennifer Steinhauer, "Can't Find the Mayor? Well, What's It To You," *NYT,* February 20, 2002; Kirsten Danis, "Mike's A Man About Town—Just Not Ours," *NYP,* February 19, 2002; Frankie Edozien, "Hidden Mike: Mayor Ducks Out Yet Again," *NYP,* February 25, 2002.

5 Jennifer Steinhauer, "Bloomberg Choices for Top Aides Set Inclusive Tone for Mayoralty," *NYT,* December 8, 2001.

6 Author's interview, Marc Shaw, July 29, 2014; Steinhauer, "Bloomberg Choices for Top Aides Set Inclusive Tone for Mayoralty," *NYT,* December 8, 2001.

7 Author's interview, Dennis Walcott, August 2, 2016; Steinhauer, "Bloomberg Choices for Top Aides Set Inclusive Tone for Mayoralty," *NYT,* December 8, 2001.

8 Steinhauer, "Bloomberg Choices for Top Aides Set Inclusive Tone for Mayoralty," *NYT,* December 8, 2001; Kirsten Danis, "Bloomy Picks His Legal Eagles," *NYP,* December 12, 2001.

9 Jonathan Hicks, "Bloomberg Names 56 to Transition Committee," *NYT,* November 20, 2001; "The Committee Members," *NYT,* November 20, 2001; Michael Cooper, "Bloomberg Appoints Five to Be City Commissioners," *NYT,* December 28, 2001; Diane Cardwell, "Bloomberg Adds Six To His Team," *NYT,* December 29, 2001; Michael Cooper, "Bloomberg Chooses Head of Fire Department," *NYT,* December 31, 2001; Adam Nagourney, "Bloomberg Fills Nine Posts With Government Veterans," *NYT,* December 20, 2001; Jennifer Steinhauer, "The Mayoral Transition; The Bloomberg Administration Emerges," *NYT,* January 1, 2002; "Bloomberg Names Special Mayoral Advisor," *NYT,* January 24, 2002.

10 Author's interview, Janette Sadik-Khan, September 14, 2016; Author's interview, Adrian Benepe, September 29, 2015.

11 Adam Nagourney, "Bloomberg Vows to Work at Center of Things," *NYT,* December 25, 2001; John Tierney, "The Big City; By the Cubicle, The Dilberting

of City Hall," *NYT,* January 4, 2002; Alan Feuer, "A Command Center Like The Mayor Who Built It," *NYT,* April 1, 2009.

12 Tierney, "The Big City; By the Cubicle, The Dilberting of City Hall," *NYT,* January 4, 2002; Author's interview, William Cunningham, May 12, 2014; Author's interview, Dennis Walcott, August 2, 2016.

13 Author's interview, William Cunningham, May 12, 2014; Author's interview, Dennis Walcott, August 2, 2016.

14 Nagourney, "Bloomberg Vows to Work at Center of Things," *NYT,* December 25, 2001; Tierney, "The Big City; By the Cubicle, The Dilberting of City Hall," *NYT,* January 4, 2002; Author's interview, Marc Shaw, July 29, 2014; Author's interview, Dennis Walcott, August 2, 2016.

15 Author's interview, Adrian Benepe, September 29, 2015; Sam Roberts, "1,000 Days Left For Bloomberg, All On His Own Terms," April 1, 2007.

16 Adam Nagourney, "Political Memo: Clouds Loom for New York, But Bloomberg Stays Sunny," *NYT,* December 7, 2001.

17 Kirsten Danis, "The Blooming of a New Era: Mike Inherits Keys to the City from Giuliani," *NYP,* January 2, 2002; "The Mayoral Transition; Mayor's Speech: 'Rebuild, Renew and Remain the Capital of the Free World,'" *NYT,* January 2, 2002.

18 "The Mayoral Transition; Mayor's Speech: 'Rebuild, Renew and Remain the Capital of the Free World,'" *NYT,* January 2, 2002; David Seifman, "Hizzoner's Long View Comes Up A Bit Short on Specifics; Cost-Cutting A Personnel Woe," *NYP,* January 2, 2002.

19 Joyce Purnick, "Recalling the 70s, Warily," *NYT,* November 11, 2001.

20 Author's interview, Marc Shaw, July 29, 2014; Editorial, "Losing Control," *NYT,* November 13, 2001; City of New York, Office of the Mayor, "The City of New York Financial Plan Fiscal Years 2002–2006"; Citizens Budget Commission, "10 Myths About Balancing New York City's Budget and 5 Ways To Lower the Cost of Government By $1 Billion Per Year," December 7, 2002; "The Mayoral Transition; Mayor's Speech: 'Rebuild, Renew and Remain the Capital of the Free World,'" *NYT,* January 2, 2002; Michael Cooper, "The Mayor's Budget Proposal: Overview; Bloomberg Seeks Cuts In Spending At Most Agencies," *NYT,* February 14, 2002; Citizens Budget Commission, "Managing the Budget in the Bloomberg Administration: A Background Paper Prepared for the Citizens Budget Commission Conference on 'New York City's Changing Fiscal Outlook,' IBM Executive Conference Center, Palisades, New York, December 7–8, 2001; Joyce Purnick, "Recalling the 70's, Warily," *NYT,* November 11, 2001; David Leonhardt, "Economic View; How a Tax on Cigarettes Can Help the Taxed," *NYT,* April 14, 2002.

21 City of New York, Office of the Mayor, "The New York City Financial Plan Fiscal Years 2002–2006"; Michael Cooper, "Mayor's Deficit Estimate Grows to $4.5 Billion," *NYT,* February 8, 2002; Cooper, "The Mayor's Budget Proposal: Overview; Bloomberg Seeks Cuts In Spending At Most Agencies," *NYT,* February 14, 2002; Author's interview, Carol Kellerman, Charles Brecher, Maria Doulis at Citizens Budget Commission, October 15, 2014; New York City Independent Budget Office, "Federal Aid to New York City in the Aftermath of September 11: How Much and for What?," Testimony of Ronnie Lowenstein, Director,

IBO Before the Joint Hearing of the City Council Finance, Lower Manhattan Redevelopment and State and Federal Legislation Committees, February 2002.

22   Jonathan Hicks, "Man in the News: An Alliance Builder; Alan Gifford Miller," *NYT*, January 8, 2002; Nicholas Confessore, "Mayor's Thorn On City Council Is Used To Low Expectations," *NYT*, August 16, 2005; New York City Council, "Fiscal 2003: Preliminary Budget Response," April 2002; Michael Cooper, "Council Seeks Tax Surcharge to Aid Schools," *NYT*, April 9, 2002; Michael Cooper, "New York City Budget; The Deal; Bloomberg and Council Agree on Budget to Close Big Deficit," *NYT*, June 20, 2002; Frankie Edozien, "Council Seeks State OK To Hike Taxes Nearly $1B," *NYP*, June 20, 2002.

23   Robert F. Pecorella, *Governing New York State* (Albany: SUNY Press, 2012), 39; Author's interview, William Cunningham, May 12, 2014; Author's interview, Marc Shaw, July 29, 2014.

24   Author's interview, Dean Fuleihan, August 12, 2015; Purnick, *Mike Bloomberg*, 13.

25   Author's interview, Dean Fuleihan, August 12, 2015; Author's interview, William Cunningham, May 12, 2014; Author's interview, Marc Shaw, July 29, 2014.

26   New York City Council, "Fiscal 2003: Preliminary Budget Response," April 2002; Michael Cooper, "Council Seeks Tax Surcharge to Aid Schools," *NYT*, April 9, 2002; David Leonhardt, "Economic View; How a Tax on Cigarettes Can Help the Taxed," *NYT*, April 14, 2002; Michael Cooper, "New York City Budget; The Deal; Bloomberg and Council Agree on Budget to Close Big Deficit," *NYT*, June 20, 2002; Frankie Edozien, "Council Seeks State OK To Hike Taxes Nearly $1B," *NYP*, June 20, 2002; Tom Farley, MD, *Saving Gotham: A Billionaire Mayor, Activist Doctors and the Fight for Eight Million Lives* (New York: W.W. Norton & Company, 2015), 31; Author's interview, Dean Fuleihan, August 12, 2015.

27   Michael Cooper, "Mayor Warns of More Belt Tightening," *NYT*, July 21, 2002; David Seifman, "Budget Critics Predict Tax Hike," June 22, 2002; City of New York, Office of the Mayor, "The City of New York Financial Plan Fiscal Years 2003–2007"; Citizens Budget Commission, "10 Myths About Balancing New York City's Budget and 5 Ways To Lower the Cost of Government By $1 Billion Per Year," December 7, 2002.

28   Author's interview, Marc Shaw, July 29, 2014.

29   Author's interview, Marc Shaw, July 29, 2014; Author's interview, Gifford Miller, October 24, 2014; Michael Cooper, "Council Affirms Deep Cuts and 18% Property Tax Rise," *NYT*, November 26, 2002; District Council 37, AFSCME, AFL-CIO, "We Can Do the Work: How the City Can Save Over $600 Million Without Cutting Services: DC 37 Recommendations for Fiscal Year 2003 Savings for the New York City Budget," Submitted by Lillian Roberts, Executive Director, May 2002; Michael Cooper, "City Budget Gap Grows, and Visions of the 70s Grow Vivid," *NYT*, October 10, 2002; Michael Cooper, "Political Memo; How Deep and How Often To Use The City Budget Knife," *NYT*, October 30, 2002; Joyce Purnick, "Metro Matters; Perfect Storm Seen Heading For the Budget," *NYT*, November 11, 2002; Steven Greenhouse, "Deal Saves City $100 Million A Year In Health Costs," *NYT*, December 19, 2003.

30   Author's interview, Marc Shaw, July 29, 2014; Author's interview, Dean Fuleihan, August 12, 2015; Michael Cooper, "Mayor Seeking Income Tax on Commuters,"

NYT, November 14, 2002; David Seifman, "Commuters Get Taken For Ride: Bloomberg Belts 'Em, But Cuts Resident Tax," *NYP,* November 14, 2002; Michael Cooper, "Shoals Ahead for Bloomberg's Budget Plan," *NYT,* November 19, 2002; Richard Perez-Pena, "The Mayor's Budget Plan; Debt; Borrowing Called Tactic Best Left in the 70s," *NYT,* November 21, 2002; Michael Cooper, "Credit Rating is On the Line, City is Warned," *NYT,* November 22, 2002; City of New York, Office of the Mayor, "The City of New York Financial Plan, Fiscal Years 2004–2008"; Michael Cooper and Edward Wyatt, "Pataki Rejects East River Tolls, Threatening City Budget and Mayoral Relations," *NYT,* October 23, 2002; Randy Kennedy, "On Bridges, Raising Money but Not Blood Pressure," *NYT,* October 24, 2002.

31 Michael Cooper, "Drastic Backup City Budget Has Up To 15,000 Layoffs," *NYT,* April 2, 2003; Jennifer Steinhauer, "Pressure Building on State to Close City's Budget Gap," *NYT,* April 10, 2003; Frederic U. Dicker, "Tax Surcharge Eyed As Apple Budget Boost," *NYP,* April 14, 2003; Nick Paumgarten, "The State We're In," *The New Yorker,* February 17, 2003.

32 Author's interview, Marc Shaw, July 29, 2014; Al Baker and James C. McKinley Jr.,"Legislators Pursue a Budget That Reverses Pataki's Cuts," *NYT,* April 30, 2003.

33 Author's interview, Marc Shaw, July 29, 2014; Author's interview, Dean Fuleihan, August 12, 2015; Baker and McKinley Jr., "Legislators Pursue a Budget That Reverses Pataki's Cuts," *NYT,* April 30, 2003.

34 Baker and McKinley Jr., "Legislators Pursue a Budget That Reverses Pataki's Cuts," *NYT,* April 30, 2003; Kenneth Lovett, "Team Mike Paints A Budget Doomsday in Bond War," *NYP,* August 20, 2003; David Seifman, "Poll: Voters Like Mike But Long For Rudy," *NYP,* July 19, 2002; David Seifman, "Gloomberg—Popularity Plummets; Budget $lash Cuts Mike's Ratings, Too," *NYP,* November 22, 2002; John Podhoretz, "Mike's Mistake; Stopping Civic Decline Requires Leadership, Not Tax Hikes," *NYP,* November 15, 2002; Elizabeth A. Roistacher, "How Much Do Taxes Matter? What Economists Can—and Cannot—Tell NYC Policy Makers," Citizens Budget Commission, December 11, 2006, 3–4; Author's interview, Peter Madonia, November 11, 2016.

35 David Seifman, "Mayor Mike in Poll Hole—Hits Rock Bottom on Job Approval," *NYP,* May 8, 2003; Jennifer Steinhauer, "The City Budget; The Mayor; A Budget Success, But Bloomberg Gets No Respect," *NYT,* June 26, 2003; Quinnipiac University Poll, "Bush Gets 3 – 1 Approval in New York City," February 6, 2002; Quinnipiac University Poll,"New York Is A Party Town, Thumbs Down On Mayor And Non-Party Election Idea," July 2, 2003; Quinnipiac University Poll, "Budget Busts Bloomberg Approval, NYC Voters Split on Higher Taxes if Commuters Pay More," November 21, 2002.

36 City of New York, "The City of New York Financial Plan, Fiscal Years 2004–2008 through 2008–2012."

37 City of New York, "The City of New York Financial Plan, Fiscal Years 2004–2008"; Mike McIntire, "Mayor Looks to Cut Spending By $750 Million Over Two Years," *NYT,* December 16, 2005.

38 Author's interview, Marc Shaw, July 29, 2014; Jim Rutenberg, "Bloomberg Keeps His Name off Rebate Checks," *NYT,* September 25, 2005.

39 City of New York, Office of the Mayor, "The City of New York Financial Plan, Fiscal Years 2002–2006 and Fiscal Years 2007–2011"; Author's interview, Carol

Kellerman, Charles Brecher, Maria Doulis, October 15, 2014; Author's interview, Ronnie Lowenstein, George Sweet, Doug Turetsky, October 15, 2014.

40 Sorkin, *Too Big to Fail,* 88 and *passim*; Ben S. Bernanke, *The Courage To Act: A Memoir of Crisis and Its Aftermath* (New York: W. W. Norton and Company, 2015, ebook edition), *passim.*

41 Patrick McGeehan, "History Hints A Recession Would Hit City Hard," *NYT,* April 28, 2008.

42 Author's interview, Off the record; David W. Chen and Michael Barbaro, "Bloomberg and Council Reach Deal on Budget," *NYT,* June 27, 2008.

43 Winnie Hu, "Next Council Speaker is a Doer and a Trail Blazer," *NYT,* January 4, 2006.

44 David W. Chen and Michael Barbaro, "Bloomberg and Council Reach Deal on Budget," *NYT,* June 27, 2008.

45 Chen and Barbaro, "Bloomberg and Council Reach Deal on Budget," *NYT,* June 27, 2008.

46 Sorkin, *Too Big to Fail, passim*; Ben Bernanke, *The Courage to Act, passim.*

47 Sorkin, *Too Big to Fail,* 368; Ben Bernanke, *The Courage to Act, passim*; Author's interview, Robert Lieber, May 21, 2015.

48 Michael Barbaro and Fernando Santos, "New York City Wants Cuts By Agencies Across the Board," *NYT,* September 23, 2008; David Chen, "City Room: Blogging From the Five Boroughs; Bloomberg Orders More Budget Cuts," *NYT,* December 10, 2008; "Memo To: Agency Heads; From: Mark Page; Subject: November 2008 Financial Plan; Date: September 23, 2008"; "Memo To: Agency Heads; From: Mark Page; Subject: January 2009 Preliminary Budget and Financial Plan; Date: December 9, 2008,"; City of New York, Office of the Mayor, "The City of New York Financial Plan, Fiscal Years 2010–2014,"; Sewell Chan, "City Projects $4 Billion Gap for Next Fiscal Year," *NYT,* January 30, 2009.

49 City of New York, Office of the Mayor, "The City of New York Financial Plan, Fiscal Years 2010–2014,"; New York City, Independent Budget Office, "Growth in New York's Medicaid Enrollment and Costs: While Enrollment Highest in the City, Recent Increases Mostly in Suburbs and Upstate" (October 2013), 5; Sewell Chan, "City Projects $4 Billion Gap for Next Fiscal Year," *NYT,* January 30, 2009; "Mike Eases Up on Pink Slips Talks of Firing 15,000 Teachers Subsides in Advance of Stimulus Money," *NYP,* March 8, 2009; David Seifman, "Pensions Will Cru$h Big Apple, Mike Warns," *NYP,* April 10, 2009; Citizens Budget Commission, "Testimony Submitted to the City Council Finance Committee," June 6, 2012, Maria Doulis, Director of City Studies; Author's interview, Carol Kellerman, Charles Brecher, and Maria Doulis, October 15, 2014.

50 Author's interview, Off the record; Author's interview, Steven Spinola, May 21, 2015.

51 Author's interview, Steven Spinola, May 21, 2015.

52 Eric Lipton and Steven Greenhouse, "Bloomberg and City Unions Draw the Lines, Far Apart," *NYT,* August 19, 2003.

53 Frank Branconi, "Municipal Employee Compensation in New York City," City of New York, Office of the Comptroller, (Winter 2011), 2; Author's interview, James Hanley, September 29, 2014; Michael Cooper, "Mayor Hints City May Cut M.T.A. Funds," *NYT,* July 18, 2002.

54 Citizens Budget Commission, "The 40 Hour-Week: A Proposal To Increase the Productivity of Non-Managerial Civilian Municipal Workers," December 2002; Citizens Budget Commission, "7 Things New Yorkers Should Know About Municipal Labor Contracts In New York City" (May 2013), 3; Eric Lipton and Steven Greenhouse, "Bloomberg and City Unions Draw the Lines, Far Apart," *NYT,* August 19, 2003.

55 Author's interview, James Hanley, September 29, 2014; Author's interview, Marc Shaw, July 29, 2014; Steven Greenhouse, "Mayor Gets Labor-Pact Savings That Eluded His Predecessors," *NYT,* April 22, 2004; Steven Greenhouse, "Teachers' Union Accuses City of Avoiding Talks on Contract," *NYT,* December 2, 2003; Steven Greenhouse, "Mayor's Goal Is 'Thin' Pact With Teachers," *NYT,* February 6, 2004; Steven Greenhouse, "Labor Talks on Stage," *NYT,* June 14, 2004; David W. Chen and Steven Greenhouse, "A Police Contract Without Tears or Arbitration," *NYT,* August 24, 2008; Steven Greenhouse, "Disappointed By Raises, Officers Praise Their Union," *NYT,* September 6, 2002; Steven Greenhouse and William K. Rashbaum, "Arbitration Panel Grants Police 10% Raise, Lifting Stakes in City Contract Talks," *NYT,* June 29, 2005; Nicholas Confessore, "Mayor Says Its Best To Let Police Control Terror Scenes," *NYT,* April 3, 2005; Michelle O'Donnell, "New Terror Response Plan Angers Fire Department," *NYT,* April 22, 2005; Michelle O'Donnell, "City Hall Limits Testimony on Emergency Protocols," *NYT,* April 28, 2005; Mike McIntire, "Bloomberg Says Fire Chief Must Support Emergency Plan Or Leave," *NYT,* May 11, 2005.

56 Timothy Williams and Sewell Chan, "State Mediators' Plan Clears Way to Resolve 60 Hour Ordeal," *NYT,* December 22, 2005.

57 Javier C. Hernandez, "Labor Seeks Influence in New York's Mayoral Race," *NYT,* June 18, 2013; Editorial, "The Storm on New York's Horizon," *NYT,* September 2, 2013; Cas Holloway, "Tough Talk With Unions," *NYT,* September 11, 2013; Kate Taylor and David W. Chen, "Bloomberg Says He'll Leave DeBlasio No Deficit," *NYT,* November 21, 2013.

58 Author's interview, Carol Kellerman, Charles Brecher, Maria Doulis, October 15, 2014; Author's interview, Ronnie Lowenstein, George Sweet, Doug Turetsky, October 15, 2014; Author's interview, Off the record; Holloway, "Tough Talk With Unions," *NYT,* September 11, 2013; Kate Taylor and David W. Chen, "Bloomberg Says He'll Leave DeBlasio No Deficit," *NYT,* November 21, 2013.

59 Citizens Budget Commission, "The Explosion in Pension Costs: Ten Things New Yorkers Should Know About Retirement Benefits for New York City Employees," April 2009; City of New York, Office of the Mayor, "The City of New York Financial Plan, 2004–2008 through 2007–2011"; Michael Barbaro, "Mayor Warns on Pension Costs But Gave Pay Deals," *NYT,* June 22, 2009; Mary Williams Walsh, "Padded Pensions Add to New York Fiscal Woes," *NYT,* May 20, 2010; Editorial, "N.Y.C. vs. N.Y.S., the Pension Battle," *NYT,* March 24, 2011.

60 Citizens Budget Commission, "The Explosion in Pension Costs: Ten Things New Yorkers Should Know About Retirement Benefits for New York City Employees," April 2009; Citizens Budget Commission, "Six Figure Civil Servants: Average Compensation Cost of New York City Public Employees," January 2009; Citizens Budget Commission, "The First Priority in the New Year—Pension Reform," January 2012; Andrew White, "How the City Pays for State's Sins," *NYT,* November

9, 2002; Editorial, "Public Pensions In Trouble," *NYT,* August 22, 2006; Editorial, "N.Y.C. vs. N.Y.S., the Pension Battle," *NYT,* March 24, 2011; Steven Malanga, "Union Power Comes in Many Forms," *City Journal* (Spring 2011), online version; Joel Siegel, "The Pataki Puzzle: Could He Actually Be Thinking About Running for President?," *New York*, July 2004; Frederic U. Dicker, "Good Riddance; Why Pataki Won't Be Missed," *NYP*, December 28, 2006; Peter Elkind, *Client 9: The Tragedy of Eliot Spitzer* (New York: Penguin Publishers, 2010), *passim*; Author's interview, Carol Kellerman, Charles Brecher, and Maria Doulis, October 15, 2014; Author's interview, Ronnie Lowenstein, George Sweeting, and Doug Turetsky, October 15, 2014; Author's interview, Dean Fuleihan, August 12, 2015.

61 Mary Williams Walsh and Michael Cooper, "New York Gets Sobering Look at Its Pensions," *NYT,* August 20, 2006; Roger Lowenstein, "The Next Crisis: Public Pension Funds," *NYT,* June 25, 2010; City of New York, Office of the Comptroller, "Comprehensive Annual Financial Report of the Comptroller, Fiscal Years 2002–2009"; "Comprehensive Annual Financial Report of the Comptroller, Fiscal Year 2013, Required Supplementary Information, Schedule of Pension Funding Progress", 127–130; City of New York Office of the Comptroller, "The $8 Billion Question: An Analysis of the NYC Pension Costs Over the Past Decade" (April 2011), 1–7; City of New York, Office of the Comptroller, "Sustainable or Not? NYC Pension Cost Projections Through 2060" (June 2011), 10; Joelle Saad-Lesser, Teresa Ghilarducci, and Lauren Schmitz, "Are New Yorkers Ready for Retirement?" (Schwartz Center for Economic Policy Analysis and City of New York, Office of the Comptroller, January 2012), 16–18; Mayor Michael Bloomberg, "State of the City Address," January 19, 2011; David W. Chen, "Bloomberg Seeks A Sweeping Overhaul of City Pensions," *NYT,* February 2, 2011; "Bloomberg's Plan on Pension Changes," *NYT,* February 2, 2011; Governor's Press Office, "Governor Cuomo Introduces Pension Reform Legislation," Press Release, June 8, 2011.

62 Thomas Kaplan and John Eligon, "New York Lawmakers Vote to Limit Public Pensions," *NYT,* March 14, 2012; Author's interview, Dean Fuleihan, August 12, 2015; Maria Doulis, "New York City Is Not Alone," Citizens Budget Commission Blog Report, November 17, 2011; City of New York, Office of the Comptroller, "Comprehensive Annual Financial Report of the Comptroller, Fiscal Year 2013, Required Supplementary Information, Schedule of Pension Funding Progress," 128; Author's interview, Dean Fuleihan, August 12, 2015.

63 Citizens Budget Commission, "Everybody's Doing It: Health Insurance Premium-Sharing by Employees and Retirees in the Public and Private Sectors," January 2013; Author's interview, Carol Kellerman, Charles Brecher, and Maria Doulis, October 15, 2014; Author's interview, Ronnie Lowenstein, George Sweeting, Doug Turetsky, October 15, 2014.

64 Citizens Budget Commission, "The Candidates on Fiscal Issues: 2001 Mayoral Election, City of New York," April 2001; Bloomberg with Winkler, *Bloomberg by Bloomberg,* 167–70; Citizens Budget Commission, "Planning After PLANYC: A Framework for Developing New York City's Next Ten Year Capital Strategy," December 6, 2013; Office of the Comptroller, Bureau of Fiscal and Budget Studies, "Fiscal Year 2014 Annual Report on Capital Debt and Obligations," December 2013; Author's interview, Carol Kellerman, Charles Brecher, Maria Doulis, October 15, 2014.

65 New York City Independent Budget Office, "Debt Affordability Metrics" special analysis in possession of the author, prepared 2014, courtesy of Doug Turetsky and Ana Champeny, all interpretations are the responsibility of the author; Office of the Comptroller, Bureau of Fiscal and Budget Studies, "Fiscal Year 2014 Annual Report on Capital Debt and Obligations," December 2013; Citizens Budget Commission, "Planning After PLANYC: A Framework for Developing New York City's Next Ten Year Capital Strategy," December 6, 2013; City of New York, "Bond Official Statement Archive, 2002–2013"; David Seifman, "City Bonds Take a Hit," *NYP,* November 27, 2002.

66 Adam Brodsky, "Not Happening in '05," *NYP,* December 26, 2004; Steven Malanga, "What Bloomberg Could Still Accomplish," *City Journal,* (Winter) 2006; Steven Malanga, "The City's Finances, Part 1: Life in Taxopolis," *City Journal,* July 10, 2009; Steven Malanga, "The Coming Budget Crunch," *City Journal,* Special Issue 2013; Citizens Budget Commission, "The Candidates on Fiscal Issues: 2001 Mayoral Election, City of New York," April 2001; Ken Auletta, "After Bloomberg," *The New Yorker,* August 26, 2013; Author's interview, Carol Kellerman, Charles Brecher, Maria Doulis, October 15, 2014; Bloomberg with Winkler, *Bloomberg by Bloomberg,* 167–70.

Chapter 4

1 Jim Dwyer, "Early Test for Bloomberg: Shaping Police Strategy," *NYT,* November 10, 2001; Kevin Flynn, "Kerik Says He Won't Stay On as Police Commissioner," *NYT,* November 10, 2001.

2 Jim Dwyer, "Early Test for Bloomberg: Shaping Police Strategy," *NYT,* November 10, 2001; William K. Rashbaum and Kevin Flynn, "Kelly Focuses on City Defense and Bolstering Shelters' Safety," *NYT,* January 5, 2002.

3 Alan Finder, "Top Deputy Named New York Police Commissioner," *NYT,* October 17, 1992; Jim Dwyer, "After Terror at His Doorstep, Kelly Returns to Public Stage," *NYT,* November 14, 2001; Eric Pooley, "Bulldog," *New York,* February 22, 1992, 33–40; McNickle, *The Power of the Mayor,* 233–6.

4 McNickle, *The Power of the Mayor,* 268–70; Jim Dwyer, "After Terror at His Doorstep, Kelly Returns to Public Stage," *NYT,* November 14, 2001; Murray Weiss, "Kelly Takes Helm Again As NYPD Faces Test," *NYP,* January 5, 2002.

5 Bratton with Knobler, *Turnaround,* 196–99.

6 Eli B. Silverman, *NYPD Battles Crime: Innovative Strategies in Policing* (Boston: Northeastern University Press, 1999), 201; Editorial, *Daily News,* October 27, 1993; New York City Police Department, Crime Statistics, 1993 and 2001; Citizens Crime Commission, "Crime, Police and the Community," July 2001, Introduction, I.

7 Citizens Budget Commission, "The Candidates on Fiscal Issues 2001 Mayoral Election, City of New York," August 2001, 4; Adam Nagourney, "Quality of Life is High Priority for Bloomberg," *NYT,* December 27, 2001; William K. Rashbaum and Kevin Flynn, "Kelly Focuses on City Defense and Bolstering Shelters' Safety," *NYT,* January 5, 2002; Murray Weiss, "Kelly Takes Helm Again As NYPD Faces Test," *NYP,* January 5, 2002; Citizens Crime Commission, "Crime, Police and the Community," July 2001, 6.

8 Joseph Goldstein, "Weekly Police Briefing Offers Snapshot of Department and Its Leader," *NYT,* February 10, 2013; "New York Police Chief Has Tough Act to Follow and It's His Own," November 15, 2005; Geoffrey Gray, "Boss Kelly," *New York,* May 16, 2010.

9 Al Baker, "Many Splendid Ties, But Just One Knot," *NYT,* August 30, 2009; Geoffrey Gray, "Boss Kelly," *New York,* May 16, 2010.

10 City of New York, Office of the Mayor, "Mayor's Management Report," 1993–2013; Stephanie Gaskell, "NYPD Ready to Make Even Bigger 'Impact'," *NYP,* January 13, 2004; Megan Golden, Cari Almo, "Reducing Gun Violence: An Overview of New York City's Strategy" (Vera Institute of Justice, 2004), 9–11; Post Staff Report, "NYPD Commissioner Touts Technology," *NYP,* June 23, 2010; Geoffrey Gray, "Boss Kelly," *New York,* May 16, 2010; Christopher Dickey, *Securing the City: Inside America's Best Counterterror Force—the NYPD* (New York: Simon & Schuster, 2009), 106–7; Judith Miller, "Counterterror and the Crunch," *City Journal* (August 14, 2009), online version.

11 New York Police Department, Crime Statistics, 2001, 2013; Office of the Mayor, "Mayor Bloomberg Announces New York City's Incarceration Rate Hits New All-Time Low," Press Release, December 26, 2013; Franklin Zimring, *The City That Became Safe: New York's Lessons For Urban Crime and Its Control* (New York: Oxford University Press, 2009), 35–40; Heather Mac Donald, "New York's Indispensable Institution," *City Journal,* July 7, 2009; James Austin and Michael Jacobson, "How New York City Reduced Mass Incarceration: A Model for Change?" (JFA Institute, Vera Institute of Justice and Brennan Center for Justice at New York University Law School, January 2013), 13, 16, 18–25.

12 Editorial, "Protecting the Bench from Politics," *NYT,* March 23, 2002.

13 Graham A. Rayman, *The NYPD Tapes: A Shocking Story of Cops, Cover-ups and Courage* (New York: Palgrove Macmillan, 2013), *passim*; David N. Kelley and Sharon L. McCarthy, "The Report of the Crime Reporting Review Committee To Commissioner Raymond W. Kelly Concerning Compstat Auditing" (NYPD, April 8, 2013), 18, 21, 55–8; Zimring, *The City That Became Safe,* 31–5; 219–221.

14 Zimring, *The City That Became Safe,* 223–5; City of New York, Office of the Mayor, "Press Release: Mayor Bloomberg Announces New York City's Incarceration Rate Hits All Time Low," December 26, 2013.

15 Author's interview, Raymond Kelly, October 3, 2016; Larry Celona, "Kelly Plans City Force to Fight Terror," *NYP,* January 16, 2002; Raymond W. Kelly, "Defying the 'Inevitable'," *NYP,* September 11, 2007; Dickey, *Securing the City,* 37.

16 Dickey, *Securing the City,* 71; Author's interview, Raymond Kelly, October 3, 2016.

17 Keane and Hamilton, et al., *The 9/11 Commission Report,* 109; Dickey, *Securing the City,* 31, 36; Michael A. Sheehan, *Crush the Cell: How to Defeat Terrorism Without Terrifying Ourselves* (New York: The Riverview Press, 2008) *passim*.

18 Author's interview, Raymond Kelly, October 3, 2016; Dickey, *Securing the City,* 72–5; 144–5.

19 Judith Miller, "NYPD's Intelligence Advantage," *NYP,* July 16, 2007; Dickey, *Securing the City,* 140–2; 159.

20 Dickey, *Securing the City,* 144–5.

21 Dickey, *Securing the City,* 148–9; Gray, "Boss Kelly," *New York,* May 16, 2010, online edition.

22 Author's interview, Raymond Kelly, October 3, 2016; N. R. Kleinfield, Al Baker, and Joseph Goldstein, "After 11 Years, A Police Leader Hits Turbulence," *NYT,* February 3, 2012; Gray, "Boss Kelly," *New York*, May 16, 2010; Michael A. Sheehan, *Crush the Cell*, 232; Dickey, *Securing the City*, 145–6; New York Police Foundation @ http://www.nycpolicefoundation.org/about-us/40-year-history/; Miller, "Counterterror and the Crunch," *City Journal*, 14 August 2009, online version.

23 Author's interview, Raymond Kelly, October 3, 2016; Murray Weiss, "Finest Race Into Action—Lightning Response Floods Apple Transit Hubs," *NYP*, July 8, 2005; Erika Martinez, "NYPD's Global Eyes and Ears; Cops Abroad on Terror Beat," *NYP,* November 28, 2005; Dickey, *Securing the City*, 147.

24 Author's interview, Raymond Kelly, October 3, 2016; Murray Weiss, "Finest Race Into Action—Lightning Response Floods Apple Transit Hubs," *NYP*, July 8, 2005; Erika Martinez, "NYPD's Global Eyes and Ears; Cops Abroad on Terror Beat," *NYP,* November 28, 2005; Dickey, *Securing the City*, 147.

25 Murray Weiss, "NYPD Mosque Spies Have Feds Irate," *NYP,* October 5, 2002; Miller, "NYPDs Intelligence Advantage," *NYP,* July 16, 2007; Judith Miller, "FBI and NYPD Bury the Hatchet," *NYT,* December 11, 2008; David Johnston and William K. Rashbaum, "New York Police Fight with US on Surveillance," *NYT,* November 19, 2008; Gray, "Boss Kelly," *New York*, May 16, 2010; Dickey, *Securing the City*, 150; Judith Miller, "New York 9/11/11," *City Journal*, (Summer 2011).

26 Gray, "Boss Kelly," *New York*, May 16, 2010; Sheehan, *Crush the Cell*, 237–8; Colleen Long, "Ray Explains Shootdown," *NYP,* September 29, 2011; Miller, "New York 9/11/11," *City Journal* (Summer 2011).

27 Dickey, *Securing the City*, 111–17.

28 Mitchell D. Silber and Arbin Bhatt, Senior Intelligence Analysts, NYPD Intelligence Divisions, "Radicalization in the West: The Homegrown Threat," NYPD, 2007; Sewell Chan, "Police Issue Report on 'Homegrown' Terror Threat," *NYT,* August 15, 2007; Al Baker, "New York City Police Report Explores Homegrown Terrorism," *NYT,* August 16, 2007.

29 Ralph Blumenthal and Sharaf Mowjood, "Muslim Prayers and Renewal Near Ground Zero," *NYT,* December 8, 2009.

30 Michael Barbaro and Javier C. Hernandez, "Mosque Plan Clears Hurdle in New York," *NYT,* August 3, 2010.

31 Michael Barbaro, "Mayor's Stance on Muslim Center Has Deep Roots," *NYT,* August 12, 2010.

32 Associated Press publication of NYPD documents: "The Demographics Unit,"; "Intelligence Division, Demographic Unit, Albanian Location of Concern Report,"; "Target of Surveillance: Majid Omar, Paterson, N.J."; Miller, "New York 9/11/11," *City Journal*, (Summer 2011); Amy Davidson, "The Koran and the NYPD," *The New Yorker,* February 22, 2012.

33 *Hasson et al. v. The City of New York*, United States District Court for The District of New Jersey, Civ. No. 2–12.341, p.10; City of New York, Department of Investigation and NYPD Department of Investigation, "An Investigation of NYPD's Compliance With Rules Governing Investigations of Political Activity," August 23, 2016 and "New York City Police Department Final Response," August 23, 2016; Matt Apuzzo and Adam Goldman, "Judge Rejects Settlement Over Surveillance of Muslims by New York Police Department," *NYT,* October 31, 2016.

34 Raymond W. Kelly, "Keeping New York Safe," *NYP,* September 8, 2011; Joseph Goldstein, "Kelly Defends Surveillance of Muslims," *NYT,* February 27, 2012; Joseph Goldstein, "City Council Grills Kelly on Police Surveillance of Muslims," *NYT,* October 6, 2011; Michael Powell, "In Shift, Police Say Leader Helped With Anti-Islam Film and Now Regrets It," *NYT,* January 24, 2012; Michael Grynbaum, "Mayor Defends Kelly, But Says Anti-Muslim Film Caused Damage," *NYT,* January 26, 2012; Mike Lupica, "Police Commissioner Ray Kelly Has Made the City Safer With NYPDs Surveillance of Muslims," *Daily News,* March 4, 2012; James Freeman, "The Saturday Interview: The Political War on the NYPD: New York's top cop Ray Kelly on fighting crime and fighting off critics of a basic police tool: stopping suspicious characters and checking for weapons," *The Wall Street Journal,* April 5, 2013.

35 Ray Kelly, *Vigilance: My Life Serving America and Protecting Its Empire City* (New York: Hachette Books, 2015), 208; Dickey, *Securing the City,* vi, 118; Author's interview, Edward Skyler, September 12, 2016.

36 Shaila K. Dewan, "Questions Swirl in Roof Shooting Inquiry," *NYT,* January 30, 2004.

37 Michael Brick, "Hundreds Attend Funeral of Rooftop Shooting Victim," *NYT,* January 31, 2004; Robert D. McFadden and Ian Urbina, "Fatal Shooting Not Justified, the Police Say," *NYT,* January 25, 2004; Author's interview, Raymond Kelly, October 3, 2016.

38 Shaila K. Dewan and Oren Yaniv, "Police Union Chief Assails Comments about Shooting," *NYT,* January 28, 2004.

39 Author's interview, Raymond Kelly, October 3, 2016; Michael Cooper, "Mayor's Response to a Fatal Police Shooting A Departure From His Predecessor," *NYT,* January 26, 2004; Murray Weiss, "Anatomy of NYPD's Tragic Bad-Raid Blunder in Harlem," *NYP,* May 30, 2003; Shaila K. Dawan, "City to Pay $1.6 Million in Fatal, Mistaken Raid," *NYT,* October 29, 2003; Author's interview, Dennis Walcott, August 2, 2016.

40 McFadden, "Police Kill Man after a Queens Bachelor Party," *NYT,* November 26, 2006; Rashbaum and Baker, "50 Bullets, One Dead and Many Questions," *NYT,* December 11, 2006.

41 McFadden, "Police Kill Man after a Queens Bachelor Party," *NYT,* November 26, 2006; Rashbaum and Baker, "50 Bullets, One Dead and Many Questions," *NYT,* December 11, 2006.

42 Diane Cardwell and Sewell Chan, "Mayor Calls 50 Shots by the Police 'Unacceptable'," *NYT,* November 28, 2006.

43 Patrick Healy, "Police Commissioner Looks Ahead and Back," *NYT,* November 30, 2006; Jamie Schram, "Rikers Plot to 'Kill Commish,'" *NYP,* March 6, 2007.

44 Matt Flegenheimer and Al Baker, "Officer in Bell Killing Is Fired; 3 Others to Be Forced Out," *NYT,* March 23, 2012; Editorial, "New Rules for Undercover Cops," *NYT,* June 20, 2007; Murray Weiss, "NYPD Hired Gun Aims at Shootings," *NYP,* January 5, 2007; Bernard D. Rostker, Lawrence M. Hanser, William M. Hix, Carl Jensen, Andrew R. Morral, Greg Ridgeway, Terry L. Schell, "Evaluation of the New York City Police Department Firearm Training and Firearm-Discharge Review Process," (Santa Monica, CA: RAND Corporation, 2008).

45 *Terry v Ohio*, 392 US 1 (1968); Author's interview, Raymond Kelly, October 3, 2016; Jeffrey Toobin, "Rights and Wrongs: A Judge Takes On Stop-and-Frisk," *The New Yorker*, May 27, 2013.

46 New York State Office of the Attorney General, "An Investigation Into the NYPD's Stop and Frisk Practices," 1999, 72; New York State Office of the Attorney General, "A Report on Arrests Arising From the New York City Police Department's Stop-and-Frisk Practices," 2013, 1–4; *Floyd et al., v. The City of New York*, 08 Civ. 1034, Opinion and Order, August 12, 2013, 6–7; Author's interview, Raymond Kelly, October 3, 2016.

47 "$100 Offered For Any Gun Turned In, No Questions Asked," *NYT*, May 8, 2002; William K. Rashbaum, "Judge Clears Way for City to Sue Gun Companies," *NYT*, December 3, 2005; Damien Cave, "With Victories, City Challenges More Gun Sales," *NYT*, December 8, 2006; Michael R. Bloomberg, Richard M. Daley, James K. Hahn, and Scott L. King, "Lawyers, Guns and Mayors," *NYT*, February 24, 2004; Alan Feuer, "US Appeals Court Rejects City's Suit To Curb Guns," *NYT*, May 1, 2008.

48 *Floyd et al., v. The City of New York*, 08 Civ. 1034, Opinion and Order, August 12, 2013, 51; Epi Research Report, "Firearm Deaths and Injuries in New York City," New York City Department of Health and Mental Hygiene (April 2013), 5–7; Al Baker, "City Is Doubling Police Program to Reduce Crime," *NYT*, December 27, 2007; Editorial, "The Police's Excellent Year," *NYT*, December 30, 2007; Citizens Crime Commission, "Police and Public Safety in New York City," January 2004, 21.

49 Philip Messing, "Study Will Eye Cops Risky 'Biz'," *NYP*, March 1, 2007; Al Baker and Joseph Goldstein, "Kelly Reacts After Stop-and-Frisk Ruling," *NYT*, May 17, 2012; Jeffrey Toobin, "Rights and Wrongs: A Judge Takes On Stop and Frisk," *The New Yorker*, May 27, 2013; Lawrence Downes, "What Ray Kelly Said About Stop-and-Frisk," *NYT*, May 3, 2013; Dr. Delores Jones-Brown, Jaspreet Gill, and Jennifer Trone, forward by Jeremy Travis, "Stop, Question and Frisk Policing Tactics In New York City: A Primer," Center for Race, Crime and Criminal Justice, John Jay College of Criminal Justice, March 2010, *passim*; Author's interview, Raymond Kelly, October 3, 2016; Greg Ridgeway, "Analysis of Racial Disparities in the New York Police Department's Stop, Question, and Frisk Tactics," Santa Monica: CA, RAND Corporation, 2007, xii.

50 "Second Supplemental Report of Jeffrey Fagan, Ph.D." in the matter of *Floyd et al. v. The City of New York* 08 Civ. 01034 (SAS), 16–21 and *passim*; Carla Shedd, "What About the Other 99%?: The Broader Impact of Street Stops on Minority Communities," Research Paper presented at Urban Institute Justice Policy Center forum on Key Issues in Police Use of Pedestrian Stops and Searches, August 2012, 24; Center for Constitutional Rights, "Racial Disparity in NYPD Stops-and-Frisks: The Center for Constitutional Rights Preliminary Report on UF-250 Data from 2005 Through June 2008" (New York, 2009), 1–5, *passim*; Andrea Bernstein, "New York Remade: Before and After Bloomberg," WNYC, December 27, 2013.

51 Jennifer Fratello, Andres F. Rengifo, and Jennifer Trone, "Coming of Age With Stop and Frisk: Experiences, Self-Perceptions and Public Safety Implications" (New York, NY: Vera Institute for Justice, 2013), 2–3, 10–20, and *passim*; Center for Constitutional Rights, "Stop and Frisk: The Human Impact: the Stories Behind the Numbers, the Effects on Our Communities" (New York, July 2012), *passim*; Michael Powell, "Former Skeptic Now Embraces Divisive Tactic," *NYT*, April 9,

2012; Jim Dwyer, "On Arrests, Demographics and Marijuana," *NYT*, April 30, 2008; Elizabeth A. Harris, "Police Memo on Marijuana Warns Against Some Arrests," *NYT*, September 23, 2011; Post Staff Report, "Pot Arrests Top 50K in 2011 Despite NYPD Order," *NYP*, February 1, 2011; Thomas Kaplan, "Bloomberg Backs Plan to Limit Arrests for Marijuana," *NYT*, June 4, 2012; New York State Office of the Attorney General, "A Report on Arrests Arising From the New York City Police Department's Stop-and-Frisk Practices," 2013, 1–4; Editorial, "No Progress on Marijuana Arrests," *NYT*, October 28, 2014.

52 Center for Constitutional Rights, "Stop and Frisk," *passim*; Dwyer, "On Arrests, Demographics and Marijuana," *NYT*, April 30, 2008; Harris, "Police Memo on Marijuana Warns against Some Arrests," *NYT*, September 23, 2011; Editorial, "No Progress on Marijuana Arrests," *NYT*, October 28, 2014.

53 Post Staff Report, "Paterson Signs Law Limiting Stop-Frisk Database," *NYP*, July 16, 2010; Bob Herbert, "Watching Certain People," *NYT*, March 1, 2010; Michael Powell, "Arguments for Most Police Stops, and the Math, Don't Hold Up," *NYT*, May 28, 2012.

54 *Floyd et al., v. The City of New York*, 08 Civ. 1034, Opinion and Order, August 12, 2013, 4–16; *Ligon et al., v. The City of New York*, No. 12 Civ. 2274 (2013), Opinion January 8, 2013; Al Baker and Aidan Gardiner, "New York Police Dept. Is Sued Over Stops in Private Buildings," *NYT*, March 28, 2012; Benjamin Weiser and Joseph Goldstein, "New York City Asks Court to Vacate Rulings on Stop-and-Frisk Tactics," *NYT*, November 8, 2013; Benjamin Weiser, "Judges Decline to Reverse Stop-and-Frisk Ruling, All But Ending Mayor's Fight," *NYT*, November 22, 2013; Author's interview, Raymond Kelly, October 3, 2016.

55 *David Floyd et al., v. The City of New York*, 08 Civ. 1034, Opinion and Order, August 12, 2013, 4–15; *David Floyd et al., v. The City of New York* and *Jaenon Ligon et al.*, Remedies Opinion *passim*; Freeman, "The Saturday Interview: The Political War on the NYPD," *The Wall Street Journal*, April 5, 2013; Joseph Goldstein, "Kelly Said Street Stops Targeted Minorities, Senator Testifies," *NYT*, April 1, 2013.

56 Author's interview, Raymond Kelly, October 3, 2016; New York City Police Department, "Stop, Question and Frisk Data," 1998–2013; New York City Police Department, "Crime Statistics," 1998–2013; Christopher Dunn, Sara LaPlante and Jennifer Carnig, "2013 Stop and Frisk," American Civil Liberties Union, New York, August 2014.

Year	2002	2003	2004	2005	2006	2007	2008	2009	2010	2011	2012	2013
Major Crime	154,809	147,069	142,093	135,475	128,682	121,009	117,956	106,730	105,115	106,669	111,147	111,135
YOY%	N/A	-5.00	-3.38	-4.66	-5.01	-5.96	-2.52	-9.52	-1.51	1.48	4.20	-0.17
Stops	97,296	160,851	313,523	398,191	506,491	472,096	540,320	581,168	601,285	685,724	532,911	191,558
YOY%	N/A	65.32	94.92	27.01	27.20	-6.79	14.45	7.56	3.46	14.04	-22.28	-64.05

57 Quinnipiac University Poll, "New York City Voters Back NYPD Monitor More Than 2–1," April 11, 2013; Raymond W. Kelly, "Heads in the Sand," *NYP*, October 25, 2012; J. David Goodman, "City Council Votes to Increase Oversight of New York Police," *NYT*, June 27, 2013; Wendy Rudman, "Mayor Vows to Veto Inspector for Police," *NYT*, March 20, 2013; Post Staff Report, "Cop Watchdog Veto," *NYP*, July 24, 2013; Post Staff Report, "Council Overrides Mayor's Vetoes and OK's NYPD Watchdog, Bloomberg Says Oversight Jeopardizes City Safety,"

NYP, August 22, 2013; Michael Bloomberg, "'Stop and Frisk' Keeps New York Safe," *The Washington Post,* August18, 2013; Heather Mac Donald, "Courts v. Cops," *City Journal* (Winter 2013); Ray Kelly, *Vigilance,* 279.

58 Kevin Flynn, "Ex-Police Head Criticizes Strategies," *NYT,* April 5, 2000; William Rashbaum and Al Baker, "Police Commissioner Closing Controversial Street Crime Unit," *NYT,* April 10, 2002; Al Baker, "Commissioner Bans Profiling Using Race By the Police," *NYT,* March 14, 2002; William J. Bratton, Commissioner, "Crime and Enforcement Activity in New York City" (Jan 1–Dec 31, 2013), Appendix C, New York City Police Department Census, C-1.

59 Michael Cooper, "Chances of a Shooting Similar to Diallo's Are Less, Mayor Says," *NYT,* February 5, 2002; Dean E. Murphy and David M. Halbfinger, "9/11 Bridged the Racial Divide, New Yorkers Say, Gingerly," *NYT,* June 16, 2002.

60 Kate Taylor, "Borough President Seeks Limits on Stop and Frisk," *NYT,* September 23, 2011; Author's interviews, Off the record; Author's interview, Raymond Kelly, October 3, 2016.

61 Author's interview, Raymond Kelly, October 3, 2016; Author's interview, Heather Mac Donald, October 6, 2016; Jeffrey Toobin, "Rights and Wrongs: A Judge Takes on Stop and Frisk," *The New Yorker,* May 27, 2013; Raymond W. Kelly, "What The Commish Told The Rev," *NYP,* April 4, 2013.

62 N. R. Kleinfield, Al Baker and Joseph Goldstein, "After 11 Years, A Police Leader Hits Turbulence," *NYT,* February 3, 2012; Freeman, "The Saturday Interview: The Politic; At War on the NYPD," *The Wall Street Journal,* April 5, 2013; Quinnipiac University, "December 14, 2011—New Yorkers Nix Mayor on Occupy Wall Street, Quinnipiac University Poll Finds; Voters Back Living Wage 4:1," Release Detail December 14, 2011; Michael Powell and William K. Rashbaum, "Kelly, Flinching a Bit, Looks Back with Head High," *NYT,* December 30, 2013; Ray Kelly, *Vigilance,* 270–282.

63 City of New York, Office of the Mayor, "Press Release: Mayor Bloomberg and Police Commissioner Kelly Announce 2013 Saw the Fewest Murders and Fewest Shootings in Recorded City History at NYPD Graduation Ceremony," December 27, 2013. Shootings were 1,093 in 2013 through December 26, down from 1,608 in 2001.

Chapter 5

1 David P. Gardner et al., *A Nation at Risk: The Imperative for Educational Reform* (Washington, D.C.: National Commission on Excellence in Education, April 1983), 5.

2 Joel Klein, *Lessons of Hope: How to Fix Our Schools* (HarperCollins Publishers, ebook edition, 2014), location 4267–4279.

3 Richard D. Kahlenberg, *Tough Liberal: Albert Shanker and the Battles Over Schools, Unions, Race and Democracy* (New York: Columbia University Press, 2007, ebook edition), location 2769–3063; Diane Ravitch, *The Great School Wars: A History of the New York City Public Schools* (New York: Basic Books, 1988), xiv–xvii; Jerald E. Podair, *The Strike That Changed New York: Blacks, Whites and the Ocean Hill-Brownsville Crisis* (New Haven: Yale University Press, 2002) *passim.*

4 Diane Ravitch, *The Great School Wars,* xiv–xvii; Joseph P. Viteritti, *Across the River: Politics and Education in the City* (New York: Holmes & Meier, 1983), 6–17; McNickle, *The Power of the Mayor,* 145.

5   Siegel and Seigel, *Prince of the* City, 114–5; Jennifer Steinhauer, "Consensus on City Schools: Political Memo; How Bloomberg Captured a Prize That Others Found Elusive," *NYT,* June 7, 2002; Jeffrey R. Henig, Eva Gold, Marion Orr, Megan Silander, Elaine Simon, "Parent and Community Engagement in NYC and the Sustainability Challenge for Urban Education Reform," in Jennifer O'Day, Catherine S. Bitter, and Louis M. Gomez, eds. *Education Reform in New York City: Ambitious Change in the Nation's Most Complex School System* (Cambridge, MA: Harvard Education Press, 2011), 36; Author's interview, Randi Weingarten, May 19, 2015; City of New York, Office of the Mayor, *Mayor's Management Report, 2002,* 18; Carl Campanile, "Secret Flunkers: Parents in Dark About Failing Schools: Poll," *NYP,* December 20, 2002; James F. Brennan, "New York City Public School Improvement Before and After Mayoral Control," in Diane Ravitch et al., *NYC Schools Under Bloomberg and Klein: What Parents, Teachers and Policymakers Need to Know* (New York: Lulu, 2009), 105–13; National Assessment of Educational Progress (NAEP), "The Nation's Report Card: Trial Urban District Snapshot Report, New York City Department of Education Public Schools, Reading Grade 4 and Grade 8 and Math Grade 4 and Grade 8," 2002, 2003.

6   Author's interview, William Cunningham, May 12, 2014; Author's interview, Dennis Walcott, August 2, 2016.

7   Bloomberg with Winkler, *Bloomberg by Bloomberg,* 245; Citizens Budget Commission, "The Candidates on Fiscal Issues 2001 Mayoral Election, City of New York," August 2001, 4; "The Mayoral Transition; Mayor's Speech, 'Rebuild, Renew and Remain the Capital of the Free World,'" *NYT,* January 2, 2002.

8   Author's interview, Marc Shaw, July 29, 2014; Author's interview, Dean Fuleihan, August 12, 2015.

9   Author's interview, Marc Shaw, July 29, 2014; Author's interview, Randi Weingarten, May 19, 2015; Author's interview, Dean Fuleihan, August 12, 2015; Michael Cooper, "Mayor Expresses Optimism On Teachers' Talks," *NYT,* March 11, 2002; Carl Campanile, "Silver Will Give Mike Schools in Exchange for Teacher Raise," *NYP,* April 27, 2002.

10 Abby Goodnough, "Union For New York City Teachers Takes First Step Toward a Strike," May 8, 2002; Carl Campanile, "It's All Talk—A Strike is Too Costly—For Teachers," *NYP,* May 8, 2002.

11 Author's interview, Marc Shaw, July 29, 2014; Author's interview, Randi Weingarten, May 19, 2015; Author's interview, Dean Fuleihan, August 12, 2015; Author's interview, Off the record; Anemona Hartocollis, "Consensus on City Schools; Outrage Leads Back to Centralized Leadership," *NYT,* June 7, 2002; Steinhauer, "Consensus on City Schools: Political Memo; How Bloomberg Captured a Prize That Others Found Elusive," *NYT,* June 7, 2002.

12 Author's interview, Marc Shaw, July 29, 2014; Author's interview, Randi Weingarten, May 19, 2015; Author's interview, Dean Fuleihan, August 12, 2015; Author's interview, Off the record; Hartocollis, "Consensus on City Schools; Outrage Leads Back to Centralized Leadership," *NYT,* June 7, 2002; Steinhauer, "Consensus on City Schools: Political Memo; How Bloomberg Captured a Prize That Others Found Elusive," *NYT,* June 7, 2002.

13 David Seifman, "Bloomy Making School History—Lands Control of Ed. Board in Deal with Silver," *NYP,* June 7, 2002.

14 Seifman, "Bloomy Making School History—Lands Control of Ed. Board in Deal with Silver," *NYP,* June 7, 2002; Jennifer Steinhauer, "2 Major Points of School Law Get Justice Dept. Approval," *NYT,* July 4, 2002; Patrick J. Sullivan, "Inside the Panel for Educational Policy," in Diane Ravitch, *NYC Schools Under Bloomberg and Klein,* 69.

15 Richard Rothstein, "Lessons; Mr. Mayor, Schools Chief. Mr. Fix-It Is Another Tale," *NYT,* April 17, 2002; Editorial, "Mayoral Control of City Schools," *NYT,* June 7, 2002; Joyce Purnick, "Consensus on City Schools; News Analysis; More Power, More Risks," *NYT,* June 7, 2002; Bob McManus, "The Battle Has Just Begun, & Here's How Mike Can Win," *NYP,* June 7, 2002; Jennifer Steinhauer, "Mayor Wants Tweed Building For School Use," *NYT,* March 19, 2002; Samuel G. Freedman, "Bloomberg's Chance to Save the Schools," *NYT,* June 14, 2002; Author's interview, Dennis Walcott, August 2, 2016.

16 Anemona Hartocollis, "Mayor Says Gerald Levin Might Be Fine Schools Chief," *NYT,* May 29, 2002; Anemona Hartocollis, "Schematic for a Schools Chancellor; Seeking Business Circuitry, a Hard Shell and 'Fire in the Belly,'" *NYT,* July 14, 2002; Anemona Hartocollis, "A Former Deputy Mayor Emerges as Front-Runner for Schools Chancellor," *NYT,* July 20, 2002; Jennifer Steinhauer, "The New Schools Chancellor: Overview; Bloomberg Picks a Lawyer to Run New York City Schools," *NYT,* July 30, 2002; Anemona Hartocollis, "The New Schools Chancellor; News Analysis, Hoping an Outsider Plus a Bottom-line Approach Equals Reform," *NYT,* July 30, 2002; Klein, *Lessons of Hope,* location 637; Author's interview, Dennis Walcott, August 2, 2016.

17 Klein, *Lessons of Hope,* location 481, 587–637; Adam Liptak, "Man in the News: Joel Irwin Klein," *NYT,* July 30, 2002; Steven Brill, *Class Warfare: Inside the Fight to Fix America's Schools* (New York: Simon & Shuster, ebook edition), 87–8.

18 Klein, *Lessons of Hope,* location 481, 587–637, 650; Adam Liptak, "Man in the News: Joel Irwin Klein," *NYT,* July 30, 2002; Brill, *Class Warfare,* 87–8; Jennifer Steinhauer, "The New Schools Chancellor: Overview; Bloomberg Picks a Lawyer to Run New York City Schools," *NYT,* July 30, 2002; Author's interview, Dennis Walcott, August 2, 2016.

19 Steinhauer, "The New Schools Chancellor: Overview; Bloomberg Picks a Lawyer to Run New York City Schools," *NYT,* July 30, 2002; Anemona Hartocollis, "The New Schools Chancellor; News Analysis, Hoping an Outsider Plus a Bottom-line Approach Equals Reform," *NYT,* July 30, 2002; Jennifer Steinhauer, "Schools Chief With Traits That a Mayor Prizes Most," *NYT,* July 31, 2002.

20 Klein, *Lessons of Hope,* location 625; Author's interview, Dennis Walcott, August 2, 2016.

21 Author' interview, Randi Weingarten, May 19, 2015; Brill, *Class Warfare,* 44, 100–101; Randi Weingarten, AFT president, biography, American Federation of Teachers, www.aft.org; Wayne Barrett, "Weingarten's War: The Teacher Boss Puts Bloomberg on the 'Bad Step,'" *The Village Voice,* May 13, 2003.

22 Brill, *Class Warfare,* 101–2; Dana Goldstein, *The Teacher Wars: A History of America's Most Embattled Profession* (New York: Doubleday, 2014, ebook edition), location 3516–3521, 3690; Author's Interview, Peter Cunningham, February 11, 2015; Barrett, "Weingarten's War: The Teacher Boss Puts Bloomberg on the 'Bad Step,'" *The Village Voice,* May 13, 2003; Jason L. Riley, "The Weekend Interview:

Weingarten for the Union Defense," *The Wall Street Journal*, March 26, 2011; RiShawn Biddle, "Randi's Tangled Vine Garden," *The American Spectator*, May 2011; Steven Greenhouse and David M. Herszenhorn, "Mayor's Fate Is Intertwined With Head of Teachers' Union," *NYT,* January 26, 2004.

23 Author's interview, Randi Weingarten, May 19, 2015; Author's interview, Joel Klein, March 2, 2015; Elissa Gootman, "Klein Assails Job Protection for Teachers," *NYT,* October 17, 2003; Hartocollis, "The New Schools Chancellor; News Analysis, Hoping an Outsider Plus a Bottom-line Approach Equals Reform," *NYT,* July 30, 2002.

24 Author's interview, Randi Weingarten, May 19, 2015; Author's interview, Joel Klein, March 2, 2015; Elissa Gootman, "Klein Assails Job Protection for Teachers," *NYT,* October 17, 2003; Hartocollis, "The New Schools Chancellor; News Analysis, Hoping an Outsider Plus a Bottom-line Approach Equals Reform," *NYT,* July 30, 2002.

25 Michael Cooper, "Bloomberg Assailed Over Layoff Stance," *NYT,* March 18, 2003; Abby Goodnough, "Teachers' Union Sues Klein, Claiming Bias in Layoff of Aides," *NYT,* May 6, 2003; Carl Campanile, "UFT Sues City Over 'Racist' Layoff Plan," *NYP,* May 6, 2003; Author's interview, Joel Klein, March 2, 2015; Author's interview, Randi Weingarten, May 19, 2015.

26 Author's interview, Randi Weingarten, May 19, 2015.

27 Randi Weingarten, "First Things First," Speech at United Federation of Teachers Spring Conference 2003, in author's possession, courtesy of Randi Weingarten; Carl Campanile, "Teachers Declare War on Bloomberg," *NYP,* May 7, 2003; Abby Goodnough, "Teacher's Union President Turns Against Schools Plan," *NYT,* May 11, 2003; Abby Goodnough, "Schools Plan Loses Ally," *NYT,* May 15, 2003; Carl Campanile, "Class Disruption—Teachers, City Take Off Gloves," *NYP,* May 11, 2003; Brill, *Class Warfare*, 103; Klein, *Lessons of Hope,* location 1643–1667; Author's interview, James Hanley, September 29, 2014; Author's interview, Joel Klein, March 2, 2015; Email from Joel Klein to Author, October 31, 2016.

28 Ravitch et al., *NYC Schools under Bloomberg and Klein*, 2.

29 Ravitch et al., *NYC Schools under Bloomberg and Klein, passim*; Parent Commission on School Governance and Mayoral Control, "Recommendations on School Governance," NYC, March 2009, final report, *passim.*

30 Steven Greenhouse, "Deep Distrust Slows Contract Talks With Teachers," *NYT,* December 15, 2004; Greenhouse and Herszenhorn, "Mayor's Fate Is Intertwined With Head of Teachers' Union," *NYT,* January 26, 2004; David M. Herszenhorn, "Teachers' Leader Hurls Criticism At Mayor," *NYT,* December 3, 2004; Brill, *Class Warfare* 101–103; Klein, *Lessons of Hope,* location 1656; Author's interview, Joel Klein, March 2, 2015; Author's interview, Off the record.

31 "Forum With New York City Schools Chancellor Joel Klein," *Carnegie Reporter,* Vol. 2, No. 2, Spring 2003, 1–2; Abby Goodnough, "Fixing the Schools," *NYT,* October 4, 2002; Joseph P. Viteritti, "Managing the City's Schools," *NYT,* November 18, 2002; Abby Goodnough, "Klein Taking Time To Make His Mark As Schools Chancellor," *NYT,* November 22, 2002; Clara Hemphill and Kim Nauer with Helen Zelon, Thomas Jacobs, Alessandra Raimondi, Sharon McCloskey, and Rajeev Yerneni, "Managing by the Numbers: Empowerment and Accountability in New York City's Schools," Center for New York City Affairs, Milano, The New

School for Management and Urban Policy, June 2010, 10; Klein, *Lessons of Hope,* location 952; Author's interview, Joel Klein, March 2, 2015; Author's interview, Dennis Walcott, August 2, 2016.

32 Klemper and Nauer, et al., "Managing by the Numbers," 1; New York City Department of Education, "Children First: A Bold, Common Sense Plan to Create Great Schools for All New York City Children, Updated 2008–2009 School Year," 3; Maureen Kelleher, "New York City's Children First: Lessons in School Reform," Center for American Progress, January 2014, 19; Childress, Higgins, et al., "Managing for Results at the New York City Department of Education," 88–91.

33 City of New York, Office of the Mayor, "Remarks by Mayor Michael R. Bloomberg: Major Address on Education at New York Urban League's Dr. Martin Luther King, Jr. Symposium," January 15, 2003; Jennifer Steinhauer, "Vision for the Schools: Assessment; Bloomberg As Strict Headmaster," *NYT,* January 16, 2003; Carl Campanile, "Bloomberg's Class Action: Launches New Era For City Schools," *NYP,* January 16, 2003; Carl Campanile, "Mayor Gets A+ For Answering Every Question," *NYP,* January 16, 2003; Klein, *Lessons of Hope,* location 1593.

34 Klein, *Lessons of Hope,* location 3310; Klemper and Nauer, et al., "Managing by the Numbers," 27–8.

35 Eric Nadelstern, *10 Lessons from New York City Schools: What Really Works To Improve Education* (New York: Columbia University Teachers College Press, 2013, ebook edition), *passim,* location 2099; Klemper and Nauer, et al., "Managing by the Numbers," 23–5; Author's interview, Joel Klein, March 2, 2015.

36 Nadelstern, *10 Lessons From New York City Schools*, location 144–265, 481; Goodnough, "Klein Taking Time To Make His Mark As Schools Chancellor," *NYT,* November 24, 2002; Stacey Childress, Monica Higgins, Ann Ishimaru, and Sola Takahashi, "Managing for Results at the New York City Department of Education," in O'Day, Bitter, and Gomez, eds. *Educational Reform in New York City,* 87; Carl Campanile, "Klein's Principal Purge," *NYP,* December 12, 2002; Carl Campanile, "Big Biz$$$ Give Schools A Boost," *NYP,* October 27, 2002; Abby Goodnough, "Executive Who Saved G.E. is to Train School Principals," *NYT,* January 14, 2003; Carl Campanile, "He'll Bring Good Things—Klein Lines Up GE's Welch To Help Schools," *NYP,* January 14, 2003; Anne Grosso Le'oacutean, "The School Leadership Crisis: Have Principals Been Left Behind?," *Carnegie Reporter,* Vol 4, No. 1, Fall 2006, 7–10; New York City Independent Budget Office, "New York City Public School Indicators: Demographics, Resources, Outcomes,*"* May 2013, 16–17; Klein, *Lessons of Hope,* location 1199, 1275–1350.

37 New York City Department of Education, "Children First, Updated 2008–2009 School Year," 10–11; Childress, Higgins, et al., "Managing for Results at the New York City Department of Education," 89; Klein, *Lessons of Hope,* locations 2111–2124; 3324–3361.

38 Klemper and Nauer, et al., "Managing by the Numbers," 15–6.

39 Klemper and Nauer, et al., "Managing by the Numbers,*"* 15–6; Ravitch et al., *NYC Schools Under Bloomberg and Klein,* 3; Elisa Gootman and Robert Gebeloff, "Principals Younger and Freer, But Raise Doubts In Schools," *NYT,* May 25, 2009; Thomas Hehir et al., "Comprehensive Management Review and Evaluation of Special Education," Submitted to the New York City Department of Education, September 20, 2005, 35; Michael Winerip, "Keeping Special Ed On The Radar,"

NYT, October 19, 2005; Author's interview, Joel Klein, March 2, 2015; Email from Joel Klein to Author, October 31, 2016.

40 Author's interview, Randi Weingarten, May 19, 2015; Author's interview, Off the record.

41 Ravitch, *The Great School Wars,* xiv–xv; Kahlenberg, *Tough Liberal,* location 792–1157; Steven Brill, "The Rubber Room," *The New Yorker,* August 31, 2009, online edition; Tamar Lewin, "A New Schools Chancellor Draws Advice, Optimism and Crossed Fingers," *NYT,* August 4, 2002; Margaret Goertz, Susanna Loeb, and Jim Wyckoff, "Recruiting, Evaluating, and Retaining Teachers: The Children First Strategy to Improve New York City's Teachers," in O'Day, Bitter, and Gomez, eds., *Education Reform in New York City,* 162.

42 New York City Department of Education, "Children First, Updated 2008–2009 School Year," 18; Klein, *Lessons of Hope,* location 3416; New York City Independent Budget Office, "Is It Getting Fairer? Examining Five Years of School Allocations Under Fair Student Funding," April 2013, 1, *passim*; Kelleher, *New York City's Children First,* 35–40; Patrick J. Sullivan, "Inside the Panel for Educational Excellence," in Diane Ravitch et al., *NYC Schools Under Bloomberg and Klein,* 71; Leanna Steifel and Amy Ellen Schwartz, "Financing K-12 Education in the Bloomberg years, 2002–2008," in O'Day, Bitter, and Gomez, eds. *Education Reform in New York City,* 61–2.

43 Steven Greenhouse and David M. Herszenhorn, "Mayor's Fate Is Intertwined With Head of Teachers' Union," *NYT,* January 26, 2004; David M. Herszenhorn, "Mayor's Goal Is 'Thin' Pact With Teachers," *NYT,* February 6, 2004; David M. Herszenhorn, "Teachers' Union Warns of an Impasse in Talks With the City," *NYT,* February 7, 2004; David M. Herszenhorn, "Outlook Dims on Deal For Teachers Pact Tied to Aid Suit," *NYT,* November 14, 2004; Klein, *Lessons of Hope,* location 2558–2570; Author's interview, Joel Klein, March 2, 2015.

44 Author's interview, Joel Klein, March 2, 2015; Author's interview, Randi Weingarten, May 19, 2015; David M. Herszenhorn, "Mayor Moves Closer To Deal On Teachers," *NYT,* September 27, 2005; Herszenhorn, "City and Teachers Union Reach Tentative Accord on Contract," *NYT,* October 3, 2005; Rutenberg and Greenhouse, "Neutralizing the Teachers: Win-Win For Mayor And The Union Chief," *NYT,* October 4, 2005; "Memorandum of Agreement Between the Board of Education of the City of New York and United Federation of Teachers, Local 2, American Federation of Teachers, AFL-CIO covering Teachers, July 1, 2003–October 12, 2007," *passim*; Brill, *Class Warfare,* 126; Klein, *Lessons of Hope,* location 2551–2614.

45 Herszenhorn, "City and Teachers Union Reach Tentative Accord on Contract," *NYT,* October 3, 2005; Klein, *Lessons of Hope,* location 2551–2614; "Memorandum of Agreement, Board of Education and UFT, 2003–2007," 105, 145–50; Kelleher, "New York City's Children First," 47; Sol Stern, "A Teacher's Contract for a New Era," *City Journal,* 21 July 2009; Klein, *Lessons of Hope,* location 3375; "Memorandum of Agreement, Board of Education and UFT, 2003–2007," 69; Author's interview, Joel Klein, March 2, 2015; Author's interview, Randi Weingarten, May 19, 2015.

46 David Andreatta, "De-Perked and Irked—Teachers Fear Raise Not Worth Givebacks," *NYP,* October 6, 2005; David M. Herszenhorn, "Metro Briefing:

New York: Manhattan: Teachers Approve Contract Deal," *NYT,* November 4, 2005; Author's interview, Joel Klein, March 2, 2015; Author's interview, Randi Weingarten, May 19, 2015.

47 Author's interview, Randi Weingarten, May 19, 2015; Author's interview, James Hanley, September 29, 2014; Author's interview, Off the record; "Memorandum of Agreement Between the Board of Education of the City of New York and United Federation of Teachers, Local 2, American Federation of Teachers, AFL-CIO covering Teachers," dated November 6, 2006 covering October 13, 2007 through October 31, 2009, 1, 75.

48 Donald Boyd, Hamilton Lankford, Susan Loeb, Jonah Rockoff and James Wyckoff, "The Narrowing Gap in New York City Teacher Qualifications And Its Implications for Student Achievement in High Poverty Schools," National Bureau of Economic Research, June 2008, 2, *passim*; New York City Department of Education, "Children First, Updated 2008–2009," 9; Klein, *Lessons of Hope,* location 3378; Author's interview, Joel Klein, March 2, 2015.

49 Author's interview, Joel Klein, March 2, 2015; Klein, *Lessons of Hope,* location 1592–1616; Abby Goodnough, "City is Converting Reading and Math to Uniform Course," *NYT,* January 22, 2003; Carl Campanile, "Back to School Basics—Klein Overhauls Math & Reading," *NYP,* January 22, 2003.

50 Abby Goodnough, "City is Converting Reading and Math to Uniform Course," *NYT* January 22, 2003; Abby Goodnough, "Bush Advisor on Phonics Casts Doubt on Benefits of Phonics Program," *NYT,* January 24, 2003; Abby Goodnough, "A Living Lab for the City's New Curriculum," *NYT,* March 10, 2003; Robert Kolker, "On the Lam," *New York* online edition, March 22, 2004; Klein, *Lessons of Hope,* location 1592–1616; Sol Stern, "Wrong on Curriculum, Wrong on Pedagogy," in Ravitch et al., *NYC Schools Under Bloomberg and Klein,*145–151; Jennifer O'Day and Catherine S. Bitter, "Improving Instruction in New York City: An Evolving Approach," in O'Day, Bitter, and Gomez, eds., *Education Reform in New York City,* 113–4.

51 Abby Goodnough, "City is Converting Reading and Math to Uniform Course," *NYT,* January 22, 2003; Abby Goodnough, "A Living Lab for the City's New Curriculum," *NYT,* March 10, 2003; Robert Kolker, "On the Lam," *New York* online edition, March 22, 2004; Robert Kolker, "A is for Apple, B is for Brawl: Why New York's Reading Wars Are So Contentious," *New York,* May 1, 2006; Klein, *Lessons of Hope,* location 1592–1616; Leonie Haimson, "'Children First': A Short History,*"* in Diane Ravitch et al., *NYC Schools Under Bloomberg and Klein,* 9.

52 Jennifer Steinhauer, "Changing the Schools: The Mayor; Bloomberg Says His Mind Was Set From Day 1 On Ending Social Promotion in Schools," *NYT,* March 17, 2004; Klein, *Lessons of Hope,* location 2347–68; Sullivan, "Inside the Panel for Educational Policy," in Diane Ravitch et al., *NYC Schools Under Bloomberg and Klein,* 73–4.

53 Klein, *Lessons of Hope,* location 2347–68; Elissa Gootman, "Metro Briefing: New York: Manhattan: Teachers Offer Alternative," *NYT,* March 3, 2004.

54 Elisa Gootman, "Changing the Schools: Reaction; Praise and Anger Over Mayor's Do-It-My-Way Decision," *NYT,* March 17, 2004; David Herszenhorn, "Changing the Schools: the Debate; Keeping Pupils in Third Grade, But Then What?," *NYT,* March 17, 2004; Arthur Levine, "The Failing Grade System," *NYT,* September 26,

2004; Klein, *Lessons of Hope,* location 2368; Email Joel Klein to Author, October 31, 2016.

55 Jennifer Medina, "Process to Escape Bad Schools Begins in Spring," *NYT,* December 10, 2002; Janet C. Quint, Janell K. Smith, Rebecca Untermann, Alma C. Moadano, "New York's Changing High School Landscape: High Schools and Their Characteristics, 2002–2008," MDRC, 2010, ES1, 39, *passim*; "Memorandum of Agreement Between the Board of Education of the City of New York and United Federation of Teachers, dated November 6, 2006," 1.

56 Jennifer Medina, "Process to Escape Bad Schools Begins in Spring," *NYT,* December 10, 2002; Janet C. Quint, Janell K. Smith, Rebecca Untermann, Alma C. Moadano, "New York's Changing High School Landscape," ES1, 39, *passim*; "Memorandum of Agreement Between the Board of Education of the City of New York and United Federation of Teachers," dated November 6, 2006, 1; David C. Bloomfield, "Small Schools: Myth and Reality," in Diane Ravitch et al., *NYC Schools Under Bloomberg and Klein,* 52; Author's interview, Gordon Berlin, September 29, 2015; Email from Joel Klein to Author, October 31, 2016.

57 Anemona Hartocollis, "At 12th Street Academy, Resistance to Being Closed Down," *NYT*, June 26, 2002; New York City Independent Budget Office, "Memorandum dated 1/25/10 To: Ronnie Lowenstein, From: James Murphy, Re: Comparisons Between Schools Slated for Closing and All Other Schools, Transmitted to Council Member Robert Jackson," January 25, 2010; New York City Department of Education email, February 17, 2015 in response to Author's inquiry; New York City Independent Budget Research Office, "New York City Public School Indicators: Demographics, Resources, Outcomes," May 2013, 29; Janet C. Quint, et al., "New York's Changing High School Levin Landscape," ES1, *passim*; Citizens Budget Commission, "Planning After *PlaNYC*: A Framework for Developing New York City's Next Ten Year Capital Strategy," December 6, 2013, 6; Author's interview, Howard Wolfson, August 4, 2016.

58 Janet C. Quint et al., "New York's Changing High School Landscape," ES1, 39; Sean P. Corcoran and Henry M. Levin, "School Choice and Competition in the New York City Schools," in O'Day, Bitter, and Gomez, *Education Reform in New York City,* 204–8, 215.

59 New York City Department of Education, email dated March 3, 2015 in response to author's query; Carl Campanile, "Classy Bigwigs To Donate Big Bucks," *NYP,* January 13, 2003; David M. Herszenhorn, "New York City Big Donors Find New Cause: Public Schools," *NYT,* December 30, 2005; Ravitch, *The Death and Life of the Great American School System: How Testing and Choice Are Undermining Education* (New York: Basic Books, 2010), Chapter 5, Chapter 10 and *passim*; Diane Ravitch, "Mayor Bloomberg's Crib Sheet," *NYT,* April 9, 2009; Sam Dillon, "Scholar's School Reform U-Turn Shakes Up Debate," *NYT,* March 2, 2010.

60 Brill, *Class Warfare,* 111; Klein, *Lessons of Hope,* location 3958.

61 Klemper and Nauer, et al., "Managing by the Numbers," 40; The Parthenon Group, "An Assessment of the New York City Department of Education School Support Structure," November 2013, 11; Leonie Haimson, "'Children First': A Short History,'" in Ravitch et al., *NYC Schools Under Bloomberg and Klein,* 9; Ravitch, *The Great School Wars,* xii–xiii.

62 Anemona Hartocollis, "Consensus on City Schools; Outrage Leads Back to Centralized Leadership," *NYT,* June 7, 2002; Jennifer Medina, "After 100 Days of Poking Around in the Schools, Klein is Optimistic," *NYT,* November 27, 2002; Jennifer Steinhauer, "Vision For The Schools; Assessment; Bloomberg As Strict Headmaster," *NYT,* January 16, 2003; Klein, *Lessons of Hope,* 797; Nadelstern, *10 Lessons,* location 170; Jeffrey R. Henig, Eva Gold, Marion Orr, Megan Silander, Elaine Simon, "Parent and Community Engagement in NYC and the Sustainability Challenge for Urban Education Reform," in O'Day, Bitter, and Gomez, eds., *Education Reform in New York City,* 38–43.

63 New York City Department of Education, "Learning Environment Surveys Citywide Results," 2007 through 2013 at www.schools.nyc.gov; Quinnipiac University Polling Institute, New York City Polls, March 14, 2012; Hemphill, Nauer, et al., "Building Blocks for Better Schools," 38.

64 LynNell Hancock, "School's Out," *Nation,* July 9, 2007 cited in Clara Hemphill, "Parent Power and Mayoral Control: Parent and Community Involvement in New York City Schools," in Joseph P. Viteritti, Editor, *When Mayors Take Charge: School Governance in the City* (Washington, D.C. Brookings Institution Press, 2009, ebook edition), location 2586.

65 David M. Herszenhorn and Elissa Gootman, "Battle Over School Bus Service in City," *NYT,* February 1, 2007; Elissa Gootman, "A Week After Changes, Parents' Complaints Continue," *NYT,* February 6, 2007; Elissa Gootman, "Council Grills City Officials on School Bus Changes," *NYT,* February 14, 2007; Klein, *Lessons of Hope,* location 3421–3444; Diane Cardwell, "For 2 Councilmen, Closed Doors at City Hall," *NYT,* April 13, 2002.

66 Winnie Hu and Steven Greenhouse, "Police Officers, Firefighters and Teachers Share A Protest," *NYT,* June 9, 2004; Jennifer Steinhauer, "Labor Demands Cast A Rich Mayor In A Miserly Light," *NYT,* June 10, 2004; Diane Ravitch and Randi Weingarten, "Public Schools Minus The Public," *NYT,* March 18, 2004; David M. Herszenhorn, "In Subway Ads, Teachers Renew Push for Contract," *NYT,* April 18, 2005; Klein, *Lessons of Hope,* location 2456.

67 Parent Commission on School Governance and Mayoral Control, "Recommendations on School Governance," NYC, March 2009, final report, 1; Jeffrey R. Henig, Eva Gold, Marion Orr, Megan Silander, Elaine Simon, "Parent and Community Engagement in NYC and the Sustainability Challenge for Urban Education Reform," in O'Day, Bitter, and Gomez, eds., *Education Reform in New York City,* 45–8.

68 Javier C. Fernandez, "Senate Impasse Forces City to Revive Old School Board in Name," *NYT,* July 1, 2009; Javier C. Hernandez, "Mayoral School Control Less Assured in Senate," *NYT,* July 5, 2009; Jeremy W. Peters, "In Albany, No Action on School Control for Bloomberg," *NYT,* July 17, 2009; Jennifer S. Lee, "Borough Presidents Seek More Say on Schools," *NYT,* July 24, 2009; New York City Independent Budget Office, "New York City Public School Indicators: Demographics, Resources, Outcomes," May 2013, 1; Paul Hill, "Leadership and Governance in New York City School Reform," in O'Day, Bitter, and Gomez, eds., *Education Reform in New York City,* 17–32.

69 Klein, *Lessons of Hope,* location 3402; Klemper and Nauer, et al., "Managing by the Numbers," 37.

70 Klemper and Nauer, et al., "Managing by the Numbers," 34.

71 Jennifer Medina, "On New York School Tests, Warning Signs Ignored," *NYT,* October 10, 2010; Leonie Haimson, "'Children First': A Short History," in Diane Ravitch et al., *NYC Schools Under Bloomberg and Klein,* 12; Editorial, "The Schools' New Carrot," *NYT,* September 28, 2002; Jane Gross, "Public Lives; A Skeptical and Distant Eye on the Schools," *NYT,* September 3, 2002.

72 New York City Independent Budget Office, "New York City Public School Indicators: Demographics, Resources, Outcomes," May 2013, 35–6.

73 Klein, *Lessons of Hope,* location 3126; Stacey Childress, Monica Higgins, Ann Ishimaru, Sola Takahashi, "Managing for Results at the New York City Department of Education," 100–3.

74 City of New York, Office of the Mayor, "Mayor Bloomberg Delivers 2007 State of the City Address: Taking the Next Step," January 17, 2007, www.nyc.gov; Susan Saulny, "Report Cards of Schools Get Grade of C-Minus," *NYT,* October 1, 2004; Klemper and Nauer, et al., "Managing by the Numbers," 49; Hemphill, Nauer, et al., "Building Blocks for Better Schools," 39; New York City Department of Education, "Children First, Updated 2008–2009," 17; Childress, Higgins, et al., "Managing for Results at the New York City Department of Education," 94–100; Klein, *Lessons of Hope,* location 3138; Steve Koss, "Test Score Inflation: Campbell's Law at Work," in Ravitch et al., *NYC Schools under Bloomberg and Klein*, 88; Aaron M. Pallas and Jennifer L. Jennings, "'Progress' Reports," in Ravitch et al., *NYC Schools Under Bloomberg and Klein*, 99–104.

75 Klemper and Nauer, et al., "Managing by the Numbers," 28.

76 City of New York, Office of the Mayor, "Mayor's Management Report, 2002–2009," Department of Education results; Jennifer Medina, "On New York School Tests, Warning Signs Ignored," *NYT,* October 10, 2010.

77 Medina, "On New York School Tests, Warning Signs Ignored," *NYT,* October 10, 2010; Author's email correspondence, Peter Cunningham, June 14, 2015.

78 David M. Herzenhorn, "Mayor Runs On Schools, But Verdict Is Still Out," *NYT,* October 27, 2005; Michael Winerip, "One Secret To Better Test Scores: Make State Reading Tests Easier," *NYT,* October 5, 2005; Diane Ravitch, "Student Achievement in New York City: The NAEP Results," in Ravitch et al., *NYC Schools under Bloomberg and Klein*, 23; Koss, "Test Score Inflation: Campbell's Law at Work," in Ravitch et al., *NYC Schools Under Bloomberg and Klein,* 87–94; Medina, "On New York School Tests, Warning Signs Ignored," *NYT,* October 10, 2010; Klein, *Lessons of Hope*, 3957–3982; Sol Stern, "Can New York Clean Up the Testing Mess?," *City Journal* (Spring 2010); Author's interview, Joel Klein, March 2, 2015.

79 Author's interview, Joel Klein, March 2, 2015; Elissa Guttman and Robert Gebeloff, "Gains On Tests In New York Schools Don't Silence Critics," *NYT,* August 3, 2009; Medina, "On New York School Tests, Warning Signs Ignored," *NYT,* October 10, 2010; Sol Stern, "Can New York Clean Up the Testing Mess?," *City Journal* (Spring 2010).

80 City of New York, Office of the Mayor, "Mayor's Management Report, 2010," department of education results; Hemphill, Nauer, et al., "Building Blocks for Better Schools," 15; Childress, Higgins, et al., "Managing for Results at the New York City Department of Education," 99–100; Jennifer L. Jennings and Aaron M. Pallas, "The Racial Achievement Gap," in Diane Ravitch et al., *NYC Schools Under*

Bloomberg and Klein, 31–38; Stern, "Can New York Clean Up the Testing Mess?," *City Journal* (Spring 2010).

81 Medina, "On New York School Tests, Warning Signs Ignored," *NYT,* October 10, 2010; City of New York, Office of the Mayor, "Mayor Bloomberg Delivers 2nd Inaugural Address," January 1, 2006.

82 Medina, "On New York School Tests, Warning Signs Ignored," *NYT,* October 10, 2010; Klein, *Lessons of Hope,* location 1478; Sol Stern and Andrew Wolf, "Institutional Cheating," in Ravitch, *NYC Schools Under Bloomberg and Klein,* 115–22.

83 Author's interview, Joel Klein, March 2, 2015.

84 Klein, *Lessons of Hope,* location 4165; Cathie Black, *Basic Black: The Essential Guide for Getting Ahead at Work (and in Life)* (New York: Crown Business, 2007, ebook edition), *passim*; Hemphill, Nauer, et al., "Building Blocks for Better Schools," 17–8; Kelleher, "New York City's Children First," 16; Author's interview, Off the record.

85 Klein, *Lessons of Hope,* location 4165; Hemphill, Nauer, et al., "Building Blocks for Better Schools," 17–8; Kelleher, "New York City's Children First," 16; Author's interview, Dennis Walcott, August 2, 2016.

86 William G. Ouchi with Lydia G. Segal, *Making Schools Work: A Revolutionary Plan to Get Your Children the Education They Need* (New York: Simon & Schuster, 2003, electronic edition), 13–4; Kelleher, "New York City's Children First," 51–3.

87 Klemper and Nauer, et al., "Managing by the Numbers," 10; Kelleher, "New York City's Children First," 51–3; Author's interview, Joel Klein, March 2, 2015; Author's interview, Dennis Walcott, August 2, 2016; Author's interview, Howard Wolfson, August 4, 2016.

88 Author's interview, Gordon Berlin, September 29, 2015; Howard S. Bloom, Saskia Levy Thompson, and Rebecca Untermann, "Transforming the High School Experience: How New York City's New Small Schools Are Boosting Student Achievement and Graduation Rates," MDRC, June 2010, iii, *passim*; Rebecca Untermann, "Headed to College: The Effects of New York City's Small High Schools of Choice on Post-Secondary Education," MDRC Policy Brief, October 2014; Robert Bifulco, Rebecca Untermann, and Howard S. Bloom, "The Relative Cost of New York City's New Small Public High Schools of Choice," MDRC, 2014, iii, *passim*; Howard S. Bloom and Rebecca Untermann, "Sustained Progress: New Findings About the Effectiveness and Operation of New Small Public High Schools of Choice in New York City," MDRC, August 2013, iii, *passim*; Adriana Villavicencio, William H. Marinell, "Inside Success: Strategies of 25 Effective Small High Schools in NYC," NYU Steinhardt School of Culture, Education and Human Development, The Research Alliance for New York City Schools, July 2014, ES1–6 and *passim*.

89 "Charter School Performance in New York City Schools," Center for Research on Educational Outcomes at Stanford University, 2013, 6–10, *passim*; Sean P. Corcoran and Henry M. Levin, "School Choice and Competition in the New York City Schools," in O'Day, Bitter, and Gomez, *Education Reform in New York City,* 222–3; Grover Russ Whitehurst with Sarah Whitfield, "School Choice and School Performance in the New York City Public Schools—Will the Past Be Prologue?," Brown Center on Education Policy at Brookings, October 2013, 2; Paul T. Hill,

"Bloomberg's Education Plan Is Working: Don't Ditch It," *The Atlantic*, October 2013, online edition; Author's interview, Joel Klein, March 2, 2015.

90 Klemper and Nauer, et al., "Managing by the Numbers," 51; Hemphill, Nauer, et al., "Building Blocks for Better Schools," 17–8; New York City Independent Budget Office, "New York City Public School Indicators: Demographics, Resources, Outcomes," May 2013, 19–22; Klein, *Lessons of Hope,* location 2968; Author's interview, Joel Klein, March 2, 2015.

91 Klemper and Nauer, et al., "Managing by the Numbers," 51; Hemphill, Nauer, et al., "Building Blocks for Better Schools," 17–8; The Parthenon Group, "An Assessment of the New York City Department of Education School Support Structure," November 2013, 9; New York City Department of Education, "Strong Schools, Strong Communities: A New Approach to Supporting New York City's Public Schools and All of Our Students," January 2015; Author's interview, Joel Klein, March 2, 2015.

92 Klemper and Nauer, et al., "Managing by the Numbers," 51; Hemphill, Nauer, et al., "Building Blocks for Better Schools," 17–8; New York City Independent Budget Office, "New York City Public School Indicators: Demographics, Resources, Outcomes," May 2013, 19–22; Klein, *Lessons of Hope,* location 2968; Margaret Goertz, Susanna Loeb, and Jim Wyckoff, "Recruiting, Evaluating, and Retaining Teachers: The Children First Strategy to Improve New York City's Teachers," in O'Day, Bitter, and Gomez, *Education Reform in New York City,* 170; Ronald Ferguson, "How Students' Views Predict Graduation Outcomes and Reveal Instructional Disparities Under Children First Reforms,'" in O'Day, Bitter, and Gomez, eds., *Education Reform in New York City,* 225–251; Author's interview, Joel Klein, March 2, 2015.

93 New York City Independent Budget Office, "New York City By The Numbers: Fiscal History Table," December 10, 2014; New York City Independent Budget Office, "Is It Getting Fairer?" 1, *passim*; Leanna Stiefel and Amy Ellen Schwartz, "Financing K-12 Education in the Bloomberg Years, 2002–2008," in O'Day, Bitter, and Gomez, eds., *Education Reform in New York City,* 72; O'Day and Bitter, "Reflections on Children First," in O'Day, Bitter, and Gomez, eds., *Education Reform in New York City,* 303–05; Citizens Budget Commission, "Planning After *PlaNYC*: A Framework for Developing New York City's Next Ten Year Capital Strategy," December 6, 2013, 6.

94 James J. Kemple, "Children First And Student Outcomes: 2003–2010," in O'Day, Bitter and Gomez, eds., 271–5, 288–9; National Assessment of Educational Progress (NAEP) "The Nation's Report Card: Trial Urban District Snapshot Report, New York City Department of Education Public Schools, Reading Grade 4 and Grade 8 and Math Grade 4 and Grade 8," 2002, 2003, 2013 and various years, US Department of Education, Institute of Education Sciences, National Center for Education Statistics; City of New York, Office of the Mayor, "Mayor's Management Report 2013," 122 and prior years education sections for comparative data; Adrian Villavicencio, Dyuti Bhattacharya, Brandon Guidry, "Moving the Needle: Exploring Key Levers to Boost College Readiness Among Black and Latino Males in New York City," NYU Steinhardt School of Culture, Education and Human Development, The Research Alliance for New York City Schools, July 2013, ES1–6; *passim*; John Kucsera with Gary Orfield, "New York State's Extreme

School Segregation: Inequality, Inaction and a Damaged Future," The Civil Rights Project, March 2014, vi–x; Lloyd Grove, "Filling Superman's Shoes," *The Daily Beast,* November 10, 2010; Quinnipiac University Poll, "Schools Chancellor Should Have Education Experience, New York City Voters Tell Quinnipiac University Poll, Bloomberg Approval At Lowest Point in Five Years," November 23, 2010; Author's interview, Joel Klein, March 2, 2015.

95   NAEP, "The Nations Report Card, New York City Department of Education," 2013 and various years; Hemphill, Nauer, et al., "Building Blocks for Better Schools," 11; James J. Kemple, "The Condition of New York City High Schools: Examining Trends and Looking Toward The Future," NYU Steinhardt School of Culture, Education and Human Development, The Research Alliance for New York City Schools, March 2013, 1–3, *passim;* Jennifer L. Jennings and Leonie Haimson, "Discharge and Graduation Rates," in Ravitch et al., *NYC Schools Under Bloomberg and Klein,* 77–85; Author's interview, Joel Klein, March 2, 2015.

96   Author's interview, Joel Klein, March 2, 2015; The New York City Department of Education, "Strong Schools, Strong Communities: A New Approach to Supporting New York City Public Schools and All of Our Students," January 2015, 2; Marist Poll, "Bloomberg, City Schools Receive Low Grades," April 24, 2012; Marist Poll, "Better Scores on Bloomberg's Handling of NYC Public Schools, But . . .," September 28, 2011; Author's interview, Randi Weingarten, May 19, 2015.

97   Hemphill, Nauer, et al., "Building Blocks for Better Schools," 3; "Reforming Underperforming High Schools," MDRC, March 2013; James J. Kemple, "The Condition of New York City High Schools: Examining Trends and Looking Toward The Future," NYU Steinhardt School of Culture, Education and Human Development, The Research Alliance for New York City Schools, March 2013, 1–3.

Chapter 6

1   Partnership for New York City, "NYC Jobs Blueprint," 2013, 17; Mitchell Moss, "A Great Mayor Says Goodbye," *New York Observer,* October 1, 2013.

2   City of New York, Office of the Mayor, "Mayor Michael R. Bloomberg's State of the City Address, Brooklyn Botanic Garden," January 23, 2003; Diane Cardwell, "Bloomberg Plans Quick Start of Citywide 311 Phone System," *NYT,* February 1, 2002; Editorial, "Mayor Bloomberg's State of the City," January 18, 2008; Jim Rutenberg, "Bloomberg Lives By Statistics and Gives Aides a Free Hand," *NYT,* October 18, 2005; Mayor Michael R. Bloomberg, Public Advocate Betsy Gotbaum, Deputy Mayor Edward Skyler, Director, Mayor's Office of Operations Jeffrey A. Kay, "NYC Feedback Citywide Customer Survey: Report of Survey Results," December 2008.

3   Author's interview, Daniel Doctoroff, September 3, 2015; Stephen Goldsmith, *The Entrepreneurial City: A How-To Handbook for Urban Innovators* (New York: The Manhattan Institute, 1999), Introduction, *passim;* Jason Hackworth, *The Neoliberal City: Governance, Ideology, and Development in American Urbanism* (Ithaca, NY: Cornell University Press, ebook edition, 2014), *passim;* Julian Brash, *Bloomberg's New York: Class and Governance in the Luxury City* (Athens: University of Georgia Press, 2011), 4–8; Tom Angotti, *New York for Sale: Community Planning Confronts*

Global Real Estate (Cambridge, MA: MIT Press, 2008), 10–13; Susan Fainstein, *The Just City* (Ithaca, NY: Cornell University Press, 2010), 1–2.

4   Charles Morris, *The Cost of Good Intentions: New York City and the Liberal Experiment, 1960–1975* (New York: McGraw Hill, 1980), *passim*; Martin Shefter, *Political Crisis/Fiscal Crisis: The Collapse and Revival of New York City* (New York: Basic Books, 1985), 127–148; Jonathan Soffer, *Ed Koch and the Rebuilding of New York City* (New York; Columbia University Press, 2010), 117–20, 148–50.

5   City of New York, Office of the Mayor, "Mayor Michael R. Bloomberg's State of the City Address, Brooklyn Botanic Garden," January 23, 2003; Diane Cardwell, "Mayor Says New York Is Worth the Cost," *NYT,* January 8, 2003.

6   Jesse Edgerton, Andrew F. Haughwout, and Rae Rosen, "Revenue Implications of New York City's Tax System," *Current Issues in Economics and Finance, Second District Highlights,* Volume 10, Number 4, April 2004; Jonathan Bowles and Joel Klotkin, "Engine Failure," Center for an Urban Future, 7; "After the Fall," *The Economist*, February 17, 2005; New York State Department of Labor, New York City Current Employment Statistics, January 2002.

7   Bowles and Klotkin, "Engine Failure," 5, 15–17; "After the Fall," *The Economist*, February 17, 2005; Thomas J. Lueck and Jim Rutenberg, "Proposed Science Park Hopes to Lure Biotech to New York," *NYT,* August 11, 2005; Edward I. Glaeser, "Start-Up City," *City Journal* (Autumn 2010), online version.

8   City of New York, Office of the Comptroller, "The City of New York Financial Plan Fiscal Years 2002–2006; "Comprehensive Annual Financial Report of the Comptroller," Fiscal Year 2002; Citizens Budget Commission, "Managing the Budget in the Bloomberg Administration: A Background Paper Prepared for the Citizens Budget Commission Conference on 'New York City's Changing Fiscal Outlook,' IBM Executive Conference Center, Palisades, New York, December 7–8, 2001; Alice Rivlin and Rosemary Scanlon, "Overview," Working Group Reports Prepared for Civic Alliance to Rebuild Downtown New York, September 2002, Section I, 1; New York City Partnership and Chamber of Commerce, "Working Together to Accelerate New York's Recovery," November 2001, *passim*; Jason Bram, Andrew Haugwout, and James Orr, "Special Issue: The Economic Effects of September 11: Has 9/11 Affected New York City's Growth Potential," *Economic Policy Review,* Vol. 8. No. 2; Adam Nagourney, "The 2001 Elections: Mayor; Bloomberg Edges Green in Race for Mayor; McGreevey Is An Easy Winner in New Jersey," *NYT,* November 7, 2001; John Tierney, "The Big City; An Outsider Comes Inside to Run Things," *NYT,* November 8, 2001; Steven Malanga, "How to Rebuild New York," *City Journal* (Autumn 2001); Editorial, "Mayor-elect Michael Bloomberg," *NYT,* November 7, 2001; Author's interview, Robert Yaro, October 1, 2015.

9   Author's interview, Daniel Doctoroff, September 3, 2015; Author's interview, Kathryn Wylde, May 8, 2015; Brash, *Bloomberg's New York,* 87.

10 Brash, *Bloomberg's New York,* 87; Jennifer Steinhauer, "A Survey Asks Companies for Opinions of New York," *NYT,* April 10, 2002; "After the Fall," *The Economist*, February 17, 2005; "Under New Management," *The Economist*, February 17, 2005; Donald J. Boyd, "A Simulation of Business Taxes in New York City and Other Locations," Citizens Budget Commission, June 2, 2007, 3–4; Elizabeth A. Roistacher, "How Much Do Taxes Matter? What Economists Can—and Cannot— Tell NYC Policy Makers," Citizens Budget Commission, December 11, 2006, 3–4.

11 Bowles and Klotkin, "Engine Failure," 2003, 15–23; "After the Fall," *The Economist,*
    February 17, 2005; "Under New Management," *The Economist,* February 17, 2005;
    Group of 35 Task Force, "Preparing for the Future: A Commercial Development
    Strategy for New York City," June 2001, 2–12; Hugh F. Kelly, "The New York
    Regional and Downtown Office Market: History and Prospects After 9/11," in
    Alice Rivlin and Rosemary Scanlon, "Working Group Reports Prepared for Civic
    Alliance to Rebuild Downtown New York," September 2002, Section IV, 1–44;
    Brash, *Bloomberg's New York,* 110–12.

12 "After the Fall," *The Economist,* February 17, 2005; "Under New Management,"
    The Economist, February 17, 2005; Diane Cardwell, "Mayor Says New York Is
    Worth the Cost," *NYT,* January 8, 2003; Brash, *Bloomberg's New York,* 105–10.

13 Cardwell, "Mayor Says New York Is Worth the Cost," *NYT,* January 8, 2003;
    New York City, "News from the Blue Room: Mayor Michael R. Bloomberg Hosts
    Summit on New York City Economic Development for Top CEOs and City
    Leaders," January 7, 2003; New York City Office of the Mayor, "Mayor Michael
    R. Bloomberg's State of the City Address, Brooklyn Botanic Garden," January
    23, 2003; Brash, *Bloomberg's New York,* 105; Email from Seth Pinsky to Author,
    October 28, 2016.

14 Jonathan Mahler, "The Bloomberg Vista," *NYT,* September 10, 2006; Jonathan
    Bowles, "Beyond the Olympics," Center for an Urban Future, 2005, 2; "Under
    New Management," *The Economist,* February 17, 2005; City of New York,
    Office of the Mayor, "Mayor Michael R. Bloomberg's State of the City Address,
    Brooklyn Botanic Garden," January 23, 2003; City of New York, Office of the
    Mayor; "Mayor Bloomberg Looks Back at New York City on September 12, 2001
    and Outlines Progress on Economic Recovery, Major Growth in Population and
    Historic Decreases in Crime," September 12, 2013.

15 Author's interview, Daniel Doctoroff, September 3, 2015; Author's interview,
    Robert Yaro, October 1, 2015.

16 Author's interview, Jonathan Bowles, May 8, 2015; Author's interview, Steven
    Spinola, May 21, 2015; Author's interview, Robert Yaro, October 1, 2015; Author's
    interview, Tom Wright, October 26, 2015; Neil Scott Kleiman, "The Sector
    Solution: Building a Broader Base for the New Economy," The Center for an Urban
    Future, January 2000, 11; Jonathan Bowles, "Economic Development Overview:
    A Look at Economic Development Issues Likely to Face our Next Mayor," Center
    for an Urban Future, May 2001; Jonathan Bowles, "A Case for a Sector Based
    Economic Development Strategy," Testimony of Center Research Director Jonathan
    Bowles before the New York City Council's Economic Development Committee,
    The Center for an Urban Future, June 2002, 1–3; Joan Fitzgerald, "Retention
    Deficit Disorder," The Center for an Urban Future, March 2002; Charles V. Bagli,
    "Bear Stearns and City Hall Hit an Impasse on Tax Breaks," *NYT,* January 6, 2003;
    Jonathan Bowles, "Beyond the Olympics," Center for an Urban Future, 2005, 2–3,
    7; Soffer, *Ed Koch and the Rebuilding of New York,* 290–304.

17 Geraldine Frabrikant, "The 2001 Election: Ethics; Bloomberg Turns Down Tax
    Break for Business," *NYT,* November 8, 2001; Bowles, "Beyond the Olympics,"
    2; Partnership for New York City, "NYC Jobs Blueprint," 2013, 17; City of New
    York, Office of the Comptroller, "Audit Report on the New York City Industrial
    Development Agency's Project Financing, Evaluation and Monitoring Process,"

March 19, 2012; Author's interview, Daniel Doctoroff, September 3, 2015; Author's interview, Jonathan Bowles, May 8, 2015.

18 City of New York, Office of the Mayor; "Mayor Bloomberg Looks Back at New York City on September 12, 2001 and Outlines Progress on Economic Recovery, Major Growth in Population and Historic Decreases in Crime," September 12, 2013; New York City Partnership and Chamber of Commerce, "Working Together to Accelerate New York's Recovery," November 2001, *passim*; Joan Fitzgerald, "Attention Deficit Disorder," The Center for an Urban Future, March 2002; Jonathan Bowles, "Testimony of Jonathan Bowles, Research Director, before New York City's IDA Board on the question of New York Stock Exchange Financing," The Center for an Urban Future, October 2001; Charles V. Bagli, "Staying or Not, Wall St. Giants Could Reap Aid," *NYT,* March 21, 2002; Michael Cooper, "Mayor Says Leaner City Must Still Invest in Economic Growth," *NYT,* October 22, 2003; Patrick McGeehan, "Officials Defend Actions to Keep Goldman Sachs Downtown," *NYT,* August 12, 2005; Jonathan Mahler, "The Bloomberg Vista," *NYT,* September 10, 2006.

19 Author's interview, Daniel Doctoroff, September 3, 2015.

20 Author's interview, Robert Steel, May 15, 2015; Author's interview, Seth Pinsky, May 12, 2015; Author's interview, Robert Lieber, May 21, 2015; Author's interview, Kyle Kimball, September 23, 2015.

21 Author's interview, Steven Spinola, May 21, 2015; Author's interview, Robert Yaro, October 2, 2015; Author's interview, Tom Wright, October 26, 2015; Author's interview, Robert Steel, May 15, 2015; Author's interview, Seth Pinsky, May 12, 2015; Author's interview, Robert Lieber, May 21, 2015; Author's interview, Kyle Kimball, September 23, 2015.

22 Brash, *Bloomberg's New York,* 96; Jennifer Steinhauer, "A Survey Asks Companies for Opinions of New York," *NYT,* April 10, 2002; Bowles, "A Case for a Sector Based Economic Development Strategy," Testimony of Center Research Director Jonathan Bowles before the New York City Council's Economic Development Committee, 2; Bowles, "Beyond the Olympics," 3; Author's interview, Jonathan Bowles, May 8, 2015.

23 Bowles, "A Case for a Sector Based Economic Development Strategy," 2; Bowles, "Beyond the Olympics," 3; Alice Rivlin and Rosemary Scanlon, "Findings and Recommendations: Working Group Reports Prepared for Civic Alliance to Rebuild Downtown New York," September 2002, Section II, 10–18; Author's interview, Kathryn Wylde, May 8, 2015.

24 Author's interview, Robert Steel, May 15, 2015; Author's interview, Seth Pinsky, May 12, 2015; Author's interview, Robert Lieber, May 21, 2015; Author's interview, Daniel Doctoroff, September 3, 2015.

25 Author's interview, Dan Doctoroff, September 3, 2015; Author's interview, Robert Steel, May 15, 2015; Brash, *Bloomberg's New York,* 96; Erica Bergen, "The Leading Lady Behind New York City's Revitalized Entertainment Business," *Digital Hollywood,* September 30, 2013; John Gapper, "Are We No Longer the World's Financial Capital?," *New York,* October 25, 2007; McKinsey & Company, "Sustaining New York's and the US' Global Financial Leadership," (2006), ii; Bowles, "A Case for a Sector Based Economic Development Strategy," Testimony of Center Research Director Jonathan Bowles before the New York City Council's

Economic Development Committee, 2; Bowles, "Beyond the Olympics," 3; Author's interview, Jonathan Bowles, May 8, 2015.

26 Thomas J. Lueck and Jim Rutenberg, "Proposed Science Park Hopes to Lure Biotech to New York," *NYT,* August 11, 2005; Daniel Hemel, "Mayor Unveils Plans for $700 Million Biotechnology Center," *New York Sun*, August 11, 2005; Jim O'Grady and Jonathan Bowles, "Building New York's Innovation Economy," The Center for an Urban Future, 8; Author's interview, Jonathan Bowles, May 8, 2015; Author's interview, Daniel Doctoroff, September 3, 2015; Partnership for New York City, "NYC Jobs Blueprint," 2013, 19.

27 Bowles, "Beyond the Olympics," 5; Erica Bergen, "The Leading Lady Behind New York City's Revitalized Entertainment Business," *Digital Hollywood*, September 30, 2013; New York State Department of Labor, Division of Research and Statistics, Bureau of Labor Market Information, "New York's Motion Picture Industry: A Statewide and Regional Analysis" (June 2014), 3; Casey Cirpriani, "Lights, Camera, Action! The Bloomberg Legacy," *New York City News Service* (undated); "City Talk: Katherine Oliver, Commissioner, Mayor's Office of Film, Theater, Broadcasting" (CUNY75), June 25, 2011.

28 Author's interview, Kyle Kimball, September 23, 2015; New York City Economic Development Corporation and Oliver Wyman, "Media.NYC.2020," 2010, *passim*; The Boston Consulting Group, "Evaluating NYC Media Sector Development and Setting the Stage for Future Growth: Final Report," May 8, 2012, *passim*.

29 Erica Bergen, "The Leading Lady Behind New York City's Revitalized Entertainment Business," *Digital Hollywood*, September 30, 2013; The Boston Consulting Group, "Evaluating NYC Media Sector Development and Setting the Stage for Future Growth: Final Report," May 8, 2012, 2, 6, 22–3; New York City Economic Development Corporation and Oliver Wyman, "Media.NYC.2020," 2010, 5; Robert Keegan, Neil Kleiman, Beth Seigel, and Michael Kane, "Creative New York," Center for an Urban Future, December 2005, 14; New York State Department of Labor, Division of Research and Statistics, Bureau of Labor Market Information, "New York's Motion Picture Industry: A Statewide and Regional Analysis," June 2014, 3; Author's interview, Robert Yaro, October 1, 2015.

30 Bob Herbert, "In America; the Tourism Crisis," *NYT,* November 29, 2001.

31 Author's interview, Off the record; Jennifer Steinhauer, "Suddenly, It's Art for Arts Stake; Bloomberg's Hearty Embrace Signals A Whole New Approach at City Hall," *NYT,* July 3, 2002; Jennifer Steinhauer, "The Arts Administration," *NYT,* October 23, 2005; New York City, Mayor's Management Report, 2002–2006; Citizens Budget Commission, "Planning After PlaNYC: A Framework for Developing New York City's Next Ten-Year Capital Strategy," 2013, 6.

32 Author's interview, Adrian Benepe, September 29, 2015.

33 Carolyn Curiel, "At Last the Gates Wave in Central Park," *NYT,* February 12, 2005; Campbell Robertson, "A Last Look at 'The Gates,'" *NYT,* February 28, 2005; Jane Isay, "The Gates in the Park: A Midwinter Day's Dream," Letters to the Editor, *NYT,* February 15, 2005; Robin Pogrebin and Michael M. Grynbaum, "Art Groups Fear Losing a Mayor and His Money," *NYT,* July 2, 2013; Author's interview, Adrian Benepe, September 29, 2015.

34 NYC & Co. "New York City Tourism: A Model for Success," 2013, 23–30; NYC & Co., "Economic Impact of Travel and Tourism," Revised September 2, 2014;

Patrick McGeehan, "Happy With Tourist Influx, City Wants Even More Visitors," *NYT,* February 20, 2013.

35 Author's interview, Kyle Kimball, September 23, 2015; City of New York, Office of the Mayor, "Mayor Bloomberg Delivers 2009 State of the City Address," January 15, 2009.

36 City of New York, Office of the Mayor, "Mayor Bloomberg Delivers 2009 State of the City Address," January 15, 2009; Author's interview, Robert Steel, May 15, 2015; Author's interview, Seth Pinsky, May 12, 2015.

37 Author's interview, Robert Steel, May 15, 2015; Author's interview, Seth Pinsky, May 12, 2015; Author's interview, Robert Lieber, May 21, 2015; Author's interview, Robert Yaro, October 1, 2015.

38 Author's interview, Robert Steel, May 15, 2015; Author's interview, Seth Pinsky, May 12, 2015; Author's interview, Robert Yaro, October 1, 2015.

39 Author's interview, Robert Steel, May 15, 2015.

40 Author's interview, Robert Steel, May 15, 2015.

41 Author's interview, Robert Steel, May 15, 2015; Richard Pérez-Peña, "Building a Better Tech School," *NYT,* April 12, 2013; City of New York, Office of the Mayor, "Press Release: Mayor Bloomberg Officially Transfers 12 Acres of Roosevelt Island to Cornell Tech," December 19, 2013; Ariel Kaminer, "New Cornell Technology School Tightly Bound to Business," *NYT,* January 21, 2013.

42 Author's interview, Robert Steel, May 15, 2015; Author's interview, Seth Pinsky, May 12, 2015; Author's interview, Off the record; YouTube Video, Mike Bloomberg Speaks at Cornell Tech Groundbreaking, January 16, 2015; City of New York, Office of the Mayor, "Press Release: Mayor Bloomberg Officially Transfers 12 Acres of Roosevelt Island to Cornell Tech," December 19, 2013; Richard Pérez-Peña, "Cornell Alumnus Is Behind $350 Million Gift to Build Science School in City," *NYT,* December 19, 2011.

43 City of New York, Office of the Mayor, "Press Release: Mayor Bloomberg Officially Transfers 12 Acres of Roosevelt Island to Cornell Tech," December 19, 2013; Richard Pérez-Peña, "Cornell Alumnus Is Behind $350 Million Gift to Build Science School in City," *NYT,* December 19, 2011; Michael Grynbaum, "DeBlasio and Bloomberg Trade Rare Praise. No Hug, Though," *NYT,* June 16, 2015; Author's interview, Robert Steel, May 15, 2015; Author's interview, Mitchell Moss, September 23, 2015.

44 Ariel Kaminer, "New Cornell Technology School Tightly Bound to Business," *NYT,* January 21, 2013; Charles V. Bagli, "Google Signs Deal to Buy Manhattan Office Building," *NYT,* December 2, 2010; Eric P. Newcomer, "Columbia Gets $15 Million to Expand a School," *NYT,* July 30, 2012; Steve Lohr, "Microsoft Taps Yahoo Scientists for New Research Lab," *NYT,* May 3, 2012; New Tech City with Manoush Zamorodi, "Google's Top NYC Engineer on City's Tech Economy," WNYC, September 18, 2013; Manoursh Zamorodi, "NYC Tech: Who's Your Daddy," WNYC, September 18, 2013; Author's interview, Kathryn Wylde, May 8, 2015; The Boston Consulting Group, "Evaluating NYC Media Sector Development and Setting the Stage for Future Growth: Final Report," May 8, 2012, 2.

45 Author's interview, Robert Steel, May 15, 2015; Author's interview, Seth Pinsky, May 12, 2015; Author's interview, Robert Lieber, May 21, 2015; City of New York,

Office of the Mayor, "Mayor Bloomberg Welcomes First 27 Start-Up Companies to City Sponsored Incubator and Announces Plans for Expansion," September 1, 2009; Author's interview, Kyle Kimball, September 23, 2015.

46 Author's interview, Jonathan Bowles, May 8, 2015; Author's interview, Kathryn Wylde, May 8, 2015; Author's interview, Robert Yaro, October 1, 2015; Manoursh Zamorodi, "NYC Tech: Who's Your Daddy," WNYC, September 18, 2013.

47 City of New York, "New York City Industrial Policy: Protecting and Growing New York City's Industrial Job Base," January 2005; Laura Wolf Powers, "Twilight Zoning," The Center for an Urban Future, November 2003; Author's interview, Amanda Burden, July 20, 2015; Author's interview, Robert Yaro, October 1, 2015; Sean Campion, "A Profile of New York City's Industrial Workforce," New York City Independent Budget Office, June, 2014; Author's interview, Jonathan Bowles, May 8, 2015; "The Start of a NYC Manufacturing Revival," Center for an Urban Future, March 2014.

48 Powers, "Twilight Zoning," Center for an Urban Future (2003); Jennifer Gerend, "The Outrage Over New York's Storefront Awning Ticket Blitz Is Justified—But So Are the Limits," The Center for an Urban Future, August 2003; Laura Vanderkam, "Where Did the Korean Greengrocers Go?," City Journal (Winter 2011); Author's interview, Robert Yaro, October 1, 2015; Amobio Morelix, Joshua Russell, Robert W. Fairlie, E.J. Reedy, "The Kauffman Index: Main Street Entrepreneurship 2015," Ewing Marion Kauffman Foundation, December 2015, 7, 10.

49 Author's interview, Amanda Burden, July 20, 2015; City of New York Planning Commission, Department of City Planning, "Zoning Handbook: Guide to the Zoning Resolution of the City of New York, 1961," 16–26; Peter D. Salins, "Liberating Development," City Journal (July 10, 2009); Amy Armstrong, Vicki Breen, Josiah Madar, Simon McDonnell, "How Have Recent Rezonings Affected the City's Ability to Grow," Furman Center for Real Estate and Urban Policy, New York University, March 2010.

50 Author's interview, Amanda Burden, July 20, 2015; City of New York Planning Commission, Department of City Planning, "Zoning Handbook: Guide to the Zoning Resolution of the City of New York, 1961," 10–14; Michael Brick, "Nancy Drew and the Hidden Loft," NYT, April 16, 2005; Peter D. Salins, "Liberating Development," City Journal (July 10, 2009).

51 Author's interview, Amanda Burden, July 20, 2015; New York City Planning Commission, "Mission," www.nyc.gov; Ralph Gardner Jr., "Social Planner," New York, May 13, 2002.

52 Brash, Bloomberg's New York, 84; Michael Cooper, "Mayor Adds Six Members to His Team," NYT, January 16, 2002; Ralph Gardner Jr., "Social Planner," New York, May 13, 2002; Author's interview, Off the record; Author's interview, Amanda Burden, July 20, 2015.

53 Author's interview, Amanda Burden, July 20, 2015; City of New York, Department of City Planning, "Zoning Handbook 2011 Edition," 2011, Preface.

54 Author's interview, Amanda Burden, July 20, 2015; Author's interview, Daniel Doctoroff, September 3, 2015; Russ Buettner and Ray Rivera, "A Stalled Vision: Big Development As City's Future," NYT, October 28, 2009.

55 Author's interview, Jonathan Bowles, May 8, 2015; Author's interview, Amanda Burden, July 20, 2015; Amy Armstrong, Vicki Breen, Josiah Madar, Simon

McDonnell, "How Have Recent Rezonings Affected the City's Ability to Grow"; City of New York, "New York City Industrial Policy: Protecting and Growing New York City's Industrial Job Base," January 2005; Janny Scott, "In a Still-Growing City, Some Neighborhoods Say, Slow Down," *NYT,* October 10, 2005; Peter D. Salins, "Liberating Development," *City Journal* (July 10, 2009), online version.

56 Author's interview, Jonathan Bowles, May 8, 2015; Author's interview, Amanda Burden, July 20, 2015; Armstrong, Breen, Madar, McDonnell, "How Have Recent Rezonings Affected the City's Ability to Grow," Furman Center; City of New York, "New York City Industrial Policy: Protecting and Growing New York City's Industrial Job Base," January 2005; Janny Scott, "In a Still-Growing City, Some Neighborhoods Say, Slow Down," *NYT,* October 10, 2005; Peter D. Salins, "Liberating Development," *City Journal* (July 10, 2009), online version.

57 Author's interview, Daniel Doctoroff, September 3, 2015.

58 Author's interview, Daniel Doctoroff, September 3, 2015; Author' interview, Adrian Benepe, September 29, 2015; Author's interview, Off the record.

59 City of New York, "PlaNYC: A Greener, Greater New York," April 2007; Julian Brash, *Bloomberg's New York*, 105–10.

60 Author's interview, Gifford Miller, October 24, 2014; "Special Report New York: Under New Management," *The Economist*, February 17, 2005; Liz Robbins and Mike McIntire, "A True Champion of Grand Plans and Tiny Details; With the Zeal of An Athlete, Doctoroff Pursues Olympics," *NYT,* May 16, 2004; Craig Horowitz, "Stadium of Dreams," *New York,* June 21, 2004; Tom Robbins, "Giving and Getting; Bloomberg and Doctoroff: Reshaping the City's Skyline for the Olympics," *Village Voice,* January 25, 2005; Tom Robbins, "The Deputy Mayor for the Olympics," *Village Voice,* January 25, 2005; Tom Robbins, "A Fool's Gold: Doctoroff's Legacy; No Olympic Medal, No Ground Zero Mettle," *Village Voice,* December 4, 2007.

61 Author's interview, Kathryn Wylde, May 8, 2015; Author's interview, Jay Kriegel, September 22, 2014; Author's interview, Steven Spinola, May 21, 2015; Moss, "How New York City Won the Olympics," Rudin Center for Transportation and Management, 2, 13; Robert Kolker, "Olympic City, N.Y.," *New York,* October 28, 2002; Jim Rutenberg, "Mayor Says Olympic Bid Was Worth a Shot," *NYT,* July 7, 2005; Robbins, "Giving and Getting," *Village Voice,* January 25, 2005.

62 Charles V. Bagli, "Chasing Dream of Olympics, Stadium and All, for New York," *NYT,* November 2, 2002; Robbins and McIntire, "A True Champion of Grand Plans and Tiny Details; With the Zeal of an Athlete, Doctoroff Pursues Olympics," *NYT,* May 16, 2004; Sewell Chan, "Doctoroff Is Leaving Bloomberg Administration," *NYT,* December 6, 2007.

63 Author's interview, Daniel Doctoroff, September 3, 2015; Bagli, "Chasing Dream of Olympics, Stadium and All, for New York," *NYT,* November 2, 2002; Robbins and McIntire, "A True Champion of Grand Plans and Tiny Details; With the Zeal of an Athlete, Doctoroff Pursues Olympics," *NYT,* May 16, 2004; Rutenberg, "Mayor Says Olympic Bid Was Worth a Shot," *NYT,* July 7, 2005; Chan, "Doctoroff Is Leaving Bloomberg Administration," *NYT,* December 6, 2007; NYC2012, "The Olympic Games in the World's Second Home," Volume 1, 2001, 11; Jan Hoffman, "Public Lives; Man with a Five Ring Dream for New York," *NYT,* March 21, 2000.

64 Author's interview, Daniel Doctoroff, September 3, 2015.

65 Author's interview, Daniel Doctoroff, September 3, 2015; Hoffman, "Public Lives; Man with a Five Ring Dream for New York," *NYT*, March 21, 2000; Kolker, "Olympic City, N.Y.," *New York*, October 28, 2002; Alexander Garvin, *The American City: What Works, What Doesn't* (New York: McGraw Hill, 1996, third edition 2014), Preface to the First Edition, xiii.

66 Author's interview, Daniel Doctoroff, September 3, 2015; Robbins and McIntire, "A True Champion of Grand Plans and Tiny Details; With the Zeal of an Athlete, Doctoroff Pursues Olympics," *NYT*, May 16, 2004; Blair Golson, "Doctoroff Olympiad," *The New York Observer*, November 29, 2004; Craig Horowitz, "Stadium of Dreams," *New York*, June 21, 2004; Rutenberg, "Mayor Says Olympic Bid Was Worth a Shot," *NYT*, July 7, 2005.

67 Robbins and McIntire, "A True Champion of Grand Plans and Tiny Details; With the Zeal of an Athlete, Doctoroff Pursues Olympics," *NYT*, May 16, 2004; Golson, "Doctoroff Olympiad," *The New York Observer*, November 29, 2004; Craig Horowitz, "Stadium of Dreams," *New York*, June 21, 2004.

68 Terry Pristin, "Zoning Changes Fail to Attract Businesses to Long Island City," *NYT*, July 6, 2002; Mitchell Moss, "How New York City Won the Olympics," 2, 46; New York City Economic Development Corporation, "Press Release: Mayor Bloomberg Joins Phipps Houses, Related Companies and Monadnock To Break Ground on First Two Residential Buildings at Hunter's Point South on Queens Waterfront," March 4, 2013.

69 Moss, "How New York City Won the Olympics," 44–6; Alexandra Lange, "The Brooklyn and Queens Waterfront in 2016," *New York*, June 5, 2006; Author's interview, Amanda Burden, July 20, 2016.

70 Tom Robbins, "Terminal Solution: Doctoroff's Developer Pal Lands a Deal in the Bronx," *Village Voice*, April 6, 2004; Joseph Berger, "Exhilaration as Giant Mall Springs Up in a Strike Against Blight," *NYT*, September 4, 2009; Jill Gardiner, "City Council Probe Set for Bronx Market As Vendors Press Lawsuit Against City," *New York Sun*, June 27, 2005; Charles V. Bagli and Robin Shulman, "Transforming Bronx Terminal Market, But At a Steep Price," *NYT*, October 24, 2005; Susan S. Fainstein, "Global Transformation and the Malling of the South Bronx," location 2699–2851 in Jerilou Hammett and Kingsley Hammet, eds., *The Suburbanization of New York* (New York: Princeton Architectural Press, ebook edition, 2007).

71 Moss, "How New York City Won the Olympics," 60–2; Michael Saul, "'Decrepit' Armory's Fresh Look," *Daily News*, September 7, 2006; Tom Perrotta, "A Tennis Renaissance Arrives in Harlem," *The New York Sun*, October 2, 2006; New York City Economic Development Corporation, "Press Release: Mayor Bloomberg, City Council Speaker Quinn, Borough President Carrion and the Related Companies Break Ground on Gateway Center at Bronx Terminal Market," August 14, 2006; Author's interview, Adrian Benepe, September 29, 2015.

72 Robbins and McIntire, "A True Champion of Grand Plans and Tiny Details; With the Zeal of an Athlete, Doctoroff Pursues Olympics," *NYT*, May 16, 2004; Moss, "How New York City Won the Olympics," 19–36; Brash, *Bloomberg's New York*, 144–55; Author's interview, Daniel Doctoroff, September 3, 2015.

73 Moss, "How New York City Won the Olympics," 19–36; Brash, *Bloomberg's New York,* 144–55; Charles V. Bagli and Mike McIntire, "Mayor and Council Reach Deal on West Side Development," *NYT,* January 11, 2005.

74 Group of 35 Task Force, "Preparing for the Future: A Commercial Development Strategy for New York City," June 2001, 2–12; Charles V. Bagli, "Schumer Proposals Address Shortage of Office Space," *NYT,* June 11, 2001; Author's interview, Robert Yaro, October 1, 2015; Author's interview, Tom Wright, October 26, 2015; Author's interview, Amanda Burden, July 20, 2015.

75 Moss, "How New York City Won the Olympics," 19–36; Brash, *Bloomberg's New York,* 144–55; "The Mayoral Transition; Mayor's Speech, 'Rebuild, Renew and Remain the Capital of the Free World,'" *NYT,* January 2, 2002.

76 Moss, "How New York City Won the Olympics," 19–36; Brash, *Bloomberg's New York,* 144–55; Richard Sandomir, "Pro Football; Johnson has the Team; Now for a New Stadium," *NYT,* January 19, 2000.

77 Author's interview, Amanda Burden, December 22, 2016; Moss, "How New York City Won the Olympics," 19–36; Brash, *Bloomberg's New York,* 144–55; Author's interview, Daniel Doctoroff, September 3, 2015; Author's interview, Amanda Burden, July 20, 2015.

78 Author's interview, Jay Kriegel, September 22, 2014; Author's interview, Dean Fuleihan, August 12, 2015.

79 Moss, "How New York Won the Olympics," 27–8; Author's interview, Jay Kriegel, September 22, 2014.

80 Robbins and McIntire, "A True Champion of Grand Plans and Tiny Details; With the Zeal of an Athlete, Doctoroff Pursues Olympics," *NYT,* May 16, 2004; Blair Golson, "Kalikow Waiting for $1.2 Billion Olympiad," *The New York Observer,* May 24, 2004; Golson, "Doctoroff Olympiad," *The New York Observer,* November 29, 2004; Marc Speigler, "A Come-From-Behind Plan to Land the Olympics," *New York,* February 21, 2005; Peter Keating, "Another Kind of Moneyball," *New York*, January 17, 2005.

81 Charles V. Bagli, "Jets and Rivals Increase Bids for Railyards," *NYT,* March 22, 2005; Tom Robbins, "Win One for the Gyppers," *Village Voice,* March 29, 2005; Susan S. Fainstein, "The Return of Urban Renewal: Dan Doctoroff's Grand Plans for New York City," *Harvard Design Magazine,* Spring/Summer 2005, 1–5; Author's interview, Richard Ravitch, May 19, 2015; George Vecsey, "New York is Jumping the Gun on a Stadium," *NYT,* January 20, 2005; Jim Rutenberg, "A Bloomberg Victory At a Price," *NYT,* April 1, 2005.

82 Craig Horowitz, "Stadium of Dreams," *New York,* June 21, 2004; Robbins, "Giving and Getting," *Village Voice,* January 25, 2005; Jim Rutenberg, "Bloomberg Lives by Statistics and Gives Aides a Free Hand," *NYT,* October 18, 2005; The Regional Plan Association, "Urban Development Alternatives for the Hudson Rail Yards," December 2004; The Regional Plan Association, "Study Shows Mixed-Use Development Outperforms Stadium on Far West Side," February 3, 2005; Author's interview, Daniel Doctoroff, September 3, 2015; Author's interview, Robert Yaro, October 1, 2015; Author's interview, Tom Wright, October 1, 2015; Quinnipiac University Poll, "Mayor Should Control Ground Zero Development, Voters Oppose Stadium But Say It Will Pass," May 12, 2005.

83 Author's interview, Daniel Doctoroff, September 3, 2015; Author's interview, Amanda Burden, July 20, 2015; Mike McIntire, "Mayor and Speaker, Face to Face but Not Agreeing," *NYT,* June 6, 2005; Brash, *Bloomberg's New York*, 239–42.

84 Peter Keating, "The Big End Run," *New York,* December 6, 2004; Michael Cooper and Charles V. Bagli, "Board's Vote on a Stadium Is Still in Doubt," *NYT,* June 2, 2005; McIntire, "Mayor and Speaker, Face to Face But Not Agreeing," *NYT,* June 6, 2005; Charles V. Bagli, Jim Rutenberg, Michael Cooper, and Jennifer Steinhauer, "Requiem for West Side Stadium: Overtures Were Made Too Late," *NYT,* June 8, 2005; Bob Herbert, "A Blessing for Bloomberg," *NYT,* June 9, 2005; Brash, *Bloomberg's New York*, 239–42; Editorial, "A Stand Against the Stadium," *NYT,* June 7, 2005; Author's interview, Off the record; Author's interview, Dean Fuleihan, August 12, 2015.

85 Keating, "The Big End Run," *New York,* December 6, 2004; Jim Rutenberg and Charles V. Bagli, "In City's Push for Stadium, Silver's District Reaps Benefits," *NYT,* April 25, 2005; Cooper and Bagli, "Board's Vote on a Stadium Is Still in Doubt," *NYT,* June 2, 2005; McIntire, "Mayor and Speaker, Face to Face But Not Agreeing," *NYT,* June 6, 2005; Bagli, Rutenberg, Cooper, and Steinhauer, "Requiem for West Side Stadium: Overtures Were Made Too Late," *NYT,* June 8, 2005; Herbert, "A Blessing for Bloomberg," *NYT,* June 9, 2005; Mike McIntire and Jim Rutenberg, "After Stadium Bid Fails, a Disheartened Bloomberg Worries for City," *NYT,* June 8, 2005; Brash, *Bloomberg's New York*, 239–42.

86 Author's interview, Marc Shaw, July 29, 2014; Author's interview, Robert Yaro, October 1, 2015.

87 Moss, "How New York Won the Olympics," 54–5; Lynn Zinser and Jim Rutenberg, "New Look at Queens Stadium Option With Mets," *NYT,* June 11, 2005; Charles V. Bagli and Mike McIntire, "Taxpayer Expense Is Less In Deal for New Stadium," *NYT,* June 14, 2005; Michael Brick, "Queens Sighs at Mayor's New Olympic Plan," *NYT,* June 14, 2005; Editorial, "Did Someone Say Queens?," *NYT,* June 14, 2005; Richard Sandomir, "Bronx Is Up as Yankees Unveil Stadium Plan," *NYT,* June 16, 2005; Geoffrey Gray, "Doctor, Doctor! PR Rx for Doctoroff," *New York,* October 24, 2007; Author's interview, Daniel Doctoroff, September 3, 2015.

88 Author's interview, Steven Spinola, May 21, 2015; Author's interview, Robert Yaro, October 1, 2015; Author's interview, Tom Wright, October 26, 2015; Author's interview, Amanda Burden, December 22, 2016; Charles V. Bagli, "No Stadium, No Problem," *NYT,* June 12, 2005; Anthony Weiss and Alex Appelbaum, "West World," *New York,* December 3, 2007; Charles V. Bagli, "West Side Redevelopment Plans in Disarray," *NYT,* April 14, 2008; Robert C. Lieber, "Letter to the Editor: Hudson Yards," *NYT,* April 25, 2008; Justin Davidson, "From 0 to 12 Million Square Feet," *New York*, October 7, 2012; Charles V. Bagli, "Time Warner Intends to Move to Planned Skyscraper at Hudson Yards," *NYT,* July 1, 2013; Katherine Clarke, "Real Estate Gain the Related Companies Breaks Ground on First Residential Towers at Hudson Yards," *Daily News,* December 4, 2014; The Related Companies, "Hudson Yards Press Kit," January 21, 2015; Department of City Planning Maps dated February 2010, in the author's possession.

89 Moss, "How New York Won the Olympics," 33–5; Kurt Anderson, "The Little Abandoned Train Line That Could, Did," *New York,* December 20, 2004; Thomas Demonchaux, "How Everyone Jumped Aboard a Railroad to Nowhere," *NYT,*

May 8, 2005; Paul Vitello, "Rusty Railroad Advances on Road to Pristine Park," *NYT,* June 15, 2005; Author's interview, Amanda Burden, July 20, 2015; Author's interview, Daniel Doctoroff, September 3, 2015; Author's interview, Tom Wright, October 26, 2015.

90   Moss, "How New York City Won the Olympics," 44–6; Alexandra Lange, "The Brooklyn and Queens Waterfront in 2016," *New York,* June 5, 2006; Robbins, "Terminal Solution," *Village Voice,* April 6, 2004; Berger, "Exhilaration as Giant Mall Springs Up in a Strike Against Blight," *NYT,* September 4, 2009; Gardiner, "City Council Probe Set for Bronx Market As Vendors Press Lawsuit Against City," *New York Sun,* June 27, 2005; Bagli and Shulman, "Transforming Bronx Terminal Market, But At a Steep Price," *NYT,* October 24, 2005; Winnie Hu, "2 Companies Plan to Expand and Add Jobs in Hunts Point," *NYT,* December 2, 2005; Robin Shulman and Diane Cardwell, "Weiner Attacks City Deal on Bronx Market," *NYT,* August 25, 2005; Juan Gonzalez, "Bronx Gateway Center Mall Has Turned Out To Be A Great Deal – For Developers," *Daily News,* June 24, 2011; Susan S. Fainstein, "Global Transformation and the Malling of the South Bronx," location 2699–2851 in Jerilou Hammett and Kingsley Hammet, eds., *The Suburbanization of New York* (New York: Princeton Architectural Press, 2007, ebook edition); Alan Feuer, "Where Will New Yorkers Go To Buy Burnt Cow Feet?" *NYT,* April 24, 2005; Damien Cave, "City Sees Growth; Residents Call it Out of Control," *NYT,* November 6, 2006; Mike Jaccarino, "Parks Near Yankee Stadium Set to Open, But Critics Say City Is Still Shortchanging Residents," *Daily News,* June 21, 2010; Author's interview, Ruben Diaz Jr., October 6, 2015.

91   Williams Cole, "Construction/Destruction of Williamsburg Continues at Frantic Pace," *The Brooklyn Mail,* December 8, 2006; Charles V. Bagli, "$1.4 Billion Development At Sugar Refinery in Brooklyn Wins Key Council Support," *NYT,* June 29, 2010; Adam Bonislowski, "Greenpoint, Get Ready to Get Williamsburg-ed," *NYP,* March 25, 2015; Stephen Farrell, "Williamsburg: Not What It Was," *NYT,* March 11, 2013; Author's interview, Adrian Benepe, September 29, 2015.

92   Chris Smith, "Mr. Ratner's Neighborhood," *New York,* November 13, 2006; Nicole Gelinas, "Eminent Domain As Central Planning," *City Journal* (Winter 2010); Michael Clancy, "Not Everyone Is Sad to See Doctoroff Go," *Runnin' Scared, Village Voice Blog,* December 10, 2007; Andrea Bernstein, "New York Remade: Before and After Bloomberg," WNYC, December 27, 2013.

93   Author's interview, Robert Yaro, October 1, 2015; Author's interview, Tom Wright, October 26, 2015; Robbins, "Giving and Getting," *Village Voice,* January 25, 2005; Golson, "Doctoroff Olympiad," *New York Observer,* November 29, 2004; Horowitz, "Stadium of Dreams," *New York,* June 21, 2004; Chris Smith, "The Stadium's Silver Lining," *New York,* June 20, 2005; Gray, "Doctor, Doctor! PR Rx for Doctoroff," *New York,* October 24, 2007; Clancy, "Not Everyone Is Sad to See Doctoroff Go," *Daily News,* December 10, 2007; Brash, *Bloomberg's New York,* 202.

94   Robbins, "Giving and Getting; Bloomberg and Doctoroff: Reshaping the City's Skyline for the Olympics," *Village Voice,* January 25, 2005; Golson, "Doctoroff Olympiad," *New York Observer,* November 29, 2004; Horowitz, "Stadium of Dreams," *New York,* June 21, 2004; Smith, "The Stadium's Silver Lining," *New York,* June 20, 2005; Gray, "Doctor, Doctor! PR Rx for Doctoroff," *New York,*

October 24, 2007; Clancy, "Not Everyone Is Sad to See Doctoroff Go," *Daily News,* December 10, 2007; Julian Brash, *Bloomberg's New York*, 202.

95 Author's interview, Daniel Doctoroff, September 3, 2015.

96 Susan Fainstein, *The Just City*, 105; Jonathan Bowles, "Giving Small Firms the Business," Testimony before the City Council by the Director of the Center for an Urban Future, June 2005; Gelinas, "Eminent Domain As Central Planning," *City Journal* (Winter 2010); Author's interview, Robert Steel, May 15, 2015; Author's interview, Seth Pinsky, May 12, 2015; Author's interview, Robert Yaro, October 1, 2015; Author's interview, Tom Wright, October 26, 2015.

97 Author's interview, Jonathan Bowles, May 8, 2015; Horowitz, "Stadium of Dreams," *New York*, June 21, 2004; Bowles, "Beyond the Olympics," 7; Author's interview, Maria Torres, October 21, 2015; Author's interview, Steven Spinola, May 21, 2015; Author's interview, Robert Yaro, October 1, 2015; Author's interview, Ruben Diaz Jr., October 6, 2015; Author's interview, Off the record.

98 Author's interview, Daniel Doctoroff, September 3, 2015.

Chapter 7

1 Author's interview, Daniel Doctoroff, September 3, 2015; Author's interview, Rohit Aggarwala, October 29, 2015.

2 Author's interview, Daniel Doctoroff, September 3, 2015; Author's interview, Rohit Aggarwala, October 29, 2015.

3 Author's interview, Daniel Doctoroff, September 3, 2015; Author's interview, Rohit Aggarwala, October 29, 2015; Bernstein, "New York Remade: Before and After Bloomberg," WNYC, December 27, 2013; Katherine Bagley and Maria Gallucci, *Bloomberg's Hidden Legacy: Climate Change and the Future of New York City* (New York: David Sasson, 2003 ebook edition), location 243–253.

4 Author's interview, Daniel Doctoroff, September 3, 2015; Author's interview, Rohit Aggarwala, October 29, 2015; Bagley and Gallucci, *Bloomberg's Hidden Legacy,* location 243–253.

5 Author's interview, Daniel Doctoroff, September 3, 2015; Rohit Aggarwala, October 29, 2015; City of New York, "*PlaNYC*: A Greener, Greater New York," April 2007, 3, 13.

6 Author's interview, Daniel Doctoroff, September 3, 2015; Rohit Aggarwala, October 29, 2015; City of New York, "*PlaNYC*: A Greener, Greater New York," April 2007, 3, 13.

7 Tom Farley, MD, *Saving Gotham: A Billionaire Mayor, Activist Doctors, and the Fight for Eight Million Lives* (New York: W. W. Norton & Company, 2015), 4; Bagley and Gallucci, *Bloomberg's Hidden Legacy,* location 358–377.

8 Tom Farley, MD, *Saving Gotham,* 10–16; Centers for Disease Control, Directors biography.

9 Author's interview, Marc Shaw, July 29, 2014; Author's interview, Edward Skyler, September 12, 2016; Jim Rutenberg and Lily Koppel, "In Barrooms, Smoking Ban is Less Reviled," *NYT,* February 6, 2005; You Tube Video, Press Conference, "Mayor Bloomberg Discusses Impact of 2003 Smoke-Free Air Act on 10th Anniversary," March 28, 2013; City of New York, Office of the Mayor, "Mayor Bloomberg, Deputy Mayor Gibbs and Commissioner Farley Celebrate Local,

National and Global Impact of Smoke-free Air Act on 10th Anniversary," March 27, 2013; Tom Farley, MD, *Saving Gotham,* 28–9, 147–9, 196–7.

10 Author's interview, Marc Shaw, July 29, 2014; Rutenberg and Koppel, "In Barrooms, Smoking Ban is Less Reviled," *NYT,* February 6, 2005; You Tube Video, Press Conference, "Mayor Bloomberg Discusses Impact of 2003 Smoke-Free Air Act on 10th Anniversary," March 28, 2013; New York City Office of the Mayor, "Mayor Bloomberg, Deputy Mayor Gibbs and Commissioner Farley Celebrate Local, National and Global Impact of Smoke-free Air Act on 10th Anniversary," March 27, 2013; Epi Data Brief, "Trends in Cigarette Use Among Adults in New York City, 2002–2010," New York City Department of Health and Hygiene, November 2011; Tom Farley, MD, *Saving Gotham,* 28–9, 147–9, 196–7.

11 Rutenberg and Koppel, "In Barrooms, Smoking Ban is Less Reviled," *NYT,* February 6, 2005; You Tube Video, Press Conference, "Mayor Bloomberg Discusses Impact of 2003 Smoke-Free Air Act on 10th Anniversary," March 28, 2013; New York City Office of the Mayor, "Mayor Bloomberg, Deputy Mayor Gibbs and Commissioner Farley Celebrate Local, National and Global Impact of Smoke-free Air Act on 10th Anniversary," March 27, 2013; Tom Farley, MD, *Saving Gotham,* 147–9.

12 Jennifer Steinhauer, "Putting City Hospitals On Firmer Footing," *NYT,* May 11, 2002.

13 Jennifer Steinhauer, "Putting City Hospitals On Firmer Footing," *NYT,* May 11, 2002; Sewell Chan, "City Hospitals May Need More Aid to Counter Deficits," *NYT,* March 13, 2006; Commonwealth Fund, "The New York City Health and Hospitals Corporation: Transforming a Public Safety Net Delivery System to Achieve Higher Performance," 2008, x; NYC Vital Signs, "Preventing Hospitalizations in New York City," New York City Department of Health and Mental Hygiene, October 2012, Volume 11, Number 3, 3; Epi Research Report, "Health Care Reform in New York City—Access to Primary Care Before Reform," New York City Department of Health and Mental Hygiene, November 2011, 2–3; New York City Independent Budget Office, "As Medicaid Enrollment Has Surged, Composition of the Caseload Has Changed," June 2003, 2; New York City Independent Budget Office, "Medicaid, Employer-Sponsored Health Insurance & the Uninsured in New York: Regional Differences in Health Insurance Coverage," October 2014, 1; City of New York, Office of the Mayor, "Mayor's Management Report," 2003, 18, 37; City of New York, Office of the Mayor, "Mayor's Management Report," 2013, 91, 145.

14 Kahliah Laney, David Giles, and Jonathan Bowles, "Innovations to Build On," Center for an Urban Future, November 2013, 12; City Health Information, "Take Care New York: A Policy for a Healthier New York City," New York City Department of Health and Mental Hygiene, September 2009, Volume 28, Supplement 5: 1–8; Author's interview, Robert Doar, July 24, 2015; Michael Powell, "In Fighting Teenage Pregnancy, the Folly of Blame and Shame," *NYT,* March 11, 2013; New York City Department of Health and Mental Hygiene, "NYC Condoms. Get Some." Health Bulletin, Volume 6 Number 1, 2007; Sewell Chan, "A New Condom In Town, This One Named NYC," *NYT,* February 15, 2007; Press Release: New York City Department of Health and Mental Hygiene, "Health Department Releases New NYC Condom Wrapper; More Than 36 Million NYC Condoms Given Out Last Year; New TV, Radio and Print Campaign Launched," February 13, 2008.

15   Commission for Economic Opportunity, "Increasing Opportunity and Decreasing Poverty in New York City," September 18, 2006, 8, 37; New York City Center for Economic Opportunity, "Strategy and Implementation Report," 2007, 4; Thomas Hilliard, "Subsidizing Care, Supporting Work," Center for an Urban Future, January 2011, 6–8, *passim*; New York City Independent Budget Office, "Early Learn Takes Its First Steps: City's Redesigned Subsidized Child Care System Still Faces Challenges," December 2012, 3.

16   "Take Care New York: 10 Steps To a Longer and Healthier Life," New York City Department of Health and Mental Hygiene, Health Bulletin, Volume 8 Number 7, 2004; W. Li, G. Maduro, E.M. Begier, "Epi Report: Life Expectancy in New York City: What Accounts for the Gains?," New York City Department of Health and Mental Hygiene, March 2013, 1–12; "New York City Community Health Survey Atlas, 2010," New York City Department of Health and Mental Hygiene, 2010; C. Gordon, N. Ghai, M. Purciel, A. Tawalker and A. Goodman, "Eating Well in Harlem: How Available is Healthy Food," New York City Department of Health and Mental Hygiene, 2007.

17   New York City Center for Economic Opportunity, "Strategy and Implementation Report," 2007, 34–5; Diane Cardwell, "A Plan To Add Supermarkets To Poor Areas, With Healthy Results," *NYT,* September 23, 2009; "New York City Healthy Bodegas Initiative," New York City Department of Health and New York City Center for Economic Opportunity, May 2010; Health Bulletin, "Choose Less Sodium," New York City Department of Health and Mental Hygiene, February/March 2006, Volume 12, Number 1; Michael Barbaro, "Mayor Doesn't Always Live By His Health Rules," *NYT,* September 23, 2009.

18   Tom Farley, MD, *Saving Gotham,* 44–5; 75–81, 85–8, 114–126; The New York City Department of Health and Mental Hygiene, "The Regulation to Phase Out Artificial Trans Fat In New York City Food Service Establishments (Section 81.08 of the New York City Health Code)," February 2007; Thomas J. Lueck and Kim Severson, "New York Bans Most Trans Fats in Restaurants," *NYT,* December 5, 2006; New York City Department of Health and Mental Hygiene, "Agency Biennial Report 2007–2008," 2009, 18; Thomas J. Lueck and Kim Severson, "New York Bans Most Trans Fats in Restaurants," *NYT,* December 5, 2006; New York City Department of Health and Mental Hygiene "Are You Pouring On the Pounds?" 2009; P. Alberti and P. Noyes, "Sugary Drinks: How Much Do We Consume?," New York City Department of Health and Mental Hygiene, 2011; Matt Flegenheimer, "Pouring It On," *NYT,* June 3, 2012; Michael M. Grynbaum, "Judge Blocks New York City's Limits on Big Sugary Drinks," March 11, 2013; Reuters, "State High Court Rules NYC Ban on Large Sodas Is Illegal," *NYT,* June 26, 2014; The Marist College Institute for Public Opinion, "Marist Poll: Put Sugary Drink Ban on Ice . . . Ban Goes Too Far, Says Majority," June 4, 2012.

19   Suraje Dessai, "The Climate Regime from The Hague to Marrakech: Saving or Sinking the Kyoto Protocol," Tyndall Centre for Climate Change Research, Working Paper No. 12, 2001, 5–8; Naomi Oreskes and Erik M. Conway, *Merchants of Doubt: How a Handful of Scientists Obscured the Truth on Issues from Tobacco Smoke to Global Warming* (New York: Bloomsbury Press, 2010), 169–216.

20   Author's interview, Rohit Aggarwala, October 29, 2015; New York City Office of the Mayor, "Address to Graduates of Johns Hopkins School of Medicine, Baltimore,

Md.," May 26, 2006; Robert T. Watson, ed., and Core Writing Team, *Climate Change 2001: Synthesis Report, United Nations Environmental Program and World Meteorological Organization* (Cambridge, UK: Cambridge University Press, 2001), 4, 5, and *passim*; Naomi Oreskes, "The Scientific Consensus on Climate Change," *Science,* December 3, 2004, vol. 306, 1686; Oreskes and Conway, *Merchants of Doubt,* 169–215.

21 Author's interview, Tom Wright, October 26, 2015; Author's interview, Daniel Doctoroff, September 3, 2015; Author's interview, Rohit Aggarwala, October 29, 2015.

22 Author's interview, Rohit Aggarwala, October 29, 2015; A Special Supplement from the City of New York, "By 2030 Will You Still Love New York? It's Up to You," *PlaNYC,* December 2006, in author's possession, courtesy of Rohit Aggarwala; City of New York, *"PlaNYC:* A Greener, Greater New York," April 2007, 3, 13; Thomas J. Lueck, "Bloomberg Draws a Blueprint for a Greener City," *NYT,* April 23, 2007.

23 City of New York, *"PlaNYC:* A Greener, Greater New York," April 2007, 3.

24 City of New York, *"PlaNYC:* A Greener, Greater New York," Update April 2011, 3, 9.

25 Citizens Budget Commission, "Planning after *PlaNYC:* A Framework for Developing New York City's Next Ten-Year Capital Strategy, 2013," 6.

26 City of New York, *"PlaNYC:* A Greener, Greater New York," April 2007, 75–97; New York City Independent Budget Office: Fiscal Brief, "Toward A State of Good Repair? City Capital Spending on Bridges, 2000–2012," April 2014; Trey Popp, "Street Fighter," *The Pennsylvania Gazette,* March/April 2016.

27 City of New York, *"PlaNYC:* A Greener, Greater New York, April 2007," 77–80; The Partnership for New York City, "Growth or Gridlock? The Economic Case for Traffic Relief and Transit Improvement for a Greater New York," December 2006, 3; Sewell Chan, "Driving Around Manhattan, You Pay, Under One Traffic Idea," *NYT,* November 11, 2005; Nicole Gelinas, "Transit for Tomorrow," *City Journal,* 8 July 2009.

28 City of New York, *"PlaNYC:* A Greener, Greater New York," April 2007, 75–97; Kim Tangley, "Tunneling Below Second Avenue," *NYT,* August 1, 2012; Nicole Gelinas, "Ungridlocked," *City Journal* (Spring 2012).

29 City of New York, *"PlaNYC:* A Greener, Greater New York," April 2007, 96; Author's interview, Seth Pinsky, May 12, 2015.

30 Author's interview, Rohit Aggarwala, October 29, 2015. Author's interview, Seth Pinsky, May 12, 2015.

31 Author's interview, Robert Yaro, October 1, 2015; Author's interview, Steven Spinola, May 21, 2015; Author's interview, Rohit Aggarwala, October 29, 2015.

32 Author's interview, Robert Yaro, October 1, 2015; Author's interview, Tom Wright, October 26, 2015; Author's interview, Daniel Doctoroff, September 3, 2015; Author's interview, Rohit Aggarwala, October 29, 2015; Winnie Hu, "Mayor Says Traffic Fees Are Not on City's Agenda," *NYT,* November 12, 2005.

33 Author's interview, Steven Spinola, May 21, 2015; Sewell Chan, "The Mayor and His Plan: Reaction," *NYT,* April 23, 2007; Bruce Schaller, "New York City's Congestion Pricing Experience and Implications for Road Pricing Acceptance in the United States," *Transport Policy* 17 (2010), 266–73.

34 Author's interview, Steven Spinola, May 21, 2015; Chan, "The Mayor and His Plan: Reaction," *NYT,* April 23, 2007; Schaller, "New York City's Congestion Pricing Experience and Implications for Road Pricing Acceptance in the United States," 266–73.

35 Schaller, "New York City's Congestion Pricing Experience and Implications for Road Pricing Acceptance in the United States," 266–73; Author's interview, Steven Spinola, May 21, 2015; Editorial, "It's Up to You, Mr. Silver," *NYT,* April 2, 2008; Chan, "The Mayor and His Plan: Reaction," April 23, 2007; William Neuman, "Some Subways Found Packed Past Capacity," *NYT,* June 26, 2007; Geoffrey Gray, "The Obstructionist," *New York,* June 1, 2008; Editorial, "Moment of Truth on Congestion Pricing," *NYT,* March 26, 2008; Author's interview, Jonathan Bowles, May 8, 2015.

36 Chan, "The Mayor and His Plan: Reaction," April 23, 2007; Neuman, "Some Subways Found Packed Past Capacity," *NYT,* June 26, 2007; Gray, "The Obstructionist," *New York,* June 1, 2008; Editorial, "Moment of Truth on Congestion Pricing," *NYT,* March 26, 2008.

37 Author's interview, Robert Yaro, October 1, 2015; Author's interview, Rohit Aggarwala, October 29, 2015; Editorial, "It's Up to You, Mr. Silver," *NYT,* April 2, 2008; Schaller, "New York City's Congestion Pricing Experience and Implications for Road Pricing Acceptance in the United States," 266–73.

38 Author's interview, Robert Yaro, October 1, 2015; Bagley and Gallucci, *Bloomberg's Hidden Legacy,* location 653.

39 Geoffrey Gray, "The Obstructionist," *New York,* June 1, 2008; Editorial, "Moment of Truth on Congestion Pricing," *NYT,* March 26, 2008; Editorial, "It's Up to You, Mr. Silver," *NYT,* April 2, 2008; Danny Hakim, "In Congestion Talks Upstate, Mayor Sends In The Surrogates," *NYT,* April 7, 2008; Editorial, "Congestion Pricing, Still Alive," *NYT,* July 29, 2007; Raymond Hernandez, "Bloomberg Steps In To Help G.O.P. In Albany Fight," *NYT,* March 1, 2008; Purnick, *Mike Bloomberg,* 160; Author's interview, Dean Fuleihan, August 12, 2015.

40 Gray, "The Obstructionist," *New York,* June 1, 2008; Editorial, "Moment of Truth on Congestion Pricing," *NYT,* March 26, 2008; Editorial, "It's Up to You, Mr. Silver," *NYT,* April 2, 2008; Danny Hakim, "In Congestion Talks Upstate, Mayor Sends In The Surrogates," *NYT,* April 7, 2008; William Neuman, "State Commission Approves A Plan For Congestion Pricing," *NYT,* February 1, 2008; Raymond Hernandez, "Bloomberg Steps In To Help G.O.P. In Albany Fight," *NYT,* March 1, 2008; Purnick, *Mike Bloomberg,* 160; Author's interview, Marc Shaw, April 21, 2015; Author's interview, Dean Fuleihan, August 12, 2015.

41 Geoffrey Gray, "The Obstructionist," *New York,* June 1, 2008; Editorial, "Moment of Truth on Congestion Pricing," *NYT,* March 26, 2008; Editorial, "It's Up to You, Mr. Silver," *NYT,* April 2, 2008; Danny Hakim, "In Congestion Talks Upstate, Mayor Sends In The Surrogates," *NYT,* April 7, 2008; Editorial, "Congestion Pricing, Still Alive," *NYT,* July 29, 2007; William Neuman, "State Commission Approves A Plan For Congestion Pricing," *NYT,* February 1, 2008; Raymond Hernandez, "Bloomberg Steps In To Help G.O.P. In Albany Fight," *NYT,* March 1, 2008; Shaunna Murphy, Shea O'Rourke, and Marguerite A. Suozzi, "Bloomberg and the Press Give Bruno a Pass on Congestion Pricing," *Village Voice,* April 15, 2008.

42 Gray, "The Obstructionist," *New York,* June 1, 2008; Purnick, *Mike Bloomberg,* 160; Author's interview, Dean Fuleihan, August 12, 2015.

43   Author's interview, Robert Lieber, May 21, 2015; Author's interview, Rohit Aggarwala, October 29, 2015; City of New York, Office of the Mayor, "Statement By Mayor Michael R. Bloomberg On the Failure Of The State Legislature To Vote Congestion Pricing," April 8, 2008; Editorial, "Mr. Silver Does It Again," *NYT,* April 8, 2008.

44   Author's interview, Kathryn Wylde, May 8, 2015; Author's interview, Robert Yaro, October 1, 2015; Editorial, "It's Not Easy Being Green," *NYT,* November 10, 2008; Diane Cardwell, "Paterson Supports Congestion Pricing," *NYT,* March 22, 2008.

45   Schaller, "New York City's Congestion Pricing Experience and Implications for Road Pricing Acceptance in the United States," 266–73; Richard Ravitch, *So Much To Do: A Full Life of Business, Politics and Confronting Fiscal Crisis* (New York: Public Affairs, 2014), 178–80; Author's interview, Richard Ravitch, May 19, 2015; Gelinas, "Transit for Tomorrow," *City Journal,* July 8, 2009.

46   Schaller, "New York City's Congestion Pricing Experience and Implications for Road Pricing Acceptance in the United States," 266–73; Ravitch, *So Much To Do,* 178–80; Author's interview, Richard Ravitch, May 19, 2015; Author's interview, Dean Fuleihan, August 12, 2015.

47   Schaller, "New York City's Congestion Pricing Experience and Implications for Road Pricing Acceptance in the United States," 266–73; Ravitch, *So Much To Do,* 178–80; Author's interview, Richard Ravitch, May 19, 2015; Author's interview, Off the record; Nicholas Confessore, "Dissidents Disrupt Plans of Democrats in Albany," *NYT,* May 10, 2009; Benjamin Weiser, "Former State Senator is Sentenced to 7 Years in Vast Bribery Case," *NYT,* April 26, 2012; Mosi Secret, "Espada to Plead Guilty to Remaining Charges After Being Convicted of Theft," *NYT,* October 11, 2012; James Fanelli, "Hiram Montserrate's Prison Stay Delayed Over Toothache," dnainfo.com, March 11, 2013.

48   City of New York, "*PlaNYC*: A Greener, Greater New York, Update," April 2011, 91; Move NY, "The Move NY Fair Plan," February 2015, 8, 25; Author's interview, Robert Yaro, October 1, 2015; Gelinas, "Transit for Tomorrow," *City Journal,* July 8, 2009.

49   Port Authority of New York and New Jersey, "The Economic Impact of the Aviation Industry on the New York–New Jersey Metropolitan Region," October 2005, 1–2; Partnership for New York City, "Grounded: The High Cost of Air Traffic Congestion," February 2009, 7; City of New York, Office of the Mayor, "One New York: The Plan for a Strong and Just City," 2015, 84–5.

50   City of New York, Office of the Mayor, "*PlaNYC*: A Greener, Greater New York, Update," April 2011, 91; Landrum & Brown, "Report Prepared for the New York City Economic Development Corporation and the Port Authority of New York and New Jersey: JFK Air Cargo Study," January 2013, Executive Summary, 1–5.

51   Charles V. Bagli and Nicholas Confessore, "Take the Number 7 to Secaucus? That's a Plan," *NYT,* November 16, 2010; City of New York, Office of the Mayor, "One New York: The Plan for a Strong and Just City," 2015, 87–92.

52   Michael Crowley, "Honk, Honk, Aaah," *New York*, May 17, 2009; New York City Department of Transportation, "Sustainable Streets: Strategic Plan for the New York City Department of Transportation for 2008 and Beyond," 2008, Letter from the Commissioner, 4, *passim*; Janette Sadik-Khan, "TED Talk: City Transportation

Expert," October 8, 2013; Author's interview, Tom Wright, October 26, 2015; Author's interview, Janette Sadik-Khan, September 14, 2016.

53 New York City Department of Transportation, "The New York City Pedestrian Safety Study and Action Plan," August 2010; Janette Sadik-Khan, "TED Talk: City Transportation Expert," September, 2013; New York City Department of Transportation, Pedestrian Plaza Sites; Author's interview, Janette Sadik-Khan, September 14, 2016; Author's interview, Robert Yaro, October 1, 2015.

54 NYC Vital Signs, "Improving Traffic Safety in New York City," New York City Department of Health and Mental Hygiene, November 2010, Volume 9, Number 6, 1; Crowley, "Honk, Honk, Aaah," *New York*, May 17, 2009; Janette Sadik-Khan, "TED Talk: City Transportation Expert," September 2013.

55 New York City Department of Transportation, "Greenlight for Midtown Evaluation Report," January 2010, 1, *passim*; New York City Department of Transportation, "Sustainable Streets: 2009 Progress Report," 2009, 6; Gelinas, "Ungridlocked," *City Journal* (Spring 2012); Michael Grynbaum, "Tourists And New Yorkers Take A Rubber Seat In Times Square," *NYT,* June 10, 2009; Author's interview, Tom Wright, October 26, 2015.

56 New York City Department of Transportation, "Greenlight for Midtown Evaluation Report," January 2010, 1, *passim*; New York City Department of Transportation, "Sustainable Streets: 2009 Progress Report," 2009, 6; Grynbaum, "Tourists and New Yorkers Take a Rubber Seat in Times Square," *NYT,* June 10, 2009; Gelinas, "Ungridlocked," *City Journal* (Spring 2012).

57 New York City Department of Transportation, "Sustainable Streets: Strategic Plan for the New York City Department of Transportation for 2008 and Beyond," 15; Michael M. Grynbaum, "In a Reprise, Saturdays With Zones Free of Cars," *NYT,* June 29, 2009; Gelinas, "Ungridlocked," *City Journal* (Spring 2012); City of New York, Office of the Mayor, "One New York: The Plan for a Strong and Just City," 2015, 84; Author's interview, Janette Sadik-Khan, September 14, 2016.

58 Author's interview, Janette Sadik-Khan, September 14, 2016; Crowley, "Honk, Honk, Aaah," *New York*, May 17, 2009.

59 Gelinas, "Ungridlocked," *City Journal* (Spring 2012); City of New York, Office of the Mayor, "One New York: The Plan for a Strong and Just City," 2015, 84; Author's interview, Janette Sadik-Khan, September 14, 2016; Quinnipiac University Poll, "New York City Voters Back Mayor's Storm Plan, 4–1, Slim Majority Backs Food Recycling, Bike Rentals," June 27, 2013; New Yorkers' Views on Their Mayor and His Programs," *NYT,* August 16, 2013; New York City, "Mayor's Management Report," 2002, 62 and 2014, 226.

60 City of New York, "*PlaNYC*: A Greener, Greater New York, April 2007," 117–29; City of New York, "*PlaNYC*: A Greener, Greater New York, Update," April 2011, 122–31; Author's interview, Rohit Aggarwala, October 29, 2015; Lisa Millay Stevens, ed., "Air Pollution and the Health of New Yorkers: The Impact of Fine Particles and Ozone," New York City Department of Health and Mental Hygiene, 2011, 3.

61 Author's interview, Rohit Aggarwala, October 29, 2015; Anthony DePalma, "Getting More Than That New-Car Smell," *NYT,* April 23, 2005; City of New York, "*PlaNYC*: A Greener, Greater New York," April 2007, 117–29; City of New York, "*PlaNYC*: A Greener, Greater New York, Update," April 2011,

122–31; City of New York, "*PlaNYC* Progress Report: Sustainability and Resiliency," 2014, 24; New York City Taxi & Limousine Commission, "2014 Taxicab Factbook," 1.

62 Author's interview, Rohit Aggarwala, October 29, 2015; City of New York, "*PlaNYC*: A Greener, Greater New York," April 2007, 101, 117–29; City of New York, "*PlaNYC*: A Greener, Greater New York, Update," April 2011, 122–31; City of New York, "*PlaNYC* Progress Report: Sustainability and Resiliency," 2014, 24.

63 Author's interview, Rohit Aggarwala, October 29, 2015.

64 City of New York, "*PlaNYC*: A Greener, Greater New York," April 2007, 100–15; City of New York, "*PlaNYC*: A Greener, Greater New York, Update," April 2011, 122–31.

65 "Case Study: New York City Green Codes Task Force," American Council for Energy Efficient Economy, January 2014; City of New York, "*PlaNYC*: A Greener, Greater New York," April 2007, 117–29; City of New York, "*PlaNYC*: A Greener, Greater New York, Update," April 2011, 122–31; City of New York, "*PlaNYC* Progress Report: Sustainability and Resiliency," 2014, 20, 24.

66 City of New York, "*PlaNYC*: A Greener, Greater New York," April 2007, 17–8.

67 Soffer, *Ed Koch*, 290–304; City of New York, "*PlaNYC*: A Greener, Greater New York," April 2007, 17–8; Josiah Madar and Mark Willis, "Creating Affordable Housing Out of Thin Air: The Economics of Mandatory Inclusionary Zoning in New York City," NYU Furman Center, March 2014, 2.

68 City of New York, "*PlaNYC*: A Greener, Greater New York," April 2007, 18; Mayor Michael R. Bloomberg, Public Advocate Betsy Gotbaum, Deputy Mayor Edward Skyler, Director, Mayor's Office of Operations Jeffrey A. Kay, "NYC Feedback Citywide Customer Survey: Report of Survey Results," December 2008, 19.

69 Jennifer Steinhauer, "Mayor Calls for Thousands of New Homes," *NYT,* December 11, 2002; Michael H. Schill, "More Housing on the Map," *NYT,* December 18, 2002; Editorial, "Mayor Bloomberg Brings Housing Home," *NYT,* December 27, 2002; Author's interview, Tom Waters, October 26, 2015.

70 City of New York Department of Housing, Preservation and Development, "The New Housing Marketplace: Creating Housing for the Next Generation 2004–2014," 2006; Association for Neighborhood and Housing Development, Inc., "Real Affordability: An Evaluation of the Bloomberg Housing Program and Recommendations to Strengthen Affordable Housing Policy," 2013, 22.

71 City of New York, Department of Housing, Preservation and Development, "Housing New York: A Five Borough, Ten Year Plan," 2014; Elyzabeth Gaumer, Assistant Commissioner and Sheree West, Ph.D., Sr. Housing Analyst, Housing Policy Analysis and Research, "Selected Initial Findings of the 2014 New York City Housing and Vacancy Survey," New York City Department of Housing, Preservation and Development, February 9, 2015; Cindy Rodriguez, "As Bloomberg Built Affordable Housing, City Became Less Affordable," WNYC, July 9, 2013.

72 Edwin G. Burrows and Mike Wallace, *Gotham: A History of New York City to 1898,* (New York: Oxford University Press, 1999), 589–98, 625–8; City of New York, "*PlaNYC*: A Greener, Greater New York," April 2007, 12, 63–71; City of New York, "*PlaNYC* Progress Report: Sustainability and Resilience," 2014, 13–16; Michael Cooper, "Water Rates Are Expected To Rise To Help Finance New

Aqueduct," *NYT,* March 7, 2003; Author's interview, Edward Skyler, September 12, 2016.

73 New York City Parks Department, "A Brief History of High Bridge"; Jim Dwyer, "A Stunning Link to New York's Past Makes a Long-Awaited Return," *NYT,* June 4, 2015; Author's interview, Ruben Diaz Jr., October 6, 2015.

74 City of New York, "*PlaNYC*: A Greener, Greater New York," April 2007, 12, 53–61; City of New York, Department of City Planning, "The New Waterfront Revitalization Plan," September 2002; City of New York, Department of City Planning, "Comprehensive Waterfront Plan," 1992; City of New York, Department of City Planning, "Vision 2020: New York City Comprehensive Waterfront Plan," March 2011.

75 City of New York, Department of City Planning, "Vision 2020: New York City Comprehensive Waterfront Plan," March 2011, 64–71.

76 City of New York, "*PlaNYC*: A Greener, Greater New York," April 2007, 41–9; City of New York, "*PlaNYC* Progress Report: Sustainability and Resiliency," 2014, 11–2.

77 City of New York City Planning Commission, "Application by the New York City Economic Development Corporation and the Department of Housing, Preservation and Development for Zoning Amendments to create a 'Special Willets Point District,'" September 24, 2008/Calendar No. 14, N080382 ZRQ , 1–9; Ray Rivera, "Groups Admit to Lobbying Illegally to Aid Mayor's Plans," *NYT,* July 3, 2012; Sarah Maslin Nir, "The End of Willets Point," *NYT,* November 22, 2013; Charles V. Bagli, "New York City Declines to Fight in Court for Complex Near Citi Field," *NYT,* August 19, 2015; Author's interview, Kyle Kimball, September 23, 2015.

78 Sarah Maslin Nir, "The End of Willets Point," *NYT,* November 22, 2013; Charles V. Bagli, "New York City Declines to Fight in Court for Complex Near Citi Field," *NYT,* August 19, 2015; Author's interview, Kyle Kimball, September 23, 2015.

79 The Trust for Governor's Island, "Press Release: Governor Eliot Spitzer and Mayor Michael Bloomberg Announce the Selection of a Team to Design Park and Open Space on Governor's Island," December 19, 2007; City of New York, Department of City Planning, "Vision 2020: New York City Comprehensive Waterfront Plan," March 2011, 42–61; Philip Delves Broughton, "New York's Glory Rendered in Glass and Steel," *Financial Times,* July 22, 2016; Michael Kimmelman, "A Step Up for Brooklyn Bridge Park," *NYT,* September 16, 2013; Author's interview, Adrian Benepe, September 29, 2015; Author's interview, Amanda Burden, January 9, 2017.

80 Author's interview, Adrian Benepe, September 29, 2015; City of New York, "*PlaNYC*: A Greener, Greater New York," April 2007, 29–38.

81 City of New York, "*PlaNYC*: A Greener, Greater New York," April 2007, 29–38; City of New York, Department of City Planning, "Vision 2020: New York City Comprehensive Waterfront Plan," March 2011, 11–2; Laura Vanderkam, "Parks and Re-creation," *City Journal* (Summer 2011); Author's interview, Adrian Benepe, September 29, 2015; City of New York Office of the Mayor, "Mayor Bloomberg Discusses the Progress Made in Each of the Five Boroughs Since 2001 in Weekly Radio Address," December 22, 2013.

82 City of New York, "*PlaNYC*: A Greener, Greater New York," April 2007, 130, 133.

83   City of New York, "*PlaNYC*: A Greener, Greater New York," April 2007, 135–9;
     City of New York, "*PlaNYC* Progress Report: Sustainability and Resiliency," 2014,
     29; Author's interview, Adrian Benepe, September 29, 2015.

84   City of New York, "*PlaNYC*: A Greener, Greater New York," April 2007, 135–9; City
     of New York, "*PlaNYC* Progress Report: Sustainability and Resiliency," 2014, 29;
     Author's interview, Adrian Benepe, September 29, 2015; New York City Comptroller
     Scott Stringer, "Press Release: Stringer Audit Reveals City Failure to Set Goals for
     Reducing Greenhouse Gas Emissions in City Buildings," September 3, 2015.

85   City of New York, Office of the Mayor, "Mayor Bloomberg Looks Back at New
     York City on September 12, 2001 and Outlines Progress on Economic Recovery,
     Major Growth in Population and Historic Decreases in Crime," September 12,
     2013; City of New York, Office of the Mayor, "One New York: The Plan for a
     Strong and Just City," (2015), 28; New York State Department of Labor Statistics,
     2013; Sam Roberts, "Fewer People Abandoning the Bronx, Census Shows," *NYT*,
     May 14, 2013; Mike Hales and Andres Mendoza Pena, "2012 Global Cities Index
     and Emerging Cities Outlook," A.T. Kearney and The Chicago Council on Global
     Affairs, 2012, 3; Partnership for New York City, "New York City Jobs Blueprint,"
     18–9; Maria Doulis, "Competitiveness Scorecard: Assessing NYC Metro's
     Attractiveness As a Home for Human Capital," Citizens Budget Commission,
     February 2013.

86   City of New York, Office of Management and Budget, "January 2013 Financial
     Plan Fiscal Years 2013–2017," 15; President Barack Obama, "Speech Sponsored
     by the Center for American Progress on the Economy and Income Inequality,"
     December 4, 2013, transcript and video recording on Politco.com.

Chapter 8

1   City of New York, Office of the Mayor, "Mayor Bloomberg Announces the
     Recommendations of the Mayor's Commission for Economic Opportunity,"
     September 18, 2006; Author's interview, Heather Mac Donald, October 7, 2016.

2   David Jason Fischer and Neil Scott Kleiman with Julian L. Alssid, "Rebuilding
     Job Training from the Ground Up: Workforce System Reform After 9/11,"
     Center for an Urban Future and The Workforce Strategy Center, August 2002;
     David Jason Fischer, "Training Wreck," Center for an Urban Future, April
     2002; David Jason Fischer, "Testimony of David Jason Fischer, Project Director,
     Center for an Urban Future, New York City Council Committee on Economic
     Development Oversight Hearing: New York City Workforce Investment Board,
     CY 2005 Strategic Plan: Where Are We Today?," Tuesday, February 13, 2007;
     Aaron Fichtner and K.A. Dixon, "Dressed to Skill," Center for an Urban Future,
     December 2003; David Fischer, "Mike Has the Right Idea on Welfare Reform,"
     Center for an Urban Future, June 11, 2002; Author's interview, David Fischer,
     May 21, 2015.

3   David Jason Fischer, "Transferring Workforce Programs to the Small Business
     Services Department, Testimony before the General Welfare Committee of the
     New York City Council," June 2003; Author's interview, David Fischer, May 21,
     2015; Author's interview, Jonathan Bowles, May 8, 2015; Community Service
     Society and the Center for an Urban Future, "Closing the Gap: A Blueprint for

Preparing New York City's Workforce to Meet the Evolving Needs of Employers," 2010, 34.

4   Community Service Society and the Center for an Urban Future, "Closing the Gap," 34; David Jason Fischer, "The Big Idea: Black Male Unemployment in NYC in 2004," Center for an Urban Future, August 2004, 29; David Jason Fischer, "Work in Progress," Center for an Urban Future, June 2007; David Jason Fischer, "The Many Faces of Poverty: Disconnected Youth," Center for an Urban Future, September 2006.

5   Brash, *Bloomberg's New York*, 229; Winnie Hu, "Two Different Kinds of Math, and Two Spins on Unemployment," *NYT*, October 15, 2005; City of New York, Office of the Mayor, "Press Release: Mayor Michael R. Bloomberg Announces Appointments to Mayor's Commission on Construction Opportunity," March 5, 2005; City of New York, Office of the Mayor, "Press Release: Mayor Bloomberg, Congressman Rangel, Comptroller Thompson, Building and Construction Trade Council President Malloy and Non-Traditional Employment for Women Board Chair Hayes Announce 10 Initiatives of Mayor's Commission on Construction Opportunity," October 5, 2005.

6   James Parrot, "Building Up New York, Tearing Down Job Quality: Taxpayer Impact of Worsening Employment Practices in New Construction in New York City," Fiscal Policy Institute, December 5, 2007, 4, 10, 23; David Jason Fischer, "Off the Cuff: Something to Build On," Center for an Urban Future, February 2008.

7   New York State Department of Labor Unemployment Statistics; The New York City Commission for Economic Opportunity, "Report to Mayor Michael R. Bloomberg: Increasing Opportunity and Reducing Poverty in New York City," September 2006, page 4, 8; Mark Levitan and Susan Weiler, "Poverty in New York City, 1969–1999: The Influence of Demographic Change, Income Growth, and Income Inequality," *FRBNY Economic Policy Review*, July 2008, 13.

8   Author's interview, Linda Gibbs, September 14, 2016; City of New York, Office of the Mayor, "Mayor Michael R. Bloomberg Delivers 2006 State of the City Address 'A Blueprint for New York City's Future,'" January 26, 2006; Commission for Economic Opportunity, "Increasing Opportunity and Reducing Poverty in New York City," September 2006, 12.

9   City of New York, Office of the Mayor, "Mayor Michael R. Bloomberg Delivers 2006 State of the City Address 'A Blueprint for New York City's Future,'" January 26, 2006; Commission for Economic Opportunity, "Increasing Opportunity and Reducing Poverty in New York City," September 2006, 12.

10   Commission for Economic Opportunity, "Increasing Opportunity and Reducing Poverty in New York City," September 2006, transmittal letter, 2; Author's interview, Linda Gibbs, September 14, 2016.

11   City of New York, Office of the Mayor, "Mayor Bloomberg Announces the Recommendations of the Mayor's Commission for Economic Opportunity," September 18, 2006; NYC Center for Economic Opportunity, "Strategy and Implementation Report," 2007, 3; Author's interview, James Riccio, October 16, 2015; Author's interview, Gordon Berlin, September 29, 2015.

12   New York City Center for Economic Opportunity, "Strategy and Implementation Report," 2007, 3, 6, 9, 30; Author's interview, Linda Gibbs, September 14, 2016.

13   New York City Center for Economic Opportunity, "Strategy and Implementation Report," 2007, 3, 6, 9, 30; Author's interview, Linda Gibbs, September 14, 2016.

14   Commission for Economic Opportunity, "Increasing Opportunity and Reducing Poverty in New York City," September 2006, 44; New York City Center for Economic Opportunity, "The CEO Poverty Measure," August 2008, 9, 10; City of New York, Office of the Mayor, "The CEO Poverty Measure, 2005–2013," April 22, 2015, iii–vi.

15   City of New York, Office of the Mayor, "The CEO Poverty Measure, 2005–2013," April 22, 2015, 13, i; Rachel L. Swarns, "With New Formula, An Official Helped Unmask the Face of Poverty in New York," *NYT,* December 8, 2013.

16   City of New York, Office of the Mayor, "The CEO Poverty Measure, 2005–2013," April 22, 2015, iii; The New York City Commission for Economic Opportunity, "Report to Mayor Michael R. Bloomberg: Increasing Opportunity and Reducing Poverty in New York City," September 2006, 1, 2.

17   Author's interview, Robert Doar, July 24, 2015; City of New York, Office of the Mayor, "Mayor's Management Report," 2002, 2013; Author's interview, David Jones, October 13, 2015.

18   Editorial, "Elusive Helping Hands in the City," *NYT,* December 5, 2003; Winnie Hu, "Bloomberg Administration Is Criticized on Food Stamps," *NYT,* November 22, 2004; Leslie Kaufman, "Fewer New Yorkers Get Food Stamps, and Critics Blame City," *NYT,* August 24, 2005; New York City Center for Economic Opportunity, "Early Achievements and Lessons Learned," 2008, 71–2; Patrick McGeehan, "In New Ads, Health Department Offers Supersized Warnings," *NYT,* January 10, 2012; City of New York, Office of the Mayor, "Mayor's Management Report," 2013, 95; Sewell Chan, "Mayor Overrules 2 Aides Seeking Food Stamp Shift," *NYT,* April 18, 2006.

19   City of New York, Office of the Mayor, "Mayor's Management Report," 2002, 27; City of New York, Office of the Mayor, "Mayor's Management Report," 2013, 95; New York City Center for Economic Opportunity, "Strategy and Implementation Report," 2007, 34–5; New York City Center for Economic Opportunity, "Early Achievements and Lessons Learned," 2008, 71–2; Author's interview, Robert Doar, July 24, 2015; Joe Coscarelli, "Bloomberg Doubles Down on Finger Printing for Food Stamps," *New York,* January 6, 2012; New York State Governor Andrew M. Cuomo, Press Release, "Governor Cuomo Announces New York State To End Finger Imaging Requirement for Food Stamp Recipients," May 17, 2012.

20   Annie E. Casey Foundation, "Building Family Economic Success: The Earned Income Tax Credit (EITC)," August 2005, 1; New York City Center for Economic Opportunity, "Strategy and Implementation Report," 2007, 15, 30, 49.

21   Kahliah Laney, David Giles, and Jonathan Bowles, "Innovations to Build On," Center for an Urban Future, November 2013, 13; City of New York, Office of the Mayor, "Mayor's Management Report," 2013, 96; Kay S. Hymowitz, "Getting Dads Back On The Job," *City Journal,* September 8, 2009; New York City Center for Economic Opportunity, "Strategy and Implementation Report," 2007, 30–3; Author's interview, Robert Doar, July 24, 2015; Rachel Pardoe and Dan Bloom, "Paycheck Plus: A New Antipoverty Strategy for Single Adults," MDRC, May 2014.

22   Commission for Economic Opportunity, "Increasing Opportunity and Decreasing Poverty in New York City," September 18, 2006, 12, 17; New York City Center

for Economic Opportunity, "Evidence and Impact," 2009, 2; Author's interview, James Riccio, October 16, 2015; Kahliah Laney, David Giles, and Jonathan Bowles, "Innovations to Build On," Center for an Urban Future, November 2013, 14; NYC.gov, "More Than 25,000 New Yorkers Have Visited NYC's Financial Empowerment Center Network," November 17, 2013; Jonathan Mintz, "Transforming the Availability of Financial Counseling Across America," *Bloomberg Philanthropies*, March 13, 2015.

23 New York City Center for Economic Opportunity, "Replicating Our Results," 2011, 3.

24 Commission for Economic Opportunity, "Increasing Opportunity and Decreasing Poverty in New York City," September 18, 2006, 13, 27; David Banks and Ana Oliveira, "Young Men's Initiative: Report to the Mayor from the Chairs," August 2011, 15; New York City Center for Economic Opportunity, "Early Achievements and Lessons Learned," 2008, 7; New York City Center for Economic Opportunity, "Evidence and Impact," 2009, 10.

25 New York City Center for Economic Opportunity, "Strategy and Implementation Report," 2007, 5; New York City Center for Economic Opportunity, "Evidence and Impact," 2009, 12, 27; New York City Center for Economic Opportunity, "Replicating Our Results," 2011, 27; New York City Center for Economic Opportunity, "Local and National Impact," 2012, 5, 65; Susan Scrivener, Michael J. Weiss, Alyssa Ratledge, Timothy Rudd, Colleen Somo, Hannah Fresques, "Doubling Graduation Rates: Three Year Effects of CUNY's Accelerated Studies in Associates Programs (ASAP) for Developmental Education Students," MDRC, February 2015; Author's interview, Gordon Berlin, September 29, 2015, and follow-up correspondence, October 24, 2016; Author's interview, Linda Gibbs, September 14, 2016.

26 City of New York, Office of the Mayor, "Mayor Bloomberg Delivers 2010 State of the City Address Detailing His Plans for the Recovery Ahead and the Details Behind It," January 20, 2010.

27 David Banks and Ana Oliveira, "Young Men's Initiative: Report to the Mayor from the Chairs," August 2011, 5, 19; New York City Center for Economic Opportunity, "Local and National Impact," 2012, 19; Kathleen Agaton and Donna Taper, "The New York City Young Men's Initiative: Working to Improve Outcomes for Black and Latino Young Men," Submitted by Metis Associates to the New York City Center for Economic Opportunity, June 2014, 14; City of New York, Office of the Mayor, "Press Release: Mayor DeBlasio Announces the Next Phase of NYC's Young Men's Initiative, Opening New Doors for Young Men of Color," January 30, 2015; Author's interview, Linda Gibbs, September 14, 2016.

28 Commission for Economic Opportunity, "Increasing Opportunity and Decreasing Poverty in New York City," September 18, 2006, 38–9; City of New York, Office of the Mayor, "Ready to Launch: New York City's Implementation Plan for Free, High Quality, Full-Day Universal Pre-Kindergarten," January 2014, 4.

29 City of New York, Office of the Mayor, "Mayor Bloomberg Announces the Recommendations of the Mayor's Commission for Economic Opportunity," September 18, 2006; New York City Center for Economic Opportunity, "Early Achievements and Lessons Learned," 2008, 51; Author's interview, James Riccio, October 16, 2015.

30 City of New York, Office of the Mayor, "Mayor Bloomberg Announces the Recommendations of the Mayor's Commission for Economic Opportunity," September 18, 2006.

31 City of New York, Office of the Mayor, "The CEO Poverty Measure, 2005–2013," April 22, 2015, iii; New York City Center for Economic Opportunity, "Replicating Our Results," 2011, 3; Press Release, "Center for Economic Opportunity Wins Harvard Innovations in Government Award," Harvard Kennedy School, Ash Center for Democratic Governance and Innovation," February 12, 2012; City of New York, Office of the Mayor, "Press Release: Mayor Bloomberg Receives Award for Anti-Poverty Efforts from Children's Aid Society, Releases New Data Showing Every Major US City Saw Increase in Poverty Rate—Except for New York City— Since 2000," November 14, 2013, based on 2000 US Census Bureau Data and 2012 US American Community Survey Data; Citizens Budget Commission, "Managing Economic Development Programs in New York City: Lessons for the Next Mayor from the Past Decade" (December 2013), 5.

32 City of New York, Office of the Mayor, "The CEO Poverty Measure, 2005–2013," April 22, 2015, iii; Mayor Michael R. Bloomberg, Public Advocate Betsy Gotbaum, Deputy Mayor Edward Skyler, Director, Mayor's Office of Operations Jeffrey A. Kay, "NYC Feedback Citywide Customer Survey: Report of Survey Results," December 2008, 4; City of New York, Office of the Mayor, "Press Release: Mayor Bloomberg Receives Award for Anti-Poverty Efforts from Children's Aid Society, Releases New Data Showing Every Major US City Saw Increase in Poverty Rate— Except for New York City—Since 2000," November 14, 2013.

33 New York City Center for Economic Opportunity, "Local and National Impact," 2012, Appendix C, Performance Data, 60–65; Dana Goldstein, "Behavioral Theory: Can Mayor Bloomberg Pay People to Do the Right Thing?," *The American Prospect*, August 14, 2009; Michael Katz, "Bloomberg, Champion of the Poor," *NYT*, November 5, 2013; Author's interview, David Jones, October 13, 2015.

34 Goldstein, "Behavioral Theory," *The American Prospect*, August 14, 2009; City of New York, Office of the Mayor, "Mayor's Management Report," 2013, 99; Glen Pasanen, "As Poverty Increases, Budget Cuts Tatter the Safety Net," *Gotham Gazette*, November 16, 2011; Author's interview, David Jones, October 13, 2015.

35 Jennifer Steinhauer, "Bloomberg Plans More Housing Aid for the Homeless," *NYT*, June 18, 2002; Jennifer Steinhauer, "Mayor's Style is Tested in Sending Homeless to Old Jail," *NYT*, August 16, 2002; Diane Jeantet, "Bloomberg's Homeless Plan Was Incredibly Ambitious," *City Limits*, March 11, 2013.

36 *Callahan v. Carey* (1981); *Eldredge v. Koch* (1983); *McCain v. Koch* (1983); City of New York, Office of the Mayor, "Uniting for Solutions Beyond Shelter: The Action Plan for New York City," 2004, 22; Leslie Kaufman, "New York Reaches Deal to End 20-Year Legal Fight on Homeless," *NYT*, January 18, 2003; Leslie Kaufman, "Deal on Legal Aid Lawsuits Breaks Down," *NYT*, February 16, 2005; New York City Family Homelessness, Special Master Panel, "Family Homelessness Prevention Report," November 2003, 1–8; The National Alliance to End Homelessness, "Community Snapshot: New York City" (July 2005); City of New York, Office of the Mayor, "Mayor's Management Report," 2006, 37–40; Sewell Chan, "City Settles Law Suit Over Homeless Families," *NYT*, September 17, 2008.

37 Diane Jeantet, "A Brief History of Homelessness in New York," *City Limits,* March 13, 2011; Jeantet, "Bloomberg's Plan Was Incredibly Ambitious," *City Limits,* March 13, 2011; Author's interview, Peter Madonia, November 11, 2016; City of New York, Office of the Mayor, *Uniting for Solutions Beyond Shelter: The Action Plan for New York City,* 2004, Appendix, D, E; Nina Bernstein, "A Plan to End Homelessness in 10 Years," *NYT,* June 13, 2002; Leslie Kaufman, "City Calls Its System of Aiding Homeless Too Broken to Fix," *NYT,* March 23, 2004.

38 Leslie Kaufman, "Billionaire Mayor Takes Up the Cause of the Homeless," *NYT,* April 28, 2005; City of New York, Office of the Mayor, *Uniting for Solutions Beyond Shelter,* 2004, 4–5, 36–8; Jeantet, "Bloomberg's Plan Was Incredibly Ambitious," *City Limits,* March 13, 2011; Leslie Kaufman, "Reining In Welfare, But At A Lower Volume," *NYT,* November 1, 2005.

39 The National Alliance to End Homelessness, "Community Snapshot: New York City," July 2005; Department of Homeless Services, "A Progress Report on Uniting for Solutions Beyond Shelter: An Action Plan for New York City" (Fall 2008); "Testimony of Brendan Cheney, Budget and Policy Analyst Before the City Council Committee on General Welfare on the Uniting for Solutions Beyond Shelter: The Mayor's Five Year Plan to Reduce Homlessness by Two-Thirds," New York City Independent Budget Office, September 23, 2008; Coalition for the Homeless, "Briefing Paper: Five Years Later: The Failure of Mayor Bloomberg's Five-Year Homeless Plan and the Need to Reform New York City's Approach to Homelessness," June 23, 2009; Jeantet, "Bloomberg's Plan Was Incredibly Ambitious," *City Limits,* March 13, 2011.

40 Diane Jeantet, "As Homeless Numbers Rose, Clashes Over Policies," *City Limits,* March 11, 2013; Coalition for the Homeless, "State of the Homeless 2013: 50,000" (March 2013), 11, 20; Robert Kolker, "A Night On the Streets," *New York,* March 16, 2008; Author's interview, Linda Gibbs, September 14, 2016; Author's interview, Peter Madonia, November 11, 2016.

41 Jeantet, "As Homeless Numbers Rose, Clashes Over Policies," *City Limits,* March 11, 2013; Coalition for the Homeless, "State of the Homeless 2013: 50,000" (March 2013), 11, 20; Robert Kolker, "A Night On the Streets," *New York,* March 16, 2008; Author's interview, Linda Gibbs, September 14, 2016.

42 Andrea Elliott, "Invisible Child," *NYT,* December 9, 2013; Howard Wolfson and Linda Gibbs, "Bloomberg's Real Antipoverty Record," *Wall Street Journal,* December 17, 2013.

43 Tom Waters and Victor Bach, "Destabilized Rents: The Impact of Vacancy Decontrol on Low-Income Communities," Community Service Society, June 2009, 5–7; Author's interview, Victor Bach, October 13, 2015; Author's interview, Tom Waters, October 26, 2015.

44 Mike Maciaga, "Governing Data: Gentrification in America Report," *Governing,* February 2015; Glenn Kenny, "From 'A Tree Grows in Brooklyn' to 'Little Men': A Borough's Real Estate Crisis on Screen," *NYT,* August 3, 2016.

45 New York City Housing Authority, "The Plan to Preserve Public Housing," April 2006, 1.

46 Nicholas Dagen Bloom, *Public Housing That Worked: New York in the Twentieth Century* (Philadelphia, University of Pennsylvania Press, 2008), *passim*; Victor Bach and Tom Waters, "Strengthening New York City's Public Housing: Directions

for Change," Community Service Society, July 2014, 2; New York City Housing Authority, "The Plan to Preserve Public Housing," April 2006, 1.

47 Oliver Plunz, *A History of Housing in New York City* (New York: Columbia University Press, 1990), 313; New York City Independent Budget Office, "Examining NYCHA's Plan to Preserve Public Housing," June 8, 2006, 1–7; Batya Ungar-Sargon, "Decisions New York's Next Mayor Will Face on Public Housing," *City Limits*, April 18, 2013; Author's interview, Victor Bach, October 13, 2015; Email correspondence, Author and Victor Bach, Community Service Society, October 28, 2015; Author's interview, Tom Waters, October 29, 2015.

48 New York City Housing Authority, "The Plan to Preserve Public Housing," April 2006, 1–6; New York City Independent Budget Office, "Examining NYCHA's Plan to Preserve Public Housing," June 8, 2006, Summary 1–2; City Council Committee on Public Housing, "Preliminary Hearing on the New York City Housing Authority's Fiscal 2011 Capital and Operating Budget," March 28, 2011, 2–3; Larry McShane, Greg B. Smith, "NYCHA Board Sitting on Nearly \$1B in Fed Cash," *Daily News,* August 1, 2012; Greg B. Smith, "NYC Housing Authority Boss John Rhea Seeks Millions for 'Desperately Needed' Repairs—2 Years Too Late," *Daily News,* October 1, 2012; The Boston Consulting Group, "Reshaping NYCHA Support Functions," August 2012, 22–38, 40; Victor Bach and Tom Waters, "Strengthening New York City's Public Housing: Directions for Change," 2, 4–12, 14–16; Ungar-Sargon, "Decisions New York's Next Mayor Will Face on Public Housing," *City Limits*, April 18, 2013; Author's interview, Victor Bach, October 13, 2015; Author's interview, Tom Waters, October 26, 2015.

49 New York City Housing Authority, "The Plan to Preserve Public Housing," April 2006, 1–6; New York City Independent Budget Office, "Examining NYCHA's Plan to Preserve Public Housing," June 8, 2006, Summary 1–2; City Council Committee on Public Housing, "Preliminary Hearing on the New York City Housing Authority's Fiscal 2011 Capital and Operating Budget," March 28, 2011, 2–3; Greg B. Smith, "NYC Housing Authority Boss John Rhea Seeks Millions for 'Desperately Needed' Repairs—2 Years Too Late," *Daily News,* October 1, 2012; The Boston Consulting Group, "Reshaping NYCHA Support Functions," August 2012, 22–38, 40; Victor Bach and Tom Waters, "Strengthening New York City's Public Housing: Directions for Change," Community Service Society, July 2014, 2, 4–12, 14–16; Batya Ungar-Sargon, "Decisions New York's Next Mayor Will Face on Public Housing," *City Limits*, April 18, 2013.

50 Victor Bach and Tom Waters, "Strengthening New York City's Public Housing: Directions for Change," Community Service Society, July 2014, 2, 7, 4–12; Author's interview, Robert Steel, May 15, 2015; Author's interview, Victor Bach, October 13, 2015; Author's interview, Tom Waters, October 26, 2015; Alicia Glen, Deputy Mayor for Housing and Economic Development, "Housing New York: A Five Borough, Ten Year Plan," May 2014, 5–13; Editorial, "To Save New York's Public Housing," *NYT,* May 26, 2015.

51 Author's interview, Robert Steel, May 15, 2015; Author's interview, Victor Bach, October 13, 2015; Author's interview, Tom Waters, October 26, 2015; Mireya Navarro, "City Slows Plans for Market Rate Housing on Public Housing Land," *NYT,* August 16, 2013; Mireya Navarro, "City Council Moves to Stall Land

Leases at Public Housing," *NYT,* October 10, 2013; Alicia Glen, Deputy Mayor for Housing and Economic Development, "Housing New York: A Five Borough, Ten Year Plan," May 2014, 5–13; Editorial, "To Save New York's Public Housing," *NYT,* May 26, 2015; Mireya Navarro, "Mayor de Blasio's Public Housing Plan to Seek City Aid and More Money from Tenants," *NYT,* May 18, 2015; Author's interview, Off the Record.

52 Alan B Krueger, "Inequality, Too Much of a Good Thing," 1–11 in James J. Heckman and Alan B. Krueger, *Inequality in America* (Cambridge, MA: MIT Press, 2005), 1–76; Thomas Piketty and Emmanuel Saez, "Income Inequality in the United States, 1913–1998," *The Quarterly Journal of Economics* 118, no. 1 (February 2003), 1–39.

53 Adam Lisberg, "Mayor Bloomberg's 'Waging' a New War Against Minimum Salary, Suggests Companies Should Pay," *Daily News,* September 12, 2010; Paul Harris, "Why Michael Bloomberg Vetoed the Living Wage," *The Guardian,* June 9, 2012, accessed through Gazette.com.

54 Fred Brooks, "The Living Wage Movement: Potential Implications for the Working Poor," *Families in Society,* 88 (3), 2007, 437–442; Robert Pollin and Stephanie Luce, *The Living Wage: Building a Fair Economy* (New York: The New Press, 1998) *passim*; Jared Bernstein, "The Living Wage Movement: What Is It?, Why Is It?, and What's Known about Its Impact," National Bureau of Economic Research, December, 2004, 99–140 in Richard B. Freeman, Joni Hirsch, and Lawrence Mishel, eds., *Emerging Labor Market Institutions for the Twenty-first Century* (Chicago: University of Chicago Press, 2004); Doug Turetsky, "Living Wage Again," New York City Independent Budget Office, November 30, 2011; Email from Doug Turetsky to Author, October 28, 2016.

55 New York City Center for Economic Opportunity, "Strategy and Implementation Report," 2007, 2, 15, 32; Commission for Economic Opportunity, "Increasing Opportunity and Decreasing Poverty in New York City," September 18, 2006, 12, 15; City of New York, Office of the Mayor, "Mayor Bloomberg Announces the Recommendations of the Mayor's Commission for Economic Opportunity," September 18, 2006.

56 Michael Powell, "In Gilded City, Living Wage Proposal Still Stirs Fears," *NYT,* December 20, 2011; Kate Taylor and Thomas Kaplan, "Bloomberg Backs Effort to Raise Minimum Wage," *NYT,* January 12, 2012; City of New York, Office of the Mayor, "Mayor Bloomberg Delivers 2012 State of the City Address –NYC: Capital of Innovation," January 12, 2012.

57 Powell, "In Gilded City, Living Wage Proposal Still Stirs Fears," *NYT,* December 20, 2011; Adam Lisberg, "Mayor Bloomberg's 'Waging' a New War Against Minimum Salary, Suggests Companies Should Pay," *Daily News,* September 12, 2010.

58 Jennifer Bleyer, "An Armory, Long on Furlough, Soon to Get Its Orders," *NYT,* November 5, 2006; Gregory Beyer, "Yet Again, A Majestic Armory Contemplates Its Future," *NYT,* October 28, 2007; Sam Dolnick, "Coalition Vows Wage Fight Over Kingsbridge Armory Mall Proposal," *NYT,* November 16, 2009; Sam Dolnick, "Council Overrides Veto, Blocking Plan for Armory Mall," *NYT,* December 21, 2009; Sam Dolnick, "Wage Proposal May Prompt Fight at City Hall," *NYT,* May 23, 2010; Author's interview, Ruben Diaz Jr., October 6, 2015.

59 Dolnick, "Coalition Vows Wage Fight over Kingsbridge Armory Mall Proposal," *NYT,* November 16, 2009; Dolnick, "Council Overrides Veto, Blocking Plan for Armory Mall," *NYT,* December 21, 2009; Dolnick, "Wage Proposal May Prompt Fight at City Hall," *NYT,* May 23, 2010; Author's interview, Ruben Diaz Jr., October 6, 2015.

60 Dolnick, "Coalition Vows Wage Fight Over Kingsbridge Armory Mall Proposal," *NYT,* November 16, 2009; Dolnick, "Council Overrides Veto, Blocking Plan for Armory Mall," *NYT,* December 21, 2009; Dolnick, "Wage Proposal May Prompt Fight at City Hall," *NYT,* May 23, 2010; "New York by the Numbers: Low Wage Jobs," Center for an Urban Future, December 2009, Vol. 2, Issue 5; Mayor Michael R. Bloomberg, Public Advocate Betsy Gotbaum, Deputy Mayor Edward Skyler, Director, Mayor's Office of Operations Jeffrey A. Kay, "NYC Feedback Citywide Customer Survey: Report of Survey Results," December 2008, 6; Bob Kappstatter, "Mayor Bloomberg Could Step in on Armory Deal," *Daily News,* November 9, 2009.

61 Dolnick, "Coalition Vows Wage Fight Over Kingsbridge Armory Mall Proposal," *NYT,* November 16, 2009; Author's interview, Robert Lieber, May 21, 2015; Author's interview, Seth Pinsky, May 12, 2015; Author's interview, Ruben Diaz Jr., October 6, 2015; Michael Powell, "In Gilded City, Living Wage Proposal Still Stirs Fears," *NYT,* December 20, 2011; Adam Lisberg, "Mayor Bloomberg's 'Waging' a New War Against Minimum Salary, Suggests Companies Should Pay," *Daily News,* September 12, 2010.

62 Michael Powell, "In Gilded City, Living Wage Proposal Still Stirs Fears," *NYT,* December 20, 2011; Adam Lisberg, "Mayor Bloomberg's 'Waging' a New War Against Minimum Salary, Suggests Companies Should Pay," *Daily News,* September 12, 2010.

63 Jim Rutenberg, "Mayor Vetoes Health Care Bill," *NYT,* September 17, 2005; Editorial, "Wrong Solution for the Uninsured," *NYT,* October 17, 2005; Patrick McGeehan, "Council Speaker Shelves a Sick-Leave Bill," *NYT,* October 14, 2010; Michael Barbaro and Michael M. Grynbaum, "Quinn Is Said To Be In Talks Over Sick Time," *NYT,* March 26, 2013; Powell, "In Gilded City, Living Wage Proposal Still Stirs Fears," *NYT,* December 20, 2011; Adam Lisberg, "Mayor Bloomberg's 'Waging' a New War Against Minimum Salary, Suggests Companies Should Pay," *Daily News,* September 12, 2010, accessed through Gazette.com.

64 Jim Rutenberg, "Mayor Vetoes Health Care Bill," *NYT,* September 17, 2005; Patrick McGeehan, "Council Speaker Shelves a Sick-Leave Bill," *NYT,* October 14, 2010; Michael Barbaro and Michael M. Grynbaum, "Quinn Is Said To Be In Talks Over Sick Time," *NYT,* March 26, 2013.

65 David Neumark, "How Living Wage Laws Affect Low Wage Workers and Low-Income Families," Public Policy Institute of California Report #156, 2002, viii; Mark D. Brenner, Jeanette Wicks-Lim, Robert Pollin, "Measuring the Impact of Living Wage Laws: A Critical Appraisal of David Neumark's 'How Living Wage Laws Affect Low Wage Workers and Low-Income Families,'" Political Economy Research Institute, University of Massachusetts, Working Paper Series Number 43, 2002, i, ii; Bernstein, "The Living Wage Movement," National Bureau of Economic Research, December, 2004, 136; T. William Lester and Ken Jacobs, "Creating Good Jobs in Our Communities: How Higher Wage Standards Affect Economic

Development and Employment," Center for American Progress, November 2010, 28; Sam Dolnick, "Voting 45–1, Council Rejects $310 Million Plan for Mall at Bronx Armory," *NYT*, December 14, 2009.

66 Thomas Piketty (translated by Arthur Goldhammer), *Capital in the Twenty-First Century* (Cambridge, MA: The Belknap Press of Harvard University Press, 2014, ebook version), location 5120, 5043, 5130; Oren M. Livin-Waldman, "Local Labor Markets, Income Inequality, and Institutional Response: The Case of New York City," *Regional Labor Review,* Fall 2001, 36–46.

67 Mark Levitan and Susan Weiler, "Poverty in New York City, 1969–1999: The Influence of Demographic Change, Income Growth, and Income Inequality," *FRBNY Economic Policy Review*, July 2008, 13, 15; Patrick McGeehan, "Most Low Wage Workers Are Cheated of Pay, Report Finds," *NYT,* January 28, 2010; Levin-Waldman, "Local Labor Markets, Income Inequality and Institutional Responses: The Case of New York City," 36–46.

68 Jonathan Bowles, Joel Kotkin, and David Giles, "Reviving the City of Aspiration: A Study of the Challenges Facing New York City's Middle-Class," Center for an Urban Future, 2009, 23–4; Citizens Budget Commission, "Managing Economic Development Programs in New York City: Lessons for the Next Mayor from the Past Decade," December 2013, 5; Max Schulz, "Energize," *City Journal,* August 6, 2009; Edward L. Glaeser, "Houston, New York Has a Problem," *City Journal* (Summer 2008); Patrick D. Healy, "As Costs Rise in Queens, So Do Doubts About Bloomberg," *NYT,* October 26, 2005.

69 Jim Dwyer, "A Different (and Surprising) Economic Tale of Two Cities Emerges," *NYT,* February 18, 2015; New York City Independent Budget Office, "Budget Outlook: A Bright Budget Picture: Jobs Increasing, Tax Revenues Rising, Budget Gaps Shrinking" (December 2014), 6; Bowles, Kotkin, and Giles, "Reviving the City of Aspiration: A Study of the Challenges Facing New York City's Middle-Class," 23–4; Christine Haughney, "Bloomberg Has Added Jobs, And Lost Some Too," *NYT,* October 14, 2009.

70 Jill Gardiner, "Bloomberg's Worth May Have Soared to near $20 Billion,"*New York Sun*, November 20, 2006.

71 Azi Paybarah, "Using Some of City Hall's Own Worst Stats Against Them," WNYC January 13, 2011; Mark Levitan and Susan Weiler, "Poverty in New York City, 1969–1999," 13, 15; Levin-Waldman, "Local Labor Markets, Income Inequality and Institutional Responses: The Case of New York City," 36–46.

72 Matt Taibbi, "The Great American Bubble Machine," *Rolling Stone,* April 5, 2010; Dealbook, "How Much Is Blankfein Worth," *NYT,* December 4, 2009; Graham Bowley and Eric Dash, "Some See Restraint in Goldman Chief's Bonus," *NYT,* February 5, 2010; Michael Powell, "Gilded Blinders to the Reality of a Collapse," *NYT,* November 7, 2011; Robert B. Avery and Kenneth P. Brevoort, "The Subprime Crisis: Is Government Housing Policy to Blame?, Finance and Economics Discussion Series: 2011–36 Division of Research and Statistics, Board of Governors of the Federal Reserve System, Washington D.C., August 3, 2011, 1; Chris Smith, "Bloomberg's One Percent Solution," *New York*, November 18, 2011; Bernanke, *The Courage to Act*, location 1635.

73 Nathan Schneider, *Thank You, Anarchy: Notes from the Occupy Apocalypse* (Berkeley, CA: University of California Press, 2013, 3–23;

74 Nathan Schneider, *Thank You, Anarchy*, 3–23; N. R. Kleinfield and Cara Buckley, "Wall Street Occupiers, Protesting Till Whenever," *NYT,* September 30, 2011; Nick Harbaugh and Jon Huang, "Wall Street Protestors Speak," *New York Times Video,* October 1, 2011.

75 Erik Eckholm and Timothy Williams, "Anti-Wall Street Protests Spreading to Cities Large and Small," *NYT,* October 3, 2011; "Occupy," *NYT,* December 25, 2011; Colin Moynihan, "Park Gives Protestors Place to Call Home," *NYT,* September 27, 2011; Kate Taylor, "For Bloomberg, Wall Street Protest Poses a Challenge," *NYT,* November 3, 2011; Nicholas Kristof, "Occupy the Agenda," *NYT,* November 19, 2011; NYPD Police Pepper Spray Occupy Wall Street Protestors (Anthony Balogna), uploaded to YouTube September 24, 2011; Associated Press, "New York City Settles with 6 Occupy Wall Street Protestors Pepper Sprayed by the Police," *NYT,* July 6, 2015.

76 "Occupy," *NYT,* December 25, 2011; Moynihan, "Park Gives Protestors Place to Call Home," *NYT,* September 27, 2011; Taylor, "For Bloomberg, Wall Street Protest Poses a Challenge," *NYT,* November 3, 2011; Al Baker and Joseph Goldstein, "After an Earlier Misstep, A Minutely Planned Raid," *NYT,* November 15, 2011; Brian Stelter and Al Baker, "Reporters Say Police Denied Access to Protest Site," *NYT,* November 15, 2011; James Barron and Colin Moynihan, "City Reopens Park After Protestors Are Evicted," *NYT,* November 15, 2011.

77 Barron and Moynihan, "City Reopens Park After Protestors Are Evicted," *NYT,* November 15, 2011; James Barron and Colin Moynihan, "Police Oust Occupy Wall Street Protestors at Zuccotti Park," *NYT,* November 15, 2011; *Waller v. City of New York*, New York State Supreme Court, Index Number 112957/2011, November 15, 2011; "A Surprise Nighttime Raid, Then a Tense Day of Maneuvering in the Streets," *NYT,* November 15, 2011; Colin Moynihan and Corey Kilgannon, "As Police Moved In, the Word Went Out: 'It's Happening,'" *NYT,* November 15, 2011; Nicholas Kristof, "Occupy the Agenda," *NYT,* November 19, 2011.

78 Taylor, "For Bloomberg, Wall Street Protest Poses a Challenge," *NYT,* November 3, 2011; Andrew Rosenthal, "NYC's Mayor Bloomberg Confronts Occupy Wall Street," *NYT,* November 15, 2011; Chris Smith, "Bloomberg's One Percent Solution," *New York*, November 18, 2011.

79 Sam Roberts, "Gap Between Manhattan's Rich and Poor is Greatest in US, Census Finds," *NYT,* September 17, 2014; "Highlights from Andrew Beveridge's Talk on Inequality at New York Law School," April 20, 2015; Powell, "Gilded Blinders to the Reality of a Collapse," *NYT,* November 7, 2011; City of New York, Office of the Mayor, "One New York: The Plan for a Strong and Just City," 2015, 30; Thomas Piketty, *Capital in the Twenty-First Century*, location 5120.

80 Thomas Piketty, *Capital in the Twenty-First Century*, location 452–571 and *passim*.

81 Thomas Piketty, *Capital in the Twenty-First Century,* 452–571; Simon Kuznets, "Economic Growth and Income Inequality," *American Economic Review* 45, no.1 (1955), 1–28.

82 Thomas Piketty, *Capitalism in the Twenty-First Century,* location 4422, 5044–5143.

83 Thomas Piketty, *Capitalism in the Twenty-First Century,* location 8993, 10093–10130.

Chapter 9

1   Quinnipiac University Poll, "Bush Gets 3–1 Approval in New York City," February 6, 2002; Quinnipiac University Poll, "New York Is A Party Town, Thumbs Down On Mayor And Non-Party Election Idea," July 2, 2003; Quinnipiac University Poll, "Budget Busts Bloomberg Approval, NYC Voters Split on Higher Taxes if Commuters Pay More," November 21, 2002; Jennifer Steinhauer, "A Mayor's Honeymoon Wanes; Bloomberg Has Enemies; It Seems Like New York Again," *NYT,* August 25, 2002.

2   Michael Cooper, "The Blackout of 2003: The Mayor; Bloomberg, Cast as a Figure of Quiet Authority," *NYT,* August 15, 2003; Winnie Hu, "The Blackout: New York City; Crisis Gives Mayor a Stage to Show Leadership Skills," *NYT,* August 16, 2003; Editorial, "Mr. Bloomberg's Moment," *NYT,* August 17, 2003; Quinnipiac University Poll, "Blackout Role Brightens Bloomberg Approval," September 9, 2003.

3   Jonathan P. Hicks, "Non-Partisan in New York: Plan Emerges," *NYT,* August 18, 2003; Jonathan P. Hicks and Michael Cooper, "The 2003 Election: City Charter; City Votes Down An Effort To End Party Primaries," *NYT,* November 5, 2003; Mike McIntire, "The 2003 Election: City Charter; Only Motivated Voters Ventured Into the Voting Booth," *NYT,* November 6, 2003.

4   The Beacon Hill Institute at Suffolk University, "The Impact of the Republican National Convention on the New York City Economy," June 2004, 2.

5   Quinnipiac University Poll, "New Yorkers Split on Mike, Give Bush a Bronx Cheer, Most Back Peaceful Protests, But Will Be Good Hosts," August 26, 2004; New York Police Department Executive Summary, "New York City Republican National Convention," June 24, 2004, 2–5; Editorial, "Surveillance, New York Style," *NYT,* December 23, 2005; Diane Cardwell, "Mayor Defends Spying By Police Before G.O.P. Convention," *NYT,* March 28, 2007.

6   Editorial, "President Bush and New York City," *NYT,* August 30, 2004; Christopher Dunn, Donna Lieberman, et al., "Rights and Wrongs At the RNC: A Special Report About Police and Protest at the Republican National Convention," New York Civil Liberties Union, 2005, 2–6; Diane Cardwell, "In Court Papers, a Political Note on '04 Protests," *NYT,* July 31, 2006; Diane Cardwell, "Mayor Defends Spying By Police Before G.O.P. Convention," *NYT,* March 28, 2007; Jim Dwyer, "Police Surveillance Before Convention Was Larger Than Previously Disclosed," *NYT,* April 3, 2007; *Hacer Dinler, et al., plaintiffs, versus The City of New York, et al.,* defendants, United States District Court, Southern District of New York, No 04 Civ. 7921 (RJS) (JCF) Consolidated RNC Cases, Opinion and Order, September 30, 2012; American Civil Liberties Union, "Victory in Unlawful Mass Arrest During 2004 RNC the Largest Protest Settlement in History," January 15, 2014; David Carr, "N.Y.P.D. Can Keep Its Secrets: 2004 Convention Arrests Remain Mysterious," *NYT,* June 11, 2010.

7   *Hacer Dinler, et al., plaintiffs, versus The City of New York, et al.,* defendants, United States District Court, Southern District of New York, No 04 Civ. 7921 (RJS) (JCF) Consolidated RNC Cases, Opinion and Order, September 30, 2012, 1, 17; Randal C. Archibald and Michael Wilson, "Police and Protestors Spar a Last Time, Over the Peace," *NYT,* September 4, 2004; Michael Slackman, et al., "The Republicans: The Convention in New York—The Demonstrations; Police Tactics Mute

Protesters and Messages," *NYT*, September 2, 2004; Editorial, "The Convention Papers," *NYT*, August 19, 2008; Jim Dwyer, "Four Years Later, Still Sorting Fall-Out of Republican Convention," *NYT*, September 6, 2008; Carr, "N.Y.P.D. Can Keep Its Secrets: 2004 Convention Arrests Remain Mysterious," *NYT*, June 11, 2010; Jason Lewis, "Federal Court Rules NYPD's Mass Arrests During Republican National Convention Unlawful," *Village Voice*, October 22, 2012; Colin Moynihan, "New York Is Said to Settle Suits Over Arrests at 2004 G.O.P. Convention," *NYT*, December 23, 2013; Erin Durkin and Daniel Beekman, "City Pays $18 Million to Settle Lawsuits Stemming from Republican National Convention at Madison Square Garden," *Daily News*, January 15, 2014; Statement by RNC Plaintiff Attorneys, "1800 People Arrested During 2004 Republican National Convention Settle Lawsuits Against NYPD," January 15, 2014.

8   Josh Barbanel, "Big Tax Increases, Small Tax Rebate," *NYT*, September 18, 2005; "Metro Briefing / New York: Manhattan: Rebate Checks Mailed to Homeowners," *NYT*, October 3, 2005; Mike McIntire, "Mayor's Ad Hints at Tax Rebate Not Yet Approved," *NYT*, October 11, 2005; Quinnipiac University Poll, "Bloomberg Approval Up As Election Year Begins, Ferrer, Undecided Lead Pack of Dem Challengers," November 10, 2004; Quinnipiac University Poll, "NYC Voters Say Ferrer Cares More than Mayor, Mayor Slips in Approval Match-ups," March 2, 2005; Author's interview, Edward Skyler, September 12, 2016.

9   Jim Rutenberg, "Spending More, Mayor Refines Voter Strategy," *NYT*, June 26, 2005; Jim Rutenberg, "Voter Profiles for Bloomberg Went Beyond Ethnic Labels," *NYT*, November 15, 2005.

10 Quinnipiac University Poll, "Bloomberg Approval Up As Election Year Begins, Ferrer, Undecided Lead Pack of Dem Challengers," November 10, 2004; Jim Rutenberg, "For Bloomberg, This Speech Is An Election Year Speech," *NYT*, January 11, 2005; Michael Slackman, "A Mayor Campaigning for Office, and Credit," *NYT*, January 12, 2005.

11 Rutenberg, "For Bloomberg, This Speech Is an Election Year Speech," *NYT*, January 11, 2005; Jim Rutenberg, "Bloomberg Claims Progress and Makes His Political Appeal," *NYT*, January 12, 2005; Joyce Purnick, "Newish Mayor Embraces An Old Game," *NYT*, January 17, 2005.

12 Author's interview, Fernando Ferrer, October 12, 2015; Michael Slackman, "Mayoral Candidates Show Early Fund-Raising Prowess," *NYT*, January 13, 2005; Author's interview, Roberto Ramirez, September 30, 2016; Author's interview, Eduardo Castell, September 30, 2016.

13 Global Strategy Group, "Fernando Ferrer Brushfire Survey," April 2005, in author's possession, courtesy of Fernando Ferrer and Jeffrey Pollock; Quinnipiac University Poll, "NYC Voters Say Ferrer Cares More than Mayor, Mayor Slips in Approval Match-ups," March 2, 2005; Diane Cardwell, "For Ferrer and Police, A Shifting Relationship," *NYT*, March 18, 2005; Author's interview, Fernando Ferrer, October 12, 2015; Author's interview, Roberto Ramirez, September 30, 2016; Quinnipiac University Poll, "Fields Is Up, Ferrer Is Down Among Dems in Diallo Flap, Miller, Weiner Trail In Dem Primary Race," March 30, 2005; Manny Fernandez and Patrick D. Healy, "Bloomberg Sets His Sights on Liberal Party Line," *NYT*, August 2, 2005; Author's interview, Fernando Ferrer, October 15, 2015; Author's interview, Roberto Ramirez, September 30, 2016.

14   Randall C. Archibald, "Rangel Backs Fields in Race to Challenge Bloomberg," *NYT,* April 1, 2005; Diane Cardwell, "Sharpton Backs No Candidate in the Primary," *NYT,* April 21, 2005; Randal C. Archibald, "As Fields Makes Strides, She Starts Feeling Sharp Elbows," *NYT,* May 17, 2005; Manny Fernandez, "Fields Seeks To Regain Momentum In Mayoral Campaign," *NYT,* August 15, 2005.

15   Winnie Hu, "Council Speaker Struggles For Broader Voter Support," *NYT,* April 9, 2005; Randall C. Archibald, "Fields Accuses Miller Of Using Tax Money To Aid Mayoral Bid," *NYT,* June 15, 2005; Nicholas Confessore, "Mailings From Miller's Office Cost Taxpayers $1.6 Million," *NYT,* July 15, 2005; Nicholas Confessore, "Mayor's Thorn On City Council Is Used to Low Expectations," *NYT,* August 16, 2005; Global Strategy Group, "Fernando Ferrer June Benchmark Study," May 31–June 2, 2005 in author's possession, courtesy of Fernando Ferrer and Jeffrey Pollock.

16   Nicholas Confessore, "Weiner Urges Increasing Police Force By 3,000," *NYT,* August 19, 2005; Robin Shulman, "Weiner Offers His Proposal For Cheaper Health Insurance," *NYT,* August 28, 2005; New York and Region, "Corrections," *NYT,* August 23, 2005.

17   Diane Cardwell, "From The Back Of The Mayoral Pack, Snarls And Snaps," *NYT,* July 15, 2005; Diane Cardwell, "Ferrer Makes His Appeal In Two Languages," *NYT,* August 2, 2005; Nicholas Confessore, "A Congressman As A Regular Guy, Twice," *NYT,* August 30, 2005; Nicholas Confessore, "From His Stoop In Brooklyn," *NYT,* September 10, 2005; Nicholas Confessore, "Weiner, Who Once Imagined A Resurgence, Now Has One," *NYT,* September 10, 2005; Author's interview, Fernando Ferrer, October 12, 2005; Author's interview, Roberto Ramirez, September 30, 2016; Sam Roberts, "A Mixed Message For Ferrer In Primary Voting Patterns," *NYT,* September 25, 2005; New York City Board of Elections, "Annual Report," 2005.

18   Sam Roberts, "Bloomberg Democrats Are A Primary Force," *NYT,* September 2, 2005; Sam Roberts, "A Mixed Message for Ferrer in Primary Voting Patterns," *NYT,* September 25, 2005.

19   Robin Shulman, "Ognibene Loses Bid for Line on Ballot against Bloomberg," *NYT,* August 4, 2005; Jim Rutenberg, "G.O.P. Rival in Mayor's Race Says Petition Is In Jeopardy," *NYT,* July 26, 2005.

20   Michael Slackman, "In New York, Fringe Politics in Mainstream," *NYT,* May 28, 2005; Nicholas Confessore, "Independence Party Gives Bloomberg Its Support," *NYT,* May 29, 2005; Patrick D. Healy, "Democrats Attack Bloomberg Over His Ties to The Independence Party," *NYT,* June 4, 2005; Mike McIntire, "Fulani Loses Independence Party Role Over Comments On Jews," *NYT,* September 19, 2005.

21   Adam Brodsky, "Sitting Pretty: 'Four More Years' Is Looking A Lot More Likely," *NYP,* June 27, 2004; David Herszenhorn, "4th-Grade Success to 8th-Grade Disappointment; Tests' Meaning Questioned," *NYT,* May 26, 2005; David M. Herszenhorn, "Democrats May Stress Schools, But Can't Attack the Mayor," *NYT,* August 26, 2005; Quinnipiac University Poll, "Schools Flunk But Bloomberg Gets Good Grades, Education Is Top Priority In Mayor's Race," September 22, 2005; James Traub, "Bloomberg's City," *NYT,* October 2, 2005; Author's interview, Edward Skyler, September 12, 2016.

22   Jim Rutenberg, "As Democrats Fight Stadium, Some Blacks Buck the Trend," *NYT,* March 24, 2005; Nicholas Confessore, "Council Approves Makeover of the

Brooklyn Waterfront," *NYT,* May 12, 2005; Jim Rutenberg, "Off the Trail: 2005 Mayor; Mr. Bloomberg's Most Consistent Supporter," *NYT,* July 11, 2005; Jim Rutenberg, "More Unions Endorse Bloomberg," *NYT,* July 15, 2005; Patrick D. Healy, "On Ground Zero Issue, a Delicate Political Calculus," *NYT,* May 7, 2005; Diane Cardwell and Jim Rutenberg, "Mayor Vows a Bigger Role in Rebuilding at Ground Zero," *NYT,* October 13, 2005; Charles V. Bagli, "Mayor Pursues Plans Outside Manhattan, And Even Critics Are Impressed," *NYT,* July 11, 2005; Author's interview, Robert Yaro, October 2, 2015; Author's interview, Jonathan Bowles, May 8, 2015; Author's interview, Edward Skyler, September 12, 2016.

23 Elisa Gootman, "Bloomberg to Give Staten Island a Package of Elite School Programs," *NYT,* January 26, 2005; Kirk Semple, "Metro Briefing: Staten Island; Mayor Says Precinct Needed," *NYT,* March 14, 2005; Jim Rutenberg, "After Earlier Veto, Mayor Backs Increased Ferry Service For S.I.," *NYT,* April 26, 2005; Sewell Chan, "M.T.A To Build Third Depot For Staten Island Bus Service," *NYT,* September 28, 2005; Jim Rutenberg, "Metro Briefing: New York: Staten Island; Bloomberg Names a Campaign Chairman," *NYT,* March 30, 2005; Jim Rutenberg, "Bloomberg Announces Plan for Fresh Kills Park On Staten Island," *NYT,* August 25, 2005; Jeff Vandam, "Recycling a Reputation," *NYT,* August 28, 2005.

24 Sewell Chan and Jim Rutenberg, "In Shift, Bloomberg Opposes Rail Tunnel," *NYT,* March 4, 2005; Editorial, "A Cross-Harbor Rail Link," *NYT,* March 13, 2005; Jim Rutenberg, "Anti-Politician Faces Reality of Realpolitik," *NYT,* April 16, 2005.

25 Michael Wilson, "Metro Briefing: New York: Manhattan: Dominican Police Dept. Liaison," *NYT,* March 15, 2005; Robin Finn, "From Harlem, For Bloomberg, With No Regrets," *NYT,* April 1, 2005; Michael Barbaro, "Bloomberg Makes Early, Aggressive Bid for Black Support," *NYT,* April 2, 2009.

26 Steven Greenhouse, "Service Agencies and City in Deal on Pay Raises," *NYT,* May 5, 2005; Robert D. McFadden, "Wall Collapses Onto a Busy Manhattan Highway," *NYT,* May 13, 2005; Sewell Chan, "City Pushing to Clear Wall Debris By Monday," *NYT,* May 14, 2005; Robin Finn, "An Architect Who Also Clears Away," *NYT,* May 20, 2005; Jim Rutenberg, "Metro Briefing: New York: Manhattan: Mayor to End Radio Show," *NYT,* August 22, 2005.

27 Michelle O'Donnell and William K. Rashbaum, "White Men Attacked 3 Black Men in Howard Beach Hate Crime, Police Say," *NYT,* June 30, 2005; Jim Dwyer, "It's Not '86 Residents Say, Seeing a River of Blame That Flows Two Ways," *NYT,* July 1, 2005; Kareem Fahim, "Restraint As Sharpton Visits Howard Beach Attack Site," *NYT,* July 5, 2005.

28 Mike McIntire, "S&P Raises City's Rating to A+, Its Best Ever," *NYT,* May 18, 2005; Jim Rutenberg and Steven Greenhouse, "Big City Union Shifts Support to Bloomberg," *NYT,* July 14, 2005.

29 Sam Roberts and Jim Rutenberg, "With More Private Giving, Bloomberg Forges Ties," *NYT,* May 23, 2005; Sam Roberts, "City Groups Get Bloomberg Gift of $20 Million," *NYT,* July 6, 2005; Thomas J. Lueck, "What's Up and Spans the City? Bloomberg's Philanthropy," *NYT,* August 17, 2005; Editorial, "$ilence Was Golden," *NYP,* June 23, 2013.

30 Sam Roberts and Jim Rutenberg, "With More Private Giving, Bloomberg Forges Ties," *NYT,* May 23, 2005; Jennifer Steinhauer, "Bloomberg's New Deputy Has a Velvet Fist," *NYT,* December 6, 2005.

31 Jim Rutenberg, "Bloomberg Tries to Woo Democratic Donors Away From His Rivals In The Race For Mayor," *NYT,* June 22, 2005; Jim Rutenberg, "Rich Democrats Are Lining Up With Mayor," *NYT,* July 26, 2005; Andrew Ross Sorkin, "Quadrangle To Manage Bloomberg Fund," *NYT,* January 15, 2008; Author's interview, Fernando Ferrer, October 12, 2015.

32 Michael M. Grynbaum, "Mayor Takes the Subway—By Way of SUV," *NYT,* August 1, 2007; Mike McIntire, "Who Has Bloomberg's Number? Anybody with a Phone Book," *NYT,* July 13, 2005; Jim Rutenberg, "A Man for All Boroughs," *NYT,* June 28, 2005; Bagli, "Mayor Pursues Plans Outside Manhattan, And Even Critics Applaud," *NYT,* July 11, 2005.

33 Jim Rutenberg, "Spending More, Mayor Refines Voters Strategy," June 26, 2005; Patrick D. Healy and Marjorie Connelly, "Big Issues Lift Mayor's Rating to a New High," *NYT,* June 29, 2005; Patrick D. Healy and Mike McIntire, "Ferrer and Bloomberg Trade Barbs on Cash," *NYT*, October 10, 2005.

34 Quinnipiac University Poll, "Bloomberg Has 14-Point Likely-Voter Lead Over Ferrer, But Democrat 'Cares' More Than Mayor Voters Say," September 21, 2005; Sam Roberts, "N.Y.'s Ever Changing Electorate: Next, The White Minority," *NYT,* September 13, 2005; Sam Roberts, "Write-In Voters Give Bloomberg A Tiny Victory," *NYT,* October 2, 2005; Jim Rutenberg and Patrick D. Healy, "Bloomberg Spends $46.6 Million On Race," *NYT,* October 8, 2005; Healy and McIntire, "Ferrer And Bloomberg Trade Barbs On Cash," *NYT,* October 10, 2005; Nicholas Confessore, "Prominent National Democrats Rally Around Ferrer," *NYT,* September 25, 2005; Diane Cardwell, "Racial Politics of 2001; Unhealed Wounds of 2005," *NYT,* May 8, 2005; Author's interview, Roberto Ramirez, September 30, 2016.

35 Patrick D. Healy, "On The Candidates' Blogs: Writing Right and Wrong," *NYT,* September 28, 2005; Patrick D. Healy and Diane Cardwell, "Ferrer Being Hurt By Self-Inflicted Wounds," *NYT,* September 30, 2005; David M. Herszenhorn, "Under Siege On Schools, Mayor Pledges New Programs," *NYT,* October 22, 2005; Thomas J. Lueck, "Seeking to Improve Standards, Mayor Offers Preschool Plan," *NYT,* October 7, 2005.

36 Michael Barbaro, "Weiner Accuses Bloomberg Campaign of Spreading Negative Stories to Press," *NYT,* May 12, 2009; Author's interview, Fernando Ferrer, October 12, 2015.

37 Winnie Hu, "Two Different Kinds of Math, and Two Spins on Unemployment," *NYT,* October 15, 2005; Diane Cardwell, "With Cleanup Crew's Arrival, Ferrer Event Is Thwarted Again," *NYT,* November 3, 2005; Thomas J. Lueck, "Taking a Cue from Ferrer, Mayor Issues Housing Plan," *NYT,* October 20, 2005; Rutenberg, "Bloomberg Keeps His Name Off Rebate Checks," *NYT,* September 25, 2005.

38 David W. Chen, "Challengers Look For An Angle On One Of The Mayor's Strengths," *NYT,* September 7, 2005; Author's interview, Randi Weingarten, May 15, 2015; Author's interview, Joel Klein, March 2, 2015; David Herszenhorn, "City Reaches Tentative Deal With Teachers," *NYT,* October 4, 2005; Jim Rutenberg and Steven Greenhouse, "Neutralizing the Teachers: Win-Win for Mayor and the Union Chief," *NYT,* October 4, 2005; Steven Greenhouse, "City Announces New Pact For Sanitation Workers," *NYT,* October 13, 2005; Kareem Fahim, "Firefighters Reach Accord With the City," *NYT,* October 28, 2005.

39 Author's interview, Fernando Ferrer, October 12, 2015; Patrick D. Healy, "The Race for Mayor Audio Slide Show," *NYT*, November 7, 2005.

40 William K. Rashbaum, "New York Named In Terror Threat Against Subways," *NYT*, October 7, 2005; James Barron, "In Skeptical New York, Terror Alert Stirs Doubts," *NYT*, October 8, 2005; William K. Rashbaum, "Threat Discounted, New York Eases Subway Alert," *NYT*, October 11, 2005; William K. Rashbaum, "A Threat's Journey From Iraq To New York," *NYT*, October 12, 2005; Author's interview, Roberto Ramirez, September 30, 2016; Kelly, *Vigilance*, 208–256; Author's interview, Raymond Kelly, October 3, 2016.

41 Quinnipiac University Poll, "Bloomberg Jumps To 28-Point Lead Over Ferrer, Mayor's Numbers Spiked After Subway Terror Alert," October 12, 2005; Author's interview, Fernando Ferrer, October 12, 2015.

42 Jim Rutenberg, "Off the Trail; 2005 Mayor; A Multi-lingual Ad Campaign," *NYT*, July 25, 2005; Marist Poll, "New York City Race for Mayor: Bloomberg Has a Formidable Lead Over Ferrer," November 4, 2005.

43 Mike McIntire and Jim Rutenberg, "Ferrer Offers a Tax Break For Less Expensive Homes," *NYT*, October 24, 2005; Quinnipiac University Poll, "Bloomberg Has 28 Point Lead In Home Stretch, No Shift In Post-Debate Voter Responses," November 1, 2005; Author's interview, Fernando Ferrer, October 12, 2015; Patrick D. Healy, "Ferrer Makes His Candidacy Look Stronger Than The Polls Suggest," *NYT*, October 31, 2005; Jim Rutenberg and Diane Cardwell, "Ads In The Mayoral Race Turn Meaner On The Eve Of The Final Debate," *NYT*, November 1, 2005; Diane Cardwell, "The Ad Campaign; Ferrer Bets Against Two Republicans On A Horse," *NYT*, November 1, 2005.

44 Sam Roberts, "Mayor Crossed Ethnic Barriers for Big Victory," *NYT*, November 10, 2005.

45 Author's interview, Roberto Ramirez, September 30, 2016; Sam Roberts, "Offers of Coal for the Mayor's Newcastle," *NYT*, December 16, 2005; Jim Rutenberg, "For Bloomberg, Victory Lap Leads Right Back to Work," *NYT*, November 10, 2005.

46 Sam Roberts, "1,000 Days Left For Bloomberg, All of Them on His Own Terms," *NYT*, April 1, 2007.

47 Michael Barbaro, "Mayor Trusts Youngest Deputy to Run the City," *NYT*, April 9, 2009; Sam Roberts and Serge F. Kovaleski, "Moving on From City Hall, A High Level Relationship That Was Built on Trust," *NYT*, December 7, 2007.

48 Dean E. Murphy, "Public Lives: A Charmed Life Leads To City Hall's Blue Room," *NYT*, January 2, 2002; Barbaro, "Mayor Trusts Youngest Deputy To Run The City," *NYT*, April 9, 2009; Adam Lisberg, "Mayor Bloomberg Deputy, Edward Skyler, Says So Long to City Hall," *Daily News*, March 30, 2010; Author's interview, Edward Skyler, September 12, 2016.

49 Murphy, "Public Lives: A Charmed Life Leads To City Hall's Blue Room," *NYT*, January 2, 2002; Barbaro, "Mayor Trusts Youngest Deputy to Run the City," *NYT*, April 9, 2009; Burk, Cruz, Lisberg, "City Hall Hero: Deputy Mayor Edward Skyler Foils Mugger In Midtown Manhattan," *Daily News*, March 4, 2009; Jaccorino, Elbert, "It's 'Cesspool to Jacuzzi': City Dries and Cleans Stinky Bronx Marsh Stretch Dubbed 'Everglades'," *Daily News*, December 22, 2009; Lisberg, "Mayor Bloomberg Deputy, Edward Skyler, Says So Long to City Hall," *Daily News*, March 30, 2010; Author's interview, Edward Skyler, September 12, 2016.

50 Barbaro, "Mayor Trusts Youngest Deputy to Run the City," *NYT,* April 9, 2009; Fernanda Santos, "City To Add 63 Inspectors for Construction Sites," *NYT,* May 19, 2008; Robin Finn, "The Hard Hat Passes To a New Commissioner," *NYT,* May 2, 2008; Charles V. Bagli, "Bloomberg Says Acting Commissioner Should Head the Buildings Department," *NYT,* August 15, 2008; Nicole Gelinas, "Construction Safety Woes," *City Journal* (Summer 2008); City of New York Office of the Comptroller, "Audit Report on the Follow-up of Violations Issued By the Department of Buildings," June 23, 2008; CTL Engineers and Construction Technology Consultants, P.C., "Report for Buildings Commissioner Robert D. LiMandri: High Risk Construction Oversight Study," June 5, 2009; City of New York, Office of the Mayor, "Mayor's Management Report," 2009 through 2013.

51 Joyce Purnick, *Mike Bloomberg,* 163; Chris Smith, "The Third Man," *New York,* April 24, 2006; Chris Smith, "Bloomberg's Enabler," *New York,* January 27, 2008.

52 Grace Rauh, "If Mayor Runs, 'Empirically He Can Win,'" *New York Sun*, February 1, 2008.

53 Douglas E. Schoen, *Declaring Independence: The Beginning of the End of the Two-Party System* (Random House, New York, 2008, ebook), location 30.

54 Smith, "The Third Man," *New York,* April 24, 2006; Editorial, "Bloomberg, On Everything," *NYT,* June 9, 2006; Diane Cardwell, "US Is 'Really In Trouble,' Says Bloomberg, Sounding Like A Candidate," *NYT,* June 19, 2007; Ray Rivera, "Bloomberg Calls For National Energy Reforms," *NYT,* May 12, 2007; Janet Elder, "Independent Label, Partisan Vote," *NYT,* June 27, 2007.

55 Joyce Purnick, *Mike Bloomberg,* 166; Sam Roberts, "Bloomberg Moves Closer To Running For President," *NYT,* December 31, 2007; Michael Bloomberg, "I'm Not Running for President, But . . ." *NYT,* February 28, 2008.

56 Raymond Hernandez and Nichols Confessore, "Obama's Surge Deflates Forum and Talk of a Bloomberg Run," *NYT,* January 8, 2008; Michael Grynbaum and John Harwood, "Mayor Quiet on Bid. Senator Not So Much," *NYT,* February 9, 2008; Michael Bloomberg, "I'm Not Running for President, But . . ." *NYT,* February 28, 2008; Diane Cardwell and Michael Powell, "An Obama-Bloomberg Ticket? No Cheers from the Mayor" *NYT,* March 28, 2008.

57 Timothy L. O'Brien, "The Company He Keeps (for Now)," *NYT,* March 20, 2005; Michael J. de la Merced and Louise Story, "Bloomberg Expected to Buy Merrill's Stake in His Firm," *NYT,* July 17, 2008.

58 Editorial, "A Campaign on the Money," *NYT,* August 14, 2005; Editorial, "Bloomberg Redux," *NYT,* November 9, 2005.

59 Raymond Hernandez, "Bloomberg Is Said To Explore a Third Mayoral Term Or a Bid for Governor," *NYT,* June 4, 2008.

60 Steven Lee Myers, "Ronald Lauder, Leader of the Term-Limit Band," *NYT,* October 24, 1993.

61 Joyce Purnick. "Speak Softly But Carry a Big Wallet," *NYT,* November 18, 1996.

62 Sam Roberts, "Council Moves Toward Easing Term Limits," *NYT,* June 11, 2005; Clyde Haberman, "Back When The Mayor Loved Term Limits," *NYT,* October 20, 2008.

63 Grace Rauh, "Top Bloomberg Aid Opposes Third Term," *New York Sun,* August 13, 2008; Michael Barbaro, "Top Bloomberg Aides Said to Oppose Third Term," *NYT,* August 29, 2008; Author's interview, Edward Skyler, September 12, 2016.

64   Hernandez, "Bloomberg Is Said to Explore A Third Mayoral Term or a Bid For Governor," *NYT,* June 4, 2008; Michael Barbaro and Jonathan P. Hicks, "Anger Rising at Wavering by Bloomberg on Term Rule," *NYT,* September 1, 2008.

65   Michael Barbaro, "Quinn's Silence on Term Limits May Reflect Conflict of Ambition and Past Stand," *NYT,* October 7, 2008.

66   Frankie Edozien, "This $$ Is Hers For The Faking," *NYP,* April 3, 2008; Post Staff Report, "Quinn's Phantom Funds," *NYP,* April 4, 2008; Ray Rivera and Ross Buettner, "Phony Allocations By City Council Reported," *NYT,* April 4, 2008; Michael Barbaro, "Quinn's Silence on Term Limits May Reflect Conflict of Ambition and Past Stand," *NYT,* October 7, 2008; Quinnipiac University Poll, "New Yorkers Want Bloomberg for Mayor, but Not Enough to Change Term Limits," July 16, 2008.

67   Michael Barbaro, "Opposition Solidifies to Change in Term Limits Law," *NYT,* September 5, 2008.

68   Post Staff Report, "Run Mike, Run," *NYP,* September 30, 2008; Editorial, "The Limits of Term Limits," *NYT,* September 30, 2008.

69   New York Times Video, "CNBC Bloomberg Announcement," October 2, 2008; Quinnipiac University Poll, "New Yorkers Tilt Against Third Term for Bloomberg, 87 Per Cent Say Let Voters Decide in Referendum," October 21, 2008; Corky Siemaszko, "We Like Term Limits—But We Like Mike Too: New Yorkers Split on Third Term for Mayor Bloomberg," *Daily News,* October 3, 2008.

70   Michael Barbaro and David W. Chen, "Bloomberg Enlists His Charities In Bid To Stay," *NYT,* October 17, 2008; Ronald Lauder, "In New York, a Willing Suspension of Term Limits," *NYT,* October 2, 2008; Michael Barbaro and Kareem Fahim, "Lauder Opposes Mayor on Change to Term Limits," *NYT,* October 5, 2008; Michael Barbaro and Sewell Chan, "Lauder and Bloomberg Strike a Deal," *NYT,* October 8, 2008; Javier Fernandez, "Once Again, City Voters Approve Term Limits," *NYT,* November 3, 2010.

71   David W. Chen and Michael Barbaro, "Council Backs Bloomberg Bid To Run Again," *NYT,* October 23, 2008; Ray Rivera, "Countering Mayor's Bid With a Bill To Put Term Limits in The Voter's Hands," *NYT,* October 4, 2008; Author's interview, Eduardo Castell, September 30, 2016.

72   David W. Chen and Michael Barbaro, "Council Backs Bloomberg Bid to Run Again," *NYT,* October 23, 2008; Michael Barbaro and Fernanda Santos, "Bloomberg Gets His Bill And A Public Earful," *NYT,* November 3, 2008.

73   David W. Chen and Marjorie Connelly, "Poll Finds Lukewarm Support For Bloomberg," *NYT,* June 8, 2009; Kathleen Lucadamo, "Mayor Michael Bloomberg's Approval Rating Drops to Three Year Low After Term Limits, Tax Hike," *Daily News,* November 21, 2008; Author's interview, Off the record.

74   David W. Chen and Michael Barbaro, "Council Backs Bloomberg Bid To Run Again," *NYT,* October 23, 2008; David W. Chen and Marjorie Connelly, "Poll Finds Lukewarm Support For Bloomberg," *NYT,* June 8, 2009; Kathleen Lucadamo, "Mayor Michael Bloomberg's Approval Rating Drops to Three Year Low After Term Limits, Tax Hike," *Daily News,* November 21, 2008; Author's interview, Bradley Tusk, September 6, 2016; Author's interview, Edward Skyler, September 12, 2016.

75   Jim Rutenberg and Raymond Hernandez, "In About-Face, Wolfson Now Works for Bloomberg," *NYT,* July 10, 2009; Author's interview, Howard Wolfson, August 4, 2016.

76 Jim Rutenberg and Raymond Hernandez, "In About-Face, Wolfson Now Works for Bloomberg," *NYT,* July 10, 2009.

77 Jim Rutenberg and Raymond Hernandez, "In About-Face, Wolfson Now Works for Bloomberg," *NYT,* July 10, 2009; Michael Barbaro, "Bad Feelings Are Not New For Rival Campaign Advisers," *NYT,* September 18, 2009; Author's interview, Howard Wolfson, August 4, 2016.

78 Michael Barbaro and Raymond Hernandez, "Sounding Like A Rival, Weiner Attacks Bloomberg," *NYT,* January 12, 2009; Jacob Gershman, "Will Weiner Blink?" *New York,* February 1, 2009; Mark Jacobson, "Anthony and the Giant," *New York,* May 11, 2009; Author's interview, Off the record.

79 Author's interview, Bradley Tusk, September 6, 2016; Author's interview, Patrick Muncie, September 6, 2016; Michael Barbaro, "Weiner Steps Back, for Now, from Mayoral Campaign," *NYT,* March 11, 2009; Raymond Hernandez, "'Survey' Calls Attack Bloomberg Rival," *NYT,* April 6, 2009; Michael Barbaro, "Weiner Accuses Bloomberg Campaign Of Spreading Negative Stories To Press," *NYT,* May 11, 2009.

80 Anthony Weiner, "Why I'm Not Running for Mayor," *NYT,* May 26, 2009; Michael Barbaro and David W. Chen, "Weiner Decides to Stay Out of Mayoral Campaign," *NYT,* May 26, 2009; Michael Barbaro, "Chief Factor In Mayor's Race: Bloomberg Influence," *NYT,* November 3, 2009.

81 Clyde Haberman, "Bad Day for Bloomberg? Or Personality Trait?" *NYT,* April 20, 2009; Jeremy W. Peters, "Awkward Confrontation at Bloomberg Speech," *NYT,* April 16, 2009; Julie Bosman, "A Bloomberg Apology (Sort of) Is Accepted (Sort of)," *NYT,* April 17, 2009; *New York Times Video,* "In A Term Limits Question, Bloomberg Sees 'Disgrace,'" *NYT,* May 28, 2009; Michael Bloomberg, "Testy Bloomberg Calls Reporter a Disgrace," *NYT,* May 29, 2009.

82 Joyce Purnick, *Bloomberg,* 176; Author's interview, Howard Wolfson, August 4, 2016; Author's interview, Bradley Tusk, September 6, 2016.

83 Michael Barbaro, "Bloomberg Spends $3 Million on TV Ads in Mayoral Race," *NYT,* April 7, 2009; Michael Barbaro, "Bloomberg's Spending on Reelection Bid Reaches $7.5 Million," *NYT,* April 23, 2009; Michael Barbaro, "Bloomberg Spending Twice As Much As He Did In '05 Campaign," *NYT,* May 15, 2009; Editorial, "Mayor Bloomberg's Rich Campaign," *NYT,* May 16, 2009; Clyde Haberman, "In Mayoral Race, No One Outspends Bloomberg, But Bloomberg," *NYT,* May 18, 2009; Michael Barbaro, "Pace Of Mayor's Spending Is Four Times His First Run," *NYT,* July 10, 2009; David Chen, "Thompson Ad Contrasts 'US' With 'Rich And Powerful,'" *NYT,* September 18, 2009; Clyde Haberman, "Mayor Gets The G.O.P. To Let Him In," *NYT,* April 13, 2009; Michael Barbaro, "Seeking 3rd Term, Mayor Stumps Across City," *NYT,* March 30, 2009; Fernanda Santos, "Bloomberg Is Endorsed By Independence Party," April 5, 2009; Sam Roberts, "Bloomberg Goes All Out To Lift Turnout," *NYT,* October 27, 2009; David W. Chen and Kate Taylor, "Mayor, Not Recalling Much, Testifies At Consultant's Trial," *NYT,* October 3, 2011; John Eligon, "Jury Convicts Consultant of Stealing Money From Bloomberg," *NYT,* October 21, 2011.

84 Michael Barbaro, "Low-Key Comptroller Promises Vigorous Run for Mayor," *NYT,* December 9, 2008; Greg Sargent, "Will Bill?" *New York,* May 3, 2004; "Brawl for the Hall: Vital Statistics for William (Bill) C. Thompson: Mayor," *Daily News,*

August 15, 2009; David Seifman, "Bloomy in 'Rally' Low Blow," *NYP*, September 3, 2009; Post Staff Report, "Meet Councilman Tony Avella," *NYP*, August 31, 2009.

85 Barbaro, "Low-Key Comptroller Promises Vigorous Run for Mayor," *NYT*, December 9, 2008; Greg Sargent, "Will Bill?" *New York*, May 3, 2004; "Brawl for the Hall: Vital Statistics for William (Bill) C. Thompson: Mayor," *Daily News*, August 15, 2009.

86 Barbaro, "Low-Key Comptroller Promises Vigorous Run for Mayor," *NYT*, December 9, 2008; Michael Barbaro, "Q. and A. With William C. Thompson, Jr.," *NYT*, December 9, 2008; Author's interview, Eduardo Castell, September 30, 2016.

87 Adam Lisberg and Bill Egbert, "City Controller Bill Thompson Says Croton Filtration Plan Project Will Be Doubly Costly," *Daily News*, September 1, 2009; David Seifman, "Hosp's Off Meds," *NYP*, June 29, 2009; City of New York, Office of the Comptroller, "Audit on the Department of Environmental Protection's Oversight of Costs to Construct the Croton Water Treatment Plant," September 1, 2009; City of New York Office of the Comptroller, "Audit Report on the Department of Health and Mental Hygiene Oversight of the Correction of Health Code Violations at Restaurants," July 20, 2009; City of New York Office of the Comptroller, "Audit Report on the Contract of Basic Housing, Inc., With the Department of Homeless Services to Provide Shelter and Support Services," July 17, 2009; City of New York, Office of the Comptroller, "Audit Report on Inventory Controls Over Noncontrolled Drugs at Coney Island Hospital," June 25, 2009.

88 Barbaro, "Seeking 3rd Term, Mayor Stumps Across City," *NYT*, March 30, 2009; David Seifman, "DC 37 Touts Thompson," *NYP*, August 14, 2009; Frederic U. Dicker, "Paterson Ripped Over 'Silence' of the Dems," *NYP*, August 31, 2009; Editorial, "For Democratic Mayoral Candidate," September 9, 2009.

89 Courier Life, "Thompson Makes His Case for City," *NYP*, September 2, 2009; Sam Roberts, "A Primary Turn-out So Low It May Be A Modern Record," *NYT*, September 16, 2009; Greg Sargent, "Will Bill?" *New York*, May 3, 2004.

90 Chris Smith, "In Conversation: Michael Bloomberg," *New York*, September 7, 2013; John Cassidy, "Bloomberg's Legacy: Plutocracy and Populism," *New York*, December 31, 2013; Author's interview, Off the record.

91 Author's interview, Off the record.

92 "Speech by William C. Thompson, Jr.," *NYT*, October 23, 2009; Carl Campanile, "Bloomberg, Thompson Go On Attack in 1st Debate," *NYP*, October 13, 2009; New York City Campaign Finance Board Video, "2009 Mayoral General Debate," October 13, 2009; New York City Campaign Finance Board Video, "2009 Mayoral General Debate," October 27, 2009.

93 Author's interview, Bradley Tusk, September 6, 2016; Author's interview, Howard Wolfson, August 4, 2016.

94 Quinnipiac University Polls, November 25, 2008, January 27, 2009, February 24, 2009, March 24, 2009, June 16, 2009, July 28, 2009, August 26, 2009, September 24, 2009, October 26, 2009, November 2, 2009; Marist College Institute for Public Opinion Poll, October 22, 2009; Michael Barbaro, "Mayor Mends Fences After Slim Victory," *NYT*, November 4, 2009; Author's interview, Howard Wolfson, August 4, 2016; Author's interview, Bradley Tusk, September 6, 2016; Author's interview, Edward Skyler, September 12, 2016.

95 Author's interview, Howard Wolfson, August 4, 2016; Author's interview, Bradley Tusk, September 6, 2016; Michael Barbaro, "Mayor Mends Fences After Slim Victory," *NYT,* November 4, 2009; Author's interview, Eduardo Castell, September 30, 2016.

96 Author's interview, Eduardo Castell, October 3, 2016; Michael Barbaro, "Bloomberg Foe's Campaign Shows Lax Management," *NYT,* October 22, 2009.

97 Author's interview, Bradley Tusk, September 6, 2016; Michael Barbaro, "Chief Factor in Bloomberg Race: Bloomberg Influence," *NYT,* November 3, 2009.

98 Author's interview, Bradley Tusk, September 6, 2016; Barbaro, "Chief Factor in Bloomberg Race: Bloomberg Influence," *NYT,* November 3, 2009.

99 Author's interview, Bradley Tusk, September 6, 2016; Author's interview, Eduardo Castell, October 3, 2016; Barbaro, "Chief Factor in Bloomberg Race: Bloomberg Influence," *NYT,* November 3, 2009; Michael Barbaro, "Council Leader Gives Thompson Endorsement, Whether He Wanted It or Not," *NYT,* October 26, 2009.

100 Edison Research Poll, "Profile of New York City Voters," *NYT,* November 4, 2009.

101 Author's interview, Eduardo Castell, October 3, 2016; Edison Research Poll, "Profile of New York City Voters," *NYT,* November 4, 2009; Michael Barbaro, "Trusted Aides To Bloomberg Get Big Bonuses," *NYT,* January 15, 2010.

102 Barbaro, "Mayor Mends Fence After Slim Victory," *NYT,* November 4, 2009; Michael Powell, "The Morning After Democrats Regret Lost Chances To Win," *NYT,* November 4, 2009; Michael Powell and Julie Bosman, "Mayor No Longer Seems Invincible," *NYT,* November 4, 2009; "Laugh Lines: He Changed The Law," *NYT,* November 5, 2009.

103 *New York Times Video,* "Incumbent Michael R. Bloomberg's Acceptance Speech," *NYT,* November 4, 2009.

Chapter 10

1 City of New York Office of the Mayor, "A Stronger, More Resilient New York," June 2013, 5–6, 12, 21–7.

2 City of New York Office of the Mayor, "A Stronger, More Resilient New York," June 2013, 11–18.

3 Author's interview, Rohit Aggarwala, October 29, 2015; City of New York, "A Greener, Greater New York," April 2007, 53–61; City of New York, Office of the Mayor, "A Stronger More Resilient New York," June 2013, 1, 21–7.

4 City of New York Office of the Mayor, "A Stronger, More Resilient New York," June 2013, 1, 416–434, 401.

5 Author's interview, Rohit Aggarwala, October 29, 2015.

6 *New York Times Video,* "Mayor Bloomberg Announces NYC Rapid Repair," November 9, 2012; Author's interview, Caswell Holloway, September 23, 2016; New York City Department of Investigation, "Status Report On Build It Back," October 9, 2014, 1.

7 Chris Smith, "Bloomberg's Inner Circle: The Lonely Mayor," *New York,* April 4, 2010; David Chen, "Top Political Advisor Leaving Bloomberg the Mayor for Bloomberg the Firm," *NYT,* March 2, 2010; Barbaro, "Key Bloomberg Aide To

Leave City Hall," *NYT,* March 30, 2010; Michael Barbaro, "Another Exit From Bloomberg's Inner Circle," *NYT,* March 30, 2010; Author's interview, Off the record.

8   Smith, "Bloomberg's Inner Circle: The Lonely Mayor," *New York,* April 4, 2010; Chen, "Top Political Advisor Leaving Bloomberg the Mayor for Bloomberg the Firm," *NYT,* March 2, 2010; Barbaro, "Key Bloomberg Aide To Leave City Hall," *NYT,* March 30, 2010; Matthew Tully, "Steve Goldsmith Wants To Reboot Local Government," *Indianapolis Star,* October 9, 2014; Author's interview, Off the record.

9   New York City Department of Investigation, "Investigation Into Allegations of Possible Slowdown By Department of Sanitation During Blizzard of December 2010," June 2011, 1–3, 21; Juan Gonzalez, "Deputy Mayor Stephen Goldsmith And His Flaky Ideas Doom New York During Storm," *Daily News,* December 30, 2010; N. R. Kleinfield, "An Off-Kilter City, Marooned In Powdery Dunes," *NYT,* December 27, 2010.

10 Juan Gonzalez, "Deputy Mayor Stephen Goldsmith And His Flaky Ideas Doom New York During Storm," *Daily News,* December 30, 2010; N. R. Kleinfield, "An Off-Kilter City, Marooned In Powdery Dunes," *NYT,* December 27, 2010.

11 New York City Office of the Mayor, "Press Release: Mayor Bloomberg and Investigations Commissioner Gill Hearn Announce $500 Million Payment By Prime CityTime Contractor SAIC To Settle City Claims," March 14, 2012; *US v. Mazer et al.* Superseding Indictment, June 20, 2011; City of New York Office of the Comptroller, "Audit Report on the Office of Payroll Administration's Monitoring of the Oversight of the CityTime Project by Spherion Atlantic Enterprises LLC," September 28, 2010, 1–3; Ronnie Lowenstein, Director, New York City Independent Budget Office, Letter dated August 25, 2010 to Hon. Letitia James, Council Member.

12 New York City Office of the Mayor, "Press Release: Mayor Bloomberg and Investigations Commissioner Gill Hearn Announce $500 Million Payment By Prime CityTime Contractor SAIC To Settle City Claims," March 14, 2012; *US v. Mazer et al.* Superseding Indictment, June 2011; *United States vs. Mark Mazer et al.,* Prepared Remarks For US Attorney Preet Bharara, June 20, 2011; Bob Hennely, "CityTime Payroll Scandal A Cautionary Tale," WNYC, June 29, 2011; Juan Gonzalez, "CityTime Consulting Company Technodyne Goes Bust, Terminates 200 Employees In Wake Of Scandal," *Daily News,* June 1, 2011; Carl Campanile, "Mayor Bloomberg: Detection Of Fraud In CityTime Scandal Saved NY Money," *NYP,* July 27, 2013.

13 Juan Gonzalez, "City's 911 Emergency System Fails Three Times In The Past Week—Overhaul Is A Must," *Daily News,* November 19, 2009; Juan Gonzalez, "Cost Of New York City's Problem-Plagued 911 System Is Skyrocketing," *Daily News,* December 28, 2011; New York City Department of Investigation, "Report on the Emergency Communications Transformation Program," February 2015, *passim*; Caswell Holloway, "Former New York City Deputy Mayor for Operations on the Emergency Services Transformation Program," January 16, 2015, in author's possession, courtesy of Caswell Holloway; Author's interview, Caswell Holloway, September 23, 2016; Author's interview, Edward Skyler, September 12, 2016.

14 City of New York, Office of the Mayor, "Press Release: Mayor Bloomberg Announces New York City's Incarceration Rate Hits New All-Time Low," December 26, 2013; Austin and Jacobson, "How New York City Reduced Mass Incarceration: A Model for Change?," The JFA Institute, Brennan Center for Justice, New York University and The Vera Institute, January 2013.

15 City of New York, Office of the Mayor, "Mayor Bloomberg Delivers 2010 State of the City Address Detailing His Plans for the Recovery Ahead and the Details Behind It," January 20, 2010; Citizens Crime Commission of New York City, "Guide to Juvenile Justice in New York City," May 2010; City of New York, Office of the Mayor, "Preventing Crime & Punishment: New York City's Historic Cuts in Crime & Adult and Juvenile Incarceration," 2011, 15; Jennifer Saltello, Annie Salsich, and Jennifer Jenson Ferrone, "Juvenile Detention Reform," Vera Institue for Justice, January 2014; Author's interview, Linda Gibbs, September 14, 2016; "Number of New York City Juvenile Delinquents and Juvenile Offenders in Placements, December 2006–September 2012," analysis in author's possession, courtesy of Linda Gibbs.

16 Michael Schwirtz and Michael Winerip, "Violence By Rikers Guards Grew Under Bloomberg," *NYT,* August 13, 2014; Preet Bharara et al., "CRIPA Investigation of the New York City Department of Correction Jails on Rikers Island," US Department of Justice, United States Attorney Southern District of New York, Letter to Honorable Bill De Blasio, New York City Department of Corrections Commissioner Joseph Ponte, and New York City Corporation Counsel Zachary Carter, August 4, 2014, 3–14, 19, 44–5; *Mark Nunez et al. v. City of New York et al.* "Memorandum of Law In Support of the United States of America Motion to Intervene," 11 Civ. 5845 (LTS) JCF), December 11, 2014; Author's interview, Off the record; Author's interview, Linda Gibbs, September 14, 2016.

17 Jennifer Wynn, *Inside Rikers: Stories From the World's Largest Penal Colony* (New York: St. Martin's Griffin, 2001), 3–4; City of New York, Office of the Mayor, "Mayor's Management Report," 2002 through 2014, Department of Corrections statistics; Preet Bharara et al., "CRIPA Investigation of the New York City Department of Correction Jails on Rikers Island," US Department of Justice, 3–14.

18 Bernard B. Kerik, *The Lost Son: A Life In Pursuit of Justice* (New York: Harper Torch, 2001), 264–5, 272–5; City of New York, Office of the Mayor, "Mayor's Management Report," 2002; Author's interview, Michael Jacobson, September 27, 2016.

19 Author's interview, Martin Horn, September 27, 2016; Author's interview, Peter Madonia, November 11, 2016.

20 Author's interview, Off the record; City of New York, Office of the Mayor, "Mayor's Management Report," 2002 through 2005, Department of Correction statistics.

21 Michael Schwirtz and Michael Winerip, "At Rikers, a Roadblock to Reform," *NYT,* December 14, 2014; Author's interview, Off the record.

22 City of New York, Office of the Mayor, "Mayor's Management Report," 2002 through 2014, Department of Correction statistics; Russ Buettner, "Jail Officers Protest Cuts as Assaults Show a Rise," *NYT,* March 30, 2010; Michael Schwirtz and Michael Winerip, "Violence By Rikers Guards Grew Under Bloomberg," *NYT,* August 13, 2014.

23 Schwirtz and Winerip, "Violence By Rikers Guards Grew Under Bloomberg," *NYT,* August 13, 2014; Author's interview, Linda Gibbs, September 14, 2016;

Author's interview, Martin Horn, September 27, 2016; Unpublished draft letter from Martin Horn to Budget Director Mark Page, dated November 1, 2008, published original in city files according to Horn, draft in possession of author courtesy of Martin Horn.

24 Schwirtz and Winerip, "Violence By Rikers Guards Grew Under Bloomberg," *NYT,* August 13, 2014; Graham Rayman, "Rikers Island Fight Club," *Village Voice,* April 8, 2008; Ross Buettner, "Rikers Extortions Noted Before Death," *NYT,* March 15, 2009; John Eligon, "Corrections Officers Accused of Letting Inmates Run Rikers Island," *NYT,* January 22, 2009; Benjamin Weiser, "Lawsuits Suggest Pattern of Rikers Guards Looking the Other Way," *NYT,* February 3, 2009; Isolde Raftery, "6-Year Sentence For Guard In Rikers Island Beating," *NYT,* August 6, 2010; Mary Murphy, "Former NYC Corrections Commissioner Knew Rikers Was Headed For Trouble," WPIX 11 News, September 22, 2014.

25 Jennifer Gonnerman, "Before the Law: A boy was accused of taking a backpack. The courts took the next three years of his life," *The New Yorker*, October 16, 2014, 26ff; Brent Staples, "Fighting Brutality at Rikers Island," *NYT,* June 11, 2015.

26 Nina Bernstein, "Immigration Offical to Run New York's Jails," *NYT,* September 8, 2009.

27 Michael Schwirtz and Michael Winerip, "At Rikers, a Roadblock to Reform," *NYT,* December 14, 2014; Paul von Zeilbauer, "Correction Officers' Union Wants Commissioner Fired," *NYT,* August 14, 2003; Steve McFarland, "Unions Hope He'll Ease Labor Pains," *Daily News,* November 8, 2001.

28 Michael Schwirtz and Michael Winerip, "Violence by Rikers Guards Grew Under Bloomberg," *NYT,* August 13, 2014; Schwirtz and Winerip, "At Rikers, a Roadblock to Reform," *NYT,* December 14, 2014; The Council of State Governments, the Justice Center, "Improving Outcomes for People With Mental Illness Involved with New York City's Criminal Court and Correction Systems," December 2012.

29 Schwirtz and Winerip, "Violence by Rikers Guards Grew Under Bloomberg," *NYT,* August 13, 2014; Schwirtz and Winerip, "At Rikers, a Roadblock to Reform," *NYT,* December 14, 2014; Collen Wright and Benjamin Weiser, "Ex-Rikers Captain Is Sentenced To 5 Years in Inmate's Death," *NYT,* June 18, 2015; Author's interview, Linda Gibbs, September 14, 2016.

30 Schwirtz and Winerip, "At Rikers, a Roadblock to Reform," *NYT,* December 14, 2014; Edna Wells Handy, Commissioner, New York City, Citywide Administrative Services, "Determination of Violation of Civil Service Law 210 By Certain Correction Officers In the Department of Correction Transportation Division," December 11, 2013.

31 Preet Bharara et al., "CRIPA Investigation of the New York City Department of Correction Jails on Rikers Island," US Department of Justice, 3–14, 19, 44–5.

32 Preet Bharara et al., "CRIPA Investigation of the New York City Department of Correction Jails on Rikers Island," US Department of Justice, 3–14, 19, 44–5; *Mark Nunez et al. v. City of New York et al.* "Memorandum of Law In Support of the United States of America Motion to Intervene," 11 Civ. 5845 (LTS) JCF), December 11, 2014; City of New York, Department of Investigation, "Report on Security Failures at City Department of Correction Facilities," November 2014; City of New York, Department of Investigation, "Report on the Recruiting and Hiring Process for New York City Correction Officers," January 2015; City of

New York, Office of the Comptroller Press Release, with Accompanying Charts, "Violence at City Jails Spikes Dramatically and Cost Per Inmate Explodes Even As Inmate Population Declines," October 16, 2015; Michael Winerip and Michael Schwirtz, "Riker's Inquiry Expands to Include Union Chief's Financial Dealings," *NYT,* June 2, 2015.

33 City of New York, Office of the Mayor, Remarks as Delivered at 7 World Trade Center at Breakfast Meeting of the Alliance for Downtown Manhattan, "Mayor Bloomberg Looks Back at New York City on September 12, 2001 and Outlines Progress on Economic Recovery, Major Growth in Population and Decreases in Crime," September 12, 2013.

34 City of New York, Office of the Mayor, Remarks as Delivered at 7 World Trade Center at Breakfast Meeting of the Alliance for Downtown Manhattan, September 12, 2013.

35 Jeffrey A. Kroessler, *New York Year by Year: A Chronology of the Great Metropolis* (New York: NYU Press, 2002), 182–3.

36 Sam Roberts, *Grand Central: How a Train Station Transformed America* (New York: Grand Central Publishing, 2013), 97–111.

37 James Glanz and Eric Lipton, *City in the Sky: The Rise and Fall of the World Trade Center* (New York: Times Books Henry Holt and Company, LLC, eBook edition, 2013), location 136–217, 380; Mitchell Moss, "The Redevelopment of Lower Manhattan: The Role of the City," 95–7, in John Mollenkopf, ed. *Contentious City: The Politics of Recovery in New York City* (New York: Russell Sage Foundation, 2005); Jane Jacobs, *The Death and Life of Great American Cities* (New York: Vintage Books, 1961), 1, 50, 154–61.

38 Glanz and Lipton, *City in the Sky*, location 506–644.

39 Glanz and Lipton, *City in the Sky*, location 664–720; Susan S. Fainstein, "Ground Zero's Landlord: The Role of the Port Authority of New York and New Jersey in the Reconstruction of the World Trade Center Site," in John Mollenkopf, ed. *Contentious City*; Paul Goldberger, *Up From Zero: Politics, Architecture and the Rebuilding of New York,* (New York: Random House, 2005), 20–3.

40 Glanz and Lipton, *City in the Sky*, location 3589–4149; Goldberger, *Up From Zero,* 28–33; Elizabeth Greenspan, *Battle for Ground Zero: Inside the Political Struggle to Rebuild the World Trade Center* (New York: Palgrave Macmillan, 2013), 473–93; Jonathan Mahler, "The Bloomberg Vista," *NYT,* September 10, 2006.

41 Glanz and Lipton, *City in the Sky*, location 3589–4149; Goldberger, *Up From Zero,* 32–33; Greenspan, *Battle for Ground Zero,* 485–94.

42 Rivlin and Scanlon, "Working Group Reports Prepared for Civic Alliance to Rebuild Downtown New York," September 2002, 11–12; Goldberger, *Up From Zero,* 32–33; Fainstein, "Ground Zero's Landlord," 76–7; Moss, "The Redevelopment of Lower Manhattan," 95–7, in John Mollenkopf, ed. *Contentious City.*

43 Lynne B. Sagalyn, "The Politics of Planning the World's Most Visible Redevelopment Project," 23–64 and Mitchell Moss, "The Redevelopment of Lower Manhattan: The Role of the City," 95–111 in John Mollenkopf, ed. *Contentious City*; Paul Goldberger, "Groundwork: How the Future of Ground Zero is Being Resolved," *The New Yorker,* May 20, 2002; Deborah Sontag, "Broken Ground: The Hole in the City's Heart," *NYT,* September 11, 2006; Charles V. Bagli, "Rebuilding at 9/11

Site Runs Late, Report Says," *NYT,* July 1, 2008; Author's interview, Robert Yaro, October 1, 2015.

44   Lynne B. Sagalyn, "The Politics of Planning the World's Most Visible Redevelopment Project," 23–64 and Moss, "The Redevelopment of Lower Manhattan," 95–111 in John Mollenkopf, ed. *Contentious City*; Paul Goldberger, "Groundwork: How the Future of Ground Zero is Being Resolved," *The New Yorker,* May 20, 2002; Deborah Sontag, "Broken Ground: The Hole in the City's Heart," *NYT,* September 11, 2006; Charles V. Bagli, "Rebuilding at 9/11 Site Runs Late, Report Says," *NYT,* July 1, 2008.

45   Kurt Andersen, "Ground Zero to Sixty," *New York,* May 23, 2005; Sontag, "Broken Ground: The Hole in the City's Heart," *NYT,* September 11, 2006; Sagalyn, "The Politics of Planning the World's Most Visible Redevelopment Project," 24, 33–6; Greenspan, *Battle for Ground Zero,* location 715; Arielle Goldberg, "Civic Engagement in the Rebuilding of theWorld Trade Center," 132, in John Mollenkopf, ed. *Contentious City;* Author's interview, Robert Yaro, October 1, 2015; Author's interview, Tom Wright, October 26, 2015.

46   Greenspan, *Battle for Ground Zero,* location 187, 566–596, 673–84, 1952; Moss, "The Redevelopment of Lower Manhattan: The Role of the City," 100, in John Mollenkopf, ed. *Contentious City.*

47   City of New York, Office of the Mayor, "Remarks by Mayor Michael R. Bloomberg: Vision for 21st Century Lower Manhattan," Regent Wall Street Hotel, December 12, 2002; Phil Hirschkorn, "Mayor Unveils $11 Billion Plan for Lower Manhattan," CNN.com, December 12, 2002; Andrea Bernstein, "Bloomberg's Plan for Lower Manhattan," WNYC News, December 13, 2002; Moss, "The Redevelopment of Lower Manhattan: The Role of the City," 104–6, in John Mollenkopf, ed., *Contentious City.*

48   City of New York, Office of the Mayor, "Remarks by Mayor Michael R. Bloomberg: Vision for 21st Century Lower Manhattan," Regent Wall Street Hotel, December 12, 2002; Phil Hirschkorn, "Mayor Unveils $11 Billion Plan for Lower Manhattan," CNN.com, December 12, 2002; Andrea Bernstein, "Bloomberg's Plan for Lower Manhattan," WNYC News, December 13, 2002; Jennifer Steinhauer, "Mayor's Proposal Envisions Lower Manhattan as an Urban Hamlet," December 13, 2002; Moss, "The Redevelopment of Lower Manhattan: The Role of the City," 95–7, in John Mollenkopf, ed. *Contentious City.*

49   Lower Manhattan Development Corporation, "A Vision for Lower Manhattan: Context and Program for the Innovative Design Study," October 11, 2002; Greenspan, *Battle for Ground Zero,* location 2156; Sagalyn, "The Politics of Planning the World's Most Visible Redevelopment Project," 23–7; Arielle Goldberg, "Civic Engagement in the Rebuilding of the World Trade Center," 112–38; Sewell Chan, "Settlement a Boon for Ground Zero," *NYT,* May 23, 2007.

50   Sagalyn, "The Politics of Planning the World's Most Visible Redevelopment Project," 23–64; Sontag, "Broken Ground: The Hole in the City's Heart," *NYT,* September 11, 2006; Author's interview, Daniel Doctoroff, September 3, 2015; Author's interview, Robert Yaro, October 1, 2015.

51   Andersen, "Ground Zero to Sixty," *New York,* May 23, 2005; Editorial, "Manhattan's Mayor Ahab," *NYT,* May 2, 2005; New York Metro American Planning Association, "A Statement from the New York Metro Chapter American

Planning Association, New York New Visions, Civic Alliance for Downtown New York, Labor Community Advocacy Network," November 1, 2005; Sagalyn, "The Politics of Planning the World's Most Visible Redevelopment Project," 23–64; Sontag, "Broken Ground: The Hole in the City's Heart," *NYT*, September 11, 2006.

52 Author's interview, Seth Pinsky, May 12, 2015; Author's interview, Robert Lieber, May 21, 2015; Greenspan, *Battle for Ground Zero,* location 2166.

53 Author's interview, Seth Pinsky, May 12, 2015; Robert Kolker, "Who Wants to Move to Ground Zero?" *New York,* April 18, 2005; John Heile, "Poker at Ground Zero," *New York,* March 27, 2006; Sontag, "Broken Ground: The Hole in the City's Heart," *NYT,* September 11, 2006; Greenspan, *Battle for Ground Zero,* location 2166–87.

54 Author's interview, Seth Pinsky, May 12, 2015; Kolker, "Who Wants to Move to Ground Zero?" *New York,* April 18, 2005; Greenspan, *Battle for Ground Zero,* location 2166–87.

55 City of New York, Office of the Mayor, "Mayor Michael R. Bloomberg Delivers 2006 State of the City Address: A Blueprint for New York City's Future," January 26, 2006; Editorial, "Down to the Wire at Ground Zero," *NYT,* February 13, 2006; Charles V. Bagli, "At Ground Zero, No End to Dispute That's Years Old and 1776 Feet High," *NYT,* February 19, 2006; Michael Cooper, "Stalled Talks Are More Bad News for Pataki," *NYT,* March 16, 2006; Editorial, "Greed vs. Good at Ground Zero," *NYT,* March 17, 2006; Charles V. Bagli, "Master of Slow and Deliberate at Ground Zero," *NYT,* March 24, 2006; Editorial, "A Ground Zero Summit," *NYP,* April 8, 2006; John Heile, "Poker at Ground Zero," *New York,* March 27, 2006; Mahler, "The Bloomberg Vista," *NYT,* September 10, 2006; Sontag, "Broken Ground: The Hole in the City's Heart," *NYT,* September 11, 2006; Greenspan, *Battle for Ground Zero,* location 2166–87, 2251.

56 Diane Cardwell and Charles V. Bagli, "Bloomberg Set to Lead 9/11 Memorial Group," *NYT,* October 6, 2006; Sontag, "Broken Ground: The Hole in the City's Heart," *NYT,* September 11, 2006; Greenspan, *Battle for Ground Zero,* location 2597–2645.

57 Jennifer Steinhauer, "Threats and Responses: Perspectives; Grieve Today, Mayor Says, And Then Grasp Tomorrow," *NYT,* September 11, 2002; Edward Wyatt, "Bloomberg Is Put on Defensive After a Remark," *NYT,* June 14, 2002; Mahler, "The Bloomberg Vista," *NYT,* September 10, 2006; Sontag, "Broken Ground: The Hole in the City's Heart," *NYT,* September 11, 2006; Diane Cardwell and Charles V. Bagli, "Bloomberg Set to Lead 9/11 Memorial Group," *NYT,* October 6, 2006; Diane Cardwell, "Bloomberg Tries to Move City Beyond 9/11 Grief," *NYT,* September 11, 2007; Greenspan, *Battle for Ground Zero,* location 2597–2645.

58 Cardwell, "Bloomberg Tries to Move City Beyond 9/11 Grief," *NYT,* September 11, 2007; David Dunlop, "9/11 Memorial Faces Setback Over Names," *NYT,* June 27, 2006; Editorial, "A Public Memorial," *NYT,* January 29, 2007; Greenspan, *Battle for Ground Zero,* location 2597–2645; 2655–2696.

59 Editorial, "A Clear-Eyed Look at Ground Zero," *NYT,* July 2, 2008; Michael M. Grynbaum, "Director Said to Be Leaving Port Authority Next Month," *NYT,* September 28, 2011; Greenspan, *Battle for Ground Zero,* location 2597–2645.

60 Author's interview, Christopher Ward, May 12, 2015.

61 Author's interview, Christopher Ward, May 12, 2015; Author's interview, Robert Lieber, May 21, 2015.

62 Author's interview, Christopher Ward, May 12, 2015; Charles V. Bagli, "Rebuilding at 9/11 Site Runs Late, Report Says," *NYT,* July 1, 2008; Editorial, "A Clear-Eyed Look at Ground Zero," *NYT,* July 2, 2008; Michael M. Grynbaum, "Director Said to Be Leaving Port Authority Next Month," *NYT,* September 28, 2011; Greenspan, *Battle for Ground Zero,* location 2597–2645.

63 Author's interview, Christopher Ward, May 12, 2015; Charles V. Bagli, "New Plan Sees 9/11 Memorial Open by 2011," *NYT,* September 26, 2008; Editorial, "Seven Years Later, Ground Zero," *NYT,* September 11, 2008; Charles V. Bagli, "New Plan Sees 9/11 Memorial Open By 2011," *NYT,* September 26, 2008.

64 Author's interview, Christopher Ward, May 12, 2015; Author's interview, Robert Lieber, May 21, 2015; Charles V. Bagli, "New Plan Sees 9/11 Memorial Open by 2011," *NYT,* September 26, 2008; Editorial, "Seven Years Later, Ground Zero," *NYT,* September 11, 2008; Charles V. Bagli, "New Plan Sees 9/11 Memorial Open By 2011," *NYT,* September 26, 2008.

65 Author's interview, Christopher Ward, May 12, 2015; Author's interview, Robert Lieber, May 21, 2015; Author's interview, Dean Fuleihan, August 12, 2015; Editorial, "Seven Years Later, Ground Zero," *NYT,* September 11, 2008; Charles V. Bagli, "New Plan Sees 9/11 Memorial Open By 2011," *NYT,* September 26, 2008.

66 Paul Goldberger, "Broken Promises at Ground Zero," *The New Yorker,* September 10, 2009; Editorial, "Ground Zero Stalls Again," *NYT,* August 10, 2009; Charles V. Bagli, "Two New Towers May End Impasse at Ground Zero," *NYT,* May 24, 2010; Charles V. Bagli, "Developer Reaches Deal to Finish 80-Story Tower," *NYT,* June 25, 2014; Author's interview, Robert Lieber, May 21, 2015; Author's interview, Christopher Ward, May 12, 2015.

67 Elizabeth Greenspan, *Battle for Ground Zero,* location 2705; Author's interview, Seth Pinsky, May 12, 2015; Author's interview, Robert Lieber, May 21, 2015; Author's interview, Robert Steel, May 15, 2015; Author's interview, Chris Ward, May 12, 2015.

68 Kolker, "Who Wants to Move to Ground Zero?," *New York,* April 18, 2005; Michael Powell, "For a Ground Zero Developer Seeking Subsidies, More Is Never Enough," *NYT,* March 31, 2014; Edwin Heathcoate, "Rebuilding the World Trade Center: A Progress Report," *The Financial Times,* December 27, 2013; Paul Goldberger, "Shaping the Void: How Successful is the New World Trade Center," *The New Yorker,* September 12, 2011; Eliot Brown, "Silverstein Loses Battle Over 9/11 Payouts," *The Wall Street Journal,* July 18, 2013; Caroline Bankoff, "One World Trade Center is Only About Half Rented (Updated)," *New York,* May 27, 2014.

69 Daniel L. Doctoroff, "New York City's Vision for Lower Manhattan: Vision to Reality in Ten Years," Speech Given on September 6, 2006, 1; Adam Gopnik, "Cities and Songs," *The New Yorker,* May 17, 2004; Alliance for Downtown New York Annual Report 2013, "Turn the Page: Lower Manhattan's Moment Has Arrived," 2013, *passim*; Mahler, "The Bloomberg Vista," *NYT,* September 10, 2006; David M. Levitt, "Lower Manhattan Revival Nears Culmination After 13 Years," *Bloomberg News,* September 10, 2014.

70 City of New York, Office of the Mayor; "Mayor Bloomberg Looks Back at New York City on September 12, 2001," September 12, 2013; Edwin Heathcoate, "Rebuilding the World Trade Center: A Progress Report," *The Financial Times*, December 27, 2013; Elizabeth Greenspan, "Mayor Bloomberg's Legacy," *The New Yorker*, September 18, 2013; Alliance for Downtown New York Annual Report 2013, "Turn the Page: Lower Manhattan's Moment Has Arrived" (New York, 2013), 10; Alliance for Downtown New York, "Lower Manhattan Real Estate Year in Review 2013" (New York, 2013), 1; Alliance for Downtown New York, "A Surge of Bits and Bytes: The State of Tech and Innovation in Lower Manhattan," October 2013.

71 City of New York, Office of the Mayor; "Mayor Bloomberg Looks Back at New York City on September 12, 2001," September 12, 2013; Edwin Heathcoate, "Rebuilding the World Trade Center: A Progress Report," *The Financial Times*, December 27, 2013; Greenspan, "Mayor Bloomberg's Legacy," *The New Yorker*, September 18, 2013.

Chapter 11

1   Citizens Budget Commission, "Managing Economic Development Programs in New York City: Lessons for the Next Mayor from the Past Decade," December 2013, 5.

2   Author's interview, Tom Wright, October 26, 2015.

3   Author's interview, Tom Waters, October 26, 2015; Bernstein, "New York Remade: Before and After Bloomberg," WNYC, December 27, 2013.

4   Emma G. Fitzsimmons, "M.T.A. Approves Budget, But Cuts 2nd Ave. Line Funding," *NYT*, October 28, 2015; Author's interview, Off the record.

5   W. Li, G. Maduro, E.M. Begier, "Life Expectancy in New York City: What Accounts for the Gains?," New York City Department of Health and Mental Hygiene, Epi Report, March 2013, 1–12; Tom Farley, MD, *Saving Gotham*, 257.

6   Li, Maduro, Begier, "Life Expectancy in New York City: What Accounts for the Gains?," New York City Department of Health and Mental Hygiene, Epi Report, March 2013, 1–12; "New York City Community Health Survey Atlas, 2010," New York City Department of Health and Mental Hygiene, 2010; Raj Chetty et al., "The Association Between Income and Life Expectancy in the United States, 2001–2014," *JAMA*, published online April 10, 2016; Neil Iwin and Quoctrung Bui, "The Rich Lived Longer Everywhere. For the Poor, Geography Matters," *NYT*, April 11, 2016.

7   Author's interview, Off the record.

8   Author's interview, Off the record.

9   Quinnipiac University Poll, June 27, 2013.

10 Author's interview, Off the record.

11 Donald T. Campbell, "Assessing the Impact of Planned Social Change," The Public Affairs Center, Dartmouth College, Hanover, N.H., Occasional Paper Series, Number 8, December 1976, 49; Author's interview, Rev. Al Sharpton, May 23, 2014.

12 Author's interview, Off the record.

13 Ken Auletta, "After Bloomberg," *The New Yorker*, August 26, 2013.

14 Author's interviews, Off the record.

15 Editorial, "$ilence Was Golden," *NYP,* June 23, 2013.

16 Nicholas Confessore, Sarah Cohen, and Karen Yourish, "Just 158 Families Have Provided Nearly Half of the Early Money for Efforts To Capture the White House," *NYT,* October 15, 2015; Martin Gilens and Benjamin I. Page, "Testing Theories of American Politics: Elites, Interest Groups and Average Citizens," American Political Science Association, September 2014, Vol. 12/No. 3, 564–581.

17 The Marist College Institute for Public Opinion, "Marist Poll: NYC Mayoralty: Quinn Leads Democratic Field . . . Lhota Ahead Among GOP," February 14, 2013; Luisita Lopez Torregrossa, "In The City, Sex Isn't Everything," *NYT,* September 3, 2013; Jonathan Van Meter, "Madam Would-Be Mayor," *New York,* February 4, 2013; Celeste Katz, "Bill Thompson Has Raised More Than $1 Million Since July But Still Trails Council Speaker Quinn in Mayoral Race," *Daily News,* January 16, 2013; Jennifer Fermino, "Poll: Christine Quinn Slipping in Mayoral Race—Support Hits Five Month Low," *Daily News,* April 10, 2013.

18 David Seifman, "Weiner Stiff Competition for Dem Foes," *NYP,* April 11, 2013; Victoria Bekiempis, "Appeals Court Upholds Fraud Convictions of Two Workers Associated With ex-NYC Controller John Liu's Mayoral Campaign," *Daily News,* January 26, 2016; Mark Jacobson, "Huma? Hey Honey? Was I Happy Before I Started Running for Mayor," *New York,* July 22, 2013; Joe Coscarelli, "Anthony Weiner, Or 'Carlos Danger,' Admits to Cybersex—But Was It After the Scandal?" *New York,* July 23, 2013; Jordan Hoffman, "Anthony Weiner's Bone-Headed Mayoral Run Has Led To One of The Best Campaign Films Ever Made," *Vanity Fair,* January 25, 2016, online edition.

19 Ford Fessenden, Haeyoun Park, Tim Wallace, and Derek Watkins, "How De Blasio Turned Conventional Wisdom on Its Head," *NYT,* September 11, 2013; Chris Smith, "The 99% Mayor," *New York,* November 4, 2013; Author's interview, Off the record.

20 Fessenden, Park, Wallace, and Watkins, "How De Blasio Turned Conventional Wisdom on Its Head," *NYT,* September 11, 2013.

21 Michael M. Grynbaum, "Taking Office, de Blasio Vows to Fix Inequity," *NYT,* January 1, 2014; "Text of Bill de Blasio's Inauguration Speech," *NYT,* January 1, 2014; Michael M. Grynbaum, "De Blasio Defends His Inauguration's Sometimes Harsh Tone Toward Bloomberg," *NYT,* January 2, 2014.

22 Ginia Bellafante, "Bloomberg's Presidential Dreams, and Past Realities," *NYT,* January 29, 2016.

23 Author's interview, Edward Skyler, September 12, 2016.

Index